Kamikaze Attacks
of World War II

Kamikaze Attacks of World War II

A Complete History of Japanese Suicide Strikes on American Ships, by Aircraft and Other Means

ROBIN L. RIELLY

McFarland & Company, Inc., Publishers
Jefferson, North Carolina, and London

The present work is a reprint of the illustrated case bound edition of Kamikaze Attacks of World War II: A Complete History of Japanese Suicide Strikes on American Ships, by Aircraft and Other Means, *first published in 2010 by McFarland.*

LIBRARY OF CONGRESS CATALOGUING-IN-PUBLICATION DATA

Rielly, Robin L.
Kamikaze attacks of World War II : a complete history of Japanese suicide strikes on American ships, by aircraft and other means / Robin L. Rielly.
p. cm.

Includes bibliographical references and index.

ISBN 978-0-7864-7303-8
softcover : acid free paper ∞

1. Japan. Kaigun. Kamikaze Tokubetsu Kogekitai. 2. World War, 1939–1945 — Aerial operations, Japanese. 3. Kamikaze pilots — History. 4. World War, 1939–1945 — Campaigns — Pacific Area. 5. World War, 1939–1945 — Naval operations, American. 6. Warships — United States — History — 20th century. I. Title.
D792.J3R523 2012 940.54'4952 — dc22 2010021494

BRITISH LIBRARY CATALOGUING DATA ARE AVAILABLE

© 2010 Robin L. Rielly. All rights reserved

No part of this book may be reproduced or transmitted in any form or by any means, electronic or mechanical, including photocopying or recording, or by any information storage and retrieval system, without permission in writing from the publisher.

On the cover: Photograph of an attack on the U.S.S. *White Plains* by a Japanese A6M Zero on October 25, 1944 (National Archives and Records Administration)

Manufactured in the United States of America

*McFarland & Company, Inc., Publishers
Box 611, Jefferson, North Carolina 28640
www.mcfarlandpub.com*

To Madeline Rose Booth

Table of Contents

Preface 1
Introduction 3

Part One — The Genesis of the Kamikazes, Their Organization, and Disposition

1. The Development of the Samurai Class and Its Ethos 7
2. Kamikaze Traditions 16
3. Special Attack Aircraft 29
4. Development of the *Tokko-tai* 42
5. Tactics 54
6. Kamikazes on Land and Sea 73

Part Two — The Kamikaze Chronicles: A Detailed Account of the Attacks

7. Prelude to Mayhem 107
8. The December Kamikazes, 1944 138
9. Lingayen Gulf 154
10. Taiwan, Iwo Jima, and Ulithi 176
11. Okinawa and the *Ten Go* Campaign 187
12. The Invasion of Okinawa, Week One 205
13. The Onslaught Continues 227
14. "...We Cleaned Up the Bodies..." 253
15. A Miserable May 273
16. The War Winds Down 288
17. *Ketsu Go*: Defending the Homeland 301

Appendix I: U.S. Navy and Merchant Marine Ships Damaged or Sunk by Kamikaze Attacks, 1942–1945 317
Appendix II: Ship Types 325
Appendix III: American and Japanese Aircraft 334

Chapter Notes 343
Bibliography 355
Index 369

Preface

For the past fifteen years or so I have focused my research efforts on American naval history in the World War II era. This research began with an interest in the ship on which my father served during that war. I thought it would be my first and last effort in the area but as time went on, one research project seemed to lead to another. I completed books on the LCS(L) ships, then the radar picket ships at Okinawa and, in this work, the kamikaze experience.

Over the years there have been a number of books published on the kamikazes. Virtually all focus on specific incidents, campaigns, or ships and their experiences as they encountered the *Tokko-tai* fliers or kamikazes. To this point no one has attempted a complete accounting of the more than 400 incidents of kamikaze attacks on American ships in World War II.

Some of the books written to date were by eyewitnesses to the carnage suffered by the United States Navy ships that were attacked by the kamikazes in the Philippines and at Okinawa. Still others were by former members of the Japanese naval and army air wings whose fate assigned them to the special attack corps. Ultimately, they survived to tell of their training and experience. A few former Japanese naval officers have written about the kamikazes and sought to rationalize their participation in the organization that sent others, much junior, to their deaths. In addition, there are works that seek to sensationalize the kamikaze phenomenon. To my knowledge, no work exists that documents the numerous attacks that took place against the American ships that served in the Pacific theater of operations. With that in mind, I have undertaken an examination of the kamikaze attacks during the Second World War.

As the reader will note, there are a number of photos in this work from the National Archives and Records Administration in College Park, Maryland. I have spent many hours of research there and have had excellent help from Rutha Beamon, Theresa Roy, Sharon Cully, and Holly Reed in the still photo section. Barry Zerbe in the textual reference branch has always been able to find materials hidden in the vast collection that have aided in my research.

Numerous veterans of the war have generously consented to interviews and have aided substantially in my understanding of the events. Their eyewitness accounts have been most helpful. For their time and eyewitness testimony I am indebted to Dr. Donald L. Ball, John L. Barkley, Frank Barnby, Ray Baumler, Earl Blanton, Dean Bell, William E. Bletso, Robert Blyth, Harold H. Burgess, William R. Christman, George E. Davis, Mel Dean, W. A. Dworzak,

Melvin Fenoglio, David Gauthier, Earl O. Griffis, Claude Haddock, Edwin Hoffman Jr., Lawrence S. Katz, Harold Kaup, James Kelley, Doyle Kennedy, Capt. Richard M. McCool, Franklin Moulton, Albert Perdeck, Harry Portolan, L. R. Russell, Mark Sellis, Tom Spargo, Robert Sprague, Harold Tolmas, and Dr. Robert Wisner.

I benefited greatly from the interviews with karate master Teruyuki Okazaki who graciously shared his views of samurai tradition as well as his experiences as a middle school student undergoing kamikaze training in Japan. Expert assistance in translating various Japanese language materials was given by Takamichi Maeshima, to whom I am indebted.

Special thanks are due to my proofreaders Lucille Rielly and Ken Thompson who made numerous invaluable suggestions about the text. In spite of their diligent efforts, the sole responsibility for the accuracy of this work rests with the author.

Introduction

It should be noted from the outset that this is a study of the kamikazes from the American perspective. Sources used consist primarily of reports from army, navy, Marine, and merchant marine units, as well as secondary published materials. Although some records exist in Japanese pertinent to the operations of the *Tokko-tai,* many were officially destroyed in the aftermath of the war, leaving large gaps in the available documentation needed to cover the subject from the Japanese perspective. Since the end of the war, many former members of the Japanese military have attempted to piece together the history of various units to which they were attached, some with great detail. *The Reports of General MacArthur* was an early attempt to coordinate the many available Japanese materials that survived in the aftermath of World War II. That work, along with the *Japanese Monograph* series, Allied Translator and Interpreter Section reports and interrogations, and *United States Strategic Bombing Survey* reports have provided a great deal of information as to how the Japanese formed and ran their special attack corps.

The presentation of this material proved problematic. The chapters relating to kamikaze traditions and the development of the special attack forces, which is covered in the first part of the book, were easiest. The second part had to be organized as a chronicle, noting the attacks on each ship in a day by day manner. There was no single ship or group of ships that encountered kamikazes in exactly the same way and location. Attacks came singly or en masse, on individual ships or groups of ships, there were few common denominators. This would have made my chore easy as I could have followed the exploits of a ship as it wandered from war zone to war zone. Since my focus was to demonstrate the extent of the kamikaze program, I had to document the attacks as they occurred. There was simply no other way to approach the task.

As time goes by, fewer and fewer of our World War II veterans are available to tell their stories. As a result, it was not possible to delve into personalities in the case of most of the ships. Accordingly, the information on most ships comes from ship action reports, war diaries, numerous government publications and some personal interviews and correspondence between me and survivors of kamikaze attacks. It was never my goal to delve into much of the personal history of the men on the ships. Rather it was to document the magnitude of the attacks during the war as this had not been done before and I thought it important to do so.

Throughout the text I have made continual use of the term "suicide." The Japanese never thought of the special attack missions as suicide. Rather, they were a means to an end, i.e., one aircraft had the ability to sink or seriously damage an enemy ship. Trading one man for one hundred seemed to be an excellent swap in a war in which human life came to mean very little. The Japanese considered that the individual airman, seaman, or soldier was using special attack tactics to defeat an enemy. The ethos and training of the Japanese army or navy man made it possible to carry out such missions. As we shall see, this training did not coincide with the formation of the *Tokko-tai* in October 1944, but rather was the result of decades of militaristic training in civilian life as well. It is my contention that, contrary to popular belief, the kamikaze was not simply a World War II phenomenon, but the culmination of centuries of tradition.

In Appendix I, I have attempted to make a comprehensive list of all ships sunk or damaged by special attack methods, including the most familiar air or kamikaze attacks. Less familiar are the attacks made by the explosive speedboats, the *Maru-re* and *Shinyo,* as well as the attacks by manned torpedoes or *Kaiten* and midget submarines. I believe the list to be complete, although there are some who might include other vessels or delete some on my list. Further, there is the possibility that a few ships that were struck by kamikazes may not be included. On a few occasions in ship and aircraft action reports I have found mention of an unnamed ship suffering a kamikaze attack for which no supporting records exist. Since it was not possible to verify the attack, I have not included them.

Gray Areas

Compiling a list of ships damaged in kamikaze attacks has been somewhat difficult. The primary problem revolves around just which ships to include. As the reader will note, my standards are broad. Some ships suffered kamikaze attacks that were near misses, but still caused damage to the ship. For instance, the destroyer *William D. Porter DD 579* was sent to the bottom on 10 May 1945 by a Val which crashed close aboard. It did not hit the ship, but its bomb passed below the destroyer's hull, where it exploded under water and opened her seams. She sank three hours later. None of her crew died, but sixty-one were wounded. *Palmer DMS 5* was sunk on 7 January 1945 in a definite suicide attack; the plane, however, missed her. Just prior to the impending crash, its pilot released two bombs which penetrated her hull at the water line. The ship made a last minute hard turn toward the plane, causing it to overshoot. The two bombs opened her hull and she went down in six minutes, suffering sixty-six casualties. Neither of these two ships was actually struck by the kamikaze plane, but were certainly sunk in a kamikaze attack. Accordingly, they qualify for inclusion in this work. On 28 December 1944 the Liberty ship *John Burke,* carrying a cargo of ammunition, was proceeding from Leyte to Mindoro as part of a supply convoy. When the kamikaze aircraft struck her the resulting explosion of the ship's cargo was so great that when the smoke cleared there was no trace of her. Following closely behind her was an Army FS ship, which was sunk when *John Burke* exploded. The army ship was not struck by the kamikaze, but certainly sank as a result of the kamikaze's attack on the Liberty ship. In addition, many ships suffered minor damage in a kamikaze attack, such as having a portion of a mast or antennae clipped off as a kamikaze scored a near miss. They reported that they had been damaged in a kamikaze attack and, therefore, are included herein.

Still other ships were so badly damaged by the kamikaze attacks that they were reduced to hopeless hulks. In all likelihood they would have gone under eventually, but they presented a hazard to navigation. American ships sunk them with gunfire or torpedoes. I have listed them as sunk by kamikaze attack as that was the primary cause of their demise. *Colhoun DD 801*, sunk on 6 April 1945, and *LCS(L) 33*, sunk on 12 April 1945, are examples of this type of sinking.

Casualty lists pose a particularly difficult problem. In the confusion attendant with a kamikaze attack, many men were blown over the side or were vaporized by the explosions and fires. Lists of dead, missing, and wounded were compiled by the ship's officers, noting that the majority of those listed as missing were presumed dead. Men were transferred off the ship in critical condition and listed as probable fatalities but were alive at the time of transfer. I have listed such cases as killed in action, since that was their prognosis. Of course, this is a judgment call, but probably accurate in most instances. Still others, listed as "serious," were expected to survive but did not. In some action reports the record of casualties is missing. In cross-checking action reports, war diaries, ship logs, and secondary sources it is obvious that the data do not exist. In such cases I have inserted a question mark in the list to note that the data are not available. In some ship documents the casualties are listed as "several," "numerous," or some other non-specific term. Accordingly, I have used these terms in my list as they represent the only data available. The resulting list of casualties in the appendices must therefore be considered to be close approximations of casualties, rather than definitive figures.

In the sources and literature pertaining to kamikaze attacks there are continual references to the number of aircraft that set out from various air bases specifically to make kamikaze attacks. However, many additional aircraft not flying a kamikaze mission made such attacks when the pilot recognized that his plane was damaged and that he would probably perish. Under those circumstances many chose to crash into an enemy ship rather than die without causing damage to the enemy. Thus they became kamikazes on the spur of the moment. This makes counting actual kamikaze missions difficult. Accordingly, I have counted any aircraft that deliberately crashed into a ship as a kamikaze even thought that may not have been the original mission. As noted in Chapter 4 the formal organization of the kamikaze units did not start until 19 October 1944, with the first successful official sorties of those units' planes on 24 October 1944. However, American naval reports after the war do not draw a distinction as to the date. As a result, the attack on *Smith DD 378* at the Battle of Santa Cruz on 26 October 1942 is listed as a kamikaze attack in the BuShips *Summary of War Damage to U. S. Battleships, Carriers, Cruisers, and Destroyers 17 October, 1941 to 7 December, 1942*. Several other officially designated kamikaze attacks also pre-date the October 1944 mark.

The reader should note that this is a listing of U.S. Navy ships and merchant ships that flew the U.S. flag. Additional ships of allied navies were also hit, but these fall outside the parameters of this work.

One final point that needs clarification relates to dates. To the west of the International Date Line are several time zones that are relevant to this work, such as time zones Item (I) and King (K). Events in these zones are one day ahead of time zones to the east, leading to some discrepancies in dates. Occasionally writers use dates relative to the American mainland, leading to some confusion. Dates and times in this work reflect those of the time zone in which the attack occurred. Hopefully, this will explain the inconsistencies in dates between this list and those published by some other researchers.

For readers who may be unfamiliar with the various ships and aircraft discussed in the text, a visual depiction of ships and aircraft is shown in the final appendices.

PART ONE
The Genesis of the Kamikazes, Their Organization, and Disposition

1. The Development of the Samurai Class and Its Ethos

The Samurai and His Ethos

With centuries of tradition behind them, Japanese kamikaze pilots hurtled from the sky into American ships during the last year of the war. The *Tokko-tai* or kamikaze did not suddenly appear in 1944 as a new feature in Japanese society, rather they were the culmination of more than ten centuries of cultural development that made such tactics possible. How these tactics became an integral part of the Japanese war machine in the later stages of the war bears some discussion.

Although Japanese history in general is relatively unknown to Westerners, the exploits of the samurai class are much more familiar. Many are not aware that the samurai class had a profound effect on the customs and culture of the Japanese. These centuries-old cultural traits are evident in the development of the kamikaze corps during World War II. To fully understand the kamikazes it is necessary to trace the development of the Japanese martial ethos through the rise and development of the samurai class, the original bearer of these traits. The modern transformation of this ethos into the actions of the kamikazes during the war are evidence of the strong tradition of the samurai that ran through Japanese culture.

The origins of the Japanese samurai class can be traced to the eighth century. Within the following four hundred years they developed from a group of armed guards and soldiers into a class that ruled Japan through its *bafuku*, or military government. Their position in Japanese society and government would be paramount until the modernization of Japan during the Meiji Restoration of 1868. Their value system, known as *bushido*, became the cultural heritage of the Japanese nation as it entered the twentieth century. What *bushido* was and how it developed is important to the understanding of the kamikazes and their actions toward the end of the war.

The First Kamikaze

The term kamikaze, or "Divine Wind," dates to the thirteenth century, and refers to the incident in which the Japanese survived the Mongol attempt at invasion through what they considered to be divine intervention. Kublai Khan launched his first, and unsuccessful, invasion of Japan in 1274. Determined to have Japan as a part of his empire, the great Khan continued to send envoys to the Kamakura Court, offering the Japanese a place under his authority in a tributary relationship. On two occasions he received the heads of his envoys as an answer. To bring the Japanese under his domination, he assembled a force of 140,000 men and launched his second assault on the island empire in 1281. Northern Kyushu was the target and some limited success in landing was achieved. However, a wall around Hakata Bay limited the Mongols' ability to land their forces for nearly two months. The end of the campaign came when a large typhoon roared in out of the East China Sea and destroyed much of the Mongol invasion fleet. Japan had been spared by the wind of the gods, a kamikaze. Only about half of the Mongol invasion force made it back to China.

"Kamikaze," used as a term to identify the Special Attack Corps, is generally thought to be an erroneous pronunciation of the Japanese characters by Japanese-Americans. In the Imperial Japanese Navy, the corps was called the *Shimpu Tokubetsu-Kogekitai*. The characters for *Shimpu* can also be read as "kamikaze," hence the commonly used name in Western works. In the Japanese Army Air Forces, the units were known as *Shimbu Tokubetsu-Kogekitai*. *Shimbu* translates as a "gathering of courageous forces." Among the pilots and other military men, the shortened name of *To*, *Tokko-tai* or *Tokubetsu-Kogekitai* was more commonly used. Intercepted Japanese messages usually referred to the units simply as *To*.

The concept of the Divine Wind was alive and well during the war years and was frequently referred to in newspaper and magazine articles. An editorial in the *Asahi Weekly* of 5 September 1943 explained how the Divine Wind worked for Japan.

> This Divine Wind does not blow only in an adverse hour in answer to prayer. Needless to say it blows in a desperate struggle in a righteous war which is waged in accordance with the Divine will, but it is certainly not limited to the last decisive battle in which the enemy receives a knock-out blow. In the first shot fired in the Great East Asia War, in the bold attack on Pearl Harbour, which was launched against the enemy's camp, and in the raid on the Philippines on the same day, a Divine Wind, which can be reckoned as providential help, arose and caused an auspicious beginning on behalf of Japan.[1]

The *Bushido* Code

The martial traditions of Japan have been handed down for over a thousand years. In order to comprehend some of the forces that made the role of kamikaze acceptable to the Japanese people, an understanding of these traditions is necessary. Japan's military class, the samurai, originated during the Nara Period (A.D. 710–784). During that time period, large landholders used their workers to defend their estates. As the estates grew in size over time, a class of full-time warriors also developed. Ultimately, the assent to power by the samurai class left the country under their control from 1185 until 1867, when four powerful clans, the Hizen, Tosa, Satsuma, and Choshu overthrew the Tokugawa clan's rule and set Japan on its road to modernization.

The new government had to cope with increased pressure from the West. With its modern armies and navies, the Western powers were deemed a serious threat. In an effort to increase their national strength, the Japanese built a new type of military force. No longer would samurai be the only bearers of weapons. Class distinctions were eliminated and the new army and navy would rely heavily on conscripts. To identify the guiding principles of the new military man, the government issued the *Imperial Precept for the Military* (1882). The document stressed loyalty and self-discipline, virtues expected of samurai but not necessarily the values of those conscripted.

The ethos of the samurai class was known as *bushido*, a set of traditions that emphasized frugality, stoicism, honor, obedience, a sense of duty, a war-like spirit, loyalty, courage, and self-discipline. Since the samurai ruled Japan for nearly seven centuries, it was natural that their ethos would filter down to the lower classes and become a common value system among the Japanese.

As Japan struggled to modernize and compete with the Western world, it realized the necessity of reinforcing the *bushido* ethos in order to sustain and safeguard its unique identity in a modern world. The well known work by Inazo Nitobe, *Bushido the Soul of Japan* (1904), was a reminder to the Japanese of their military traditions and an attempt to keep the Japanese in touch with their heritage. The idea of self-sacrifice and the belief that the individual existed to serve the Emperor and the nation was inherent in the *bushido* code. Diving a bomb-laden fighter or *Oka* into an enemy ship was an ideal demonstration of the spirit of the warrior. In the *Suicide Force Combat Methods Training Manual* (1945), the Inspectorate General of the Army Air Force asserted:

> The essence of a "TO" [kamikaze] Force is complete disregard of life. Its unique power in combat will be developed to the full by superlative skill in tactics and by a spirit which throws away life for certain death. Enemy vessels at anchor or under way will be sunk without fail by a reckless collision, thereby the plans of the enemy will be confounded and the way to the total victory of our army will be opened. The basis for victory of this kind of attack will depend absolutely on the spiritual strength of our flying personnel.[2]

The idea of committing oneself completely to the attack was not a new one in Japanese culture. In the traditional Japanese martial art of jujitsu the concept of *taiatari o kurawasu*, which meant to charge against the opponent with one's body, was well known. It implied that success in a fight would come from complete commitment to the attack. In the mid–1920s Capt. Yamaki, who later became Deputy Superintendent and Chief Instructor of the Kasumigaura Naval Flying School, wrote:

> They [the Americans] know nothing about the real strength of Japan's weapons. Then through that dreadful flack our gallant airmen, imbued with the spirit of Bushido, will pierce their way unwaveringly. Even though wounded by enemy bullets, they will stagger on, release their bombs and torpedoes and crash headlong on the enemy's battleships.... It can be assumed that America and Britain will endeavor to gain a victory by an all-out air attack on a large-scale. Japan therefore will make every effort to meet this attack by sending out an overwhelming number of airmen prepared to charge headlong and crash themselves on the decks of the enemy's ships.[3]

Many militaristic works were popular during the pre–World War II era and the emphasis on the *bushido* code was strong throughout the educational system. Eiji Yoshikawa's serialized novel on the life of the famous swordsman, Miyamoto Musashi, ran in the *Asahi Shimbun* newspaper from 1935 to 1939. It romanticized the life and ideals of Japan's samurai class and helped foster a military spirit in youth of the times. The modern conscript army was not the samurai class of old but it embraced its traditions proudly.

Education for Death

The changes in the Japanese educational system that were instituted shortly after the Meiji Restoration of 1868 became important factors in training the populace to accept a role that would make it possible for them to sacrifice their lives in the name of the emperor.

Early attempts to revamp the educational system met with resistance from those who feared that the Japanese would lose their national identity. This was further complicated by the fact that the Japanese had a number of different educational models from which to choose. Among them were the school systems of France, Germany, Russia, England, Holland, and the United States. Attempts in the 1870s and early 1880s to adapt the French and then the American models met with failure. It was reasoned that the systems of Western education were in conflict with Japanese traditions and any successful modernization of the education system would require that Japanese tradition and Western-styled modernization be melded. This was spelled out in *The Great Principles of Education* put forth by the Emperor in 1879.

Faced with the reality that Japan lagged behind the Western nations in her political, military, and educational development, the Japanese set out to adapt what was useful from the West. This led to a wholesale attempt to adopt Western thinking and was reflected in the curriculum of the schools. No centralized authority controlled the content of the curriculum and, in short order, a wide range of textbooks reflecting Western democratic thought appeared in the schools. The People's Rights Movement was seen as the major influence causing these changes. An alarmed Meiji government reacted to what they perceived as a threat and compiled a list of books that would be proscribed in the schools. The trend toward governmental control of the curriculum then gained momentum.

By 1885, the Japanese had begun to follow the highly centralized Prussian system. It was seen as a vehicle by which the state could effectively conduct a program of political socialization within the country which was based on traditional Confucian thought. The role of the state in the educational system would be to preserve tradition and foster an increased sense of nationalism in the face of Westernization. The beneficiaries of this system of education would realize that their role was to serve the state. By 1886, textbooks to be used in the schools had to be approved by Japan's Ministry of Education. From that point on state-approved texts became the norm.

The Imperial Rescript on Education (1890) was the next step in solidifying governmental control of the Japanese mind. That document, along with later government decrees such as the *Educational Reform of 1941 (Imperial Ordinance No. 1483)*, fostered militaristic outlooks and group cohesiveness. They would be useful tools of the Japanese government as it set about unifying the country. The Emperor became an ultimate authority figure imbued with religious sanction that was backed by Japanese tradition found in the sacred books of Shinto mythology, the *Kojiki* and the *Nihon Shoki*. Photographs of the Emperor were placed in each school. Annual ceremonies were conducted to reinforce the *Imperial Rescript* and develop an increased reverence for the Emperor and his line. In this manner, the education to which elementary and middle school children were subjected inculcated upon them a reverence for both Emperor and nation that could not be separated.

The outbreak of the Sino-Japanese War in 1894 accelerated the militarization of the curriculum. This received another boost in 1904 with the beginning of the Russo-Japanese War. Teachers in the elementary and middle schools stressed war and patriotic themes in their lessons. Among these was the concept that duty to the Emperor and nation were primary. Mathematics and science classes used military examples for their study. Jingoistic themes prevailed throughout the period and military indoctrination of the children was accomplished. As the years passed, the ethics classes that had stressed loyalty to both Emperor and nation soon began to emphasize devotion to the Emperor and his line above all else. By the end of World War I, forces were at work within Japan that would change the role of Emperor to one in which he would become the state.

In 1925, a new figure entered the Japanese school, the military officer. Military officers were placed in all middle and high schools and military training subjects were introduced into the curriculum. Students were required to participate in military drills for two hours each week. By the time that Japan attacked Pearl Harbor, this had increased. Writer John Morris reported, "The amount of time devoted to military instruction is supposed to be about five or six hours a week, but 'special' periods of instruction are often added.... The military instruction included lectures on discipline and the merit of dying for one's country. There is also a certain amount of field work, which includes route marches of anything up to twenty-five miles."[4] Students were given instruction in bayonet fighting, the use of hand grenades and other modern military subjects. Additionally, students were required to attend a military camp for a week each year where more intense military training was accomplished.

Shigeo Imamura, who eventually became a kamikaze pilot, related how this worked:

> Another new subject for us was Military Training. Every boys' secondary school had retired army officers and non-commissioned officers on the faculty. In the first year we had mostly basic training: marching, handling of the rifle and the like. The rifles we used were Model 38 Infantry Rifles, the same ones used by the army. The training was very strict and in compliance with army regulations. On rainy days, the officers lectured to us in classrooms on bits of military history and strategies. We didn't necessarily like the training, but we all took it seriously as a matter of course. Speaking out against it in any way would have been interpreted as a traitorous act. In our fifth year, we were marched about an hour to the Matsuyama Regiment's shooting range to practice shooting with real bullets.[5]

He recalled that as early as the fourth grade there was a required class in ethics. Students were taught a series of lessons on nationalistic themes, which increased in detail and intensity as the students worked their way through the first phase of their education in primary school.[6] By 1937,

> schools at all levels in Japan could not be and were not immune to the rising national and international tensions. Young children were told to finish breakfast early, assemble at certain spots in their neighborhood and march to school in formation. Secondary school boys were made to wear military-style leggings when coming to school and to salute any military officers they might pass on their way.... In short, schools became semi-army camps, in form and in atmosphere.[7]

Forward-looking recruiters for the kamikaze programs extended their searches for candidates. Teruyuki Okazaki recalled his days as a student at Kurata Middle School in Nagaoka City on Kyushu. Okazaki entered the school in 1941 at the age of 10. In 1943, the curriculum became militarized under the control of the army. Students there were taught military tactics to be used against an American invasion force. This included how to attack a tank by jamming an explosive pole charge into its side. Another method involved hiding in a spider hole until a tank passed over. The student would then pop up from the hole in which he had been crouching and set off a mine under the tank. Both methods involved the death of the student.[8] Older students were screened for kamikaze pilot training and, at the age of fourteen, Okazaki began elementary training in the *Tachikawa Ki-9*. Nagaoka City had a small army airfield on the side of town and the student pilots were taken there for flight training. Training consisted of practicing take offs and diving on targets. No attempt was made to teach the prospective pilots to land; the instructor took over and brought the plane down. The youth of the students made it easy for them to accept the role of kamikaze pilot; for them it seemed a glorious way to serve their country. The number of training hours was limited by the availability of fuel and also by the danger from patrolling American fighter aircraft, particularly during 1944–1945 when Okazaki undertook flight training.[9]

By 1911 training in traditional martial arts such as kendo and judo had been introduced into the normal and middle school curriculum as electives. Their popularity increased in the 1930s and, by the outbreak of the war with the United States, kendo was a requirement for students in the fifth grade and above.[10] The martial arts were seen as important vehicles through which the martial spirit and sense of self-sacrifice that would be required of the students once they had reached draft age would be achieved. An emphasis on spirit was the result of the realization that Japan lagged behind the Western powers in material strength. To compete, the Japanese emphasized the importance of spirit in winning battles. In that manner, they justified their expanding role in wars that had become increasingly dependent on mechanization and scientific advances.

The *Tachikawa Ki-9 KAI Army Type 95-1* Medium Trainer Model B aircraft carried the Allied code name "Spruce." NARA 80G 169925.

Shigeo Imamura recalled that, upon entering Matsuyama Middle School, students were required to participate in a one hour class of either judo or kendo every other week, a practice that continued throughout their middle school experience. By the end of the three year period many of the students had achieved black belt rank.[11]

In addition to indoctrinating children into the war effort, the Japanese went to great lengths to convince the general population that war was necessary and desirable. Increasing control of the media by the military was a part of Japanese society in the 1930s. By the time of the Pearl Harbor attack, the military had virtually complete control of the newspapers,

Japanese middle school boys practice sword techniques using the wooden practice sword (*bokken*). NARA 306-NT-1155-L-2.

Top: In this photograph, taken on 28 October 1936, elementary school girls practice sword techniques with wooden practice swords to encourage their "Japanese spirit." This type of training became the norm for physical education classes in the 1930s. NARA 306-NT-1155-I-6. *Above:* Japanese college girls visit the Headquarters of the 3rd Infantry Regiment in Tokyo for rifle training. This photograph was taken on 19 May 1934. NARA 306-NT-1156-A-9.

Top: School girls were also required to participate in military training drills. NARA 306-NT-1156-A-8. *Bottom:* Students rest after a military style march on 31 May 1934. This was a regular part of the military preparedness regimen in Japanese schools. NARA 306-NT-1156-A-12.

1. The Development of the Samurai Class and Its Ethos 15

magazines, radio and movies. Numerous laws authorized this control and it became the conduit through which war propaganda was funneled to the populace. Most of the people possessed a minimal education and were unsophisticated with regard to international relations and domestic politics. The propagandists put forth false information about non-existent victories, minimized the reporting of losses and generally led their citizens to believe that the war was going well. As the end drew near and even the least sophisticated Japanese became aware of the destruction visited upon their homeland, the propaganda told them that part of the problem came from their lack of effort and patriotism and they were urged to work harder and keep their martial spirit in readiness for the final battle.[12]

Shortly after the official beginning of the kamikaze corps in the Philippines in October 1944, the Imperial Headquarters Naval Information Department released a propaganda article to the newspapers praising the kamikaze flyers and submariners and urging the workers to emulate their sacrifice. It stated:

> And so, you who strive day and night on the ramparts of production behind the guns must remember that even one plane more is a sacred plane which rushes to destroy the enemy, when that one plane has aboard the sacred spirit of a master of the KAMIKAZE Force. The young eagles of the KAMIKAZE Special Attack Force who dare to dash headlong and happily to the destruction of the enemy are waiting anxiously for that plane to fly to the front lines, saying to themselves, "I too shall go." So it is, the brave, ruddy-faced warriors with handkerchiefs tied about their heads at peace in their favorite planes, sailing happily as if gathered to the fond bosoms of their mothers and the forms which dash out spiritedly to the attack along a path of assault from which there is no return, do they not appear vividly before us? Increase production! Stand firm! Drive on![13]

2. Kamikaze Traditions

Kamikaze Rituals and Traditions

Kamikaze pilots, prior to their take off, participated in a number of rituals and ceremonies, designed to both bring them success in their missions and provide an opportunity to express their feelings to the families and friends they were leaving behind. They included the wearing of various articles of clothing and adornment, some of which allowed the kamikaze pilot to have remembrances of his loved ones with him at the time of his death. Among these were the headband (*hachimaki*), thousand stitch belt (*sen-nin-bari*), and mascot dolls (*masukotto ningyo*). Many of the kamikazes carried swords with them, some of which were family heirlooms and some that had been presented to them by their unit commanders. In some cases other items were carried in the plane that were somewhat unique. As an example, the ashes of Lt. Cmdr. Tsutomu Kairya, who had been killed during the training of the Thunderbolt Corps, were placed in a white silk pouch and carried by Lt. Kentaro Mitsuhashi on his *Oka* mission on 21 March.[1]

Death Before Dishonor

The view of Americans toward the Japanese who participated in special attacks is varied. There is a certain respect of the adversary based on the assumption that, as a group, the kamikazes would perform acts that most Americans would not. There were several factors that influenced the Japanese military men and made them capable of committing themselves to the ultimate attack. They were: (1) tradition and group values, (2) a sense of obedience to higher authority and (3) peer pressure.

Throughout the long history of Japan, the samurai class had a great influence. Although the traditional class structure had been abolished during the Meiji Restoration, the ethos of the samurai was carried forward into the new conscript army. Education in the pre-war era included military drills and martial arts education. The values of the Japanese in the twentieth century became imbued with archaic ideas that placed the Emperor and state first and subjugated the will of the individual to group consensus. When asked to volunteer for a kamikaze mission, it was virtually impossible for the individual pilot to go against what he perceived as group approval of the mission. For the Japanese military man to question or disobey higher authority was unthinkable. Throughout his basic military training, he had been subjected to punishment for even the slightest infraction of the rules. It had been drilled into him time

Japanese Navy Lt. Kentaro Mitsuhashi salutes as he receives his orders for the ill-fated *Oka* mission of 21 March 1945. The silk pouch carrying the ashes of Lt. Cmdr. Tsutomu Kariya hangs from his neck. Photograph courtesy the Naval History and Heritage Command. NH 73095.

and again that orders must be obeyed without question. Japanese as individuals sought the approval of their peers more so than those living in western cultures. Conformity was valued over individualism and the nail that stuck up was hammered down. It was not acceptable to go against the perceived beliefs or values of the group. As a result, Japanese pilots, sailors, and infantrymen accepted the idea that their lives belonged to a power outside themselves which was free to use it as it saw fit.

Hachimaki and Robes

The *hachimaki*, or headband, was frequently a part of the kamikaze's wardrobe. These originated with the samurai who tied them around their heads in order to keep hair and sweat out of their eyes during battle. Adm. Soemu Toyoda, Commander in Chief of the Combined Fleets, reinforced the tradition for the kamikazes when the first *Oka* mission was flown on 21 March 1945. He inscribed the words "Thunder Gods" on fifteen *hachimaki*, which were then given to the *Oka* pilots. Occasionally these headbands were inscribed in blood. Navy Lt. Yasuo Ichishima wore one on his mission on 29 April; it had been given to him by a friend.[2]

Reports from American fighter pilots indicated that on at least one mission Japanese suicide pilots wore white robes. One pilot from the carrier *Bennington* reported:

> Almost as soon as I opened fire the Jap pilot opened the cockpit cover. Another burst from my guns apparently killed him. I saw him slump forward, head down. A white material flowed from his person and streamed in the wind. It appeared to be an Arab-type robe with large sleeves. As I came up beside him and flew wing on his plane I could see the robe type suit flowing a foot

A pilot fastens a *hachimaki* around the head of his comrade. This photograph was taken in late 1944 or early 1945. Photograph courtesy the Naval History and Heritage Command. NH 73096.

behind him in the wind. I could not see his head.... It is possible that the robe suit had a white hood attached but of this I could not be certain. Then I saw another trio of ZEKES. I started for one head on.... The Jap pilot was wearing an outfit similar to the first pilot.³

Thousand Stitch Belt

The *sennin-bari*, or thousand persons' stitches, was another good-luck item worn by the kamikaze, as well as by other members of the military. This was a white cloth about four to five inches wide with a thousand stitches in red thread. On each end were cotton strings that could be used to fasten it tightly about the pilot's waist. Each stitch had been sewn on by a different person, indicating their wishes for the success of the pilot on his mission. Usually this was produced by a family member who asked the help of friends and other family members in obtaining the stitches. Each pilot wrapped this long cloth around his waist. On occasion, they sewed two five-sen coins into the *sennin-bari*. The value of each coin was one more than four. Four in Japanese is read as *shi*, which also means death. Accordingly, the superiority of the number five brought good luck as it was more than the death number.

Shigeo Imamura recalled that on his last visit home his mother presented a *sennin-bari* to him as he was preparing to return to base. It had been produced by a young woman named Michiko, who was a family friend.⁴

As he prepared for his kamikaze mission on 9 August 1945, navy Lt. (jg) Tohimasa Hayashi, of the Shinpu Special Attack Unit, wrapped a *sennin-bari* around his waist that had been sent to him by his mother. Flight PO 2d Class Tomio Matsuo did also. On 21 March he wrote, "I am going, but I am not feeling lonely because I have the *haramaki* (stomach-band) which mother made to protect me."⁵ Although these *sennin-bari* did little to protect their wearers from enemy aircraft or anti-aircraft barrages put up by the picket ships, they did have another function. According to Richard J. Smethurst they "did serve to comfort the soldiers, however, and made them feel that loved ones and friends in the community cared for them."⁶ Still other items of cloth might be worn. Japanese flags might be inscribed with good

In this 1937 photograph the girl on the left is adding a stitch to a "thousand stitch belt" on the Ginza in Tokyo. Such belts were worn as good luck omens by Japanese military men as they went to war.

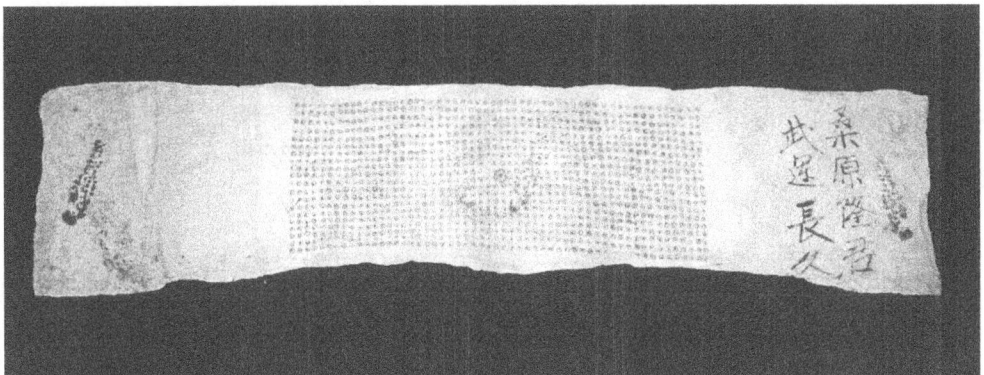

A *sennin-bari* from World War II. A five sen coin is sewn into the center of the belt. The inscription on the right reads *Kuwahara Takashi-kun*, the owner's name. To its left is the slogan *bu-un-cho-kyu* or "eternal good luck in war." This *sennin-bari* is from the Teri Jane Bryant collection. Photograph courtesy Teri Jane Bryant.

luck messages from family and friends and given to the pilot at the last family meeting. These were frequently carried on the mission, as well as smaller flags that were sewn to the uniform.

Dolls

Kimono-clad dolls were sometimes stitched to the pilot's uniform or attached to his belt to bring good luck. Referred to as *masukotto ningyo* (mascot dolls) or *imon ningyo* (keepsake dolls), they were hand-made by Japanese women and sent to servicemen. It was considered that they had a spirit of their own and would bring good luck to the kamikaze pilot. The harshness of the pilot's life left little room for beauty or anything that reminded him of the softer side of life. A doll kept as a mascot in the pilot's quarters and carried in the kamikaze plane was a reminder of the better things in life. Some kept them as a memory of family members they had left behind. Particularly touching were the words penned by Lt. Masahisa Uemura to his infant daughter Matoko: "When you grow up and want to know about me, please ask your mother and grandmother. I have left my album for you to see.... I am going to take your doll with me as a charm to ward off any danger to my plane. This means that you are with me."[7] Still other dolls had been sent to the pilots to demonstrate the peoples' support of their efforts. Found in the wreckage of a kamikaze plane that crashed near *LCI(G) 567* on 8 April was a doll and a letter from schoolgirl Tsuko Miwachi. She wrote:

> Even the hearing of this name arouses a deep emotion. Of the acts of the American and British devils, attacking and surrounding on all sides our army, poor in material resources at this time of fierce decision in the war. We are raging at the unspeakable destruction. We also as students and laborers give help to the men. With a clear mind, daily to be able to rush forth to the destruction of the American ... is happiness. Of the spirit of the SPECIAL ATTACK FORCE, not stopping till it strikes! In this is the thought of the Gods I believe. I believe it is the lofty state of mind which will make an eternal future of great righteousness for the Emperor's sake. Ah, this time, thinking, "if I were only a boy." I grow more

A pilot climbs into the cockpit of his plane prior to the interception of a B-29 raid. Hanging from his harness are two *masukotto ningyo* dolls carried for good luck.

envious; when I think of making a mascot to send to the men of the SPECIAL ATTACK FORCE I am filled with a great happiness. With this mascot the fierce spirit which will crumble the enemy ships into small pieces boils passionately, positively attack! Can you bear defeat? The foolish rascals of America and Britain! I am in a mood to shout these things aloud. Since I made the "mascot" in this spirit, it is doubtless unskillful, but please sink the enemy ships together with the "mascot." This is my greatest request.

Soon the mascot will take off gaily with the SPECIAL ATTACK FORCE. What will this be but the greatest happiness? Though I myself am not in the attack, my spirit will be serving as a member of the SPECIAL ATTACK FORCE.

Be of good health. I pray for great war results.[8]

Superstitions

Although Japan had entered into a period of modernization after the Meiji Restoration of 1868, there was still an undercurrent of superstition that permeated Japanese thought. How much any individual soldier or sailor believed in good luck or bad luck is subject to question. However, it may be considered that those with lesser educations may have been more adversely affected by the concept. Certain days of the year were considered to bring bad luck. These were termed the *Jippogure* days.

> JIPPOGURE means that all ten directions are closed and dark. These ten directions are the eight horizontal directions and the up and down directions. The JIPPOGURE are the days when the ten signs of the Element Zodiac and the twelve signs of the Animal Zodiac clash and become dangerous for mankind.... They are considered the worst of all unlucky days and are sometimes called KURO-BI, or dark days, meaning that death is certain on these days.[9]

The dates listed as *Jippogure* days for 1944 were January 21, March 21, May 20, July 19, September 17, and November 16. For 1945 they were January 15, March 16, May 15, July 14, September 12, and November 11.

In addition to the *Jippogure* days, Japanese superstition held there were the *To Shi Bi*, or death days each year. In 1944, they were January 10 and 22; February 11 and 23; March 2, 14, and 26; April 3, 15, and 27; May 5, 17, and 19; June 6, 18, and 30; July 8 and 20; August 9 and 21; September 10 and 22; October 12 and 24; November 1, 13, and 25; and December 3, 15, and 27. In 1945, the days were January 4, 16, and 28; February 5 and 17; March 9 and 21; April 10 and 22; May 12 and 24; June 1, 13, and 25; July 3, 15, and 27; August 4, 27, and 28; September 5, 17, and 29; October 7, 19, and 31; November 8 and 20; and December 10 and 22.[10]

While some of the superstitions may have made the lower and less educated ranks uneasy, it did little to affect the planners in the high commands of the army and navy.

The Farewell Ceremony

Prior to leaving on their last flight, the kamikaze pilots participated in a farewell ceremony. Yukihisa Suzuki, a kamikaze pilot who survived the war, described the activity.

> I recalled the farewell ceremony at Himeji: Under the bright sunshine of April, all the personnel of the air base gathered in front of the airplane shed and waited for the arrival of the members of the Special Attack Corps from their rooms. In front of the sheds on a long table covered with a white tablecloth were various foods ready to serve in honor of their heroic departure and for the purpose of wishing them good luck: many bottles of sake, sake cups, dishes of dried cuttlefish, dried chestnuts, sea weed, and balls of rice with red beans....
>
> As we waited near the warming-up planes, our classmates appeared wearing new flight clothes on the back of which was painted a small national flag, a crimson disk on a white ground. They had green parachute belts. White silk scarves were around their necks. Some of them wore a white cloth around their flight helmets. Some had sprays of cherry blossoms which was the symbol of young and vigorous soldiers, especially young pilots, as the beautiful but fragile blossoms

A group of the earliest kamikaze pilots receives a ceremonial cup of saki from VAdm. Takajiro Onishi in late 1944. Photograph courtesy the Naval History and Heritage Command. NH 73097.

bloomed for only a few days and then fell just like the young men who died in their prime. Some had small dolls or other mascots hanging from their belts."[11]

Once the pilots had assembled near their aircraft, a senior ranking officer usually made a short patriotic speech praising their courage and devotion to the Emperor and the country. The officiating officer might be quite high in the chain of command, depending on the importance of the mission. When the first *Oka* attack took off on 21 March 1945 from Kanoya, Corps Cmdr. Okamura gave the speech and VAdm. Matome Ugaki attended to wish the attackers well. These speeches usually included the prophecy that they would all meet in the future at Yasukuni Shrine. As time wore on and kamikaze missions became common, fewer high officials attended. In the final stages of the battle for Okinawa, the speech was frequently given by the flight leader. The pilots drank a cup of saki and departed the field.

The Last Letter Home

Young men about to die had to say their farewells. In many cases they had seen their families for the last time somewhere in the few months preceding their missions. All felt inclined to leave their thoughts and wrote letters home advising their families not to worry, that they were willingly going to their fate. Mixed in with their philosophy of life and death were personal messages to fathers, mothers, siblings and friends. Frequently the pilot included nail clippings and locks of his hair with the letter. Some also included a whole finger or a part of one. These body parts could then be cremated and the ashes placed in the family shrine. During *Kikusui 4*, navy Lt. (jg) Akio Otsuka met his death on 28 April 1945 off Kadena. In his letter, penned the morning of his final mission, he wrote:

> Believing in the certainty of our victory in the Great East Asia War, praying for your happiness, and apologizing for all the deeds I did contrary to filial piety, I shall set off for the mission with a smile on my face.

Tonight there is a full moon. While viewing the moon over the shore of Okinawa's main island, we will search for the enemy, and will carefully strike once he is sighted.
I shall die very courageously and, you will see, thoughtfully too.[12]

The attitude of some was fatalistic. One of the Betty crewmen on the ill-fated 21 March *Oka* mission was Flight PO 2d Class Naokichi Kameda. He wrote, "A man will die sooner or later. The value of being a man is given at the time of his death."[13] Perhaps all of this was just bravado or perhaps he truly believed it. However, with their leader, VAdm. Ugaki, writing in his diary, "Oh, what a noble spirit this is!"[14] any self-respecting military man had to express similar sentiments. These letters, as well as all correspondence, were censored. Pilots writing to their families could not express their true feelings. After the war, Flying Officer Ryuji Nagatsuka wrote:

My only excuse was that I could not write down my true thoughts because I knew that these private memoirs would be read after my death, which would doubtless occur quite soon. Indeed, I considered them as a sort of testament, which I was keeping for my nearest and dearest, and so they contained only half-sincerities, carefully embroidered.[15]

Haruo Araki, an army officer who commanded the Eternity Air Unit which flew from Chiran on 11 May 1945, wrote to his wife Shigeko:

Tomorrow I will dive my plane into an enemy ship. I will cross the river into the other world, taking some Yankees with me. When I look back, I see that I was very cold-hearted to you. After I had been cruel to you, I used to regret it. Please forgive me.
When I think of your future, and the long life ahead, it tears at my heart. Please remain steadfast and live happily. After my death, please take care of my father for me.
I, who have lived for the eternal principles of justice, will forever protect this nation from the enemies that surround us.[16]

Yasukuni Shrine

Early in the Meiji Restoration, the government began to exercise increasing control over religion in Japan, with an eye toward making Shinto the state religion. However, the Japanese had long before combined elements of both Buddhism and Shinto in their personal beliefs and governmental attempts to place Shinto above Buddhism met with rejection. By 1877 the Japanese abandoned the effort and disbanded the Religious Ministry that had been instrumental in the program. Even attempts to control Shinto met with resistance and the government finally divided Shinto into what they termed Shrine Shinto and Sectarian Shinto. The government would maintain control over Shrine Shinto and use it as a means to foster allegiance to the Emperor; they held that it was the bearer of the true Shinto traditions. Shinto shrines were under the control of the local, prefectural or national government, which would maintain them and control their affairs. Tying all this together was the *Imperial Rescript on Education* (1890) which identified the shrines as the center of Emperor worship. Governmental officers officiated at each of the shrines, with Ise, Kashiwara and Meiji shrines among the most prominent in the celebration of Emperor worship. Hachiman shrine, which celebrated the god of war, was also one of the most important.

On Kudan Hill, near the Imperial Palace in Tokyo, sits the revered Yasukuni (Peaceful Country) Shrine. Established in 1868 to commemorate those who gave their lives in the struggle to build a new nation, it is the meeting place for the spirits of Japan's war heroes. In 1879 it came under the authority of the Ministries of the Army and Navy. Shinto mythology held that the spirits of Japanese warriors who die in battle are linked eternally to the shrine. They reside there as god-like figures who guard the Empire and are the pillars upon which the nation rests. By the early 1930s, as Japan engaged in war with China, the shrines took on increasing importance. The annual day of celebration at the shrine became a national holiday

Children gather at Yasukuni Shrine to honor their fathers and brothers who died in the war with China. This photograph was taken in the late 1930s. NARA 306-NT-1156-C-28.

Japanese airmen frequently paid their respects at local shrines prior to making their last sortie. In this photograph, four pilots perform a ceremonial bow at a shrine. This photograph was a staged re-enactment of the ceremony taken in November 1945 for the USSBS film *Strategic Attack*. NARA 342-FH-3A-3250.

and the military encouraged school children, their parents, and teachers to attend the ceremonies. Celebrations to honor the war dead were held regularly at Yasukuni and morning prayers for victory were a daily occurrence. The Emperor or his representative made regular visits with donations for the upkeep of the shrine.

In the last days before their final missions, kamikaze pilots often referred to their meeting at Yasukuni. Farewells by kamikaze pilots and speeches by their leaders frequently advised them that they would all be together there at some point in the future. Common last words between kamikaze pilots and their squadron mates often mentioned the eventual meeting.

Japanese Pilots' Thoughts and Reflections on Kamikazes

It is logical to question the motives and feelings of those Japanese airmen who were willing to sacrifice their lives in the service of their country. Generals and Admirals claimed that the men were proud to die for their country and that, rather than committing suicide, they were committing themselves to the destruction of the enemy. According to Lt. Gen. Masakasu Kawabe, Commanding General of the General Air Army, "No matter how you look at it, everyone who participated in these attacks died happily in the conviction that they would win the final victory by their own death."[17] This may have been the view from above, but it was not necessarily shared by the pilots themselves. Writings about the kamikazes in English have not presented an accurate view. Many of their writings, such as the work by Rikihei Inoguchi, echo the philosophy of the officers who sent the men to their deaths.[18] Others' writings selectively quote from diaries and letters sent by *Tokko-tai* pilots that demonstrate their disillusion with the program.[19] Recent scholarship by Emiko Ohnuki-Tierney has shed new light on the process by which young men were convinced that participation in the special attack program was acceptable.[20] According to her, they were the victims of a carefully orchestrated government propaganda program that utilized the cherry blossom as a symbol of both nationalism and their youth.

Among the Special Attack Corps pilots were many who felt that the mission was a great honor and that it was the best course of action. Labeled as *kichigai* (madmen) by their fellow pilots, these fliers lived for the mission. To them there was no better way to express loyalty and the *bushido* code than by crashing their plane into an enemy ship. One of these men, Yoshi Miyagi, whose kamikaze plane was shot down on 19 May 1945, wrote of his pride in the corps and the role that it played in the military traditions of his country. He rejected the American notion that it was suicide and asserted that Special Attack Corps pilots were motivated by patriotism and idealism.[21] Navy Lt. (jg) Takuji Mikuriya of the Shinpui Special Attack Unit, asserted that they would die happy, having given their lives for their country.[22]

Others fell into the category of *sukebei* (liberals). These pilots were also willing to die for their country but viewed the Special Attack Corps as a last resort rather than a preferred method of combat. Hachiro Sasaki, a member of the Showa Special Attack Unit, evidenced still another, more pragmatic, philosophy. According to him, it was a matter of fate. He had been born Japanese and the role assigned to him in life was a responsibility to be accepted.[23] Sasaki went down off Okinawa on 14 April. *Oka* pilot Keichi Itoh of the 722nd Tornado Corps, reasoned that he was going to die in the war. If that were to be the case, he was consoled by the fact that he would be making a contribution.[24] Yasuo Ichijima, a member of the Special Attack Corps who died piloting his plane in late April 1945, wrote:

> I cannot believe that I shall die within a week. I feel neither depressed nor nervous.
> When I try to imagine what my last moments will be like, everything seems like a dream. I am not sure whether I will remain as calm as I am now when the time comes, but it seems to me that it ought to be easy.[25]

Some airmen were not opposed to flying such missions but remained realistic about their chances for success. Yukihisa Suzuki described the special attack planes as being in such poor condition that they would have a difficult time completing their missions. In addition to flying antiquated aircraft, the kamikaze pilots also had to fly through large numbers of American fighters just to reach their targets. The intense anti-aircraft fire from the ships made it nearly impossible to crash into one. He was willing to go but not optimistic about his chances for a successful mission. He referred to the obsolete and poorly maintained Kate which he was assigned to fly as a "miserable coffin."[26]

Others openly resented the decision to use the Special Attack Corps as a weapon. Flying Officer Fujisaki, prior to flying his Sonia from Chiran at the end of April 1945, wrote his last letter home. He accused the military leaders of "incompetence and stupidity,"[27] and claimed that they were exploiting the patriotism of the young pilots. Lt. Yukio Seki was more realistic. He told his compatriots that he flew his upcoming suicide mission from Mabalacat for his wife, not his Emperor.[28]

It has been frequently asserted that all Japanese kamikaze pilots were volunteers, but not all researchers seem to agree on this point. In an article on kamikazes in *Air Power History* (1996), Professor Shogo Hattori asserted that there is evidence that "in the last few months of the war about one third of them were not volunteers."[29] Yukihisa Suzuki reported the words of his fellow pilot, Lt. Kawashima who stated: "I won't volunteer to be a member of the Special Attack Corps, but if I am selected and am obliged to go, I'll do the best in my power. But I don't want to die. As I was born a man, I want to die as a man."[30]

When asked if the pilots who flew kamikaze missions had volunteered, Superior Pvt. Guy Toko answered, "I never knew any."[31] He did, however, indicate that there were many who did. He and one friend, both of whom were university educated, did not want to volunteer. According to him, the volunteers were mostly from those who had attended military schools or who had very little education.

Maj. Gen. Miyoshi, Commanding General of the 30th Flying Group, indicated that the early kamikazes were all volunteers, but that later "it was made compulsory and that was bad."[32] The first army kamikazes in the Philippines were mainly officers from the Army Air Academy. At Okinawa they were mainly non-commissioned officers (NCOs) who were ordered to become kamikazes. He claimed that they were not good pilots.

Perhaps the most coherent explanation of why pilots volunteered for kamikaze missions was expressed by 1st Class PO Takao Musashi, a member of the 105 Fighter Flying Unit on Cebu Airfield in the Philippines. Musashi stated that

> no JAP pilot would volunteer for such a mission of his own free will, yet if volunteers were called for, practically all pilots would volunteer. He explained by adding that no JAP would question an order, and signified that the matter would be put to them in such a way that no one would dare to do other than put his hand up. Apart from this, if a pilot did not volunteer, his life would be made unbearable by other pilots.[33]

At the Tokyo detachment of the Kasumigaura NAC, Lt. (jg) Shigeo Imamura was working as a flight instructor when the decision was made to organize a special attack unit from the base's pilots.[34] After the commanding officer announced that there was to be the formation of the unit and that married pilots, only sons, or oldest sons were exempt, he paused for a few seconds and then asked for volunteers.

> There was a big thud. It seemed like just about everyone stepped forward, cadets as well as instructors. I was among them. It seemed that I gave no consideration to the fact that I was the first son of the Imamura family. As a matter of fact, I don't think I gave consideration to anything. At the command, my body moved forward automatically. To volunteer to die for the country seemed to me the only right thing to do. Was I scared? No, not at all.[35]

Families of the pilots of the Special Attack Corps were justifiably proud of their sons, brothers and family members who had made the supreme sacrifice, however, not all were satisfied that the government had used them wisely. Many felt that it was a waste of patriotic young men, and others were harshly critical of those who had ordered their loved ones to their deaths. Those who had served and survived remembered their comrades with special feelings since they were the only ones who could understand what they faced.

For those left behind, emotions ran the gamut from pride to a feeling of waste. Kunihei Kobayashi, whose son Tsunenobu had died as an *Oka* pilot, wrote "How completely empty it all was!"[36] In a letter written on 6 January 1951, Motoji Ichikawa, a surviving member of the Thunderbolt Corps, wrote:

> The souls of the young men will never be able to rest in peace no matter how much the creators of the Special Attack Forces tactics acclaim the gallant deeds of the dead. They took the utmost advantage of the young men's sincere desire to sacrifice themselves upon the alter of their country's cause by covering their eyes and stopping up their ears.[37]

With so much dissension among the Japanese pilots, it is easy to understand how the Americans could fail to comprehend the kamikazes' motives. For the American sailors on the ships and the pilots flying combat air patrol over their stations, the motives of the Japanese were hard to fathom. Sonarman 2/c John Huber, who served on the destroyer *Cogswell*, reported his feelings on the *Oka*:

> Rumor has it that the Nips are using something like a flying torpedo, called a "Baka" bomb. It takes one man to operate it. It is released from a heavy high flying bomber and the suicide pilot aims it at a ship. Those guys must be nuts.[38]

Long after the war ended, many of the Americans who served on the radar picket stations at Okinawa were able to reflect on the situation. It was not infrequent to hear words of respect for the kamikazes. As Bob Rielly, Quartermaster on *LCS(L) 61* put it, "Those were brave men."[39] Sailor Charles Brader, on *LCS(L) 65*, summed up the experience from American eyes:

> They came in droves daily, sometimes hourly. And they were shot down in droves. Only on rare occasions did the Kamikazes get through our defenses to crash with explosion and burning slaughter into one of the ships at Hagushi or Buckner Bay [Nakagusuku Wan].[40]

No matter how Americans viewed it, it was still difficult to understand. Sonarman 1/c Jack Gebhardt, who was on the destroyer *Pringle* when it was sunk by a kamikaze on 16 April 1945, said: "It was horrifying to try and comprehend someone intentionally diving through a hail of deadly anti-aircraft fire with the sole purpose of killing themselves in a blinding explosion."[41] As a final note, Japanese historian Saburo Ienage later wrote: "Legions of promising young men were sent off to meaningless deaths."[42]

Japanese Bodies

After a kamikaze attack had taken place there was usually a period of time during which the American ships' officers could assess the performance of their crews and the enemy, repair equipment, care for the dead and wounded, and search for bodies. On some occasions, the bodies of kamikaze pilots were recovered and examined for information. The light minelayer *Aaron Ward* reported:

> It appears that at this time a description of the Japanese Kamikaze pilot, his personal equipment, apparent skill and tactics is in order. (a) Equipment — Three bodies of pilots were recovered on board ship and thoroughly examined. They were all found to be very young, although the mutilated condition of the bodies was such that an exact estimate as to age was not possible. All pilots were definitely identified as males.

All pilots were wearing parachutes. As a matter of fact, the pilot of the first plane shot down off our starboard quarter, bailed out just prior to the plane's crash, was seen to catapult from the cockpit across the ship with his chute partially opened, and fall into the water, attempting to gather the shrouds of his chute together as he hit. The three pilots found on board were fully equipped, even to the extent of oxygen masks, still on the faces of two of them.

Pilots were carrying very few personal effects, except one, who had two booklets; one on suicide tactics and the characteristics of our own fire power, and the other one a personal notebook. These were turned in to the Office of Naval Intelligence and proved to be of value to their representative.[43]

It was not infrequent for American ships at Okinawa to find Japanese airmen floating in the ocean. Many of those airmen were from planes that had accompanied the kamikazes on missions as escorts or guide planes and had either bailed out of their planes or crash-landed in the water. In some cases they were taken alive, but others killed themselves before being taken aboard. On 5 May, the light minelayer *Henry A. Wiley DM 29* spotted a Japanese flier in the water. As the ship approached to capture him, he removed his life jacket and slipped beneath the waves rather than be captured.

3. Special Attack Aircraft

In the beginning stages of the kamikaze program, front line fighters were the primary types of aircraft used in the special attacks. At Mabalacat, Philippines the first kamikaze aircraft were Zekes in good condition flown by experienced pilots. Their successes led to an expansion of the program. With Japan's declining resources and her inability to train replacement pilots expeditiously due to fuel shortages, inexperienced pilots ultimately became the cutting edge of the kamikaze sword. The planes they flew were not the best; those were reserved for the more experienced pilots and saved for defense of the homeland. Appearing in the skies over the Allied ships were a variety of army and navy types. Some were current models in poor condition; some were obsolete types, while still others were trainers. Interestingly enough, some of the trainers had good success at Okinawa. Their fabric over wood frame construction made them hard to detect on radar, and the proximity fuses used in the U.S. Navy guns would not detonate near them as they would with metal aircraft. The most commonly used planes in the special attacks were the Val, Sonia, Tony, Kate, Oscar, Dave, Pete, Nate, and older Zekes, as well as trainers such as the Willow and the *Shiragiku*. The attributes of the kamikaze aircraft varied so greatly that gunners on the ships might face anything from an incoming *Oka* piloted bomb making 450 knots to a Willow trainer doing eighty knots.

Oka Program

Although many aircraft were used for suicide missions against the American ships, none had been specifically designed for the task. Zekes and other aircraft mentioned above, loaded with extra bombs, were the main type of kamikaze encountered by the Americans. However, one airplane was designed as a suicide plane from the beginning, the *Oka* or Cherry Blossom.

By mid–1944, the situation was becoming desperate for the Japanese and naval officers began to consider new methods of driving off the Americans. One of them, Lt. (jg) Mitsuo Ohta, developed the concept of the piloted bomb. Ohta was a transport pilot with the 405th Kokutai and was not an experienced aeronautical engineer. Ohta brought his plans to the Aeronautical Research Institute at the University of Tokyo where he received expert help in its design. These were refined and the plans were presented to the *Dai-Ichi Kaigun Koku Gijitsusho* (First Naval Air Technical Arsenal) at Yokosuka in August of 1944. There Lt. Cmdr. Tadanao Miki, head of the Futuristic Aircraft Design Section, was called in to examine the plans. At first Miki rejected the idea, believing that the guidance system of the plane was to be based on current technology, which was not effective. He was shocked when Ohta described the ultimate guidance system, a human pilot. Miki refused to consider the idea but, when Ohta volunteered to pilot the plane himself, he realized that the concept was viable. Later, when the Americans became aware of the plane and the nature of its mission, they gave it a new name, the *Baka* (fool). Since higher authority was supportive of the project, Miki turned it over to his engineering team. Under Masao Yamana, Tadanao Mitsugi, and Rokuro Hattori, the design was refined and a prototype made ready. By the end of September, 1944, ten *Oka Model 11*s were ready for flight. Testing proceeded for the next four months, but production began before the trials were completed. A total of 755 *Oka Model 11*s were built prior to the beginning of the assault on Okinawa.

The *Oka* had a very limited range and had to be carried to the target by a mother plane, usually a Betty bomber, although other types were capable of the task and sometimes used. Since it weighed nearly two tons, the *Oka* cut the range of the mother plane and its speed. The range of the Betty was normally about 2,000 miles. With the *Oka* on board it would be about a quarter of that, and the Betty's maximum speed declined from 230 to 140 knots. Its maneuverability was also affected. As soon as a mother plane came under attack, the first thing it did was to jettison the rocket powered craft in order to save itself. American aircraft action reports indicate that this was done frequently.

At least a dozen *Okas* were captured on the first day of the invasion of Okinawa. Some showed damage sustained during the initial onslaught. However, one perfect example was shipped to the Technical Air Intelligence Center at Anacostia, Maryland for testing. The Division of Naval Intelligence reported:

> The theoretical maximum horizontal range of BAKA [*Oka*] when released at 27,000 feet is 55 miles. Fifty-two of these miles would be traveled at a glide speed of 229 miles per hour and at a glide angle of 5 degrees 25 minutes. During the remaining three miles, the use of rockets would accelerate the speed to 535 miles per hour in level flight with a corresponding increase in speed as the diving angle was increased.
> At a 50 degree or greater diving angle, maximum speed would be 618 miles per hour....
> In attacking ships protected by heavy deck armor, it is presumed the rockets would be used at the end of the run in a torpedo approach in order to score a close to the water line hit. If launched from a distance, however, BAKA would be vulnerable to attack by fighters before reaching a position to effectively complete its own attack. Lacking maneuverability, BAKA could take but little evasive action in its unpowered glide and its only method of escape would be to fire one or more of its rockets. In this event, and also in the case of BAKA using its rockets at the start of the glide, the increased velocity secured from the rocket would dissipate before BAKA could reach its target and its final terminal velocity would be substantially decreased.[1]

In addition, the canopy on the *Oka* studied at Anacostia could be jettisoned, leading the TAIC to speculate that it might have been designed for training or testing.

The *Oka* had a wingspan of 16' 5" and length of 19'10". Its fuselage was constructed of aluminum alloy and the wings were made of stressed-skin plywood, with a fabric covering. After dropping from the mother ship and gliding an appropriate distance, the pilot would ignite the *Oka's* rocket engines and hurtle toward his target. The 2,645 pound warhead was packed with trinitro-anisol, a high explosive which would detonate upon impact with the target vessel. Igniting the engine at the correct time was vital, since a high speed at impact was desired in order to penetrate the hull of larger warships.

Recruitment for the *Oka* program began in August 1944. Volunteers were solicited from all naval units, and from them was formed the 721st Naval Air Corps. The navy did not accept sole surviving sons, elder sons or those with only one surviving parent. Applicants who had families dependent on them were also not accepted. In addition, there were specific skills that

Angle of Dive (Prior to Levelling Out)	Terminal Speed in Dive (Initial Speed Level Run) mph	Horizontal Range from 27,000' Glide miles	Level Flight Impact Speed after Firing Rockets			Horizontal Distance Travelled Under Rocket Power (S.L.)			Total Horizontal Range
			1 Rocket	2 Rockets	3 Rockets	1	2	3	
5°24'	230	52.0	350	455	535	0.6	1.3	2.3	54.3
30°	280	9	375	465	535	0.75	1.6	2.6	11.6
45°	325	5	400	475	535	0.75	1.75	3.0	8.0
60°	365	3	430	500	535	1.0	2.1	3.4	6.4
70°	420	1.8	475	520	535	1.0	2.3	3.8	5.6
80°	535	0.9	535	535	535	1.7	3.4	5.1	6

The above chart shows speeds for the *Oka* piloted bomb at various angles of attack.

had taken many hours of flight time to develop. Pilots skilled at dive bombing and torpedo bombing were not accepted because it would take too long to replace them.

The 721st transferred from Konoike Naval Air Base to Hyakurigahara Naval Air Base on 7 November 1944. Six hundred volunteers were selected for the unit and placed under the leadership of its commander in chief, Cmdr. Motoharu Okamura. Spirit was high among the men and within a short time they had taken the name of *Jinrai Butai* (Divine Thunderbolt Corps) for themselves. Lt. Cmdr. Goro Nonaka was appointed as the Chief Flight Officer.

Pilots who volunteered for the *Oka* program found that their training was limited. *Oka* pilots did most of their training in the Zeke. After they had completed enough flight hours to solo, they were given practice in the glide procedure. This consisted of flying a Zeke to a high altitude and then gliding it downward toward the field at a 7:1 angle, which approximated the glide path of the *Oka*. During the dive, the engine was throttled down to make the glide more realistic. To give the pilots additional experience an *Oka* glider, the K-1 model, was developed. It had no engine and used water ballast to represent the weight of engines and explosives. A retractable skid was used to land the glider after the pilot had slowed its speed by jettisoning the water ballast. Usually each pilot was allowed two or three runs in the training *Oka* and then had to practice further in a Zeke.

Lt. Cmdr. Ohira, a test pilot attached to the Yokosuka First Naval Air Technical Arsenal, assisted in the training of *Oka* pilots. According to him, the air speed at which the *Oka* was released from the mother plane was crucial; it had to be close to 140 knots. Speeds greater or lesser than that could result in a collision between the *Oka* and the bomber. He also noted that the release altitude had to be at a 7:1 angle to the target.[2]

It is frequently assumed that pilots of the *Okas* and other suicide planes were of like mind, that they all volunteered for the duty and willingly went to their deaths. In actuality, the pilots had differing views. *Oka* pilot and commander of the 3rd Cherry Blossom Squadron,

Marines inspect a captured *Oka* Type 11 at Yontan Airfield, Okinawa, 11 June 1945. NARA 80G 323641.

An *Oka* unpowered trainer shown after the war. Water ballast was used in place of the heavy explosive charge and jettisoned just prior to landing. The skid was used in place of wheels. NARA 80G 193349.

The *Oka* Model 22 was powered by a turbojet engine. The air intakes for the jet may be seen on the side of the fuselage. NARA 80G 193444.

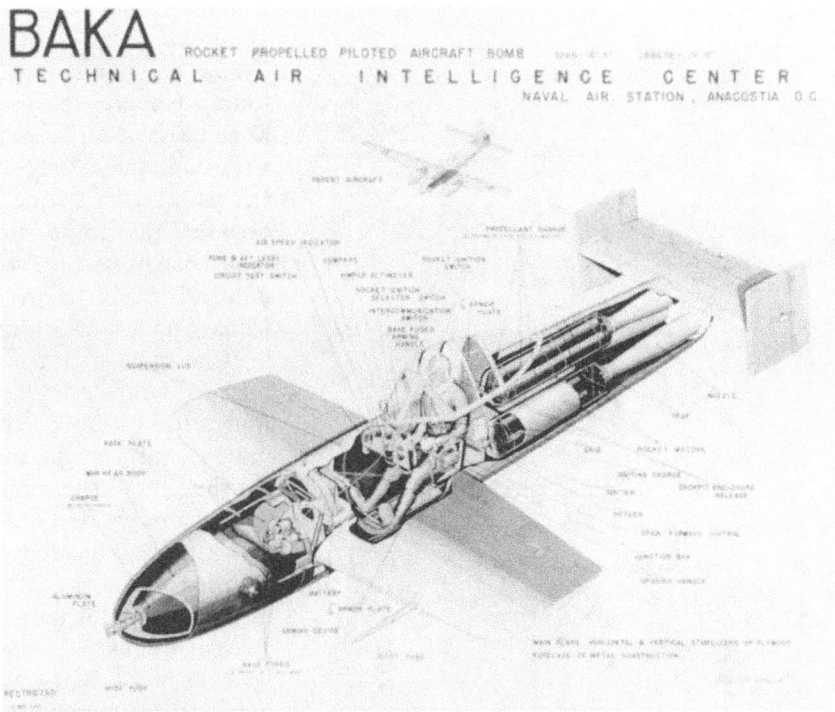

This technical drawing of the *Oka Model 11* from the Technical Air Intelligence Center in Anacostia, D.C. was based on the *Oka* captured at Yontan Airfield during the invasion of Okinawa in April 1945. NARA 80G 192694.

721st Naval Air Corps Lt. Morimasa Yunokawa, described himself as awestruck when he first saw the *Oka*.[3] Yunokawa survived the war, never having had the experience of flying the rocket plane into an enemy ship. Others, however, were not so awe-inspired by the prospect of flying it. Another pilot, Masazo Okubo, questioned whether the Imperial Japanese Navy had deluded itself. He doubted that the *Oka* had the ability to make a decisive contribution to the Japanese war effort. If the rocket plane were truly the super weapon that the Japanese high command claimed, he could have accepted the mission. His view was that the *Oka* program was not significant and that his death would be a waste.[4] Flight Chief PO Konichi Okabi claimed that suicide pilots preferred an *Oka* assignment over conventional types of kamikaze aircraft. According to him, "In discussing the type of duty most preferred, all trainees come out for duty in the BAKA-bombs [*Oka*]. Second choice was any sort of duty which offered an opportunity to go out on a suicide attack."[5]

When the situation in the Philippines grew steadily worse for the Japanese, it was decided to use the *Oka* against the American forces there. Fifty *Oka Model 11s* were loaded on the new aircraft carrier *Shinano* for transport to the Philippines, departing from Tokyo on 28 November 1944. However, she was intercepted by the American submarine *Archerfish* and sunk by torpedoes 138 miles southeast of Honshu. With her went the plans to send the Cherry Blossom Squadrons into action in the Philippines.

Re-deployment of the squadrons began at the end of January 1945, with some assigned to the Naval Air Bases at Izumi and Miyakonojo. Their final destination would be the base from which they would launch their attacks. These bases included Tomitaka, Usa, Oita, and Kanoya Naval Air Bases. First Lt. Akira Hirano remained at Konoike Naval Air Base to begin a new unit, the 722nd Naval Air Corps. Like the Divine Thunderbolts, this corps also gave itself a nickname, the *Tatsumaki Butai* (Tornado Corps). From January until mid–March 1945, the Cherry Blossom Squadrons prepared for their destiny. With American Task Force 58 operating 360 miles to the south of Kyushu, it was determined that an *Oka* attack was in order. The 1st Cherry Blossom Unit reported to Kanoya on 21 March in preparation for the mission. Taking off at 0945 that morning were eighteen Betty medium bombers carrying fifteen *Okas*. Fifty-five Zekes accompanied the bombers to fly cover. Shortly after taking off, a number of the

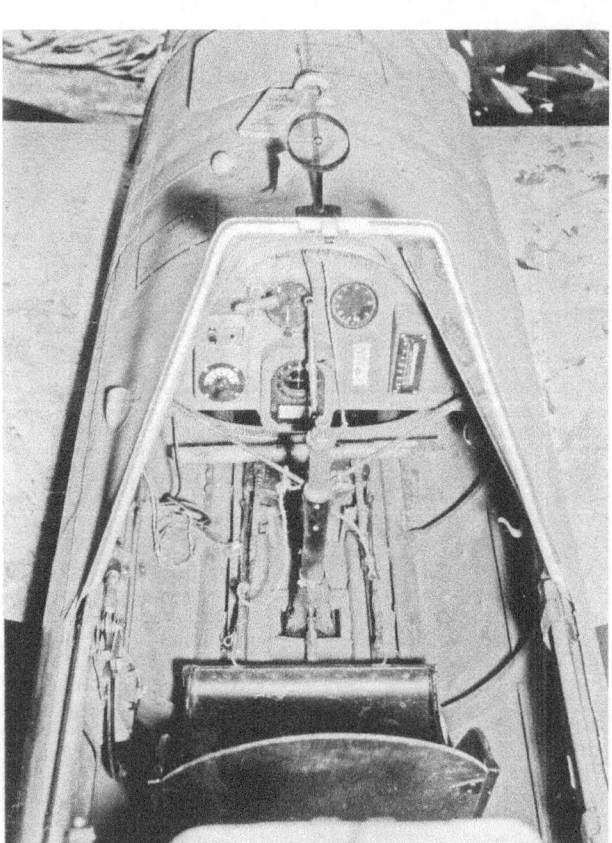

The piloted bomb had few controls as its function was simple. Ten minutes was probably the maximum flight time as it hurtled toward its target. NARA 342-FH-3A-3211.

The scene at Kanoya, just prior to the ill-fated mission of Lt. Cmdr. Goro Nonaka on 21 March 1945. Nonaka led the flight of eighteen Bettys, fifteen of which carried *Okas*. They were all shot down by carrier fighters from TF 58. To the right is Nonaka's banner which reads *Hi-Ri-Ho-Ken-Ten*, an acronym for a historical saying dating to the fourteenth century. For a further discussion see Naito, page 70. Photograph courtesy the Naval History and Heritage Command. NH 73101.

Japanese crew members of the 721st Naval Air Corps relax prior to taking off in their Betty bomber. Underneath the bomber is an *Oka*. The photograph was taken at Kanoya Naval Air Base in early 1945. NARA 80G 90097.

This series of photographs was taken from the gun camera of an American fighter. It shows a Betty carrying an *Oka* as it is being shot down. NARA 80G 185585. These photographs were shot on 1 April 1945 and probably show the first use of an *Oka* at Okinawa. At the time, the reports indicated that the Betty was carrying a *Henschel 293*. See National Security Agency *"Magic" Far East Summary # 389.* 13 April 1945, B-3.

fighters developed problems with their fuel pumps and had to return to base, leaving only thirty Zekes to protect the bombers. Leading the attack was Chief Flight Officer Lt. Cmdr. Goro Nonaka, a flamboyant and experienced squadron leader who commanded the bombers. His plane did not carry an *Oka*. Since this was the first attack of the new piloted bombs, VAdm. Matome Ugaki came to the field to see them off. *Oka* pilots penned their last words and boarded their bombers. Typical were the words of Flight PO Ataru Shimamura who wrote: "I shall fall, smiling and singing songs. Please visit and worship at Yasukuni Shrine this spring. There I shall be a cherry blossom, smiling, with many other colleagues. I died smiling, so please smile. Please do not cry. Make my death meaningful."[6]

At about 1400, the light carrier *Langley* picked up the incoming attack when it was eighty-five miles northwest of the task force. With such a large raid approaching, 150 fighters were ordered aloft. Hellcats from VF-17 and VBF-17 off *Hornet* and VF-30 Hellcats from *Belleau Wood* intercepted them sixty miles out. The fighter planes were soon joined by other Combat Air Patrol (CAP) planes, bringing the total number of American fighters at the scene to twenty-four. Burdened by their heavy cargo and making only 110 knots, the Bettys stood no chance. Ten minutes into the battle eleven of them had been shot down. The others jettisoned their *Okas* in a desperate attempt to escape, but of the total flight of forty-eight fighters and bombers, only two badly shot up Zekes made it back to Kanoya.

Hellcats from VF-30 reported that "when attacked, the enemy bombers, and their low fighter cover, dove and headed north, while the high cover came down on our fighters. As soon as the enemy force was attacked the fighters deserted the BETTYS, despite their large numerical superiority, leaving the bombers to shift for themselves as best they might."[7] With so many planes in the air, confusion reigned. American reports claimed that the raid consisted of twenty-four Bettys and about twenty-four fighters flying cover. With so many aircraft in the air, conflicting claims for shoot downs were inevitable. CTG 58.1 claimed that a total of twenty-six Bettys, twelve Zekes and two Jacks had been shot down, with another two Zekes, a Betty and a Tony damaged in the melee. The reports assert that Ens. W. H. Smith, Jr., from VF-30 shot down three of the Bettys and Ens. J. V. Reber, Jr., got two Bettys and two Zekes. Squadron mates Lt. (jg) H. W. Sturdevant and Ens. J. G. Miller each shot down four fighters. Lt. (jg) Murray Winfield of VF-17 was credited with four and one-half Bettys. Pilots from VF-86 reported shooting down eight Bettys and several Zekes. Ship and squadron action reports described it as a "turkey shoot." The raid had come no closer than thirty miles from the ships.

The next attempted use of the *Oka* came during the battle for Okinawa. On 1 April 1945, six Bettys with *Okas* departed from Kanoya Airfield. Among the *Oka* pilots was Flight Chief PO Keisuke Yamamura. The Betty in which he was flying was shot down near Okinawa by an American fighter and crashed in the water after jettisoning its *Oka*. Yamamura survived and later found that only one of the six Bettys had made it back to base after becoming lost.[8] No American ships were hit by *Okas* on that date. From that point on, a number of missions were launched from the bases on Kyushu with a few successes and many failures. Gradually, the number of trained pilots diminished and the plan to replace them with an entirely new unit was scrapped. The 722nd Naval Air Corps, which had been formed in January of 1945, was not quite ready, and selected members of the three hundred man corps were sent to the Divine Thunderbolts as replacements.

As the months wore on, it was painfully obvious that the battle for Okinawa was not going well for the Japanese. They decided to keep their *Okas* in reserve for the anticipated assault on the homeland. Komatsu Naval Air Base on Kyushu became the new home of the Divine Thunderbolt Corps, with some units going to Matsuyama West Naval Air Base on Shikoku. With the end of the battle for Okinawa came the last flight of *Okas* from Kanoya. Participating in *Kikusui* 10 from 21 to 22 June were six *Okas* carried by Betty bombers. The mission was led by Lt. (jg) Toshihide Fujisaki. Two of the *Oka*-carrying Bettys made it back to base, unable to complete their mission. The four remaining Bettys with *Okas* fell victim to Marine Corsairs. Of those, one made it to Radar Picket Station No. 15A, where it was shot down by fighters from VMF-224. The other three were shot down near Radar Picket Station No. 16A by VMF-314.

After recognizing that they were facing a new weapon, American navy leaders began to evaluate the *Oka*. They noted that its extreme speed of 400 to 600 knots and small control surfaces limited its maneuverability. In the early part of the Okinawa campaign, the *Oka* attacks seemed to have been coordinated with attacks by other aircraft. This was designed to distract the ships' lookouts so that they missed the *Oka's* approach. One of the warning signs was the appearance of Betty bombers flying at a high altitude and then turning away from the ships at a distance of about five miles. No standard approach was noted with *Okas* coming in at an angle or skimming the water.

In practice, the most difficult part of the mission was probably delivering the *Oka* to an area near enough to launch it. The Betty was not capable of flying very fast or well with its payload. Once it neared the target area, at about 20,000 feet, the *Oka* pilot climbed into the rocket glider and prepared for launch. When the mother plane was ready to drop the *Oka*, it signaled to the pilot: "dot dot dot dash dot (*o-wa-ri-ma-a-a-ku*), this is the end."[9] The *Oka* was then released from the mother ship and fell several thousand feet, picking up speed on the way down. As it leveled out and headed toward the target ship, the pilot ignited the rocket engines to increase the impact speed. The most crucial time to intercept the *Oka* was during the initial drop, before it had picked up enough speed to outrun American fighters.

Having identified the new enemy weapon, the Americans began to consider various strategies to combat it. Since the *Oka* could not turn easily, a ship might avoid being hit by radical maneuvering. Adjustments to the VT fuses could also be made, with settings to compensate for the rocket plane's speed. Gunners would probably have a greater chance of hitting an *Oka* if they relied on tracers rather than trying to track it with their Mark 14 sights.

Most reports on the use of the *Oka* indicate that it was carried by Betty bombers. Early in the Okinawa campaign 1st Lt. Dewey F. Durnford, Jr., of VMF-323, encountered a Helen carrying an *Oka* thirty miles north of Ie Shima and shot it down.[10] On 4 May 1945, pilots of VC-90 reported one carried by a Dinah near Radar Picket Station No. 12. In all likelihood, the parent plane was not a Dinah. Allied intelligence reports at the beginning of the Okinawa campaign had indicated that any of the Japanese medium bombers could probably carry the *Oka*.[11] Later reports stated that "a Sky [*Ten*] Air Force order of 7 July discloses that the Japanese are planning to use the twin-engine bomber Frances as a mother plane for *Baka* [*Oka*]. The order directs the commander of Air Group 762 to use 12 plane crews to form a suicide attack unit which will include about 9 Frances 'capable of carrying' *Baka* [*Oka*]." In addition, tests were being carried out with the Peggy medium bomber as well.[12] Some models of the Peggy and Frances had dorsal turrets, however, the *Mitsubishi Ki-67-I Hiryu* (Peggy) probably bore the closest resemblance to the *Mitsubishi Ki-46-II* (Dinah), but was nearly twice the size. The Dinah was just too small an aircraft to carry the heavy *Oka*. It seems obvious that the pilots misidentified the mother plane.[13]

By this time, American intelligence had studied the *Oka* closely. It was evident that the piloted bomb could be carried by any of the medium bombers with some modifications to the parent plane. They concluded:

> In addition to BETTY, the following aircraft are believed to be suitable for launching BAKA or could be made satisfactory without major modifications:
>
> PEGGY 1 — Satisfactory. May need extended tail wheel.
> HELEN 2 — Possible. Would need longer tail wheel assembly or cut in bomb bay for horizontal stabilizer. (A recent report indicates that BAKA may also have been launched from HELEN).
> SALLY 2 — Possible. Would need extended (back) bomb bay and longer tail wheel assembly.
> TAIZAN — 16 Exp. Land Attack Plane. Expected successor to BETTY and could undoubtedly be used. May be in limited production.
> RITA 11 — Possibly more than one BAKA.
> FRANCES 11 — May carry modified version of BAKA.[14]

During the period of the Okinawa campaign, between 18 March and 22 June 1945, American forces encountered a total of fifty-seven *Okas*. Of these, forty-two of the mother planes were shot down before they could launch their deadly cargo. Four of the rocket powered gliders actually hit American ships, but only one sinking was achieved when the destroyer *Mannert L. Abele* was hit on 12 April. Two of the *American* reports might not have been accurate. American intelligence speculated that the mother planes may have been carrying torpedoes, not *Okas*.[15]

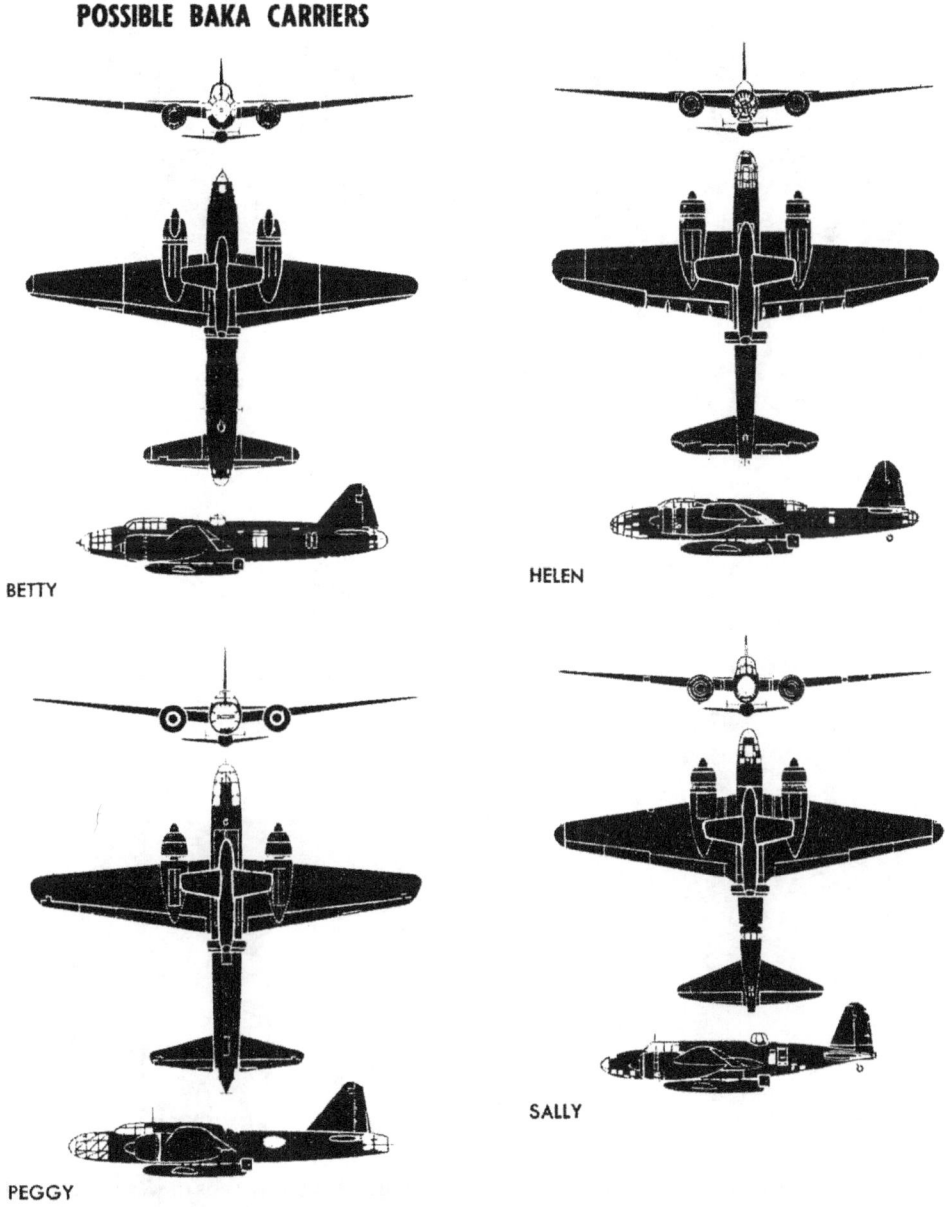

By May of 1945, the Allied forces had encountered the *Oka* piloted bomb and identified several planes as possible carriers. Among them were the bombers Betty, Peggy, Helen, and Sally. War Department — Navy Department *Recognition Journal*. Number 22, June, 1945, p. 5.

Last Chance Weapons

The *Oka* was not the only potential rocket powered aircraft. As early as April 1945, the Japanese were experimenting with rocket units added to Zekes in order to increase their speed as they approached targets in their suicide runs. They found that it was too difficult to mount them in the plane's fuselage; however, two small rocket units, known as *Funshinki*, might be mounted under the wings. Test results showed that "although there is a loss of speed of about

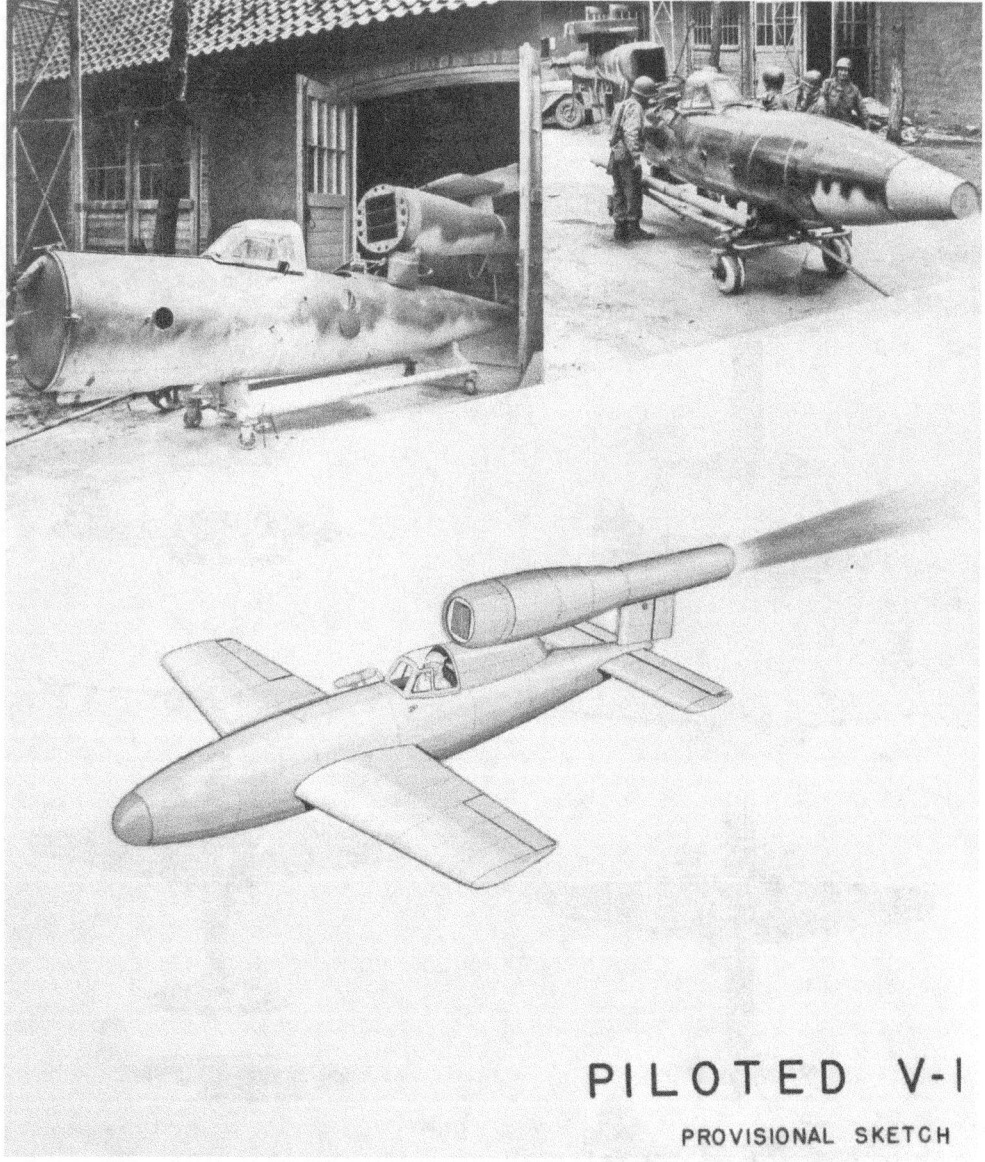

One of the special attack weapons under development at the end of the war was the *Kawanishi Baika* (Plum Blossom). This was to be a manned version of the German V-1 buzz bomb that plagued London during the war. It was in the last stages of development when the war ended. This model was found at the end of the war and taken to the Technical Air Intelligence Center in Anacostia, D.C., for study. The wingspan was 18'10", LOA 26'3", and the fuselage length 24'3". NARA 80G 400870.

The *Nakajima Ki-115a Tsurugi* (Sabre) was designed as a low cost kamikaze plane for defense of the home islands. Although 105 were produced by the end of the war it never became operational.

five knots when they are not in operation, there is about a 30-knot gain in speed at an altitude of 6,000 meters when they are put into operation."[16] During the Okinawa campaign, there were no reported uses of such rockets on Japanese special attack planes.

Had the war continued and had Japanese production not been severely hampered by American air attacks, the *I-Go* guided bomb, under development, might have replaced the *Oka*. Two models of this were being tested, with warheads of 660 and 1,760 lbs. The mother plane, a Peggy or Lily, released the rocket bomb at about 5,000 feet and then guided it by radio control to the target. Difficulties with the guidance system and army opposition slowed its development.

The Japanese were also in the process of adapting the German V-1 "buzz bomb" for their own uses. Their version, called the *Baika* or Plum Blossom, was still under development at war's end. This was to be a piloted version used in suicide attacks.

Japanese army planners took a practical approach to the problem. Recognizing that additional special attack planes would be needed in the defense of the home islands, they consulted with the Nakajima company on the production of a new airplane that was specifically designed for kamikaze attacks. Their initial charge to the company was on 20 January 1945. This plane would be known as the *Nakajima Ki-115 Tsurugi* (Sabre). Specifications called for an airframe that could mount a variety of engines, giving the Japanese the flexibility to use whatever was at hand. Cheap, rapid production was the goal, and the new aircraft was to be capable of carrying a single bomb at a good rate of speed. Lightness would be achieved by using a wood structure and dispensing with the added weight of guns and landing gear. The landing gear would be jettisoned after take off since there would be no use for it. For training purposes the aircraft was fitted with a crude set of landing gear which made ground handling characteristics problematic. The *Tsurugi* was to have a top speed of around 342 miles per hour with a range of 745 miles. This would be sufficient to fly from the home islands against any American invasion force. It would carry a single 1763 lb. bomb. Poor handling and flight characteristics slowed production of the aircraft and by war's end only 105 had been produced, none of which became operational.[17]

4. Development of the *Tokko-tai*

Kamikaze History and Development

Although kamikaze actions by Japanese fliers became well known during the battle for the Philippines, there had been isolated incidents of special attacks prior to the fall of 1944. Pilots whose planes had been damaged beyond repair and who had no chance of making it alive back to their base sometimes attempted crash dives into enemy ships. These were individual actions and decisions and not official Japanese military policy. Ens. Sadeo Nakamura, a member of the 293rd Naval Air Unit at Nichols Field in Manila, asserted:

> These attacks were made when pilots knew that escape was impossible, as for instance when parts of structures were shot off or the airplane was in flames. They would then attempt to ram ALLIED airplanes or ships, damaging them as much as possible, rather than crash uselessly. These attacks depended on the feelings of the individual pilot at a given moment.[1]

Japanese fighter ace Saburo Sakai further claimed that this sort of action was an "unwritten convention"[2] that was practiced by all pilots, be they Japanese, American, German, or British.

Early examples of such actions were fairly well-known in military circles, although they were singular in nature and not an organized program. According to Capt. Mitsuo Fuchida, one such incident took place at the battle of Midway. As the attack progressed and the Japanese carriers *Akagi*, *Kaga*, and *Soryu* were destroyed, only the *Hiryu* remained operational. Lt. Cmdr. Tomonaga, commanding the air group on *Hiryu*, made preparations for take off. According to Fuchida:

> Before the take off, one of the gas tanks of his airplane was found to have been punctured by a shell hit received in the first attack. However, because of the pressing need for immediate tactical action there was no time to repair it. Moreover, since there was enough fuel for a one-way flight, he took off for the torpedo attack with his plane in that condition. He did not leave any word behind as he took off, but it was fully surmised that he had silently resolved to make his a suicide attack.[3]

There are no U.S. Navy records indicating a kamikaze attack on American shipping that day.

The first recorded successful kamikaze attack came on 26 October 1942 when the destroyer *Smith DD 378* was hit during the Battle of Santa Cruz. She was part of Task Force 61, which included *Enterprise CV 6*, *South Dakota BB 57*, *Portland CA 33*, *San Juan CL 54*, *Porter DD 800*, *Conyngham DD 371*, *Shaw DD 373*, *Cushing DD 797*, *Preston DD 795*, and *Mahan DD 364*. At 0800 the task force was maneuvering to allow *Enterprise* to launch her aircraft. *Cushing* and *Smith* were providing anti-submarine screening. At 0944 radar picked up incoming enemy aircraft and the ships began to take evasive maneuvers. Japanese torpedo bombers plagued the ships between 0944 and noon. At 1148 the ships fired on and hit a Kate. The gunfire set the plane afire. In all probability its pilot realized that he would not survive and chose *Smith* as his target. *Smith's* action report details the attack:

> At 1148 a flaming Japanese torpedo plane dived from slightly abaft the starboard beam, hit the shield of Gun Number 2 and crashed on the forecastle deck port side and abreast Gun Number 1. There was an immediate flash and the forward part of the ship was enveloped in a sheet of flame and smoke apparently caused by the bursting of gasoline tanks. The major portion of the fuselage fell over the side, passed to port in flames and sank astern. At 1149 abandoned the bridge.[4]

Firefighting commenced, but at 1153 a large explosion took place which spread small fires over the decks. These were soon extinguished. In order to prevent additional ammo from cooking off and her magazine from exploding, the forward magazine was flooded. She approached *South Dakota* and the battleship was able to help extinguish her fires. At 1212 the four forward torpedoes were jettisoned to prevent them from exploding and the ship began to make headway, resuming its screening duties. About that time twenty more dive bombers attacked the task force, but *Smith* had survived the crash and was not damaged further. She suffered twenty-eight dead and twenty-three wounded. Although the concept of a kamikaze attack was unknown to Americans at the time, later reports described this attack as such.[5]

In the fall of 1943 and for about a month at the beginning of 1944, Lt. Col. Koji Tanaka, a staff officer of the Imperial General Headquarters, surveyed the situation in New Guinea.

Smith DD 378 explodes as she is hit by a kamikaze during the Battle of Santa Cruz, 26 October 1942. American documents claim that this is the first kamikaze attack on an American ship. NARA 80G 33333.

Damage to *Smith DD 378*'s turret is in evidence as she refuels from *South Dakota BB 57*. NARA 80G 20675.

According to him, the army air units there suffered from a lack of operational aircraft, which was caused by continual difficulties with the Type III Tony Fighter, the training of replacement pilots, and command and infrastructure problems. In an effort to stop the constant raids, some Japanese army pilots had resorted to crashing their planes into American B-17s and B-24s. The use of these special attack methods by the army began in 1943 and lasted into the spring of 1944. For example:

> Sgt. Ono, attached to the 8 Air Div. and assigned to escorting convoys crashed his plane into an enemy B 17 north of MADANG, NEW GUINEA, causing the enemy plane to crash and thus accomplishing his mission of protecting convoys. In the latter part of May 1944, four fighter planes under the command of Maj. TAKATA of the 5 Air Regt. decided to crash into an enemy vessel off the southern shore of BIAK and sink it. It was believed that three of the four planes crashed into the enemy destroyer, and the remaining one was believed missing.
>
> The above two incidents were formally reported by wire to the Imperial General Headquarters and the War Ministry by the Army commander of that area, and it is believed that rewards were given.[6]

Although Takata's flight came close to the American destroyer *Sampson DD 394*, the results were not as successful as the Japanese reported. Takata's flight consisted of four twin-engine Nicks escorted by five Oscars. In the early evening of 27 May 1944, about 1641, *Sampson* was covering the landing area on Biak Island when she was attacked by four single-engine fighters which came in from the East. One was shot down by the ship and one by shore fire. Almost simultaneously with the first attack, a second attack came in from the northeast at treetop height. This raid consisted of the four Nicks led by Takata. They strafed the beach and dropped bombs which missed the nearby LSTs. The lead plane, probably Takata's, was shot down and crashed close to the LSTs and a second was shot down near the jetty. The third plane passed over the ship and 20mm and 40mm fire from the destroyer hit an engine and set it afire. The damaged plane circled and made a run on the *Sampson*, but heavy fire from the ship shot off part of one wing and the plane passed over the bridge, narrowly missing it. It hit the water about 400 yards off the destroyer's starboard side, spreading flames onto *SC 699*, which was cruising nearby. The fourth plane was driven off.

On board the sub-chaser, commanding officer Lt. (jg) J. W. Foristel watched as the third plane circled and headed for his ship. After it was hit by fire from several ships, the plane's left wing hit the water about thirty yards off the port side. The Nick bounced off the water and struck the ship near the water line, starting a raging gasoline fire which enveloped the central part of the ship and reached to mast height. Eighteen men where either blown overboard or jumped, including the commanding officer. Confusion made it difficult to determine what had happened. *Sonoma* came alongside and assisted in putting out the fires. Two men were killed, including William H. Harrison RM 2/c who was killed when the plane hit his 20mm gun station. Harrison's body was found still in his harness. He had fired his gun until the end.

Tanaka returned to Japan and reported his findings to the highest echelon of the Army and recommended that the use of special attack operations be considered. Philosophical disagreements sprang up among the top army officers. The discussion centered on whether or not special attack tactics and squadrons should be under a mandate from the Imperial Army or whether they should be strictly volunteer. Both the Inspector General of Aviation, Gen. Korechika Anami and his deputy chief, Lt. Gen. Torashiro Kawabe, felt that they should be strictly voluntary. After conversations with Maj. Gen. Shuichi Miyazaki, the Chief of the First Bureau, General Staff Headquarters, it was decided not to order army pilots to engage in special attack training.[7] Shortly thereafter, in July 1944, the army "Aviation Inspector-General sent a letter to all flight school superintendents requesting a list of special attack volunteers be submitted. (A similar letter was sent from the War Minister to all air group commanders.)"[8] Within a short period of time the army had selected fifty volunteers. Bomber pilots trained at Hamamatsu and Hokoda Army Flight Schools and the fighter pilots at Hitachi and Akeno Army Flight Schools. The following month, another sixty volunteers were accepted for special attack training and the program began to grow. By fall of 1944, the army pilots were still undergoing training, but the navy had also been considering special attacks. The program was initiated by the navy using regular pilots who were asked to volunteer.

Japanese sources frequently credit RAdm. Masafumi Arima as the inspiration for the beginning of the suicide attacks at the Philippines. Arima commanded the 26th Air Flotilla which was based at Manila. On 15 October 1944, he decided to lead a strike against American carriers near Luzon, an unusual undertaking for an officer of his high rank. Japanese reports claim that Arima crashed his Zero into the carrier *Franklin CV 13*, but this is unlikely. Neither *Franklin* nor the other carriers in the American force were hit by kamikazes that day.

The official beginning of the Japanese Navy's kamikaze units came on 19 October 1944 when VAdm. Takijiro Onishi toured the base of the 201st Air Group at Mabalacat, Philippines. Onishi had just been appointed commander of the First Air Fleet and recognized that Japan's position in the war was tenuous. He suggested to the air group's leaders that suicide crashes were their only chance to defeat the enemy. Within the hour the determination had been made to use this extreme attack method and twenty-seven members of the 201st volunteered for the mission. These men were not poorly trained beginners but were ranked among the best pilots in the air group. Lt. Yukio Seki, a graduate of the Naval Academy, was selected as their leader.

What took place at Mabalacat was a new strategy, one that would plan, organize and coordinate this attack method. A new strategy was timely after the loss of 1,500 Japanese airmen in the Marianas. With so many capable pilots gone, it would not be possible to replace them in a short space of time.

The First Shimpu Special Attack Corps, having been formed at Mabalacat, soon went into action. They consisted of four groups, the *Asahi, Shikishima, Yamato,* and *Yamazakura* Units. On 21 October 1944, the corps began conducting unsuccessful sorties over the ocean searching for American ships. On the morning of 25 October 1944, at about 0730, six Zekes and their four escorts from the *Asahi* and *Yamato* Units found RAdm. Thomas Sprague's group of escort carriers off Samar. About the same time, Seki led the *Shikishima* Unit's five bomb-laden Zekes and four escorts off the field at Mabalacat and, at 1045, spotted another carrier group under RAdm. Clifton Sprague. Their attacks were successful and one carrier was sunk and several others damaged. With the success of these attacks in the Philippines, Onishi's strategy was validated. From this point on, the use of special attack units would be given serious consideration in any operation.

The experiences of the Japanese during the Philippines' campaign demonstrated that the use of kamikaze planes was a viable alternative. It had proven to be the most effective attack method, with a high percentage of hits on American vessels. Of the 650 suicide missions flown during the Philippines' campaign, nearly 27 percent were deemed successful.[9] Part of this success may be attributed to the use of the Zeke. Its good speed and maneuverability gave it an advantage over the many obsolete types that would be flown on the missions at Okinawa. In addition, the first of the kamikaze pilots were veterans with significant flying skills. This would stand in sharp contrast to the kamikaze pilots utilized during the Okinawa campaign, many of whom had only basic flight training.

One might question how the Japanese expected to win the war by the use of such tactics. By the time the American forces invaded Okinawa, it was obvious to the Japanese that the possibility of victory had vanished and that it was only a matter of time before the home islands were targeted for invasion.

VAdm. Takajiro Onishi. Photograph courtesy the Naval History and Heritage Command. NH 73093.

What did the Japanese high command hope to accomplish by sending its young pilots to certain death? When faced with catastrophic losses, they had few options. In an interview conducted by the Americans at the end of the war Capt. Rikihei Inoguchi, of the Tenth Air Fleet, discussed the program's goals. Inoguchi had been present at the inception of the kamikaze program in the Philippines. He asserted that the Japanese never expected to win the war using such methods. What was possible, however, was the achievement of acceptable conditions for its termination. If the Americans were to sustain unacceptable losses from the special attack units, then they might be willing to end the war with terms more favorable to the Japanese.[10] Lieutenant Col. Naomichi Jin, who served as Chief of Liaison Staff in the Thirty-Second Army Intelligence during the battle for Okinawa, identified four reasons for the adoption of kamikaze tactics:

1. There were no prospect of victory in the air by employment of orthodox methods.
2. Suicide attacks were more effective because the power of impact of the plane was added to that of the bomb, besides which the exploding gasoline caused fire—further, achievement of the proper angle effected greater speed and accuracy than that of normal bombing.
3. Suicide attacks provided spiritual inspiration to the ground units and to the Japanese public at large.
4. Suicide attack was the only sure and reliable type of attack at the time such attacks were made (as they had to be) with personnel whose training had been limited because of shortage of fuel.[11]

Propaganda value was certainly a consideration. Capt. Katsuo Shima, head of the propaganda section of the Naval General Staff, instituted a program that was aimed at convincing the Allies that the Japanese would commit national suicide rather than surrender. The Special Attack Corps was held up as an example of what the Allies could expect. In addition, Japanese news sources wrote compelling stories of the heroism and successes of the kamikaze pilots. In their desperation, the Japanese desire for a weapon that would end the American threat overrode their common sense. The impetus toward further development of the kamikaze concept was spurred on by exaggerated reports of their early success. Civilian workers on the home front were encouraged to emulate the sacrifice of the kamikazes in their daily tasks. If men could willingly go to their deaths for the nation, surely workers at home could be expected to make great sacrifices as well. Pilots committing themselves to the ultimate sacrifice could also look forward to a reward. Almost from the beginnings of the kamikaze campaign in the Philippines, the pilots were given posthumous promotions. At first these were only one-rank promotions but soon a two-rank promotion became the norm.

One of the curiosities of the kamikaze experience was the appearance of a small number of Koreans among the ranks of the *Tokko-tai*. Crewmen on the destroyer *Luce* picked up a Korean pilot after they had shot down his plane. He indicated that he was a farmer who had been drafted into the military and forced to become a kamikaze pilot.[12] The Japanese had been accepting Koreans for military service since 1938 and began drafting them in April of 1944. According to some sources, eleven Koreans eventually became members of the *Tokko-tai*.[13] Among them were Capt. Kim San Phil, 2d Lt. Tak Kyon Hyen and Sgt. 1st Class Park Ton Fun, all of whom are honored at the Yasukuni Shrine and the Chiran Peace Museum.[14]

Okinawa and the *Ten Go* Campaign

In order to achieve maximum success against the American invasion of Okinawa, it was imperative that both the Japanese army and navy cooperate. Although both branches drafted plans for the joint venture, the army plan was adopted. Col. Ichiji Sugita, former Operations

Staff Officer at Imperial General Headquarters, would later claim that "the Navy took an extremely negative and indifferent attitude in formulating the *Outline of the Operations Plan of the Imperial Army and Navy* in January 1945. The new operations plan was formulated with the agreement of the Navy only after enthusiastic suggestion by the Army."[15] This was also the case with the planning for the *Ten Go* Operation. Capt. Toshikazu Omae, who served as Planning Section Chief, Naval General Staff during that period, later reported:

> The actual condition of the Navy's air strength at that time (especially from the viewpoint of training) regrettably would not allow the Navy to participate in the OKINAWA Air Operations which were expected to occur in March or April. The Navy generally desired to avoid the hitherto gradual attrition of semi-trained personnel and did not wish to engage in operations at OKINAWA and other fronts, much less the homeland, until about May, by which time it would have accumulated sufficient fighting strength.[16]

Although both branches of the Japanese military were committed to cooperate against the Americans at Okinawa, the planning ran into problems. Targets to be attacked by the army forces were convoys and troop carriers. These vessels were easier to hit and pilots required less training for the missions. By comparison, the navy targets were the carrier task forces, which were more difficult to attack and required greater flying skills. Japanese navy planning called for additional special attack training. According to Cmdr. Yoshimori Terai, former officer in charge of Air Operations, Naval General Staff, "From the beginning, air preparations (special attack planes) were not expected to be completed until the end of May. Although we desired to delay the American advance on OKINAWA through the Second TAN Operations (attack on ULITHI Base), but as a result of their failure, we were forced to face the Okinawa Operations unprepared."[17]

The situation was no better for the army. With the failure of the operations against Ulithi and the accelerated advance of the American forces toward Okinawa, the army was caught in the time trap as well. According to Japanese naval officers involved in the planning for *Ten Go*, "the preparations of the 6 Air Army were even more behind schedule than those of the Navy."[18] Still, cooperation between the branches was necessary. *Navy Directive No. 540* of 1 March 1945 detailed the extent of that cooperation.

The Army-Navy Joint Central Agreement on Air Operations

1. Policy

To destroy the enemy, who is expected to invade the East China Sea and the vicinity, with a display of the combined air strength of the Army and the Navy and at the same time to strengthen the direct Homeland defense. In order to execute the above-mentioned operations, emphasis will be placed on build-up and use of the special attack strength.

2. The principle of air operational guidance in each area:

a. Air operations in the East China Sea and the vicinity (Formosa, the Nansei Islands, Southeast China, Kyushu and Korea).

The Army-Navy air forces will immediately deploy in the East China Sea and the vicinity and destroy enemy invading units.

The chief targets for the Navy air forces will be enemy carrier striking task forces, and for the Army, enemy transport convoys. However, the Army will cooperate as much as possible in the attack against enemy carrier striking task forces.[19]

Navy Directive No. 513, issued by Adm. Koshiro Oikawa on 20 March 1945, spelled out the goals of the *Ten Go* Operation. Its first priority was the destruction of the American carrier task forces that had been attacking Japan. This was to be accomplished by the mass use of kamikaze aircraft, suicide boats, manned torpedoes, and midget submarines. A secondary target was the American invasion fleet operating in and around Okinawa. Of particular importance were the air bases on Okinawa. Should they fall into American hands, the security of the home islands would be further imperiled.[20]

Training Program for Naval Aviators

The selection process for naval aviators was extremely rigorous. After enduring the brutal discipline of recruit training, which included many physical beatings by petty officers, the new seamen were assigned to a ship or unit. Beatings there continued until the individual became a petty officer, then conditions improved a bit. Escape from the ranks of the common seaman was by application to a specialist's school and the passing of admission tests. In the late 1930s, this was the procedure for becoming a pilot. Students enrolled in the Naval Academy at Eta Jima also received harsh physical treatment, but not quite as brutal as that given to enlisted men.

Tsuchiura, located fifty miles northeast of Tokyo, was the site of a Navy Fliers School. There, selected members of the Imperial Japanese Navy underwent a rigorous program in flight training. Famous Japanese Navy ace, Saburo Sakai, reported that when he was accepted for pilot training in 1939, only seventy applicants out of 1,500 were admitted. Those selected were a mixture of graduates of the Naval Academy at Eta Jima, enlisted non-commissioned officers, and new recruits. Training there was even more brutal than basic training and other specialized schools. Daily regimens of wrestling, swimming, pole climbing, one-hand hanging for over ten minutes, gymnastics, springboard diving, and other forms of physical exercise were utilized to improve balance, coordination and spirit. Dismissal was possible at any time and Sakai reported that of his original class of seventy, only twenty-five graduated from the ten-month course.[21] These men became extremely talented and capable pilots. Once their training had been completed, the navy pilots were frequently referred to as *Umi no Arawashi* or Sea Eagles. This label was first used by Capt. Yamaki of the Kasumigaura Naval Flying School.

Another base used for pilot training was Mie Naval Air Station. Shigeo Imamura reported that in September 1943, 5,000 men were accepted into the Naval Air Reserve. Of this number, half were sent to Tsuchiura and half to Mie for basic training. After Mie, Imamura went to Isumi Naval Air Center and trained on the Willow intermediate trainer, a fabric covered biplane.

Yukihisa Suzuki, who underwent special attack training at Hyakurigahara Air Base, did his training in the same aircraft that would be used for the special attack mission. These were Nakajima B5N2 torpedo bombers (Kate). Fuel was in short supply and the amount of training time severely limited. Suzuki reasoned that it did not matter much as the flight was one way. Taking off and being able to fly the plane would be sufficient. While at Hyakurigahara, Suzuki and his fellow cadet officer pilots experienced the same type of brutal discipline that was common in the training procedure. On one occasion, following a day of mediocre practice, the student pilots were lined up in several rows. After the chief flight instructor had expressed his disappointment with the training, he left and four of his assistants took over. They upbraided the cadets for several minutes and went through the ranks, punching each in the face several times. Those who staggered or fell were beaten more severely, either by punches to the face or by being beaten with sticks. This was a typical end to the daily training regimen. Suzuki reported that in his earlier training at Himeji, he had seen a trainee beaten to death by the administration of numerous punches to his face.[22] Apparently this was common throughout the navy. Shigeo Imamura related how the same type of treatment was meted out to students at Izumi as well.[23]

Another Japanese navy pilot, Flight Chief PO Konichi Okabe, began his training in 1943. He spent three months in pre-flight training at Tsuchiura, after which he went on to Yatabe for elementary flight training. After five months at Yatabe, he went to Nagoya for training as a dive bomber pilot. After three months of training at Nagoya, he became an assistant flight instructor. Three months of work as an assistant flight instructor qualified him as a full instructor and he remained there until 1945. On 1 March 1945, he was transferred to the No. 1 Attack Flying Unit which was based at Kanoya. On 16 March, the unit transferred to Oita for practice against ship targets. His Judy 33 was shot down over Okinawa a month later after flying a kamikaze mission from Kanoya.[24]

One of the important factors influencing the outcome of any battle is the training of the combatants. In the case of the Japanese army and navy air forces, the training began to decline as the war progressed. At the beginning of the war with America, the Japanese had a number of well-trained pilots. Prior to joining a combat unit, the average navy flier had completed 650 hours of flight time and the army pilots 500. This intensive training, along with the exclusive admission requirements, weeded out all but the most talented candidates. Such a rigorous and selective process, coupled with combat experience in China, meant that the Japanese fighter pilots at the beginning of the war were equal or superior to their opponents. Added to a pilot's training experience was the superiority of the Zeke over its adversaries. It is easy to see why the Japanese pilots enjoyed great success in the early stages of the war. However, one problem for the Japanese was that they did not increase the pilot recruitment and training programs early on and failed to recognize just how valuable their experienced pilots were. When they lost a large percentage of them during the first year and a half of the war, they had to scramble to train replacements. Aircraft flown by these men had little protective armament and, if they were shot down, it was unlikely that they would be rescued. The Japanese system of air-sea rescue was poor. A second problem hinged on the production and development of new aircraft. Believing in the superiority of the Zeke, navy planners continually called for improvements and modifications to the plane instead of pushing for newer designs. When superior fighter designs were developed, it was too late in the war to produce them in the numbers required to turn the tide of battle. An additional problem that they faced was the decline in the amount of aviation gas available, making it difficult for student pilots to amass the number of hours needed to polish their flying skills. Where once the Japanese pilots had an equal amount of flying experience, by the end of the war, most Japanese kamikaze pilots had less than one hundred hours in the air. Shigeo Imamura reported that by the time of his graduation from Oita, his group had logged only seventy flight hours in Willows and Claudes. This stood in sharp contrast to American pilots, who averaged 600 hours, making air combat a very one-sided affair. During his interrogation at the end of the war, Cmdr. Yoshimori Terai indicated:

> Until December 1940, the Japanese Naval Air Force training program consisted of the following phases:
> 1. Elementary or basic training for 30 hours in Type-3 trainers or Type-90 seaplane trainers. Following completion, candidates went to:
> 2. Intermediate training using Type-90 land trainers and Type-93 (WILLOW). After 40 hours, trainees moved to:
> 3. Advanced combat training where combat and obsolete combat type aircraft were employed. 30 hours flight time in ZEKES, CLAUDES, KATES, VALS, ALFS, PETES, and NELLS was required before candidates were assigned to:
> 4. Operational units. If selected for ship borne air groups, personnel had another 50 hours training before leaving operational units.
>
> In December 1940, elementary and intermediate training were combined but total flight time of the two reduced by 10 hours.
>
> ... In the spring of 1944 the "skipping" of advanced combat training was stopped by the naval General Staff and restored for all trainees because, (1) operational losses were excessive, (2) longer period of training in the newer combat types consumed more aviation gasoline than training in the less modern aircraft assigned to advanced combat training units and (3) tactical units were then beginning to employ new plane types such as GEORGE, JILL, JUDY, MYRT, and FRANCES which were "too hot" for any but experienced pilots to fly.[25]

During the summer and fall of 1943, as the First Air Fleet was being organized, its commander in chief had eliminated advanced training because he wanted to supervise his new pilots in their advanced combat training. This practice lasted about a year and was scrapped for the reasons cited above.

Apparently there was some variation in the training curriculum. One captured navy pilot claimed that his first flight training was in a Type 96 Nell and that his training time was longer than usual. American military intelligence interviewers speculated that this may have been done as an experiment.[26]

The reduction in the number of training hours left large gaps in the hierarchy of skilled pilots. Normally, those with many hours of flight time would be given the task of training others and would serve as flight instructors. By the time of the Okinawa campaign, these pilots were in short supply. Many students who had just finished their own flight training were pressed into service as instructors. While experienced pilots might be able to do a good job, these new instructors found themselves with about twice the student load of their predecessors. Some of the students recruited during the Okinawa campaign were as young as fourteen. Still other pilots with more flying time were too valuable to expend in the kamikaze program and were kept back at the bases. There they could train others and assist in the defense of the homeland when it became necessary.

Fuel shortages sharply reduced the number of hours pilot trainees could practice in the air. During training one might find that his aircraft's engine was fueled by low octane gasoline or a mixture of gas and alcohol, which did not allow for consistent running of the engine. As the need for kamikaze pilots grew, some basic subjects such as navigation were dropped from the curriculum. Kamikaze planes could be led to the target area by one plane piloted by an experienced aviator. In short, as the Okinawa campaign wore on, the pilots flying missions to Okinawa became increasingly less proficient than those who had fought the Americans in other areas of the Pacific.

If better pilots were used on the kamikaze missions, it would be to provide escort fighter protection and to report back on the results of the attack. Since the pilots flying the kamikaze planes were relatively inexperienced, it was not long before the Americans recognized that they were not the best of the Japanese airmen. According to Lt. A. P. Glienke, the commanding officer of *LCS(L) 115*:

> Suicide pilots do not seem to be experienced flyers, and have probably never had the experience of operating an aircraft at the rate of speed attained in a suicide dive, from a position angle of thirty degrees. They tend to overshoot, and if overshooting, depend on throwing the stick forward to crash down on their target. If they are off the target, forward or aft, they will try a wing over to crash down on their target.[27]

Training Program for Army Aviators

Training procedures for the Imperial Japanese Army Air Force were no less harsh than what was previously described for the navy. Generally speaking, enlisted recruits were brutalized by their training NCOs much more than those who were destined to become officers. Yasuo Kuwahara, who won Japan's National Glider Championships in 1944 when he was fifteen years old, was quickly recruited by the army for its enlisted pilot program. During his three months of basic training at Hiro Air Base, he and his fellow recruits were continually beaten and tormented by the NCOs in charge of them. So brutal was their treatment that, by the end of his three months at Hiro, nine of the recruits had committed suicide.[28]

Basic training at Hiro was three months of hell, interspersed with military subjects. Following that, the recruits went on to a six-month period of intermediate training. The first three months of this intermediate training was filled with the study of aeronautics and other military subjects related to flying. During the second half, the students had their first flying experiences, training in the *Tachikawa Ki-9* (Spruce) biplane. After three months of flying the biplane, they moved on to single seat fighter trainers and finally on to the *Nakajima Ki-43 Hayabusa* (Oscar).[29]

Not all training went smoothly. Those going through the program in the later stages of the war sometimes found that it was interrupted. Ryuji Nagatsuka, in training to become an officer in the Japanese Army Air Force, was in the second phase of his training in September 1944, when a fuel shortage hit and flying was suspended for ten days. A mixture of gas and alcohol was substituted and the class got through a couple of more months. The training cycle was cut short by one month and the student pilots were sent to the front lines to complete their next phase in twin engine *Ki-45 Toryus* (Nick). After a month and a half there, they were then sent back to Ozuki for further fighter training in *Nakajima Ki-27 Type 97s* (Nate). In their last stage they also flew the advanced *Nakajima Ki-43* fighters (Oscar) at Kumagaya Flying School at Kagohara.[30]

In general, pilots training for the Special Attack Corps had to learn a variety of skills. The army was the first to devote training time to kamikaze tactics. However, both army and navy used similar methods. According to a report entitled "The Japanese Air Force," by Col. N. Brunetti:

> Proof of the excellent maneuvering skill of which the Japanese pilots are capable is furnished by the type of training the volunteer suicide pilots go through (Army school at ATSUGI, Navy school at KANOYA). The most intricate piece of exercise consisted in hitting an air filled rubber balloon which was towed by a plane. The pilot had to hit the balloon at the very closing phase of any acrobatical maneuver.[31]

Fighters equipped with bombs were frequently used in the kamikaze attacks, but this was an unusual configuration for many of the light fighter planes. The fighter pilots had to

The *Mitsubishi Type 97* "Nate" was a front line fighter in the 1930s. By the time of the Philippines campaign it was primarily used as a trainer. It also saw use as a kamikaze at Okinawa. NARA 342 FH 3B 35009.

practice with dummy weights attached to the fuselage to get used to the additional take off space needed when carrying bomb loads. At some bases a log was affixed under the plane to simulate the bomb.

Nagatsuka claimed that there were two approaches for the Oscars and similar types of fighter planes, one from a high altitude and one from low on the water. The high altitude approach, from 16,000 to 20,000 feet, enabled the kamikaze pilots to use the clouds for cover. Then they dove on their target at an angle of forty-five to fifty-five degrees. Once committed to the dive, there was no turning back and no margin for error. The low level approach enabled the planes to evade radar, as well as fire from the bigger guns on the ships, which could not depress sufficiently to hit them.[32]

Pilot training in the Japanese Army Air Force came to an abrupt halt in April 1945. Continued bombing and strafing of the training fields made it difficult to get anything accomplished. Karasehara, on Kyushu, was the largest training center for kamikaze pilots; however, it was high on the list of bases to be hit by American bombers. In addition, pilot shortages made it necessary to utilize many of the instructors for combat missions. Fuel shortages continued to plague the air installations. Fields such as Chiran were difficult to supply since the rail lines to the area had been bombed. Limited training was resumed in July, but it was too late to be of any use to the war effort.

Pilot quality continued to decline. Lower admission standards were required in order to get the necessary number of pilot recruits. Additionally, the standards for graduation were relaxed. Col. Junji Hayashi, who served as Chief of Staff of the 51 Training Flying Division at Gifu on Honshu, stated that the failure rate for pilot trainees was only ten percent, however, of those who graduated, about twenty percent were ill-prepared. They were permitted to graduate in spite of their weaknesses since the Japanese sorely needed pilots.[33]

5. Tactics

Kamikaze Tactics

Organized kamikaze attacks began during the Philippine campaign, but by the time of the Okinawa campaign, the attacks were much more intense and better planned. In the Philippines, attacks by three to four planes were the norm. Japanese aviation strategists felt that a small number of special attack planes, accompanied by a few escorts, had the best chance of approaching the American ships undetected. The massed attacks at Okinawa were much larger and better executed. Discussing the attack at Radar Picket Station No. 1 at Okinawa on 4 May, the destroyer *Ingraham* reported

> an estimated forty to fifty planes were thrown into the attack. The first planes were modern fast types, appearing in small groups, or singly, and approaching from several widely separated sectors. These attacks built up until the CAP had more than it could handle, at which time the enemy began to slip through. Soon enough attackers had shaken free of our fighters to saturate AA defense. At this period the enemy began attacking from all directions at different altitudes, pilots apparently attacking independently as opportunities were offered. It was at this stage that MORRISON took her first two hits and that the first formation of float planes put in their appearance. The float planes came in from the north flying low and attracted many of our fighters. Following the float plane attack came an intensified attack by fast land planes. Observers state that the coordinated attack made upon this vessel came from a loose formation from which each plane peeled off to attack from different directions as simultaneously as possible. After the fast planes had expended themselves two more formations of float planes approached. Those two formations did not reach attack positions until well after the enemy's major effort had been exhausted.[1]

The tactics employed by the Japanese airmen in their kamikaze attacks were determined, in large part, by the types of planes available and the relative amount of training completed by their pilots. As previously noted, the Japanese had lost many experienced pilots by the time of the Okinawa invasion. Training time had been cut considerably by the shortages of aviation gas and pilots preparing for kamikaze missions were given the minimal training needed to accomplish their goal. By the end of the war, army pilots training for the Special Attack Units had only seventy hours of flight time and navy pilots only thirty to fifty hours.

An analysis of the different types of approach was offered by American naval intelligence. The approaches fell into three categories. The single approach consisted of a single plane or a single group of planes coming in from the same altitude. Ships operating near shore might find this approach being used, as the enemy aircraft could utilize the land mass to confuse radar. The double approach consisted of two groups of suicide planes which approached from different altitudes and directions. One group was usually larger and served as a decoy. With this approach, it would be difficult for the ships' gunners to concentrate on both groups at once. The larger group would occupy the ships' gun crews while the smaller group slipped in from the opposite side. Multiple approaches might be undertaken by a single group or multiple groups that would break into individual attacks. It was difficult for the ships to defend themselves effectively with the attacks coming from numerous altitudes and directions. This was deemed to be the most dangerous type of attack because some of the kamikazes were sure to slip through.[2]

Destroyers and other ships on the screening stations preferred to take planes under fire on the beam, or in the case of ships like the LCS(L)s from about 45 degrees off the bow. This allowed maximum use of their guns. Recognizing this, the Japanese frequently tried to attack from astern. The radar picket destroyer, *Pritchett*, reported that this was the tactic used during the attack on Radar Picket Station No. 9 at Okinawa on 29 May 1945. *Pritchett*, *Dyson*, and *Aulick* were patrolling in a column with the *LCS(L)s 11, 20, 92,* and *122* in formation nearby when they were attacked by three Zekes. The Japanese planes were flying toward the ships on the port beam and circled to make an attack from astern. As the destroyers turned to meet them broadside, the planes turned again to keep their stern position.[3]

The Attack

A standard attack by a group of kamikaze planes involved three elements: the special attack planes, direct escort planes and intermediate escort planes. The direct escort planes were responsible for providing close cover over the air base as the special attack planes took off. As the mission progressed toward the ships at Okinawa, the direct escort planes stayed

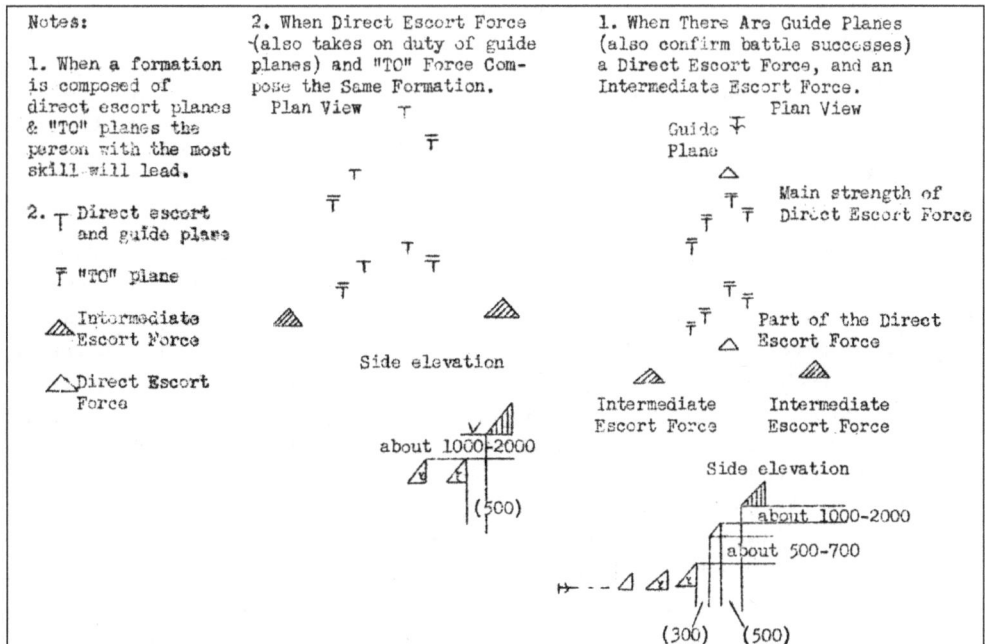

Depending on the number and type of planes in the attacking unit, as well as the opposition they expected to encounter, kamikazes used a variety of formations. The drawing above depicts two that were commonly used. Since this was translated from Japanese, the reading begins at the upper right and goes to the bottom left. CinCPacCinCPOA Bulletin No. 129–45. *Suicide Force Combat Methods Special Translation Number 67.* 27 May 1945, p. 7.

with the special attack planes to provide cover and keep the attack together. Prior to their arrival at the scene of the attack, the direct escort planes had been preceded by the intermediate escort planes. The job of the intermediate escort planes was to engage the enemy aircraft that stood between the special attack group and the target. Once the path had been cleared of enemy fighters and the special attack planes had crashed into their targets, the intermediate force was to confirm their success. In some cases, the intermediate escort planes flew a different route to the target in order to draw American fighters away from the special attack and direct escort planes.

The pilot of the kamikaze plane had to arm his bomb once he sighted the enemy forces. In early attacks in the Philippines, kamikaze planes carried a variety of explosives, including mortar and artillery shells, as well as bombs. By the time of the battle for Okinawa, each type of plane carried a specific bomb load.

Bombs Carried by Japanese Army Air Force Kamikaze Planes[4]

Type of Plane	Type of Bombs Used	Number of Bombs Carried	Loading Position
Ki-46-1 Dinah	No. 80 GP Bomb (Navy)	1 × 800 kg [1,763 lbs.]	Beneath Fuselage
Ki-8 Frank	250 kg bomb [551 lbs.]	2 × 250 kg	Beneath Wings
Ki-43 Model 3 Oscar 3	250 kg bomb	2 × 250 kg	Beneath Wings
Ki-27 Nate	250 kg or 500 kg bomb [1,102 lbs.]	1 × 500 kg 2 × 250 kg	Beneath Fuselage
Ki-45 Nick	250 kg bomb	2 × 250 kg	Beneath Wing
Ki-51 Sonia	250 kg or 500 kg bomb	1 × 250 kg or 1 × 500 kg	Beneath Fuselage
Ki-36 Ida	250 kg or 500 kg bomb	1 × 250 kg or 1 × 500 kg	Beneath Fuselage
Ki-54 Hickory	No. 80 GP Bomb (Navy)	1 × 800 kg	Beneath Fuselage
Ki-79 Improved Nate	250 kg bomb	1 × 250 kg	Beneath Fuselage
Ki-9 Spruce	100 kg bomb [220 lbs.]	2 × 100 kg	Beneath Fuselage
Ki-86 Cypress	50 kg bomb [110 lbs.]	1 × 50 kg	Beneath Fuselage
Ki-48 Lily	No. 80 GP Bomb (Navy)	1 × 800 kg	Bomb Bay
Ki-67 Peggy	No. 80 GP Bomb (Navy)	2 × 800 kg	1 in Bomb Bay, 1 in Fuselage

Bombs normally carried by army aircraft were smaller than those carried by navy aircraft which were designed to sink ships. Since Allied shipping had become a primary target, the army had to borrow larger bombs from the navy. This led to some problems fitting them to army aircraft. Army fighters normally could carry a 1,102 lb. bomb but, with the change in their mission at Okinawa, borrowed the 1,763 lb. bomb from the navy. Some army units began to train in the use of torpedoes in May 1944 and used them at Okinawa beginning in April 1945. The navy continued to develop larger bombs, but there was a limit to their size since they did not have the heavy bombers which could carry the additional payload.

Various conditions, such as weather, aircraft type, or the presence of enemy fighters would determine if the attack were to be conducted at a low or high altitude. In the case of individual attacks, the pilot's altitude, speed and angle of attack had been predetermined by various studies. One of the more important factors that a pilot had to consider was his plane's speed at the moment of impact. If his aircraft did not have sufficient speed it would lessen the effect and the plane and bomb might not penetrate the ship's hull or deck. If the air speed was too great, such as in a diving attack, it might make the plane rise and throw off the pilot's aim. Kamikaze pilots had been trained to know the characteristics of their aircraft.

When kamikazes attacked in force they had additional considerations. Guide planes played an important role in a kamikaze attack, keeping the planes from getting in the way of each other and insuring that the force operated with maximum effectiveness. *The Suicide Force Combat Methods Training Manual* stated:

> As soon as the attack is ordered the planes will form a fairly extended column, following the plane of the commander, and will begin to approach the enemy at top speed. Then, when the plane of the commander makes its final run-in (TOSSHIN) the pilots, without additional orders, will pick their targets from those assigned previously and will make their attack runs. At this moment they must strive to attack one ship with one plane.
>
> At the time of the attack run the conditions encountered by the "TO" Force will usually be extraordinarily difficult and violent. All sorts of confusion and error must be anticipated. Even at this time each pilot must burn with the desire to sink his target and fulfill his mission by bravely and calmly making an attack run which means certain death.[5]

Pilots were further directed to attack the target ships using a variety of different altitudes and bearings in their final run.

Many of the kamikaze attacks were attempted at a low level, perhaps only twenty to thirty feet off the water. As the planes approached at this low altitude, they skimmed under radar detection. However, at that angle they were easier to hit. Planes attacking from an extreme high angle were more difficult targets, and it was one of the most effective of the attack positions. When directly overhead, it was almost impossible for a ship to fire on them. At Okinawa Cmdr. R. H. Holmes, commanding officer of the destroyer *Bennion*, found his

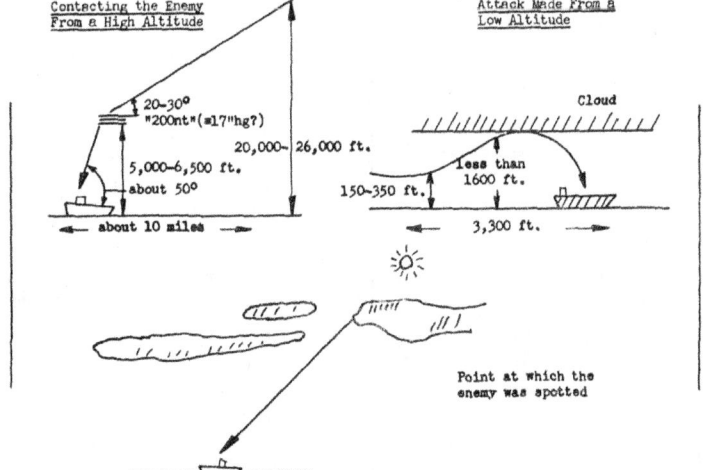

Kamikaze units varied their approaches to take advantage of existing conditions. This diagram, reproduced from captured Japanese documents, illustrates the use of cloud cover and surprise attacks using low level flying. *Suicide Weapons and Tactics "Know Your Enemy!"* CinCPac-CinCPOA Bulletin 126–45. 28 May 1945, p. 6.

58   Part One — The Genesis of the Kamikazes, Their Organization, and Disposition

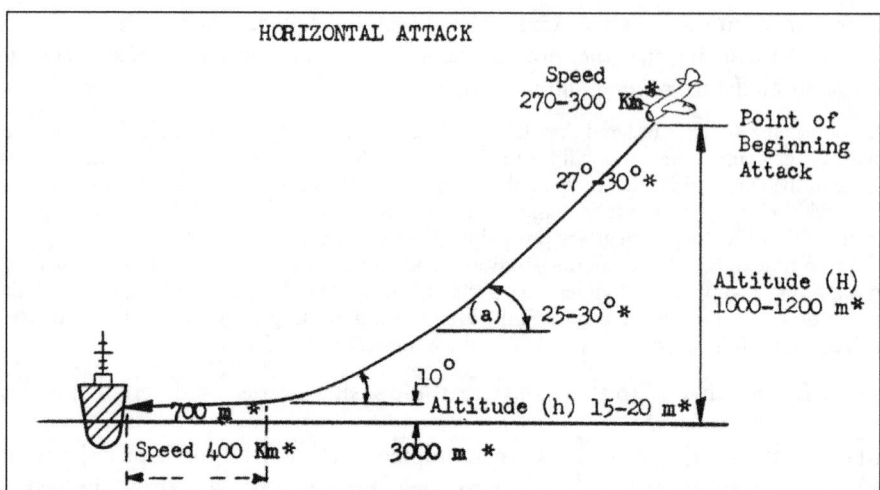

HORIZONTAL COLLISION

Standard Data for Various Types of Planes

Data	Point of beginning peel off and run in.			On entering extreme low altitude.			Remarks
Type of Planes	Altitude (H) (meters)	1 Km (Speed)	Angle (a)	Altitude h(meters)	1 Km (Speed)	X meters	
Fighters	1000 to 15 (Ill.) Probably 1500	320–350	25°–30°	Below 20	450–450 (TN:Sic)	30–35	It is important to decrease the altitude of the point of the beginning peel off and run in even more depending on weather and atmospheric conditions. In such circumstances, when colliding, it is especially important to maintain sufficient colliding power.
Hq Recce Plane (DINAH)	800 to 1000	"	25°		"		
Ki 45 (NICK 1)	"	300	25°–30°		"		
Ki 48 (LILY 1)	1200	270–300	20°–30°		"		
Ki 51 (SONIA 1)	"	270	30°		400–450		
Ki 67 (PEGGY)	800 to 1000	320–350	"		450–500		
Ki 27 (NATE)	1200	300	20°–25°		450		
Ki 79 (Type 2 Advanced Trainer)	"	250	30°		350		
Ki 36 (IDA)	"	"	"		"		
Ki 59 (THERESA)	"	"	"		"		
Ki 9 (SPRUCE)	"	180	"		250		

Horizontal attacks were preferred when surprise was a possibility. *Suicide Weapons and Tactics "Know Your Enemy!"* CinCPac-CinCPOA Bulletin 126–45. 28 May 1945, p. 10.

ship under attack by several kamikazes at Radar Picket Station No. 1 on 28 April 1945. *Bennion*'s lookouts spotted one circling directly over their heads and watched in frustration as it spiraled downward. "At this point the plane was circling at 80°–90° position angle making a track impossible and allowing the guns to bear only seconds at a time.... Extreme difficulty in loading was experienced due to the maximum elevation and slewing in train of the 40 MM guns."[6] It was not until the plane entered a steep glide to make a run from astern that *Bennion*'s gunners were able to hit it.

Japanese air commanders had given a great deal of thought to the types of approaches and the angles of attack of their kamikaze planes. Their knowledge had been formalized in manuals developed by both the Japanese Army Air Force and the Japanese Navy Air Force. One of these, developed by the army and published in February 1945, gave detailed descriptions for the ideal angle of attack for aircraft such as the Nick, Lily, Sonia, Peggy, Nate, Ida, and

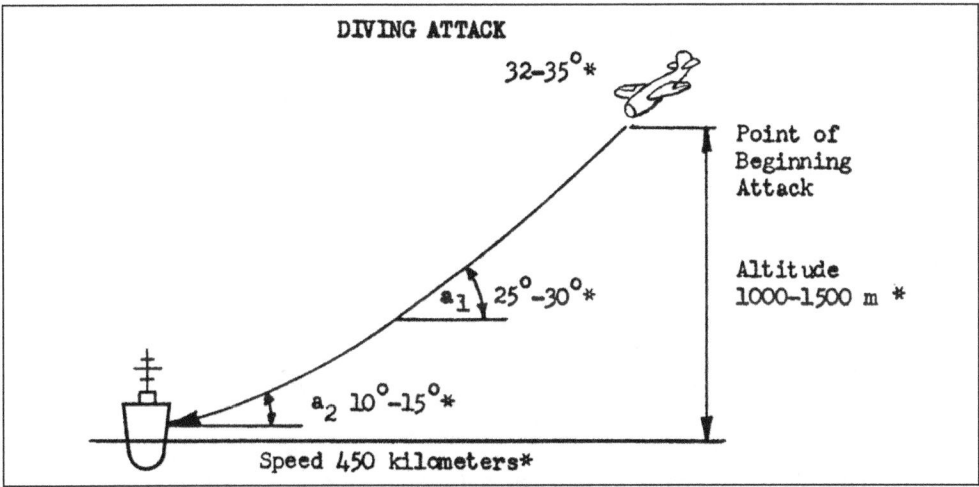

DIVING COLLISION

Basic Data / Plane	When beginning attack.			When colliding.
	Altitude	Speed	Angle (a_1)	Angle (a_2)
Fighters	500–1000	320–350	25°–30°	10°–15°
Hq Recce Plane (Dinah)	800–1500	"	25°	"
Ki 45 (NICK 1)	"	300	25°–30°	10°
Ki 48 (LILY 1)	1200	270–300	25°–30°	10°
Ki 51 (SONIA 1)	1200	270	30°	10°
Ki 67 (PEGGY)	500–1000	320–350	30°	10°
Ki 27 (NATE)	1200	300	20°–25°	10°
Ki 79 (Type 2 Advanced trainer)	1200	250	30°	10°
Ki 36 (IDA)	1200	250	30°	10°
Ki 55 (Type 97 Heavy Trainer)	1200	250	30°	10°
Ki 9 (SPRUCE)	1200	250	30°	10°

Diving attacks from a high altitude were preferred, particularly when the attacking formation included a large number of aircraft. *Suicide Weapons and Tactics "Know Your Enemy!"* CinCPac-CinCPOA Bulletin 126–45. 28 May 1945, p. 10.

Spruce. Details for the attack included the altitude and speed at which to begin the attack, as well as the angle of attack for each plane.[7]

The low angle approach was used for surprise attacks or in conditions of low visibility, such as dawn, dusk or poor weather. A high angle approach was more frequently used when the raid was large. By May 1945, American naval intelligence noted that the Japanese were emphasizing the low altitude approaches with greater frequency. In many cases, they skimmed the waves on the way in. This made it difficult to pick them up, either visually or by radar. Combat air patrol planes flying at a higher altitude had a difficult time shooting them down, as they had to dive to get near them. Corsairs in particular, because of their weight, might have difficulty in pulling out of their dives and risked crashing into the ocean. If the kamikazes

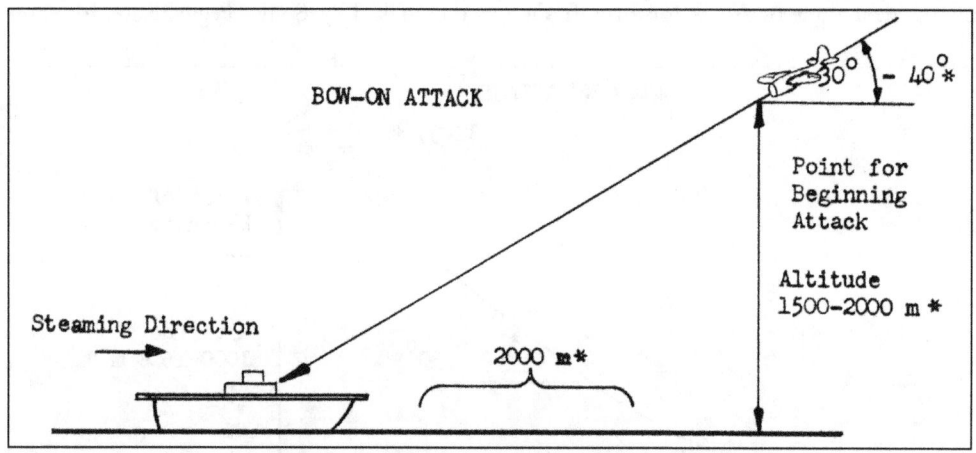

Basic data for beginning of attack for each type of plane are as follows

Type of Plane	Altitude (meters)	Speed (Km) (Instrument)	Angle (a)
Fighters	1500	320	35°-40°
Hq Recce Plane (Dinah)	1200	"	35°
Ki 45 (NICK 1)	1500	300	35°-40°
Ki 48 (LILY 1)	1200	"	35°
Ki 51 (SONIA 1)	1200	"	40°
Ki 67 (PEGGY)	1200	320	30°
Ki 27 (NATE)	1200	300	25°
Ki 79 (Type 2 Advanced trainer)	1500	250	35°
Ki 36 (IDA)	1200	250	30°
Ki 55 (Type 97 Heavy Trainer)	1200	250	30°
Ki 9 (SPRUCE)	1200	180	30°

The bow-on attack was frequently used against American carriers. *Suicide Weapons and Tactics "Know Your Enemy!"* CinCPac-CinCPOA Bulletin 126–45. 28 May 1945, p. 10.

were low enough, the guns of the target ship might not be able to depress sufficiently to fire on them and, if they did, they risked hitting other ships on patrol in the area. In addition, it was much more difficult to maneuver away from a plane approaching at a low altitude.[8]

Part of the decision to utilize the lower approaches might have stemmed from the difficulties encountered when pilots put their planes into a steep dive. Heavily laden with a bomb and diving at full throttle, the plane would encounter two problems. The first was increased pressure on the control surfaces, making it difficult for the pilot to adjust his course toward a moving target. The second problem was the high speed increase in lift and its effect on accuracy mentioned above.

Cpl. Yasuo Kuwahara, after having flown escort for several kamikaze missions, wrote:

> In my own estimation, the best procedure was to descend anywhere from ten to five thousand feet, the sun at our tails. The dive varied from forty-five to sixty degrees, leveling out at about five hundred yards from the target, striking for the stern as low to the water as possible.
> Thus an approach was effected below the angle of the bigger guns. It was advantageous for another reason: that way ships were in danger of hitting each other with their own ammunition.[9]

Advantages of the lower approach were noted by Cmdr. Bruce McCandless, CO of the destroyer *Gregory*. He claimed that the "steep diving attacks are more spectacular and probably more damaging when successful, but [the] tendency is to overshoot. The more nearly horizontal runs, or shallow glides, appear to have a higher percentage of hits."[10]

Additional skills had to be learned by kamikaze pilots, among them the identification of ships and enemy aircraft. Each type of ship was given a different priority, with both army and navy identifying aircraft carriers as the most important target. The priority after that was given to battleships, cruisers and transports. Carriers could be put out of action if hit in the forward elevator. Kamikazes attempted to approach the carrier from astern, giving the ship a limited ability to avoid the crash. At Okinawa the radar picket ships noted that kamikazes seemed to pick the amidships sections or the bridge as the target, hoping to cause the most damage there. According to the *Suicide Force Combat Methods Training Manual*:

> The collision point will vary with the type of plane, kind of target, its size, and speed, but in the event of a steep diving collision it will be on the deck, amidships, if possible between the stack and the bridge, and for carriers, at the elevators. In case of an extreme low altitude horizontal collision, the best point will generally be amidships slightly above the water line.[11]

During the final dive, some of the kamikazes strafed the intended target, but many did not. This sometimes proved confusing to men on the ships. They did not understand that many of the kamikaze planes were not equipped with machine guns since their pilots had little or no experience using them. *LCS(L) 85* noted further:

> The pilots are either not well trained or their judgement is bad, for they miss many ships, even if it is by a close margin. Some suicide planes do not carry bombs, but just rely on their gasoline to create a fire and the plane to do damage. Also most of them do not carry machine guns, or else they would do more strafing.[12]

Inexperienced pilots had a difficult time identifying various types of American ships and also had difficulty in zeroing in on a specific part of a ship. It was not unusual for pilots to confuse oilers, LCTs and LSMs with carriers. With numerous American CAP planes in the air near the targets, many kamikazes opted to crash into the nearest available target rather than be shot down while searching for a carrier. What frequently occurred at Okinawa was that the first ships encountered by the kamikazes were the ships on the radar picket stations and screens. Therefore, destroyers, destroyer escorts, LSM(R)s and LCS(L)s became prime targets of opportunity.

Guide Planes

Kamikazes heading for the Okinawa area were usually guided and covered by more experienced pilots whose job it was to ensure that the kamikaze got through to the target. American planes intercepting them would have an easy time shooting down the kamikazes, which were piloted by men with far less experience and training. Additionally, their aircraft were poorly equipped for dogfighting Hellcats and Corsairs. Many ship action reports indicated that a couple of Japanese planes kept their distance and seemed to be directing the kamikazes in their attacks. *Ingraham* reported:

> Furthermore, the airmanship displayed by the pilots of these two formations was of low order. These two formations reminded one of flocks of pelicans—each bird following the leader in a loose, ragged file and flying very close to the water. Only one individualist broke away to approach independently. All fell easy prey to our fighters. The impression gained was that the leader of each formation was an experienced aviator, but that all of the others had barely enough flight time to solo.[13]

As the kamikaze campaigns against Okinawa began, the suicide planes had a great deal of support. Many Japanese fighter aircraft flew protective cover for them so they could reach their targets. As the months wore on, the fighter strength of the Japanese was diminished, as well as the quality of the planes employed by the special attack units. Where air superiority once insured some success in the kamikaze attacks, the Japanese now found themselves in the position of frequently sending single planes on the missions or using training planes for nighttime attacks since they did not have the ability to protect them.

As noted above, in the earlier stages of the *Kikusui* attacks on the American forces at Okinawa, more planes were available and more of them of a high quality. As the campaign wore on, the Japanese kept their better fighters for defense of the home islands. Occasionally more advanced planes appeared over Okinawa, but the outmoded Zeke was the most frequently used. Because of its good speed and maneuverability it was probably the most successful of the kamikaze planes in the Philippines and at Okinawa.

Use of Window

In order to cover their approach, designated aircraft in the kamikaze attack group dropped "window," a cloud of small metal strips designed to confuse radar. In an attack on 16 April, three Judys left Kanoya to attack American shipping at Okinawa. When they came in sight of their target and were fired upon by the ship, the lead plane dropped window. No special device was used, the observer in the rear cockpit area simply opened a box and scattered it over the side of the plane. This type of defensive maneuver was effective in many cases. The destroyer *Morrison*, attacked at Radar Picket Station No. 1 on 4 May 1945, was totally confused by the use of window, a major factor leading to her sinking.

Timing the Attack

Since the protective combat air patrol planes were most numerous during the daylight hours, the kamikazes planned their attacks to coincide with the return of the planes to their bases or carriers. This was just at sunset, as the CAP had usually been sent back to base and there was enough light to see the target. Men on the destroyers were well aware of this. With regard to the attack on his ship at Radar Picket Station No. 9 at Okinawa on 17 May, Lt. B. M. Demarest, fighter director officer on the destroyer *Douglas H. Fox*, reported that within a few minutes after the *Eldorado* had ordered the CAP back to base, the enemy began to appear.

It seemed obvious that they were monitoring the Fighter Director (FD) and Identification Friend or Foe (IFF) networks and were just waiting for the CAP to leave the area. Demarest elaborated:

> The enemy stayed low over the horizon to the west, out of sight of our radars and CAP until the latter was ordered to base. Darkness was falling rapidly, and although surface targets were clearly visible, aircraft were but small black dots on the refraction blurred evening sky. With suspicious promptness a bogey appeared within two minutes after our F.D.O. had reported our Dusk CAP on steer for base. He was shot down, but not before he had drawn into the attack at least ten more planes. DOUGLAS H. FOX seemed to be singled out as the principal target for the group, either as the leading ship or the larger DD present. For a minute or two, every plane maneuvered for position in all quadrants and then, obviously on signal, a coordinated attack was launched. One and perhaps two planes are known to have withdrawn and heckled later but these made no attempt at the use of suicide tactics.[14]

Cloudy, rainy nights were welcomed by the ships as the poor weather kept the kamikazes away. Most dreaded of all were bright, moonlit nights, which made the ships highly visible and perfect targets. Enemy planes were hard to see in the night sky, particularly if they approached from a low angle. The phosphorescent wake of the ships was also a dead giveaway, pointing at their sterns like a giant arrow on the ocean. Attacks during daylight hours exposed the kamikazes to the fire of the ships and the threat of interception by the combat air patrol. Rainy days held the best promise for the Japanese, as their planes were able to use cloud cover to hide their approach.

The primary means that Americans had of determining if a plane was friendly was by Identification Friend or Foe (IFF), but this was not always reliable. According to the commanding officer of the light minelayer *Shannon*, Lt. Cmdr. W. T. Ingraham:

> On several occasions it has been proven conclusively that the enemy has in their possession our Mk.6 IFF system. Several times have planes showed "lights" and proved themselves to be bogies by suiciding into ships. Up until this time [15 July 1945] we have been almost correct in assuming that any plane showing lights was friendly. Now our primary means of identification during darkened hours is of doubtful value.... It is believed that Jap suicide planes often turn on their running lights when in a Kamikaze attack so as to draw fire from the 40mm. The aviator is then able to ride in on the tracers. Tracer ammo should be reduced to a minimum at night and 40mm radars installed as fast as possible so effective control of 40mm fire may be had.[15]

Although the Japanese were able to rationalize the need to use the extreme methods of the Special Attack Corps, American commanders did not feel they were justified. Their success would be determined by pilot training and expertise. Cmdr. L. E. Schmidt, Commanding Officer of the destroyer *Isherwood*, commented:

> The percentage of successful suicide attacks is probably about the same as the percentage of successful glide-bombing, dive bombing and torpedo attacks. An enemy who has the requisite experience, skill, and lack of understanding of the principles of longevity to crash his aircraft into a target undoubtedly could conduct a successful attack by, to us, more conventional methods.... The suicide pilot who is not endowed with the prerequisites necessary for conducting a successful bombing or torpedo run is considered hardly capable of carrying through a properly executed suicide attack.
> It may be concluded, therefore, that the primary value of the suicider is his psychological effect upon our combat personnel.[16]

In this respect, Schmidt had identified the psychological impact of suicide attacks as a primary reason for the use of the Special Attack Corps. Japanese planners knew that the poorly trained pilot was likely to be shot down before reaching his target. Therefore, the only sure way to overcome the awesome material advantage of the American forces was by psychological means. For the individual Japanese airman, the use of such tactics was considered acceptable. Capt.

Rikihei Inoguchi explained, "We must give our lives to the Emperor and Country, this is our inborn feeling. I am afraid you cannot understand it well, or you may call it desperate or foolish. We Japanese base our lives on obedience to Emperor and Country. On the other hand, we wish for the best place in death, according to Bushido. Kamikaze originates from these feelings."[17] It should be noted that Inoguchi did not pilot a special attack plane and that he survived the war.

Problems Identifying Japanese Aircraft

The identification of ships and aircraft was of paramount importance. Only by visual means could one be certain if the aircraft approaching his ship was friendly or not. Numerous training aids and manuals were developed to assist American personnel in the identification of aircraft. Many instances of American aircraft being shot down by gunners on American ships had been recorded. Further, determining if the aircraft belonged to the Japanese army or navy could assist in revealing their base of origin, be it a land base or carrier.

Japanese aircraft appearing over the American ships were numerous and of varied models, particularly during the Okinawa campaign. It was frequently difficult, in the heat of battle, to determine just which type of aircraft the Japanese were flying. Confusion of identification

Top: The *Mitsubishi A6M5 Reisen*, or Zero, was also known by the Allied code name Zeke. NARA 80G 248975. *Bottom:* The Allied code name for the *Nakajima Ki-44 Shoki* was Tojo. NARA 80G 192160.

was common, with ships and pilots alike reporting differences in the planes encountered. In many cases, Oscars, Zekes and Tojos were mistakenly identified. At other times, spatted, fixed-gear Japanese aircraft such as Vals, Sonias and Anns were frequently confused. This led CinCPac-CinCPOA to state, "It appears that perhaps VALS have been used in the greatest number of suicide attacks. This may be explained partly by the confusion between VAL and other planes with landing gear down."[18]

At Radar Picket Station No. 11A off Okinawa on 3 June 1945, the destroyer *Cassin Young*, the light minelayers *Thomas E. Fraser*, *Robert H. Smith*, and *LCS(L)s 16*, *54*, *83*, and *84* were

Top: The *Nakajima Ki-43-IIb Hayabusa* was assigned the code name Oscar. NARA 80G 167062. *Bottom:* This *Mitsubishi Ki-30* light bomber photographed in December 1944. The code name for this aircraft was Ann. NARA 80G 169802.

on patrol when they were attacked by two Japanese planes. One plane was shot down by the CAP and the other crashed into *LCS(L) 16*. *Robert H. Smith* and *LCS(L) 16* reported both planes as Zekes, but *LCS(L)54* reported that the plane hitting the *16* was an Oscar. *LCS(L) 84* reported that one was a Zeke and one an Oscar and *LCS(L) 83* described the one shot down as an Oscar.

The action report of the destroyer *Anthony* for 7 June 1945 indicated the approach of two planes, but the observers could not determine if they were Nates or Vals. In a later incident, the aircraft action report for CAG-40 identified five enemy planes as Vals. A study of the gun camera film after the incident showed that four of them were Sonias.

The *Kawasaki Ki-45 Toryu* (Nick), a twin engine fighter, was easy to confuse with another

Top: The *Aichi D3A1* dive bomber was code named Val. NARA 80G 345604. *Bottom:* The *Mitsubishi Ki-51* was code named Sonia. NARA 80G 169862.

twin engine plane, the *Mitsubishi Ki-46-11* (Dinah). On 4 May, the destroyers at RP Station No. 2 at Okinawa, *Lowry DD 770, Massey DD 778, James C. Owens DD 776*, and the support ships *LCS(L)s 11, 19, 87* and *LSM(R) 191* reported an attack on them by a Dinah, but the *Action Report of VF-85* for that day claimed it was a Nick. Confusion over the identification of plane types was common. In the case of some of the larger attacks a variety of planes were used, both army and navy, adding to the problem of identification.

Declining Resources

Japanese aircraft used at the beginning of the Okinawa *Ten-Go* campaign were diverse but most were combat types specially adapted for use as special attack planes. With parts in short supply, the Japanese began to prioritize their repair procedures. By the beginning of the Okinawa campaign Japan's aircraft situation was serious. American naval intelligence intercepted a transmission from Japan's Bureau of Aeronautics dated 30 March 1945. Apparently the strain of war was having its effect on the air depots. The bureau put forth a list of aircraft and aircraft repairs that were prioritized. The Third and Fifth Air Fleets were directed to recondition land planes and seaplanes, and the Tenth Air Fleet was directed to recondition land planes, operational trainers and intermediate land trainers in that order. Only minor plane repairs were to be made on the Betty, Jack, Irving, Kate, Grace, Val, Tess, Jake, Pete, Alf, Dave, Susie, Rufe, Rex and the land transport version of the Betty and the Nell. The only aircraft to receive major repairs were the Zeke, George, Judy, Jill, Frances, and Myrt as these were most important to the Japanese war effort. Major repairs that had begun on the Emily and the Mavis were to be completed.[19]

> Still another intercepted message from the headquarters of the Tenth Air Fleet to five of its Naval Air Depots on 18 April 1945 continued to give evidence of problems: With the decrease in production of new aircraft, the parts and materials allotted to this Fleet have been used in repairing planes. At present, however, we have on hand only enough planes for about 70% of our suicide attack personnel. Under present war conditions we deem it essential that this deficiency be speedily overcome. Do everything, therefore, to speed up repair work, and advise us of the types and number of planes which can be delivered.[20]

Aircraft slated for use against the allied forces at Okinawa were sent from the factory to air depots for testing and preparation for delivery to operational units. Two problems faced the depots working on these new planes. To begin with, poor production made it necessary for new aircraft to undergo additional work before they could be sent on to a squadron. Secondly, a shortage of qualified mechanics to work on the planes meant that the repairs would not be as good and would take more time to complete.

The engine was the most critical element to be tested on a new airplane. Before 1945, the engine would be run for five hours at the factory and then the plane flown for another ten hours. Decreases in the amount of fuel available for testing began to take a toll. By 1945 the engine would have a two hour test at the factory. It would be run for an hour and a half and then disassembled to insure that there were no defective parts. It would be reassembled and run again for another half hour. The plane was then assembled and given a two hour flight test. After delivery to the air depot it was flown for an additional three hours. The plane was then delivered to the transport unit to be flown to the fields on Kyushu. It would arrive there with less than ten hours on the engine. Japanese experience had shown that any problems with the engines would develop after ten hours. Therefore, the planes delivered to front line units had a high failure rate. Many crashed en route to their units or shortly after having been put into service.

As the battle for Okinawa raged and incessant raids on the homeland increased, the situation began to change. American estimates of the effectiveness of raids by B-29s and other aircraft indicated that the Japanese ability to launch attacks against the ships at Okinawa was seriously hampered. As a result of these raids the repair and maintenance facilities at Tachiarai, Oita, and Omura were damaged, severely hindering the ability of the Japanese army and navy to repair aircraft. With the extensive damage to hangars and other repair facilities at many of the bases, it became difficult to service aircraft as would normally be done. Serviceability rates dropped to almost forty-five percent. Squadrons at Kanoya in particular, as well as many other bases, found themselves unable to launch raids. Just as they were preparing strikes, the B-29s came in and disrupted their operations. With so many American aircraft attacking the bases, it was necessary to divert four of Kanoya's fighter units scheduled for use against Okinawa to CAP duties over Kyushu.

One of the means that the Japanese used to protect their dwindling air forces was the "fly away" strategy. If American bombing raids were detected soon enough, Japanese aircraft units could be redeployed to bases in Shikoku, Honshu and Korea to avoid destruction. In addition, daily life at the bases was strained by constant calls to alert. This limited the ability of the Japanese to complete repairs to runways, hangars and other facilities that had been previously bombed. With all these difficulties at the bases, it was not possible to launch the concerted attacks that had been planned by the army and navy.[21] The overall effects of these raids

Kanoya Airfield on Kyushu was considered to be one of the most important airfields in Japan, making it a constant target for American planes. Here, two SB2C Helldivers and an F4U Corsair from Task Force 58 strike the field on 13 May 1945. U.S.S. *Bennington CV 20* Serial 0021 3 June 1945. *Action Report of USS Bennington (CV 20) and Carrier Air Group Eighty-Two in Support of Military Operations at Okinawa 9 May-28 May (East Longitude Dates) Including Action Against Kyushu.*

diminished the ability of the Japanese to fly their aircraft against American ships at Okinawa. As terrible as the ordeal of the American ships was, it would have been far worse if the Kyushu bases had not been attacked regularly by both army air force bombers and other aircraft from carriers and the bases on Okinawa and the Marianas.

As the Okinawa campaign reached its finale, it was obvious that the Japanese were not giving up. In spite of great losses to their industrial production, there were no signs that they would surrender. Their military leaders were convinced that the Japanese spirit, *Yamato daimashii*, would overcome the material advantages of the Allied forces. No matter how outnumbered, some still felt that victory was possible. Shortly after the war, Lt. Gen. Masakazu Kawabe told his interrogator, Col. Ramsey D. Potts,

> The Japanese, to the very end, believed that by Spiritual means they could fight on equal terms with you, yet by any other comparison it would not appear equal. We believed our Spiritual conviction in victory would balance any scientific advantages and we had no intention of giving up the fight. It seemed to be especially Japanese.... That's probably a contention that you cannot understand — that's the Japanese feeling; we'd made up our minds to fight to the very last man and thought we still had a chance.[22]

To the south, the airfields on Taiwan and in the Sakishima Gunto were attacked by aircraft from the British carrier task force under VAdm. H. B. Rawlings. These raids took place between 26 March and 20 April 1945, as well as from 3 to 25 May. Also from 8 April on into June, American escort carriers under RAdm. Durgin regularly attacked the fields in the Sakishima Gunto.

By the end of April 1945, parts shortages and attrition from combat activities had severely strained the regular combat units. The Japanese began to use aircraft from naval training units for special attacks. Reports by the United States War Department's Military Intelligence Service indicated that 1,550 biplane trainers and 650 monoplane trainers were being readied for use as special attack planes by the Imperial Japanese Navy's Tenth Air Fleet.[23] Estimates in early May revised the number of these aircraft upward. According to Maj. Gen. Kazuo Tanikawa:

> In addition to combat planes in tactical units, the Japanese have an estimated total of 1,460 combat planes in training units, and 2,655 advanced trainers and 3,100 elementary trainers. Combat planes from both Army and Navy training units have been used for operations; in a few instances Army advanced trainers have appeared in combat.... The Japanese Navy has been preparing to use a substantial number of trainers in the Ryukyus operations, and operational reports state that a few biplanes have been seen in the Ryukyus area. Moreover, two new

VAdm. Jisaburo Ozawa. NARA 890JO 63425.

air flotillas scheduled to be formed on 5 May were to include ten training air groups and to be assigned to the Third Air Fleet.... An estimated 500 trainers were thus to be transferred to tactical command, presumably in preparation for tactical deployment.[24]

By mid–May, a new air flotilla had been formed to participate in *Kikusui No. 7* and included a single-engine trainer unit. Still another unit, flying elementary trainers, participated in night attacks during that period.[25] *Kikusui No. 8*, which took place from 27 to 29 May, included the use of navy trainers as suicide planes.

By the end of May, it was obvious that the battle for Okinawa was a lost cause. The army became less enthused about continuing special attacks against the Americans and preferred to maintain their strength in preparation for the coming battle for the homeland. With the last offensive of the 32nd Army from 4 to 5 May a failure, "the Army abandoned hope in the outcome of the Tengo Air Operation."[26] From that point on, the army would focus its efforts on homeland defense. About that time, Adm. Toyoda received a new assignment. He was promoted to Chief of the Naval General Staff and VAdm. Jisaburo Ozawa was appointed to replace him as Commander in Chief of the Combined Fleet. Ozawa was one of the best fleet commanders in the Japanese Navy and an excellent strategist. Careful planning was a hallmark of his strategies and, once committed to a course of action, he was persistent in its completion. His promotion caused a problem in protocol as Ozawa was junior in rank to Lt. Gen. Sugawara. Accordingly, the 6th Air Army was released from the jurisdiction of the combined fleet and was once again under the authority of the Commanding General of the General Air Army, Gen. Masakazu Kawabe, as required by Imperial General Headquarters, Army Department

The ungainly *Kyushu K11w1 Shiragiku* trainer became increasingly useful as a kamikaze during the latter stages of the Okinawa campaign. This plane, shown at Sasebo Air Base on Kyushu in September 1945, is painted white with green crosses by American direction. Planes painted in this manner were used for courier service from mid–September to mid–October 1945. NARA USMC 138377.

Directive No. 1336 of 26 May 1945.[27] VAdm. Takajiro Onishi replaced Ozawa as the Vice Chief of the Naval General Staff.

In early June 1945, reports about another training plane to be used for suicide attacks began to circulate. According to the Military Intelligence Service, "Recent messages have disclosed Japanese plans for extensive tactical use of Shiragiku trainers.... MIS estimates that total current production of Shiragiku is at the rate of about 100 per month."[28] Still more trainers would be used as suicide planes in other parts of Japan in response to the anticipated American invasion of the homeland. Reports in early June indicated the construction of ten new airfields in central Honshu and a total of 6,170 trainers of various kinds in both army and navy training units.[29] This change in the use of training units had been ongoing through-

Japanese naval air cadets prepare their *Yokosuka K5Y* intermediate trainers for flight. The aircraft carried the code name Willow. In the latter stages of the war the aircraft became an effective kamikaze weapon.

out 1945 but, by mid–June, American reports asserted that "the distinction between tactical and training units has largely broken down."[30]

Biplane trainers had been used as kamikazes at Okinawa but an intercepted message from the Japanese Bureau of Aeronautics to navy bases on 13 June stated that "'in view of the present war situation,' the elementary trainer Willow hereafter will be considered one of the more important types of planes to be used as suicide planes."[31]

6. Kamikazes on Land and Sea

Explosive Speedboats

The best known of the special attack methods involved the use of aircraft to attack ships. The Japanese, however, had developed several other weapons to commit the ultimate sacrifice. The most effective of these tactics were the explosive speedboats, which were considered a serious threat in the Philippines and at Okinawa. Piloting some of these special attack speedboats were young men only fifteen or sixteen years of age. They had been recruited from junior and senior high school and were promised special privileges and posthumous promotions. Others were a few years older and had more of an education.

Both the Japanese army and navy had special attack boats, but their method of attack differed. The army boats were commonly known as *Maru-re* (liaison boats). This was a general term that was used to describe both the boats and their units. At Imperial Headquarters the units were referred to as *maru-ni* or *Renraku Tai* (Liaison Unit). Army boats carried two depth charges on racks behind the driver. In theory, the driver of the *Maru-re* approached the target at a high speed, swerved at the last moment and dropped the depth charges alongside the target ship. Set to explode three to four seconds after release, the explosives would only sink about ten feet before detonating. There was no depth charge mechanism for detonation. The depth charges might explode before the boat could escape, killing the pilot. In addition, many died as the ships they just attacked sank them with gunfire as they attempted their getaway.

Navy special attack speedboats were known as *Shinyo* (ocean shakers), and operated in a different manner. In the bow of a *Shinyo* was a 595 lb. explosive charge that would go off as the boat rammed into the side of a target vessel. On 16 February 1945, the Japanese sank three LCS(L)s at Mariveles Harbor in the Philippines in this manner. LCS(L) and LCI gunboats and PT boats were particularly watchful for these enemy speedboats and hunting them was one of their important duties in the Philippines. As the invasion of Okinawa was underway, the gunboats once again resumed their suicide boat hunting duties.

The speedboats were produced in numerous small shipyards, therefore their construction, size and engines varied slightly. They were constructed of wood and were from sixteen and one-half to twenty-one feet in length, with a beam of about six feet. Speeds differed according to the engine, but their designed speed was in the twenty to twenty-five knot range.

The Navy Shinyo Program

The Japanese navy designed seven *Shinyo* boats for these missions, designated as Types 1, 2, 3, 5, 6, 7, and 8. "Type 4 was never designated because of the superstition attached to "shi," its Japanese pronunciation, which can also mean "death."[1] Of the two types, the Type 1, Model 1 and Type 5 were the only ones to become operational.

The beginnings of the navy program can be traced to experiments in the late 1930s, during which time the Japanese studied various hull designs developed by American, British, and Italian designers. Their primary concern at that point was the development of torpedo boats and the eventual design of their 18-meter torpedo boat was based on these efforts. As the war with America reached its third year, the Japanese began to experiment with various weapons that would produce maximum effect for less cost and effort, both financially and in terms of manpower. This resulted in the beginnings of the *Shinyo* program in March 1944. The *Shinyo* fit the bill since a successful strike by a small motorboat might sink an enemy transport or troop carrier, exchanging the loss of one *Shinyo* pilot for many enemy troops.

The first design was designated the *Shinyo* Type 1 and involved scaling down the 18-meter torpedo boat. However, the torpedo boat was designed as a planing hull and had to operate at high speeds. The *Shinyo* would need to move into position stealthily and slowly before opening up to full speed during the final attack. Planing hulls do not operate all that well at slower speeds, particularly in a chop; they take water over the bow. This was discovered when the first models were tested on 27 May 1944. The Japanese had produced two at Tsurumi, made of wood, and six of steel plate at their facilities in Yokosuka. As a result, the bow section had to be redesigned to correct this tendency. In addition, the use of steel in the production was problematic, given the shortage of steel supplies and skilled steel workers. Producing them in wood was the only practical method, as they could be built and repaired locally, wherever they were to be used. The redesign of the bow section resulted in the first model, the *Shinyo* Type 1, Model 1.

The *Shinyo* Type 1, Model 1, was constructed of wood and had an inboard engine mounted for direct drive. It was first tested in July of 1944 and proved acceptable. It measured 16' 8" in length and was designed for a maximum speed of twenty-three knots. Powered by a Toyota six cylinder automobile engine, the craft would prove to be reliable. An explosive charge of 595 lbs. was mounted in the bow. It was sufficient to damage or sink many smaller vessels. This charge could be set to detonate on impact or the pilot could set it off himself at the appropriate time. Models produced near the end of the war also had two rudimentary rocket racks mounted on either side of the pilot's seat, which were capable of firing 4.7-inch rockets, each of which weighed about fifty lbs. The two rockets carried an anti-personnel load similar to shotgun pellets that would be used against automatic weapons crews on board the ships they were attacking.

Organization and Deployment in the Philippines

The original plans for stationing *Shinyo* units on Corregidor called for seven units and a headquarters platoon. These were sent to Corregidor at various times from September through December 1945.

> Plans formulated in August called for the construction of Navy surface raiding bases at Davao and Sarangani Bay on Mindanao, at Tacloban on Leyte, and at Lamon Bay on Luzon. The boat units and maintenance personnel began arriving on Luzon early in September, but the projected bases in the southern and central Philippines were not completed in time to permit deployment

before the invasion of Leyte. On Luzon the surface raiding forces were concentrated at four main points of anticipated invasion — Lingayen Gulf, Manila Bay, Batangas, and Lamon Bay.[2]

By the time of the re-capture of Corregidor in Manila Bay, the Japanese had organized their remaining forces in the area into the Manila Bay Entrance Defense Force. This was commanded by navy Capt. Takashi Itagaki, who was also the senior staff officer of the 31st Base

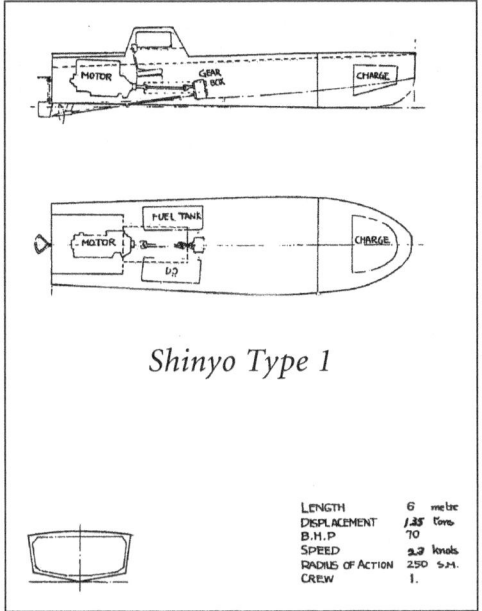

Shinyo Type 1

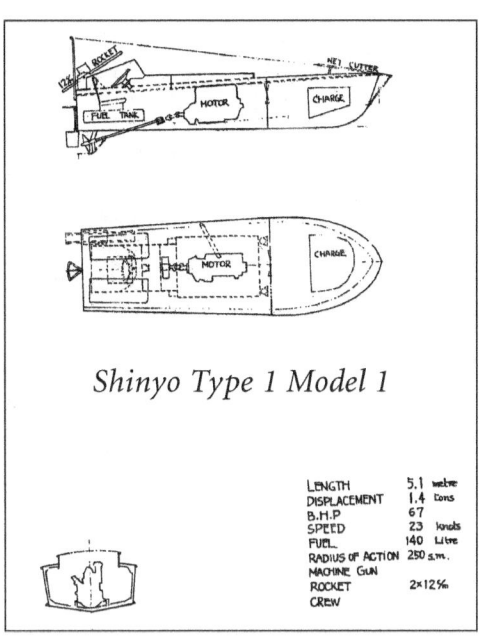

Shinyo Type 1 Model 1

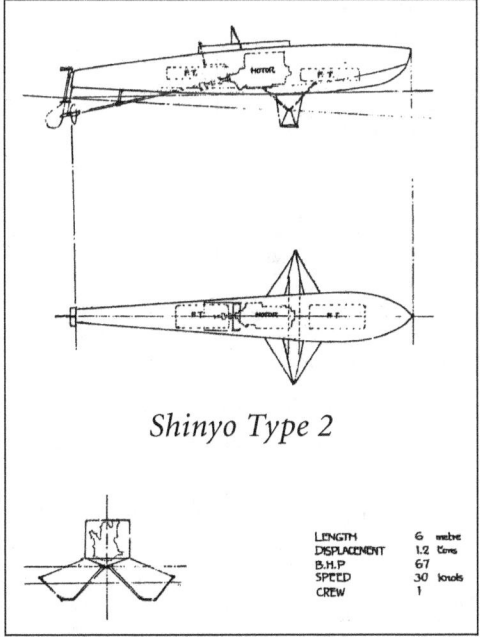

Shinyo Type 2

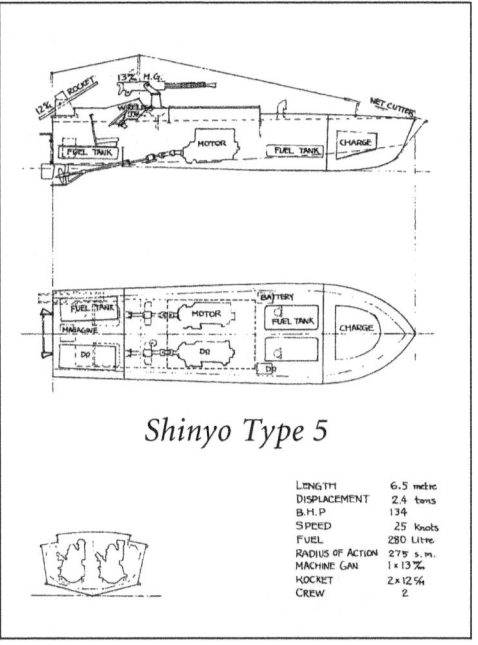

Shinyo Type 5

Above and following page: U.S. Naval Technical Mission To Japan. *Ships and Related Targets Japanese Suicide Craft.* January 1946, pp. 10–21.

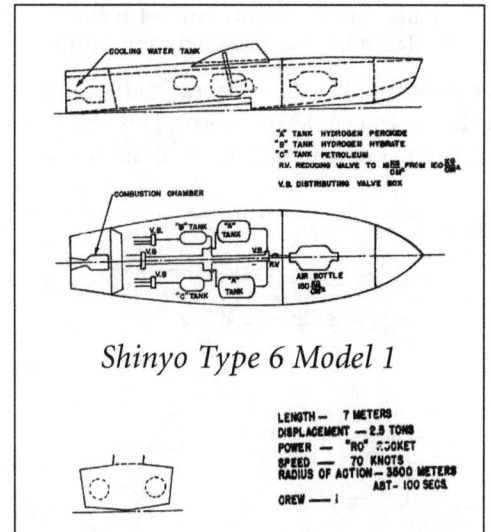

Shinyo Type 6 Model 1

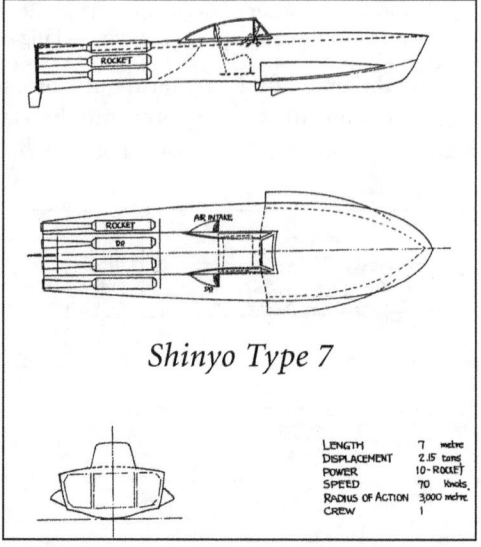

Shinyo Type 7

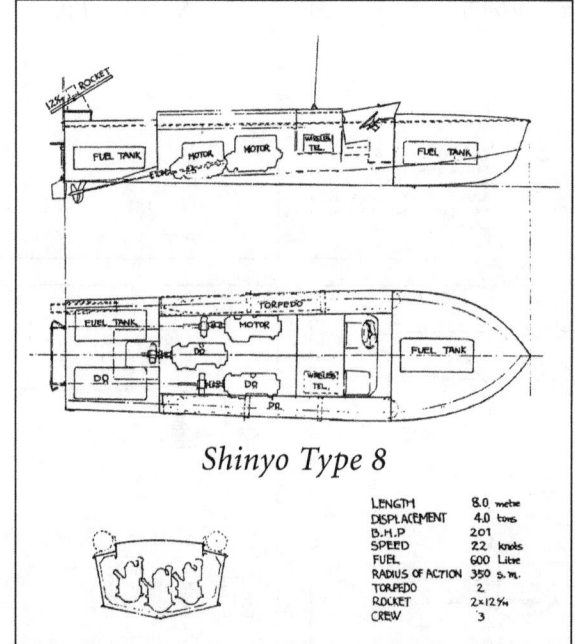

Shinyo Type 8

Force. The officer in charge of the surface special attack forces, consisting of the *Shinyo*, was Lt. Cmdr. Shoichi Oyamada. The *Shinyo Tai* Forces stationed on Corregidor included the following:

Unit No.	Commanding Officer	Officers	NCO & EM	Total
Headquarters Platoon Suicide Unit (*Shinyo-tai*)	-	0	18	18
9th Suicide Unit	Lt.(jg) Kenjiro Nakajima	7	169	176
10th Suicide Unit	Lt. Ishikawa	8	175	183
11th Suicide Unit	Lt. (jg) Shigeo Yamazaki	7	194	201
12th Suicide Unit	Lt. (jg) Yoshihisa Matsueda	7	192	199
13th Suicide Unit	Lt. (jg) Horikawa	6	181	187[3]

Shinyo Type 5s built near the end of the war were equipped with rocket racks on either side of the pilot. These are shown at Sasebo, Japan on 18 October 1945. Army Signal Corps Photograph.

One of the units so dispatched was the 13th Special Attack Unit under Lt. (jg) Horikawa which set sail from Japan in early November 1944. It was torpedoed by an American sub on 14 November and all of its boats and many of its men were lost. Survivors of the sinking finally made it to Corregidor where their unit was reconstituted. The *Shinyo Tai* units suffered additional losses while on Corregidor. Their boats were stored in tunnels at the base of Corregidor and that led to several disasters. On 23 December 1944, as *Shinyo Tai* units were preparing to attack approaching American forces, one boat caught fire. The fire quickly spread and when the disaster was over, fifty boats and one hundred men had been lost. American sources claimed that these explosions took place because "personnel were so little trained in the wiring of the explosive that several accidents occurred."[4] This was followed a couple of weeks later when, on 23 and 24 January 1945, American air raids hit the tunnels and destroyed about twenty-five boats. An explosion in the tunnels on 10 February wiped out another forty-five boats. Remaining boats were shifted to the Malinta Tunnel, a huge complex beneath the rock that had been constructed in 1922 and originally used by the American forces as an arsenal. Later, when the Japanese attacked Corregidor, MacArthur used the tunnel as his headquarters and also as the location for the hospital. It had several entrances, one of which was near the water and used by the navy for storage and launching of *Shinyo*. By the time of the actual assault on Corregidor and Manila, the *Shinyo* units were seriously under strength, with the number of boats down to about one hundred.

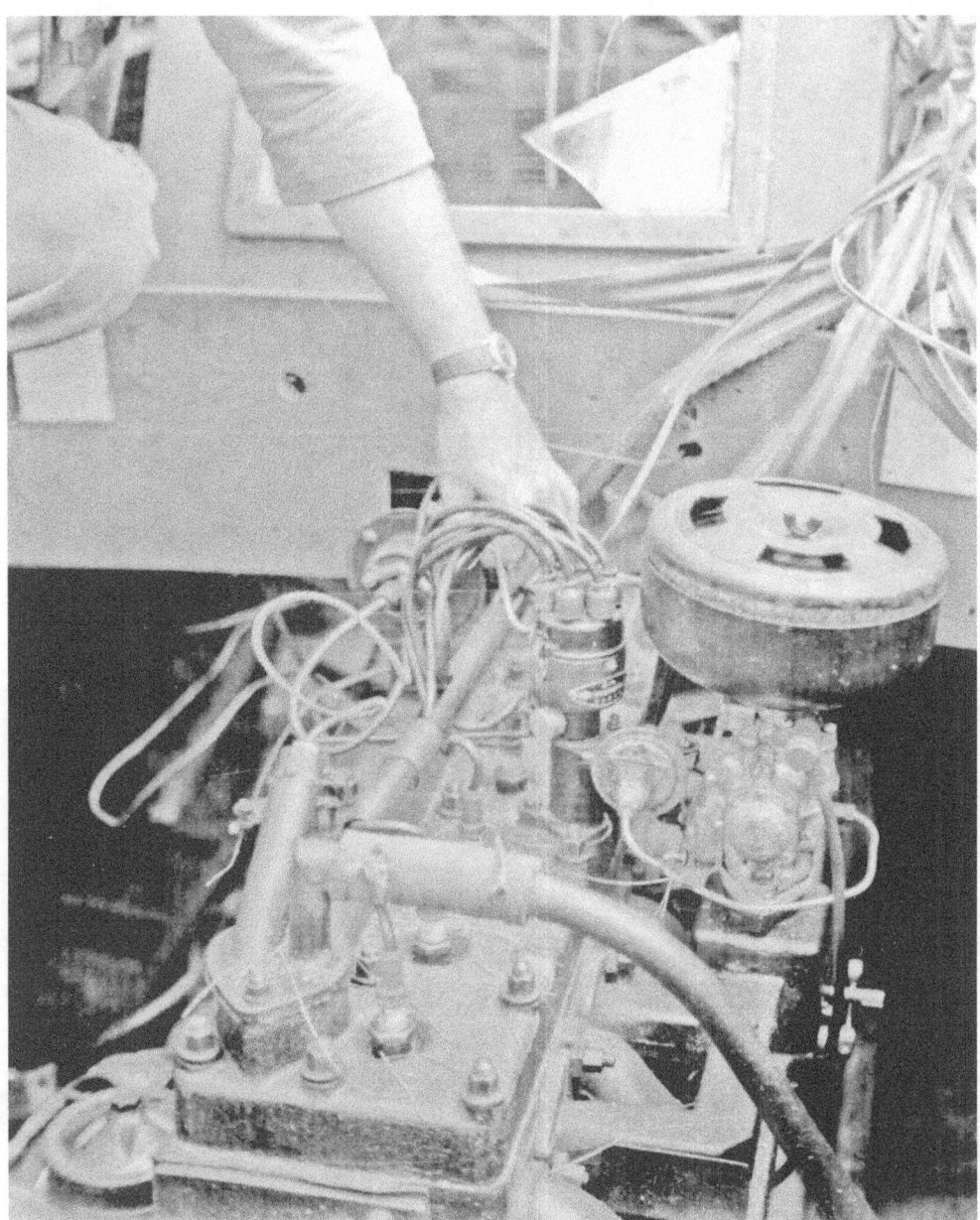

Shinyo Type 1 engine on a boat captured at Okinawa. NARA 80G 31429.

In addition to the boats, the *Shinyo* units had additional weaponry issued to them for use as the situation required. For example, on 8 February 1945, the 12th *Shinyo* Unit on Corregidor was estimated to have:

Unit Weapons:

Suicide crash boats	55
Rifles (Type 38)	63
13mm rapid fire guns	4
Pistols	15
Hand grenades	4 per person[5]

This *Shinyo*, on tracks outside its cave on Corregidor, was part of the 9th Suicide Boat Unit under Lt. (Jg) Kentaro Nakajima. The forward hatch of the vessel may be seen lying on the ground next to it. Commander Task Force SEVENTY-EIGHT. Serial 0907. *Action Reports, MARIVELES—CORREGIDOR Operation, 12–16 February 1945.* Enclosure (G).

Once Corregidor was captured, American forces got their first good look at the way in which the *Shinyo* explosives were set up. The charge itself was circular in shape with a row of spikes on its forward surface. Separated from the spikes was a circular metal band covered with rubber to prevent corrosion. The band carried current from the fuse inserted into the rear of the charge. As the boat crashed into its target, pieces of wood in front of the band pushed the band into the spikes, completing the circuit and causing the electric detonator to go off. A second hand-activated detonator was inserted in the rear of the charge. If the electric circuits failed, the explosive charge could be set off by hand. A switch box which monitored the circuitry was near the driver's seat, allowing him to test the circuits and resort to the manual detonator if need be.[6]

With the forward hatch removed, it is possible to see the 595 lb. explosive charge in the bow of the *Shinyo*. Commander Task Force SEVENTY-EIGHT. Serial 0907. *Action Reports, MARIVELES—CORREGIDOR Operation, 12–16 February 1945.* Enclosure (G).

Left: Metal spikes in the front of the charge were linked to a trigger mechanism. As the boat made contact with its target, the spikes were driven into the metal band in front of it, making contact and completing the explosive circuit. The metal band was rubber covered to prevent corrosion, necessitating the use of spikes to puncture the rubber. Commander Task Force SEVENTY-EIGHT. Serial 0907. *Action Reports, MARIVELES—CORREGIDOR Operation, 12–16 February 1945.* Enclosure (G). *Right:* This is a view of the explosive charge after it has been removed from the *Shinyo*. Commander Task Force SEVENTY-EIGHT. Serial 0907. *Action Reports, MARIVELES—CORREGIDOR Operation, 12–16 February 1945.* Enclosure (G).

Organization and Deployment at Okinawa

Two *Shinyo Tai* Units, Numbers 22 and 42, were assigned to the defense of Okinawa. These two units were based at Chinen and Yonabaru respectively. Both bases were in the southeast part of Okinawa, and these small vessels frequently attacked American ships in Nakagusuku Bay. In early attacks on the island, prior to its invasion, many of the boats were destroyed by air raids.

By comparison, the Imperial Japanese Army's suicide boats were more numerous. Eight suicide boat regiments were assigned to the Okinawa area They were Nos. 1, 2, 3, 4, 26, 27, 28, and 29. Suicide Boat Regiments Nos. 1, 2, 3, and 4 were based on several islands of the Kerama Retto group. Although they launched some attacks prior to 1 April, they were captured early in the campaign so that use of them was denied to the Japanese. Other units continued to attack American shipping where possible, but vigilant LCS(L) and LCI(G) gunboats destroyed many. Patrolling against the *Shinyo* and *Maru-re* was officially known as "fly-catching." The sailors soon referred to it as "skunk patrol."

The Army *Maru-re* Program

By late 1943, Japanese army planners, as well as those of the navy, had recognized that the fortunes of the Japanese empire were in decline.

> In April, 1944, Lieutenant General Suzuki, then Commander-in-Chief of the Army's Shipping Headquarters in Ujina, won a resounding support of his staff officers when he openly insisted that the defense of the small islands should not be left solely to their air corps, and the naval defense matters be dealt with directly by his own troops on site. The new tactical concept as drawn up by General Suzuki called for quiet deployment of a countless number of light-weight, manned torpedoes in their simplest mechanical form along selected beaches near anticipated enemy landing zones.[7]

The specifics laid out by Suzuki were approved by Imperial Headquarters and research on the new weapon commenced. The result was the development of torpedo and explosive boat prototypes in May of 1944, with continued testing for the next month or two. Shortly thereafter, with the fall of Saipan, it became army policy to adapt special attack methods to bolster their sagging air defenses. This was particularly important for many of the islands could not expect significant air support in the face of an American invasion. This policy was spelled out in the *Guidelines Pertaining to Military Operations Covering Smaller Islands*.[8]

Two types of explosive boats were developed by the army, one utilized primarily for training, and the second for actual combat missions. The training boat was designated as the *Ujina* model and was about 16'5" in length with a 5' beam. It was constructed of cyprus or other suitable wood. The second boat was the operational model and known as the *Heihon* model. *Heihon* boats were slightly longer and beamier and constructed of plywood veneers, in what was basically a cold-molded process. Both could be powered by one of several engines, usually dependent upon availability. Most prevalent were the Toyota and Nissan engines, developing 60 and 70 hp respectively. The Toyota was preferred over the Nissan as the former had less of a problem with spark plugs getting wet. With these engines, the maximum speed of the boats was in the twenty to twenty-two knot range. In addition, six cylinder Chevrolet auto engines were also used on some models. The Chevrolet engine put out 85 hp and could power the boat at an estimated speed of thirty-five knots.[9] Directions issued to the harbor construction units which oversaw the maintenance of the boats indicated that the engines could easily catch fire and had to be checked after each run of one to five hours. In addition, high speeds would throw spray into the engine area and damage the starter motor. If it were to get wet it would be ruined within a month.[10]

Armament

Unlike the navy boats which carried an explosive charge in the bow area, the primary means of attacking an enemy ship was by the use of two depth charges. These were dropped next to the hull of an enemy ship. The targets were troop transports, supply ships and other similar, unarmored ships as the depth charges were of such a size that they would not do much damage to an armored warship. The early model *Heihon* boats carried two seventy lb.

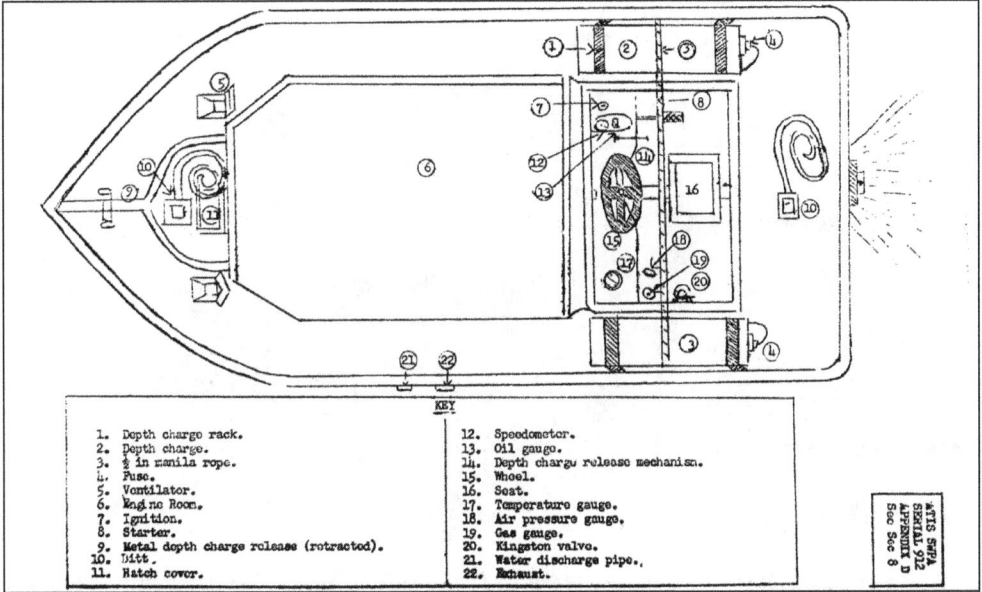

This overhead drawing of a Japanese army *Maru-re* explosive speedboat shows the early version which carried a depth charge on either side of the pilot's position. Allied Translator and Interpreter Section South West Pacific. *Interrogation Report No. 749. Corporal Nobuo Hayashi.* Appendix D.

depth charges, one on either side of the pilot's seat. However, they soon proved to be too small and the later boats carried two charges of 265 lbs. each. These depth charges were not pressure activated, but rather utilized a timer which would allow them to sink to a depth of about ten feet prior to exploding. Timing on these attacks was critical as the pilot had to approach the target vessel at high speed, swerve at the last moment and release the charges. In later models the two depth charges were mounted on racks aft the driver's seat. No other armament was carried on the boats, but pilots were encouraged to carry hand grenades which might be used for close in attacks if other means were not available to them.

The pilot of the boat risked death as he dropped the charges. A mistake in his timing would leave him too close to the explosion to escape, and many of the pilots were killed or thrown into the water after the depth charge had destroyed their suicide boat. It was possible

American personnel inspect a Japanese *Maru-re Type 5* suicide boat at Kerama Retto on 10 April 1945. This model was used by the Japanese army. The racks aft the driver's compartment held two depth charges. Attacking the target, the pilot would swerve next to the ship and drop the depth charges which were set to go of at a shallow depth, blowing a hole in the ship. Official U.S. Navy Photograph.

to survive, as many ships reported seeing a *Maru-re* making its escape. Lookouts on the *Charles J. Badger DD 657*, which was attacked on 9 April 1945 at Okinawa, saw their attacker head away from the destroyer at high speed before they could react. In that case, the pilot made good his escape as well as his attack.

Tactics

Japanese explosive speedboats were used for night attacks. During the day they remained hidden in small streams, on river banks, or near the beaches where they could be camouflaged

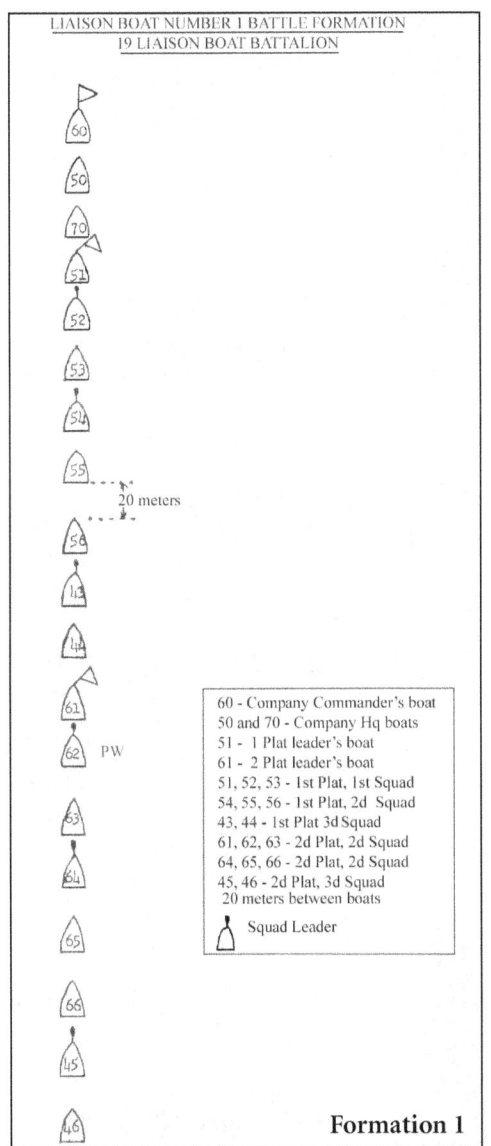

Formation 1

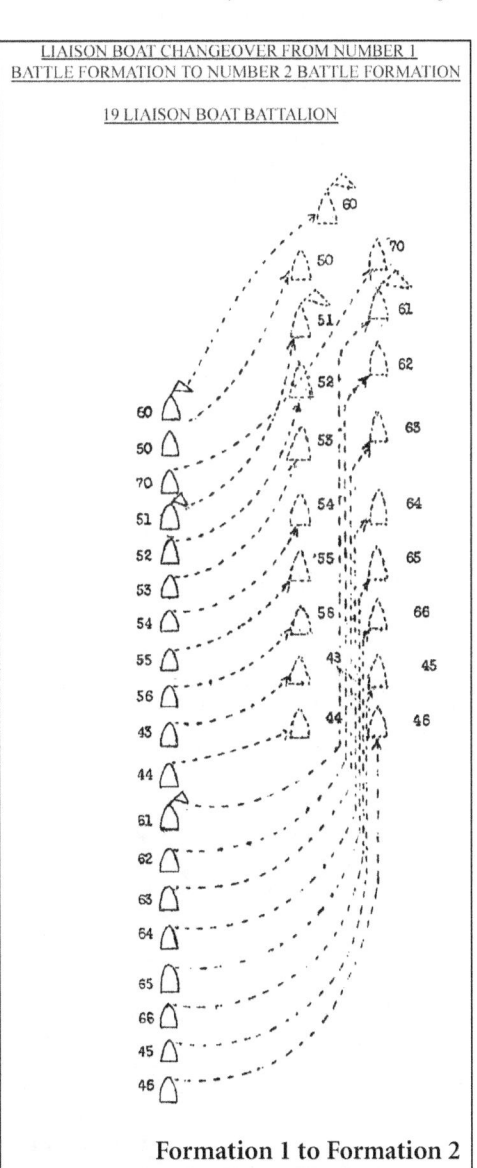

Formation 1 to Formation 2

Maru-re boats would move from their hiding places and follow Formation 1 until they reached open water, at which time they would shift to Formation 2. *Allied Translator and Interpreter Section—Southwest Pacific Area Serial 912*. Appendices F and G.

with tree branches, foliage, grass, or whatever material was at hand to keep them secure from aircraft, gunboats, and PT boats. After dark they were launched and proceeded in single file (Formation 1) down the river until they reached open water. At that point they formed into two columns (Formation 2) for the approach to the enemy ships. Signals for the formation changes were made utilizing a white light from the commander's boat, moved in various directions to indicate position changes among the *Maru-re* fleet. The change to attack formation was signaled using a red light. This generally took place about one hundred meters from the target ships. Individual boats would take on a target. If the number of boats was greater than the target vessels, two would participate in the attack, approaching from opposite sides in order not to get in each other's way. The final attack run saw the boats moving in at fifteen knots with the closest boat of the leaders going after the farthest targets. At five meters from the target vessel, the *Maru-re* made a ninety degree turn, cut loose the depth charges and increased to top speed in hopes of escaping the explosion; few did.[11] This was the general practice for the 19th Liaison Boat Battalion which was stationed at Binubusan, Luzon. Other tactics would be used if the number of enemy ships was smaller, including the sending of only one or two boats to attack the transports. Enemy shipping coming within one hundred miles of the base was fair game, as that was the extreme range for the boats. At that distance, no return to base was anticipated. Long range missions would see the boats cruising toward the target at about five knots so as to conserve fuel and not cause attention to themselves by excessive engine noise.

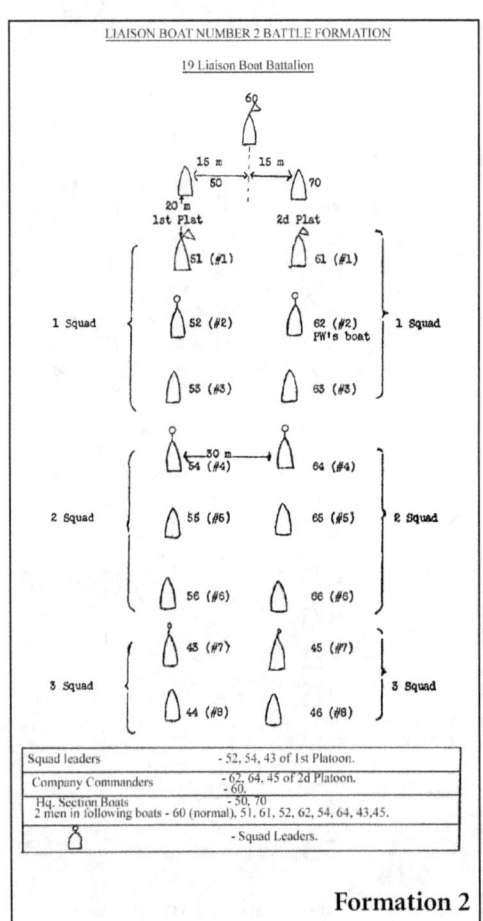

Formation 2

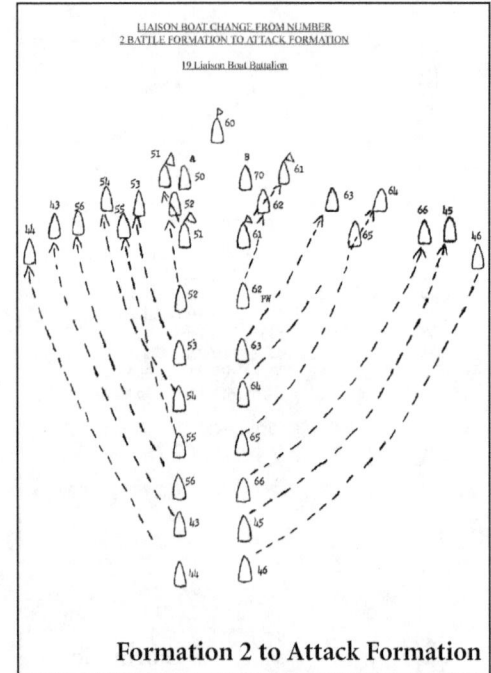

Formation 2 to Attack Formation

After proceeding toward the target vessels using Formation 2, the boats would shift into Formation 3 in preparation for the attack. *Allied Translator and Interpreter Section—Southwest Pacific Area Serial 912.* Appendix K.

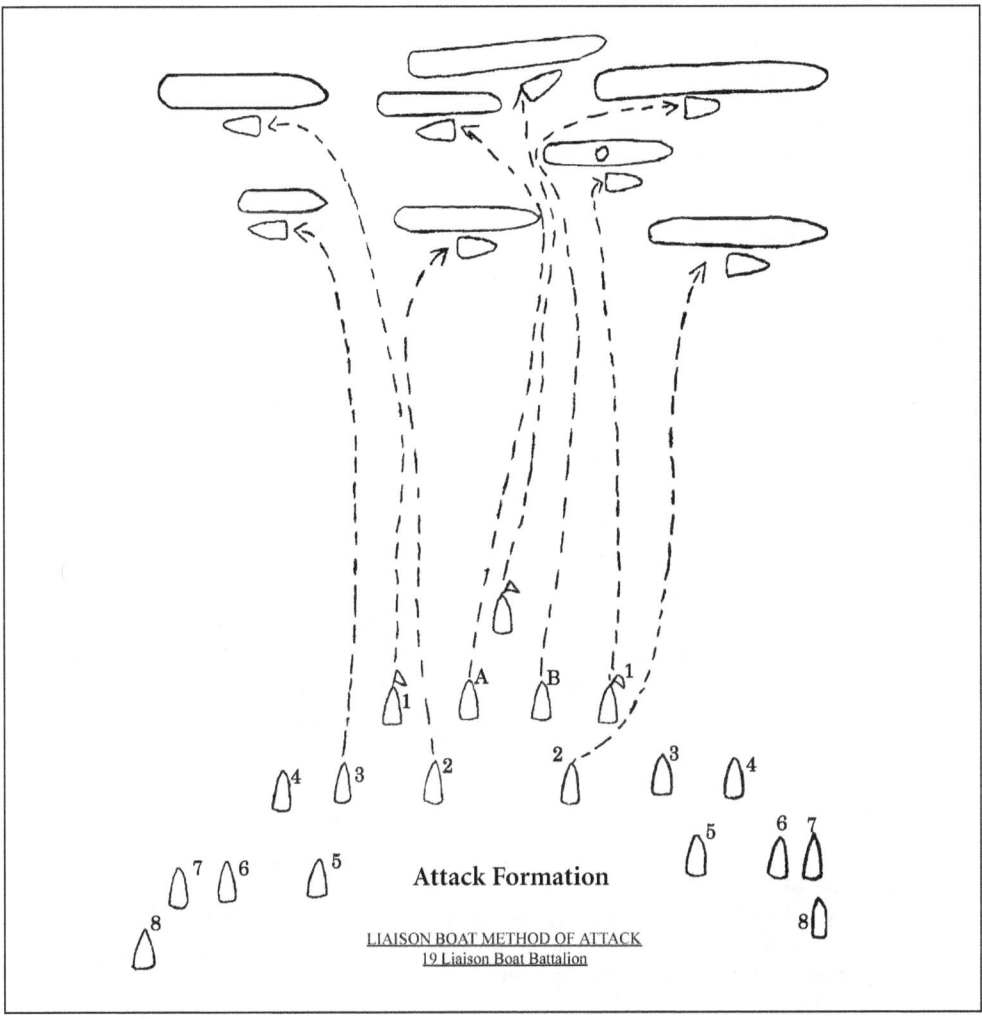

After proceeding toward the target in the Number 3 Formation, the boats would attack. At this point target selection would be based on the number of target vessels as compared to the number of *Maru-re* available for the attack. Where possible a target vessel would be approached by two boats, one from port and one from starboard. *Allied Translator and Interpreter Section—Southwest Pacific Area Serial 912.* Appendix K.

Training

Interviews with captured Japanese *Maru-re* pilots revealed their training program. Cpl. Nobuo Hayashi, a squad leader for the 19th Liaison Boat Battalion, was captured near Tigbulan, Luzon on 1 February 1945. He discussed the training program that he had undergone after volunteering for the liaison boat program.

> The training program started approximately July 1944 at TESSHIMA (TOYOSHIMA) in the Inland Sea. Training ground was later removed to UJINA Area August 1944. Boat operators would receive from one to three months training.... In the middle of August 1944, boat operators assembled at UJINA, where they were outfitted. Then proceeded to KONOURA, ETAJIMA Barracks where they were organized. They received one week's basic training ashore. Then they were sent to TAIBI, east of ETAJIMA, where the unit's boats were assembled.... They remained

there for approximately 10 days, receiving simple instructions concerning motors and motor repairs from an Army sergeant. Returned to ETAJIMA. At first they boarded a UJINA Model Liaison Boat, along with the platoon leader as instructor, and four other men. They took turns as helmsmen for a period of one week. Then each was assigned a UJINA Model boat and practiced following the leader's boat on very erratic courses for two days. The number of boats in this stage of training was not fixed. Then for one week, they practiced number 2 formation.... This part of the training was continued by First Lieutenant NAKAMURA. Upon completion of this and, until he left ETAJIMA, he received training in attack formation, in changing from number 2 formation to attack formation, and in actual attack runs.[12]

Subsequent sessions saw the trainees practicing their attack runs against various types of Japanese landing craft and merchant ships. Of course, no actual depth charges were used in these practice runs. At other times the depth charges were dropped when no ships were in the vicinity. At the completion of the training, Hayashi was "issued a new uniform, sword, canteen, helmet, life jacket, dog tag, and eight inch wide band to be wrapped around the body as a precaution against underwater explosions."[13]

Organization and Deployment in the Philippines

Army *Maru-re* boats were organized into battalions, with each battalion consisting of approximately 100–150 men divided into three companies of thirty each. Assigned to the battalion would be between seventy-five and one hundred boats, depending on the availability of the boats and the area the battalion needed to cover. In order to keep the existence and purpose of these battalions as secret as possible, they were referred to officially as "Fishing Battalions." Accompanying each "Fishing Battalion" was a maintenance and service battalion, referred to as "Harbor Construction Battalions."[14] This unit was responsible for building the base, maintaining it, and keeping the boats in good repair. Orders for the harbor construction battalions read:

> When the unit CO is informed of the plans where the unit will be stationed, he will receive detailed instructions. He will then reconnoiter the area and lay his plans.
>
> a. Points to be observed when reconnoitering the selected position.
>   (1) How easily boats and supplies can be brought ashore
>   (2) Slope of shore line and general terrain featured
>   (3) Waves, tide, and wind
>   (4) Obstacles at water's edge
>   (5) Difficulties of construction and extent of necessary construction
>   (6) Equipment and personnel necessary for the construction
>   (7) Water supply (boiled or distilled)
>   (8) Billeting facilities (caves)
>   (9) Protection from air attacks
>   (10) Presence of local repair shops
>   (11) Condition of repair and supply facilities of other forces
>   (12) Local technicians available
>   (13) Facilities for camouflaging
>   (14) Ease with which depth charges, fuel, etc. can be accumulated.[15]

These were serious considerations given that many of the boats were lost to American air attack, as well as the shore bombardment of PT boats and LCI type gunboats.

In early 1945 Allied intelligence identified locations for some of the army battalions in the Philippines as follows:

Fishing Battalion Number	Date	Location
1	January 1945	San Fernando
2	3 January 1945	Batangas
3	21 January 1945	Pangasinan

Fishing Battalion Number	Date	Location
9	22 November 1944	San Fernando
11	[no date given]	Ternate
12	2 January 1945	Port Sual
13	Transport sunk en route P.I. remaining company at Binubusan with 19th Battalion	
15	December 1944	Manila
16	[no date or location given]	
17	26 December 1944	Obando
18	19 January 1945	Dampalit
19	1 February 1945	Binubusan
20	[no date or location given]	
105	January 1945	Batangas
106	January 1945	Batangas
107	[No date]	Ternate
111	February 1945	Legaspi
112	17 January 1945	Port Sual
114	January 1945	Batangas
115	25 November 1944	Talin Bay
117	February 1945	Obando and Bulacan
118	13 February 1945	Obando[16]

Organization and Deployment at Okinawa

Army *Maru-re* boats were organized into battalions consisting of about one hundred boats each with 104 pilots. Each battalion was divided into three boat companies. Additional support and command personnel were included with each company. After the organization of the first thirty battalions at Etajima in late 1944 was completed, they were given their assignments.

> A total of sixteen out of these thirty battalions were assigned to the Philippines as follows: 5 to Ramon Bay on the eastern coast, 1 to Manila, 1 to Lingayen Bay, 1 to Ternate and 8 to Bandagas on the southern coast. For Okinawa, nine SBRs [battalions] were deployed as follows: 3 in the Kerama Archipelago, 4 on Okinawa Island, and 2 on Miyakojima Island. The remaining 5 of the 30 SBRs [battalions] were posted to Taiwan. In addition, another 12 regiments [battalions] (31st through 40th, 51st and 52nd SBRs [battalions]) completed their deployment across Japan for homeland defense.[17]

An assessment of the situation at Okinawa had been made earlier on, with prospective enemy landing zones identified. Assignment of the battalions to specific areas reflected these expectations. In order of probability the landing zones were identified as "(1) Hagushi-Oyama Beach, (2) Naha-Itoman, (3) Kadena Beach, (4) Minatogawa, and (5) Nakagusuku Bay. In order to facilitate a timely scramble which could cover any one of these five districts, the First Special Boat Battalion was deployed on Zamami Island, the Second on Akajima Island and ... the Third on Takashiki Island."[18] Located in the southern section of Okinawa were the 26th, 27th, 28th, and 29th Special Boat Battalions. The first three Special Boat Battalions were all located on islands of the Kerama Retto, a string of islands to the south west of Okinawa that would be the site of the first American landings at Okinawa. In the opening days of the campaign the three battalions were put out of commission. Approximately three hundred boats were captured by the Americans, and the battalion personnel retreated to the hills where they continually launched attacks and harassed the Americans until the end of the war.

Army Suicide Boat Regiments (SBRs)* at Okinawa

SBR Number	Commanding Officer	Date Arrived	Location at Okinawa
1st SBR	Capt. Hiroshi Umezawa	10 Sept. 1944	Zamami Island, Kerama Retto
2nd SBR	Capt. Yoshihiko Noda	Late 1944	Akajima and Keruma Islands, Kerama Retto

SBR Number	Commanding Officer	Date Arrived	Location at Okinawa
3rd SBR	Capt. Yoshitsugu Akamatsu	26 Sept, 1944	Tokashiki Island, Kerama Retto
26th SBR	Capt. Mutsuo Adachi	14 Dec. 1944	Tokashiki Island, Kerama Retto
27th SBR	Capt. Shigami Okabe	Dec. 1944–Jan. 1945	Yonabaru, Nakagusuku Bay
28th SBR	Capt. Toshio Honma	Mid-Feb. 1945	Minatogawa and Naha
29th SBR	Capt. Hisanori Yamamoto	17 Feb. 1945	Chatan, NE of Naha

*In the report by Lt. CO. Masahiro Kawai, the units are referred to as Suicide-Boat Regiments. However, their size indicates that they were probably equal in size to what would be considered a company.[19]

Organization and Deployment at Taiwan, Iwo Jima and Japan

Both *Shinyo* and *Maru-re* boats were sent to Iwo Jima and Taiwan, however, their use was limited at those two islands. On Iwo Jima there was little cover for the boats and the two units sent there, *Shinyo* Squadrons 3 and 4, were decimated in preliminary air raids against the island in preparation for the invasion.

Taiwan was bypassed as MacArthur had determined that his main focus was to be the recapture of the Philippine Islands. This strategy was favored by the navy as well, as they saw no need to concentrate forces on the island. It was too far from the Japanese home islands to be of any use in a final invasion of Japan. This did not mean that the Japanese forces there were any less prepared for an invasion. After forming in Japan, the suicide boat units were transferred to Taiwan, Okinawa, and the Philippines. Originally scheduled to arrive in Taiwan in October 1944, they did not arrive until December 1944 and January 1945. The poor results shown by the suicide boats in the Philippines were attributed to a lack of time for proper preparation. Planning for the invasion of Taiwan would be more thorough, as there was more time and valuable lessons had been learned from the experience of the suicide boats in the Philippines. Both the army and navy had agreed on a plan for defense of the island which included the use of suicide boats. It assigned units as follows:

Local Military and Naval Agreement on
Sea Offensive Operations
Commander of the Tenth Regional Army
Commandant of the TAKAO district

No. I. Policy.

The army liaison vessels [*Maru-re*] and the naval one-man torpedo boats [*Shinyo*] will be secretly based in the southern part of FORMOSA under a unified program in order to make sudden attacks and destroy any enemy convoy attempting to land. This operation is called Operation 8.

No. II. Designated Points.

1. The disposition of units of Operation 8 is as follows:
   20th Naval Raiding Unit — HIGASHIISHI Vicinity.
   21st Naval Raiding Unit — BOSAN Vicinity
   22nd Naval Raiding Unit — SHISHI GASHIRA (Area between BOSAN and BORYO).
   23rd and 8th Naval Raiding Units — Outer harbor of TAKAO
   24th Naval Raiding Unit — Between TAINAN and TAKAO (Southern side of the mouth of NISOKOKEI River.)
   25th and 5th Naval Raiding Units — Vicinity of the NISOKOKEI River south TAIWAN.
     One unit of one-man torpedo boats — KAIKO, KOSHUN-GUN
     One unit of one-man torpedo boats — TOKO Vicinity
     Two units of one-man torpedo boats — Northern foot of JUZAN, SAEI
     One unit of one-man torpedo boats — BOKOTO.
2. The army liaison ship unit will be under the command of the commandant of the TAKAO Naval Guard District for the operation.
3. The time for the execution of Operation 8 will be early morning (by dawn) of the next day after the enemy convoy has anchored. However, if circumstances permit, the operation may be carried out on the same night that the enemy anchors.

4. The objectives of the attack will be the anchored enemy transports. However, depending on the circumstances, the smaller ships may be attacked.
5. The purpose of the attack is to make one mass attack to avoid successive attacks utilizing complete surprise.
6. The detailed points of attack will be decided by the attacking unit, under naval coordination. However, several plans may be prepared according to the expected anchorage position of the enemy and will be simple instead of being tactical and complicated.[20]

It was expected that the American invasion would take place in southern Taiwan, so the suicide boats were concentrated there. However, strategic planning for an invasion included the possibility that the actual invasion of Taiwan could be in the north, where there were more important air bases. To cover that contingency, half of the suicide boat units could be shifted to the north. There they would establish bases further inland to avoid losses that might come from pre-invasion bombardment. In *Japanese Monograph No. 52*, it was reported that an estimated 450 *Maru-re* and 900 navy *Shinyo* were available in Taiwan for use against American transports.[21]

Invasion of the home islands was of greater concern to the Japanese. To defend against the coming invasion the Japanese began to hold back on the expenditure of their forces toward the end of the Okinawa campaign. In addition to aircraft, numerous *Shinyo* and *Maru-re* units were stationed throughout Japan in preparation for the assault on Japan proper.

Cmdr. Liui F. Kuo of the Chinese navy and John Keinle F 2/c from *LCS(L) 96* inspect the engine of a Japanese *Shinyo* at Amoy on 6 April 1945. Official U.S. Navy Photograph.

Kaiten

The concept for the development of the manned torpedo came from two junior officers, Ens. Sekio Nishina and Lt. (jg) Hiroshi Kuroki. The two were midget submarine pilots who recognized both the value of the midget submarine and its shortcomings. A new type weapon was needed, one that combined the attributes of the midget submarine with that of the faster torpedo. They evolved plans for utilizing the Type 93, Model 3 "long lance torpedo" as its base.

As junior officers, they had little ability to influence naval planning and policy, so they sought expert help. It was their good fortune to make contact with Hiroshi Suzukawa, a designer at Kure Naval Arsenal. Looking over their sketches, Suzukawa saw an opportunity for the creation of a new weapon. The three men combined their skills and spent the latter months of 1942 working up plans for the new vessel. Rejection by the Naval General Staff was not enough to halt the progress of the three men. They continually revised and fine tuned their plans for the new weapon. In February 1944, their efforts were finally rewarded when they were afforded the chance to build a prototype. Concerned that the new weapon was a suicide weapon, the navy high command required the installation of an escape hatch. While this seemed to alleviate their concern, any pilot close enough to leave the manned torpedo would not be able to survive the nearby detonation of its massive warhead. Production of the prototype was to take place at the secret naval base at Kure.[22]

Actual work on the prototype *Kaiten* manned torpedo began in March 1944 and by August of that year it had gone into production. Based on the Type 93 Model 3 torpedo, the *Kaiten* would be the ultimate torpedo, one that would be guided to its target by a pilot. Its 3,418 lb. explosive warhead insured that a successful attack would result in the sinking of most any ship in the U.S. fleet. In all, four different types of *Kaiten*, Types 1, 2, 4, and 10 were designed, but only the Type 1 became operational.

Kaiten Type 1 utilized parts of the Type 93, Model 3 torpedo. Warhead size was increased and a control compartment for the pilot was fitted between the forward section housing the warhead and air tanks and the torpedo body. This model was fueled by oxygen as was the original torpedo. A manually operated periscope was fitted into the sail. Hatches above and below the pilot allowed access to the steering compartment. Since four to six *Kaiten* were carried on the deck of an I-Class mother sub, access to the *Kaiten* from the mother sub was effected through the use of a tube between two of the *Kaiten* and the sub. Access to the others required the sub to surface so the pilots could use the upper hatch. The pilot could manually set his course or use an electric gyroscope to guide his hand-controlled steering apparatus. The explosive charge could be detonated by either a built in inertia-type pistol or electrically by the pilot.

Type 1 *Kaitens* were designed to reach a depth of one hundred meters, however they leaked at that depth but were able to withstand the pressures at sixty meters. The run toward the target vessel would usually be at periscope depth until the course could be determined, at which time the *Kaiten* make the final run to the target at a depth of about five meters. Speed was controlled by the pilot, and the manned torpedo could reach speeds of thirty knots. At that speed its range was about fourteen miles. A longer range of forty-eight miles was possible if the *Kaiten* were run at twelve knots. In practice, a combination of various speeds would be tested, with the slower speeds used in the early part of the approach and an increase to maximum speed once the *Kaiten* was within striking distance.[23]

Kaiten Type 2 was a dedicated model, that is, it was designed as a manned torpedo, not adapted from the regular naval torpedo. It was a much larger vessel than the Type 1 and designed to have a maximum speed of forty knots at a range of fifteen miles. Powered by an engine designed to run on a combination of hydrogen peroxide and hydrogen hydrate, it was vastly different from the oxygen fueled *Kaiten* Type 1. Difficulties in engine development

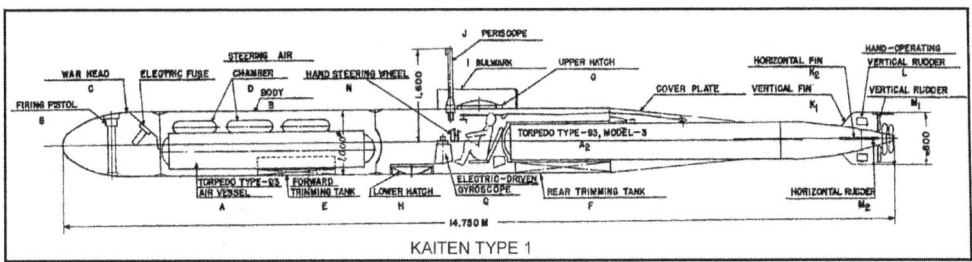

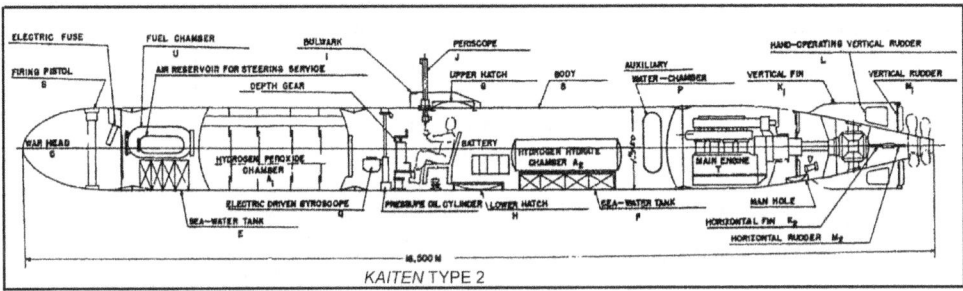

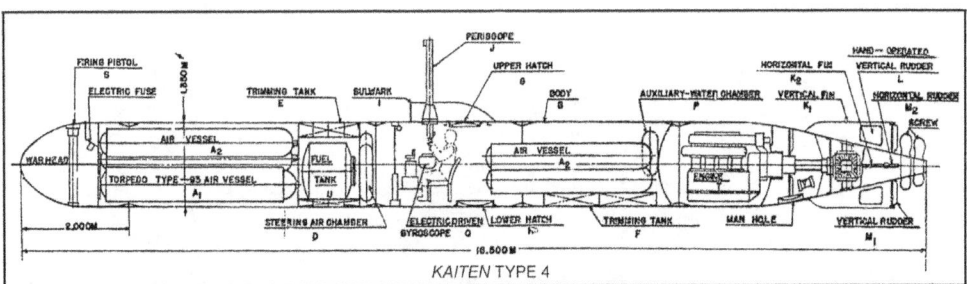

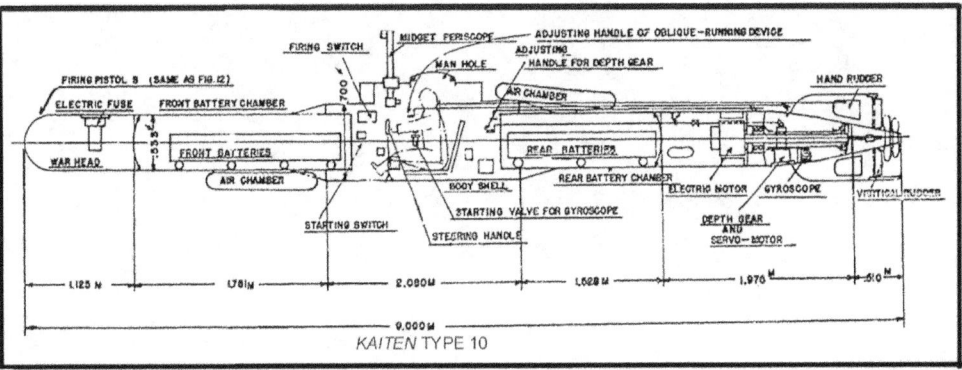

Kaiten Models *1, 2, 4,* and *10.* U.S. Naval Technical Mission to Japan. *Ships and Targets Japanese Suicide Craft.* January 1946, pp. 23, 26.

slowed production of the vessel, however, by December 1944, the Japanese had two ready for testing. Constant problems developed during the testing phase of the *Kaiten* Type 2 and the project was halted in favor of still another model, the Type 4.

The *Kaiten* Type 4 model was designed as an improved Type 2, however, it also ran into problems. The engine was modified to run on a combination of kerosene and oxygen, a modification that would decrease the weight of the fuel and allow the size of the war head to be increased to 3,968 lbs. Between January and March of 1945, five of the model were produced and tested. Engine problems once again proved to be the major difficulty. Although the redesign of the *Kaiten* Type 4 had the desirable effect of increasing the size of the warhead, the engine problem could not be overcome and the project had to be abandoned.

Kaiten Type 10 was the final attempt at an improved model. New developments in storage batteries made the use of electric motors a possibility. However, their relative lack of power made it necessary to downsize the vessel to about "one-third the size of the Type 1 and to have only 300kg [661 lbs.] of explosive."[24] The lack of a lower escape hatch made it impossible to carry it on a submarine for underwater launch. It is surmised that this model was probably to be launched from shore at invading American ships or carried on a surface ship and launched on the water's surface. There are no production figures available for this type and it is likely that it was in the planning stage at war's end.

This *Kaiten* variant was probably designed to launch from shore to be used against amphibious assaults or anchored transports. It was captured at Truk. NARA 809G 276351.

American sailors inspect a *Kairyu* submarine at Yokosuka Naval Yard, 11 September 1945. These subs were fitted with an explosive warhead. NARA 80G 338383.

Selection of *Kaiten* Personnel and Their Training

As compared to the pilots of the explosive speedboats, the *Kaiten* pilots were older and better trained. Shortages of available aircraft for kamikaze missions had left a surplus of trained pilots, men whose skills and qualifications could be transferred to the newly developing *Kaiten* corps. Presented to trainee pilots at both the Tsuchiura and Nara Naval Air Bases in August 1944, was a new prospect, one that would make use of their burgeoning talents. The *Kaiten* was described to the trainees as a super weapon that would easily annihilate an enemy ship. Although over a thousand trainees volunteered for the new mission at Tsuchiura, only one hundred were chosen. Candidates selected for the new weapon had a combination of physical strength and strong will, fighting spirit, and minimal family responsibilities. At the conclusion of their training at Tsuchiura and Nara, the prospective *Kaiten* pilots were shipped off to the next stage of their training at Otsujima Island.[25]

Once established at Otsujima, pilots undertook training in the manned torpedo. They quickly learned that the project was top secret and that the weapon was not to be described in regular terms. It was known as the "circle six metal fitting,"[26] a term so nondescript that it could have been used to describe basically any type of hardware. All of the manned torpedoes and midget submarines would use this type of label in order to prevent the enemy from learning of their existence. Although there were numerous *Kaiten* pilots in training, their progress was hampered at first by a shortage of vessels in which to train. Classroom lectures, information sharing meetings, and lectures of various types on the mechanics of the *Kaiten* occupied the first stage of their training, which lasted for a couple of months.

Training in the *Kaiten* was hazardous. Each of the manned torpedoes had its own idiosyncrasies which required constant attention. Tight controls, greased fittings, and the close proximity of controls to one another was problematic. But the naval high command had cor-

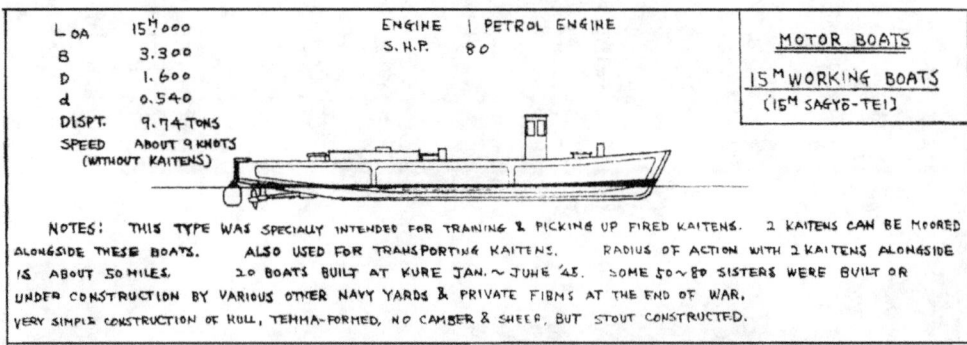

Top: Practice runs for the *Kaiten* involved tying one or two of them to the *Kaiten* chaser boat. This fifteen meter long boat would take them out into the bay where the trainee would climb aboard. Once all systems were checked, the *Kaiten* would be released and the chaser boat would follow, sometimes helping to locate the *Kaiten* if it sank, or warning it if it was about to hit something. Shizuo Fukui, Compiler. *Japanese Naval Vessels at the End of War.* Administrative Division, Second Demobilization Bureau, Japan. April 25, 1947, p. 165. *Bottom:* Cradles to hold *Kaiten* are shown on the Japanese submarines *I-58* and *I-53*.

rectly deduced that aircraft pilots would be able to handle them. The *Kaiten* were prone to dive or climb without warning. Sometimes they launched themselves downward and stuck in the mud at the bottom of the bay. Launching the *Kaiten* for practice runs was effected by lashing one or two of them to a fifteen meter work boat, which transported them out into the bay. After an early mishap and loss of life, the work boat was assigned to follow the trail of the *Kaiten* through practice. If it did not surface when it was supposed to, bubbles emitted from the sub might help in determining its location. It was not infrequent for a diver to descend to the bay bottom, hook cables to a *Kaiten* and raise it to the surface, in that manner saving the student pilot for another day. Pilots manning these torpedoes knew that they were on their own and that rescue might not be possible. During *Kaiten* training, fifteen prospective pilots lost their lives, including the co-creator of the *Kaiten*, Lt. Hiroshi Kuroki, who met his fate on 6 September 1944.

Kaiten Missions

In spite of the intense training undergone by the *Kaiten* pilots, their success rate would be dismal. A number of missions were sent out, but the missions were either unsuccessful or the mother subs were sunk with all hands lost. Only *Mississinewa AO 59*, sunk at Ulithi on 20 November 1944, and *Underhill DE 682*, sunk off the Philippines on 24 July 1945, were successful missions for the manned torpedoes. The liberty ship *Pontus H. Ross* was struck at Hollandia, New Guinea on 11 January 1945, but it suffered very little damage. Some *Kaiten* which launched at target vessels were spotted and blown up by enemy fire, while still others hit reefs or were otherwise unable to complete their missions. Japanese sources indicate that in the

Japanese submarine *I-47* is shown with *Kaiten* on her decks as she departs from Otsujima on 20 April 1945. She was headed for Okinawa where she launched two of her *Kaiten*. Neither was successful in striking an American ship.

After the loss of Guadalcanal and other islands in the south, the Japanese recognized the need for ships which could rapidly transport men and material to their island strongholds. The 1st Class Transport, shown above, was designed in mid-1943. In addition to troops and other supplies they could carry either four *Daihatsu* landing barges, two *Koryu* midget subs, or six *Kaiten*. Transport No. 5, shown above with a *Koryu* on her deck, was lost in the Philippines.

course of these missions approximately seventy-five *Kaiten* pilots were killed, along with the entire crews of the eight *Kaiten* carrying subs that were sunk.[27]

Fleet submarines, *I-36, 37, 44, 47, 48, 53, 56, 58, 156, 157, 158, 159, 162,* and *165* were modified to carry the *Kaiten*. Transport subs *I-361, 363, 366, 367, 368, 370, 372,* and *373* were also converted. The last year of the war also saw surface combatants modified to carry *Kaiten*. The largest of these was the cruiser *Kitakami*, which was capable of carrying eight *Kaiten* that could be launched off her stern. The destroyers *Namikaze* and *Shiokaze*, along with several *Matsu* class destroyers such as *Take* were also converted. Many of these ships had suffered war damage and were converted while under repair.[28] None of them ever went into battle to launch *Kaiten*.

After the fall of Guadalcanal it became apparent to the Japanese that they had a need for high speed transports that could deliver men, supplies, and equipment to their numerous island strongholds. In mid-1943 they designed the 1st Class Transport, which could carry needed troops and equipment. An additional feature of the ships was that they could also carry either six *Daihatsu* landing barges, two *Koryu* midget subs, or six *Kaiten*. The *Koryu* could be launched while the ship was underway, making for a speedy delivery. Most of the transports were lost during the war. Additionally Light Escorts Types A and B were under construction at the end of the war. One of their functions would be the local delivery of *Kaiten* throughout Japan.

KAITEN CARRYING SUBMARINES

Submarine	Type	Length	Date of Conversion	No. of Kaiten
I-8	J3	323'	1944	4
I-36	B1	356'	1945	6
I-37	B1	356'	1945	4
I-44	B2	356'	1944	6
I-47	C2	358'	1945	6
I-48	C2	358'	1944	4
I-53	C3/4	330'	1945	6
I-56	B3/4	356'	1944	4
I-58	B3/4	356'	1944	6

Submarine	Type	Length	Date of Conversion	No. of Kaiten
I-156	KD3A/B	330'	1945	2
I-157	KD3A/B	330'	1945	2
I-158	KD3A/B	330'	1945	2
I-159	KD3A/B	330'	1945	2
I-162	KD4	320'	1945	5
I-165	KD5	320'	1945	2
I-361	D1/2 Transport	248'	1945	5
I-363	D1/2 Transport	248'	1945	5
I-366	D1/2 Transport	248'	1945	5
I-367	D1/2 Transport	248'	1945	5
I-368	D1/2 Transport	248'	1945	5
I-370	D1/2 Transport	248'	1945	5
I-372	D1/2 Transport	248'	1945	5
I-373	D1/2 Transport	248'	1945	5

Some subs, such as *I-47, 53, 58* and others, were initially fitted to carry four *Kaiten* and later refitted to carry more. Figures above reflect the final configuration.[29]

Kairyu and *Koryu*

Successes at Pearl Harbor and the limited successes of the *Kaiten* spurred further development of the small submarine projects. These midget submarines were generally referred

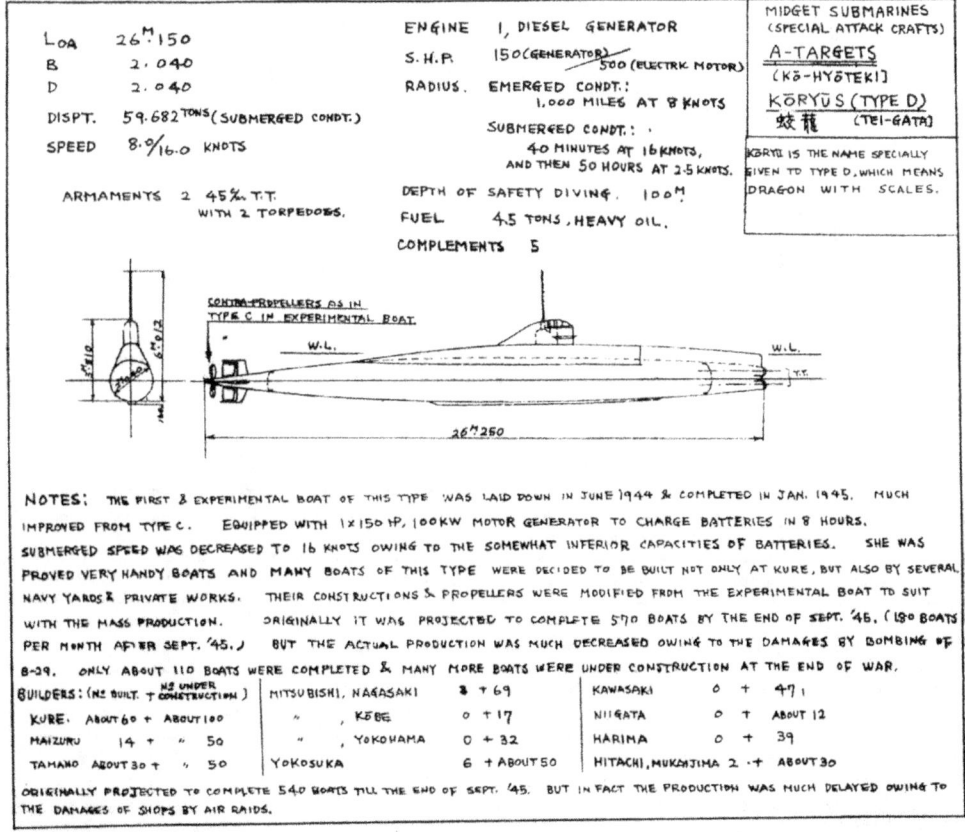

Koryu midget subs were designed to carry two conventional torpedoes in their bow. Shizuo Fukui, Compiler. *Japanese Naval Vessels at the End of War*. Administrative Division, Second Demobilization Bureau, Japan. April 25, 1947, p. 197.

to as *Ko-Hyoteki* (A-targets), to disguise their existence, and were of two types, the *Kairyu*, or Sea Dragon, and the *Koryu*, or Scaly Dragon. It is probable that their planned use was for defense of the home islands in the face of an American invasion.

The *Koryu* measured eighty-six feet in length with a beam of nearly seven feet. Two 18" torpedoes were mounted in its bow tubes. This was a true submarine with long distance capabilities. Its five man crew could take it to depths of 330 feet and, on the surface, its cruising speed of eight knots gave it a range of one thousand miles. Capable of sixteen knots submerged, it did not become operational until early 1945, as its first model was completed. By war's end only 110 of a projected 540 had been built,[30] none of which became operational. The major production center was at Kure, with others constructed at Maizuru, Tamano, Nagasaki, Kobe, Yokohama, Yokosuka, Kawasaki, Niigata, Harima, and Hitachi. The scarcity of torpedoes toward the end of the war would probably have led to its use as a suicide weapon, however, American air raids continually interrupted production.

A smaller sub, the *Kairyu*, was also developed at war's end. This vessel had a crew of two and was fifty-seven feet long. Although it could dive to 650 feet, it was slower than the *Koryu* and only had a range of about 450 nautical miles. Originally designed to carry two 18" torpedoes on the outside of their hulls, they also fell victim to the torpedo shortage that plagued the *Koryu*. Models were found in Yokosuka Naval Yard after the war with 1,300 lb. explosive

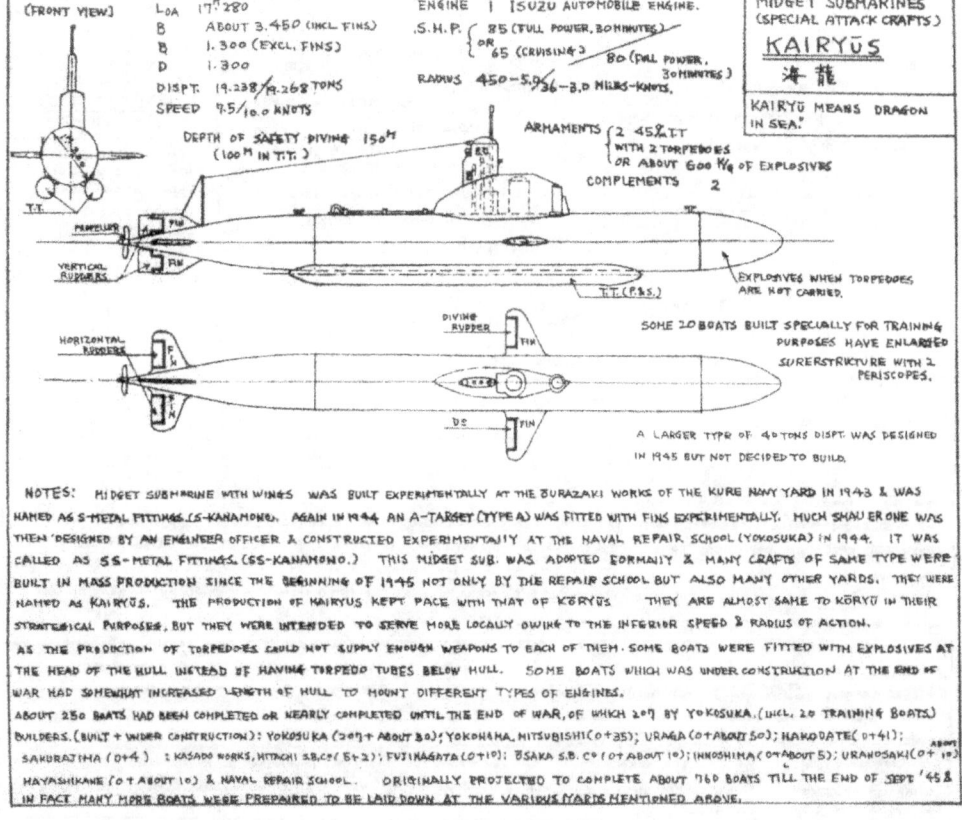

The *Kairyu*, or Sea Dragon, was originally designed to carry a single torpedo. Shortages of torpedoes at war's end made the mounting of an explosive warhead the logical progression. This turned it into a suicide weapon. Shizuo Fukui, Compiler. *Japanese Naval Vessels at the End of War*. Administrative Division, Second Demobilization Bureau, Japan. April 25, 1947, p. 198.

Kairyu submarines at Yokosuka shipyard on 11 September 1945. Subs numbered *4018* and *4016* can be identified as training subs because they have two periscopes and a longer sail. NARA 80G 338384.

warheads fitted, indicating that they would be used in ramming attacks like the *Kaiten*. Production figures for this sub were 250 of a projected 760 by September 1945. The major production center for these was Yokosuka, followed by Yokohama, Uraga, Hakoate, Sakurajima, Fujinagata, Osaka, Innoshima, Uranosaki, and Hayashikane. Some of the subs at Yokosuka were built as training subs with an extended superstructure and two periscopes.[31]

An even smaller sub, the *Shinkai* (sea vibrator), was not put into use. To keep its existence secret it was referred to as the *Maru-Kyu Kanamono* or "Number 9 metal fitting." This forty-foot-long sub carried a two-man crew and was designed to attach magnetic mines to the underside of ship hulls. When this proved impractical a contact warhead was fitted to the vessel. Its electric motors limited its speed to about nine knots and its development and production was abandoned after only one was completed at Ourazaki Works, Kure Naval Base.

Another small sub, about forty-six feet long, was never given a name. It was simply designated as the U-Metal Fitting (*U-Kanamono*) in keeping with the secrecy surrounding the development of these types of vessels. It carried two men and could only make about three knots. One torpedo was mounted in its nose. This limited its use to local defense. Fourteen were built at Kure in the spring and summer of 1944, but they never became operational.[32]

One other midget sub, the *M-Kanamono* or "M-Metal Fitting," was about the same size as the *U-Kanamono*. It had tracks and was designed to crawl along the bottom and attach magnetic mines to enemy vessels. One experimental model was produced at Ourazaki Works, Kure but never saw production.

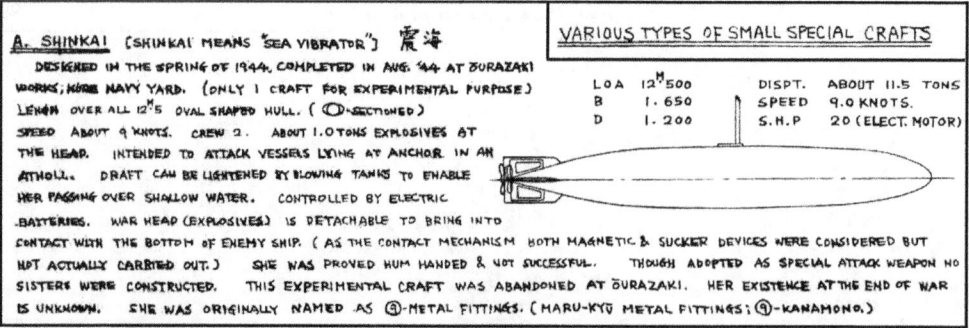

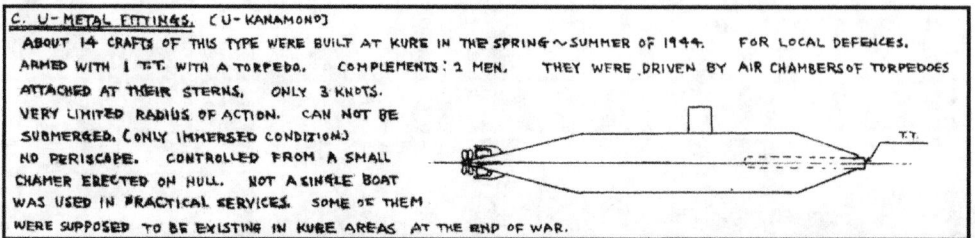

As the war entered its final stages, more emphasis was placed on the development of new special attack weapons. Two smaller special attack vessels were developed at the end of the war but not put into use. The *Shinkai* (top) was about forty feet in length and designed to attack ships anchored near shore. It carried a two man crew and could make nine knots. Only one of these was produced at Kure Naval Yard and proved unwieldy in sea trials. The *U-Kanamono* or U-Metal Fitting never had a name other than its secret developmental designation. It was about thirty feet in length. Fourteen were produced at Kure Naval Yard, but they were never put into service. Shizuo Fukui, Compiler. *Japanese Naval Vessels at the End of War.* Administrative Division, Second Demobilization Bureau, Japan. April 25, 1947, p. 204.

By the end of the war the Japanese, in desperation, created a number of special attack weapons out of whatever materials were available. This one appears to be made from an aircraft fuel drop tank. This vessel, described as a "human torpedo," was found on Saipan. Its diving planes indicate that it could partially submerge, but the design of the canopy could not take much water pressure. It probably ran just under the surface. The photograph was taken on 6 January 1949 at NAB Saipan. NARA 80G 452861F.

The Suicide Soldier

The discussions preceding this section have referred to the use of a variety of mechanical weapons designed to wreak havoc on American and Allied forces during the course of countless battles. Not mentioned previously are the tactics used by individual Japanese soldiers on the battlefields of Asia during the Second World War. These ranged from massed infantry group charges into waiting death, which was considered preferable to waiting for the enemy to annihilate them in their bunkers, caves, and foxholes, to the use of small explosives to disable American armor. Reports from numerous Japanese units indicate that the formation of "suicide squads" was a common tactic. The *Antitank Combat Reference*, issued by the Japanese army, indicated:

> Antitank combat is based principally on close-quarters assault, the essence being thorough training in and the execution of suicide tactics.... In attacking, the assailant carrying explosives must dash against the tank in a spirit of self-sacrifice, while the antitank weapons must engage the tank. If one man and one antitank gun can destroy one tank and its crew, their mission will be well accomplished, especially if the tank is a heavy or super heavy tank.[33]

The simplest weapon devised to combat American tanks was the lunge antitank mine. This was a cone-shaped explosive charge attached to the end of a six foot pole. The mine contained about twelve pounds of explosive and could penetrate six inches of armor plate if it were to strike at a ninety degree angle. American military intelligence described its use:

> Perhaps the oddest of these antitank charges is the so-called "Lunge Mine" encountered on Leyte Island. This weapon—an armor-piercing charge on the end of a pole—derives its name from the way in which it must be thrust against the side of a tank in order to detonate.
> The mine is an explosive-filled, sheet-steel cone, about 12 inches long and 8 inches in diameter at the base. As in all hollow charges, the cavity in the bottom of the cone tends to guide the force of the explosion out from the bottom of the cone and against the armor plate of the target. A metal sleeve extends from the top, or point end, of the cone and houses the simple firing device—a nail on the end of the broomstick-like handle which fits into the sleeve. The detonator is a little more than an ordinary blasting cap set into the top of the cone, where the nail will strike the cap if the handle is jammed down in the sleeve.... Three legs, 5¼ inches long, are attached to the bottom of the cone; the Japanese claim that these legs increase the penetrating power of the weapon. The penetrating effect of the charge is greater when the explosion occurs a few inches away from the armor.
> The Japanese suicide soldier has been taught to wield this weapon as he would a rifle and bayonet. The prescribed method of operation is for the soldier to remove the safety pin as he approaches the tank to be attacked, and to grasp the center of the handle with his left hand, and the butt end with his right. Then, holding the stick level, with the mine to the front, he lunges forward as in a bayonet attack, thrusting the three legs on the mine base against the side of the tank. The shock of contact will break the shear wire and the striker nail will be shoved into the detonator cap, thus exploding the mine as it is held against the armor. At this point the Jap soldier's mission ends for all time.[34]

According to military intelligence the lunge mine was a "pure suicide weapon."

Still another method of self-annihilation practiced by the Japanese Army involved the use of mines, or satchel charges against tanks. On the island of Biak in late May 1944, "a Biak Jap, who was lying in the road in front of tanks, was discovered and shot, an antitank mine tied to his body exploded. In the Central Pacific, a Japanese prisoner explained that his job was to climb on an advancing tank and hold a demolition charge against its side until it exploded."[35] These tactics became noticeable during the battles in the Philippines and at Okinawa, where American tanks became increasingly effective against Japanese positions.

Emphasis on the development of new weapons in the Japanese arsenal focused on aircraft and ships, leaving little development of weapons for the individual soldier. As a result, Japanese military technology had not kept pace with the development of American armor, leading to an increase in the use of individual soldiers to attack tanks with explosive charges.

By early 1945 Japanese suicide attacks against tanks were well known. In this drawing, a Japanese soldier is about to thrust a pole charge against the side of the tank. The ensuing explosion would ensure his demise. War Department, Military Intelligence Division. *Intelligence Bulletin Vol. III*, No. 2, March 1945. Washington, D.C., p. 65.

The *Kirikomi Tai*, or suicide assault units, were originally developed with each unit having an officer at its head. As the campaign for the Philippines and later Okinawa wore on, this put a serious dent in the number of infantry officers available. As a result, the units were organized with superior privates as their leaders, thus slowing the loss of officer personnel.

Japanese Army officers were not lacking in methods of sacrificing their troops. According to a War Department intelligence bulletin:

> Jap combat troops have been instructed to use what actually amounts to a human antitank minefield. If Japanese troops in defensive positions use this tactic as Tokyo directs, ten-man tank-assault units will be organized from reserve troops for every platoon in the line. These units will be deployed in two ranks, 100 yards in front of their respective platoons. There will be a distance of about 30 yards between ranks, and an interval of 50 yards between individuals. The rear rank will be staggered to cover the intervals in the front rank. When so deployed, each man will dig a spider hole with a carefully camouflaged cover. When a U.S. attack is anticipated, these suicide units will take their positions in the spider holes, and each man will be armed with a shoulder-pack box mine, a small smoke candle, two hand grenades, and a pistol, if he has been carrying one.[36]

As an American tank passed over his spider hole or nearby, the soldier would emerge from the hole and detonate the mine under or near the tank. These spider holes were well camouflaged to prevent discovery by American infantry accompanying the tanks.

When encountering possible American minefields, the Japanese sometimes resorted to the most expedient method of finding the mines. Under normal circumstances, mine detecting equipment would be used and mines dug up individually. Two American soldiers who had served in the Solomons, reported a novel Japanese approach to finding mines: "Some Japanese commanders would line up a detail of soldiers the entire length of the field, and walk them across. As the soldiers detonated the mines, replacements would be sent in to continue the

In this Japanese propaganda photograph from around 1942 Japanese infantrymen attack an American *Stuart M3* tank. The date and location of the photograph is unknown, but the *Stuart* tank was used only in the battle for Bataan Peninsula in 1942 and also by Australian troops in New Guinea. The Japanese characters read from right to left "*Gunjin wa Buyu o Sho Fuheshi*," which translates as "One must respect the soldier's military tradition."

path. This form of human mine detection was used by the Japs so that their main force could go through quickly."[37] How widespread this practice was remains to be seen, however, it is indicative of the mindset of the Japanese soldier and his commanders.

In addition to targets on land, the individual army or navy man went after American shipping. Swimming from shore to an anchored American ship armed with a mine, small explosive charge or even hand grenades was a common occurrence. These methods were described in the *Allied Land Forces S.E.A. Weekly Intelligence Review* in early January 1945:

> A new type of Japanese "suicide platoon" has come to light on PELELIU Island. The organization was made up of Japanese and locals who were drafted into the unit. Among them was 2nd Class Pfc TOKUSABURO, Uehara, who was captured by Allied forces.
>
> The PW's unit was made up of good swimmers to begin with and, in addition, was given time to practice free style swimming under water. Members were taught to swim under water towards the enemy landing craft until they were within distance to throw hand grenades into the boats. They were instructed to throw their grenades, which were timed for four to five seconds, immediately after removing the pins. (the means whereby the grenades were kept dry is not recorded).
>
> The men were also instructed to swim with mines in front of them for attacks against landing craft. Single-horn type anti-boat mines which were used were supported in the water by wooden frames to which they were connected with wire. Showing themselves as little as possible, the swimmers pushed the mines against oncoming boats.
>
> The unit was to be employed only at night, so it was not believed that the swimmers would be able to approach the boats during daylight. However, because of the severe bombing and naval

A definite suicide attack involved a soldier hiding in a "spider hole" with an anti-tank explosive charge. As the tank passed over his hole the soldier emerged and detonated the mine, destroying both the tank and himself. War Department Military Intelligence Division. *Intelligence Bulletin Vol. III*, No. 11, July 1945, p. 1.

fire which proceeded the Allied landing on PELELIU Island, the PW's unit was never able to assemble.[38]

Numerous ship action reports describe attacks by swimmers and their annihilation by rifle and pistol fire. *LCI(G) 404*, patrolling near Yoo Passage in the Palau Islands on 8 January 1945, received a message that swimmers were attacking ships in the area. She was soon under attack herself.

> The Commanding Officer of LCI(G) 404 later stated that during this period all hands including himself were engaged shooting swimmers and in damage control.... By 0300(K) sufficient information was received from LCI(G) 404 to learn that swimmers carrying explosive charges had attacked her. Enemy swimmers approached the ship toward the bow and stern. All the enemy were killed with the exception of one who was seen to dive under the fantail. Immediately afterwards, an explosion occurred hitting the steering engine room. Flooding was controlled and watertight integrity was maintained. Shortly after the explosion LCI(G) 404 sighted and destroyed and empty enemy raft two hundred feet astern of them.[39]

No casualties resulted from the attack, but the ship reported that her port rudder was blown off and her starboard rudder damaged beyond repair. Her skegs were torn loose and her aft hull plating was seriously damaged also. Such attacks were not unusual in the islands of the Pacific and American shipping would also undergo swimmer attacks at Okinawa.

Although the spectacular crashes of a kamikaze aircraft into a ship was the most notable of the suicide attack methods, it is probable that more Japanese servicemen met their deaths by simpler means. Countless thousands, armed with mines, satchel charges, pole charges, and their government issued rifles, went to their deaths in the service of the Emperor by dashing into enemy fire to plant their explosives against American tanks or swimming toward an American ship carrying explosives. Still others furiously charged into American guns rather than face capture. The number of men who died in such endeavors will never be known.

PART TWO
The Kamikaze Chronicles: A Detailed Account of the Attacks

7. Prelude to Mayhem

The possibility of a war between Japan and America had long been considered by American planners beginning shortly after the end of the Sino-Japanese War of 1894–1895. Japan's burgeoning power, as demonstrated in the Russo-Japanese War of 1904, gave added impetus to the need for contingency plans should the United States and Japan go to war at some point in the future. This planning, known in general as War Plan Orange and in the later 1930s as the Rainbow Plans, proved to be a close predictor of American activities in the war. Fortunately, the Americans were not caught totally unprepared as the possibilities of war with Japan had long been considered.

During the course of World War II, two major American thrusts toward Japan had developed. In the southern Pacific areas, General Douglas MacArthur's forces had moved across the islands in a semi-circular route heading toward the Philippines and the islands to the north, leading to the home islands of Japan. In the central Pacific, the American naval forces under Admiral Chester Nimitz had forged ahead, staging amphibious assaults on one island after another. By early 1944, the two arms of the pincer were rapidly closing in on the inner defense line of the Japanese Empire.[1]

At that point the next target became the subject of debate. MacArthur, his vision colored by his close affinity to the people of the Philippines, saw retaking the islands as the logical next step. Naval planners disagreed, believing that the Philippines could be bypassed in favor of an assault on the Marianas, Taiwan, and China, placing the Americans in a better position to attack Japan proper. At a meeting held between MacArthur, Nimitz, and President Franklin Roosevelt in Honolulu on 26 July 1944, MacArthur's view prevailed, in part because Japanese advances along the coast of China had made that an even more difficult target. The next assault on Japanese held territory would come on the island of Leyte in the Philippines.

Air Cover

The invasion of the Philippines presented numerous problems, among them the threat from Japanese air attacks. Carrier aircraft, including both Hellcats and Wildcats, were usually the first line of defense for the ships. In addition, the navy was responsible for supporting the landings at Leyte. However, once the invasion forces had gained a foothold, additional aircraft from the Far East Air Forces, under Lt. Gen. George C. Kenney, joined the fray.

The landings at Leyte centered around the northern end of Leyte Gulf near the town of

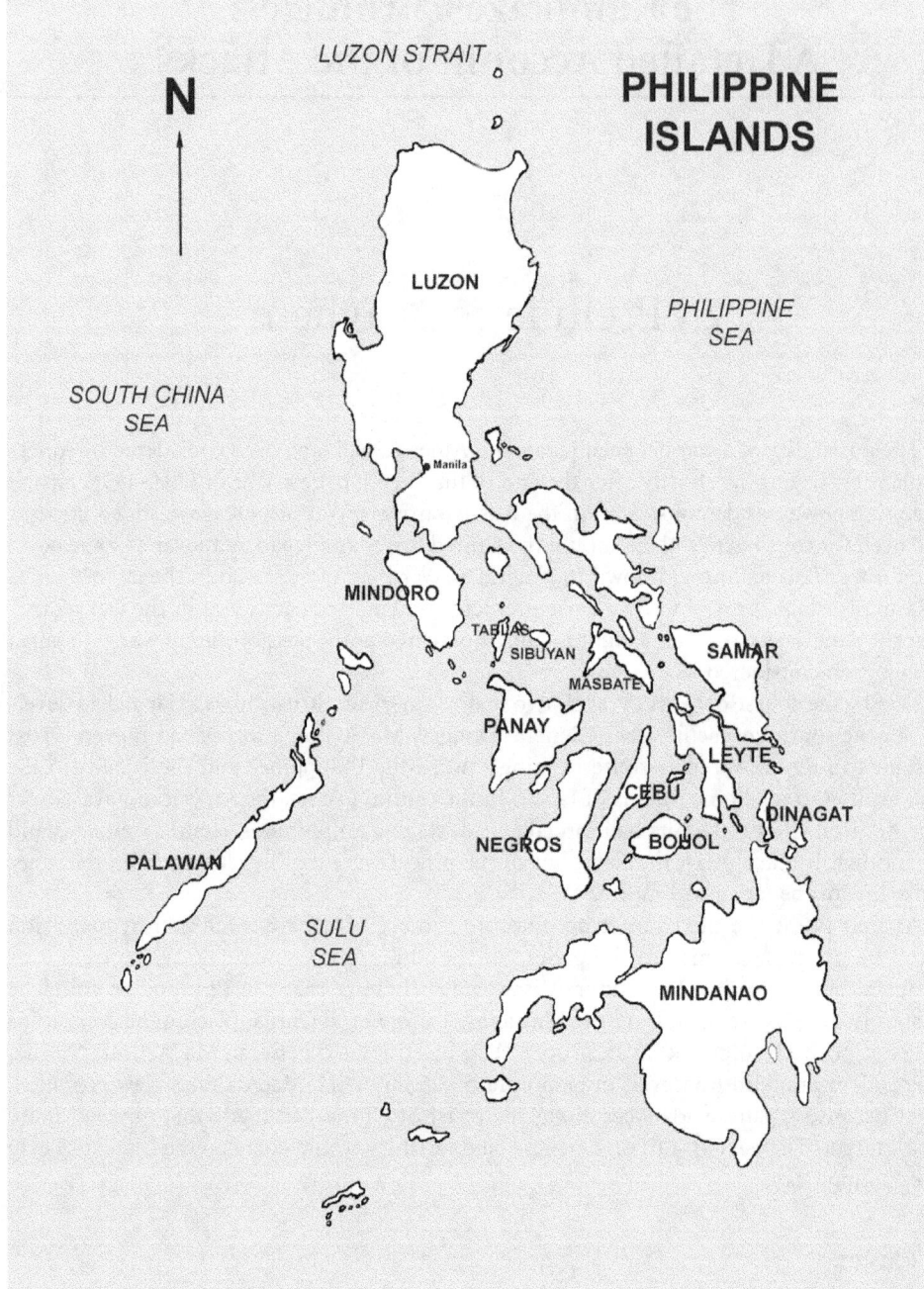

San Jose and to the south at Dulag. Both areas had airfields that were important to the support of troops and the suppression of enemy aircraft. Immediately to the north of the San Jose landing area was Tacloban air strip, a spit of land which jutted out into the water. The strip proved ideal for the landing of supplies from the LSTs. However, the mountain of material stacked on the airfield made it nearly impossible for the soon-to-land ground echelons to prepare the field for their aircraft. In frustration, Lt. Gen. George C. Kenney, commander of the Allied Air Forces, issued a threat to bring in bulldozers to clear out the area, even if it meant

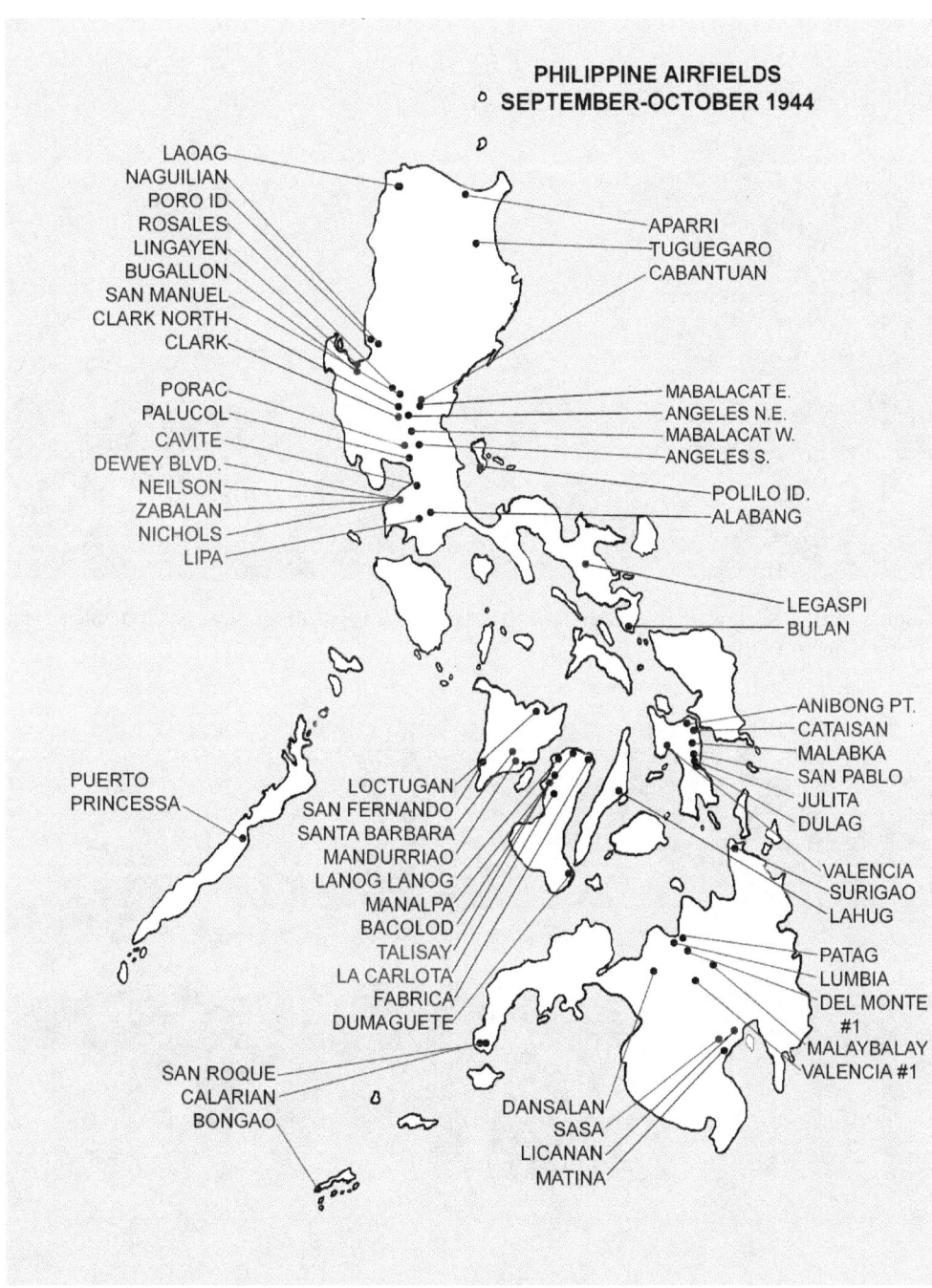

By the time of the invasion at Leyte Island, the Japanese had developed numerous airfields throughout the Philippines. This Philippine airfield map is based on General Staff, Supreme Commander for the Allied Powers. *Reports of General MacArthur The Campaigns of MacArthur in the Pacific Vol. 1* (Washington, D.C.: U.S. Government Printing Office, 1966), pp. 177, 248.

Landing craft streak toward the beach during the landing at Leyte, Philippines on 20 October 1944. Official U.S. Navy Photograph.

LSTs landing supplies near the airstrip at Tacloban, Leyte Island. The piles of supplies on the airstrip made it nearly impossible for the ground crews to prepare the airstrip. Lt. Gen. Kenney threatened to bulldoze the supplies into the ocean if they were not removed promptly. U.S. Coast Guard Photograph.

During the battle off Samar, the unfinished Tacloban airstrip provided refuge for Navy fighters from the beleaguered escort carriers that could not make it back to their ships. At Tacloban they landed under bad conditions, were refueled, and headed back to the battle. This FM-2 Wildcat had a rough landing. NARA 342 FH 4A 40839.

Tacloban airstrip was located on Cataisan Point, a spit of land just to the north of the town of San Jose and across the water from the town of Tacloban. This photograph, taken during late October 1944, shows the airstrip from the north looking south. NARA 80G 102183.

pushing the supplies back into the water. It is not clear how seriously Kenney's threat was taken, but within four days of the initial assault on the beaches at San Jose, the Far Eastern Air Forces (FEAF) sent ground echelons for the 49th and 475th Fighter Groups, the 421st Night Fighter Squadron, and the 305th Airdrome Squadron to establish the base at Tacloban. On 27 October 1944, thirty-four P-38 Lightnings of the 9th Fighter Squadron, 49th Fighter

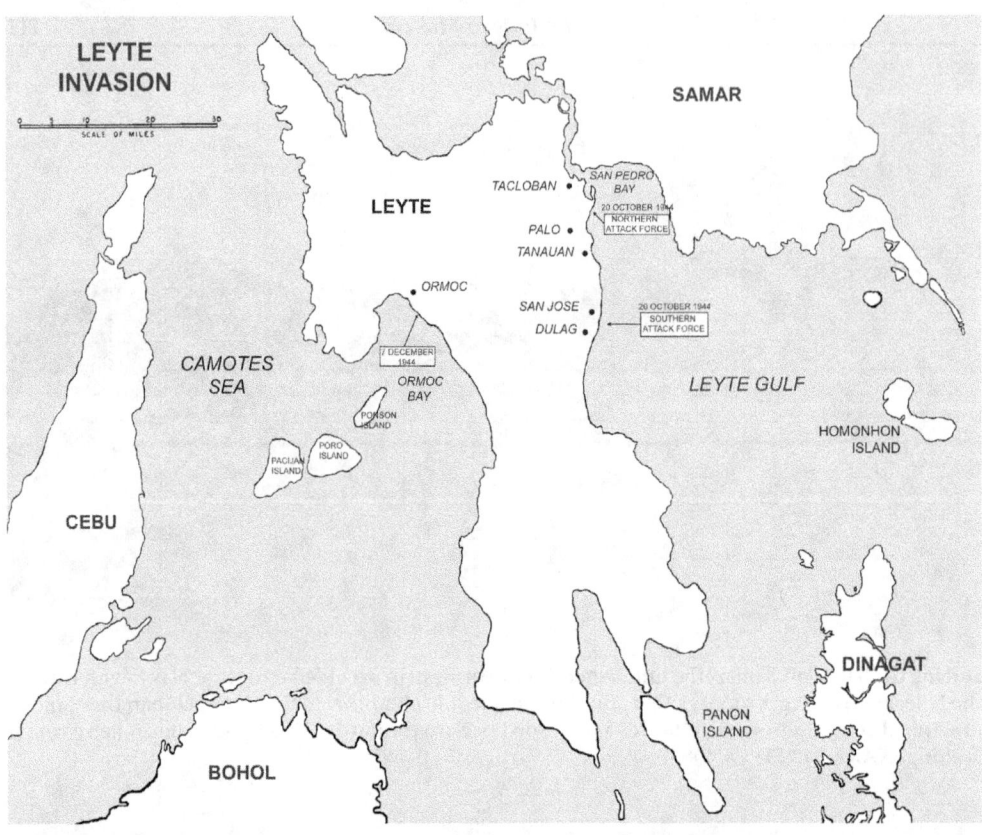

The initial landings at Leyte Island took place on the eastern side and were followed shortly thereafter by landings on the western side of the island.

Maj. Richard I. Bong poses next to his P-38 Lightning "Marge." Bong was the war's leading ace with forty confirmed kills. He died test piloting a P-80A jet fighter on 6 August 1945. NARA 342 FH 4A 06742.

Maj. Thomas B. McGuire, Jr., poses on the wing of his P-38 Lightning "Pudgy." McGuire, flying with the 432nd Fighter Squadron, was the war's second leading ace, with thirty-eight kills. He died while flying a mission in the Philippines. NARA 342 FH 4A 10405.

Cmdr. David McCambell, of *Essex CV-9's* VF 15, is shown in the cockpit of his F6F Hellcat on 29 October 1944. McCambell finished the war with a total of thirty-four kills, fifteen of which were made in the skies over the Philippines during the Leyte Operation. NARA 80G 258195.

Three kamikazes crash near ships at Leyte after being shot down. This photograph was taken in November 1944. NARA 80G 1022358.

Group, arrived at Tacloban and would attack Japanese airfields and intercept their aircraft attempting attacks on the fields and American ships. Within the next several weeks other squadrons would arrive so that by mid–November two P-38 fighter groups would be operating over Leyte.

Dulag Airstrip was taken on 21 October 1944, but conditions there were not as favorable as those at Tacloban, and the field did not become operational until 21 November 1944 when the 475th FS moved there from Tacloban.

In spite of the early difficulties in establishing air bases, the American flyers were formidable adversaries for the Japanese. Some of the leading aces of the war operated in the skies over the Philippines. Among them were Majs. Richard I. Bong and Thomas B. McGuire. Flying their P-38s, Bong finished the war with forty enemy aircraft kills to his credit and McGuire close behind with thirty-eight. The navy ace, Cmdr. David McCambell of VF-15, had thirty-four kills to his credit. McCambell flew his F6-F Hellcat off *Essex CV-9*.

The Kamikazes Appear Off Taiwan

Several kamikaze attacks took place just prior to the actual invasion of the Philippines at Leyte, even though the formal kamikaze program would not begin for several days. On 13 October 1944, *Franklin CV 13* was operating off Taiwan as the flagship of TG 38.4 under RAdm. Ralph E. Davison. Also included in the task group were *Enterprise CV 6, Belleau Wood CVL 24, San Jacinto CVL 30, New Orleans CA 32,* and *Biloxi CL 80*. Screening for the group were ten destroyers. The carriers had busied themselves for two days, sending 254 sorties to attack targets in the Toshien-Takao area of Taiwan. *Franklin* had already recovered its planes when, at 1825, four Japanese Betty bombers made it through the screening destroyers to launch an attack on the carriers. Their low altitude of about fifty to seventy-five feet off the water probably was the primary factor that allowed them to escape detection. *Franklin* and the other carriers let loose with their 20mm and 40mm anti-aircraft guns. One of the Bettys dropped its torpedo 500 yards out and *Franklin*'s CO, Capt. J. M. Shoemaker, ordered full left rudder. The torpedo passed under the carrier's fantail, missing the ship by yards. The Betty, hit numerous times by anti-aircraft fire, went out of control. The bomber's shallow dive caused it to strike a glancing blow on the flight deck abaft the carrier's island, and it went over the side of the ship without causing any significant damage. *San Jacinto* and *Franklin* took a second plane under fire. Lt. A. J. Pope, of *Franklin*'s VF-13, was approaching the carrier for a landing. He was able to maneuver his plane to get a burst of gunfire into the Betty, assisting in its destruction. *Enterprise* and *Belleau Wood* combined their fire to shoot down the third Betty. The fourth, now on track to attack *Franklin*, launched its torpedo and then passed closely over *Franklin*'s bow where it was taken under fire and shot down. Again *Franklin*'s CO handled his ship perfectly. He "ordered right full rudder and personally rung up 'Back Full' on the starboard engine. This maneuver caused the ship to slow its forward motion and pull the bow away from the on-rushing torpedo. The torpedo finally passed within 50 feet of FRANKLIN'S bow and continued on through the Task Group."[2] Damage to *Franklin* was minimal, but she suffered one dead and ten wounded.

Reno CL 96 was operating off Taiwan as part of TG 38.3 from 12 to 14 October 1944. Taiwan was alive with Japanese airfields and they responded with heavy air raids against the ships attacking them. *Reno* had shot down six enemy planes before a Jill attempted to crash her. At 1711 on 14 October it made it through her anti-aircraft fire to hit the aft part of her main deck, damaging turret six and nearby parts of the ship. Damage to the ship was minimal, although the crash wounded nine of her crew. The turret was able to resume firing, but there was some question as to whether its fire was accurate at that point as the crash had altered its alignment.

Kamikazes in the Philippines

Although there had been kamikaze attacks off Taiwan, the major kamikaze assault in 1944 would come in the Philippines. Larger ships had been the targets at Taiwan, but in the Philippines everything from PT boats to carriers would be attacked. *Sonoma ATO 12*, was not so fortunate as other, larger ships. The little fleet tug was already forty-two years old as she faced her greatest challenge of the war, survival in the face of an enemy air attack. To her went the dubious distinction of being one of the first American ships sunk by a kamikaze in World War II. *Sonoma* was operating as part of Task Unit 78.2.9 as the invasion of Leyte began and, with her task unit, entered San Pedro Bay on 20 October. At 0805 on the morning of 24 October 1944, she sent her small boat with seven men to dive for an anchor which had been lost by *LSM 21*. She then headed for the merchant ship *Augustus Thomas* to resupply her fresh water stores.

Augustus Thomas had steamed from Hollandia, New Guinea to San Pedro Bay in Leyte Gulf. She arrived in San Pedro on 20 October and was anchored, awaiting her turn to offload her cargo. Beginning around 0820, enemy planes began to attack ships in the area. A Sally passed by her stern and was shot down by a nearby ship. At 0839 four more Sally bombers attacked the ships and were hit by gunfire and set aflame. One, damaged by fire from *Thomas*, passed in front of her and crashed into *LCI(L) 1065* to her port, exploding and setting it afire.

The Sally bomber, which had a loaded weight of over 21,000 lbs. and whose fuselage was one-third the length of the LCI(L) proved to be too much for the small amphibious ship. The troop carrier went down within minutes. Thirteen men died and at least eight were injured. *Sonoma* began to fire on the incoming planes as well. She was about to cast off from the merchant ship, but it was too late. Before she could get underway she was crashed at 0845. Explosions shook her 175' frame and she began to ship water. According to her action report:

> The plane had gone completely through the deckhouse wiping out the forward engine room bulkhead sections of both starboard and port outboard bulkheads and two intermediate longitudinal bulkheads. Burning gasoline was sprayed into the engine room and throughout the midship section setting the radio shack, directly overhead, afire. Two bombs must have been released just before the plane struck, and it is believed these went beneath the hull exploding between the SONOMA and the AUGUSTUS THOMAS, causing the deluge of water from the port side which in momentarily beating down the flames, allowed many personnel time to escape.[3]

LCI (G) 72 came to her aid along with *Chickasaw ATF 83* and assisted in extinguishing the fires. Once they had been extinguished, *LCI(G) 72* pulled away and *Quapaw ATF 110* came alongside to assist with pumping. It was decided to get her into shallow water before she sank. *Chickasaw* attempted to push her into the beach at nearby Dio Island but ran the risk of running aground. All of the gear and guns that could be salvaged were stripped off her. *Sonoma* was fast losing the battle and finally sank in eighteen feet of water, her main deck only two feet under water.

The tug *Sonoma ATO 12* rests off Dio Island, San Pedro Bay, Philippine Islands, on 20 October 1944. She was one of the first two ships sunk by a kamikaze in World War II. NARA 80G 325819.

The bombs released by the plane caused significant damage to *Augustus Thomas*. Subsequent investigation by divers revealed a hole ten by sixteen feet in the bilge, along with several other smaller holes. Within minutes her engine room had twenty six feet of water and attempts were made to pump her out. On 3 November, after unsuccessful attempts to clear the water from her engine room, she was beached nearby.[4]

Also hit that day in San Pedro Bay was the liberty ship *David Dudley Field*. A kamikaze crashed her starboard bridge, ricocheted off her No. 7 and 6 gun tubs and went over the side. *Field* was particularly vulnerable to serious damage as her cargo included 4,500 tons of gasoline and other supplies. Fires started by the plane were quickly extinguished and damage to the ship was minor. Four men were injured.

The Surigao Strait Attacks

The opening salvo of what was to be the beginning of the formal kamikaze attacks took place on 25 October 1944 in the Philippines. American forces had made their main landings on Leyte beginning on 20 October 1944. Recognizing the importance of the establishment of an American beachhead in the Philippines, the Japanese formulated an appropriate response. In order to disrupt the landings and supply of troops, the Japanese planned to send a massive force into Leyte Gulf to destroy transports and their supporting gunships. VAdm. Jisaburo Ozawa would lead a decoy group of carriers to the north of the invasion site in order to draw off Adm. William Halsey's carriers. Ozawa's carriers were actually no threat as the number of planes they carried had been diminished since their sortie and by 25 October they had only twenty-nine aircraft left. To the south, a force led by VAdms. Shoji Nishimura and Kiyohide Shima would enter the area by means of a run through Surigao Strait, which ultimately was halted. The Central Force, commanded by VAdm. Takeo Kurita, included the mega-battleships *Yamato* and *Musashi* accompanied by three other battleships, thirteen cruisers and nineteen destroyers. They approached Leyte through San Bernadino Strait. This Central Force came under heavy air and surface attack by American forces and was weakened somewhat by the loss of *Musashi* and four of the cruisers. It seemed as though Kurita would retreat, but he maneuvered and headed for the American jeep carriers of Task Unit 77.4.2 (Taffy 2) and their escorts operating off Samar. Heavy damage was inflicted on the American ships, particularly the destroyers as they attempted to thwart the attack on their carriers. With Halsey decoyed to the north and VAdm. Jesse B. Oldendorf regrouping from his battle with the Japanese Southern Force, the escort carriers and their destroyers took the brunt of the assault, with *Gambier Bay* CVE 73 sunk by enemy gunfire. At the moment when the prospects for survival of the carriers seemed in doubt, Kurita withdrew his forces, leaving the carriers to survive for another day. However, as the carriers were fighting off Kurita's force, they came under attack by kamikazes.

Task Group 77.4, which contained a number of escort carriers under the command of RAdm. Thomas L. Sprague, was divided into three parts, each commonly known by their call sign "Taffy."

> Taffy 1—Task Unit 77.4.1—RAdm. Thomas L. Sprague commanding
> *Sangamon* CVE 26 (Flagship)
> *Suwannee* CVE 27
> *Chenango* CVE 28
> *Santee* CVE 29
> *Saginaw Bay* CVE 82
> *Petrof Bay* CVE 80
> Screen: *McCord* DD 539, *Trathen* DD 530, *Hazelwood* DD 531, *Edmunds* DE 406, *Richard S. Bull* DE 402, *Richard M. Rowell* DE 403, *Eversole* DE 789, *Coolbaugh* DE 217

Taffy 2 — Task Unit 77.4.2 — RAdm. Felix B. Stump commanding
Natoma Bay CVE 62 (Flagship)
Manila Bay CVE 61
Marcus Island CVE 77
Kadashan Bay CVE 76
Savo Island CVE 78
Ommaney Bay CVE 79
Screen: *Haggard* DD 555, *Franks* DD 554, *Hailey* DD 556, *Richard W. Suesens* DE 342, *Abercrombie* DE 343, *Oberrender* DE 344, *LeRay Wilson* DE 414, *Walter C. Wann* DE 412

Taffy 3 — Task Unit 77.4.3 — RAdm. Clifton A. F. Sprague—commanding
Fanshaw Bay CVE 70 (Flagship)
St. Lo CVE 63
White Plains CVE 66
Kalinin Bay CVE 68
Kitkun Bay CVE 71
Gambier Bay CVE 73
Screen: *Hoel* DD 768, *Heermann* DD 532, *Johnston* DD 821, *Dennis* DE 405, *John C. Butler* DE 339, *Raymond* DE 341, *Samuel B. Roberts* DE 823

Each of the three units was assigned to a different sector in Leyte Gulf, however, the kamikazes had no problem locating them and began their attacks even as the ships were escaping from Kurita's force. "Their regular operating areas were 30 to 50 miles apart; that of Taffy 1 to the southward, off northern Mindanao, that of Taffy 2 (Rear Admiral Stump) in the center of the entrance to Leyte Gulf, and that of Taffy 3 (Rear Admiral Clifton Sprague) to the northward, off Samar."[5]

The ships of Taffy 1 came under attack early in the morning. *Santee CVE 29* took the first kamikaze hit at 0740 as a Japanese plane managed to sneak in over the formation and dive into her flight deck on the port side. It struck forward of the elevator and did not disable its function, although it started fires as it went through the deck and into the hangar area. These were quickly brought under control and by 0751 the ship was fully operational. Sixteen men had been killed and twenty-seven wounded. However, her ordeal was not over, as within a few minutes, she took a torpedo hit from Japanese submarine *I-56*, which had been stalking the ships. This caused some hull damage and the carrier took a six degree list to starboard, which was righted by 0935. *Santee* was soon back in action and kept station with the other ships in the group.[6]

About the time that *Santee* was hit, *Suwannee*'s gunners spotted a kamikaze plunging toward her. Shells from *Suwannee*'s anti-aircraft guns struck the plane and it plunged downward, narrowly missing *Sangamon*. Twenty-four minutes after *Santee* was hit, *Suwannee* came under attack. At 0804 an enemy torpedo bomber made a successful dive, crashing through her deck just forward of the aft elevator and putting it out of commission. Its 551 lb. bomb went off between the flight deck and the hangar deck killing, and wounding a large number of the crew. The explosion tore a hole twenty-five feet in diameter in the hangar deck. Damage control parties put out the flames and made emergency repairs to the flight deck. *Suwannee* was able to launch her planes within a short time. In the midst of the action, *Petroff Bay CVE 80* shot down another kamikaze that tried to crash her.

Taffy 3's carriers did not avoid the kamikazes that day. After they had escaped the attentions of the Kurita's Central Force, they came under air attack from land based aircraft of the 201st Air Group from Mabalacat. Once they had launched their aircraft to attack elements of the Kurita's force, lookouts on *Kitkun Bay CVE 71* spotted five Zekes heading their way. This was the flight of the Shikishima Unit, which had left its field at about 0725. Let by Lt. Yukio Seki, the flight consisted of five bomb-laden Zekes with four more Zekes flying cover. At 1049 gunners on *Kitkun Bay* opened fire on the enemy aircraft.

7. Prelude to Mahem

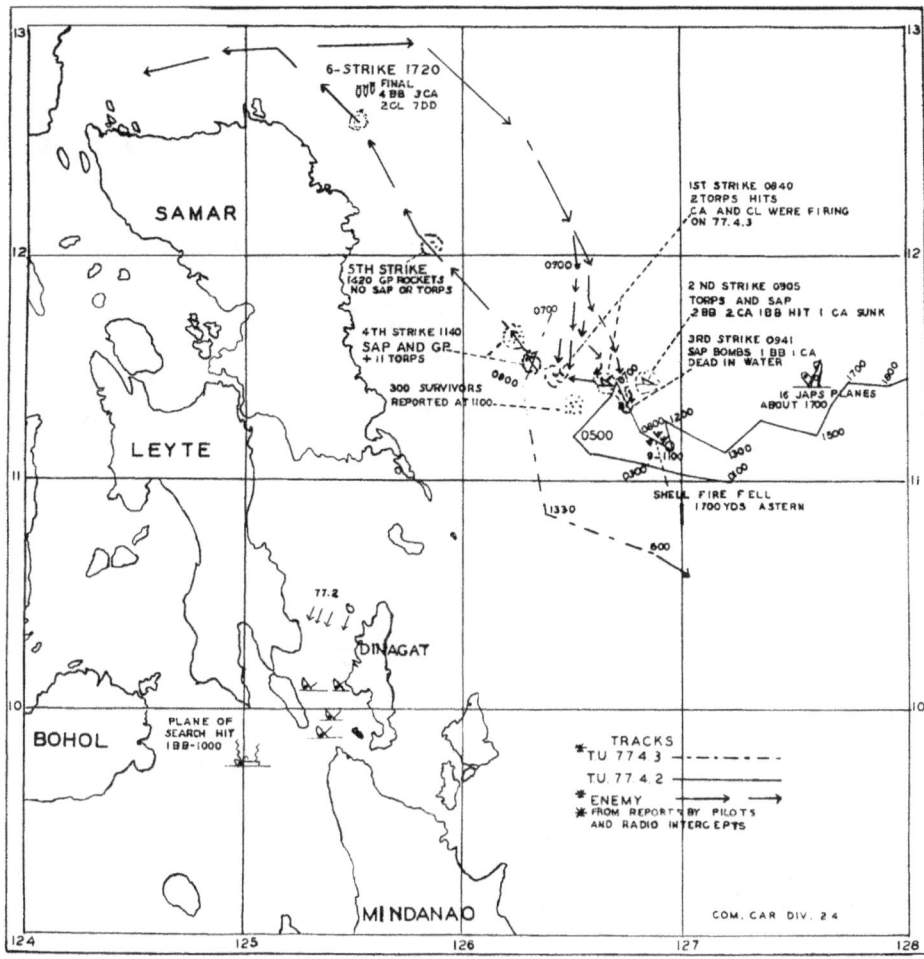

The battle off Samar on 25 October 1944 pitted major elements of the Japanese navy against the forces covering the landings at Leyte. Success by the Japanese would have doomed the invasion. It was during this battle that the first massed kamikaze attacks began. Commander Task Unit 77.4.2 (Commander Carrier Division 24) Serial 00114. *Reoccupation of Leyte Island in the Central Philippines During the period from 18 October 1944 to 29 October 1944, including the Air-Surface Engagement with Major Units of the Japanese Fleet on 25 October 1944.* 2 November 1944, p. 24.

> One Zeke crossing ahead of the ship from port to starboard, upon being brought under fire, climbed rapidly, rolled and made a suicide dive directly at the bridge strafing as it came down. This plane passed over the island, crashed into the port catwalk and fell into the sea about 25 yards on the port bow. Its fragmentation bomb exploded as the plane crashed, causing fires and other damage to the ship.[7]

The resultant blast killed one man and wounded another twenty. At 1052, as they watched the sky for other enemy assailants, they observed a Japanese plane crash through the flight deck of the *St. Lo CVE 63*, which was cruising nearby. Flames burst from the flight deck and smoke billowed, followed by several explosions. The plane's bomb had set off the carrier's torpedo and bomb magazine; *St. Lo* was finished. At 1104 her crew began the sorry task of abandoning her and, at 1121, she went to the bottom. The jeep carrier suffered 114 killed and an unknown number of wounded in this action.

St. Lo CVE 63 burns after being hit by a kamikaze on 25 October 1944. This photograph was taken from ***Kalinin Bay CVE 68***. NARA 80G 270511.

Shortly after *St. Lo* was hit, a Zeke made a run on *White Plains*. *White Plains* turned sharply to port as the plane made its dive. Her maneuvers were successful and the plane narrowly missed her, splashing close aboard her port side. The ensuing explosion sent parts of the plane and pilot up onto the deck. Although the plane had missed her, eleven of her crew suffered injuries.

Kitkun Bay formed up with the other remaining carriers, *Fanshaw Bay CVE 70*, *White Plains,* and *Kalinin Bay*. She sent two FM-2 Wildcats from VC-5 aloft to act as CAP over the ships. At 1123 a Judy came in from the stern and made a suicide run on *Kitkun Bay*. Accurate fire from the carrier shot both wings off the plane and it spiraled in fifty yards off the port bow. Its bomb hit the water twenty-five yards off the starboard bow and exploded. Debris from the plane rained down on the carrier's forecastle, but the damage to her was not substantial.

Kalinin Bay came under attack about the same time as *Kitkun Bay*. In her case, three Zekes were the perpetrators. The first was spotted to starboard at an altitude of 5,000–6,000 feet and dove downward toward the ship. Although hit repeatedly, the Zeke managed to get through the hail of fire and crashed into the flight deck, tearing a large hole and starting fires. Most of the plane failed to penetrate the deck and went over the side. Shortly thereafter, a second Zeke was sighted making a similar dive. This plane was hit and on fire as it "struck the after port stack, catwalk, and 20 millimeter mount"[8] before crashing into the sea. Damage to the ship was minimal. Following closely on the heels of this Zeke was another which missed the ship completely. It hit the water fifty yards off the port quarter and its bomb exploded, but there was no effect on the ship. Five men died and fifty-five were wounded in the attacks on *Kalinin Bay*. *Heermann, Dennis, John C. Butler,* and *Raymond* patrolled the area picking up survivors.

Sequence photographs showing an attack on *White Plains CVE 66* on 25 October 1944. In the top photograph crewmen crouch as they spot the approach of a Japanese Zeke. In the bottom photograph the Zeke is about to crash close astern. Although it did not hit the carrier, the explosion damaged her enough to send her to the States for repair. Top — NARA 80G 272870, Bottom — NARA 80G 272842.

Suwannee CVE 27 burns after a Zeke crashed through her flight deck on 25 October 1944. NARA 8OG 270662.

The carriers of Taffy 1 came under attack again the next day as twelve Judy dive bombers and a number of Zekes went after them starting about noon. A combat air patrol from *Santee* drove many off, but *Suwannee* suffered her second crash in as many days. Prior to her being attacked, one of *Suwannee*'s torpedo bombers shot down a Tony which had lined up an attack on *Petrof Bay*. *Suwanee* was landing her planes when the Japanese aircraft made their attack.

> A VT landed at 1238I, shortly before three enemy planes were spotted astern three or four miles out, at 10,000 feet. One "Zeke" made a slow slight turn, and came right in, at a 45 degree dive, started strafing at 3000 feet and crashed into the VT, landed a half minute before, parked on the forward elevator, causing an instantaneous explosion of both planes. The pilot, Lieutenant Beidelman, and two crewmen are missing.... One to three minutes later there was a second explosion in the catapult machinery space, in all probability caused by a second bomb from an enemy dive-bombing plane, starting a fire in the elevator well.[9]

Suwannee's forward elevator was smashed in the explosions, and within a short time, seven of her Wildcats and two Avengers burst into flame and blew up. It took several hours before the flames were under control. Her total casualties for the attacks on 25 and 26 October were eighty-five dead, 102 missing, and fifty-eight wounded.

Leyte

Benjamin Ide Wheeler, carrying a load of troops and general supplies including gasoline, was hit at 1045 on 27 October as she was anchored at Leyte. A Japanese bomber, on fire from anti-aircraft guns on other ships, crashed her waterline, holing it and setting off part of her cargo of gasoline. Quick work by her firefighters and damage control crew limited the damage. She had two killed and three wounded.[10]

Intrepid CV 11 had been operating off the Philippines as part of RAdm. Gerald F. Bogan's Task Group 38.2, along with the carriers *Hancock CV 19*, *Bunker Hill CV 17*, *Cabot CVL 28*, and *Independence CVL 22*. On 30 October she sent her CAG-18 planes to attack Clark Field. As the CAG-18 planes were on their mission the Japanese struck back. A kamikaze hit one of *Intrepid's* port gun tubs, killing ten men and wounding another six. Fortunately, the damage was slight and within a short time she resumed normal activities. *Franklin CV 13* was operating nearby as part of RAdm. Ralph E. Davison's Task Group 38.4, along with *Enterprise CV 6*, *San Jacinto CVL 30*, and *Belleau Wood CVL 24*. Five kamikazes eluded the CAP and two made it through to crash *Franklin* and *Belleau Wood*. One crashed close aboard *Franklin* and a second crashed her and holed her flight deck. A third dropped a bomb which missed its target. It peeled off and crashed into *Belleau Wood* holing her flight deck. *Belleau Wood's* losses were twelve CAG-21 planes, ninety-two killed and fifty-four wounded. *Franklin* lost thirty-three CAG-13 planes, fifty-six men dead and fourteen wounded. Both carriers made it back to Ulithi for repairs.

Franklin CV 13 and *Belleau Wood CVL 24* burn after being hit by kamikazes off Luzon on 30 October 1944. Both ships had extensive damage and had to be escorted back to Ulithi for repairs. NARA 80G 326798.

Fire fighting teams fight blazes on *Belleau Wood CVL 24* after she was crashed by a kamikaze off the Philippines on 30 October 1944. Official U.S. Navy Photograph.

TOTAL DAILY SORTIES BY JAPANESE ARMY
AND NAVY, 25–31 OCTOBER 1944

Date	Fourth Air Force (Army)	First Combined Base Air Force (Navy)
25 October	162	195 (18)
26 October	161	70 ((5)
27 October	70	52 (14)
28 October	98	51
29 October	43	31 (14)
30 October	2	6 (6)
31 October	51	28

Figures in parentheses represent kamikaze aircraft.[11]

On 1 November 1944, kamikazes attacked elements of the Seventh Fleet Task Group 77.1 on patrol in Leyte Gulf. The task group consisted of *Mississippi BB 41* as the flagship of RAdm.

G. L. Weyler, Commander Task Group 77.1, *California BB 44, Pennsylvania BB 38, Phoenix CL 46, Boise CL 47, Nashville CL 43, H.M.A. S. Shropshire, Killen DD 593, Abner Read DD 526, Ammen DD 527, Bush DD 529, Leutze DD 481, Newcomb DD 586, Bennion DD 662, Heywood L. Edwards DD 663, Richard P. Leary DD 664, Robinson DD 562, Bryant DD 665, Claxton DD 571,* and *H.M.A.S. Arunta.* The kamikaze's targeted *H.M.A.S Shropshire,* but gunners on board the ship drove them off. *Ammen DD 527* was the next target. At 0952 a twin-engine Frances hit the destroyer amidships between her stacks and then careened off the ship and into the sea. Significant damage and fires were the result but she kept station. The attack caused the death of five men and the wounding of another twenty-one. *Bush DD 529* and *Killen DD 593* sustained damage from bombs but remained in the fight.

Around 1339 Cmdr. A. M. Purdy, the CO of *Abner Read DD 769,* was guiding his ship near *Claxton.* Two Vals were spotted incoming at ten miles. *Abner Read* went to general quarters and began to maneuver. As the planes came into range, she opened fire, but to no avail.

> Despite heavy and accurate fire from 40mm and 20mm guns, the plane, in flames and with the port wing shot away, dived steeply downward across 40mm mount No. 3 and the after torpedo mount, then went over the portside. The starboard wing or the engine hit the 40mm director platform on the starboard side of the after stack, the breech end of the after torpedo tubes (trained 275 degrees relative) and the port 20mm machine guns. The latter were knocked over the side. An intense fire immediately engulfed the surrounding area.[12]

A bomb carried by the Val and released just prior to impact, penetrated the forward starboard side of the ship, exploding in the after fireroom. Fires quickly spread in spite of the CO's orders to stop and back the ship in order to prevent fanning the flames. *Claxton* moved in to assist but had to stand off as a huge explosion took place in the after part of *Abner Read.* Preparing for the worst, the crew disarmed depth charges and torpedoes and jettisoned them to prevent their exploding. However, five torpedoes in the after mount could not be reached and their impulse charges cooked off and launched them. For the next several minutes, both ships had to dodge the erratic torpedoes as *Abner Read* neared her fate. Internal explosions rocked the ship as various magazines and other combustibles burned. Damage to the fire mains and pumps prevented adequate water pressure from being achieved, and fighting the rapidly spreading fires became increasingly difficult. With fires continuing unchecked and the ship down by the stern and listing, Cmdr. Arthur M. Purdy gave the order to abandon ship. By 1358, the destroyer was listing twenty degrees when she was abandoned. *Abner Read* rolled over to ninety degrees and sank stern first at 1417 in thirty-five fathoms of water.[13]

Patrolling the area near *Abner Read* was *Claxton DD 571.* She came to the aid of *Abmer Read* and began picking up survivors. About 0950, as she pursued her rescue duty, a kamikaze exited from the cloud cover and then made a successful dive on her. The plane hit the water and exploded close aboard, causing her seams to open and flooding the after living quarters. Five of her men were killed and twenty-three wounded. In spite of her damage, she continued her rescue mission, eventually picking up 187 survivors from *Abner Read.*

Later that day, at 1812, *Anderson DD 411* took a kamikaze hit. Three Oscars came in at the ship from over Panaon Island. She took them under fire and they turned away. However, one turned back and made a dive on her. In spite of being hit by 20mm and 40mm gunfire, the plane got through, caught its right wing tip on the ship's stack and hit the port side. Burning gasoline covered the deck in the area of the crash and the number 1 and 2 boilers were put out of commission by the impact. With fires spreading the destroyer jettisoned her torpedoes. The fires were out by 1855 and *Anderson* was covered by *Bush,* which supplied extra medical assistance. She had sixteen dead and twenty wounded.[14]

Liberty ships and the later victory ships, along with official U.S. navy and army ships such as attack transports and cargo carriers, were an essential part of the invasion fleet. To land troops and cargo was an indispensable mission and these ships came under attack as well.

During World War II, 2,751 liberty ships were built, with the first launched in 1941. They were 441 feet long and could make ten to twelve knots. Since more speed was desirable, a new and similar ship was designed, the victory ship. Victory ships were 455 feet long but could make an estimated fifteen knots. The first of the 534 victory ships built was launched on 28 February 1944. Armament for the ships was varied, but most carried a 4" or 5" stern gun, a 3" bow gun, six to eight 20mm guns, with some of the liberty ships also mounting a pair of 37mm bow guns. Manning these guns was an Armed Guard consisting of twenty-eight men and one officer.[15] The rank of the officer was usually from ensign to lieutenant. Still another type of freighter was in the group. These were the United States Maritime Commission C1 and C1-M types, of which 173 were built during World War II. At 412' and 418' l.o.a. respectively, they could make fourteen knots. A number of these cargo carriers participated in the landings at Leyte, Mindoro, and Lingayen Gulf. During November of 1944, many of them were damaged in kamikaze attacks.

Matthew P. Deady, under the command of Master K. D. Frye, had arrived in San Pedro Bay, Leyte Gulf on 29 October, after steaming from Hollandia, New Guinea with ten other freighters and their seven escorts. She was anchored in Tacloban Bay when, at 0535 on 3

A member of the Armed Guard on board a liberty ship practices sighting in the five inch rifle. The Armed Guard was composed of members of the U.S. Navy assigned to each liberty ship and victory ship to man the weapons which were essential to the defense of the ship. Photograph from the Library of Congress — Farm Security Administration — Office of War Information Photograph Collection.

Liberty and victory ships were produced in a number of shipyards such as this one at the Bethlehem Fairfield shipyards near Baltimore, MD. Visible behind the flag on the bow is the tub for the five inch gun. Photograph from the Library of Congress — Farm Security Administration — Office of War Information Photograph Collection.

November, she came under attack. A Japanese dive bomber dropped a stick of bombs which missed her. It then turned around and made a strafing run on her from astern. The ship's gunners nearly emptied their 20mm magazines into her and may have wounded the pilot. This may have been a kamikaze crash as the last act of a dying pilot. He crashed his plane into the No. 2 gun tub and exploded in a ball of fire. Nearby oxygen and acetylene tanks exploded from the fire and a number of men were blown overboard. It had been a costly attack from the standpoint of personnel losses. In addition to two Navy Armed Guard members who were missing and presumed dead, four had been burned. Army troops on board counted twenty-two dead, thirty-five missing and over one hundred injured in the attack. Shortly after the initial attack, five more Japanese aircraft strafed the men in the water and dropped anti-personnel mines on them as the smaller ships attempted to rescue them. Two of them were shot down by fire from the ships.[16]

The next day, on 4 November, *Cape Constance,* carrying a load of general supplies, was anchored in Tacloban Bay when she was attacked. A twin-engine bomber made a run on her but, under fire from the ship's armed guard, it crashed into one of the ship's booms, disintegrated and its parts skidded off the deck into the water. Debris was everywhere but the crew quickly extinguished the fires and cleaned up. Her damage was insignificant and only one man received minor injuries.

Lexington CV 16, operating as a part of RAdm. Frederick C. Sherman's Task Group 38.3, had just finished the final stages of attacks on the withdrawing Japanese fleet. Her CAG-19 planes assisted in the sinking of the heavy cruiser *Nachi* on 5 November. Around 1300, seven Japanese aircraft were reported approaching the ships. One was shot down by the CAP but the others ducked into cloud cover and escaped destruction. At 1325 a Zeke made a dive on *Lexington* and was shot down a thousand yards away. Her action report for the day indicates:

> Shortly thereafter, another enemy plane, identified also as a Zeke, was sighted making a similar attack. This plane was also taken under fire and although hit many times by 20MM and 40MM shells and afire, managed to drop its bomb and crash the ship on the starboard side of the island structure aft. The bomb exploded against the armor plate of Battle Two completely shattering it and destroying all of the Secondary Conn equipment and communications in the area. The plane completely disintegrated upon striking the island. The resulting fragments and gasoline explosion along with the bomb blast and bomb fragments caused serious damage to the signal bridge, several 30MM and 40MM batteries and caused many casualties. Damage control measures were immediately taken to extinguish the fires and within twenty (20) minutes, in spite of exploding ammunition and electrical arcing, all fires were out.[17]

When the struggle was finally over, she counted her dead and wounded. Fifty had perished in the attack and another 132 were wounded. Although she was capable of continuing flight operations, she headed back to Ulithi with her group on 7 November.

The liberty ships *Leonidas Merritt, Thomas Nelson, William A. Coulter, Morrison R. Waite, Matthew P. Deady,* and *Alexander Majors,* all of which had transited in convoy from Hollandia, New Guinea to Leyte without incident, were anchored in Dulag Harbor, Leyte on 12 November 1944. Also sailing that route was the liberty ship *Jeremiah M. Daily* which anchored nearby in Leyte Gulf. In addition to a variety of supplies, the *Alexander Majors* and *Thomas Nelson* had gasoline as part of their cargoes and *Nelson* also carried some ammunition. The worst disasters of the day would be *Thomas Nelson* and *Jeremiah M. Daily*

Thomas Nelson was at anchor off Dulag on Sunday, 12 November 1944, along with about twenty or so other cargo carriers. At 1127 three kamikazes approached the ships from the west northwest and dove on them. One struck *Leonidas Merritt* and a second clipped *Matthew P. Deady.* The third crashed into the aft end of *Thomas Nelson.* It struck the jumbo boom on *Nelson*'s No. 4 hatch and pieces of the plane continued on through the port side bulwark. Its bomb penetrated the deck and exploded. Fires raged on deck and between decks and it took four and one-half hours to put them out. The crash killed 136 men, including 133 troops on board, and injured an additional eighty-eight.[18] *Leonidas Merritt* was hit on her forward deck, causing severe damage to the ship but only lost only three men, with another thirty-six reporting various injuries. *Matthew P. Deady,* already damaged from a kamikaze crash on 3 Novem-

Gunners on *Lexington CV 16* fire on a Zeke as it makes its kamikaze attack on the carrier on 5 November 1944. The successful kamikaze attack killed fifty men and wounded another 132. NARA 80G 270495.

ber, had another close call. As the planes approached her, she successfully fired on them and drove one off course. It narrowly missed the bridge and clipped the ship's antennae before plunging into the sea thirty feet of her port beam.

Jeremiah M. Daily, carrying troops, was hit at 1420 when four enemy aircraft appeared over the anchored ships. With over one hundred ships anchored in the area, her chances were good that she would not be singled out, however, that was not to be the case. One of the planes dropped a bomb on another ship, peeled off, and headed for *Daily*. It crashed into her wheelhouse spreading flaming gasoline over the decks and igniting fuel stowed nearby. Reports credited the CO of the Armed Guard with extreme bravery. According to the report:

> Carl Mather Kube Lt. (jg) U.S.N.R. Service no. 342997, after ringing the General Alarm on the flying bridge, put on the phones to give orders to gunners that were manning their guns. Louis C. Tyus manned his gun and opened fire under Lt. Kube's orders. Despite the fact that the plane was flying straight for them both, Lt. Kube and Louis C. Tyus never moved from their battle station until after the explosion. When the plane crashed the explosion blew Lt. Kube across the bridge. He received burns on 90% of his body and a cut above the left eye. He walked off the bridge a few minutes later unassisted to get first aid for his burns and wound.
>
> Louis C. Tyus was burned from his waist up. The gun tub he was in was demolished. He came off the bridge without help.[19]

Fires spread by the fuel caused extensive loss of life until they were finally extinguished after 1800. The crash killed one hundred-six men, including one hundred troops. Forty-three others on board the ship were injured.[20]

Damage to *Lexington CV 16's* 20mm Group 7 starboard mounts is seen after the kamikaze attack of 5 November 1944. NARA 890G 270499.

In mid-morning on 12 November, at 1029, *Morrison R. Waite* came under attack as a flaming Zeke headed toward her in a crash dive. "S1c William H. MC NEESE, No. 1 20 mm gun position, continued to fire at the aircraft until it struck the ship which blew him out of the gun tub."[21] The Zeke hit the port side and holed the ship. Within fifteen minutes the fires were under control and she could tend to her dead and injured. Twenty-one died and forty-three were injured.

Alexander Majors, carrying trucks, troops, oil, and gas was potentially a floating bomb.

However, the Zeke that attacked her at 1718 hit the mainmast and exploded above the deck. Fires were started in gasoline drums stored on her deck, but since the blast had not penetrated the deck they were brought under control with assistance from a nearby LCI. Two died and fifteen others were injured.[22] At various dates, the ships completed unloading, making temporary repairs and then headed back to San Francisco for final repairs.

William A. Coulter, carrying 3,500 tons of general supplies, took a hit in her aft end from a Zeke at 1745, but the plane skidded off the deck and into the water. Minor damage to the ship occurred but no one had been killed. Minutes later a second Zeke crashed close aboard after being hit by the ship's gunfire, but its explosion caused no further damage. Sixty-nine of the officers, crew, armed guards, and passengers reported injuries.

The landing craft repair ships *Egeria ARL 8* and *Achilles ARL 41* were also struck that day, with *Achilles* losing thirty-three men and suffering another twenty-eight wounded. At 1300, *Achilles* lookouts spotted three Zekes. The second of the planes peeled off and, in spite of being under fire, crashed into the foredeck and penetrated it. Pieces of the plane's fuselage bounced along the deck and went over the stern. Within minutes fires were raging and the crew had all they could do to keep them under control. Their efforts were hampered since, as in many cases of kamikaze crashes, the impact and subsequent explosions knocked out fire mains. By 1900 the fires were nearly out and the grim task of counting the dead began in earnest. She remained in San Pedro Bay until 27 November and then departed for Hollandia and repairs.

Egeria ARL 8 was at anchor about a thousand yards from *Achilles* when that ship was hit. Moored on her port side was *LSM 138* and *LCI(L) 430*, and moored on the starboard side of the ship was *LCI(L) 364*. The four ships made a tempting target. A Zeke with a bomb made a run on *Caribou IX 114*, anchored nearby, and was turned away by gunfire. It then headed for the *Egeria* and her three companions. The only one of the three ships able to fire on the plane was the *LCI(L) 430*. Its fire caused the plane to veer off and circle around the three ships, coming in to attack the *LCI(L) 364* from the port side. Fire from the *430* destroyed the plane about twenty-five feet off *LCI(L) 364*. Its bomb went off and opened a large hole in the port side of the *364*. *Egeria* had minor damage but twenty-one of her men, who had been working on *LCI(L) 364*, were wounded in the attack. With her flooding on the increase, *LCI(L) 364* was towed into shallow water to be beached by *LCI(L) 977*.

Alpine APA 92 was struck by a kamikaze at 0729 on 18 November. She was in the process of debarking troops at Leyte when two Japanese planes approached her position. She fired on and shot down one of the planes off her starboard quarter, but the second made it through a hail of anti-aircraft fire to crash flaming into her port side. The twin explosions of the aircraft and its bomb spread fires over the ship but they were out within a half-hour. Once the fires were out, she continued the task of getting her troops ashore and then left for Manus and repairs. Her casualties were five dead and twelve injured.[23]

Four more of the merchant ships, *Nicholas J. Sinnett, Gilbert Stuart, Alcoa Pioneer,* and *Cape Romano* suffered at the hands of the kamikazes 18–19 November. The first two were liberty ships and the latter two CI types. On 12 November, at 0724, *Nicholas J. Sinnett* had a close call at Leyte as a kamikaze made an attempt on her but struck the freighter only a glancing blow before hitting the water. She had no damage and no casualties. At the same time that *Sinnett* was attacked, *Gilbert Stuart* was hit by another of the planes in the group. She was another potential floating bomb. Along with general supplies and troops, she also had on board 6,000 barrels of gasoline stored in her hold. Fortunately for them, the troops had already left the ship. The kamikaze attacked the ship from dead ahead, striking the ship's funnel and the starboard gun tub. It eventually came to rest on the aft end of the ship. Her bombs went off, burning gasoline flowed down into the ship, and fires began to spread. Luck was on her side and the fires never reached the hold where the gas was stored.[24] *Chickasaw ATF 83* helped her extinguish her fires. She lost six men and had eleven injured. *Alcoa Pioneer* was the biggest concern in the group with her cargo of 1,200 tons of gasoline. She was crashed at 0710, but the fires were contained on deck and put out within five minutes. All hands recognized the necessity of extreme measures in their firefighting and they responded magnificently. Six died and thirteen were injured, a small toll for a potentially large disaster. The courage of her Armed Guard unit was noted by the ship's master, Lt. Cmdr. Andrew W. Gavin USNR (inactive), when he wrote:

> The following report is from my own observation, and I have approximately 30 feet of moving pictures that I took only a few seconds after the crash, which I am sending to the Armed Guard Center at San Francisco. If the pictures turn out alright, you will see courage and fortitude that is beyond description. You will see 20 mm gun tub No. 2 practically a sieve from shrapnel and still burning, and S1c Patrick Henry Stevens, No. 306-32-38, still pointing his gun although badly burned and one arm almost severed.
>
> You will see in gun tub No. 4 and No. 6, Ottis B. Caraley, S1c No. 938-61-47, William Ellis York, S1C, No. 932-59-12, Carl Winton Lee, S1c, No. 861-17-31 all standing at their guns although the entire part of the gun platform is ablaze. Caraley and Lee are wounded.
>
> In gun tub No. 3, Leroy Vincent Kirk, S1c No. 313-27-62, is critically wounded, and Edward Larcy Grigchy, S1c, No. 382-99-75, although badly burned, and tub full of shrapnel holes, is still occupying his gun. The same is true at all the guns.
>
> At guns No. 5 and No. 7 which are abreast of the stack on the starboard side, Lloyd Earl Chapde, GM — No. 613-13-16, Edward Henry Kocardora, S1c — No. 661-46-34, and Gilbert C. Baker, S1c No. 867-25-92, were still at their stations, although the entire vicinity is a shamble, Chapda and Kocardora are injured. It was their gun that hit the plane diving on the GENERAL FLEISCHER [anchored nearby and unhit].[25]

Cape Romano was the least likely to suffer any loss to the invasion effort. She had been bombed three weeks prior to this attack and was laying at anchor with an empty hold when a plane struck the port side of her bridge, hit a gun tub, and went over the side. The explosion caused some minor damage but there were no casualties.[26]

James O'Hara APA 90 arrived in a convoy of fifteen transports from Guam, carrying the army's 77th Division. They anchored at Leyte on 22 November and the following day began to disembark their troops. At 1114 a Zeke, under pursuit by four P-38 Lightnings, appeared two miles from the ship and turned toward her in a suicide run. It was taken under fire and lost a wing about one hundred feet from the ship, causing the pilot to lose control. The remainder of the plane struck the side of the transport and disintegrated in an explosion. Its remains went into the water and minor gasoline fires spread in the immediate area but were quickly put out. The ship had minimal damage and no casualties.[27]

The Task Force 38 carriers would once again feel the wrath of the kamikazes as the Philippine campaign wore on. On 25 November RAdm. Gerald F. Bogan's TG 38.2 carriers were operating about sixty miles due east central Luzon. Their planes were busy attacking Clark Field and the area around Manila when, at 1253, a Zeke made it through the combat air patrol and crashed one of *Intrepid*'s port gun tubs, killing ten and wounding six of her men. The plane continued on its path, holing her flight deck before its bomb went off. Fires started by the crash were extinguished and the ship resumed station. Her action report indicates that this was not the end of the action:

> At 1258 the task group changed course to 175°T. The enemy plane, a Zeke, bore in on this vessel firing 7.7 MM and 20 MM machine guns. At 1259 he landed on the port side about frames 140–142 and skidded all the way to the bow, where part of the engine, the pilot's torso, and plane wreckage remained on the flight deck. This plane also had been armed with a bomb, which passed through the flight deck and exploded on the hangar deck about frame 107. This explosion killed several officers and men, set fire to aircraft in the hangar deck and in the surrounding

area. After the last crash, ceased firing. Although enemy planes were in the vicinity for some time afterward, none approached within range of this ship's guns.[28]

By the time the attacks ended, *Intrepid* had shot down five enemy aircraft, including the two that crashed her. At the end of the day her casualties included sixty-nine dead and thirty-five wounded.

At 1254 a Zeke came at *Cabot* high from astern and hit the edge of her flight deck on the port side. Three minutes later a second Zeke came in from high on her port bow and exploded

This is the first in a sequence of two photographs showing a *Yokosuka D4Y2 Suisei Model 33* (Judy) bomber about to hit *Essex CV 9* on 25 November 1944. NARA 80G 270710.

This is the second in a sequence of two photographs showing a *Yokosuka D4Y2 Suisei Model 33* (Judy) bomber about to hit *Essex CV 9* on 25 November 1944. NARA 80G 270649.

Essex CV 19 is on fire after the kamikaze attack of 25 November 1944. This photograph was taken from *South Dakota BB 57*. NARA 80G 270748.

Damage to *Essex CV 9* after the kamikaze attack of 25 November did not stop her and she was soon back in action. NARA 80G 270731.

close aboard the port side. *Cabot*'s deck was showered with bomb fragments and debris from the plane. Minor fires were quickly extinguished and a survey of the ship indicated that her damage was slight.[29] She wound up with two small holes in her flight deck, thirty-six dead and sixteen wounded. Of the TG 38.2 carriers, *Hancock* fared the best. The Zeke that attacked her was blown apart about a thousand feet over the ship. Debris rained down on the flight deck starting small fires, and ten to twelve feet of its fuselage fell on her deck amidships. Small fires started by the debris were quickly extinguished but no serious damage was incurred. She had two men injured.[30]

Essex CV 9, a part of RAdm. Frederick C. Sherman's Task Group 38.3, was hit at 1255 when a Judy crashed her port side flight deck. The plane did not carry a bomb, however, its gasoline exploded, setting fires on the deck and catwalk. Her flight deck was damaged in the crash, along with her Group 4 20mm battery and hangar deck in the area of the impact. The fires were brought under control and by 1326 she was able to resume flight operations. Damage to the carrier was minor, but fifteen men were killed and forty-four wounded.[31]

27 to 29 November 1944

Task Group 77.2 under RAdm. T. D. Ruddock was stationed in Leyte Gulf awaiting new orders. On 29 November, as the ships were preparing to refuel they were attacked by an estimated twenty-five to thirty planes. *St. Louis CL 49* was hit by two, *Colorado BB 45* and *Mont*-

pelier CL 57 by one, and *Maryland BB 46* by another. The most serious casualties were incurred by *Maryland* when a kamikaze struck her between her number one and two turrets killing thirty-one and wounding thirty of her men.

The sub-chaser *SC 744*, commanded by Lt. Donald S. Stroetzel, was escorting a barge full of high octane gasoline from Tacloban Harbor to Liloan where a PT base was under construction. At 1133 the ship received a radio call that Japanese aircraft were in the area and they went to general quarters.[32] Within minutes a Zeke was spotted with two P-38s hot on its tail. Crewmen watched as the Zeke outmaneuvered the Lightnings; it shot down one and then turned to make a strafing run on the sub-chaser. The little wooden ship responded with anti-aircraft fire and the plane seemed to lose control. The sub-chaser was riddled with bullets from the Zeke as it made its dive. It seemed to the crew that their fire had killed the pilot, but it made no difference. Already on a crash course, the Zeke flew right into the *SC 744*, striking it near the stern. Its bomb, released prior to the crash, missed the ship, blowing up in the water off the bow. As the smoke settled it was obvious that the ship was still afloat and not on fire, but there were casualties. Six men were missing and two on the starboard 20mm gun were seriously wounded. The final toll for the sub-chaser was seven dead and three wounded. The tug *TP 114* picked up one man who had been blown overboard and then came to the aid of the *SC 744*. The ship was towed back to Tacloban, but sank at 0420 on 30 November while tied up at a dock. Her wounds had been too severe for her to survive.[33]

Colorado BB 45 was in company with *Maryland BB 46, West Virginia BB 48, New Mexico BB 40* and the cruisers *Minneapolis CA 36, Columbia CA 56, Denver CL 58, Montpelier CL 57,* and *St. Louis CL 49* as part of RAdm. T. D. Ruddock's Task Group 77.2. Screening for the group were the destroyers *Mustin DD 413, Lang DD 399, Aulick DD 569, Saufley DD 465, Renshaw DD 499, Waller DD 466, Conway DD 507, Pringle DD 477, Eaton DD 510, Cony DD 508, Nicholas DD 449, Jenkins DD 447,* and *Laffey DD 724*. With the initial invasion of Leyte completed, the task group was assigned to provide security for convoys transiting the gulf.

A combination of no perceived action, impending foul weather and the need to replenish fuel supplies, placed the ships at a disadvantage the morning of 27 November. The task group was circling the tanker *Caribou IX 114,* and *West Virginia* was taking on fuel as the attacks began. At 1125 a large group of approximately thirty bogeys were picked up as they closed on the ships. *West Virginia* was targeted by a bomber but escaped damage. *Colorado* took the first hit when a kamikaze crashed her port side. "The plane and its bomb exploded on 5"/51 caliber gun No. 8, destroying the gun and inflicting numerous casualties among personnel in the casemate and on 40mm mounts No. 6 and No. 18. The second plane and bomb exploded in the water but inflicted no damage to the ship or personnel."[34] A second plane was a narrow miss but crashed in the water close enough to cause additional damage. Nineteen men were killed and seventy-two wounded, but damage to the battleship was minor. At 1145 *Montpelier* came under attack by four planes. Three were shot down at a distance from the ship but one kamikaze crashed short, bounced off the water and hit her side. *Montpelier's* damage was minimal but she had eleven wounded. In all, the ships shot down a total of eleven planes during the raid.

St. Louis became the next target with the attack of a Judy at 1112. The plane dropped a bomb and then spun into the water 1,500 yards away from the cruiser.

> At 1137 St. Louis opened fire with port anti-aircraft battery at a group of four enemy planes. Subsequent to this the action was rapid and continuous with six successive diving attacks upon this ship [*St. Louis*] until approximately 1215, commencing with a suicide dive from well aft on the port quarter and almost astern which plane, at 1138, although on fire and upside down, managed to crash at about ten feet inboard from starboard at frame 128, the forward starboard corner of the hangar area. At this time the ship was slowly turning right at a formation speed of fifteen knots, conforming to the circular formation. The bomb of the plane is believed to have

had instantaneous fusing and the mutilated remains of the pilot, together with his engine, parachute, scarf, back armor, one tire, two machine guns of about 12.7 calibre, self-sealing gas tank material and various other miscellaneous items, came to rest in the after end of the GSLK storeroom on the third deck level, having penetrated bulkhead 126 at the forward lower starboard corner of the hangar space. The gasoline fire from the plane and the fire from other materials in the hangar which were ignited thereby caused a considerable fire and this, it is believed, may have attracted the succeeding attacks on the ship by indicating a damaged ship and the possibility of "finishing her off."[35]

Five more kamikazes dove on *St. Louis*, most splashing far enough from the ship as not to damage her. One, however, crashed close aboard the port side and ruptured the ship's hull just below the armor belt. Planes identified by the ship's observers included Judys, Hamps, Jills, and Vals, indicating that this was an attack by Japanese navy aircraft. Casualties aboard *St. Louis* were sixteen dead and forty-three wounded.

The task group had a break on 28 November, but the kamikazes returned the next day. The ships were under orders to depart the area and had just begun their trip back to Manus when the Japanese attacks began. Just after sunset, a kamikaze made it through the overcast sky and hit *Maryland* between her No. 1 and No. 2 turrets, causing heavy casualties and exploding in a fiery ball of flame. When her fires were eventually brought under control, the battleship continued on her way. Thirty-one died and thirty were injured by the crash. Simultaneous to this attack, two nearby picket destroyers, *Saufley DD 465* and *Aulick DD 569*, came under attack. Both were on anti-submarine screen at the entrance to Leyte Gulf. *Saufley* had minor damage when one plane crashed her and killed one crew member, but *Aulick* fared much worse. At 1750 she was attacked by six Oscars. One made it through the hail of anti-aircraft fire, dropped a bomb which missed, and crashed close aboard. Expert ship handling by *Aulick*'s CO, Cmdr. J. D. Andrew, helped his ship escape a strike. He ordered that the ship's engines be backed full, which probably threw off the pilot's timing and caused him to overshoot. A second came in from aft of the ship and was taken under fire by 20mm, 40mm, and 5" guns. It was hit numerous times probably killing the pilot. Its wing clipped the starboard side of the bridge and it spiraled down to explode on the foredeck. The force of the explosion sent shrapnel flying throughout the area, killing thirty-two men and wounding another sixty-four. *Aulick*'s No. 2 gun was put out of commission. With the immediate threat gone, she was able to come to the aid of *Saufley*, whose condition was still being evaluated.[36]

8. The December Kamikazes, 1944

Although the initial assaults on the eastern side of Leyte had been completed by early December, the assault on the opposite of the island was just underway. Beginning on 7 December, additional American army units would land in Ormoc Bay. The vast number of ships transiting from Leyte Gulf to Ormoc Bay would prove to be irresistible targets for the Japanese air forces and their kamikaze units.

The liberty ship *Marcus Daly* was heading for Leyte as part of a convoy of forty-one ships that had steamed from Hollandia, New Guinea escorted by five navy ships. Off Mindanao the ships came under air attack on 5 December. One Japanese plane dove on *Marcus Daly* at 1500 and was hit repeatedly by her fire. It is not clear if the plane was on a kamikaze run as it was strafing the ship, however, the plane was damaged severely. In all likelihood the pilot recognized that he would crash and decided to ram his plane into the ship. It came in from behind the cargo carrier, its wing clipped part of the foremast and hit the foredeck. Its bomb, estimated to be a 500 lb. device, exploded along with the airplane. *Marcus Daly* became a ball of fire with flames reaching one hundred feet. Her bow area had severe damage and both sides near the bow were blown out. Firefighting commenced and within a few hours the fires were under control. In addition to her cargo she carried 1,200 troops, sixty-two of whom were killed in the crash. Three others died and forty-nine more were wounded.[1] Although damaged, she made it to Tarragona Gulf at Leyte under her own power.

At 1515, *John Evans* came under attack when a Zeke made a run on her. Reports indicate that the plane was hit a number of times. The pilot was believed to be dead when his plane crashed into *Evans* atop her deck house, between the main mast and her stack, and went into the water off her starboard side. The explosion from its bomb caused minimal damage but four men were wounded.[2]

On 5 December 1944, as the third anniversary of Pearl Harbor approached, ships off Leyte had little time for remembrance. *Lamson DD 367, Flusser DD 368, Shaw DD 373,* and *Drayton DD 366* were operating as part of Task Group 78.3 engaged in landing the Seventy-Seventh Division in Ormoc Bay. The troops were carried on LSTs. Included in the group were twelve destroyers, nine high speed transports, four LSTs, thirty-one LCIs, twelve LSMs, nine fleet minesweepers, two sub-chasers and one rescue tug. It would prove to be a successful day for the Japanese aviators. Elements of three Special Attack Units had recently arrived in the Philippines. Active in the kamikaze effort this day was the army's Fugaku Special Attack Unit, which would see action for the first time.[3]

Enemy aircraft had been in the area the previous evening, but weather conditions pre-

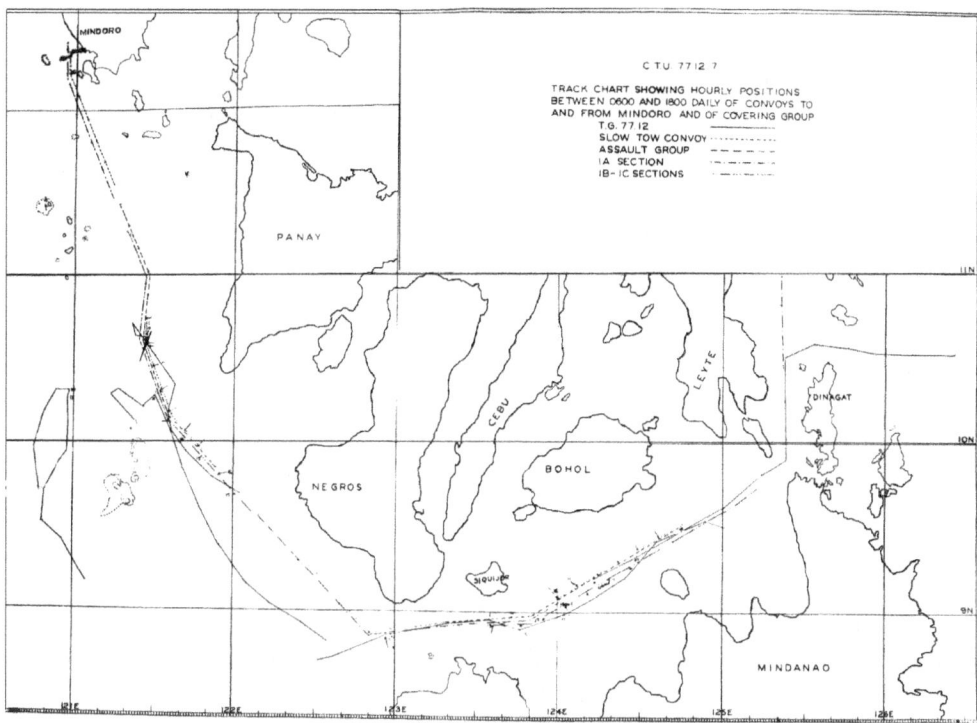

This map shows the supply route from the Leyte area to the Mindoro attack area, 13–17 December 1944. Ships plying this route were under constant threat of kamikaze attacks. Commander Task Unit 77.12.7 (Commander Carrier Division 24) Serial 00130. *Action Report Covering Operations in Connection with Occupation of Mindoro Central, Philippine Islands, 13 December 1944 to 17 December 1944, Inclusive.* 25 December 1944, p. 14.

vented them from attacking. At 0105 on 5 December the ships came under attack as an enemy plane bombed the area but missed their targets. This continued to be the pattern for the next few hours. At 0450 an enemy plane tried to bomb *Drayton*, but it was a close miss. The explosion killed two men and wounded seven more. It was a precursor of things to come. At 0900 a Dinah conducted a reconnaissance of the ships but was shot down by fire from *Lamson*. *Drayton's* action report details the events of the day:

> By 1100 the Task Unit had arrived and was proceeding northbound through Suragao Strait to the westward of Dinagat Island. Cloud cover was nearly 9/10, about 6500 feet. SC radar range was restricted to about five miles because of land interference. DRAYTON was in condition I-Easy. Four P-38s were overhead as CAP, controlled by the LAMSON. At about 1103 two groups of bogies were reported over the inter-fighter director circuit. These plotted nearly overhead. Almost simultaneously a suicide plane was observed to crash near the SHAW. DRAYTON opened fire on a diving plane on the port quarter and shot it down in flames. Several other planes were fired upon with unobserved results. A Val with fixed landing gear approached in a dive from the starboard quarter. All batteries took this plane under fire. Left full rudder was applied (speed 25 knots) and the plane passed down the starboard side with the wing tip just missing the bridge. His speed was in excess of 350 knots. When it appeared the plane would miss completely it stood up on its left wing and struck in the vicinity of gun No. 1. Most of the wreckage of the plane passed clear of the ship but part of the wing and landing gear caused damage to the ship. A serious fire was started from burning gasoline and the powder and projectile ready service boxes were broken open and powder and projectiles strewn around the deck within the flames. In spite of the intense heat none of the projectiles exploded. Some of the pow-

der went off but with a burning rather than explosive force. All powder and projectiles were jettisoned immediately and the fire extinguished using water and CO_2.[4]

Drayton suffered minor damage in the attack, but had six killed and twelve wounded. As her crew fought the fire other planes attacked her and were disposed of handily. She shot down at least one and damaged three others. As the attack on *Drayton* was taking place, an Oscar crashed into *LSM 20*, killing eight of her men and wounding nine. It was a fatal blow and the landing ship was sunk by the attack. Within minutes a Val made a run on *LSM 34* and missed, but a second Val targeted *LSM 23*. The ship's CO, Lt. K. K. Hickman, ordered flank speed and right full rudder in order to avoid the attack. The Val bounced off the water fifty feet from the starboard beam and crashed into the superstructure at deck level. Its 551 lb. bomb penetrated the LSM's hull about a foot above the water line. Fortune shone upon the landing ship as the bomb was a dud. However, the impact of the plane turned the chart house and radio room into a raging inferno, but the fires were brought under control in fifteen minutes. She had eight dead and another seven wounded.[5] The P-38s of the 9th Fighter Squadron, who were flying CAP, took their toll on the enemy aircraft by shooting down three Vals and three Oscars. Estimates of twelve to fifteen enemy planes in the area had made their numbers inadequate for the task. The surviving ships began the trip back to their base.

Conducting anti-submarine and radar picket patrol between Amagusen Point on Leyte and the mid-channel in south Surigao Strait on 5 December was *Mugford DD 389*. She observed the attacks on the LSMs and *Drayton* and, along with *LaVallette DD 448*, sped to the aid of the stricken ships. *Drayton* and *Shaw* escorted the undamaged LSMs back to Leyte. *LaValette* headed for Surigao Strait to patrol there and *Mugford* joined *Flusser* to screen for the remaining ships. In short order another air attack developed. At 1710 a Val attempted to bomb *Mugford*, but missed by two hundred yards. It flew off but returned a few minutes later and made a run on the destroyer. *Mugford*'s gunners were on target, but they failed to bring it down. The Val crashed into the port side of *Mugford* at 1716. A couple of minutes later another Val approached the ship but was shot down by two P-38s. *Mugford* temporarily lost power and was taken in tow by *LSM 34*. Within the hour her fires were under control and she was once again to able to proceed under her own power. She had eight dead and sixteen wounded.

On 7 December *Mahan DD 364* was patrolling off Ormoc Bay between Ponson Island and the western tip of Leyte Island on anti-submarine and picket duty for the group. She was equipped with a fighter director team and had seven army P-38 Lightnings overhead on combat air patrol. At 0943 enemy aircraft were reported in the area, and within five minutes they made their appearance near the ships. *Mahan* went to flank speed and prepared to engage them. The attacking planes consisted of nine twin-engine bombers, accompanied by four fighters which approached from eighty degrees on *Mahan*'s port bow. She took them under fire but ceased when three P-38s engaged the Japanese aircraft. One fighter was quickly shot down by a P-38 and a second Lightning got two more. The third P-38 shot up two of the bombers, one of which banked right and made a dive on *Mahan*, followed by several other bombers. *Mahan*'s action report reveals:

> The first plane to attack leveled off about fifty feet above the water, broad on the starboard beam, at a horizontal range of about 2000 yards, and headed for the bridge structure. Others followed the first plane at intervals of about 1,500 yards. The first plane to come in burst into flames and blew up about fifty yards from the ship, abreast 5" gun No. 3, about 30 feet above the water, as a result of the ship's 20 MM and 40 MM fire, the concussion knocking four men overboard off Gun 3 but otherwise doing no damage. The second bomber to come in apparently misjudged his altitude or was momentarily blinded by the explosion of the first plane. In any event, he passed overhead, just above the stacks, went out about 2000 yards on the port beam, low over the water, and came back in, hitting the ship abreast 5" Gun No. 2, between the water-

line and the forecastle deck level. A P-38 came in, trying to shoot him down before he reached the ship but was unable to do so. In the meantime, the third bomber to start in was shot down by the ship's 5" gun fire about 2500 yards on the starboard beam, the fourth bomber was shot down by 20mm and 40mm fire about 200 yards off the starboard side, abreast the after deck house, the fifth bomber hit the ship just abaft the bridge, starboard side, at the forecastle deck level, knocking down the forward stack and foremast, and the sixth bomber to come in hit on the starboard side, abreast 5" gun No. 2, about at the waterline. About the same time, the second bomber, that had passed overhead, hit on the port side as previously explained. The seventh bomber to come in either lost his nerve or decided that the ship had already been sufficiently damaged as he did not attempt to crash the ship. Instead, he came in strafing the after part of the ship from starboard, passed astern, and came back strafing the bridge and forward part of the ship from port.[6]

Three other bombers made strafing runs on the ship. Two of them crashed in the water after being hit by the ship's fire and fire from P-38s and another was driven off. Army P-40s of the 110th Tactical Reconnaissance Squadron joined the fray and a sizeable dogfight ensued.

Mahan, separated from the other ships by the action, bent on thirty-four knots to rejoin them. Recognizing that the high speed was fanning the flames, the CO, Cmdr. E. G. Campbell, took into account the fact that the fires below were out of control and that the forward magazine could not be flooded due to a break in the fire main. At 1001 he gave the order to get all wounded and unnecessary personnel off the ship. Depth charges were put on safe and torpedoes were jettisoned in preparation for the worst. At 1020 the forward magazine blew and the ship had to be abandoned. *Walke DD 723* and *Lamson* arrived on the scene and began rescuing survivors. RAdm. A. D. Struble, Commander of the Ormoc Attack Group, recognized that

P-38 Lightnings of the 36th Fighter Squadron, 8th Fighter Group at the airfield at San Jose, Mindoro Island, 20 December 1944. NARA 111-SC-A30104.

the situation for *Mahan* was hopeless. Rather than leave her burning hulk as a hazard to navigation, he ordered *Walke* to sink her. Gunfire and torpedoes did the job and, at 1150, *Mahan* slipped beneath the waves. She suffered six dead and thirty-one wounded.

Ward APD 16, had landed four officers and 104 enlisted men of the 77th Division. She recovered her boats and took station near *Mahan*, *Scout AM 296*, and *Saunter AM 295*, assisting them as they conducted anti-submarine patrols. The nine bombers that attacked *Mahan* passed over her and she took them under fire but no hits were scored. Shortly thereafter, she noticed that they were attacking *Mahan*. A few of the bombers survived the encounter with *Mahan* and the P-38s and made a run on *Ward*.

> The leading plane appeared to have been hit as it was trailing smoke. The WARD commenced firing at these planes with both 3" 50 cal. and 20MM batteries. The 20MM appeared to be hitting but the leading plane continued to close the ship leveling off somewhat just before striking the portside of the WARD in the vicinity of the troopspace and the boiler room. Serious fires immediately broke out in the WARD fuel tanks under the troopspace having been ruptured and ignited. When it became evident that the fires could not be controlled with the available equipment aboard, orders were given to abandon ship because of the danger from unflooded magazines.[7]

For the second time in the space of an hour, RAdm. Struble gave the order to sink one of his ships. *O'Brien DD 725* opened fire on the transport and sank it. As a result of the attack, several men were badly burned but none died.

Ward APD 16 burns in Ormoc Bay on 7 December 1944 after being hit by a kamikaze. *Ward* was so badly damaged that she was abandoned. *O'Brien DD 725* sank her with gunfire shortly after. NARA 80G 270774.

As news of *Mahan*'s plight reached the group, *Lamson* was ordered to replace her on picket duty. As she approached the area she saw the aerial battle over the ships and was soon sending fighters to intercept enemy aircraft. Between 1045 and 1145, she vectored her aircraft to intercept five bogeys. By 1130 the landing ships had finished disembarking troops and prepared to leave the area. Fortunately, *Lamson* experienced a lull in the aerial attacks until around 1400. About that time, a Dinah made a run on the ship and dropped a bomb which missed. Sharp-eyed gunners on *Lamson* hit the plane with a number of shells and it crashed into the water after passing over the ship. At that point *Lamson* had twelve P-38s under her control, but the Dinah had evaded them. *Lamson*'s action report states:

> Following this attack there was a lull of about one minute and we came to the ready. Then three planes made a low fast torpedo approach on the U.S.S. EDWARDS coming in over HIMUQUITAN ISLAND. Two of three planes were seen to be shot down and the third went over her mast, possibly hitting it and disappeared. At the same time a Tony came around from behind HIMUQUITAN ISLAND and made a low fast approach on our starboard quarter. Control managed to get on the plane at about a range of 1,000 yards, but guns one and two were in the blind. The plane came in weaving and strafing. Its approach was on our starboard quarter thirty feet off the water but it crossed slightly to amidships as we went hard left. It hit number two stack with its right wing and spun around crashing into the after port corner of the transmitter room and drove on in until the propeller was impeded in the portside of the after Combat bulkhead.[8]

Lamson's midship area was engulfed in flame and survivors of the crash were driven to the extreme ends of the ship to escape the fires. To the men on either end it seemed as if the entire ship beyond their view was engulfed in flames. As the rescue tug *ATR 31* came alongside to assist with the firefighting, the ship's First Lieutenant, Lt. Edgar H. Woods, organized firefighting parties and began the task of saving the ship. Hampered by shrapnel wounds in both legs, he managed to start the work that would eventually prove essential to the ship's continued existence. The firefighting teams could do little since the ship's water pressure was too low to be effective and the handy billys were not adequate enough to do the job. *Lamson*'s fires were soon deemed to be out of control and Capt. W. M. Cole, CO of DesRon 5, determined that she should be sunk. After her crew had been taken off, *ATR 31* continued to fight the fires and eventually succeeded. The decision to sink the destroyer was reversed and *ATR 31* took her under tow. The ships began to make their way back to safety accompanied by *Flusser DD 36*. However, another air attack soon began and *Flusser* had to maneuver to protect herself. In the melee that followed, the destroyer was narrowly missed by four bombs but managed to shoot down a Dinah. After dark the attacks subsided and the CO of *Lamson*, Lt. Cmdr. J. V. Noel, Jr., along with two officers and four crewmen, went back on board *Lamson* to assist in her tow back to San Pedro. The remainder of her trip was uneventful, but the attacks had killed four men and wounded seventeen.

Noel reported that the kamikazes apparently had devised new tactics:

> During the first part of December it was noted that the Japanese were using a new method of approach from their suicide attacks. In November these planes would come in high and dive in a manner very similar to dive bombers. However, starting about the first of December their approach was low, fast, and weaving, similar to that of a torpedo plane, but from the quarter or stern. This new approach has four very definite advantages:
> (1) Evades early radar and visual detection.
> (2) Makes director tracking difficult due to blind.
> (3) Forward guns unable to bear.
> (4) Results in greater percentage of hits.[9]

The Japanese were refining their special attack methods. Ships covering the withdrawal of the transports from the beach were also under attack. Destroyers *Smith DD 378*, *Hughes DD 410*, and the destroyer transport *Cofer APD 62* all dodged kamikazes, but *Liddle APD 60* was not so lucky. She shot down one Zeke only thirty feet off her port side but shortly thereafter, at 1120, a Zeke crashed her flying bridge. The CO of *Liddle*, Lt. Cmdr. L.C. Brogger, was killed immediately in the blast. Between the strafing attack of the first Zeke and the crash of the second, thirty-six men were killed and twenty-two wounded. After tending to the damage, the ship got underway and headed back to the convoy.

It seems strange that kamikazes would select a minor combatant as a target, but several did so in the early afternoon of 10 December when they went after four PTs on patrol at Leyte. *PT 323* was crashed amidships, nearly cutting the small boat in half. Her CO, Lt. (jg) Herbert Stadler, was killed in the impact, along with the second officer, Ens. William Adelman. Eleven more were wounded. Being small and fast, the PTs were a hard target but another plane attempted to crash *PT 532*. The PT went to flank speed and made a hard turn, leaving the kamikaze to splash in its wake.[10]

LST 737 had landed troops of the 718th and 536th Amphibian Tractor Battalions at Ormoc beginning at 0740 on 7 December. She had avoided any direct attacks during her unloading of the troops and their equipment, but the day was not over. From 1434, as she maneuvered to keep station in her convoy, the ships were under continual threat from Japanese aircraft. At 1619 a Zeke approached her from astern. She fired on it and set it ablaze. When the plane was only 500 yards away it dropped its bomb, which fell short and exploded in the water one hundred yards aft of the ship. Although damaged, the Zeke continued on course and crashed into her on the starboard side. Two men were killed and four wounded, but the crash did not seriously damage the LST and it maintained course. At 1626 another enemy plane attacked the LST and her gunners demolished it off the starboard bow.[11]

LSM 318 had successfully discharged her cargo when she came under attack as she attempted to retract from the beach. Three Betty bombers and four Oscar fighters overflew the area and dropped some bombs, but they missed the ships. *LSMs 18* and *19,* along with an LCI, were similar sitting ducks, but they all escaped damage. Once the ships had retracted from the beach they maneuvered to join their convoy. Army P-38s kept the enemy planes at bay until around 1525 when four Oscars went after the ships. As one Oscar attacked the *LSM 18*, two made a run on *LSM 318* and were taken under fire. *LSM 318*'s gunners were on target and shot down one of the Oscars bound for her and also the one that was going after *LSM 18*. According to *LSM 318*'s action report: "the third OSCAR passed overhead (it appeared that he overestimated the height of the target and overshot). He continued out over the water, flying low on a course that took him out on our Starboard beam for a distance of about 8000 yards (estimated). He then went into a climbing turn to Port, apparently to gain altitude for his next attack."[12] As he turned a P-38 tried to shoot him down but missed. The Oscar came in low on the water, followed by the P-38. Gunners on the *318* tried in vain to shoot the plane down, but it crashed into the starboard side of the ship at the waterline. Its bomb penetrated the ship's side and exploded in the engine room. *LSM 318*'s steering was disabled, along with her port engine and both generators. With her rudder jammed to full right, the LSM circled and attempted to put out her fires. As frequently happened with ships attacked in this manner, her fire-fighting equipment, lines, pumps and other apparatus were damaged, making effective fire-fighting problematic. Other ships attempted to assist in fighting her fires, but persistent enemy air attacks prevented their success. The order had to be given to abandon ship and, in the early hours of 8 December, she sank.

William S. Ladd was part of the same convoy of forty ships that included *Marcus Daly*. They had left Hollandia on 29 October and headed for Leyte. *Ladd* was anchored south of Dulag on 10 December when she came under attack at 0858. Her cargo was particularly hazardous, consisting of 600 tons of gas and explosives. As *Marcus Daly* was under attack, another Val from the group of four made a run on *Ladd*, crashing into her. Its fuselage and bomb went down into the No. 4 hold, causing an explosion. Two and one half hours of firefighting commenced, but it was a losing battle. Drums of gasoline began to explode one after another, and the ship began to take on water. As flames approached the ammunition stores, her Master, Nels F. Anderson, gave the order to abandon ship at about 1000. Her hulk continued to burn until it settled by the stern. By 2100 she was still burning with her stern resting on the bottom in about ten fathoms of water. She was later sunk. Miraculously only sixteen aboard had been injured.[13]

Marcus Daly, which had been severely damaged on her way to Leyte on 5 December, was hit again at 1700 on 10 December as she was in the process of offloading supplies in Tarragona Gulf, Leyte. Four enemy aircraft, described as either Zekes or Tojos, approached the ships in the area and two were shot down. One plane crashed her port side and parts of it hit *LCT 1075* which was alongside receiving cargo. Fires were quickly extinguished and overall damage was not heavy, but *Marcus Daly* had another eight men wounded.[14] On board *LCT 1075*, one man died instantly and ten were wounded, one of whom later died. The 119" LCT was a mass of flames and beyond saving. Its burning hulk was towed to the beach after the fires were extinguished.

Hughes DD 410 was crashed by a Betty on 10 December off the southern tip of Leyte. The plane demolished her engine room and caused severe damage to the ship. She was towed back to San Pedro Bay where she underwent temporary repairs. Her dead and wounded numbered twenty-three.

Reid DD 369 was part of Task Unit 78.3.8 charged with escorting ten LSMs and three LCI(L)s to Ormoc Bay to resupply American forces there. Other destroyers in the task unit were *Caldwell DD 605*, *Coghlan DD 606*, *Edwards DD 619*, *Smith DD 378*, and *Conyngham DD 371*. Flying overhead was a CAP of four Corsairs. At 1500, snoopers began to appear on the radar screens, but turned away out of gun range. Around 1700, twelve bogeys approached the convoy from dead ahead. They were tentatively identified as Jills and the ships went on alert. The Corsairs swung into action and went after them. As *Reid* was in the leading edge of the convoy, she took the Japanese planes under fire at 10,000 yards and turned to starboard to bring her guns to bear. Two of the Corsairs got behind the Jills and began to attack them as the ships fired on the enemy planes. *Reid* shot down three enemy aircraft before one hooked its wing in the starboard whaleboat, pivoted over, and crashed into her waterline. Its bomb exploded, opening her seams. A fifth plane strafed her and crashed close aboard her port bow. Another plane strafed her, passed over her superstructure and crashed close aboard the starboard bow. The plane that delivered the *coup de grace* came in from astern, crashed the No. 3 gun and slid forward to the port side 40mm gun tub where it came to rest in a flaming ball of fire. Its bomb penetrated the hull and blew up in the after magazine room, effectively ripping apart the entire stern section. In the space of about fifteen seconds, *Reid* had suffered two hits and five close crashes. Her action report revealed:

> The ship began lurching to starboard, it was much faster than a roll. The first indication of instability was a violent lurch to about sixty degrees, the ship whipped back to about thirty then to seventy back to fifty and then to 89° still making twenty knots. The firerooms had cut their fires and had opened the safety valves. In the engine room both ahead and astern throttles were jammed. The word to abandon ship was passed by the commanding officer locally but could not be given over any telephones or P.A. system. The commanding officer [Cmdr. Samuel A. McCornock] was the last person as far as is known to leave the ship. He stood on the port side of the director trunk and carefully looked over the ship which at that time was lying on the starboard side down by the stern with the entire ship under water up to No. 1 stack down which water was pouring, the ship still had a slight headway. The survivors were strung out astern a distance of about three hundred yards. The ship sank about fifteen seconds later in 600 fathoms of water.... A member of the gun crew of gun No. 1 was knocked down by the upper half of the Jap pilot's body whose plane crashed at the waterline at gun No. 2.[15]

Her depth charges went off, injuring and killing some of the men in the water. Others fell victim to Japanese planes which strafed them until they were driven off by Corsairs. *Reid* lost about 150 men in the attack.

The End of December

On 13 December, the kamikazes did not sink any ships, but took a heavy toll of dead and wounded in their attacks on *Nashville CL 43, Caldwell DD 605,* and *Haraden DD 585.* With the landings at Ormoc completed, the American forces turned their attention to Mindoro. RAdm. A. D. Struble, Commander Task Group 78.3, was escorting a group of ships for an assault on Mindoro. *Nashville CL 43* with RAdm. Struble and various navy and army officers on board led the attack force which consisted of *Nashville,* twelve destroyers, nine destroyer transports, thirty LSTs, twelve LSMs, thirty-one LCI(L)s, sixteen minesweepers, and additional supporting craft. Accompanying them was a Close Covering Group led by RAdm. Russell S. Berkey. This consisted of three cruisers, seven destroyers and twenty-three PTs. In order to deceive the Japanese, the two groups split apart and made a feint toward Palawan. Once darkness fell, the two resumed their original course at flank speed and made for the beaches at Mindoro. There they would establish an airfield that would prove useful in the remainder of the campaign for the Philippines. To support the landing further, a Heavy Covering and Carrier Group under RAdm. L. Theodore D. Ruddock, Jr., joined them. It included six escort carriers, three vintage battleships, three light cruisers and eighteen destroyers. Air cover was provided by a CAP of Lightnings and Corsairs.[16]

Although they had made an attempt to deceive the Japanese, a grouping of that many ships was hard to conceal. Japanese reconnaissance planes and subs had spotted the force as it moved toward Mindoro. At 1415, as the ships passed the southern tip of Negros, a Japanese fighter with two 110 lb. bombs slipped in over Siguijori Island and crashed *Nashville* in the port main deck waist. Both bombs went off on deck and gasoline fires engulfed the area near the crash. Ammo in the 5" service boxes cooked off, along with 40 mm and 20 mm ammo from nearby gun mounts.[17] Although damage to the ship was not severe, *Nashville* had to head back to Leyte with *Stanly DD 478* as an escort. Struble transferred his flag to *Dashiell DD 659* and the group continued on its way to Mindoro. One hundred thirty-five men had died and another 190 were killed. Wounded in the attack was the head of the army forces, BGen. William C. Dunckel. His Chief of Staff, Col. Bruce C. Hill, died, along with Struble's Chief of Staff, Capt. Everett W. Abdill, and several other senior officers.[18] Although only a single plane had slipped through, the toll was deadly.

Haraden DD 585 was also headed for Mindoro as part of Ruddock's Heavy Covering and Carrier Group. At 1715, as the destroyer was making twenty-five knots, she encountered four aircraft coming at her on her starboard beam. One was identified as an American navy Wildcat which was in pursuit of a Val and two Oscars. *Haraden* took them under fire but scored no hits; the Wildcat did. It shot down the Val and then one of the Oscars. According to the ship's action report:

> The remaining Oscar banked sharply to his left, gained a little altitude and then headed directly toward this ship, bearing about 060 relative. He was smoking, and receiving 20mm and 40mm hits. The approach was very shallow glide—almost at constant altitude. Just before the plane crashed, it banked to the left, the right wing striking the pilot house and torpedo director—the fuselage crashing into the forward stack where it exploded.[19]

Her topsides were severely damaged as was her forward engine room. *Twiggs DD 591* came alongside to assist in firefighting on *Haraden* which was dead in the water. Within a couple of hours *Haraden*'s condition was stable and she headed back to San Pedro for preliminary repairs. Fourteen of her men had been killed and another twenty-four wounded. From San Pedro she headed back to Hawaii and then to Puget Sound for further repairs.

Caldwell DD 605 had a close call on 11 December when she shot down a suicide Zeke only twenty feet off her starboard beam. The ship was covered with water and gas, but had no damage or casualties. At 0805 on 12 December she was escorting landing craft at Ormoc when she was jumped by several enemy planes. She fired on several Dinahs and drove them off. The destroyer then caught the attention of three Zekes which were escorting the Dinahs and they made a run on her. Her action report details the attack:

> Two Zekes peeled off for dive-bombing and were kept under fire by the main battery. The third Zeke came down the port side, under continual machine gun fire, crossed the stern in a steep bank. One landing gear was flopping out. He went into a vertical bank and at 0807 hit the ship just as he was turning over on his back. One wing hit the bridge, one the break of the forecastle, and the fuselage in Main Radio. Simultaneously, the ship was straddled with several bombs (according to observers on the other ships), one striking and exploding No. 2 Handling Room. A bomb from the suicide plane glanced off No. 2 Gun and exploded just to the starboard of No. 1 Gun. This was a perfectly planned and excellently coordinated attack.[20]

Fires broke out but were soon extinguished by her damage control parties, however, the damage was extensive. Thirty-three of her crew were killed and another forty wounded. With her temporary repairs completed, she headed for San Francisco and an overhaul.

Further attacks continued from 15 through 28 December 1944. The kamikazes damaged the destroyers *Ralph Talbot DD 390*, *Foote DD 511*, *Bryant DD 665*, the escort carrier *Marcus Island CVE 77*, *PT 84*, and *Southard DMS 10* and the merchant ships *Juan De Fuca* and *William Sharon*. Sunk were *LSTs 460, 472, 479,* and *738* along with *PT 300*. Typical of the experiences of the landing ships were those of the *LSTs 738* and *472* on 15 December.

LST 738 was operating as part of a group of thirty LSTs in Task Unit 78.34 under Capt. Richard Webb during the landings at Mindoro on 15 December 1944. As the LSTs in the unit jockeyed for position to make their landings, they came under attack by a group of approximately ten Zekes, Kates, Tojos, and Oscars. At 0850, *LST 605* had a close call as she shot down a Zeke which subsequently crashed into the water twenty feet off her port quarter after missing the ship by only five feet. As it exploded in the water, the force of the blast slightly injured men on the fantail. Shortly after 0900 the ships opened fire on the planes and shot several down with their combined fire. In the midst of the air attack, two Kates were seen making a run on *LST 738* from a low altitude. Fire from the *738* and nearby *Moale DD 693* hit the planes but did not shoot them down. The first crashed the LST hitting it "amidships just above the waterline. Explosion and fire resulted ... the plane was carrying bombs at the time. The second plane which dove for LST 738's bridge and Conn missed and was shot down by DD693 to the port of LST 738."[21] Repair parties went to work fighting fires but were hampered by the damaged fire mains caused by the crash. Confusion reigned among the army troops and they were ordered by the commanding officer to abandon the ship. To prevent explosions the LST's crew flooded her magazines, making firefighting even more difficult. Added to this was the problem of her cargo. Nestled in her hold were drums of aviation gas and a load of oxygen bottles, the perfect combination for massive explosions. In due course a second explosion ripped through the ship and most of the crew abandoned it.

> At this time the Captain [Lt. J. T. Barnett], the Pharmacist Mate, first class; and one radioman were all that could be observed aboard. The Captain personally destroyed the IFF radar and the SOS radar. The radioman was then ordered to stern and he went over the side. Another heavy explosion shook the ship throwing the Captain and Pharmacist Mate to the bridge deck. Decision was then made that all hope was gone and that even efforts of DD693 to come alongside would be useless. The Captain then went to the main deck and waited to see if the DD693 wished to come alongside but a final blast again threw him to the deck and caused the DD693 to

back off rapidly. Oil on the water about LST 738 was burning by this time and a few personnel were observed working hard to get away. After ordering the Pharmacist Mate, first class, over the side, both sides of the ship at water line were checked for personnel on lines. Several were observed and were ordered away. When they were away from the ship, the Captain then went over the side.[22]

The final blast was severe enough to put a hole in *Moale*'s bow. One of her men was killed and ten wounded. On board *LST 738* no one had died, but several men were injured. The landing ship was a burning hulk; the next morning she was sunk by gunfire.

LST 472 underwent a similar experience as she stood by in preparation for landing her troops and supplies. The same attack that saw the demise of *LST 738* finished her also. Her action report noted:

> The formation [of Japanese planes] appeared to be heading towards the beach where the other landing craft were unloading but made a sharp bank and headed towards the ships standing by in the waiting area. One plane headed for the subject ship's bow, coming in on the starboard side, was fired upon by her guns and splashed in the water on the port side of the ship. At the same time two more planes were coming in on the starboard beam, the foremost heading for the stern, was fired upon and splashed on the port quarter hitting the after gun tubs and leaving part of her wing in the tub as the plane went over. Following this plane, and lower over the water, was a third plane which was headed directly for the starboard side. This plane appeared to commence the long low dive at approximately 3500 yards and was taken under fire by the ship's guns at that time. All guns that could bear on her were firing up until the time the plane crashed

Moale DD 693 stands by **LST 738** after she was hit by a kamikaze on 15 December 1944. A number of men may be seen in the water between the ships. NARA 80G 294593.

into the side of the ship at deck level just forward of the main deck superstructure. The plane's engine and parts of the burning ship were scattered from starboard to port across the main deck, while the bomb apparently landed in the tank deck and exploded there. The plane appeared to be badly shot up as it approached the ship with parts of its wings and tail dropping off while still in flight.[23]

Several other planes strafed the ship and then tried to crash her. Under fire from the LST's guns, they were damaged and crashed close aboard. Meanwhile, fires from the crash and the subsequent explosion of the bomb reached her hold where she was carrying a supply of gasoline. The explosion and another that soon followed spelled the death knell for the ship. At 1100, her wounded skipper, Lt. John L. Blakley, was able to give the order to abandon ship. Her condition was hopeless and she was sunk by gunfire around midnight.

Howorth DD 592 was in Magarin Bay, Southwest Mindoro Island on 15 December. She had been assigned to bombard the shore in preparation for upcoming amphibious landings. At 0850 her lookouts spotted a Paul II in the area and the ship headed for deeper water in order to be able to maneuver in case of an air attack. At 0855 seven Zekes made their appearance and the ship opened fire a minute later. Three more Zekes approached the ship from another direction and *Howorth*'s gunners turned one away on fire with the likelihood that it crashed. The two remaining Zekes made a suicide run on the ship which went to twenty knots and made a hard left turn in order to bring its guns to bear. One Zeke was hit at a range of

Fires blaze on *LST 472* at Mindoro after she was hit by a kamikaze on 15 December 1944. NARA 80G 294601.

PT 297 picks up survivors from ***LST 472*** after the kamikaze attack of 15 December 1944. NARA 80G 294583.

500 yards, and the pilot lost control. His plane passed closely over the ship and crashed twenty feet off the starboard side. Its bomb went off underwater but caused no damage to the ship. Parts of the plane and its pilot were later found on the ship. *Howorth*'s action report detailed the next attack:

> The Commanding Officer [Lt. Cmdr. E. S. Burns], upon seeing that the first plane had missed, reversed the rudder (giving full right rudder). About 20 seconds to 30 seconds later, the second plane crashed into the air search radar antenna with his undercarriage, opening his gasoline tanks and spraying the ship with gasoline. The plane continued its dive with the right wing glancing off the port bow carrying away the life lines on the port side from frame 8 to 33 and putting a slight dent in the forecastle deck at frame 14 about three feet from the ship's side; luckily no fire resulted. He crashed into the water just off the port bow sending up a column of water which covered the ship including the director. The ship continued in its right turn and proceeded to a northerly heading then turning left, standing about a mile west into an area with more sea room and covering AMs in area. At 0900 two LSTs No. 738 and No. 472 were observed burning in the transport area about three miles northwest from the ship's position at this time. Three destroyers were attempting to assist them in putting out the fires and rescuing survivors.[24]

Ralph Talbot DD 390 was screening in the Sulu Sea for Task Group 77.12 between 13 and 16 December. They were providing air cover for Task Group 78.3 during the landings on Mindoro. *Haraden* was part of this group and had been crashed by a kamikaze on 13 December. On 15 December the task group again came under attack by a total of at least fifteen planes, nine of which were shot down by the ships and their CAP. The attacks began at 0400 and continued on into the morning hours. At 0813 observers on *Ralph Talbot DD 390* picked up an incoming Oscar at 1,100 yards and took it under fire. It exploded 300 yards from the ship, its debris striking the starboard side and main deck of the destroyer. Damage to the destroyer was minimal and only one man was injured.[25]

A number of PT boats were operating in Mangarin Bay by this time. On 15 December some of them dodged kamikazes. Last minute maneuvers and sharp boat handling by their skippers saved *PTs 77, 223, 230,* and *298*. A couple of days later, on 17 December, *PTs 75, 84,* and *224* came under attack by three planes. Two missed their targets and crashed into the sea and the other was shot down. *PT 75* had the closest call when one of the planes missed her by only fifteen feet. The explosion blew five men overboard, four of whom suffered shrapnel wounds.[26] On 18 December the PTs luck ran out. According to *PT 300*'s action report:

> At approximately 1600 on 18 December 1944 PT boats of TASK GROUP 70.1.4 WERE ATTACKED BY THREE (3) ENEMY AIRCRAFT, TYPE Val, approximately three hundred yards off shore of Camimanit Point, Mindoro Island, Philippine Islands. While maneuvering to meet the attack U.S.S. PT 300 was hit by enemy aircraft, which made a suicide dive on the boat, coming in low from the PT's starboard quarter, hitting the PT amidship of the engine room causing the boat to break in two. The stern sank immediately but the bow remained afloat for about eight (8) hours with about two (2) feet of the forepeak showing above water enveloped in flames from the burning gasoline around it.[27]

The entire crew, with the exception of three men, were blown over the side by the crash. Eight men died and seven were wounded, including her skipper, Lt. Cmdr. Almer P. Colvin.

Resupply of the Mindoro invasion force was a top priority. On 19 December a convoy "consisting of 25 ships, 14 LST and six chartered freighters, escorted by eleven destroyers departed Leyte Gulf,"[28] bound for Mindoro. The convoy came under attack at 1600 on 21 December in the Sulu Sea, west of Panay. At 1705 ten Japanese aircraft were sighted, among them a number of Betty bombers. Shortly thereafter, a number of single-engine fighters identified as Oscars and Tojos, made their appearance. Armed Guard gunners on the liberty ship *Juan de Fuca* brought down one of the planes and then watched as two Oscars crashed into *LSTs 460* and *479*. *LST 460* was carrying a large supply of gasoline and ammunition. The kamikaze's crash set off fires that were impossible to stop and she had to be abandoned. *LST 479* was crashed amidships. The Oscar that hit her carried a pair of bombs that set the aft end of the ship ablaze and knocked out her steering. In the midst of this, other planes attacked and disrupted the firefighting efforts. Finally she had to be abandoned. Casualties were high among the LST's crews, but an additional 107 of the 774 soldiers on the LSTs were killed also. *Juan De Fuca* was crashed next in spite of her anti-aircraft fire. She was crashed by a plane that hit her No. 2 hatch. Fortunately her cargo was not explosive and the fires were put out in short order. Her casualties included two dead and seventeen wounded.[29] *Foote DD 511,* acting as escort for the convoy, was attacked at the same time. She shot down one Tojo and the second crashed into the water close aboard her port side. At 1738 she shot down a Lily. Her damage in these attacks was minimal and she had no casualties.

Bryant DD 665 was screening off the southern tip of Mindoro Island with seven other destroyers of Task Group 78.3.13 on 22 December. At 0945 a lone Zeke came in on her starboard bow. The ship's CO, Cmdr. P. L. High, ordered flank speed and left full rudder. The plane responded by banking right to target the ship's starboard quarter. Again the CO ordered right full rudder to keep his guns bearing on the Zeke. Numerous hits from the ship's 20mm and 40mm guns threw the plane off course and it disintegrated in an explosion fifty yards off the port beam. A shower of debris and shrapnel descended upon the deck, wounding one man. It had been a close call for *Bryant* but she was unscathed.[30]

The southwestern part of the nearby island of Mindoro offered an excellent location for an airfield, particularly since there were already four fields in the area that had fallen into disuse. The American forces did not need to capture the entire island but needed to establish a perimeter around the town of San Jose for the purpose of ensuring security for the airfield. On 15 December 1944 BGen. William C. Dunckel watched as his troops made an unopposed landing on the beaches off San Jose. Included in the landing was the 19th Regimental Combat Team of the 24th Division and the 503rd Parachute Regimental Combat Team. Although their landing was unopposed, they would be in need of supplies, which would put navy ships in peril.

Pringle DD 477 and *Gansevoort DD 608* were operating as part of Task Group 78.3.15 which was screening the Mindoro Resupply Unit. This was a group of sixty ships of various kinds, including LSTs, LCIs, liberty ships, seaplane tenders and about thirty PT boats. Other destroyers in the screen included *Bush DD 529*, *Stevens DD 47*, *Philip DD 498*, *Edwards DD 619*, *Sterret DD 407*, and *Wilson DD 408*, along with the high speed minesweeper *Hamilton DMS 18*.

The Mindoro Supply Unit left the Dulag anchorage in Leyte Gulf, formed up, and headed for Mindoro through Surigao Strait on 27 December 1944. The following day, at 1020, the kamikazes made their first attack. The liberty ships *John Burke* and *William Sharon* both took hits. *William Sharon* was cruising with the convoy when, at 1022, three Vals appeared over the ships. One dove on *William Sharon* and strafed her decks. The ship's Armed Guard returned fire and set the plane ablaze, but it hit the No. 4 gun tub and bounced into the port side of the flying bridge. The commanding officer of the ship's armed guard, Lt. (jg) Gerhardt E. Ernst, was killed in the action. His decapitated body, minus one arm and one leg, was identified after the action ended. Raging fires gutted the ship as *Wilson* came alongside to assist. After four hours the fires were finally extinguished, but the ship was in no condition to continue. Survivors were transferred off the ship and she was abandoned. The following day her dead were removed by *Spencer WPG-36* and she was towed back to San Pedro by the tug *Grapple ARS-7*. Among her crew, eleven men died and eleven were wounded. *John Burke*, carrying a full load of ammunition, was not so fortunate. The Val that hit her caused explosions that disintegrated the ship and killed all sixty-eight men on board. "The debris from this ship killed and wounded over two dozen men on other ships nearby."[31] Following close behind in the convoy was an unidentified army Freight and Supply ship. The enormity of the explosion sank her as well. Rescuers pulled two of her survivors from the water, but one died shortly thereafter.[32] Also damaged in the explosion was *LST 750*, which had a large number of casualties in addition to some damage to the ship. She dropped back from the convoy and fell victim to a torpedo from a Betty. Damage to her was so severe that she had to be abandoned. Her hulk was sunk by *Edwards*. *Francisco Morazan*, shielded by nearby ships also suffered some slight damage and had three men wounded. *PT 332* had her seams opened by the blast.

At 1845 four planes attacked the convoy and *Pringle* shot down a Betty at 1901. On the 29 December the Japanese continued to stalk the convoy. Zekes attacked the ships between 0716 and 0722 before they were driven off. *Pringle* had a close call at 1703 when a Zeke tried to crash her, passed between her stacks, and crashed in the water fifty yards to port. A Betty then tried to torpedo her, but it missed and was shot down.

The fleet made it to Mindoro on 30 December and the ships began unloading their supplies. Enemy aircraft had been in the vicinity since early morning. *Gansevoort* shot down one at 0416 and fired on another at 0707. At 0700 the LSTs began to beach themselves in Mangarin Bay and the destroyers took up screen. By 1530 reports began to come in of approaching enemy aircraft and the ships readied themselves. *Pringle* spotted a Val making a suicide run on her, but her fire was too late and the plane crashed into her No. 5 40mm mount. The fires were quickly extinguished and the destroyer resumed station. Eleven of her men were killed and twenty were wounded. At 1548 observers on *Gansevoort* watched as a Japanese fighter dropped bombs on *Porcupine* and then turned toward them. The destroyer went to flank speed and turned to bear all guns on the incoming kamikaze, but to no avail. It struck the port side of the ship near the loading machine. Its bomb exploded below decks near boilers 3 and 4 and the plane itself started fires. Within a few minutes the destroyer was listing six degrees to starboard. *Philip* and *Wilson* came alongside to assist with firefighting, and by 1620 the fires were out. Seventeen men were killed and fifteen wounded. *Gansevoort* was towed to a nearby anchorage, but she was not finished.[33]

Porcupine, carrying a load of aviation gasoline for the forces at Mindoro, had no luck at all that day, save the bad kind. When the ammo carrier *John Burke* was hit on 28 December, she was one of the nearby ships that sustained damage and also had one man killed as the liberty ship blew apart. Concern for her safety led to her movement to a supposedly safer anchorage, but it was not to be so. Around 1550 on 30 December, reports came in of twelve enemy aircraft approaching the ships. According to *Porcupine*'s action report:

> Our P-38 interceptors engaged the enemy planes but four dive bombers broke through. One of these enemy dive bombers came in low over the water on our port beam and we opened fire with all of our port guns. The four port 20mm guns were scoring hits on the plane but were unable to divert it from its course. The plane, identified as a Japanese Val, was strafing as it came in. At about 1555 the plane's bomb was dropped on the main deck a few feet aft of the mid-ships deck house and the plane crashed in after it. The explosion of the bomb and the crash of the plane caused the number two deep tanks to be ruptured, the generators and switchboards to be knocked out, and the engine room was flooded with black oil and diesel. The plane tore out the after bulk heads of the mid-ships house which immediately caught fire and spread rapidly. The engine of the plane went through the hull of the ship a few feet aft of the engine room on the starboard side near the water line, tearing a large hole and rupturing number six cargo tank. Personnel casualties included everyone in sick bay, two men from damage control and one man who had been hit by strafing and was being treated in sick bay.[34]

In short order it was determined that no help was available and that the fires had spread out of control. The ship was abandoned and the damaged destroyer *Gansevoort*, which was anchored nearby, was ordered to torpedo the stern of the ship in order to bring the fires under control. The shallow water prevented a successful hit and fires spread to the gasoline tanks. *Porcupine* was engulfed in flames and burned to the water line, a total loss. Seven of her men were listed as missing and presumed dead and another eight were wounded. On 1 January 1945, the remaining members of the crew were air-lifted from Mindoro to Leyte. As they flew over their ship they noted that she was still burning.[35]

The thirty PT boats in the convoy were serviced by *Orestes AGP 10*. Around 1600, as *Pringle, Gansevoort,* and *Porcupine* were under attack, a Val crashed into *Orestes*' starboard side amidships, causing extensive damage and fires. Its bomb exploded inside the ship, causing heavy casualties. Nearby LCIs helped put them out, but the PT tender was put out of action. She was beached nearby for repairs and then towed back to Leyte. Temporary repairs allowed her to depart Leyte on 27 February 1945 and she arrived in San Francisco on 13 May. After extensive repairs she returned to Samar, but the war had just ended. The kamikaze attack had effectively terminated her war career. Her heavy casualties included fifty-nine dead and 106 wounded.

9. Lingayen Gulf

Having established beachheads at Leyte and Mindoro, the American forces next targeted Lingayen Gulf, in the northwestern part of the island of Luzon. A successful landing there would give army troops the ability to form up and maneuver as they marched the one hundred miles south to capture Manila. Task Force 77, under VAdm T. C. Kincaid, was scheduled to attack the Lingayen Gulf area. It consisted of 685 ships, not counting minor combatants. The landing was scheduled for 9 January 1945. Prior to that, Adm. William F. Halsey's Third Fleet would unleash their fast carriers for air strikes in the area around Lingayen Gulf on 6–7 January. Immediately following those strikes would be an attack by Task Group 77.2, the Bombardment and Fire Support Group and also the Lingayen Fire Support Group under VAdm J. B. Oldendorf. Oldendorf's fleet consisted of 164 ships including the battleships *California BB 44* (flag), *Colorado BB 45*, *New Mexico BB 40*, *Mississippi BB 41*, *West Virginia BB 48*, and *Pennsylvania BB 38*. Also a part of the fleet were cruisers, escort carriers, destroyers, and numerous other ships and smaller craft.

Within the next few days additional ships would be hit and sunk. The various task groups began departing Leyte for Lingayen Gulf on 2 January, with the slower ships leaving first. The next day the fleet was spotted by the Japanese who sent a Val crashing into the deck of the oiler *Cowanesque AO 79*. She suffered minimal damage, but had two men killed and one injured. *Orca AVP 49* had a kamikaze splash close aboard. The seaplane tender was not damaged but six of her crew were wounded.

The escort carriers put up a sizeable combat air patrol to thwart further attacks. Once in the Sulu Sea, however, the attacks began in earnest. On 3 January, kamikazes from the field at Sarangani nearly hit *Makin Island CVE 93*. Combat air patrol planes accounted for fifteen to twenty Japanese aircraft during the period from 3 to 5 January. On 4 January, at 1712, a twin-engine bomber dove successfully on *Ommaney Bay CVE 79*. Prior to hitting the escort carrier's starboard side, the plane released two bombs. One penetrated the flight deck and exploded on the hangar deck below among fully-gassed aircraft. The second bomb penetrated through the hangar deck and damaged fire mains, making the fighting of fires impossible. Fires raged throughout the ship, cooking off ammunition as they approached the torpedo warhead storage area. With no way to extinguish the flames, the ship had to be abandoned. Her torpedo warheads finally went off, dooming the ship. She was finished off by a torpedo from the destroyer *Burns DD 588*. Ninety-three of her men were killed and sixty-five wounded. The following day her sister jeep carrier *Savo Island CVE 78* had a close call, but the kamikaze that attempted to crash her struck a glancing blow, causing little damage and no casualties.

9. Lingayen Gulf

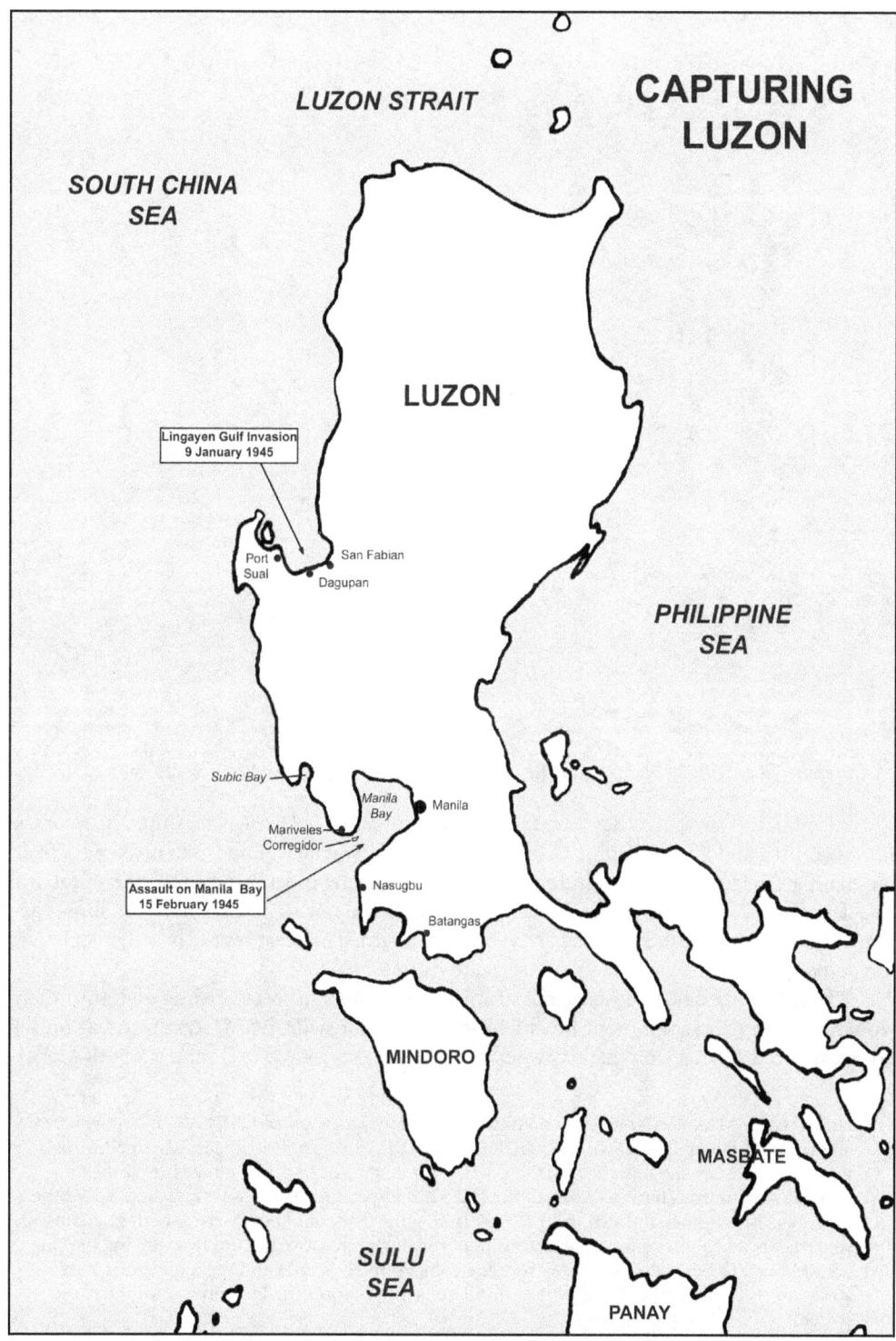

The capture of the island of Luzon began with the landings at Lingayen Gulf. Once the area had been captured American army units moved south toward Manila while the American navy moved down the western coast of the island and closed on Manila Bay from seaward.

Ommaney Bay CVE 79 burns after the kamikaze strike of 4 January 1945. NARA 80G 273153.

Also hit and sunk that day was the liberty ship *Lewis L. Dyche*. The ship, a part of the Minesweeping and Hydrographic Group, under Cmdr. Wayne R. Loud, had broken off from the main group to anchor at Mindoro. At 0820 a Val came in twenty feet off the water and struck her amidships. The ammo carrier and her men did not stand a chance. The ship evaporated in a giant fireball, killing all sixty-nine on board. The blast sent debris flying all over the harbor, killing or wounding men on nearby ships.

The following day, 5 January, the kamikazes were out in force. Falling victim to them would be seven more ships, none of which were sunk. *Louisville CA 28*, serving as flag for the group, suffered an attack on that day when three kamikazes roared in from the field at Mabalacat.

> One struck HMAS ARUNTA stationed in the screen just forward of LOUISVILLE's port beam; one was shot down close aboard the DD on LOUISVILLE's port bow; the third came through the screen and headed straight for LOUISVILLE. It could not be taken under fire by the LOUISVILLE until after it had passed the DD. At the speed the plane was travelling, very little time was left to knock it down. All LOUISVILLE guns that could bear were shooting. Plane was smoking, but kept on coming, headed straight for the foremast structure. By swinging the ship hard to port, CO diverted the blow from the comparatively fragile and vulnerable foremast structure to Turret 2 and the pilot house. All guns' crews continued to shoot until the plane struck.[1]

The plane crashed into the starboard side of the ship forward of amidships. Its two bombs detonated, blowing holes in the deck and damaging the side of the chart house. The cruiser's CO, Capt. R. L. Hicks, was burned in the attack and incapacitated. Cmdr. W. P. McCarty, the ship's XO, took command. Fifty-eight others were injured. It did not prevent the cruiser from completing her mission. In his endorsement to the ship's action report, J. R. Hamly, Chief of Staff Cruiser Division Four, suggested that the kamikaze attacks were flown by skilled pilots and represented a serious threat to the ships. He further suggested the development of a new weapon to combat them. This would be a "super type flame thrower that has a range of 300–400 yards which might explode the plane or burn the wing coverage sufficiently to cause the plane to drop in to the sea before it can strike the ship."[2] Although it sounded interesting, the weapon was not developed.

The escort carrier *Manila Bay CVE 61* was operating as a part of the San Fabian Carrier Group T.U.77.4.2 under RAdm. F. B. Stump. Late in the afternoon a group of Zekes, estimated at between six to eight in number, attacked the carriers and their screen.

> It is believed that at least one of these was shot down by the screen; one hit the H.M.A.S. AUSTRALIA amidships; one clipped the radar antennae of SAVO ISLAND and plunged into the sea alongside; one was shot down just before reaching NATOMA BAY, crashing alongside that ship; and two attacked MANILA BAY. The first of these last two scored a direct hit on the flight deck; the second hit the starboard yardarm and plunged into the sea about thirty feet off the starboard quarter.[3]

Both planes were handled by experienced pilots. They weaved in toward the carrier, evading anti-aircraft fire and strafing the ship on their approach. The first plane hit at the base of the island structure and its bomb penetrated the deck, exploding in the hangar and the radar

A Japanese kamikaze dives on *Natoma Bay CVE 62* on 5 January 1945. The plane missed the carrier. NARA 80G 273553.

Manila Bay CVE 61 burns after being hit by a kamikaze on 5 January 1945. NARA 80G 337999.

transmitter room. Fires enveloped the area but were quickly extinguished. Within twenty-four hours the escort carrier was back in action. She lost twenty-two dead and fifty-six wounded.

The small combatants were not spared either. On the morning of 5 January *LCI(G) 70* had been covering the activities of Underwater Demolition Team No. 8 as they attempted to reconnoiter the beach at Lingayen White Beaches One and Two. That task accomplished, the gunboat attacked various targets on the beaches. Later in the afternoon, at 1974, a Zeke approached from the stern, clipped off her mast and antenna and dug into her three inch gun tub near the forecastle area. The gun was rendered inoperable and her communications were knocked out. Six of the crew were killed and nine injured.

The tug *Apache ATF 67* took a minor hit from a kamikaze but only had three men wounded. She continued on duty after some minor patch work. The destroyer escort *Stafford DE 411* was screening the escort carrier *Tulagi CVE 72,* along with *Helm DD 388* and two other ships when the kamikazes roared in. *Stafford* took a crash in her starboard side and lost two dead and twelve wounded. Nearby *Helm* had a close call as another kamikaze narrowly missed her important parts, took off a mast and searchlight and crashed alongside the ship, wounding six men.

January 5 had been a bad day for the ships, but 6 January would prove even more deadly. Fifteen ships would suffer at the hands of the divine wind flyers, one of which would be sunk. It would tough going for the "big boys" with two battleships and four cruisers taking the brunt of the assault along with five destroyers and several other ships.

New Mexico BB 40, in the midst of shore bombardment off San Fernando Point and the Poro Isthmus area with other ships of Task Unit 77.2.1 the San Fabian Fire Support Unit, came under kamikaze attack at 1159 on 6 January. A Zeke came in from astern and crashed her on the port wing of the navigation bridge. Its bomb, judged to be a 551 pounder, killed the CO, Capt. R. W. Fleming, along with several other officers and visiting dignitaries. Damage to the superstructure was significant but did not impede the battleship's mission. The ship's Executive Officer, Cmdr. J. T. Warren, assumed command and within minutes other planes attacked. At 1209 the ship was hit by an Oscar which crashed on its port bow. At 1305 the ship resumed shore bombardment, but kamikazes still continued to plague her. She was strafed by another Japanese plane at 1437. From around noon until 1939 there were continual flights of enemy aircraft in the area, along with the American combat air patrol, making the situation confusing. The battleship fired on and hit a number of these, but none came close enough to crash the ship. *New Mexico* suffered thirty dead and eighty-seven wounded in the attacks of 6 January. At 1719 *New Mexico* received word that *California BB 44* had been hit by a kamikaze.

California was the flagship of VAdm. J. B. Oldendorf's Task Group 77.2 Bombardment and Fire Support Group. The group was cruising in Lingayen Gulf when, at 1718, two Zeke 52s appeared near the island on a parallel course to the ships. Within minutes the aircraft, which seemingly had come out of nowhere, were on a collision course with the ships, flying only twenty-five feet off the water. *California* knocked one down with her 5"/38 battery but "the plane that crashed the CALIFORNIA was hit several times. At 1720 this plane turned toward the ship in a steeply banked climbing turn and came over the starboard beam striking the after side of the mainmast tower at the 05 level a little to port of the centerline. At the same time mount number 4 was penetrated by a 5" shell which exploded inside the mount."[4] Although no bomb was observed on the Zeke, the magnitude of the explosion made it likely that it carried one. The blast, accompanied coincidentally by the ship's own 5" shell explosion, caused extensive fires. When the toll was taken, it was found that forty-eight men had died and another 155 were injured. Expert fire control and damage control parties stabilized the situation, but a number of the ship's guns had been knocked out. Her action report for the incident indicates that her "Battle Efficiency is estimated to have been reduced to 75%."[5]

Walke DD 723 was attacked about the same time as *New Mexico*. At 1155 her lookouts spotted four enemy planes, judged to be Oscars, coming in at a low altitude approximately six miles distant. *Walke* took them under fire. The first Oscar was hit by the ship's guns and disintegrated and the second crossed over the ship and crashed in the water nearby. The third, strafing on the way in, crashed into the port side of the ship's bridge and the fourth was shot down off the port quarter. Within a short time the fires caused by the plane were under control and the destroyer resumed station. The kamikaze had killed twelve men and injured another thirty-four. Among the dead was her CO, Cmdr. George F. Davis. *Walke*'s action report noted that a variety of approaches were being used by the kamikazes, with the low level attack being the most successful. It also noted that kamikazes seemed to have ships' bridges as their primary targets.[6]

Early in the morning, at 0130, *Allen M. Sumner DD 692* replaced *Barton DD 722* which had been in charge of the minesweeper support unit working the area. Within an hour enemy aircraft were stalking the ships. Over the next couple of hours the skies were active as she and nearby ships fired on and drove off Japanese aircraft. At 1158 three Japanese planes identified as Zekes or Judys, made runs on her. The first two were successfully avoided, but the third approached on her port bow, strafing her on the way in. It hit the No. 2 stack and crashed into the after torpedo mount. The plane's bomb hit torpedo mount No. 2 and exploded on the starboard side of the main deck. The plane skidded off the deck and landed in the water on the starboard side of the ship. About the same time another plane hit her on the port side of the bridge. Damage to the ship was not serious but fourteen men died and nineteen were injured. The damaged *Sumner* was relieved by *Ingraham DD 694*.

Long DMS 12 was one of the old four-stack destroyers launched in 1919 that had been converted to a high speed minesweeper. She was engaged in sweeping activities in the gulf when two Zekes roared in. Her CO, Lt. Stanly Caplin, ordered her to twenty-five knots as they took the enemy planes under fire. One missed but the other crashed her port side amidships only a foot above the water line. With the ship effectively sectioned off by flame and the danger of the forward magazine exploding, Caplin gave permission for men in the forecastle to get off the ship. This was mistakenly interpreted as an abandon ship order and all vacated the vessel. *Hovey DMS 11,* another of the former four-stack destroyers, stood by to assist and picked up her crew and officers. Regrouping on the *Hovey,* Caplin and his men prepared a boarding party to fight the fires but were slowed by constant enemy air attacks. After a few hours of waiting for a break in the action, another plane hit *Long* in the same spot and broke her back. She rolled over and went under the following morning. One of her men died and thirty-five were wounded.

Brooks APD 10 was put out of action that day as well when a kamikaze crashed her portside starting fires and disabling her. Three of her men were killed and eleven wounded. She was towed back to San Pedro for repair by the merchant ship *SS Watch Hill* and decommissioned at the beginning of August.

Columbia CL 56 was operating as part of the Lingayen Fire Support and Bombardment Unit. At 1424, an enemy plane made a dive on her, narrowly missing the cruiser and crashing close aboard. The ship was jolted as its bomb went off underwater. The only damage was to an antenna which had been clipped off as the plane passed over. At 1730 a Val dodged through her hail of anti-aircraft fire and struck her on "the main deck on the port side of number four turret; the engine penetrated the main deck, and the bomb penetrated to the first platform deck where it struck the barbette turret 4 and exploded. A very serious fire resulted in the main and second decks. Casualties and damage were very heavy."[7] Her No. 4 turret was put out of commission and the magazines of turrets Nos. 3 and 4 were flooded. With the fires out and damage temporarily repaired, *Columbia* took station with her group. Thirteen men had died and forty-four were wounded.

Minneapolis CA 36 was operating as part of TG 77.2.1 San Fabian Fire Support Unit and, along with *New Mexico BB 40, Mississippi BB 41, West Virginia BB 48,* H.M.A.S. *Australia,* H.M.A.S. *Shropshire* and several destroyers, was en route to the eastern side of the entrance to Lingayen Gulf to bombard San Fernando and Poro Point. Air attacks developed around the ships starting at 1121 and lasted until 1829. Observers on *Minneapolis* watched as a kamikaze crashed on *New Mexico* at 1159.

At 1157, lookouts on *New Mexico* spotted four enemy aircraft closing on her from astern and the ship took them under fire. One went down off a nearby destroyer, but one managed to get through her fire and crashed the port outboard corner of the bridge. Its bomb, estimated at 500 lbs., went off and caused heavy casualties on the bridge and nearby areas. Her commanding officer, Capt. R. W. Fleming, sustained mortal injuries in the attack and *New Mexico's* XO, Cmdr. J. T. Warren took command. The battleship had thirty dead and eighty-seven wounded but continued on her mission.[8]

At 1437 *Minneapolis* was attacked by a plane that crossed her bow and then passed down her port side. It crashed close aboard her starboard side, taking with it her starboard paravane and causing superficial damage to the ship. Two men were wounded in the attack.[9]

Louisville, which had suffered two kamikaze hits the previous day, came under attack again on 6 January. At 1731 a Japanese plane crashed her starboard side near the bridge structure, causing heavy damage to the bridge and surrounding area. The severe fires were extinguished quickly before they could cook off the ammo in the Mount No. 41 clipping room. As they fought the fires caused by this plane, they discovered that another plane, which they had shot down close aboard, had set fire to the starboard side of the ship. This fire was quickly put out. In addition to putting the cruiser out of action, the attack killed thirty-six and wounded fifty-six. Among the dead was RAdm. Theodore E. Chandler.[10]

Richard P. Leary DD 664 was part of the anti-submarine screen for Task Group 77.2. A kamikaze came in on her port bow, apparently heading for the larger ships nearby. *Leary* took it under fire and the plane banked and made a run on her. It was hit with 20mm and 40mm gunfire and one hundred yards from the ship, it went slightly off course, its wing clipping the ship and splashing close aboard. It was believed that the pilot had been killed and that his death saved the ship from serious damage. Only one man was injured.[11] *Newcomb DD 586* was also screening nearby when she came under attack at around 1700. Heavy air attacks in her area kept her gunners busy, and they took two Tonys under fire as the planes tried to crash their ship. One hit the water twenty-five yards off her port quarter, showering the ship with shrapnel which killed two men and wounded fifteen.

O'Brien DD 725 took a kamikaze hit at 1427 as she was providing cover for a minesweeper group consisting of *Southard DMS 10, Hopkins DMS 13,* and *Chandler DMS 9*. Two planes dove on her as she was passing the destroyer *Barton*. One crashed close to *Barton* but missed. The second hit *O'Brien's* fantail and tore off a large chunk. The luck of the Irish was on her side and she suffered no casualties, although she had to retire from the area for repairs. *Southard,* one of the minesweepers being screened by the ships, took a kamikaze hit on her port side at 1732, which started fires. Within a half hour the fires were out and *Breese DM 18* towed her to safety. She was back in action the next day in spite of the loss of six of her men who were wounded in the attack.

Palmer DMS 5 was engaged in mine sweeping along with *Hopkins* in Lingayen Gulf on 7 January. At 1834 the ships went to general quarters with bogeys reported heading in their direction. *Palmer* was attacked by a twin-engine Frances. At 1837 the plane made its run at masthead height. The assumption on the part of the ship's Commanding Officer, Lt. W. E. McGuirk, was that this was a suicide run and he acted accordingly. He ordered emergency full speed and full left rudder in order to get under the path of the incoming plane. His strategy worked, the flaming plane narrowly missed his ship and crashed 150 yards to starboard of the ship. However, in spite of his plane being in flames and on its way down, the Japanese pilot had the presence of mind to release his two bombs about a hundred feet from the ship.[12] They were right on target and hit the ship on the port waterline, blowing a huge hole in its side. The ship quickly flooded and within six minutes went down by the stern.[13] *Hopkins* and *Breese DM 18* picked up the survivors. *Palmer's* casualties were twenty-six dead and thirty-eight wounded.

The ships had a brief respite from air attacks the following day, 8 January, but *Callaway APA 35* took a hit on her starboard bridge which killed twenty-nine of her men and wounded twenty-two. Her damage temporarily repaired, she discharged her troops and headed back to Ulithi for repairs.

On the by-passed Palau Islands, ships were still in grave danger. The ability of the Japanese to launch attacks with aircraft or ships was long gone in this area, however, simpler methods of attack prevailed. Japanese swimmers managed to successfully attack *LCI(G) 404* in the early morning of 8 January 1945 as she was anchored in Yoo Passage. Dean DeSirant and Ray Vayda were on watch at 0208 when they spotted a small light off the ship's stern. They shined their searchlight on the water and spotted about a dozen Japanese swimmers near the stern of the boat. They sounded general quarters and began firing at the Japanese swimmers. A few minutes later the water erupted with a large explosion. Robert F. Heath, a S1/c on board *LCI(G) 404*, would later write:

> I just got off my 2000–2400 watch when a big explosion knocked me out of my bunk. It was about 0200 when GQ sounded. We all raced to our gun stations. The Japs had floated a magnetic bomb out to our ship. They secured a line onto our anchor housing and lowered the bomb into the water and pulled the fuse. It blew open the rear bottom of the ship and buckled the entire deck and destroyed our two propellers. It messed up our engine room and the engines did not work. The hole was big enough to drive a Jeep through.[14]

By the time the shooting was over, the swimmers had all been killed and *LCI(L)404* was disabled. Fortunately there had been no casualties. She was towed to Peleliu for repairs, then on to Ulithi and finally back to the states. Her wartime career was over.

At 0545, *LST 912* was making smoke to cover the ships in her area. Noise from her fog generator drowned out the sound of an approaching Val, and her smoke made it impossible to spot the incoming plane. This may have been an accidental kamikaze crash as the ship's action report indicated that "although it may have been a suicide dive, it is believed that the Val was forced down by one of our night fighters reported in the air and thought he was going into a cloud and crashed this ship by accident. One of the DD's of the escort reported that the plane appeared to head for our fog generator."[15] Pilot error or not, the result was the same. The landing ship had damage to her boat deck and suffered four dead and four wounded. Also hit that day were the two escort carriers *Kadashan Bay CVE 76* and *Kitkun Bay CVE 71*. The attacks began early in the morning with a group of Zekes going after the escort carriers. One broke through the CAP and made a bombing run on *Marcus Island CVE 7*. Its bomb missed and it turned off heading for *Kadashan Bay*. It struck the carrier amidships, adjacent to the bridge area, tearing a hole in the carrier's side. The ship began to flood and was soon down by the bow. With her fires out and temporary repairs complete, the carrier managed to stay with the group but sent her planes to *Marcus Island* for recovery. On 12 January she headed back to Leyte for repairs and then on to San Francisco for an overhaul. Her duties as a warship were over and her next assignment would be to ferry new planes to the war zone for other carriers. The attack, although severe for the ship, had cost her only three wounded men.

Kitkun Bay and *Shamrock Bay CVE 84* were providing air cover for VAdm. T. S. Wilkinson's Task Force 79 as it headed for the Lingayen landings. Late in the afternoon the group was attacked by six Japanese aircraft. H.M.A.S. *Westralia* seemed to be a prime target and was narrowly missed by a bomb. However, an Oscar dove into *Kitkun Bay* at 1857, striking her portside amidships at the waterline. About the same time, she was hit by fire from the shore on her port side, resulting in a double hit. She managed to keep station, but within a short time she was listing thirteen degrees to port. Her casualties were sixteen dead and thirty-seven wounded. *Chowanoc ATF 100* towed her out of the area. With temporary repairs completed, she made it back to Leyte for more work and then on to San Pedro, California for a total overhaul.

The following day, *Hodges DE 231* had a close call at 0650 when a twin-engine kamikaze from Nichols Field clipped off her foremast and crashed off the side of the ship. No casualties resulted from the attack and *Hodges* continued on her mission. *Columbia CL 56*, found herself surrounded by landing craft as they made their way to shore for the invasion. Unable to maneuver in the congested area, she was a set up for a kamikaze attack. Her action report indicates that at 0745 on 9 January:

> a Japanese Tojo, with a 250 kgm [551] bomb, crashed the forward main battery director. The director and plane carried completely over the side clear of the ship. His bomb exploded on impact resulting in a very serious fire, heavy damage and many casualties in the forward superstructure. The forward fire control stations were demolished and the gunnery and air defense officers were wounded, but control was taken aft by assistants and the scheduled bombardment was commenced at 0818 in preparation for the landing which took place at 0930.[16]

Within the space of a few hours she was able to complete her mission. Her casualties, twenty-four dead and sixty-eight wounded, were taken off by *Harris APA 2*.

Mississippi BB 41 was operating nearby. Her mission was to fire on targets in the towns of Dagupan and Calasiao. With her bombardment activities finished for the day, *Mississippi* stood by for call fire. Shortly before, four Vals had set off from Tuguegarao Field on a kamikaze mission escorted by four fighters. With haze obscuring the nearby land, they were able to approach the gulf undetected. At 1303 *Mississippi*'s lookouts spotted one of the Vals above as it released its bomb, which missed the ship. A second Val came at her out of the sun and the ship's anti-aircraft batteries took it under fire. Apparently the ship's fire hit the Val's engine as it was reported that its motor was out. "This plane leveled off in a shallow glide as it passed over forecastle and struck the ship on port side below bridge level, proceeding in a straight line until it was brought up against AA gun No. 6 and fell clear of the ship over the port side. A bomb carried by the plane exploded shortly after hitting the water."[17] The battleship soon had other kamikazes to fire upon, one of which hit H.M.A.S. *Australia* operating nearby. *Mississippi*'s fires were quickly put out and medical assistance was provided for her casualties. She had twenty-six dead and sixty-three wounded.

On anti-submarine patrol off the western entrance to Lingayen Gulf was the destroyer escort *LeRay Wilson DE 414*. Early in the morning at 0710, on 10 January, a twin engine kamikaze bore in on her about twenty-five feet off the water from dead ahead and was not spotted until it was almost too late. Fire from the ship set its port wing and engine on fire, but did not deter the plane from its goal. It crashed into *Wilson*'s port side, its starboard wing doing much of the damage to the gun tubs in that area. Six of her men were killed and seven wounded by the attack. The next day her CO, Lt. Cmdr. M. V. Carson, headed her back to Manus Island for repairs.

The ships had a brief respite from airborne kamikazes. However, they were not safe. The Japanese focused their efforts at Lingayen Gulf on waterborne kamikazes, with the suicide boats hitting nine ships, sinking one.

The transport ship *War Hawk AP 168* steamed into Lingayen Gulf on 9 January 1945 to deliver her troops and cargo. Little did her commanding officer and crew know what lay ahead. Port Sual, on the southwest side of the gulf, was home to the 12th Fishing Boat Battalion under the command of Capt. Isao Takahashi. Originally composed of nearly one hundred *Maru-re* suicide boats, attrition had diminished the attacking force to about seventy. During the night of 9–10 January 1945, the entire battalion sortied to attack American ships in the gulf. The boats were from three companies led by 2nd Lts. Hayashi, Uemura, and Tahara.

At about 0320, the destroyer *Philip DD 498* picked up the incoming boats on her radar and sounded the alarm. From that point on, and for the next hour and a quarter, alert gun crews on *Philip*, *Robinson DD 562*, and *Leutze DD 481* began firing on targets of opportunity. The crowded anchorage and the large number of anchored ships made it difficult for the destroyers to move at their customary speed. Additionally, the close proximity of many of the *Maru-re*, made it impossible for the ships' guns to depress sufficiently to take them under fire. One exploded only twenty-five yards off *Philip*, having been hit by 20mm gunfire. Many of the boats made it through the anchored ships and struck home.

LST 925, anchored in the area, was among the first to be attacked by *Maru-re*. At 0335 her lookouts spotted a boat approaching from the port side while another approached from starboard. Realizing that she had been detected, the boat on the port side, turned away, but the boat to starboard made its attack, dropping its depth charges and turning away. They did not get far as the ship's gunners hit the boat and killed its occupants. They reported that the *Maru-re* carried a crew of six, which was unusual for the boats. About the time that the gunners fired on the *Maru-re*, its depth charges went off. The ship suffered extensive damage and the crew went rapidly to work to effect repairs. To add to her problems, she was attacked by a Val at 0705 but shot it down. Three days later she was able to land her troops and cargo and head for repairs.

At 0410 *War Hawk* took a suicide boat hit which opened a twenty-five foot hole in her side and killed sixty-one of her men.[18] Quick work by her repair crews saved the ship for further service. *Robinson DD 562* reported being attacked by a small boat at 0414 which came along her port side. It dropped its depth charges and sped away. There was no damage to the ship and only some minor injuries to the crew.

LST 610 was at anchor in Lingayen Gulf on 10 January 1945. At 0436 she was attacked by an undetected *Maru-re*. The blast knocked out one of her engines, which led to later problems when she attempted to beach and discharge cargo. As she fought to repair the damage, her lookouts spotted another *Maru-re* heading for *LST 735*. They took it under fire and sank it. None of her crew was seriously wounded, suffering only superficial cuts and bruises.

LST 1028 was about 450 yards east of *LST 925* when she was hit. She weighed anchor and got underway with the objective of coming alongside the *925* to assist her. By 0358 she was in the process of tying up to her port side and checking her condition when she was relieved by a tug. *LST 1028* backed off and anchored 250 feet away. At 0441 her lookouts spotted a small craft off the starboard quarter at a distance of 800 yards. The ship's gunners were put on alert and within minutes the sound of a small boat engine could be heard; the *Maru-re* was making a run on the landing ship. At 300 yards the LST opened fire but her guns could not depress sufficiently to hit the boat. Rifle fire failed to stop it either. Her action report indicated that

> the Torpedo Boat seemed to hit side of Ship on Port side at frame 31, lurched out about 10 yards then headed back jugging skin of Ship on Port side going towards Bow. When the enemy Torpedo Boat was about even with forward Port Booby Hatch, a terrific explosion rocked the Ship fairly lifting it out of the water on Port side as objects and tons of water blew straight up in the air past the Conn. Almost everyone in the Ship was knocked violently down, some being hurt seriously being thrown against bulkheads, gun tubs and other objects. In the Conn we were knocked down, signal light blown off to deck below, binnacle compass sheered off its stand, etc. When over effects of blast we saw the torpedo Boat on Starboard side racing down towards stern about 50 feet away.[19]

Within a few minutes the *Maru-re* had distanced itself far enough from the LST as to be vulnerable to her gunfire. It was hit in a cross-fire by the ship's forward and aft guns and blew up. Power was out throughout the ship, and a tug towed her in to the beach where she underwent repairs. Fourteen of her men had been injured in the attack.

LCI(G) 365 was anchored about three miles off shore in Lingayen Gulf on 10 January. At 0430 her Officer of the Deck reported a huge explosion about 800 yards off her starboard beam. *LCI(M) 974* had been hit and sunk by a *Maru-re*, although they did not realize it at the time. Gunfire from the destroyers *Robinson, Leutze,* and *Philip* was observed, but the men on board the gunboat could only guess at the cause. Radio transmissions picked up by the *365* indicated that there were survivors of her sister gunboat in the water, and all eyes turned to the water's surface in search of them. At 0443 lookouts spotted a small craft about 150–200 yards off the port beam. It was challenged as it slowly approached the *365* but did not respond. The 20mm gun crews were ordered to open fire and hit the boat a number of times before their gun jammed. It was too late. The *Maru-re* made its final run and dropped its depth charges alongside the gunboat at about 0445. Lt. (jg) John M. Hoctor, the CO of *LCI(G) 365* was injured when the blast tore the binnacle loose on the conn. Below decks three men were injured but none seriously. Men were ordered to stand by to abandon ship as the *LCI(G) 442* came alongside to render assistance. By 0720 the ship was listing to port and pumps were unable to keep up with the flooding. *LCI(L)s 442* and *676* began to tow her toward the beach to prevent her loss in case she sank. The fleet tug *Hidatsa ATF 102* arrived to assist at 1530. After all hands had been transferred off the ship and she was stabilized, a skeleton crew remained aboard for the long tow back to Pearl Harbor. She was out of the war.[20]

Eaton DD 510 became aware of the presence of *Maru-re* about 0320, as they began their attacks on *LST 925*. At 0439 her lookouts sited an unidentified object to port and she changed course to investigate. Her challenges went unheeded and "at 0500, after maneuver had put small craft on port bow, illuminated with signal searchlight and discovered a small boat with two men in enemy uniform bent over a large object, similar to a depth charge, high in the stern. Opened fire with automatic weapons at 0519, when boat was abeam to port, and saw it destroyed by an explosion after first few bursts had hit."[21] The blast sent numerous pieces of shrapnel flying toward the ship, killing one man and wounding fourteen. In addition to *Maru-re*, *Eaton* also had to contend with suicide swimmers. At 0830 her lookouts spotted two swimmers in life jackets to port. They appeared to be swimming along with a bundle, possibly containing hand grenades or other explosives. As *Eaton* maneuvered to close in on the swimmers, one pulled out a pistol, shot his companion and then himself rather than be captured.[22]

LST 610 suffered serious damage when she was struck by *Maru-re* at 0436. Elsewhere in the area, *LST 548* was hit on her port side by a *Maru-re* at 0524, but had little damage. More Japanese suicide swimmers were in the area, and between 0946 and 1310, *Belknap APD 34* reported a number of them in the water with explosives tied to their backs. None were able to get near the ships and many were machine gunned and killed in the water.[23]

Wading ashore later that evening was Probational Officer Toshio Taniguchi of the 12th Fishing Boat Battalion. At 0300 that morning he had set out with his battalion to attack the ships anchored in Lingayen Gulf. As his boat approached the ships it was fired upon and tracers from the American guns severed the ropes that held his depth charges in place. His *Maru-re* had only gone a short distance before the jettisoned depth charges went off, overturning his boat. Taniguchi clung to a floating box and eventually made it to shore that evening north of Port Sual. The following day, tired and hungry, he made the mistake of asking a Filipino native for food. After feeding him and watching him fall asleep, the Filipino called in the local guerrilla forces, which took him into custody and turned him over to the American navy. Taniguchi was a platoon leader in the 12th Liaison Boat Battalion. Contrary to popular belief, many of the explosive boat pilots had finished their high school education or technical educations and were in college. Taniguchi had finished one year at Kyoto University when he was drafted into the army.

He was inducted in December 1943 and spent the following year in various training assignments until he was sent to the Liaison Boat School at Kondura on Etajima. He was there from 10 September 1944 to 1 October 1944. Upon graduation as a probational officer, he was sent to Luzon in the Philippines and then on to Port Sual as part of the 12th Liaison Boat Battalion. There he headed a platoon with eight NCOs and nine boats. His battalion "consisted of three companies each of three platoons, and had 100 liaison boats."[24] Prior to the attack on 9–10 January, his battalion had lost about thirty of its boats to air raids and coastal shelling. The group that sortied that night was the entire remaining force. Apparently this was the end of the battalion, as the evening's combat destroyed most of their boats.

DuPage APA 41 had landed her troops on the shore near San Fabian on 9 January. The following day she was scheduled to depart the area for Leyte carrying casualties from ships and army units. As she maneuvered to join the departing convoy she was the target of a kamikaze. The plane was identified as a twin-engine Nick that crashed into her navigation bridge at 1915. Flaming debris was scattered down the deck as the transport lumbered forward. Quick action by her fire control parties put the fires out and *DuPage* continued on her way.

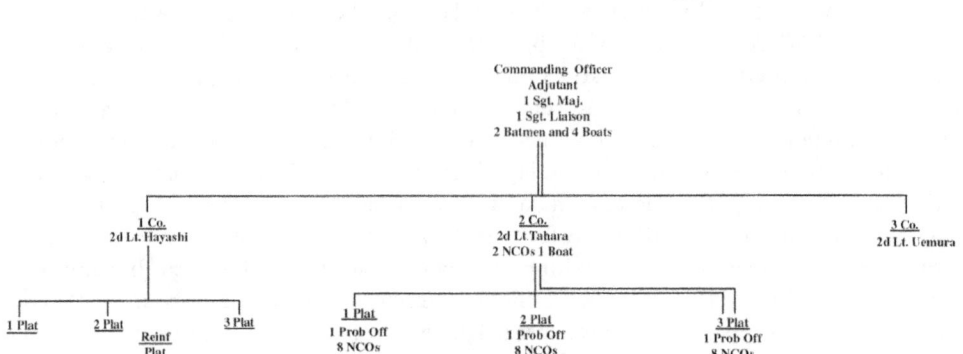

This chart shows the organization of the Army Liaison Boat Battalion Number 12, which was stationed at Port Sual on Lingayen Gulf, Philippines. Adapted from Allied Translator and Interpreter Section South West Pacific. Serial No. 938 *Interrogation Report No. 775*, p. 12.

Although her structural damage was not heavy, her personnel losses were. She had taken 189 casualties, thirty-two of whom were dead.

Although the war front had moved on, ships away from the front lines were still in danger. This threat came from Japanese submarines and *Kaiten* which were still able to operate in rear areas. A near miss was scored by a *Kaiten* from the *I-47* which sortied with the Kongo Group heading for Hollandia, New Guinea in late December, 1944. *Kaiten* pilots Lts. (jg) Teruo Kawakubo and Atsuro Hara, Flight PO 1st Class Katsumi Sato and Chief PO Minoru Muramatsu were on board to attack enemy shipping with their manned torpedoes. Lt. Cmdr. Zenji Orita guided his submarine into the harbor at Hollandia among the anchored American ships. Four of the *Kaiten* were launched but only one caused some minor damage. On board the *Pontus H. Ross,* a liberty ship carrying trucks, ammunition, gas and food supplies, men went about their business. It was early in the morning of 11 January, around 0615, when they heard a scraping noise on their port side. The *Kaiten* had struck the ship a glancing blow and finally exploded off the port bow. Although the hull plating was dented, no serious damage to the ship occurred. Although they were shaken by the nearby explosion, the crew was uninjured.[25] Another *Kaiten* exploded nearby, but of the four launched, only one had come close and it failed to sink a ship. The Japanese claimed that they had sunk four transports, but the report was inaccurate as usual.

January 12–13 saw the resumption of air attacks in force, with another thirteen ships suffering at the hands of the kamikazes. Particularly hard hit were the liberty ships and transports. Early in the morning at about 0658, the destroyer escorts *Gilligan DE 508* and *Richard W. Suesens DE 342* came under attack as they performed their anti-submarine screening duties at the western entrance to Lingayen Gulf. *Gilligan*'s lookouts spotted a twin-engine Betty only about a thousand yards away. Quickly turning to port to bring her starboard batteries under fire, the ship fell victim to a crewman's error as he deserted his post and knocked over the operator of the nearby 5" battery director. As a result, fire from that gun was limited to only fourteen rounds. More might have made the difference, but the Betty bore straight in, hitting the 40mm gun tub and director, killing twelve men and wounding thirteen more. It was a costly error, with the aircraft's gasoline igniting in a giant fire ball which eventually was put out. *Gilligan* returned to Leyte for repairs on 17 January and went back to Pearl Harbor for complete repairs a few weeks later. *Richard W. Suesens* came under attack a few minutes later at 0729. Accurate fire from the destroyer escort probably killed the pilot, threw the plane off course, and caused it to narrowly miss the ship. It crashed close aboard but still managed to wound eleven of her men.[26] Also suffering an air attack was *Belknap APD 34*. At 0750 four Tonys appeared near the transports and one made it through the hail of anti-aircraft fire to crash into *Belknap*'s No. 2 stack. Thirty-eight of her men were killed and forty-nine wounded.[27]

The first of the cargo carriers to be hit was the *Elmira Victory*. At 0800, a kamikaze appeared through the smoke screen in the transport area and caused some minor damage as it struck her No. 5 hatch. This was not the case with the second plane, which made it through the combined gunfire of the surrounding ships to crash into *Elmira Victory*, holing her just above the waterline. Fires started by the crashes were quickly extinguished, a fortunate thing as the ship was carrying 7,542 tons of ammo and an additional seventy-five torpedoes on deck. Had she gone up, her entire crew would have died and ships near her would have suffered heavy casualties. Her injuries were light, with only six wounded. Next on the list was the liberty ship *Otis Skinner*, another ticking bomb with its load of 7,000 tons of explosives and gasoline. At 1253 she was struck on her starboard side, starting fires and holing the hull. Fires raged throughout the area and below decks, but miraculously they were put out before her cargo could explode. Only two of her crew were injured, another miracle. Early in the evening, more of the liberty ships had to endure kamikaze attacks. Lookouts on *Edward N. Westcott* spotted an incoming kamikaze at around 1800. Her armed guard took it under fire with the bow gun and 20mm guns and hit it, blowing it apart a scant thirty yards from the ship. Although it had missed, the debris from the plane caused damage in the after deck area, but injured only eleven men. *Kyle V. Johnson* took a hit at 1830 when a kamikaze struck her starboard side and passed into the interior of the ship. Among the cargo carried by the ship was gasoline, and the crew flooded the compartment to keep it from exploding. Although the fires were out within an hour, the explosion of the plane had taken its toll on the troops. Quartered below deck were 506 troops bound for the invasion beaches at Lingayen. One hundred twenty-eight of them died in the crash, along with one crew member. Nine crew members were wounded as well as two members of the Armed Guard. In spite of her damage the ship made it to port where she disembarked her troops and cargo.[28] *David Dudley Field* took a kamikaze hit about the same time. Her cargo was less hazardous than some of the other ships, consisting of general army supplies and pontoons. Her would-be attacker was driven off course by fire from the ship's Armed Guard, its wing tip hitting the ship. The bomb that it carried exploded in the water on the port side of the ship, but no serious damage was caused by the attack. Minor injuries were sustained by eight of her crew.[29]

LST 700 came under attack at 0810 on 12 January. She was part of a convoy of LSTs heading back to Leyte from Lingayen Gulf after having discharged their supplies. Seven Zekes headed in toward the convoy and one attempted to drop a bomb on *Gage APA 168*, but missed. It followed up with a suicide run but crashed harmlessly into the ocean. A second plane made a run at *LST 268* but was shot down by gunfire from the *268* and the *700*. Another Zeke made a run on *Gage*, but between her fire and that of four CAP fighters, it was driven off. A fourth Zeke came in on the *700*, was driven off and pursued by a CAP plane. Both the CAP fighter and the *700* scored hits on it, and it appeared as though the kamikaze was finished. However, at the last moment, its pilot gained control and headed for a nearby YMS. It crashed before it could hit the ship. By 1015 the attack was over and the ships resumed course. On board *LST 700*, several men had been injured by shell fragments, but the ship had only minor damage. However, the next morning would be different. At 0800 on 13 January, a lone Zeke crashed her amidships on her starboard side. Her action report stated:

The plane was in a dive coming fast towards the portside of this ship, apparently towards the bridge. As the plane closed, two 20mm and one 40mm on the port side opened fire. Several hits were observed on the plane.... Plane flew over port side and crashed into weather deck 10 ft. inboard of starboard side, between frame No. 27 and No. 28. Ship lost headway immediately. Auxiliary and main engine rooms were flooded. Signal was sent to LST 268 to take us under tow. LST 911 stood by. Two of the crew were observed in water and were picked up by an SC. OTC dispatched tow DMSs to screen us. Ship started to list to starboard and steadied when list approximated 15 degrees.[30]

Minor fires caused by the crash were quickly put out. *YMS 47* and *Monadnock CM 9* assisted the LST, which had been holed from her deck to her side, below the waterline. *LST 268* began to tow her back to Mangarin Bay, Mindoro Island and *Jicarilla AT 104* completed the tow. She had eight wounded and two dead.

On the morning of 13 January, a convoy under RAdm. R. L. Conolly made preparations to leave Lingayen Gulf. Included in the group was the *Mount Olympus AGC-8* with VAdm. T. S. Wilkinson aboard. At 0821 an enemy plane appeared to be making a dive on *Mount Olympus* but swerved off at the last moment and crashed into *Zeilin APA 3* which was steaming nearby. The ensuing crash and fires killed eight and wounded thirty-two, but the ship resumed station.

The kamikaze threat at Luzon had just about run its course, but they would have one more victim, the escort carrier *Salamaua CVE 96*. She had been operating off Lingayen Gulf from 6 through 13 January, providing air support for the infantry that had landed, as well as the ships in the gulf. Her action report describes the attack:

13 January dawned, a dull day with heavy cloud cover at 8,000 feet. Our Combat Air Patrols were orbiting at 20,000 feet and at 7,000 feet, and we were engaged in routine flight operations, when without warning, about 0858, an enemy suicide plane, carrying two 200 Kilo [440 lb.] bombs, one under each wing, plunged through the flight deck, and penetrated to the Tank Tops. One bomb exploded and fires were started on the Flight Deck, Hangar Deck, and spaces below. The second bomb failed to explode and went through the starboard side of the ship at the water line. The bomb which exploded holed the starboard side below the water line in some ten places. There was immediate loss of power, communications, and steering. The after engine room and the compartment next aft were flooded, putting the starboard engine out of commission. The Ship's Company went immediately to General Quarters, and in the following ten minutes shot down two enemy aircraft. SALAMAUA proceed independently on the port engine, but in company with T.U. 77.4.1 until ordered to retire that night about 1925.[31]

The speed with which the attack had developed had left little time for the ship's gunners to draw a bead on the incoming plane. The best that they could was prevent the next two from hitting her. With temporary repairs keeping the flooding at bay, she limped back to Leyte, the last kamikaze victim of the campaign for the Philippines.

With the attacks of 12 to 13 January the airborne kamikaze threat ended. The Japanese realized that the Philippines were lost and began evacuating their aircraft to Taiwan in an attempt to save the remaining ones. Some of the units spent all their aircraft in the effort and then disbanded their air organization to fight as ground troops. Cmdr. Tadashi Nakajima of the 201st Air Group, stationed at Mabalacat, described the last attack on the ships heading for Lingayen as taking place on 5 January 1945. Forced to disband at that point, the mechanics managed to patch together five more Zekes for a final mission, which took off on 6 January, only about a week prior to the ending of the attacks.[32]

Suicide Boats Resurface

Army *Maru-re* boats were stationed throughout the Philippines and attacks on American shipping continued. The 19th Liaison Boat Battalion was headquartered at Binubusan, just south of Manila Bay. This battalion had been seriously weakened when the transport carrying them to the Philippines was sunk in November 1944, taking with it most of the men and all of their boats. Only a few of the original men from 19th Liaison Boat Battalion survived. Once settled in Binubusan, the Second Company from the 15th Liaison Boat Battalion was transferred to the 19th, giving them only one company with a total of nineteen boats and twenty-eight pilots.

The 19th Liaison Boat Company left its river hideout about midnight on 31 January 1945 headed for American ships anchored near Nasugbu. Amphibious Group 8 had just arrived carrying 11th Airborne Division troops on LSTs. Among the ships patrolling the anchorage were the destroyers *Russell DD 414*, *Conyngham DD 371*, *Shaw DD 373*, and *Flusser DD 368*, destroyer escorts *Lough DE 586*, *Presley DE 371*, and *Richard W. Suesens DE 342*, along with *PCs 1129* and *623*.

Piloting one of the *Maru-re* was Cpl. Nobuo Hayashi. His rank made him a squad leader in the battalion, although the shortage of boats was such that the distinction meant little. Hayashi was twenty-one years old and had volunteered for the army in April 1944, giving him only about ten months from his entrance into the military to his capture. After leaving the base at Binubusan, Hayashi headed his boat out into the gulf and turned toward the ships anchored off Nasugbu, north of Talin Point. He was accompanied by a second member of his platoon. In the dark, he thought that he was aiming for a transport but soon found out it was an American warship. Hayashi went on the attack. He put his throttle in and headed for the ship at high speed, dropping his depth charges near the ship's hull. His *Maru-re* had not traveled far before the charges went off, destroying his boat and killing his companion. He found himself in the water while men on the warship fired rifles at him. He managed to swim clear and made it to shore. Once there he headed back along the beach to his base, where he found it deserted. Hayashi rounded up some supplies and headed for the battalion's river hideout but was captured by Filipino guerrillas the following day and turned over to the Americans.

The *Maru-re* of the 19th Liaison Boat Company had a busy night. *PC 1129* had been the first to spot the incoming suicide boats at about 2230 and notified the destroyer escort *Lough*, which ordered the PC to investigate. Within minutes she was surrounded by a swarm of *Maru-re*.

Earl O. Griffis, Sr., a native of Mercerville, NJ, had enlisted in the navy on 15 December 1942 at the age of eighteen. After going through basic training at Great Lakes, he found himself in Florida, attending seamanship school and preparing for the delivery of his new ship, the *PC 1129*. The ship had been built in Bay City, Michigan and sent down the Mississippi River to meet her new crew. Griffis became a plank owner and his journeys on the ship had taken him from Miami to the islands of the Pacific, where the sub-chaser would see action at Green Island, Bouganville, Peleliu, New Guinea, and finally the Philippines where she met her end.

Griffis, who served as a cook on board the ship, had just finished baking bread in the galley and went on deck to get some fresh air. He was standing near the port 40mm gun tub when he spotted the *Maru-re* approach. Moments later he felt an explosion and was blown back to the fantail. The *Maru-re* had dropped its charges amidships, holing the ship near the engine room and trapping Motor Machinist's Mate Mack McGuire below. Within seconds the ship began to list. A ship's electrician, who had both legs broken in the blast, made it up the ladder hand over hand and escaped death. The order was given to abandon ship, and men went over the side in life preservers and life rafts. They watched from the water as their ship rolled over, and went under. Griffis recalled swimming to a life raft and hanging on for the next four hours until they were picked up by *Lough*.[33] The destroyer escort picked up seven of her officers and fifty-six enlisted men who had survived. The PCs normally had a complement of sixty-four men, but only one had died in the attack.[34] The following day they were transferred to *Anderson DD 411* for their trip to safety. How many of the survivors were wounded was never determined, as they were quickly sent back for rest and rehabilitation.

Lough spotted a number of the boats about 1000 yards ahead and went to twenty knots to close the distance, firing on the boats with her 20mm and 40mm guns. In the process she sank at least six of the boats and was unharmed during the action. *Claxton* had a torpedo launched at her during the fray but it missed. It is probable that the *Maru-re* were supported by Japanese torpedo boats since the *Maru-re* did not have the ability to carry or launch torpedoes. The following morning a search of the shore line was made with the intent of finding and destroying the *Maru-re* base. It resulted in the destruction of another two boats.[35]

The problems caused by the *Maru-re* led to the assignment of a number of PT boats and LCI gunboats to seek out and destroy them. From that point on, the small American combatants would be on "skunk patrol," as the chore came to be known. Motor Torpedo Boat Squadrons 28 and 36 had begun operations in the area in mid–January and were primarily concerned with intercepting and destroying barges. However, the events at Nasugbu led to increased patrols, which resulted in the destruction of many other beached suicide boats by the PTs. Between 14 January and 11 February 1945, the PTs destroyed another twenty-four suicide boats, fifty-one barges, three luggers, a forty-foot motor launch, and a 6,000 ton freighter.[36]

Once the immediate threat from the *Maru-re* was over, destruction of any remaining boats in the area became of paramount importance. Detailed to ferret out the boats in the vicinity of Talin Bay were the *LCI(G)s 73, 442*, and *558*. The difficulty of finding the *Maru-re* hideouts was pointed out in the action report of *LCI(G) 558*:

> At 1210, 1 February, 1945, entered Talin Bay in company with *LCI(G) 442* and *LCI(R) 73*. Destroyer support unit cruised at the head of the bay. Our mission was to discover and destroy enemy small craft. We did not discover any suspicious craft but destroyed three baroque [sic] canoes that might have served for an enemy suicide attempt on our ships when anchored at night. There were numerous groups of bushes overhanging the water edge where enemy craft may have been concealed from us. It was impossible to penetrate the thick foliage with our binoculars even at 200 yards. We strafed one large growth of suspicious overhanging bushes but the effective results are dubious. Returned from the mission at 1350.[37]

As the American army drove southward from Lingayen toward Manila, additional American navy units began the task of developing their attack on Corregidor and nearby islands as a prelude to landing troops to take the city. To slow the American advance, the Japanese once again resorted to the use of their suicide boats. One of the most successful of the Japanese navy *Shinyo* attacks came at Mariveles Harbor, near Corregidor, early in the morning on 16 February 1945. Six LCI(R) gunboats and six LCS(L)s had participated in the attack near Mariveles and on Corregidor during the daylight hours. Their task was to provide close inshore fire support in preparation for the landing of American troops. Included in the ships from Group 1, Flotilla 1, were six of the newly designed LCS(L)s, numbers *7, 8, 26, 27, 48, 49*. As dusk fell, the LCS(L)s were ordered to anchor across the mouth of Mariveles Harbor between Gorda Point and Cockines Point as a screen for the beached landing craft. Unbeknownst to them, a fleet of approximately forty-one navy *Shinyo* boats had left their caves in Corregidor, only four miles away, to attack them. Thirty-three of these were from the 12th *Shinyo-tai* Unit under the command of Lt. Yoshihisa Matsueda. The other eight were from the 9th *Shinyo-tai* unit under Lt. (jg) Kenjiro Nakajima. At about the same time, thirty-three more *Shinyo*, under the command of Lt. Cmdr. Shoichi Oyamada set out from Corregidor. Eight were to join in the attack at Mariveles and the remaining twenty-five were to proceed to Subic Bay. It is likely that the twenty-five boats did not make it to Subic Bay and fell victim to PT boats and other American warships. Later interrogations of survivors of the suicide boat units indicated that

LCI(G) 442 fires its port 40mm gun at suspected suicide boat locations on beach at Talin Point, near Nasugbu, Philippines on 31 January 1945. This area is just to the south of Manila Bay. Accompanying her on the mission were *LCI(G)s 72* and *558*. NARA 80G 273135.

"on the night of 15 February 1945, all boat operators got drunk first, and 10 of the boats returned giving various excuses for not attacking."[38] *LCS(L) 7,* under Lt. Franklin L. Elder, was hit and sunk by two boats at 0305. She went down within minutes. At about the same time the *27, 26,* and *49* were also crashed by *Shinyo.*

Claude Haddock, S 1/c, on board the *LCS(L) 49,* was on watch on the conn and Lt. Harry W. Smith, CO of the *49,* was asleep below. When Haddock saw *LCS(L) 7* hit, he immediately wakened the CO who sounded general quarters. About that time, the *49* suffered its first hit. Haddock went to the engine room to assist in fighting fires but was told that power had been knocked out. A second *Shinyo* hit on the port side, dooming the ship. The life raft had been blown overboard, its bottom knocked out by the blast. Haddock went over the side, swam to it, and with some other members of the crew, managed to paddle in to shore. He was not wounded but recalled that his ears rang for a couple of weeks.[39] The *49* and *26* exploded, rolled over and went under.

Dean Bell, S 2/c, on board *LCS(L)26,* was in the crew compartment when his ship was hit. The rear portion of the compartment was set afire and two men tried to go up the ladder to escape. Each burned to death before he could make it out. At that point, the water was up to Bell's chest. He was about to go up the forward ladder and someone told him to wait. In a few minutes he was told to go. He grabbed the handrail, which was extremely hot, and the flesh on his hands was burned away. He made it to the top and onto the deck. Immediately in front of him he saw his life jacket on the deck. Officers were trying to free the life raft. Bell

Three Imperial Navy *Shinyo* suicide boats are shown on tracks leading from their cave to the water on Corregidor. A series of caves may be seen in the cliff side. This made it difficult to eradicate the boats with air or naval attack, but left them vulnerable to disaster if one caught fire in the tunnel. This photograph was taken on 27 February 1945. NARA 111-SC-263697.

tried to put his life jacket on, but with his badly burned hands he could not tie it. He was told to jump. When he hit the water the jacket came off since it was not tied. A shipmate swam over, held him in a scissors with his legs and tied the life jacket on him. He told him to swim to a nearby life raft, but when they got there it was sinking under the weight of too many men. They were then told to swim to shore and, once there, found that many other survivors had made it to the same spot on a rocky shoreline. An LCT later picked them up and Bell was sent to a hospital ship. He would spend two years in the hospital before being discharged with a disability from the burns.[40]

Lt. Risley Lawrence, CO of *LCS(L) 27*, had managed to get his ship underway. His sharp-eyed gunners destroyed three of the boats before the fourth hit her a few feet off the port beam. Risley's quick thinking saved his ship, he ran it up on the beach to prevent its sinking. Along the way his gunners finished off a fifth *Shinyo*.

Harry G. Meister, who served as Engineering Officer on the *LCS(L) 27*, would later write:

> It was at the time the *LCS(L)(3) 49* took her hits that the Commanding Officer of this vessel realized that suicide boats were ramming these ships and orders were immediately passed to heave around on the stern anchor and prepare to get underway. Word was given to all gun stations to watch for small boats and their wakes and fire at anything. By this time all machine guns of this vessel were firing at targets and suspected targets. At approximately 0326 the *LCS(L)(3) 26* was hit on her port side and within 30 seconds on her starboard side. It turned keel up and sunk

This tunnel on Corregidor housed Imperial Navy *Shinyo* boats that were used to counter the American assault on the Manila Bay area. NARA 111-SC-263698.

within one minute of the first hit. Several boats were seen in the water approaching this vessel at this time. One persistently bore in on the port side and was engaged first by rifle fire and its occupant was hit, several men hearing him scream. His boat then turned away and was then sunk by 40mm machine gun. Boats were observed on both sides and one on the port side was caught in concentrated 40mm and 20mm machine gun fire and was seen to sink. At this time one on either side was observed to be bearing in amidship. The one on the port side was engaged by both forward and aft 40mm and 20mm machine guns on that side but even though hit many times, it bore in below the depression possible by all guns and was seen to explode approximately 3 feet from this vessel.... Ship had gotten underway and headed for nearest land at this time.... Boat on starboard side was hit by 20mm machine gun fire repeatedly but closed in. For some reason, probably because of the slow speed, this boat did not explode but lay along side, under the depression angle of the machine guns.... Boat was seen to come out from the starboard bow and as soon as it could be engaged by 20mm on that side, it was hit again and seen to sink.[41]

When the battle was over, *LCS(L)s 7, 26,* and *49* had been sunk and *LCS(L) 27* was severely damaged but salvageable. Sixty men had died in the suicide boat attacks, making it a very successful night for the 12th *Shinyo-tai* Unit.

The *Shinyo* attack at Mariveles was the last major attack of the suicide boats in the Philippines. Sporadic attacks continued at various places in the Philippines as the Allied forces continued to subdue Japanese resistance on many of the islands. As the struggle for the island of Davao was under way, the suicide boats struck again. In the evening of 10–11 May 1945, ships anchored in Taloma bay, Davao Gulf were attacked by the boats. Army *FS 225* was hit and

Mariveles Harbor was the scene of a deadly attack on the LCS(L) ships on 16 February 1945. Sunk in the attack were *LCS(L)s 7*, *26*, and *49*. In addition, *LCS(L) 27* was badly damaged. Commander Task Force SEVENTY-EIGHT (Commander SEVENTH Amphibious Force) Serial 04. *Action Reports—Special MARIVELES-CORREGIDOR Operation, 12–16 February 1945.* 12 April 1945, p. 31.

LCS(L) 27 shown shortly after her commissioning near Portland, Oregon. Official U.S. Navy Photograph.

sunk. This act was akin to swatting a hornet's nest and for the next several days *LCI (G)s 21, 22, PTs 106, 342, 343* and *335* joined with *Howard DE 346, Key DE 348, Flusser DD 368,* and *Leland E. Thomas DE 420* to attack various suspected bases in the area. They sank several enemy PT boats and destroyed PT and suicide boat bases.[42] This put an end to the special attack threat in Davao Gulf.

10. Taiwan, Iwo Jima, and Ulithi

The kamikazes had regrouped and reorganized after their exodus from the Philippines and were ready for action off Taiwan. Although the airfields on the Philippines were no longer active bases for action against the American fleet, those on Taiwan were. Shortly after arriving on Taiwan, the Japanese navy's First Air Fleet formed a new special attack unit based at Tainan on 18 January. It was to be known as the Niitaka Unit.[1] Adm. Halsey led the fast carriers of Task Force 38 in attacks against the Taiwan air bases in an attempt to suppress their ability to launch kamikaze attacks against American shipping in the Philippines

On 21 January 1945 Halsey's carriers, positioned one hundred miles to the east of the southern part of the island, made their strikes, hitting major air bases and accounting for 104 enemy aircraft on the ground, as well as shipping in several of their ports. Little air opposition was encountered, with two of three Japanese planes shot down as they attempted to intercept the navy fighters.[2]

The presence of enemy carriers off their coast had not gone unnoticed by the Japanese. Earlier in the morning on 21 January, the Niitaka Unit sent six Judy single-engine bombers and eleven Zekes on a kamikaze mission. They flew from the bases at Shinchiku, Tainan, and Taichu. All six of the Judys and four of the Zekes were designated as kamikazes, while the remaining Zekes flew escort.[3]

Ticonderoga CV 14 had been conducting normal flight operations with her CAG-80 aircraft when she was struck by a kamikaze at 1208. The plane crashed through her flight deck and its bomb went off just above the hangar deck. Aircraft stored on the hangar deck were set afire and a number of her men were killed by the blast. Although many of her crew were casualties, the pilots of CAG-80 managed to escape unharmed. Fire-fighting occupied the carrier's crew for the next fifty minutes. According to the ship's action report:

> A second kamikaze, believed armored because of its apparent ability to withstand many hits, struck the ship from the starboard side at the base of the forward 5-inch director on top of the island structure, starting severe fires in that vicinity. Its bomb apparently exploded just inboard of the island, firing planes and ripping holes in the flight deck, and killing and wounding upwards of one hundred personnel. The Captain was severely wounded and the Air Officer killed by this second bomb explosion. No trace of the Gunnery Officer has been found and he is considered missing in action. The Executive Officer was severely wounded by shrapnel apparently from another ship in the formation shortly before the second plane crashed.[4]

Within two hours the fires were brought under control and the crew set about tending to the dead. Wounded men had been under care since the beginning of the attacks and many had

10. Taiwan, Iwo Jima, and Ulithi

Ticonderoga CV 14 burns after being hit by two kamikazes off Taiwan on 21 January 1945. This photograph was taken from *Miami CL 80*. NARA 80G 273151.

been saved through the efforts of the ship's medical team. *Ticonderoga*'s CO Capt. Dixie Kiefer, in spite of his severe wounds, remained on the bridge until he was assured of the safety of the carrier and its men. Twelve hours would elapse before he would be taken to sick bay. The big carrier had suffered 143 men killed or missing and 202 wounded in action. Late in the afternoon she was escorted back to Ulithi for repairs.

The destroyers *Brush DD 745* and *Maddox DD 731* were acting as pickets for the carriers. At 1310, about an hour after *Ticonderoga* received her second hit, *Maddox* was crashed by a Zeke. The plane had managed to sneak toward the destroyer by accompanying a returning flight of Hellcats. Her action report indicated:

> Analysis indicated that enemy suicide plane returned from strike with friendly fighters, taking advantage of broken cloud cover to prevent detection and at all times sufficiently close to friendly planes that no unfriendly indications were apparent on radar.... At the instant the suicide plane commenced his dive, there was a 4 plane CAP overhead at about 1,000 feet and two returning strikes of about 11 F6F's at 1500 feet. The planes were all considered friendly. About 10 seconds before the crash, the suicide plane wiggled his wings and was at that time the middle plane of three; the two outboard planes being friendly F6F's in the process of orbiting at 1500 feet. This plane commenced a steep dive firing machine guns. He leveled off just aft of radio antennae marked No. I, [in the following drawing] his left wing clipped this antennae, driving him down through No. 41 40mm, marked II which his undercarriage struck and upsetting the plane to superstructure deck position III at frame 68, where the explosion took place. His bomb, estimated at 132 kg. [291 lbs.] was delayed a split second only.... Had the plane landed 10 feet further aft, the ship would have broken in two.[5]

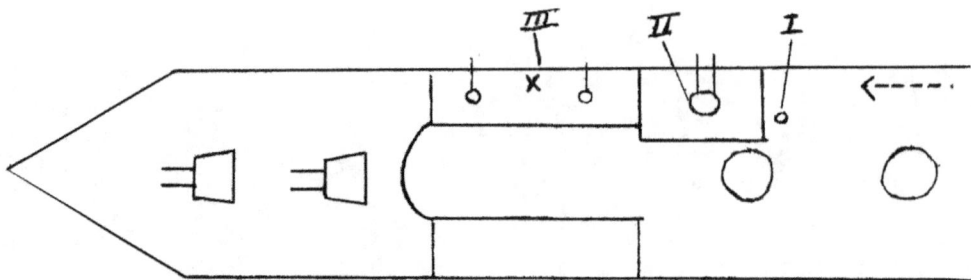

This sketch from the action report of *Maddox DD 731* shows the areas referred to in the report above. USS *Maddox DD 731* Serial 0010. *Action Report 21 January 1945—Forwarding Of.* 26 January 1945, p. 4.

Maddox's casualties of seven killed and thirty-three wounded would have been much higher had the plane hit almost anywhere else on the ship. As it was, there were serious concerns about her hull strength. She formed up with the convoy heading back to Ulithi along with *Ticonderoga*.

Iwo Jima

As the attacks at Lingayen were underway, final preparations for the assault on Iwo Jima were taking place. By the end of 1944, American bombers were flying regular missions over Japan from their bases on Saipan. However, the lengthy trip was made difficult by the prospect of no safe place to land between Japan and Saipan if the planes ran out of fuel or were damaged. Iwo Jima would serve as a safe haven for planes which could not make it back to base. Additionally, fighter aircraft, which had shorter ranges than the bombers, could be stationed there to provide escort service on the bombing missions. As a result, Iwo Jima was added to the list of islands scheduled for invasion. The story of that endeavor takes much telling, however, this work is only concerned with the instances of kamikaze attacks during that epic struggle. Two carriers would be struck by kamikazes at Iwo Jima, owing in large part to the annihilation of Japanese air forces by American naval ship bombardment and air action. Both attacks took place from 20 to 21 February 1945.

The kamikaze aircraft attacking the American ships came from the Mitate Unit No. 2, 601st Air Group, Third Air Fleet. The unit was based to the west of Yokohama, Japan, in the Kanto Plains area at Katori Naval Air Base. VAdm. Kimpei Teraoka had authorized the formation of this special attack unit on 16 February 1945. Divided into six units, the Mitate force totaled twelve fighters, twelve carrier bombers, and eight torpedo bombers divided into five groups. They sortied from their base on 21 February, refueled at Hachijo Jima, and headed for Iwo Jima.[6]

Bismarck Sea CVE 95 was part of RAdm. C. T. Durgin's support group providing air support and cover for the invasion. Other carriers in the group were *Makin Island CVE 93, Lunga Point CVE 94, Saginaw Bay CVE 82, Rudyerd Bay CVE 81,* and *Anzio CVE 57. Bismarck Sea* had just recovered her planes when, at 1730, she was ordered to scramble them again to intercept incoming bogeys which later proved to be friendly. After once again recovering her own planes, she found it necessary to take on three additional planes from other carriers and had to send four of her fighters below to the hangar deck without degassing them. This would prove to be a serious problem in the coming minutes. At about this time incoming raids were reported and, at 1845, the enemy planes were spotted approaching the ships. In the poor visibility at dusk it was difficult to see them until a Betty was spotted making a low altitude run on *Lunga Point*. Gunners on *Bismark Sea* took it under fire and shot it down.

Lunga Point CVE 94 came under attack again at 1846. She was about twenty-one miles east of Iwo Jima. Eight of her fighters were in the area flying CAP and four of her torpedo bombers were on anti-submarine patrol. When reports of the incoming raid came in, she launched an additional four fighters to augment the CAP. Five Jills approached her from the northeast and *Bismarck Sea* and a destroyer took them under fire. One of the planes made a torpedo run on *Lunga Point* and its torpedo passed closely by her bow. The plane crashed into the sea 200 yards to port. A second plane followed the first and its torpedo passed by as well. It escaped destruction and flew off. Immediately following the first two planes, a Jill dropped its torpedo off the starboard beam of *Lunga Point* and was hit by her gunfire. This torpedo passed astern of the jeep carrier, which scored many hits on the plane. In flames and severely damaged, the plane made a kamikaze run on *Lunga Point*. It exploded right next to the ship and lost a wing. The remaining parts of the plane crashed on the deck and skidded overboard to splash on the port side of the carrier.[7] Damage to the ship was light, but eleven of her crew were wounded. A fourth plane, following closely behind the other three, took a direct hit from a 5" gun and disintegrated. *Lunga Point* had escaped with minimal damage.

Although gunners on *Bismarck Sea* had shot down a plane headed for *Lunga Point*, they missed another plane heading directly for the starboard side of their own carrier. Hits were

Crewmen from *Lunga Point CVE 94* examine wreckage from a Jill that crashed her on 21 February 1945. *U.S.S. Lunga Point (CVE 94) Serial 020. Action Report—Occupation of IWO JIMA, 10 February 1045 to 11 March 1945.* 11 March 1945, Enclosure I.

scored on the plane from the time it was 1,000 yards out, but it could not be shot down. Its low level attack made it impossible for the ship's guns to depress sufficiently, so the final part of its run was unimpeded. The ship's action report reveals:

> This plane struck the ship abeam of the after elevator. On entering the ship it knocked four torpedoes from the starboard rack and scattered them about the hangar deck. The elevator cables were parted and the elevator fell to the hangar deck. The after fire main was damaged. The conflagration station turned on the water curtains and sprinklers. There was no supply to the after curtain and sprinklers.... This fire appeared controllable until a second heavy explosion occurred about two minutes later just forward of the elevator which killed a large number of the fire fighters. Eye witnesses report that this explosion was caused by a second plane which came through the flight deck and exploded among the fighters parked at that spot. These planes were full of gasoline and the fire became intense and uncontrollable. This second explosion blew the entire rear of the hangar deck out and bulkheads on the gallery deck were blown in. The decks of the clipping rooms above were apparently ruptured and a quantity of 20 or 40 mm ammunition, or both, began exploding and made the area untenable.[8]

The entire aft end of the ship was on fire and the crew had little ability to extinguish the flames. It was obvious that she was doomed. Her CO, Capt. J. L. Pratt, gave the order to abandon ship at 1905. Men went into the dark water, but it was not a good night for picking up survivors. Rough seas hampered recovery and Japanese planes strafed the men in the water. As the CO prepared to leave the ship it was rocked by a huge explosion, which may have been torpedoes cooking off. The stern section of *Bismarck Sea* disappeared in the blast and the ship took a heavy list to starboard. She rolled over and sank at 2115. Her casualties included 119 dead and ninety-nine wounded.

Saratoga CV 3, operating as the flagship for Task Unit 52.2.4 under Capt. L. A. Moebus, came under attack about the same time as the other carriers. The first attack on her was at 1700, when she was jumped by six Zekes and Judys. According to her action report:

> Coordinated attack by 6 Japanese suicide planes commenced coming in from out of the clouds to the east. Opened fire. Planes (1 or 2) strafed ship while coming in fast. No. 1 plane hit and on fire, crashed into starboard side, frame 104, penetrated into hangar deck. Violent explosion. No. 2 plane, hit and on fire, hit water and bounced into starboard side, frame 147, at water-line. Violent explosion. 5 degree list to starboard. No. 3 plane shot down clear of the ship. No. 4 plane from astern updeck dropped bomb into anchor windlass through port catapult and crashed into water. 1703 ... No. 5 plane, hit and burning, headed for bridge, carried away antennae and signal halyard, crashed into port catapult and exploded violently. No. 6 plane hit and burning, crashed into airplane crane on starboard side, dropped bomb at frame 25, starboard flight deck, parts of the plane landing in number one gun gallery, rest of plane went over the port side.[9]

Men fought fires for the next hour and a half until the next attack developed. At 1846 three more kamikazes made runs on the ship. The first two were shot down, but the third dropped a bomb on the flight deck, crashed into the deck and skidded off into the sea. Expert firefighting saved the ship and by 2031 she was landing aircraft again. Her casualties were heavy, 143 dead and 202 wounded. At 2130 she headed back to Eniwetok for repairs.

Kamikazes made their last effort at Iwo Jima on 21 February. At 1718 five Hamps flew over the island. *LST 477* was the first ship struck as one made a crash dive into her starboard side forward. Its 551-lb. bomb caused significant damage below, but the ship was not mortally wounded. However, her casualties numbered nine dead and five wounded. Immediately thereafter she shot down another Hamp making a run on a sister LST on her port beam and drove away a third. Firefighting on board the ship was made difficult as approximately 3,000 rounds of 20mm ammunition was cooked off by the fires.[10] Another Hamp picked *LST 809* as a target and made its attack from out of the sun on the ship's port quarter. Fire from the LST killed

On 21 February 1945 *Saratoga CV 30* took a kamikaze hit on her forward flight deck while participating in the invasion of Iwo Jima. This photograph was taken seconds after the crash. NARA 80G 273674.

the pilot and his plane narrowly missed the conning tower, clipping some halyards and insulators on the mainmast stay.[11]

Ulithi

Ulithi Atoll was considered to be one of the most important bases for the United States fleet during World War II. Positioned near enough to the enemy to be used as an advanced base for staging attacks at the Philippines, Okinawa, and eventually Japan, it had a huge harbor and a number of islands that could be used for supply purposes. Ships damaged in the active war areas frequently headed to Ulithi for repairs, and many invasion forces utilized the base as their staging area. It was taken over by U.S. forces on 22 September 1944, and by early 1945 was taking in over 300 tons of supplies daily. An area on the island of Mog Mog was set aside for recreation and fortunate sailors could get a couple of warm beers, swim, and play ball if they wished. Bands frequented the island and it provided a brief respite from the tension of war. However, it was not untouchable. Only the severe losses of the Japanese air arms prevented them from giving it more attention. This did not apply to the submariners who piloted the *Kaitens*.

In the course of *Kaiten* missions between 8 November 1944 and 18 August 1945, the *I-37, 44, 48, 56, 165, 368,* and *370* were sunk by American attacks. Targets for these sorties

Ulithi Atoll possessed a lagoon which could contain a large number of ships. This photograph was taken on 15 March 1945 as the American forces prepared for the invasion of Okinawa. Official U.S. Navy Photograph by Ensign Steinheimer. NARA 80G 305606.

included Ulithi Atoll, the Admirality Islands, Hollandia, New Guinea, Apra Harbor, Guam, Iwo Jima and, as the invasion of Okinawa began, the waters around Okinawa. Only two of the missions were successful, the first claiming the fleet oiler *Mississinewa AO-59* at Ulithi Atoll on 20 November 1944 and the second the destroyer escort *Underhill DE 682* on 24 July 1945. Earlier, the liberty ship, *Pontus H. Ross* had been lightly damaged by a *Kaiten* at Hollandia, New Guinea on 11 January, but it was not much of a victory for the Japanese submariners.

Departing on their mission to Ulithi on 8 November 1944 were the *I-36*, *I-37* and *I-47*, which carried four *Kaiten* each. This was the *Kaiten* group known as *Kikusui* or "Floating Chrysanthemums." *I-37*, under Lt. Cmdr. Nobuo Kanemoto, carried *Kaiten* pilots Ens. Kazuhiko Kondo and Hideichi Utsunomiya, Lt. Yoshinori Kamibeppu, and Lt. (jg) Katsutomo Murakami. She was to attack American shipping in the Kossol Passage at the northern end of the Palau Islands group. Surfacing to check her bearings just before 0900 on 19 November 1944, *I-37* was spotted by the net-layer *Winterberry AN 56* which quickly radioed her position to the destroyer escorts *McCoy Reynolds DE 440* and *Conklin DE 439*. Both ships dropped depth charges which sank the sub with all hands. She had no chance to launch her *Kaiten*.

The sub *I-36*, commanded by Lt. Cmdr. *Iwao Teramoto*, carried *Kaiten* which were to be piloted by Ens. Taichi Imanishi and Yoshihiku Kondo and Lts. (jg) Kentaro Yoshimoto and Kazuhisa Toyozumi. Their target was the northern section of the Ulithi Atoll anchorage.

One *Kaiten*, piloted by Imanishi, was launched on 20 November, but was not successful. His *Kaiten* may have run into mechanical difficulties, surfaced, and been bombed by aircraft from Marine Air Group 45. In any event, he was unsuccessful in striking an American ship and was killed during the mission. The other three *Kaiten* malfunctioned and were not launched. The sub returned to its base at Otsujima.

On board the sub *I-47* were the *Kaiten* pilots Ens. Akira Sato and Kozo Watanabe, along with Lts. (jg) Sekio Nishina, and Hitoshi Fukuda. Theirs would be the only successful mission in the *Kikusui* group. The commanding officer, Lt. Cmdr. Zenji Orita, was the overall commander of the *Kikusui* group. At 0930 on 19 November, *I-47* went to periscope depth inside the Ulithi anchorage to observe potential targets. The atoll was full of ships of varying descriptions, from carriers and cruisers to smaller ships. The next day's attack was sure to be successful.

At 0415 on 20 November 1944, the *Kaiten* piloted by Lt. (jg) Sekio Nishina slipped away from the *I-47*. On board were the ashes of the co-inventor of the *Kaiten*, Lt. (jg) Hiroshi Kuroki, which his friend Nishina carried with him. Within the next fifteen minutes the other three manned torpedoes were underway as well.[12]

On the anchored fleet oiler, *Mississinewa AO 59*, men shook the sleep out of their eyes and answered reveille. It was 0530 on 20 November 1944. At about that time the *Kaiten*, supposedly piloted by Nishina, hit the *Mississinewea*.[13] Within minutes fires and secondary explosions rocked the ship and the call to abandon ship was given. Men jumped overboard, only

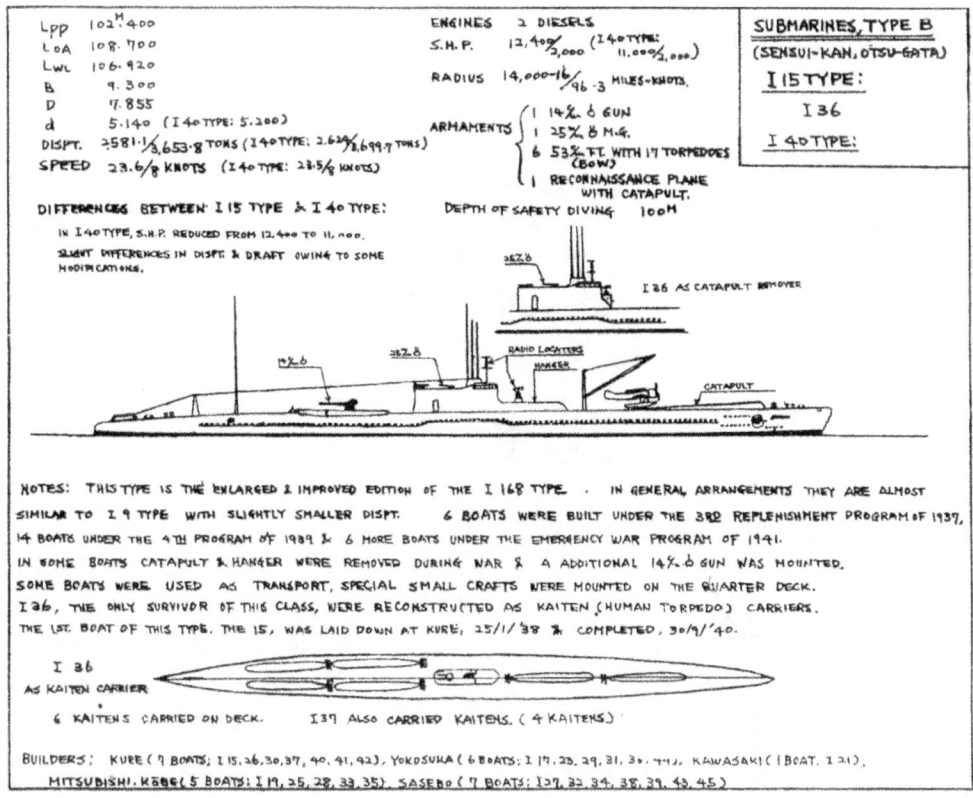

This sketch shows the plans for converting an I-15 type submarine to carry *Kaiten*. Shizuo Fukui, Compiler. *Japanese Naval Vessels at the end of War.* Administrative Division, Second Demobilization Bureau, Japan. April 25, 1947, p. 142.

to be engulfed by flames from burning oil, while others managed to fight their way to safety. At 0900 the ship rolled over and sank. Miraculously only sixty officers and crewmen of her complement of 298 had perished.

In the meantime, the destroyer *Case DD 370* had spotted and rammed another of the *Kaiten* in Mugai Channel as it attempted to attack the cruiser *Chester CA 27*. The ramming

The fleet oiler *Mississinewa AO 59* is obscured by smoke from massive explosions after being hit by a *Kaiten* manned torpedo at Ulithi Atol on 20 November 1944. This photograph was taken from *Patoka AO 49*. NARA 80G 272777.

broke the *Kaiten* in two and it sank. A third *Kaiten* nearly hit the light cruiser *Mobile CL 63*. It was sunk by depth charges shortly thereafter by the destroyer escorts *Rall DE 304*, *Weaver DE 741*, and *Halloran DE 305*. Still another of the *Kaiten* hit a reef and exploded. Thus ended the sortie of the *Kikusui* Group. Although one sub had been lost and four of the five *Kaiten* failed, the sinking of the *Mississinewa* had been successful. As usual, exaggerated reports went back to fleet headquarters, claiming that the manned torpedoes had sunk three carriers and two battleships.

The Japanese decided to give Ulithi some further attention on 11 March 1945, as they launched an air attack. Noting the extreme number of ships at Ulithi, VAdm. Matome Ugaki, commander in chief of the Combined Fleet, had been planning an attack for some time. Japanese reconnaissance planes checked Ulithi on 9 March and reported the presence of six carriers and nine escort carriers. Ugaki correctly surmised that Task Force 58 had returned and directed that the second Operation *Tan* be implemented. He gave the order for the Azusa Special Attack Unit to take off for Ulithi as soon as possible, but incomplete weather reports delayed the start of the operation until the next day. Taking off from Kanoya at 0900 were twenty-four twin-engine Frances[14] medium bombers. Many experienced mechanical problems during the long flight and reported back to base that they had been forced to make emergency landings. Ugaki waited patiently until about 1900 when reports were radioed back that the planes were diving on American carriers at Ulithi. These reports may have pleased Ugaki, but in fact only six of the planes had made it to the atoll. Subsequent reports to the CinC of the Combined

Randolph's flight deck is in disarray after the kamikaze attacks of 11–12 March 1945 at Ulithi. *USS Randolph CV 15* Serial 004. *Action Report for 11–12 March 1945, Attack by Enemy Plane at Ulithi*. 20 March 1945.

Fleet led him to recognize the failure of the operation. Reconnaissance aircraft checking Ulithi the next day reported that it looked as though it had not been hit at all.[15]

Randolph CV 15 had returned to the lagoon on 1 March after completing missions against Japan in the area of Tokyo and supporting the landings on Iwo Jima. While at Ulithi, her crew had time to train, get off the ship for some much needed R & R and replenish the ship's supplies. She sat comfortably at anchor, under condition II, which meant that her anti-aircraft guns were manned, including two 5"/38 twin mounts and five 40mm quad mounts. *Hancock CV 19*, anchored nearby, first picked up the incoming raid of four planes around 1945 and the ships went to general quarters. According to *Randolph*'s action report:

> At 2007 RANDOLPH was struck by a Japanese twin-engine Navy bomber, type Frances, which approached at low altitude and high speed from a bearing relative to the ship of 120 degrees to 140 degrees. The angle of glide was very slight if any. Impact occurred at the edge of the flight deck on the starboard side about 15 feet from the stern. The bomb load, which possibly may have been previously released, penetrated the hull and interior bulkheads several feet below the flight deck before exploding violently.... Parts of the plane were seen to fall in the water, others fell through the hole in the flight deck caused by the explosion, and still others were found in various places on the flight deck. Three bodies were found and identified as Japanese, one of which wore the insignia of a lieutenant in the Navy.[16]

In the area where the plane struck, men had just finished watching a movie on the hangar deck and had cleared the area. Another show was about to begin and men lounging on the fantail were beginning their walk to the movie area. Had the plane hit in the middle of a show, the casualties would have been much higher. Flames from the crash and explosion were intense, and ammunition began to cook off. In time the fires were brought under control and by 0050 they were out. Repairs and care for the wounded and dead became the dominant order. Twenty-five men died and 106 were wounded in the attack. Ulithi was not the safe haven many thought it to be.

11. Okinawa and the *Ten Go* Campaign

The inter-service rivalry between the Japanese army and navy had to be set aside if success was to be achieved against the American forces invading Okinawa. Both branches had plans that would include cooperation with the other, however, the army plan was eventually selected and put into action. The *Outline of the Operations Plan of the Imperial Army and Navy* was put forth in January of 1945, but only by great pressure was the army able to get it adopted. Col. Ichiji Sugita, who served as Operations Staff Officer at Imperial General Headquarters, noted that there was a great deal of resistance from the navy staff over its adoption.[1] Planning the specialized *Ten Go* Operation was no different. At that time, the Planning Section Chief of the Naval General Staff was Capt. Toshikazu Omae. It was his assertion that the navy had lost so many of its experienced pilots that the next generation, still in the training phase, would not be ready to participate in the operation at Okinawa until May of 1945.[2]

An additional problem for the two branches had to do with their traditional missions. Army aviators usually operated against ground forces and targets, which did not require as much training as did that of the naval aviators. Navy airmen usually attacked ships, which were moving targets. This required more training time, hence the inability to produce pilots ready for the Okinawa campaign. Additionally, the navy wanted more time to train special attack pilots. This problem of cooperation was not a question of willingness as much as a practical consideration.

Cmdr. Yoshimori Terai, one time head of Air Operations, Naval General Staff, indicated that training of the special attack pilots would not be completed until the end of May 1945. The best that the navy could do was the attack on American forces at Ulithi on 10–11 March 1945 which failed. This put the navy in the position of sending their flyers against the Americans at Okinawa before they were ready.[3]

Although they had prevailed in the planning for the Okinawa operations, the army was similarly unprepared along with the navy. They had hoped to slow the American advance by striking a significant blow against the Americans at Ulithi. With the acceleration of the American timetable, the army also found itself unprepared for Okinawa. Naval officers asserted that the 6th Air Army was even less prepared than the navy's air arm.[4]

The major air assault against the Americans at Okinawa was termed the *Ten Go* Operation. The operation featured a series of ten massed aircraft attacks against the ships in the Hagushi anchorage and the waters surrounding Okinawa. Flying a combination of bombers and fighters the *Kikusui,* or "Floating Chrysanthemum," raids were designed to overwhelm

American defenses. In between these large raids would be a number of smaller attacks that would seek out specific targets.

The goals of the *Ten Go* operation were detailed in *Navy Directive No. 5410* of 1 March 1945. It called for the cooperation of both the army and navy in defeating the approaching American forces in the East China Sea. Further, both branches were to cooperate in bolstering the defense of the home islands. At the center of the attacks on the Americans would be the varied special attack weapons that had proved effective in the Philippines. Army units were assigned the primary task of attacking troop and supply convoys, while the navy would go after the American carriers. This seemed a practical plan as the carriers would be harder targets to hit, and skilled navy torpedo and dive bombers would have a better chance of success against that type of ship. Of course, if army planes happened to have a clear shot at the carriers, they would seize the opportunity.[5]

It is obvious that the planning for *Ten Go* followed the traditional concept of the "decisive battle," that Japanese planners continually sought. If the American forces were placed in a position that could be overwhelmed by a superior, or better spirited Japanese force, then the war would end in a manner favorable to Japan. In this vein, *Navy Directive No. 513*, was issued by Adm. Koshiro Oikawa on 20 March 1945. Oikawa identified the first priority of the campaign to be the American carrier forces that ranged up and down the coast of Japan wreaking havoc on her cities and military installations. All types of attacks were to be used in this campaign, with heavy reliance on special attack methods. This would include the use of aircraft, suicide boats, manned torpedoes and midget submarines. Once the carrier forces were dealt with, the next priority would be assigned to the invasion forces which were poised ready to strike at Okinawa. The airfields at Yontan and Kadena were particularly important as they would serve as perfect bases from which the Americans could launch attacks on Japan's home islands.[6] Once the carrier forces had been eliminated, the American forces at Okinawa would become the first priority. Subsequent developments after the initial invasion of Okinawa on 1 April 1945 forced Japanese planners to alter their view of the situation. No longer was a decisive battle possible, and the emphasis shifted from the concept of the decisive battle to one in which the Americans would be bloodied in such a way as to discourage them from proceeding further. RAdm. Sadatoshi Tomioka, Chief of the Operations Bureau of the Naval General Staff, envisioned it as a war of attrition.[7]

To maximize the use of their assets during the *Ten Go* Operation, the 6th Air Army, commanded by Lt. Gen. Michio Sugawara, was placed under the jurisdiction of Adm. Soemu Toyoda, Commander in Chief of the Combined Fleet. This consolidation of the two air forces became effective 19 March 1945.

Cooperation between the two branches was furthered by *Navy Directive No. 516* of 8 April 1945, which put forth a plan for sharing airbases in both Korea and Japan. Army air bases at Iwaki, Togane, Oshima, Yabuki, Yokoshiba, Miyakonojo East, and Niijima, would be shared with the navy. The army would have access to navy air bases at Kanoya, Kochi, Oita, Saishu-To and the islands of Hachijo-Jima, and Tanegashima. The army's 7th and 98th Air Regiments, as well as some of the navy's units, would utilize the fields at Tachiarai, Hamamatsu, and Nittagahara. Navy forces based on Kyushu and under attack by American aircraft, could temporarily evacuate their planes to Gunzan and Keijo army air bases in Korea.[8]

The swiftness of the American thrust toward Okinawa was anticipated by the Japanese, but their state of readiness precluded a prompt response. This led American commanders to an uneasy sense of security, although they knew that the Japanese were capable of much stiffer resistance. Reality set in with the advent of the first of the *Kikusui* raids which began on 6 April Nine additional massed raids would last until 22 June, at which time the Americans declared the battle for Okinawa over. A variety of bases were used to generate these raids and

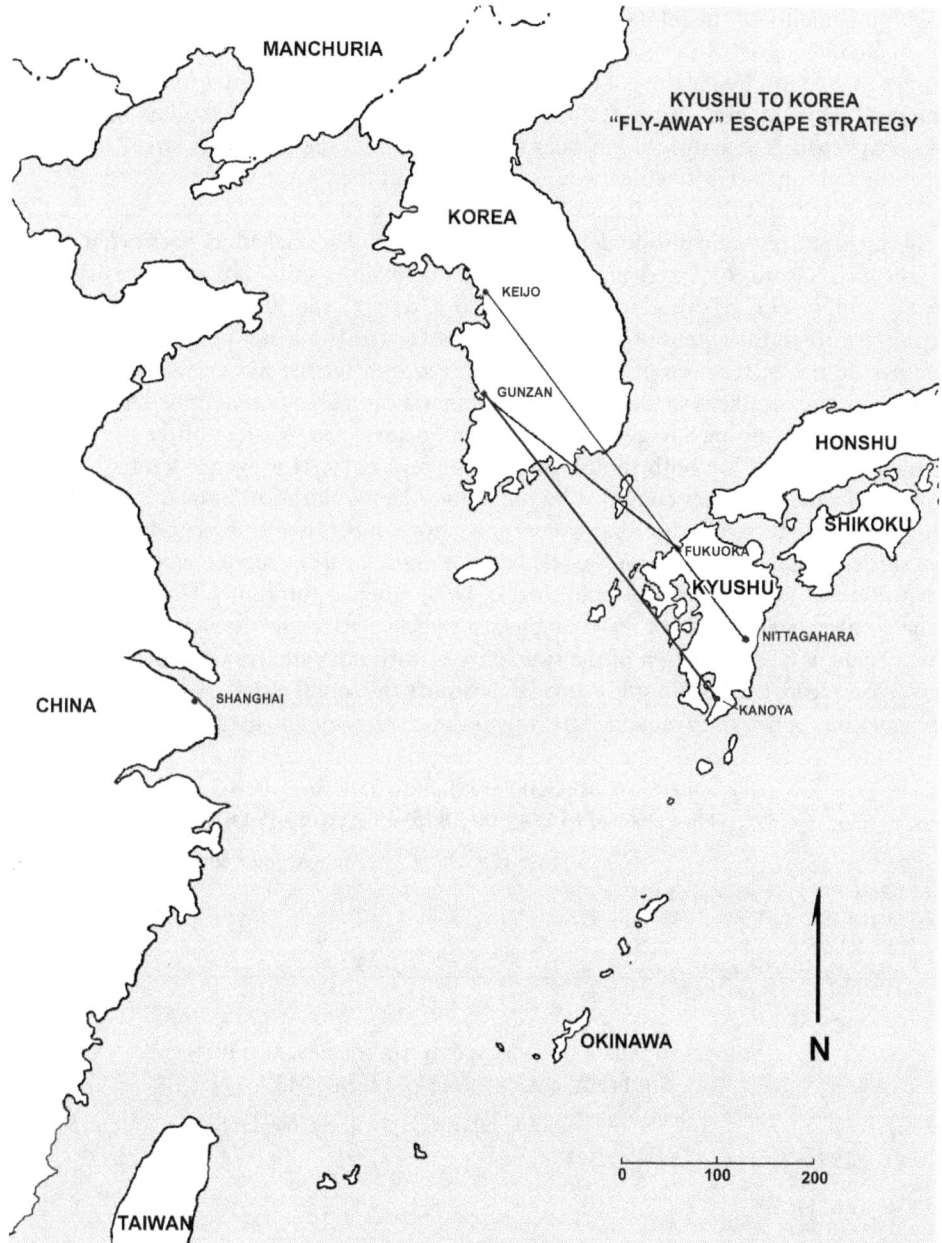

Japanese air bases in Korea were used as places of refuge when American aircraft attacked their home bases on Kyushu. Aircraft would use the "fly-away" tactic to avoid being destroyed. The route shown here is typical for aircraft stationed at Kanoya, Nittagahara, and Fukuoka. Adapted from *Magic FES 421*, 15 May 1945.

included those of the Third, Fifth and Tenth Air Fleets and the Sixth Air Army on Kyushu, as well as the Fifth Air Army at Keijo, Korea. From Taiwan, elements of the First Air Fleet and Eighth Air Division sent their planes aloft and headed them toward Okinawa. The kamikaze attacks in the Philippines, while greatly successful, would pale in comparison to the magnitude of those launched against the Americans at Okinawa. Part of this strategy had to do with the quality of the pilots engaged in the campaign. In the Philippines, top pilots flew well-maintained aircraft in small groups and managed to sneak through American defenses to strike their ships. By the time of the campaign for Okinawa, fewer of the experienced pilots remained and many of the aircraft flown by the relatively inexperienced pilots were obsolete or in poor repair. The only way for them to get through to the American forces would be to launch them in mass raids, which would ensure that at least some would succeed.

In researching this topic the author has attempted to compile a comprehensive list of actual suicide attacks and also to determine the number of special attack sorties launched by the Japanese. Records of American naval ships are accessible, and it is possible to make a reasonably complete list of ships attacked using action reports, war diaries, and ship logs. However, determining the extent of Japanese special attack sorties is not possible. This is due in large part to the destruction of many Japanese records after the war ended. An early list of statistics for the kamikaze sorties during the Okinawa campaign was compiled by The United States Strategic Bombing Survey and included in *Japanese Air Power*, published in 1946. This list included figures for both the Japanese army and navy. However, a later study in the *Japanese Monograph* series compiled by the Second Demobilization Bureau, working under the General Headquarters Far East Command, shows much higher figures for the Japanese navy sorties. *Japanese Monograph No. 141 Okinawa Area Naval Operations Supplement Statistics on Naval Air Strength* which was published in 1949, differs significantly. Unfortunately there are no similar, later studies of the Japanese army special attack sorties. As a result, the chart shown below is a combination of the two sources, with navy figures taken from *JM 141* and army figures from the USSBS study. In all probability the actual numbers for the army sorties are higher but, given the available data, this is the most complete list possible.

Sorties of Aircraft — 1st, 3rd, 5th, and 10th Air Fleets, 14 February 1945 – 19 August 1945

Date	Navy Special Attack	Navy Regular Sorties	Total Sorties
14 February 1945 to 5 March 1945	259	520	779
26 March 1945 to 4 May 1945	1,207	2,529	3,736
5 May 1945 to 22 June 1945	368	1,609	1,977
23 June 1945 to 19 August 1945	62	5,195	5,257
Total Naval Sorties for the period	1,896	9,853	11,749

Sorties of Aircraft — 5th, 6th Air Armies, and 10th Air Fleet, 6 April 1945 – 22 June 1945

Date	Army Special Attack	Army Regular Sorties	Total Sorties
6–7 April 1945	125	*	*
12–13 April 1945	60	*	*
15–16 April 1945	45	*	*
27–28 April 1945	50	*	*
3–4 May 1945	50	*	*
10–11 May 1945	80	*	*
24–25 May 1945	100	*	*
27–28 May 1945	50	*	*
3–7 June 1945	30	*	*
21–22 June 1945	15	*	*
Total Army Sorties for the period	605[9]	*	*

*Data not available

The chart for Navy sorties takes in a much greater period from the inception of American attacks around Okinawa until the end of the war. The Army statistics reflect only numbers for the ten massed *Kikusui* raids from April through June of 1945.

Japanese Naval Air Force

By the time the Okinawa campaign began at the end of March 1945, the Japanese had reorganized their aerial attack efforts against the American forces. Taiwan, to the south of Okinawa, was in an important strategic position. Its proximity to the island would make it possible to launch kamikaze raids against the invasion forces at Okinawa. Between Taiwan and Okinawa was a string of islands, the Sakishima Gunto, which included the islands of Ishigaki Shima and Miyako Jima. Aircraft flying from Taiwan to Okinawa would be able to refuel on these islands or wait there for an opportune moment to complete their missions. The First Air Fleet under VAdm. Takajiro Onishi was based on Taiwan. Bases for the First Air Fleet on Taiwan included Taichu, Kobi, Matsuyama, Takao, Shinchiku, Tainan, and Giran. Units of the Third, Fifth and Tenth Air Fleets flew from Japan proper. The Third Air Fleet was commanded by VAdm. Kimpei Teraoka, while the Tenth was under VAdm. Minoru Maeda. VAdm. Matome Ugaki commanded the Fifth Air Fleet. They were under the overall direction of the Commander of the Combined Fleet, Adm. Soemu Toyoda.

Toyoda had graduated first in his class at the Naval Academy in 1905 and became an admiral in 1931. He was one of the most capable of the Japanese naval officers and, by the mid–1930s, was the head of the Naval Affairs Bureau. In that capacity he encountered problems with the Japanese army's high command, and from that point forward he maintained an adversarial relationship with the army. His ascent to the position of Chief of the Naval General Staff came during the Okinawa campaign.

VAdm. Matome Ugaki's

This photograph of Adm. Soemu Toyoda was probably taken in September 1944. NARA 80JO 63365.

Fifth Air Fleet, based at Kanoya Naval Air Base on Kyushu, operated directly under the orders of Adm. Toyoda. In order to coordinate the attacks against the Americans at Okinawa, some consolidation of the air fleets and armies was necessary. On 1 April, Toyoda placed the Tenth Air Fleet under Ugaki's operational control, and on 16 April he added the Sixth Air Army as well. As the Okinawa campaign wore on, the Third Air Fleet also came under his jurisdiction,

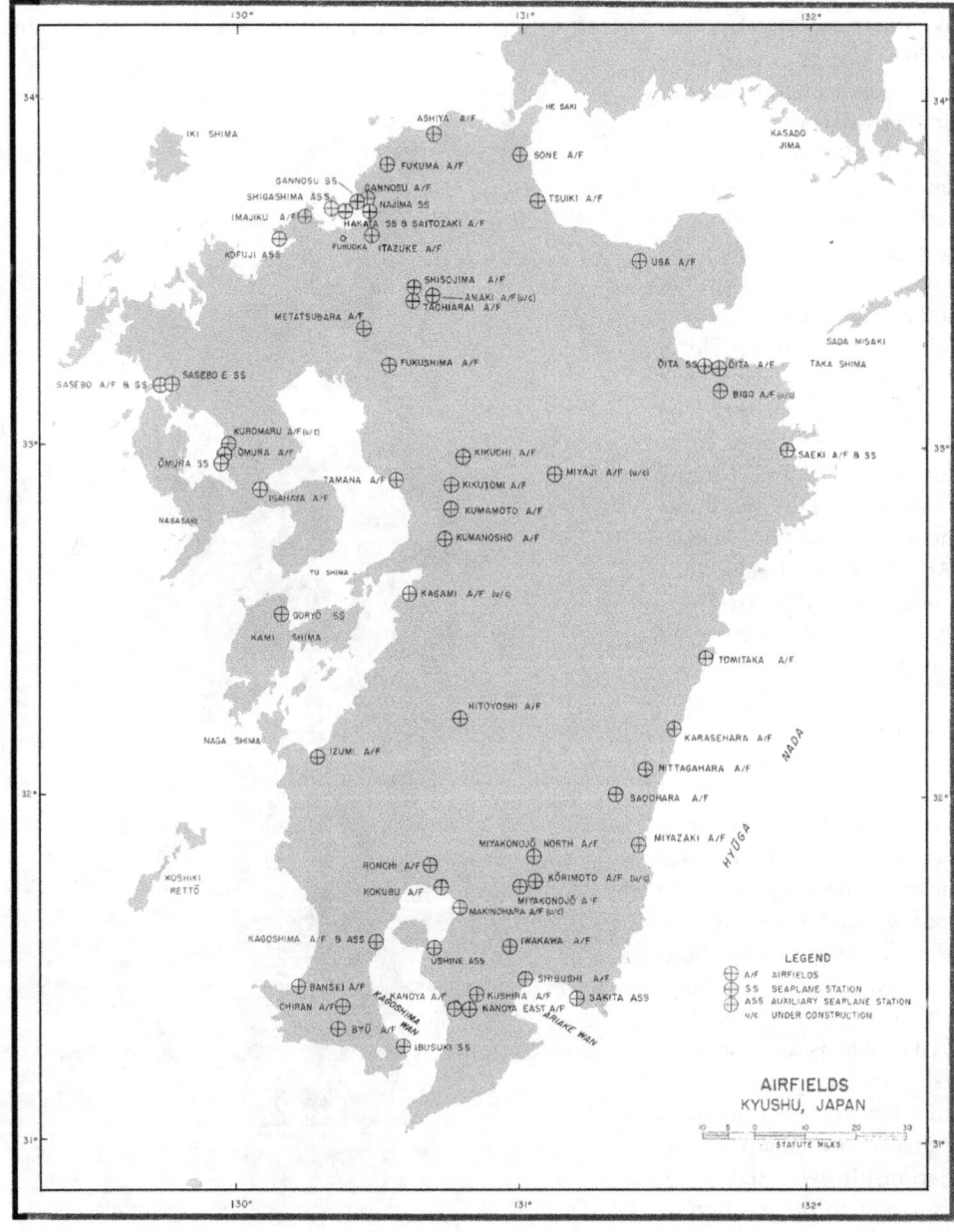

Airfields used by the Imperial Japanese Navy and the Imperial Japanese Army Air Force during the battle for Okinawa. Adapted from CinCPac-CinCPOA Bulletin No. 166–45. *Airfields in Kyushu.* 15 August 1945.

giving him a large force at his disposal. This combination of navy and army units was known as the First Mobile Base Air Force.

The First Mobile Base Air Force, comprised of the aforementioned units, operated from various airfields on Kyushu, which was the southernmost island of Japan. Ugaki's headquarters was at the main base of Kanoya, but others such as Kagoshima, Hakata, Omura, Hitoyoshi, Miyakonojo, Miyazaki, Kokubu, Kushira, Kasanohara, Ibusuki, Iwakawa, Tsuiki, Oita, Izumi, and Usa launched both orthodox and kamikaze raids against the Americans at Okinawa. At times the American forces had difficulty determining the sources of the raids, as the Japanese pilots flying off Kyushu's bases flew circular routes designed to confuse them as to their origin.

Kanoya was considered to be the most important of the Japanese air bases. Training and repair facilities at the base were extremely important to the war effort. So extensive was the technical side of the base that aircraft could readily be assembled after parts had been shipped there. Adjoining the base were satellite fields whose functions were integrated with that of Kanoya.[10] The Amami Archipelago stretches from the southernmost tip of Kyushu to Okinawa proper. Airfields on these islands, including Amami-O-Shima, Kikaiga Shima, and Tokuno Shima, were ready-made pit stops for the planes transiting from the Kyushu fields to the battle front at Okinawa. During the course of the campaign these fields became increasingly important targets for the American forces in their attempt to thwart the kamikaze attacks.

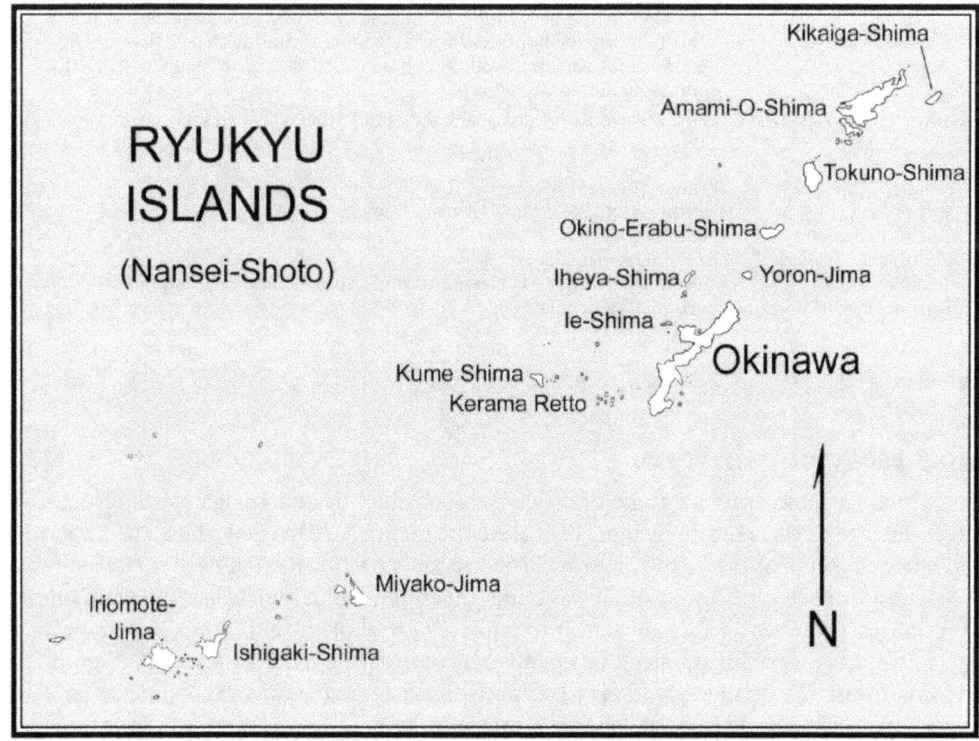

Bases to the north and southwest of Okinawa were forward staging areas for attacks on American forces at Okinawa. Planes flying from bases on Taiwan used Ishigaki Shima and Miyako Jima. Aircraft flying from Kyushu used Kikaiga Shima and Amami O Shima.

NAVY AIR FIELDS AND PRINCIPAL USES

Kyushu

Amakusa (Goryo)	Rear base for suicide seaplanes
Hakata	Important rear base for seaplanes such as Paul bombers, suicide Jakes, and Alfs normally stationed at Ibusuki
Ibusuki	Seaplanes such as Paul bombers, suicide Jakes, and Alfs
Izuki	Alternate field for fighters
Izumi	Twin-engine bombers of Tenth Air Fleet
Kagoshima	Alternate field for fighters
Kanoya	Headquarters Fifth Air Fleet, fighters, interceptors, Zeke fighter-bombers employed to attack US task forces, twin-engine bombers in tactical units including Betty/Oka
Kisaratsu	Headquarters Third Air Fleet
Kasanohara	Fighters
Kasumigaura	Headquarters Tenth Air Fleet
Kokubu No. 1	Fighters, Tenth Air Fleet suicide Zekes and Vals
Kokubu No. 2 (Ronchi)	Tenth Air Fleet suicide Zekes and Vals (satellite base)
Komatsu	Rear base for twin-engine bombers in tactical units including Betty/Oka
Kushira	Single engine torpedo bombers in tactical units and also Tenth Air Fleet training units
Miho	Rear base for twin-engine bombers in tactical units including Betty/Oka
Miyazaki	Twin-engine bombers in tactical units including Betty/Oka
Oita	Airfield and seaplane base
Omura	Interceptors, patrol planes, suicide planes
Saeki	Rear base for Kushira units, training and maintenance base for Fifth Air Fleet
Takuma	Important rear base for seaplanes such as Paul bombers, suicide Jakes, Alfs normally stationed at Ibusuki
Tomitaka	Zeke fighter-bombers employed to attack US Task force, earlier use as base for twin-engine bombers in tactical units including Betty/Okas
Usa	Rear base for Kushira units, rear base for twin-engine bombers in tactical units including Betty/Oka
	Rear base for Betty/Oka Units at Kanoya and Miyazaki

Taiwan

Karenko	Primary fighter base
Shinchiku	Headquarters First Air Fleet from mid–April 1945, fighters
Taichu (Toyohara)	Fighters
Matsuyama (Taihoku)	Reconnaissance planes
Takao (Shozokan)	Headquarters First Air Fleet until mid–April 1945, medium bombers
Tansui	Reconnaissance planes

Korea

Genzan	Zeke fighters and trainers[11]

Japanese Army Air Force

Three Japanese army air force units were responsible for attacks against the American forces during the Okinawa campaign. They were the Eighth Air Division, the Sixth Air Army, and a few elements of the Fifth Air Army. The headquarters for the Eighth Air Division was at Matsuyama (Taipei), Taiwan and it was under the command of Maj. Gen. Kenji Yamamoto. Additional army bases on Taiwan were at Karenko, Toen, Shoka, Heito, Choshu, Giran, Ryutan, Ensui, Mato, Hachikai, and Kagi. It was not unusual for aircraft from the Eighth Air Division to use the smaller island air bases on Ishigaki-Shima and Miyako-Jima as forward staging areas for their attacks on American forces at Okinawa.

The Sixth Air Army had moved its headquarters to Fukuoka on 18 March 1945. There Lt. Gen. Michio Sugawara, the head of the Sixth Air Army, planned his strategy. Other Sixth Air Army bases on Kyushu included Kikuchi, Tachiarai, Nittagahara, Chiran, Miyakanojo, Kumamoto and Kumanosho. Sugawara operated under his immediate superior, Gen.

Masakazu Kawabe, who served as commander of the Air General Army. The army shared use of the fields at Tokuno Shima, Ammami-O-Shima, and Kikaiga-Shima. There they were able to refuel aircraft that had flown south from bases on Kyushu and wait for the opportunity to launch their attack. These bases were vulnerable to attack by the American carrier task forces, and planes stationed there frequently used Korean airfields as a refuge, withdrawing to them when they sensed an imminent American attack such as that on 18 March 1945. Bolstering these Korean bases became imperative as America stepped up its air attacks. Some air units, previously stationed in China and Kyushu, were moved to airfields such as Gunzan and Keijo to prepare them should their presence be needed at Okinawa or in defense of the Kyushu bases.[12] As the invasion of the home islands loomed in the not too distant future, the preservation of the remainder of Japan's air forces became increasingly important. Withdrawal of Sixth Air Army aircraft to Korea would further that goal. Gunzan served as a base of refuge as well as the headquarters for Lt. Gen. Takuma Shimoyama's Fifth Air Army. Although their attacks on American forces at Okinawa were not that numerous, the 16th and 90th Fighter Regiments and the 8th Fighter Brigade managed to send their Lily bombers on an estimated thirty to forty sorties against the Americans.[13]

As noted previously, special attack aircraft units frequently flew from Kyushu to the island bases to the south. This enabled them to have a greater range, however, the increasing air superiority of the American forces made this more difficult as the Okinawa campaign progressed. Tokuno Shima was a favorite target of the Americans, and the Japanese suffered significant losses when they attempted to use the island base. Fitting extra fuel tanks on the aircraft made it possible to extend their range and fly directly from Kyushu, but the extra flight time wore on the pilots and their poorly maintained aircraft.

The organization of the special attacks differed between army and navy. Whereas the navy had special attack aircraft in each of their units, the army had complete units consisting of all kamikaze aircraft. These were "volunteer" units, however, in time volunteers became difficult to find. Men were transferred from training and tactical units into the special attack units, bypassing the volunteer procedure.

As the impending invasion of Okinawa loomed near, the Sixth Air Army had assembled nine special attack units on Kyushu to combat the Americans at Okinawa. This gave the army's air force sixty kamikazes to add to those of the navy. Six additional units remained in eastern Japan. Of the units sent to the Kyushu bases only three, the 20th, 21st, and 23rd *Shimbu* Units, were fully operational and combat ready. This number did not seem up to the task, and within a short time ten additional units were added, placing a strain on human as well as material resources. Pilots just out of flight school were assigned to the new special attack units with little hope of getting through American air cover to make successful sorties against the massive forces arrayed at Okinawa. Their obsolete aircraft, poorly maintained and equipped, further added to the great odds stacked against them. Nonetheless, they endeavored to make the best of a bad situation and carried out their orders faithfully.

Army special attack units consisted of twelve airplanes, but the rigors of the Okinawa campaign soon lessened the number to an average of six by June of 1945. Japanese planners envisioned up to two hundred units by the end of the battle for Okinawa, but the decline in Japan's prospects kept about two-thirds of these in reserve for homeland defense. The concept of the decisive battle no longer applied to Okinawa. If it was decisive, then victory had fallen to the Americans.

On 19 March 1945, the Commander of the Mainland Defense Army had placed the Sixth Air Army under the command of the Combined Fleet Commander, Adm. Toyoda to improve cooperation between the two rival branches. Toyoda's staff planned the attacks and then informed VAdm. Ugaki and Lt. Gen. Sugawara . The two would then consult on the specifics

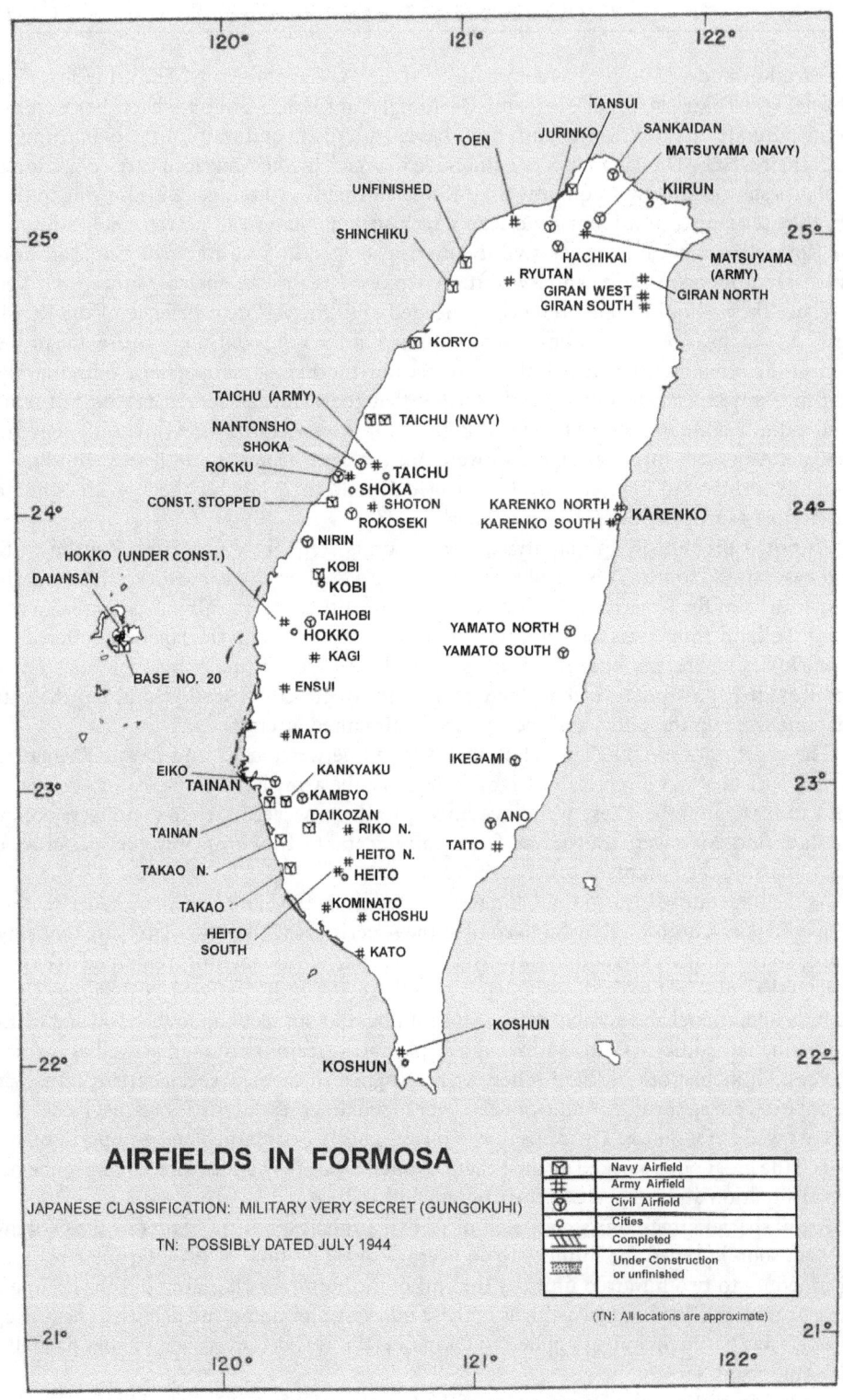

Airfields on Taiwan served as bases for the Japanese Army Air Force 8th Air Division and the Imperial Japanese Navy First Air Fleet. Adapted from CinCPac-CinCPOA Bulletin No. 102–45. *Translations Interrogations Number 26 Airfields in Formosa and Hainan.* 25 April 1945, p. 6.

of the attack. Although he operated under Ugaki's authority, Sugawara could determine the number of aircraft to be used, their tactics, and other details. A crucial aspect of the kamikaze attack was support by fighter escorts. The number of navy aircraft available for this task was greater than that of the army. A major problem in regard to this joint venture turned out to be communications. Neither branch was comfortable having to work with the other, particularly given their traditional rivalry for resources and their differing ideas of strategy.

A meeting of army air brigade commanders at Fukuoka on 25 March 1945 set the stage for the army's participation in the defense of Okinawa. Their planning for the upcoming struggle saw the assignment of various air groups to specific bases. Initial attacks would be instituted by the 1st Attacking Group (59th Air Regiment, 5 suicide plane units). This group was assigned to Kikai-ga-Shima and would be closest to the invasion forces. Moved there in secret, it was hoped that their attacks would come as a surprise to the Americans. Following that was the 2nd Attacking Group (101st Air Brigade, 102nd Air Brigade and 2 suicide units) which had transferred to Miyakanojo. Their attacks would follow closely on the heels of the 1st Attacking Group. Future sorties would be performed by the 3rd Attacking Group (103 Air Regiment, 65th Air Regiment, 66th Air Regiment, and 2 suicide units) based at Chiran and Bansei. All of these bases were in southern Kyushu and within ready striking distance of Okinawa. Two heavy bomber regiments were held in reserve at Tachiarai and Kumamoto in northern and central Kyushu respectively.[14]

Drawing on their distinct expertise, navy flyers would attack enemy warships, while the army would concentrate on transport shipping. The navy fliers, trained at hitting faster targets, would stand a better chance of hitting a destroyer or cruiser than would the army pilots. The slower transports were better targets for the less experienced army aviators.

As previously noted, neither branch was ready for action at the beginning of the invasion of Okinawa. This led to constant delays and the inability of the branches to carry out plans. Two regiments of the Sixth Air Brigade, Third Attacking Group would fly the first missions to Okinawa using Tokuno Shima as their staging area. To prepare for the attacks on 28 March, some of the brigade units advanced planes to the island's airfield. Eight of the planes came from the 103rd Air Regiment and the 66th Air Regiment supplied ten. The remainder came from the 65th Air Regiment. At 0600 on 29 March, they sortied to attack American ships in the Okinawa area.

Japanese reports were exaggerated as usual, claiming that they had hit three warships and a transport,[15] but this is not reflected in American reports for the day with only *LSM(R) 188* and *LCI(G) 560* noting damage. The Japanese continued to advance aircraft to the islands to the south of Kyushu in preparation for further attacks.

The next Japanese attack took place on 1 April 1945, as the American invasion of Okinawa commenced. On Tokuno Shima, twenty-five aircraft from the 65th, 66th, and 103rd Air Regiments, and an additional eight special attack planes from the 20th *Shinbu* Unit, were poised for the dawn attack. They took off at dawn and headed for Okinawa and their destiny.

JAPANESE ARMY AIR FIELDS AND PRINCIPAL USES

Kyushu

Chiran	Army reconnaissance and suicide planes
Fukuoka	Headquarters Sixth Air Army
Karesahara	Transports and Army airborne training base
Kumamoto	Alternate field for twin-engine bombers
Kumanosho	Alternate field for twin-engine bombers
Miyakanojo	Principal Army fighter base
Nittagahara	Alternate field for twin-engine bombers
Tachiarai	Major base for twin-engine bombers[16]

Taiwan

Ensui	Training base
Giran	Fighters
Kagi	Medium bombers
Taichu (Toyohara)	Fighters
Taihoku (Matsuyama)	Headquarters Eighth Air Division, twin-engine bombers and reconnaissance planes
Tansui	Reconnaissance planes[17]

Korea

Gunzan	Fighters, training center
Keijo	Headquarters Fifth Air Army, fighters

Types of Planes

The Imperial Japanese Army Air Force flew the fighters Tojo, Oscar, Nate, Frank, Tony, and Nick, reconnaissance planes Dinah and Sonia and the bombers Lily, Helen, Sally, Peggy, and Mary. These were good aircraft designs and many Japanese naval officers considered them superior to those of the navy. Kamikaze missions frequently used the Sally, Oscar, and Sonia, however, American reports indicated that Oscars and Tonys were the army planes most frequently encountered.[18] Nates were used on many of the missions but their age and general condition made them a poor choice. Frequent breakdowns, the difficulty of obtaining parts, and worn out engines made them problematic. Added to this was the shortage of maintenance and repair people, as many had been stranded on by-passed islands during the island-hopping strategy of the Allied forces. A number had been lost in the Philippines as well. Poorly trained replacements had difficulty keeping up with the work and many performed it badly due to their inexperience. Aircraft production facilities in Japan were under constant attack by American bombers and that, coupled with the shortage of skilled aircraft laborers, made them put out products of inferior quality. As the end of the war approached, both the production and quality declined.

The army units on Kyushu faced additional problems. They were plagued by continual attacks from American aircraft off the carriers, as well as the fields on Okinawa, Iwo Jima, and the Marianas. The bombing of rail lines slowed the delivery of aviation gas and limited their ability to launch missions. Gas had to be trucked in, and frequently the gas that did arrive was of poor quality, mixed with various other combustibles that limited the flying range and performance of the aircraft.

In like manner, the Imperial Japanese Navy Air Force also had problems. They used a variety of aircraft for the kamikaze missions: fighters, dive bombers, and trainers. The Zeke (Zero), Jack, Rufe, Irving, and George fighters were commonly seen at Okinawa. Bombers such as the Betty, Frances, Val, Judy, Kate, the reconnaissance plane Pete, and the *Shiragiku* and Willow trainers were commonly used to attack American forces. The Zeke was the most effective of the planes used on the suicide missions because of its great maneuverability and speed. However, the addition of a bomb to increase the effect of its attack made it less maneuverable and difficult to handle. The Val dive bomber, equipped with dive brakes, was also a very successful kamikaze plane. A late addition to the kamikaze force was the Willow trainer. These wood and fabric biplanes were slow but maneuverable. Radar had a difficult time picking them up and VT fuses used by the Americans would not detonate near them. Their only drawback was the size of the bomb load they could carry, since they were not designed as war planes. The destroyer *Pritchett*, under attack at Radar Picket Station 9A on 29 July, noted: "They were, however, highly maneuverable and used effective evasive tactics when under fire."[19]

Since none of the conventional aircraft were designed to be used as kamikazes, they had to be specially modified for the mission. Kasumigaura Naval Air Depot modified the Willows by adding bomb racks to enable them to carry 250 kg. [551 lbs.] bombs. Their engines were also modified to allow them to run on alcohol. Since it was difficult to start their engines on alcohol, they were primed with regular gas to get them started.

In surveying the suicide attacks at Okinawa, American reports asserted that the most numerous of the Japanese aircraft used in suicide missions was the Val, followed by the Zeke and then the Judy.[20] Many of them were in poor repair due to the shortage of parts. Still others had come from the production lines with defects. Quality control was deficient and many of the parts that went into the aircraft were faulty. For instance, the George had many problems with landing gear. According to Capt. Minoru Genda, "It was very poor. Much worse than the average Japanese plane. In dive bombing or strafing, if the plane reached a speed of 420 M.P.H., the gear was apt to fall apart in the air. About one-fourth of the pilots we lost in combat were lost for this reason. It got to be a better plane toward the end."[21] Another problem with the George was that its engine sometimes stopped dead in mid-flight, causing many crashes.

Prelude to the Invasion

Although the actual invasion of Okinawa, code named Operation Iceberg, began on 1 April 1945, the weeks leading up to the landings were fraught with danger as ships performed various duties in the Okinawa area in preparation for the assault. Task Force 58, under VAdm. Marc Mitscher was assigned to attack Japanese airfields on Kyushu as a prelude to the landings on Okinawa. If the Japanese aircraft could be destroyed on the ground, there would be less of a chance for them to attack American ships during the invasion. *Intrepid CV 11* was operating along with *Yorktown CV 10, Langley CVL 27*, and *Independence CVL 22* as a part of RAdm. A. W. Radford's Task Group 58.4. A dud bomb did no damage to *Enterprise*, but a Betty made a run on *Intrepid* and nearly succeeded. It was shot down close aboard and the explosion from the plane set fires on the carrier's hangar deck. Although the ship itself suffered little damage, two men died and forty-three were wounded.

On 19 March, the ships again came under attack as their planes were in the process of carrying out missions against Japanese shipping near the Inland Sea and the ports of Kure and Kobe. *Wasp CV 18*, commanded by Capt. O. A. Weller, took a bomb at 0710 which smashed through her flight deck into the hangar deck before exploding on the Number 3 deck, killing 101 men and wounding another 269. Her action report reveals that shortly thereafter at 0834

> a JILL was sighted high overhead as he started a 50° dive between clouds at this ship. Sky One controlling Mount No. 51 and Sky three controlling Mounts No. 43 and No. 53 in barrage commenced fire at about 4000 yards followed immediately by Sky Four controlling Mounts No. 52, 54 and 44 and all 40mm and 20mm on the ship that could bear. This plane came down dead center until hit in the engine by a 5" VT projectile at about 2500 yards. Successive repeated hits by all calibers set the plane aflame all over and put him out of control. This destructive fire combined with an emergency turn to the right by ship control caused this Kamikaze attacker to crash close aboard the port side and abreast of the deck edge elevator.[22]

This crash caused minor damage to the carrier, and no personnel casualties occurred.

The following day 20 March, the destroyer *Halsey Powell DD 686* came under attack. She had been part of the screen covering the Fast Carrier Task Force. Around 1400 she was alongside the carrier *Hancock CV 19* topping off her fuel tanks. Enemy raids had been in the area most of the morning but seemed to abate at that time. She had just cast off from the carrier when an air attack developed. A Zeke made a dive on *Hancock*, overshot the carrier and crashed

The hangar deck of *Intrepid CV 11* is on fire after a Betty crashed close aboard while operating off Shikoku as part of TF 58 on 18 March 1945. This photograph was taken from *Enterprise CV 6*. NARA 890G 274205.

into *Halsey Powell*. It was not clear if the engines of the destroyer were damaged and they were stopped momentarily for a check. Unfortunately for *Halsey Powell*, her steering had been knocked out by the Zeke, which had penetrated her deck after hitting near her No. 5 5" gun. With no control of her steering, the destroyer was nearly run down by *Hancock*, but a last minute burst of speed put her in the clear. *Stephen Potter DD 538* and later *The Sullivans DD 537* stayed with *Halsey Powell* for cover. Enemy planes continued to plague the ships, and several were driven away after being hit by fire from *Halsey Powell* and *The Sullivans*. It was determined that the ship could make way by steering with her engines and she began the slow trip back to safety. Twelve of her men had died and twenty-nine were injured in the attack.[23]

Biloxi CL 80 suffered minor damage on 26 March. She was operating northwest of Okinawa when, at 0618, a kamikaze crashed her port water line and holed her. Its bomb was a dud, sparing the cruiser serious damage, but two of her men were injured. Also suffering minor damage on 26 March was the light minelayer *Robert H. Smith DM23*, when a kamikaze crashed about twenty-five yards on her port beam after passing closely over the ship.

As the invasion of Okinawa drew near, numerous ships were involved in shelling the island prior to the landing of troops. *Callaghan DD 792* had a close call at 0605 on 27 March when a Val's landing gear clipped her mast as it attempted a crash. It crashed fifty feet to port of the ship. *O'Brien DD 725* was cruising near Kerama Retto at 0624 on 27 March when a large formation of aircraft appeared overhead. Most turned out to be American, however, at least two were not. The first, described as a fighter type, made a run on the ship and was hit

Crewmen examine the hole in the deck of *Halsey Powell DD 686* after she was struck by a kamikaze while screening off Kyushu on 20 March 1945. Official U.S. Navy Photograph.

by 20 mm and 40 mm fire when it was only 300 yards away. It flamed and went into the sea only seventy-five yards from the destroyer's starboard beam. A Val dove on the destroyer from nearly overhead. *O'Brien*'s action report indicates that

> another enemy plane was sighted well in a dive on the ship. Ship was maneuvered radically in an attempt to bring the forward battery to bear, and all available guns opened fire. Although hit many times by 20MM and 40MM shells, the plane continued to dive and crashed into the ship forward of amidships on the port side, passing through the superstructure deck to the starboard side.... The plane is believed to have carried a 500 pound bomb which exploded on the starboard side just aft of the bridge structure.... Fires were started throughout the damaged area. Changed speed to 10 knots and came around into the wind to aid in firefighting. All available repair parties and non-essential gun personnel were engaged in firefighting and rescue and care of wounded personnel.[24]

The explosion of the Val's bomb set off a magazine. *Gwin DM 23* and *Shannon DM 25*, cruising nearby, approached the destroyer to offer assistance, but it was determined that it would be best if they remained close by for anti-aircraft support. The firefighting by *O'Brien*'s crew proved effective, and within the space of twenty-five minutes her fires were brought under control. In the ensuing carnage, fifty men had been killed and seventy-six wounded. *Shannon* escorted her back to the transport area and *Gwin* continued to patrol for survivors. *O'Brien* was sent back to Mare Island for repairs. About the same time that *O'Brien* was under attack, *Gilmer APD 11* was crashed by a Val with minor damage and light casualties.

Operating off Okinawa was RAdm. Morton L. Deyo's Task Force 54 Gunfire and Covering Force. One of the larger ships, *Nevada BB 36,* suffered a kamikaze crash on 27 March. Seven kamikazes appeared overhead in the morning. At 0621 three Nates headed in toward the ships. One selected *Nevada,* which promptly took it under fire. Her action report indicated:

> The "NATE" was first sighted almost dead ahead at about 0621. The 5"/38 battery opened fire just prior to his making a 90° turn and starting a "suicide glide" headed directly for the foremast of the ship and ending on the NEVADA'S main deck aft. Fire was maintained when the plane turned while a new solution was obtained. One hit was observed and the plane left a trail of smoke. The 40MM and 20MM batteries commenced firing as the enemy plane came within their range. 5" bursts obscured the plane momentarily. The plane commenced burning fiercely and the 40's and 20's were observed to hit.[25]

The effect of the fire was that part of the plane's starboard wing was shot off and it crashed into the main deck aft. It really didn't matter if the plane was whole or in parts, the result was the same. Burning gasoline made a mess of things, the plane's bomb caused additional damage and, when it was over, *Nevada* had eleven dead and her main battery turret had been damaged.

At about the same time that *Nevada* was under attack, *Dorsey DMS 1* was also struck. She was underway to Kerama Retto for logistics when three Vals approached her starboard bow. She took them under fire and the formation split into two. One Val passed down her starboard side, circled aft and dove on her from astern. In spite of being hit numerous times, the Val made it through the ship's fire and crashed the port side of *Dorsey*'s main deck at 0620.

Flames and smoke billow from the hole in *Nevada BB 36*'s aft deck after she was crashed by a Nate off Okinawa on 27 March 1945. Official U.S. Navy Photograph.

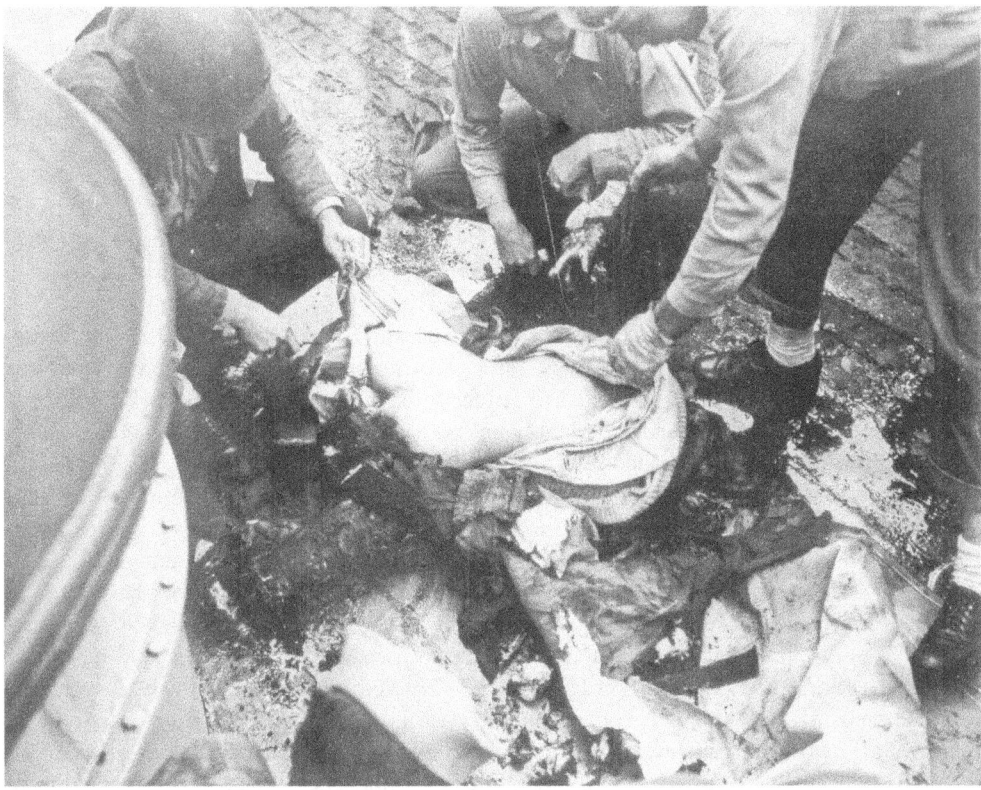

The torso of the Japanese pilot who crashed *Nevada BB 36* on 27 March is recovered in the wreckage of his airplane. NARA 80G 274504.

Several men were blown overboard but were subsequently picked up. Damage to the ship was minor, but *Dorsey* suffered three dead and two wounded. Within minutes a Betty dropped two bombs on *Dorsey* which missed. The plane was shot down by other ships in the vicinity.[26] Also suffering damage that day was *Foreman DE 633*. She had a Val crash close aboard at 0623 after grazing her starboard bow. One of her crew was injured.

Japanese suicide boats, which had proved troublesome in the Philippines, made their debut at Okinawa. During the evening of 27 to 28 March 1945, *LCI(G) 461* was on patrol near Tokashiki Shima when she spotted a *Maru-re* at 0515. She opened fire with her 20mm guns and hit the boat, effectively putting it out of action. Seconds later, there was a massive explosion. Apparently during the attack, the trigger for the depth charges carried by the boat had been set off and exploded. Shortly thereafter the gunboat fired on a raft, destroying it. Two Japanese were seen swimming to shore to escape.

From 28 to 29 March, several gunboats from Flotilla 6 were assigned to anti-small boat screening west of Okinawa. At 0037 on 29 March, they were on patrol just west of Okinawa when they came under attack. *LCI(G)s 452, 558, 559,* and *560* fired on and drove off a twin-engine plane. At 0300 lookouts on *LCI(G) 558* spotted a *Maru-re* headed in her direction on the starboard side. The ship took it under fire at a distance of 1,000 yards. Her 40mm gunfire threw it off course but it continued its attack. As it closed the gunboat at an estimated twenty knots, the ship's .50 caliber machine gun scored a number of hits on it. The OOD ordered flank speed and full left rudder, causing the suicide boat to strike a glancing blow amidships. Apparently the pilot of the boat was unable to loosen his depth charges at the appropriate time and they exploded fifty yards astern of the *LCI(G) 558*. The *Maru-re* disappeared when the depth charges went off. The gunboat fired on and turned away several other boats in the following hours, but none approached her. One pilot, apparently with a healthy respect for the ship's gunfire, dropped his charges at a distance and took off, opting to fight another day.[27] That same morning at 0330, as *LCI(G) 452* was patrolling off the Hagushi beaches, she was attacked by a *Maru-re*. It was driven off by the ship's intense 40mm and 20mm gunfire. At about the same time, *LCI(R) 646* was on patrol further west off Kerama Retto. At daybreak the gunboat spotted three suicide boats and challenged them. One turned toward the ship and was demolished by 40mm gunfire. Additional gunfire from a nearby destroyer, combined with fire from her sister gunboats, sank the other two.

Shortly thereafter, as *LSM(R) 189, Barton DD 722,* and *Henry A. Wiley DM 29* were cruising near the LCI(G)s, lookouts on *LSM(R) 189* saw a *Maru-re* drop its depth charges near the bow of *LCI(L) 560*. The *189* approached to render assistance, at which time the suicide boat turned toward her to make a run. A shell from her 5" gun blew it out of the water. A short time later another boat approached the LSM(R) and was sunk by 40mm fire. *LCI(G) 560* was not damaged but soon had a closer call. At 0615 three Nates attacked the gunboats. One went down off the bow of *LCI(G) 560*, a second passed over and flew away, and the third grazed her conn and took off her mast. It caused some minor damage and injured one man.

LSM(R) 188 was one of twelve newly-converted landing ships medium (*188–199*). The LSM(R)'s task was inshore fire support and she was ideally suited for the role. With her draft of only 7'9" fully loaded, she was capable of getting close inshore to bombard a landing area or shore target with rockets and gunfire. *LSM(R)s 188–199* were all assigned to the Okinawa campaign as their first war effort. Their armament consisted of a single 5"/38 dual purpose gun mounted aft, two 40mm anti-aircraft guns, three 20mm anti-aircraft guns, seventy-five 4-rail MK36 rocket launchers and thirty 6 rail MK30 rocket launchers. In the ships numbered from *196* to *199*, the rocket launchers were improved and those ships carried eighty-five automatic MK 51 rocket launchers. For its intended purpose it was a fearsome ship. However, many met their fate at Okinawa because they were used in roles other than shore attack. Their 206' length, coupled with their relatively slow speed of thirteen knots and poor anti-aircraft capabilities, made them easy targets for the kamikazes. The rationale for placing them on the radar picket stations was that since they were larger than the LCS(L)s they would be more capable of towing damaged destroyers. *LSM(R) 188* would be the first of the group damaged at Okinawa.

During the evening of 28–29 March, three days prior to the actual invasion of Okinawa, the *188* was patrolling about eight miles east of Naha when she came under attack. At about 0600 on 29 March, the ship's lookouts spotted enemy aircraft to starboard and took them under fire. One plane appeared to be hit by the ship's fire. A second plane, although hit, circled around and came at the rocket ship. It was on fire as it passed over the ship. Pieces of the aircraft fell off, hitting the ship and causing an explosion on deck before the plane crashed seventy-five yards to starboard. It had been a close miss but the damage was still extensive, she was out of the war. Fifteen men had died and thirty-two were injured.

Indianapolis CA 35, in the company of *Salt Lake City CA 25*, was cruising eleven miles west of Zampa Misaki at 0708 on 31 March when she came under attack. An Oscar emerged from cloud cover and made a run at her starboard side. Although it was hit by 20mm gunfire from the ship, it managed to pass over most of the cruiser before crashing into the port side of the main deck near the side of the ship. Its bomb penetrated the deck and then passed through the side of the ship to explode alongside. She was repaired the next day at Kerama Retto and was soon back in action. Her casualties were nine dead and twenty wounded.

The invasion had not yet taken place, but ships and men had already suffered at the hands of the *Tokko-tai* fliers.

12. The Invasion of Okinawa, Week One

Having secured a substantial foothold in the Philippines, the American leadership determined that the next goal for the combined navy and army forces would be the island of Okinawa, situated only 350 miles south of Japan's island of Kyushu. Defense of the island was sure to be intense and the attacking ships and troops could expect regular air attacks from the island of Taiwan to the south, as well as Kyushu to the north. To assault the island, the navy would commit 1,213 ships with still another 104 as support vessels. The number of army, navy, and Marine personnel assigned to the task was over 450,000. With the importance of the island uppermost in the minds of both adversaries, the battle was destined to be bloody. As usual, the focus here will be on the ships and their struggles against the kamikazes.

On 1 April 1945, the attack transport *Alpine APA 92* was operating as part of Task Group 51.13 carrying troops for the invasion of Okinawa. In addition to her cargo of 117 combat vehicles, she also carried fifty-nine tons of gas, 125 tons of explosives and eleven tons of demolition explosives. *Alpine* was a bomb waiting to go off. It is unclear if the embarked army troops knew this, but it did not add to their sense of well-being if they did. They numbered forty-eight officers and 828 enlisted men of various units, including infantry, field artillery, medical detachments, and others. Fortunately, *Alpine* had already landed them and was retiring off shore when she was hit by a kamikaze. Her action report of 10 April 1945 indicates:

> At approximately 1904 "FLASH RED — CONTROL YELLOW — All ships make smoke" was broadcast over voice circuits. About 1905 "stop smoke — do not make smoke unless ordered by me" received over voice circuit from CTF 51. All guns were alerted and immediately thereafter two (2) planes were reported approaching from just abaft the starboard beam, position angle twenty-five degrees. Planes were sighted and identified as enemy (low wing, single engine fighters — probably ZEKES or TOJOS). At the same time the planes were sighted they were taken under fire by many ships, much of the fire being indiscriminate and directed at other tracer streams rather than the targets.... Orders were issued at that time for all gunners who were on the target to commence firing. 20MM guns No. 1 and 3 opened fire, expending thirty (30) rounds before losing the target. Planes were seen to diverge, one going into a dive on our starboard beam and the second sheering off to the left and passing astern. Sight of the second plane was momentarily lost as attention was directed to the first and closer plane. Almost immediately attention was brought back to the second plane by firing of the after 20MM guns ... the plane which ultimately crashed into the ship was approaching in a steep dive from one point on the port quarter, altitude then about 1,000 ft. First impression was that the plane would overshoot the ship. The plane then went into a half roll to the left that brought the wings into a vertical position and the under side of the fuselage towards the starboard side of the signal bridge.[1]

The crash into *Alpine*'s starboard side at the main deck started fires and set off several explosions. Within a short time she was listing seven degrees to port. However, the firefighting efforts of her crew were effective and by 2300 the ship was secure. None of her cargo of gas, ammo, or explosives had been set off. Nonetheless, sixteen of her men had died and nineteen were wounded. After off-loading the remainder of her cargo, she headed back to the U.S. for repairs.

The light minelayer *Adams DM 27* was patrolling southeast of Kerama Retto when she was attacked by Japanese aircraft. A Japanese plane made a run on her, was hit by her gunfire, went out of control and crashed just aft of the ship. Its two bombs went off under the ship, jamming the rudder, and she was unable to maneuver. As she steamed in right hand circles, two other planes attacked her. *Mullany DD 528* shot one down and *Adams* the other. She was towed back to Kerama Retto for repairs.[2]

Simultaneously with the landings at the Hagushi area, the American forces faked a landing at the southeastern part of Okinawa. A number of landing ships and transports from Task Group 51.2 were engaged in the "demonstration landing." *LST 884*, carrying 300 Marines to the demonstration, was hit at 0549 when a kamikaze crashed her port quarter and set off her ammo stores. With fires raging, *Van Valkenburgh DD 656* and *LCS(L)s 115, 116, 118*, and *119* came alongside to render aid. Parties went aboard to assist in fighting the fires, and hoses from these ships provided water to extinguish the flames. Earl Blanton, who served as a gunner's mate on the *LCS(L) 118*, later wrote:

> Then we had a boarding party to board the LST to fight fire below decks and I honestly wanted to go but they wouldn't let me. I had to stay with my gun and a couple men in case of further air attack. The fellows had a steady battle below decks and when things started looking pretty good the ammo started going off. It's lucky it didn't all go off at once. And for the first time I was a little scared. It went off in small explosions and bursts but yet powerful enough to blow stuff all over the ship. It sounded like a regular battle going on with the shells dinging around inside the ship. The boys cut a hole in a bulkhead next to a magazine and stuck a hose through with a fog nozzle and cooled it down. After this magazine was cooled down most of the fire was out. It started at 0600 and it was now 1200. The LST had a good bit of water in her from the hoses and had a bad list to the starboard which was good. It raised the hole on the port side up from the water.[3]

Beginning at 1225 they started pumping her out to correct the list. Twenty-four men had died and twenty-one were wounded in the attack.

LST 724, cruising just ahead of the *884*, also came under attack about the same time. The Tony that attacked her fell under her guns and crashed only fifty feet from the ship, blowing two men overboard and littering the port quarter with engine parts. She suffered no damage and the two men were recovered by a small boat from *LST 884*.

Also crashed by a kamikaze during the demonstration was the attack transport *Hinsdale APA 120*, which was carrying units of the Second Marine Division. In the early morning hours, as she maneuvered to take her place for the bogus landing, she came under attack. At 0550 she was crashed by a Tony carrying three bombs which struck her at the waterline on her port side. One bomb exploded in the engine room and another in the fire room. A third bomb did not go off and was removed a few days later. Fires broke out and the crew set about working to save their ship as she lay dead in the water. The fires were quickly extinguished and the ship stabilized. She was towed back to Kerama Retto for preliminary repairs. Her casualty list was sixteen dead and thirty-nine injured.[4]

West Virginia BB 48 had been bombarding the beaches and inshore area near the Hagushi beachhead in support of the landings. At about 1910 three bogeys were reported approaching the area. An Oscar with a 551-lb. bomb made it through her anti-aircraft fire at 1913 to crash her superstructure deck. Its bomb penetrated the deck, but it was a dud, saving the battleship

12. *The Invasion of Okinawa, Week One*

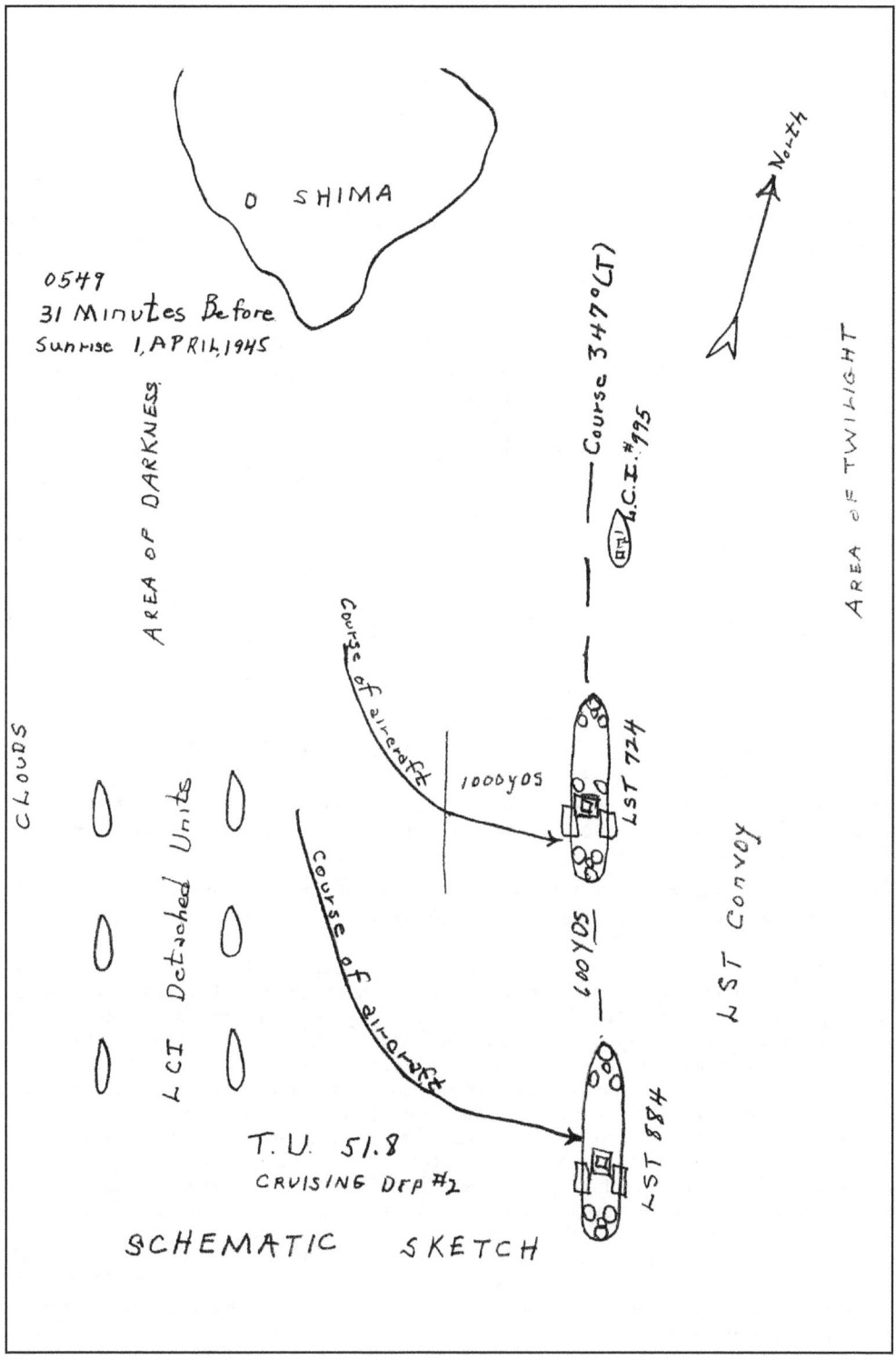

This sketch, from the action report of *LST 724*, shows the attack on *LSTs 724* and *884* on 1 April 1945. U.S.S. *LST 724* Serial 121. *Anti-aircraft Action Report—submission of.* 3 April 1945, p. 5.

from further damage. Nonetheless, four men had died and twenty-three were injured in the attack. She repaired her damage and was able to continue on her mission.[5]

The following day, 2 April, would see several more of the transports hit by kamikazes. Included in the lot were *Achernar AKA 53*, *Tyrrell AKA 80*, *Dickerson APD 21*, *Telfair APA 210*, *Goodhue APA 107*, and *Henrico APA 45*.

Early in the morning of 2 April at 0043, *Achernar* was struck as she headed for night retirement south of Kerama Retto. She had transported personnel from VMF(N)-543 to Okinawa. The Marine fighter squadron would be based at Kadena air field. A Sonia struck her starboard side above the main deck, its bomb penetrating below. According to Japanese records, this was one of the first kamikaze attacks carried out by the Japanese army air forces. Capt. Minoru Hasegawa and 2nd Lt. (jg) Nishi Yamamoto piloted the two special attack aircraft. Their flight had taken off from Tokuno Shima and was escorted by nine fighters from the 66th and 103rd Air Regiments of the Army Third Attack Division.[6] The crash caused two explosions, one from the plane and the second from its bomb. They were nearly simultaneous and started fires through the area of the impact. Expert firefighting measures by the crew soon had the blaze under control. The ship had taken a list to port which was soon corrected, and the ship looked after its casualties of which there were five dead and forty-one wounded.

Tyrrell AKA 80 had finished landing her troops at the Hagushi beachhead and had remained in the area to support the landings. She had a close call at 0555 when a twin-engine bomber attempted to crash her but narrowly missed the bridge. It clipped off the antenna, struck a boom, and careened into the water before exploding close aboard. Debris rained down upon the ship's deck, but it was not seriously damaged.

Dickerson had been operating with Task Unit 51.7, landing troops and supplies at Keise Shima in the Kerama Retto islands. The invasion attempt was completed and some of the troops of the 77th Division had been taken back on board for transport elsewhere. *Dickerson* retired to Transport Area Fox, which was about twenty miles southwest of Okinawa to await further orders. Nearby, *Shannon DM 25* had fired on and driven off a twin engine plane. It had been hit by her gunfire and was smoking as it headed for other ships in the area. About 1830 *Dickerson*'s lookouts spotted three Zekes and two Nicks converging on the transports. The Nick that had been hit by *Shannon* circled over the ship and came in on the *Dickerson* from astern. It was taken under fire by the ship's stern guns but to no avail. Lt. (jg) James D. Ebert, who had just been relieved as Officer of the Deck at 1825, related what happened next:

> I saw the plane hit the top of number one stack. At that point I was thrown to the deck by a loud blast. Upon recovering my senses undoubtedly only a few seconds later, I found the situation to be grave. Two fire-controlman, Lt. (jg) GEORGE, and myself were apparently the only men alive forward of the galley deck house. The plane had swept the galley deck, killing most of the two gun crews there; a few had jumped just before the crash and were saved. It evidently then crashed into the base of the bridge structure, toppling the mast over towards the after end of the ship. The entire well deck and bridge structure below me were a mass of flames. The four of us, unable to move aft, turned forward for a means of escape. Jumping from the flying bridge to the twenty millimeter platform forward of the bridge, we then jumped to the deck of the forecastle. There we found a scene of almost indescribable horror. An explosive force, of undetermined origin, had completely eliminated number one three inch gun, leaving a hole in the deck twenty to twenty-five feet wide, across the forecastle, and twelve to fifteen feet in length. The C.P.O. quarters below was a mass of rubble. The men serving on number one gun were horribly mutilated; from the devastation wrought, it is my opinion that a bomb, very likely dropped from a plane above was the cause. It could have hardly come from the suicide plane, considering the angle of his approach.[7]

Bunch APD 79 came alongside to assist in firefighting and *Herbert APD 22* picked up survivors. Confusion reigned as both the ship's CO, Lt. Cmdr. Ralph E. Loundsbury, and its XO, Lt. A.

G. McEwen, had been killed. The remaining officers led the crew in firefighting, but with the fires approaching the ship's magazine and the nighttime conditions, it was determined that it was necessary to abandon ship. *Bunch* continued fighting the fires until they were under control. Reboarding the ship the next day, the surviving officers with a skeleton crew stayed on board as she was towed back to Kerama Retto. *Dickerson* was declared a total loss, towed out to sea and sunk on 4 April 1945. Her casualties were fifty-four dead and ninety-seven wounded.

The attack transport *Henrico APA 45* was hit about the same time. She was part of Task Group 53.4 and was carrying reserve troops of the 305th Regimental Combat Team and the Headquarters Company of the 77th Division. As with *Dickerson*, she was retiring to a night position to the southwest of Kerama Retto when she was hit by a twin-engine Frances.

At 1830 four planes were spotted at a distance of about seven miles from the ships but were soon lost in the cloud cover. Within minutes a Tony appeared and headed for *Henrico* but turned away. At 1836 a Frances came out of the clouds and made a run on the transport. Army gunners manning the starboard 40mm took it under fire along with one of the ship's 20mm guns, but they failed to stop its progress. Two minutes later it crashed into *Henrico* on the starboard side of her bridge deck. As with most kamikazes, this one carried a bomb which penetrated the deck and exploded below. Fire mains were damaged in the impact and the subsequent explosion which made firefighting a problem. Power to the engines was soon out and the ship went dead in the water. *Hobson DM 26* and *Suffolk AKA 69* stood by to assist as the crew fought the fires. By 2100 they were under control, but the ship was unable to move under her own power. *Hobson* began to tow her back to Kerama Retto at 2330 and *Yume ATF 94* took over at 0530. It was a costly crash for the American forces, forty-nine had died and 125 were wounded in the attack. Her action report for the incident revealed that the crash killed *Henrico*'s temporary Commanding Officer, Capt. W. C. France, the Commander Transport Division Fifty, Capt. E. Kiehl, the Commanding Officer of the 305th Regiment, Col. V. J. Tanzla, and Col. L. O. Williams, Executive Officer of the 305th Regiment.[8] *Henrico* was put out of the war.

Telfair APA 210 and *Goodhue APA 107*, which were in the company of *Henrico*, were also in retirement the evening of 2 April when they were both struck by kamikazes. At 1830 an estimated ten Japanese aircraft assaulted ships in the area of which three made runs on the two transports. One crashed into the sea after being struck by the combined fire of the two ships, but the second and third found their marks. *Telfair* was crashed by a Sally between her starboard and port kingposts before the plane skidded off the side of the ship to land in the water.[9] At 1849 *Goodhue* took the hit on her aft 20mm gun tub as a Nick struck her a glancing blow and then crashed close aboard. On board *Telfair* one man died and sixteen were wounded, whereas *Goodhue*'s losses included twenty-four dead and 119 wounded.

LCI(G)s 568 and *465* also came under kamikaze attack on 2 April. The two gunboats were on "skunk patrol" in the area between Motobu Peninsula and Ie Shima looking for suicide boats, PT boats, and midget subs. Daylight hours on 2 April had seen the ships identifying onshore targets and firing on them as they were discovered. At 1845 a Japanese plane, either a Tony or a Judy, crashed into the aft gundeck of *LCI(G) 568*. The ship's gunners had taken it under fire on the way in and it seemed as though the damage threw the plane off target. The impact and subsequent explosion knocked out the ship's two 20mm guns. One man died and four others were injured. At about the same time another plane dove on *LCI(G) 465*, but fire from the ship caused it to crash short of its target.[10]

Task Unit 51.92 (Gunboat Division Six) was on patrol on the eastern coast of Okinawa on 3 April 1945. Included were *LCI(G)s 79, 82, 347, 453, 455* and *725*. Each of the gunboats was operating in assigned sections about three miles long and two miles wide, with the *Tracy*

DM 19 overlapping their patrols to seaward. The sky was dark with no moon. The following morning, at about 0125, a *Shinyo* was observed forward of *LCI(G) 82* making a run on the gunboat from seaward.

> The order to open fire was given. Approximately fifty rounds were fired from the 30 caliber machine gun on the conning tower; but the fire was believed to have gone astern of the boat. The 40mm and 20mm gunners were unable to get off any fire at all. The 20mm gunner states that he was unable to loosen the retaining clamp and train the gun around in time to fire. The 40mm pointer either froze in his seat or did not see the target (which is improbable considering that the boat was approaching from the moonlit side.) (The 40mm pointer is still missing and consequently a statement from him cannot be presented.)
> The boat approached rapidly, turned, and crashed into the ship on the port side just forward of the conning tower. A double explosion resulted, tearing a large hole in the side of the ship.... The explosion knocked out all the ship's lights and the ship immediately heeled to starboard.[11]

Flames began shooting out from forward areas of the ship and ammunition soon began to explode. Water mains had been ruptured by the blast and fighting fires was not possible. The CO, Lt. (jg) Theodore Arnow, gave the order to abandon ship. Wounded men were put in life rafts and *LCI(G) 347* picked up a number of them twenty minutes later. *Tracy* picked up others. At 1500 an inspection party reboarded the gunboat and found her to be nearly broken in two forward of the conning tower. The blast had ripped a hole in the port side approximately twenty feet long. After destroying sensitive paperwork and equipment the party left the ship. At about 1600 the ship rolled over, broke in two and went under. Eight men had died in the attack and eleven were wounded.

On 3 April *Hambleton DMS 20* was steaming with *Lindsey DM 32, Ellyson DMS 19, Rodman DMS 21,* and *Emmons DMS 22* when she was damaged by a kamikaze. At 1745 a Val came

Number	Date (1945)	Navy planes	Army planes	Total
1	6–7 April	230	125	355
2	12–13 April	125	60	185
3	15–16 April	120	45	165
4	27–28 April	65	50	115
5	3–4 May	75	50	125
6	10–11 May	70	80	150
7	24–25 May	65	100	165
8	27–28 May	60	50	110
9	3–7 June	20	30	50
10	21–22 June	30	15	45
Total		860	605	1,465

> In addition to these "Kikusui" attacks, sporadic small-scale suicide attacks were carried out during this period by 140 Navy and 45 Army planes. From Formosa 250 suicide attacks were conducted, 50 by Navy planes and 200 by Army planes. The total suicide sorties against United States surface forces during the Okinawa campaign was 1,900, by Navy planes 1,050 and by Army planes 850.
> In addition to these suicide sorties, orthodox torpedo and dive bombing attacks were carried out; the total number of sorties is, however, not known except for Navy aircraft with a reported 3,700 sorties.
> Of interest is the effectiveness of these suicide attacks, considering the number of ships sunk and damaged and the number of suicide sorties carried out. During the period of the Kikusui operations, 26 ships were sunk and 164 damaged by suicide planes as reported by Commander in Chief, Pacific Fleet.

The above chart shows the numbers of aircraft active in the ten *Kikusui* attacks at Okinawa from 6 April through 22 June 1945. United States Strategic Bombing Survey (Pacific) Naval Analysis Division. *The Campaigns of the Pacific War.* (Washington, D.C.: U.S. Government Printing Office, 1946), p. 328.

at her from dead ahead and was taken under fire by all the ships in the group. The pilot made a run on her bridge but apparently was hit by fire from the ships. The plane struck *Hambleton* a glancing blow with its right wing and hit the water off her port quarter. Damage to the ship was minimal and there were no casualties.

Wake Island CVE 65 was operating southeast of Okinawa on 3 April. At about 1730 enemy aircraft were picked up on radar approaching her position. Simultaneous with this she hit some rough water which flipped two of her Wildcats overboard and tossed several more around. Two kamikazes attempted to crash her, one splashing close aboard her port bow and the other just off her starboard side. The starboard plane exploded and opened her hull below the waterline, causing flooding. Significant damage was done to her hull and areas below deck, but by 2140 she was heading to Kerama Retto under her own power. She received temporary repairs and headed to Guam on 6 April for five weeks of additional repair work. She had no casualties from the attack.[12]

LST 599, carrying personnel of VMF-322, was anchored off Kerama Retto when she was crashed by a Tony at 0715 on 3 April. The plane that hit her was one of a flight of eight Tonys operating as special attack aircraft and escorted by five additional Tonys. They were from the 105th Air Regiment at Matsuyama Air Base on Taiwan. The Tony penetrated her deck and caused massive damage to the ship and its cargo. VMF-322 suffered the loss of most of its equipment and had twenty-one wounded.[13] This attack was a double hit for the kamikaze pilot. Stored on the deck of *LST 599* was *LCT 876*, which also sustained serious damage in the attack. On board the LST twenty-one men were injured while the LCT crew had two injured.

Kikusui No. 1

Beginning on 6 April 1945, the Japanese launched a series of ten massed raids against the American forces at Okinawa. The combined operation was known as the *Ten Go* Campaign and each of the ten raids were referred to as *Kikusui* 1 through 10. The first and largest of these raids was from 6 to 7 April and, according to the USSBS study, consisted of 230 kamikazes from the navy and 125 from the army, escorted and supported by 344 other aircraft from both the Japanese army and navy air wings. They would take their toll on the ships at Okinawa with a total of twenty-six ships damaged or sunk by kamikazes in the two-day raid. Of these, *Bush DD 529*, *Colhoun DD 801*, and *LST 447* would be sunk and *Leutze DD 481*, *Morris DD 417*, *Mullany DD 528*, *Newcomb DD 586*, *Witter DE 636*, *Rodman DMS 21*, *Defense AM 317*, *Maryland BB 46*, and *Bennett DD 473* suffered heavy damage.

The destroyer *Newcomb DD 586* was screening for *St. Louis CL 49* on 6 April when she came under heavy attack Although the combat air patrol, coupled with the radar picket ships, had managed to intercept and shoot down a large number of incoming planes, the magnitude of this raid was such that it was impossible to get them all. Many slipped through the big blue blanket and made it to the Hagushi area where ships of every description were busy supplying and supporting the invasion. *Newcomb* estimated that there were at least forty enemy aircraft in the area near her. She was attacked by seven of them, four of which struck her. The other three fell under her guns.

She was patrolling about six miles south of Ie Shima in the company of *Howorth DD 592* when the first enemy planes appeared. The combat air patrol could be observed over and near the island as they shot down many aircraft. *Newcomb* noted that the Japanese pilots seemed to be inexperienced. They apparently were incapable of any but the most elementary evasive maneuvers, and the Hellcats pursuing them had no problem closing on them and shooting them down. At 1612 *Howorth* took the first hit as a kamikaze struck her 5"/38 director and superstructure, killing nine men and wounding fourteen. A few minutes later, at 1624, it was *Newcomb*'s turn. She combined fire with *Howorth* and shot down a Val. A minute later another Val made a dive on her and crashed into the water only twenty feet off her starboard beam. Together the destroyers shot down two more attackers. *Howorth* seemed to be their first choice as a target and four more planes were shot down by the two destroyers. At 1710 the ships were ordered to their night retirement positions, but within a half hour two more planes made a try at *Howorth* and missed, splashing into the sea. *Newcomb* took her first kamikaze hit at 1800. A minute or so before the crash, her lookouts observed a plane coming in low on the water headed for her port beam. Although the ship's gunners fired on the kamikaze they couldn't stop it. It crashed into *Newcomb*'s after stack, starting fires in the upper handling room of nearby 5"/38 mount No. 3. Within minutes a second plane tried for her and was shot down, however, a third could not be stopped and crashed her amidships near the torpedo workshop. The bomb from this plane caused a massive explosion. She reported:

> All power was lost at this time as both engine rooms and the after fireroom were blown into a mass of homogeneous rubble. The after stack, both torpedo mounts, all amidship superstructure work, 40 mm mounts and magazines were disintegrated and blown over the side. The decking from frame 102 to 137 was ruptured longitudinally and blown up to port at a 45 degree angle and down to starboard. A huge fire was raging through the after deck house area, including number three upper handling room and the crew's after head. Smoke and flames towered over NEWCOMB to heights of over 1000 feet. The situation was grave as NEWCOMB slowed and came to rest dead in the water on an approximately easterly heading 3000 yards from the screening ships of TG 54.2. With intentions of polishing NEWCOMB off a fourth plane raced towards NEWCOMB from the port beam and although under fire by her forward batteries came through to crash into the forward stack spraying the entire amidship section of NEWCOMB, which was a raging conflagration, with a fresh supply of gasoline.[14]

Leutze DD 481 came alongside to render assistance at 1811. As she was preparing to assist in firefighting, another plane made a run on *Newcomb*, struck her a glancing blow and plowed into *Leutze* at the waterline. The bomb went off underwater and the effect on *Leutze* was the same as if she had been torpedoed. She cleared away from *Newcomb* to tend to her own damage and *Beale DD 471* took over her firefighting duties. The bomb had effectively put her out of commission. In addition to extreme flooding in her aft section, *Leutze*'s two shafts were bent and only her starboard engine had limited power to move the ship. *Leutze* was in danger of sinking and all topside material that could be jettisoned went over the side in order to improve her stability. Her commanding officer, Lt. Leon Grabowski, rallied his men and, through a superhuman effort, *Leutze* remained afloat. *Defense AM 317* towed her back to Kerama Retto.[15] The fleet minesweeper had her share of action earlier in the day. Around 1800 she had been attacked by four Vals. One went down under her guns, but two crashed her, wounding nine men. Damage to the ship was minimal and she remained in the area, rescuing men from *Newcomb* and *Leutze*.[16] *Newcomb* was taken in tow by *Tekesta ATF 93* and screened by *Twiggs DD 591* and *Porterfield DD 682*. She arrived at Kerama Retto around 0930 the next morning and dropped anchor. *Newcomb* and *Leutze* looked as though they were ready for the scrap yard, but they were repaired and eventually returned to duty.

Morris DD 417 was on patrol off Ie Shima on 6 April and encountered enemy aircraft throughout the day. At 1330 a Sally made a run at her but was driven off after *Morris*' gunners scored some hits on it. Seconds later the Combat Air Patrol dove on it and shot it down. At 1640 she fired on three Vals that approached her position.

Witter DE 636 was on patrol southeast of Okinawa when she came under attack. At 1611 she was approached by two Japanese aircraft and took them under fire. Both were hit by her guns and one crashed a distance from the destroyer escort, but his companion made it through to crash into *Witter* at the starboard waterline. As with most attacks, the plane released its bomb just prior to the impact, allowing it to penetrate the side of the hull and explode below. The site of the crash was perfect for the kamikaze, and *Witter* immediately began taking water. Fires started by the attack were quickly extinguished and, with the help of *Morris, Richard P. Leary DD 664, Gregory DD 802*, and *Arikara ATF 98*, she eventually made it back to Kerama Retto under her own power. *Witter* numbered six dead and six wounded among her casualties.[17]

The destroyer *Newcomb DD 586* was attacked by a kamikaze on 6 April 1945 as she was screening for the cruiser *St. Louis CL 49* off Okinawa. NARA 80G 330100.

Damage to *Newcomb DD 586* is in evidence after the attack of 6 April 1945. NARA 80G 330105.

Griffin APD 38 and *Gregory* were under attack and managed to shoot down three planes, one of which narrowly missed *Griffin*. At about that time, *Hyman DD 732* came under attack. She shot down several kamikazes, but a Hamp got through and crashed near her torpedo tubes, setting the area on fire. She managed to extinguish the flames as even more kamikazes attacked her, two of which she shot down. *Sterrett DD 407*, cruising nearby, shot down a Val at 1725. At 1811, it was *Morris*' turn. She picked up an incoming Kate at twenty miles and followed it on her radar. At 10,000 yards she opened fire with her main battery, and shortly thereafter, with her 40mm and 20mm guns. Although the plane seemed to be hit, it made it through to crash into *Morris* between her No. 1 and No. 2 5" guns, causing an immediate explosion and fires. As with many kamikaze crashes, the impact and explosion damaged fire mains and firefighting ability was compromised. *Griffin* came alongside to assist in firefighting. By 2030 *Morris*' fires were out and she began the trip back to Kerama Retto under diminished speed with the other damaged ships. Her losses were thirteen dead and forty-five wounded.[18]

Mullany DD 528 was in company with several other ships patrolling to the east of Okinawa when she was hit by a kamikaze at 1745. The plane was a low wing fighter described as either a Tojo, Oscar, or Zeke. The destroyer took it under fire at 6,000 yards and scored some hits but not enough to stop the attack. It crashed *Mullany* on the port side of the after deck house. Her action report indicates that

> the plane hit at about 1746, exploded with a spray of gasoline, and started large fires. The area between 5" mount No. 3 and mount No. 5 was ablaze, 40mm ammunition was exploding about the burned area. The deckhouse, 40mm mount and director, were a mass of torn wreckage.

12. The Invasion of Okinawa, Week One   215

Leutze DD 481 was damaged by a kamikaze as she came to the aid of *Newcomb DD 586* on 6 April 1945. *USS Leutze DD 481* Serial 0080. ***Action Report, War Damage Report, 6 April 1945.*** 5 May 1945. Enclosures.

Leutze DD 481 suffered heavy damage to her port side aft in the attack.

Steering control and other communications to the part of the ship abaft the after deck house were lost. Power throughout the 5" and 40mm battery was temporarily lost, but shift to emergency power was carried out, and in about twenty seconds control of 5" mounts No. 1 and No. 2, and 40mm mounts No. 41, No. 42, No. 43, and No. 44 was recovered.... The initial explosion carried away parts of the after bulkhead of the after engine room, spraying the engine room with fuel oil and scalding water from auxiliaries adjacent to that bulkhead. This drove the engine room personnel forward, and after clearing debris from the top of the main deck hatch, they abandoned the engine room, with all hands safe, one man receiving first degree burns on neck and ears. The after generator failed at this time.[19]

A kamikaze attack on 6 April 1945 caused this damage to *Morris DD 417* as she patrolled off Ie Shima. NARA 80G 330109.

In an attempt to safeguard the ship, torpedoes and depth charges were jettisoned. However, some of the depth charges could not be reached and, before long, they began to cook off. The first exploded at 1809 killing a number of the crew and damaging the ship further. Seeing an opportunity, another kamikaze lined up for a run on the ship but was hit by fire from the ship's 5" guns and shot down. This plane was followed by a third which was also destroyed. *LCI(G) 461* was the first ship to come to *Mullany's* aid. She played water on the fires with her hoses and assisted in the firefighting. *Gherardi DMS 30, Purdy DD 734, Execute*

Morris DD 417's starboard side was severely damaged. NARA 80G 330101.

AM 232, and *PGM 10* soon arrived on the scene to assist *Mullany*. At 1829, with ammunition continuing to cook off and the fires spreading, her CO, Cmdr. Albert O. Momm, gave the order to abandon ship as *Gherardi* stood by. Capt. Frederick Moosebrugger, in command of the destroyer screen, had ordered *Purdy DD 734* to assist *Mullany*. Momm reported on board *Purdy DD 734* and after consultation with *Purdy*'s CO, Cmdr. Frank L. Johnson, it was determined that further efforts should be made to save *Mullany*. *Purdy* set about pouring water on the flaming destroyer and finally managed to extinguish the fires. Momm reboarded his ship with a skeleton crew and the ship limped back to Kerama Retto. *Mullany* had thirty dead and thirty-six wounded.

Emmons DMS 22, *Rodman DMS 21* and *Macomb DMS 23* were supporting Sweep Unit 11 which was clearing the channel between Okinawa and Iheya Retto on 6 April. At 1515 *Macomb* reported two enemy aircraft approaching their position and the ships went to general quarters. A large flight of enemy planes headed for Okinawa passed near the ships. The presence of Tonys, Vals, and Zekes, indicated that both Japanese army and navy air arms were active in the attack. One made a dive on *Rodman*, crashing into her port bow. Its bomb was released just before the impact and exploded under the ship. Fortunately *Rodman*'s engineering plant was undamaged by the crash and she was still able to maneuver. A second plane dropped a bomb which missed. *Emmons* came to the aid of her sister ship to assist in firefighting, but *Rodman*'s crew had everything under control. *Emmons* and *Macomb* circled the area providing anti-aircraft support for the damaged minesweeper. Later estimates of the number of bogeys in the area ran from fifty to seventy-five. A number of them attacked the three ships, and *Rodman* sustained two more crashes but remained afloat. *Emmons* came under attack next. Her action report indicated:

> As we supported the USS RODMAN many attacks were directed at us. Tonys, Vals and Zekes were identified. The USS EMMONS definitely "splashed" six planes before suffering the first of five hits. During this time four other attacks missed the ship by a matter of a few yards. All five hits occurred in rapid succession, almost instantaneously, and were well coordinated. The first hit was taken on the fantail at about frame 175; the second on the starboard side of the pilot house; the third on the port side of Combat Information Center; the fourth on the starboard side of number three five-inch gun; and the fifth near the water line at frame 30, starboard side.... All of the hull aft of frame 175 was entirely missing and serious damage was inflicted on the port screw rendering it inoperable. The entire bridge structure was destroyed and fire raged in all spaces from frame 67 forward to gun one, from the main deck up. Little or nothing remained of the decks from the main deck to the bridge overhead in that area.[20]

Wounded in the attack on *Emmons* was her skipper, Lt. Cmdr. Eugene N. Foss, and command of the ship passed to Lt. John J. Griffin, Jr. Maximum damage to the minesweeper was caused by the combination of aircraft crash and the accompanying bomb, as each of the planes was judged to carry a bomb in the attack. Extinguishing fires in the aft section of the ship was problematic as the heat continually cooked off ammo in the ready boxes. Water pressure in the mains was lowered and many of the hoses were punctured by shrapnel from the crashes and explosions. With so much damage, flooding began to increase and *Emmons* was down by the stern with a ten degree list to starboard. After the second and third crashes, men began to abandon the ship even though the order had not been given. Lt. Griffin, upon getting to the main deck, came to the realization that he was the senior officer aboard. The crew remained on board with the exception of the wounded, who were placed in life rafts and put over the side. Those seriously wounded were kept aboard as transferring them was too difficult. By 1800, with the fires out of control and the ship continuing to settle, Griffin gave the order to abandon ship. At 1930, as *PGM 11* came alongside for the transfer of casualties, a heavy explosion rocked the interior of *Emmons* signaling its doom. She was abandoned and her hulk was sunk the next morning by *Ellyson DMS 19*. The attacks on these ships was costly. *Rodman* had

The bow of *Rodman DS 21* shows extreme damage after the kamikaze attack on 6 April 1945. Official U.S. Navy Photograph.

sixteen dead and twenty wounded and *Emmons* suffered sixty-four dead and seventy-one wounded. *Rodman* was towed back to Kerama Retto for temporary repairs and then sent back to the states. She was out of the war.

Ammunition carriers were particularly valuable targets for the kamikazes, and on 6 April three of them came under attack at Kerama Retto. *Las Vegas Victory* escaped damage but *Hobbs Victory* and *Logan Victory* were both destroyed. At 1645 enemy aircraft dove on the three ships at Kerama Retto. *Las Vegas Victory* shot one down and was not hit, however, *Logan Victory* was. *Logan Victory* was carrying 9,033 tons of explosives plus drums of oil. Her attacker came in low on the water and crashed her amidships. Its explosion spread fire over the deck and into the hold where it ignited some of her stores. With the threat of a super explosion and the fires raging out of control, her Master, Charles Hendrickx, gave the order to abandon ship. Fifteen of her crew died in the attack. Hendrickx was wounded by a 20mm shell that cooked off; he died later. With the possibility of a massive explosion threatening the harbor, the ship was sunk by gunfire. As soon as these attacks began, Master Kenneth F. Izant ordered *Hobbs Victory* to weigh anchor and get underway. She did not get far as two hours later she came under attack by a pair of kamikazes. Her Armed Guard report for the action revealed:

> One (1) aircraft was shot down by intense fire from the harbor area and crashed into the water inside the harbor nets. The second aircraft changed course and approached on a course of 265 degrees relative, and headed directly into the ship. All guns were manned and intense fire was maintained throughout the encounter. The aircraft was smoking but apparently under complete control. The approach of the aircraft was about 30 or 40 feet from the water level. Pilot crashed the aircraft into the side of the ship just forward of the midships at boat deck level. The crash caused a terrific explosion, and flames covered the deck. No strafing was apparent. No. 6 20MM

tub was immediately aft of the point of impact. Russell LeRoy Evjen S1c USN-I 869 71 53 who was in No. 6 tub, was blown into the water and received injuries from which he died a short time later aboard the AM 310. Chester Lee McNealy S1c V-6 USNR 982 08 58, who was also in No. 6 tub, was blown into the water and was not recovered. From the flame enveloping the gun tub and the nature of the explosion, it is felt that the subject man was killed. At 1915 the same day, on orders from the Master and approved for the Armed Guard crew by the Armed Guard Officer, all personnel abandoned ship in life boats and life rafts.... Merchant radioman Gordon Brown was killed and Merchant radioman Charles Hickman received severe leg injuries. It is felt that Mr. Hickman's life was saved by the quick thinking of Grady Driver GM2c 311 79 84, Don Taylor Combs S1c 803 45 86, and Roy Cleo Goldman S1c 624 77 72. These Navy personnel applied a tourniquet to the injured leg while Mr. Hickman was in the life boat, and thereby prevented him from bleeding to death.[21]

Izant gave the order to abandon ship at 1855 and everyone went into lifeboats, rafts, or over the side. *Success AM 310* picked up survivors, but thirteen men had died in the attack. She continued to burn through the night until she blew up at 0300 the next morning and sank.

LST 447 had landed her cargo at the Hagushi beachhead and was heading to an anchorage at Kerama Retto at 1627 when she spotted a pair of Zekes heading for the harbor. She scored hits on one, which then turned and crashed into her just above her waterline at 1630. Its bomb penetrated below and exploded. Fires raged and, with her firefighting capabilities compromised, her CO, Lt. Paul J. Schmitz, gave the order to abandon ship at 1640. *Willmarth DE 638* and *ATR 80* made a valiant attempt to extinguish the flames but it was a futile exercise. *LST 447* burned for the next day and finally sank. Her casualties included five dead and seventeen wounded.[22]

Facility AM 233 came under attack at 1710 when a Val and a Zeke made a run on her. The 185' minesweeper shot one down and drove the other off. At 1723 a Zeke was shot down twenty feet off her bow; its wreckage passed under the ship and damaged her screw. Two more Zekes were lining up for another attack at 1833 but were shot down by the CAP. Her damage in the attack was minimal and she had no casualties. At about the same time, *Fieberling DE 640* dodged a kamikaze's crash. The plane passed closely over her superstructure and clipped her mast. She had no casualties.

Haynsworth DD 700 came under attack at 1250 on 6 April. The ships in her task group had been under attack sporadically all morning. A bogey was detected approaching the formation, and within minutes, a Judy with two Corsairs on its tail appeared and dove on the destroyer. *Haynsworth* unleashed its anti-aircraft batteries and the plane turned away. A few minutes later it made a violent turn back toward the ship, this time with three or four Corsairs in pursuit. The force caused by the turn made its bomb drop off and it crashed harmlessly in the ocean, but the plane continued on course. In spite of heavy anti-aircraft fire from the ship, it crashed into *Haynsworth*'s main radio transmitter room. Fires erupted on and below decks. The destroyer's CO, Cmdr. Robert A. Brodie, Jr., stopped the engines and turned out of the wind to ease the effect of the wind on the fires which were gaining in intensity. It took nearly an hour to extinguish the flames. Part of the problem in fighting the fire was the intense smoke which obscured the area of the fires. Brodie turned the ship from time to time so that the smoke did not block firefighting efforts. *Haynsworth* had fourteen dead and twenty wounded.

The *Yamato* Mission

The American attack on Okinawa forced the naval high command to make decisions that did not always seem to make sense. One such decision was to send their largest warship, the *Yamato*, on a suicide mission. This mission was to coincide with the beginnings of the first *Kikusui* Operation which was scheduled for 6–7 April 1945. The *Yamato* and her fleet would be considered a part of this special attack operation. The Second Fleet and its flagship, the battleship *Yamato*, was ordered to attack the American invasion fleet lying off the Hagushi[23] anchorage at Okinawa. Prospects of the fleet actually reaching the island were slim, however, the Combined Fleet Headquarters felt that her presence at sea would attract numerous enemy planes from Okinawa, that would take the pressure off the 32nd Army there and allow them to resist the American invasion and inflict greater losses on the Americans. It was a true suicide mission.

At a meeting prior to the sortie, commanding officers of the ships in the Second Fleet voiced their objections. They did not mind sacrificing themselves and their ships in battle but saw little chance that they would even reach their assigned target at Okinawa. American air power was overwhelming, and the chances of success for ships without air cover was slim. Steaming for Okinawa on the morning of 6 April 1945 would be *Yamato*, accompanied by the light cruiser *Yahagi* and the destroyers *Fuyutsuki, Suzutsuki, Yukikaze, Isokaze, Hamakaze, Kasumi, Hatsushimo,* and *Asashimo*. Only enough fuel for a one way trip was allotted to the ships. If they reached Okinawa they would beach themselves and act as stationary artillery platforms to support Japanese ground troops ashore.

The ships left their anchorage around in the Inland Sea around 1500 on 6 April 1945. Within hours they were spotted by American B-29s and American submarines which shadowed the fleet as they went out to sea. Air cover was provided by ten Japanese aircraft which soon went back to their bases. It would not have mattered, as the attack on the fleet would encompass hundreds of American aircraft. They would have been but a slight nuisance.

Hancock CV 19, steaming with TF 58, had sailed north to intercept the Japanese force heading for Okinawa. It included the battleship *Yamato*, along with the light cruiser *Yahagi* and eight destroyers. *Hancock*'s planes were launched at about 1000 but could not locate the Japanese ships. At 1212 she was bombed by a Japanese plane, which then turned and crashed into her flight deck, holing it and setting fire to aircraft parked nearby. Her damage control parties soon had the fires under control and the ship was able to resume her duties. She landed her aircraft at 1630. Her dead numbered sixty-two and her wounded seventy-one.

American aircraft began to appear on the scene by 1230 and, within ten minutes, carrier planes from *Bennington* had struck the battleship with the first bombs and torpedoes. This was followed by numerous other bombs. Within the space of the next three hours the ship was hit by fifteen torpedoes and still more bombs. Capt. Kosaku Ariga chose to go down with his ship which slid beneath the waves at about 1500 on 7 April 1945. The mighty battleship had not been able to get more than about ninety miles south of Japan on her way to Okinawa. *Yahagi* was hit by bombs and torpedoes from *San Jacinto*'s planes. After suffering strikes from twelve bombs and seven torpedoes, she went to the bottom. *Hamakaze*, given equal attention by the carrier aircraft, went under as well. *Asasimo, Kasumi,* and *Isokaze* were so badly damaged in the attacks that they were scuttled and sunk north of *Yamato*. Only *Fuyutsuki, Suzutsuki, Yukikaze,* and *Hatsushimo* managed to limp back to their base in Japan, all heavily damaged.

Maryland BB 46 was operating as part of Task Force 54 to the west of Okinawa. She had been sent to intercept the *Yamato* force also. At 1846 on 7 April the ships went to general quarters with enemy aircraft reported in the area. A few minutes later *Maryland* opened fire on an attacking plane. Her gunners managed to knock out the plane's engine, but it continued to glide in and crashed on top of turret No. 3. Its 551-lb. bomb exploded, adding to the carnage. Her medical officer reported:

> The plane burst into flame and was demolished, the bomb exploding. The 20 millimeter antiaircraft mounts, located on top of the turret were demolished, and burning fragments and 20

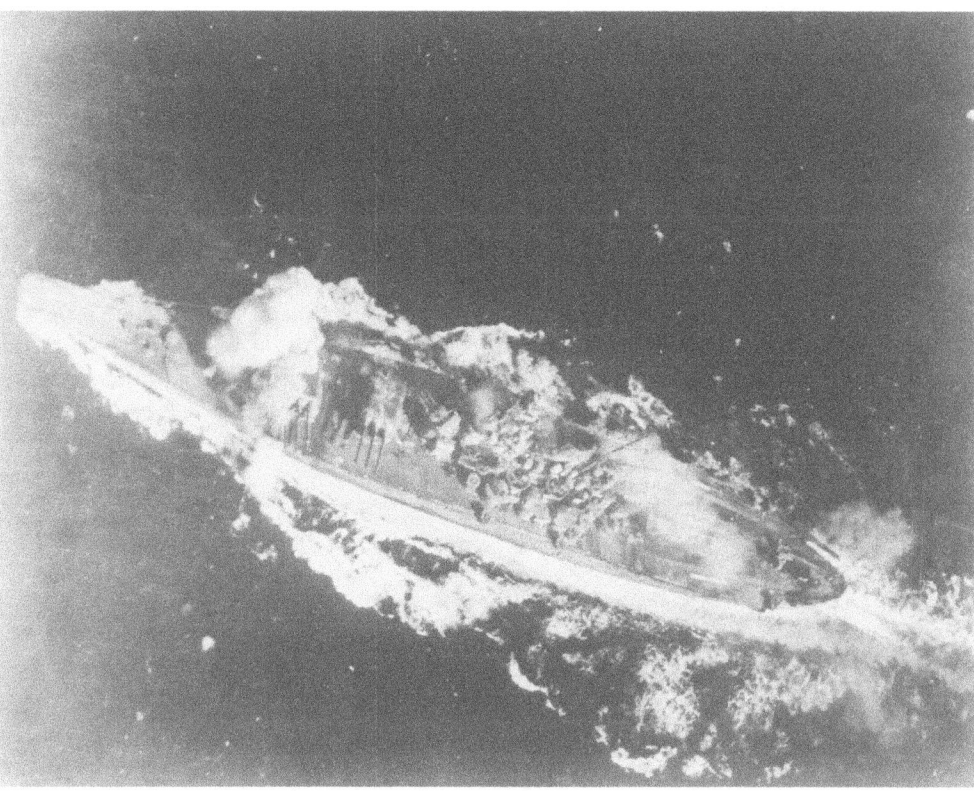

The Japanese super battleship *Yamato* receives two direct bomb hits from the Curtis Helldiver flown by 3rd Fleet pilot Lt. Cmdr. Arthur L. Dowling. *Yamato* was hit many times and sunk in this engagement. NARA 80G 349726.

millimeter shells were strewn about the quarterdeck. Most of the personnel attending the battery were blown from their stations. Apparently, some were blown overboard. Fragments of others were scattered over the quarterdeck and were hanging from the mainmast.

Great flames, covered with clouds of black smoke, leaped from the top of turret three, and extended down to its base. In the glare of the flames, the quarterdeck was littered with debris, dead, and wounded men. In addition to this, there was the exploding of 20 millimeter ammunition, from the heat of the flames. The flame and flying fragments from the explosion, extended to the top of the mainmast, and to the anti-aircraft battery on the quarterdeck, burning and wounding men attending these stations....

Owing to the close proximity of the burning plane and the bomb explosion to the men in the anti-aircraft batteries atop of turret number three, the number of missing and killed in relation to the number of surviving wounded, was comparatively high. Of the eighteen men atop of turret three, all were killed or missing, except four. One, who was blown off the turret, had a traumatic amputation of the right arm, about three inches from the shoulder joint, severe intracranial injuries, blast and burns. He never regained consciousness, and expired about fifteen minutes after the explosion. The second, was seen to arise from the top of the turret after the explosion, and walk off into space — amid the smoke and flames, landing on the quarterdeck below. Besides severe burns and blast, he had multiple compound fractures of the extremities, and evidences of intracranial injuries. He never regained consciousness, and expired about midnight, in spite of heroic treatment. The third man was lowered from the top of the turret by means of the canvas, parachute harness, stretcher. He suffered from partial traumatic amputation of the right leg, shrapnel wounds, burns, and blast. The fourth man climbed down from the turret without help, and was suffering from blast, burns, and shrapnel wounds.[24]

Maryland extinguished the fires, collected her dead and wounded and resumed her station. She had suffered thirty-dead and thirty-six wounded. On 14 April she departed Okinawa and escorted other ships back to the states where she was repaired at Puget Sound.

The Ordeal of the Radar Picket Ships

Many ships, performing various duties at Okinawa, came under attack by kamikaze aircraft. Among the greatest losses of life and shipping were those that took place on the radar picket stations (RP) surrounding the island. In the Philippines the Japanese had made ample use of their new special attack methods, and the navy high command anticipated that the situation at Okinawa would be much worse. In order to intercept the kamikaze raids coming in from southern Kyushu and Taiwan, they devised a plan to ring the island with a series of radar picket stations. Steaming on each station would be a destroyer, specially equipped with radar to detect incoming raids before they could reach the main body of American ships and

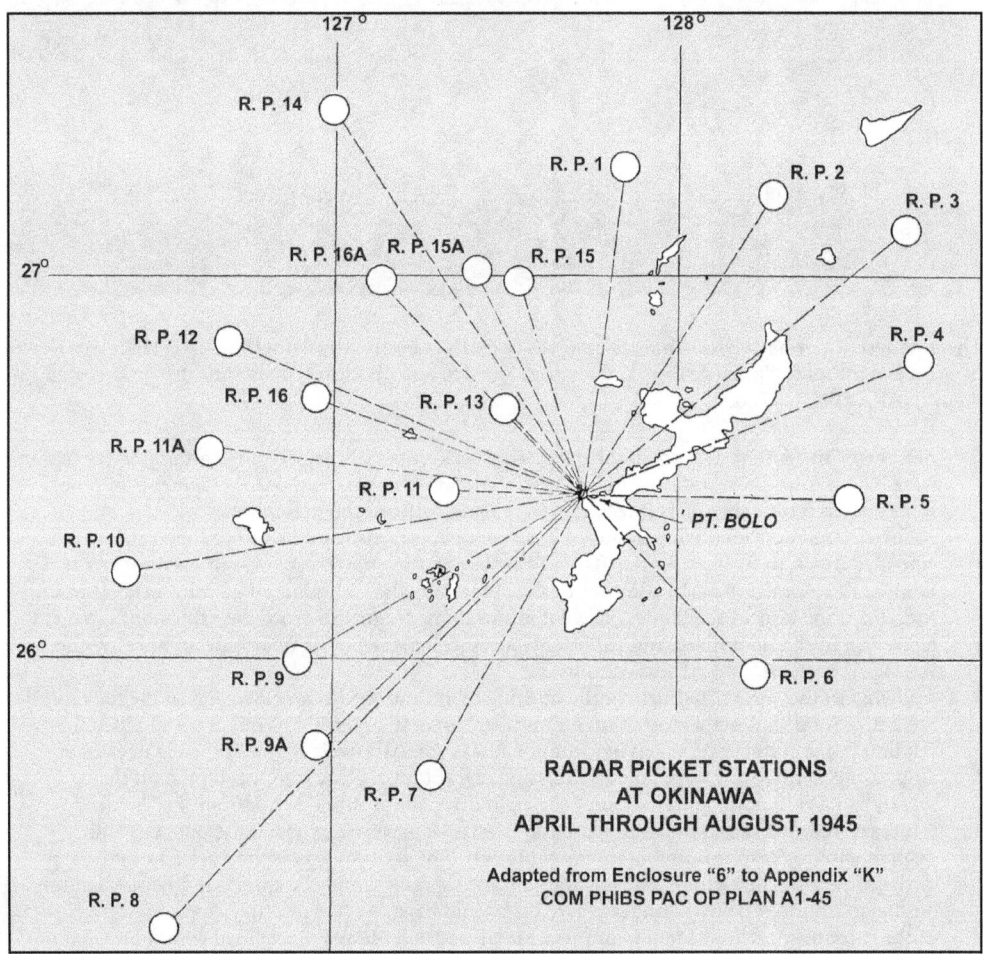

One of the important screens, and one that saw a great deal of action during the campaign for Okinawa, was the special radar picket screen. On each station a fighter director destroyer, accompanied by other destroyers and support gunboats, alerted the combat air patrol to the approach of Japanese aircraft from Kyushu and Taiwan.

troops at Okinawa proper. Working in conjunction with these radar picket destroyers would be a combat air patrol. In theory, the radar picket destroyer would detect an incoming raid and vector the combat air patrol to intercept it, thus preventing the raid from reaching Okinawa. The effectiveness of the combat air patrol was excellent and, although many aircraft did slip through the net, many did not. Within a brief time, the Japanese began to recognize the effectiveness of the radar picket ships and targeted them so as to knock out the eyes and ears of the early warning system. Within a week or two of the inception of the radar pickets, it became necessary to bolster the radar picket destroyer with additional support, and a combination of other destroyers and destroyer types, as well as LCS(L) gunboats, LSM(R)s and PGMs were on patrol. In all, a total of 206 ships served on this duty. Of that number, sixty were either sunk or damaged in kamikaze attacks,[25] making it arguably the most hazardous surface naval duty of World War II.

Radar picket duty at Okinawa began on 26 March 1945 and lasted until 14 August 1945. In the opening days of the ordeal, *Kimberly DD 521* was the first casualty, taking a hit from a kamikaze at RP No. 9 on 26 March. Two Val dive bombers from the First Air Fleet on Taiwan zoomed in for the kill. *Kimberly*'s gunners were on their mark and, although the Val was hit a number of times, it still managed to crash into the destroyer's aft 40mm gun mount. Four men were killed and fifty-seven wounded. A few days later, *Kimberly* headed back to the states; for her the war was over.

The invasion of the main island of Okinawa took place on 1 April 1945, and within the week, the radar pickets again suffered casualties. Patrolling RP No. 1 on 6 April 1945 were *Bush DD 529* and *LCS(L) 64*, while on nearby RP No. 2 *Colhoun DD 801* kept a lonely vigil. Headed for the picket stations was the first massed *Kikusui* raid of the Okinawa campaign, with a combination of nearly 700 Japanese kamikazes and conventional aircraft. The attacks began early in the morning on 6 April, and by day's end both of the destroyers would be sunk.

The first bogeys appeared at 0245, attacking all three of the ships intermittently for the next three hours. With daybreak came combat air patrol coverage and the situation eased for a few hours, in spite of continual raids approaching the ships. Finally, at about 1420, radar on the ships picked up numerous flights of Japanese aircraft and, by 1500, the ships were swarmed by fifty to sixty Japanese aircraft. They were focusing on *Bush* and also on *Cassin Young DD 793* on nearby RP No. 3. After driving off a number of Japanese aircraft, *Bush* was crashed by a Jill flying from Kushira Naval Air Base on Kyushu. It hit her amidships on the starboard side and its bomb went off. The forward engine room was damaged and within a short time the destroyer had taken on a ten degree list to port.

On nearby RP No. 2, *Colhoun* received word that *Bush* was hit. Combat air patrol planes from the carriers *Belleau Wood, San Jacinto, Hornet, Anzio,* and *Bennington* swarmed overhead, knocking out numerous Japanese aircraft, but there were too many. *Colhoun* headed for RP No. 1 to assist *Bush* and *LCS(L) 64*. Arriving at RP No. 1 at 1600, *Colhoun* found *Bush* "dead in the water smoking badly and down by the stern. The destroyer still had remains of what appeared to be a Betty plastered on her starboard side amidships. She was being circled by a group of enemy planes, consisting of three Zekes at angels 10, [10,000 feet altitude] seven Vals at angels 7 and two Zekes at angels 5."[26] *Colhoun* directed *LCS 64* to remove personnel and provided covering fire by placing herself between *Bush* and incoming aircraft. After shooting down a Val and then a Zeke, *Colhoun* took her first hit when a Zeke crashed her port bow. Its bomb went through the deck and blew up in the after fireroom. *Colhoun* was holed below the waterline and on fire. As firefighting was underway, another Zeke and two Vals made their suicide run. *LCS(L) 64* and *Bush* shot down one of the Vals and *Colhoun* shot down the Zeke. The second Val hit on the starboard side, its bomb breaking the destroyer's keel. Fires raged throughout *Colhoun* and she was soon dead in the water. Additional aircraft bombed and crashed the two destroyers. At about 1800 *Bush* went under, her crew having been rescued by *LCS(L) 64*.

Meanwhile the situation on board *Colhoun* had grown desperate. She had been crashed, bombed, and strafed by additional aircraft and was beyond hope. With no chance of saving the ship, the CO, Cmdr. G. R. Wilson, ordered his men to abandon ship. *LCS(L)s 84* and *87* removed crewmen as *Cassin Young DD 793* stood by. *Cassin Young* attempted to tow *Colhoun*, but the heavy seas soon parted the line. By the time a fleet tug arrived on the scene, *Colhoun* had a twenty-three degree list which was increasing by the minute; half the ship was awash. Unable to save the destroyer, *Cassin Young* sank her with gunfire around midnight.[27]

As all this was taking place, *Bennett DD 473* had moved from her assigned position at RP No. 4 to cover RP No. 2, which had been vacated by *Colhoun* in her attempt to assist *Bush*. With the sinking of the two vessels, she shifted over to RP No. 1 to aid in searching for survivors. Patrolling at RP No. 4, *Bennett* and *LCS(L) 39* had been busy driving off kamikazes with their gunfire when *Bennett* was crashed by a Val at 0857. The plane slammed into her side, bounced off and sank. Its bomb penetrated the hull near the waterline and exploded inside. Damage was not severe, although the destroyer suffered three dead and eighteen wounded. *LCS(L)s 109, 110, 111*, and *114* had been support firepower in these stations and drove off or shot down several enemy aircraft.

Hyman DD 732 was operating about five miles north of Ie Shima on anti-small boat patrol on 6 April. She went to general quarters at 1553 with enemy aircraft reported in the area. American and Japanese aircraft engaged in dogfights over Ie Shima and at 1615 a Zeke,

Bush DD 529, at left, maneuvers to escape kamikaze attacks at RP No. 1 on 6 April 1945. Her maneuvering was unsuccessful and she was sunk that day. *Colhoun DD 801*, at the bottom right, is obscured by smoke from fires caused by a kamikaze hit. NARA 80G 317258.

Colhoun DD 801, having suffered a kamikaze crash, attempts to evade further attacks at RP No. 1 on 6 April 1945. She was subsequently hit again and sank later that day. NARA 80G 317257.

under pursuit by two Hellcats, headed for the destroyer. Her 5" gun disintegrated the plane at 2,500 yards. During the next five minutes *Hyman* shot down a Zeke and a Nick, but, at 1626, a Hamp made an attack on her. This plane's attack was coordinated with the Nick that had just been shot down. Gunners from *Hyman* shot a wing off the plane, but it still managed to hit the destroyer's forward torpedo tube between the two stacks. A large explosion followed quickly, either from a bomb carried by the plane or the ship's torpedoes cooking off. The plane's engine careened across the deck, exploded, and blew a hole in the deck. Gasoline fires consumed the area and 40mm ammo was jettisoned to prevent it from exploding. At about this time another Zeke made a dive on the ship, shifted its attack in the face of *Hyman*'s fire, and crashed into *Howorth DD 592* which was coming to aid her. *Howorth* was struck in the main battery director but her fires were soon extinguished. The crash caused her nine dead and fourteen wounded. Gunners on *Hyman* then shot down what they identified as a Fred, which was a German designed FW 190. Whether this identification was accurate remains to be seen. It crashed off *Hyman*'s port bow. *Sterrett DD 407*, *Rooks DD 804*, *Howorth*, and *Hyman* combined fire to account for another two Vals.[28] *Hyman* extinguished her fires, tended to her casualties and headed back to Hagushi to transfer them. She had ten dead and forty wounded. *Howorth* headed for Kerama Retto and repairs.

The destroyer escort *Wesson DE 184* was screening with *LCI(G) 452* and *LCI(M) 588* off Ie Shima on 7 April when she came under attack. Three enemy aircraft passed her bow at 0917 and she took them under fire. They may have been a diversion, as almost immediately another plane dove on her from starboard, striking her amidships. Its crash caused fires and

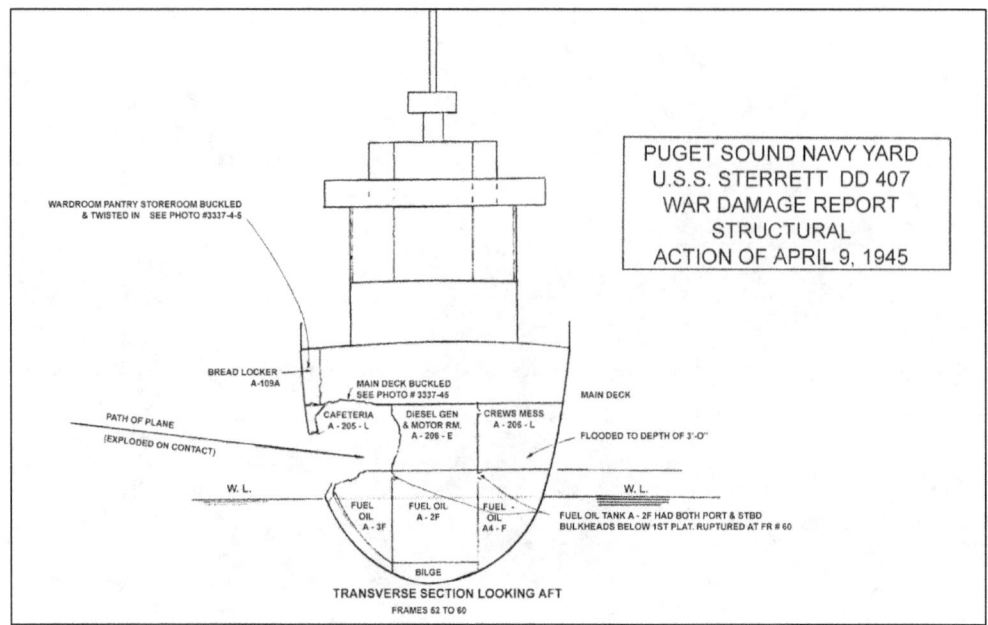

This drawing indicates the nature of the damage sustained by *Sterrett DD 407* in the kamikaze attack at Okinawa on 9 April 1945. Industrial Department, Scientific & Test Group, Puget Sound Navy Yard. *War Damage Report—USS Sterrett (DD407) Action of 9 April 1945.* Appendix B.

flooding which the destroyer escort soon brought under control. *Lang DD 399* assisted her in pumping and escorted her back to Kerama Retto. Her casualties included eight dead and twenty-three wounded.[29] *YMS 81* had a near miss that day as well. Her attacker crashed close aboard, causing minor damage. No one was injured in the attack.

Gregory DD 802, patrolling on RP No. 3 along with *LCS(L)s 37, 38,* and *40,* came under attack on 8 April. At about 1830, one of four Sonias made a suicide run on *LCS(L) 38*. Under fire by the gunboat and the destroyer, she was turned away as were two other planes attacking the ships. At 1813, one of the Sonias hit *Gregory*'s port side amidships near the water line. Fortunately the ship's gig took the hit, saving the destroyer from serious damage. Some flooding occurred, but the destroyer was soon back in action with only two men wounded in the attack.

Sterrett DD 407 was patrolling Radar Picket Station No. 4 along with *LCS(L)s 24* and *36* on 9 April when she was hit by a kamikaze. At 1825 *Sterrett*'s radar picked up incoming bogeys and the ships went to general quarters. Within minutes, five Vals were spotted approaching the ships. Four headed for *Sterrett* and she shot down three. The fourth made it through to crash into her starboard side in spite of being hit by the ship's 20mm and 40mm guns. The fifth headed for *LCS(L) 36*, but the gunboat's fire caused it to overshoot. It clipped off the top of the mast and crashed close aboard. Five of her men were wounded in the attack. On board *Sterrett* two men were wounded in the attack and the damage was quickly brought under control. She had been struck in a non-vital area and was soon underway for Pearl Harbor and repairs.[30]

Kikusui No. 1 had been the first of what would be ten raids. It was the largest series of air attacks that the Japanese would launch at Okinawa and it was deadly. Six ships were sunk and another nineteen hit with varying degrees of damage. Over fifteen hundred men were casualties, with just over half that number killed.

13. The Onslaught Continues

The American forces had landed *en masse* on the beaches at Hagushi and quickly captured the airfields at Kadena and Yontan. Awaiting the chance to attack them were the *Maru-re* pilots of the 26th SBB which was based at Itoman under Capt. Mutsuo Adachi. Their order to attack came at midnight on 8 April 1945.

> The regiment commander then gave more specific orders as follows: "All operating units to commence attack at 23:00 hours, April 8. The First Company is to take the Itoman-Kerama-Kadena route, the Second Company the Itoman-Oroku-Naha-Kadena route, and the Third Company the Itoman-Kerama-Aampa-Kadena route. All the three companies left Itoman for the assigned operations at 23:00 hours as scheduled. Although the Regiment suffered great casualties en route, its command post received a report from a company commander of the 62nd Division, who was on patrol duty on a beach north of Naha, that about 10 transports and also about 10 destroyers, minesweepers, etc. had been sunk or damaged by the Regiment's [battalion's] suicide-boats."[1]

Japanese reports were extremely optimistic. American records reveal that the only ships damaged were the destroyer *Charles J. Badger DD 657* and the transport *Starr AKA 67*.

Charles J. Badger was on a fire support station just north of Naha and about 8,000 yards off shore at 0405 on the morning of 9 April. Her main battery pointer reported:

> No reports on JP circuit in advance. Heard what sounded like two (2) cylinder engine close aboard. My impression was that it was a small plane. Explosion followed almost immediately. Silent period on JP circuit; then came report "Small craft bearing 090 heading out." Made this report to control officer. Climbed out of Director, looked on that bearing but saw nothing.[2]

The destroyer had its engines temporarily knocked out by the attack, as well as hull damage. Nearby, the destroyer *Purdy* fired on one of the boats and drove it away. A third target, the cargo ship *Starr,* was undamaged when some of her landing craft moored alongside took the brunt of the explosion. Many of the boats had been destroyed en route to the target area and still others were fired upon and sunk in the anchorage.[3] In spite of the size of the attack, the Japanese had failed to make a dent in the invasion force.

Kidd DD 661 was part of the screen covering Task Group 58.3, which was providing air support for the landing zone at Hagushi. The ships were steaming east of Okinawa when, at 1346 on 11 April, an incoming raid was picked up by *Black DD 666*. At 1354 a kamikaze dove on *Black* but was shot down by her fire and the combat air patrol. Overhead other enemy planes fell victim to the CAP flyers. At 1408 *Kidd* fired on another Japanese plane and drove it off. About the same time two enemy aircraft:

were seen in a mock dogfight behind the stern of the BLACK, which was then 1500 yards on our starboard beam. Immediately one of them began a diving turn, descended to water level and began a run on the BLACK, coming in so as to keep the BLACK directly in the line of fire of this ship. It was taken under fire by the BLACK, and upon reaching that ship pulled up sharply to clear, then resumed his course, again getting as close to the water as possible. At this time it was taken under fire by the starboard machine guns of the KIDD, but that fire, though hitting, and causing the plane to start smoking did not succeed in destroying the plane, and it crashed into the forward fireroom at the water line.[4]

The kamikaze, carrying a 551 lb. bomb, crashed the ship and penetrated its interior. The plane's bomb continued through, passing out the port side of the ship before exploding. As usual with these attacks, the plane's impact and subsequent explosion damaged fire mains and set off fires. Within five minutes the damaged area of the ship had been isolated and she was able to make twenty-two knots. *Hale DD 642* came alongside in an attempt to transfer her medical doctor to *Kidd*. At 1639 both ships came under attack by another kamikaze, but their gunfire drove it away smoking. *McNair DD 679* relieved *Hale* at 1930 and escorted *Kidd* to Task Unit 50.18.7 which was headed for Ulithi. Pumping continued for the next day or two as the ship made its way back for repairs. Among the seriously wounded in the kamikaze's crash was the ship's CO, Cmdr. H. G. Moore. Lt. B. H. Brittin, although wounded himself, was able to take temporary command and rallied the crew to fight the fires and tend to the wounded. As the ship was en route to Ulithi, Brittin's wounds finally disabled him and Lt. R. L. Kenney took temporary command. It had been an expensive event for the destroyer; thirty-eight had died and fifty-five more were wounded in the crash. *Bullard DD 660*, cruising with *Black*, watched as the destroyer was hit. She fired on *Black*'s attackers but failed to shoot any down in spite of hitting both. At 1357 an enemy plane made a run at her and passed behind her superstructure, clipping off antennae and lifelines before plummeting over the side. The destroyer escaped with minimal damage and no casualties. *Hank DD 702*, acting as a radar picket for the Task Group, was attacked by a Zeke about 1640. Her gunfire drove it off course and it crashed close aboard. Her damage was slight, but three of her men were killed and one wounded in the attack. She joined the other ships heading for Ulithi and repairs. *Bullard DD 660* also had a close call. She was operating near *Kidd* when she was attacked at 1357. Her damage was minor and she continued her operations. Also hit that day with minor damage was *Missouri BB 63*. The battleship was part of Task Group 58.4 and was near *Intrepid CV 11* and *Yorktown CV 10* on 11 April when the ships encountered enemy aircraft. The air raids began at 1110 and lasted until nearly 2400. CAPs from *Intrepid* and *Yorktown* were kept busy and shot down a number of enemy aircraft during this period. One Zeke finally got through to *Missouri* and struck her at 1440. Her action report detailed the event:

> The pilot, flying low, attempted to lift the plane above the main deck and crash. The left wing tip struck the side of the ship at frame 169 starboard about three feet below the main deck edge. The plane was then deflected towards the ship and the nose hit the ship on a butt strap at frame 160½. The propeller cut the main deck beading about frame 159. The pilot and canopy were thrown on deck and crashed into the floater net stowage aft of Quad Mount 17. Parts of the engine, ratio equipment and a machine gun were thrown about the deck. The right wing of the plane was torn loose and catapulted into the air moving forward along the starboard side; the rest of the plane falling into the water. The wing passed over the forward corner of 5" mount No. 7, damaging the left gun bloomer, across 20 mm group 11, landing on the 01 level at frame 102, inboard of 5" mount No. 3.[5]

Fires from the crash were quickly extinguished and the damage to the battleship was minor. She had one man wounded in the attack.

About the same time that *Kidd* was struck by a kamikaze, another crashed *Enterprise CV 6*, which was operating as part of Task Group 58.3. At 1410 she was struck a glancing blow by

This Japanese Zeke hit *Missouri BB 63* on 11 April 1945 causing minimal damage to the ship and wounding one man. Official U.S. Navy Photograph.

a Judy, which hit her port quarter and then crashed close aboard. Damage from this crash was slight, but another Judy hit her at 1510 starting fires which were quickly extinguished. Although she was able to resume duty two days later, she joined the group heading for Ulithi where she underwent repairs.[6] Also damaged that day was the destroyer escort *Samuel Miles DE 183*. She incurred some light damage on 11 April when a kamikaze crashed close aboard killing one of her crew.

Kikusui No. 2 savaged the ships at Okinawa on 12 April. Included in the attack were 185 kamikazes, along with 195 conventional aircraft flying escort missions and attack missions. Standing between them and the other ships at Okinawa were the radar pickets.

Purdy, *Cassin Young*, and *LCS(L)s 33, 57, 114*, and *115* patrolled RP No. 1 on 12 April. By the end of the day five of the ships would be hit by kamikazes and one sunk. Directly in the path of the Japanese aircraft flying from Kyushu, the ships at RP No. 1 began to pick up raids around 1112 on 12 April. Coming in on the radar picket station was a combination of forty Japanese aircraft, including Vals, Kates, Zekes, Oscars, and Bettys. The combat air patrols from the carriers *Petroff Bay*, *Intrepid*, *Langley*, and *Bunker Hill* were working in conjunction with the ships. In spite of their valiant efforts they would not be able to save the ships below.

Purdy and *Cassin Young* took a flight of three Vals under fire at 1337. Their combined fire shot one down, but a second dove to about five hundred feet and then headed for *Cassin Young* which maneuvered wildly to keep its guns to bear on the plane. It crashed fifteen feet off its port quarter. The third Val was shot down by the two destroyers as it prepared for a run on *Purdy*. At 1334 a fourth Val was shot down off *Purdy*'s starboard bow. Still another Val made a crash dive on the *Young*, crashing into the foremast. "This plane had strafed in its dive and exploded in mid-air forty feet above the ship, causing numerous personnel and ship casualties."[7] Within minutes another Val was shot down off the starboard beam. Overhead the combat air patrol accounted for another ten enemy aircraft. *Cassin Young* headed back to Kerama Retto. On board the destroyer one man had died and fifty-nine were wounded.

Purdy came under attack from her starboard quarter. *LCS(L) 114* and *Purdy* combined fire to shoot down the Val. Within the space of the next twenty minutes the destroyer shot down an additional three Vals. Finally another Val managed to evade the blanket of fire laid down by *Purdy* and *LCS(L) 114* and get through to the destroyer. It hit the water twenty feet off the destroyer's starboard side, bounced up and crashed into her. Its bomb was released in the action and penetrated the hull. It exploded inside the ship killing thirteen men and wounding twenty-seven. *Purdy* lost steering control, most of her internal communications, and partial power as a result of the bomb. She headed back to the anchorage to tend her wounded and repair the ship.

While *Purdy* and *Cassin Young* were fighting off kamikazes, *LCS(L) 57* came under attack as well. At 1347 the first of eight aircraft made runs on her. One was shot down fifty yards from the gunboat. Shortly thereafter, another plane began a strafing run on the ship and sharp-shooting gun crews killed the pilot. His out-of-control plane hit the forward 40mm gun tub, putting it out of action. At 1352 three Nates made a run on the ship. Two were shot down, but the third, after being hit numerous times, exploded only ten feet from the ship. The explosion blew an eight foot hole in its side. Lt. Harry L. Smith, CO of *LCS(L) 57*, took stock of his ship. Two of its three 40mm guns were out of action, the steering was out, and she was beginning to list to starboard. Emergency steering measures were taken and the ship prepared to head back to Okinawa, but her ordeal was not over. Another Nate closed on the ship, hotly pursued by CAP fighters. It went down under the combined fire of the *57* and the CAP. At 1430 another Nate slipped through the fire from the ship and the CAP and crashed

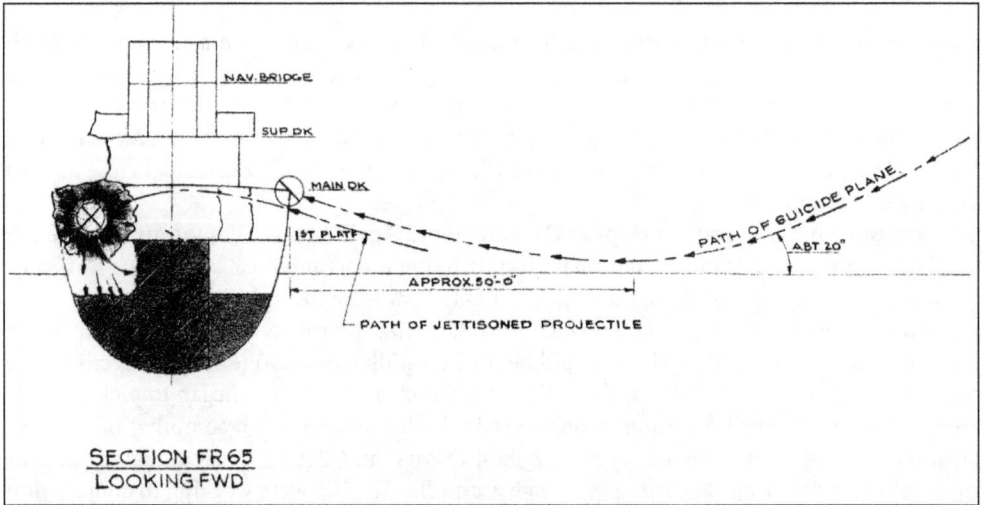

This sketch shows the damage to **Purdy DD 734** from a kamikaze bomb at Radar Picket Station # 1 off Okinawa on 12 April 1945. The Val carrying the bomb was shot down twenty feet off the ship, ricocheted off the water and hit **Purdy** in the side. Its bomb penetrated the destroyer and exploded inside. Commandant, Navy Yard, Mare Island. *U. S. S. Purdy (DD734)—War Damage Report*, 11 September 1945.

into the bow of the gunboat, disabling the 40mm bow gun and killing two men. Listing heavily to starboard, the 57 started on her journey back to Okinawa.

LCS(L) 33 had been standing by the 57 and *Purdy* and picking up men who had been blown overboard when she came under attack herself. At 1500 two Vals attacked her, one from port and one from starboard. Her gunners downed the Val to port, but the Val on the starboard side crashed her amidships and exploded. The impact broke the fire main and made firefighting impossible. The ship, a ball of fire, began to list heavily to port and the order to abandon ship was given. Her magazines began to explode from the fires, and within a short while she was barely afloat. *Purdy* sank her flaming hulk with two five-inch rounds and headed back to Okinawa.

LCS(L) 115, coming to the aid of the 33, was strafed by a Val as she attempted to pick up survivors. Although she shot the plane down twenty-five feet off her port side, two of her men were wounded. LCS(L) 114 managed to escape damage and was able to rescue men from *Purdy*. Twenty men had died and 175 were wounded on the ships at RP No. 1 that day.

On Radar Picket Station No. 2, *Stanly DD 478* was on patrol with *Lang DD 399*, *LSM(R)s 197* and *198* and *LCS(L)s 31, 52,* and *116*. At 1351 she was directed to assist *Cassin Young* at Radar Picket Station No. 1. At 1426 a Val made a suicide attempt on her but was shot down off her starboard quarter. About twenty minutes later, her lookouts were amazed to see a small aircraft approaching the ship at an extremely high rate of speed. Her action report indicated that it "outran our Combat Air Patrol."[8] Her gunners were unable to score a hit on the plane and it crashed through her bow and exploded in the water on her port bow. She had been struck by an *Oka* piloted bomb. The relatively thin plating on her hull had saved her, as the *Oka* was designed to punch through heavy armor plate prior to detonating. *Shea* was left with a hole through her bow and three men injured. Moments later, a second *Oka* was observed headed toward the ship. It was taken under fire by automatic weapons and hit several times. A tip of its wing came off and it passed just over the ship clipping off the ensign. Two to three hundred yards past the ship the pilot tried to bank for another run but hit the water and exploded. *Stanly* had a lucky day; the potential for disaster had been great.

Other radar picket stations were to prove hazardous on 12 April as well. Patrolling Radar Picket Station No. 14 was *Mannert L. Abele DD 733*, along with *LSM(R)s 189* and *190*. At 1320 an incoming raid of three Vals was reported closing on the station. Within minutes the aircraft were spotted and dove on the ship. One was hit by both *Abele* and *LSM(R) 189* before it crashed into the sea close aboard the LSM(R). *LSM(R) 190* shot down a second Val which narrowly missed her. Shortly thereafter two Kates tried to crash the *189* but were shot down close aboard. One clipped the ship's conning tower, knocking two men overboard. *LSM(R) 190* then successfully fired on another Val, sending it into the sea. *Walter C. Wann DE 412* had a close scrape at 1418 when she shot down a Val which tried to crash her. The plane hit the water twenty feet off her port bow. One man was injured but the ship was unharmed in the attack. By 1400 the air was abuzz with numerous enemy planes and the destroyer radioed for additional CAP planes to cover her. Four Lillys appeared and one made a run on the destroyer. However, it gave up in the face of the ship's fierce gunfire. Shortly thereafter, three Zekes had better luck. Two tried to crash the ship which successfully shot one down. At 1445 the second hit the ship's after fireroom on the starboard side causing serious damage. Its bomb went off inside the ship's engine room and the destroyer began to lose headway. Still another attack awaited the destroyer.

A few hours earlier a flight of nine Betty bombers had taken off from Kanoya Air Base in Southern Kyushu. Each carried an *Oka* and they were headed directly for the ships at RP No. 14. Arriving overhead near the radar picket station, the crew on one of the Bettys prepared to launch its flying bomb. At about the same time that the Zeke hit the *Abele*, the *Oka* dropped from the Betty and headed in toward the destroyer. Once glide speed had been attained the pilot, Lt. (jg) Saburo Doi, fired its rocket engines. It accelerated to over 400 miles per hour within a minute or two. Cmdr. A. E. Parker, the CO of *Mannert L. Abele*, later wrote:

> 1446 — A second plane was sighted skimming water at a terrific speed on starboard beam. This plane was a small mid wing job with no projections, large fuselage, stubby wings and painted light blue-grey or aluminum. By this time ship had lost nearly all headway. This missile hit at waterline abreast No. one fireroom causing another terrific explosion and shock. Ship was felt to buckle rapidly. Executive Officer who had appeared on bridge was sent below to direct Repair Parties and abandoning ship.
>
> 1448 — Bow and stern sections parted and sinking rapidly with bow and fantail rising. The bow section took an initial list to port on parting from stern section. Bridge personnel were directed to abandon ship. In a matter of seconds water was up to after bridge deck gratings at which time the last of bridge personnel pushed themselves out into water.
>
> 1449 — Bow and stern sections disappeared below water.[9]

Those who escaped from the ship faced additional danger. A Zeke strafed the survivors and dropped a bomb on them, wounding more of the men. Nearby, *LSM(R) 189* shot down a Kate which was making a run on her. In spite of being hit by fire continuously, the Kate persisted and crashed into the ship's conning tower wounding a number of men. With the immediate action over, the two LSM(R)s picked up survivors from *Abele*. At 1646 *Jeffers DMS 27* and *LCS(L)s 11* and *13* arrived on the scene to assist in rescue attempts. *Jeffers* had narrowly escaped an *Oka* attack at RP Station No. 12 about the same time that *Abele* was hit. She collected survivors from the two LSM(R)s and headed back to the anchorage. *Mannert L. Abele* was the first ship to be sunk by an *Oka* but would not be the last.

The destroyer escort *Rall DE 304* was operating as part Task Group 51.5, the anti-submarine screen, off the Hagushi landing beaches on 12 April. This was a crucial task as the supplies and reinforcements for the troops ashore were continually unloaded in that area. By early afternoon many planes had managed to slip past the radar picket ships and their accompanying CAP to make it to the Okinawa area. *Rall* went to general quarters at 1335 and saw no less than twelve raids approach the area during the next hour and a half. The tenth raid was the one that caused her trouble. Corsairs were seen shooting down enemy aircraft to the north, and as the planes came into range, they were tracked and then fired upon. A Nate peeled off from the group of enemy planes and came at *Rall* from her starboard side. True to kamikaze tactics, a second plane made a run on her from port. Both planes were taken under fire and the ship increased its speed to eighteen knots. The plane to port was shot down, but the plane to starboard came in only ten feet off the water, made it through the ship's fire, and crashed into the starboard side of the DE just under the deck level. Its 551-lb. bomb penetrated the ship and passed completely through, exploding fifteen feet off the port side. Two Vals then dove at the ship; one was shot down and the other turned off smoking. A third Val approached from the starboard bow, ran into a shell from the ship's 3"/50, and disintegrated 300 yards away. Almost simultaneously the ship was strafed by an Oscar. Its shells hit a depth charge locker and caused an explosion that blew three men off the ship. In the space of about three minutes, *Rall* had suffered a number of kamikaze attacks, but had survived. *Rall*'s CO, Lt. Cmdr. C. B. Taylor, Jr., led his men in quickly extinguishing the ensuing fires. *Rall* had twenty-one dead and thirty-eight wounded. She tied up to *Pinkney APH 2* to transfer her wounded and moved to *Clamp ARS 33* for temporary repairs the next day. On 15 April she went to Kerama Retto for further repairs and then on to Ulithi to complete them.[10]

The light minelayer *Lindsey DM 32* was also a part of Task Group 51.5 screening the Hagushi area. She was heading for the area near Zampa Misaki, north of the Hagushi landing beaches, to aid *Jeffers DMS 27*. *Jeffers* had been assisting *LSM(R) 189* after she was hit by a kamikaze. At 1445 she observed the ships of Task Force 54, just east of her, come under attack.

Within minutes she had three torpedo bombers off her starboard bow and took them under fire. These were followed by four Vals which she also fired on. The first group turned off, but the Vals split into two formations and came at her from port and starboard. At 1450 one of the Vals crashed her starboard side and, in less than a minute, a second Val hit her port bow near her No. 1 gun. The force of the second explosion blew out the fires from the first, and about that time the ship went dead in the water. However, the blast had basically demolished her bow. Burning gasoline covered the surface of the sea and her CO, Cmdr. C. E. Chambers, ordered her full astern to back out of the conflagration. At this point, *Lindsey* was only six miles from Aguni Shima and began to back towards that island. *Champion AM 314* closed on the ship to lend medical assistance and, at 1701, the fleet tug *Tawakoni ATF 114* arrived to tow her in. This was a slow process as a large piece of the ship's plating hung off the starboard bow into the water, acting as "a sea anchor and as a huge rudder."[11] The wounded were transferred to *PCE 853*. She listed eight known dead, forty-six missing, and sixty wounded.

The transports were also hit on 12 April. *Minot Victory,* under Master A. Jensen, had arrived the day before as part of a convoy. She was anchored at Hagushi when she came under attack at 1455 by a single engine kamikaze that approached her from starboard, only twenty feet off the water. She opened fire with her starboard 20mm guns when the aircraft was only 1,500 yards out. Her gunfire was effective and the aircraft went out of control, rising enough to miss the hull and crash into the ship's No. 4 kingpost. The ensuing crash sent flaming gaso-

The bow of *Lindsey DM 32* was demolished when she was crashed by a Val on 12 April 1945. NARA 80G 330108.

line over the bridge area, burning several members of the armed guard, of whom five were wounded. In spite of the crash, the ship suffered little damage aside from a number of .30 caliber bullet holes resulting from the plane's strafing.[12]

Zellars DD 777 had been part of Task Force 54 sent to intercept the *Yamato* force. With the possibility of large air attacks, the Task Force remained together. At 1443 the first enemy planes were detected at a range of nine miles. *Zellars*' action report revealed that

> at 1450 observed three Jills, 15 feet above the water, making a coordinated attack on this vessel from port quarter. Commenced firing, rang up 25 knots, and put rudder hard left to bring all guns to bear. Planes were sighted at about 5000 yards, fire was opened at 4500 yards; the first plane was splashed about 1800 yards from the ship, the second was splashed about 3000 yards from the ship and rudder shifted to hard right. Fire was shifted to the third plane and hits were observed with 40MM but the computer solution had not caught up to him when he crashed into the port side of Mount Two handling room.... The plane carried a bomb estimated at 500 KG [1,102 lbs.] which crossed the ship through several light bulkheads, penetrated the main deck on the starboard side and exploded in the scullery passage adjacent to plotting room.[13]

Firefighters effectively put out the ship's fires within a short period of time. However, in the midst of her recovery, another plane made a run on the ship but was brought down by the combined fire of *Zellars* and surrounding ships. *Bennion DD 662* came alongside and transferred her medical officer to assist with the wounded. Within an hour after her kamikaze attack she was heading for Kerama Retto and repairs. In the "Recommendations and Conclusions" section of her action report for the attack she noted that a lone destroyer might be able to shoot down two attacking aircraft, but if there were three, one was sure to make it through. Also suggested was that a new "weapon be developed, such as a cluster of rockets, with range of about 500 yards, locally trained and elevated, to take care of planes inside of 5" gun range."[14] Suggestions like this one were sometimes seen in action reports, but little could be done with only a few months left in the war.

Tennessee BB 43 was the flagship of Task Force 54 and was near *Zellars* when that destroyer was crashed. Soon it was her turn. Her lookouts observed a group of around seven Vals and Kates operating in the skies near her. Five of these made a run on the battleship and four were shot down close aboard. However, one Val made it through and struck the ship on the starboard side aft, wiping out a quad 40mm gun and hitting two 20mm guns and then another quad 40mm before sliding over the side. Its bomb, estimated to be a 250 lb. device, penetrated the deck and exploded below. Sheets of flame rose from the area and many were killed. For Cpl. W. H. Putnam, one of the ship's Marine contingent, it was to be an interesting time. Putnam was at his battle station as pointer on the Quad 40mm mount No. 9 when the kamikaze hit. He later reported:

> Myers, first loader, told me to jump down in the bucket. I couldn't get out of my seat, so I grabbed hold of the sight (ring sight) and tried to jump over it. My intentions when I jumped was to land in the bucket, but I went over the side, not realizing it until I hit the water. As I came up from the water there was the plane, or what was left of it, burning on the water. I couldn't swear it was the plane, probably part of it or pieces of it. The whole area around me was on fire. Kept my eyes closed and dove under and came up where the water wasn't burning. That was the last thing I saw until I got on this raft. The raft was a long piece of 12 × 12 and I think it might have been a raft from the ship. It was all broken up. I don't know how long it was before I got on the raft, maybe five or ten minutes, maybe longer than that. When I saw a parachute was hanging on the raft with a headless body on it (body identified by the destroyer that picked me up as the Jap pilot). That's the only body I saw.[15]

Putnam was picked up later by a destroyer. *Tennessee* lost twenty-two men and had seventy-three wounded.

At about the same time that *Zellars* and *Lindsey* were attacked, *Whitehurst DE 634* was also struck. She had been on anti-submarine patrol to the southwest of Kerama Retto when she was crashed by a Val. At 1442 her lookouts spotted four Vals approaching the area, one of which attacked *Crosley APD 87*. Two others were engaged by the CAP, but the fourth turned off and made a run on *Whitehurst*. It dove on her from port, and her 20mm guns scored a number of hits but could not stop it. It crashed into the port side of *Whitehurst's* bridge. As the Val was in its final moments, two other planes attacked *Whitehurst*, one from aft and one from the starboard beam. Both went down after being hit by the destroyer escort's guns. The entire bridge area was engulfed in flames and communications were out. Everyone in the Combat Information Center (C.I.C.) and the pilot house was killed in the crash, as were most in the radio room below. The forward gun crews had lost a large percentage of their men, and those not killed outright were seriously injured. For the next hour her crew fought the fires, and by 1610 had them all out. In the meantime, *Crosley APD 87* and *Vigilance AM 324* had come alongside to render aid. Emergency steering measures were put into use and *Whitehurst* made it back to Kerama Retto at 1745 where she would undergo repairs.[16] Thirty-seven had been killed and the same number wounded in the attack.

On 13 April, *Connolly DE 306* had a near miss as a group of five Vals appeared overhead under attack by Hellcats. One broke away and made a dive on the destroyer escort. Sharpshooting gun crews hit the plane and caused it to go out of control, splashing only thirty feet off the starboard bow of the ship. The ship suffered minor damage to her sound gear and surface search radar when the Val's bomb went off, but repairs were quickly made and the ship continued operating.

April 14 to 15 gave the ships at Okinawa a brief respite from the *Kikusui* attacks, but *New York BB 34* had a narrow miss on April 14 as a kamikaze hit her catapult and spotting plane but caused no further damage. *Sigsbee DD 502* was not so fortunate; the kamikaze that hit her killed twenty-two of her men and injured seventy-four. *Sigsbee*, *Harrison DD 573*, *Hunt DD 674*, and *Dashiell DD 659* were on patrol with two other destroyers of Task Group 58.8 northeast of Okinawa when incoming Japanese planes were reported. At 1355 a twin-engine bomber approached the ships followed by a CAP fighter. The fighter was seen to flame and go down, probably from the bomber's tail gun. A few minutes later four aircraft appeared on *Sigsbee's* port beam and seemed to engage in a dogfight. A Judy broke away from the melee and made a dive on *Hunt*, cruising nearby. Four CAP planes followed it and then turned away, as it looked as though it was about to crash into the sea. This was not to be so. The plane recovered from the dive and headed for *Hunt* at only twenty-five feet off the water. *Sigsbee* and *Hunt* both fired on the plane which grazed *Hunt* as it crashed close aboard at 1348, wounding five of her crew. Other enemy planes were under attack by the CAP fighters. A Zeke closed on *Sigsbee* from her starboard bow and the ship took it under fire. Cmdr. G. P. Chung-Hoon ordered full left rudder and flank speed to bring all his guns to bear on the approaching plane. Unfortunately, the kamikaze came too close before the guns could train on it. It hit *Sigsbee's* fantail and its bomb caused a large explosion. The destroyer's engines were stopped and she went dead in the water. Her aft guns were mostly damaged and of no use in the following minutes. She jettisoned her depth charges and torpedoes in order to maintain stability. As she sat dead in the water, four more planes tried to finish her off. A Zeke peeled off from the group and attacked her, but fire from *Sigsbee* and her companion destroyers shot down the would-be kamikaze. Another Zeke closed on her starboard quarter and was shot down. The remaining two Zekes made runs on the destroyers but both went down in flames. *Sigsbee* had lost steering control, and her port engine was out of commission. Her main deck from frame 170 aft was gone and her stern began to settle, but pumping stabilized the situation. *Dashiell* began to tow her back to safety at 1623 and was soon relieved of the task by *Miami CL 89* and then *Munsee AT 107*.[17] She arrived at Apra Harbor, Guam, on 20 April with her main deck

Sigsbee DD 502 is down by the stern after a kamikaze strike on 14 April 1945. This photograph was taken from *Miami CL 89*. NARA 80G 328580.

awash. She would undergo temporary repairs in safety. After repairs at Guam made her seaworthy again, she made her way to Pearl Harbor where a new sixty-foot section of stern was welded on. Her losses were twenty-two dead and seventy-four wounded.

Gladiator AM 319 escaped serious damage on 12 April. She fired on and destroyed a kamikaze, splashing it off her starboard beam. The resulting rain of debris caused some minor damage to the ship.

YMS 331 was sweeping in the area between Kerama Retto and Okinawa with CTG 52.6.3 at 0120 on the morning of 16 April when she was attacked by a *Shinyo*. It approached from her port quarter, swung astern, and came in on her starboard quarter. The ship's 20mm guns hit the boat and blew it up only ten feet off the ship. The concussion rocked the ship but no one was injured and no damage to the ship occurred.[18]

Kikusui No. 3 was launched on 16 April and involved 165 planes sent to attack the American ships at Okinawa. *Wilson DD 408* was on patrol off Kerama Retto when she observed two Japanese aircraft and took them under fire. One made a run on her and was shot down seventy-five yards to starboard, ricocheted off the water and hit *Wilson* in her 40mm gun tub. It then spun across the deck and landed in the water on the port side. Its 220-lb. bomb penetrated the ship, but only the booster charge went off, causing slight damage. It was removed intact from the ship a couple of days later. *Wilson* had five dead and three injured in the attack, but damage to the ship was minimal. She was repaired and back in action within a few days.

LCI(G) 407 was on patrol east of Okinawa the morning of 16 April when she came under attack. A Val was spotted flying low over the island of Taka Hamare and circling toward the gunboat. She brought all guns to bear on the plane, which now approached from her starboard side. "The Val was hit repeatedly as he came in and 40 mm shells were observed striking the engine of the plane when it was as close as 50 yards.... The Val did not catch on fire but lurched when hit by 40mm. The plane crashed into the starboard ramp forward and the forecastle. Gasoline and water sprayed the ship when the plane hit, but there was no fire."[19] The plane's bomb went off close aboard, holing the ship, but damage was minimal. Only one man had a minor injury. The pilot's lifeless body was found in the boatswain's locker after it was ejected from his plane.

Bowers APD 40 was operating in the anti-submarine screen about six miles north of Ie Shima. She had shot down one plane early in the morning, but around 0939 was attacked by two Vals. Her action report reveals the details:

> When the two aircraft bore 320 relative and at a range of 4–5 thousand yards, they separated. One approached directly toward the ship. This one was shot down at a range of about 1000 yards. In the meantime the other aircraft, later identified as a Val, was on a course parallel with but opposite to our own, flying down our port beam. This aircraft remained at a range of about 4000 or 5000 yards. All three guns of the main battery and the 1.10 quad mount were firing at it. On reaching a point just abaft the port beam, the aircraft turned directly toward us. All port side guns opened fire. Some 20mm and 1.10 projectiles could be seen bursting in the plane, but no flame resulted nor were any parts shot away. The plane attacked in a glide strafing the decks. One man was wounded from the machine gun fire. It is this observer's opinion that the pilot intended to crash into the ship on this run, but in the face of heavy A/A fire became confused and missed by a scant few feet. The enemy plane passed directly over the after 3"/50 gun so low that if the gun had been elevated a little more, it would have crashed. The aircraft almost struck the water on the starboard side, but regained control and commenced gaining altitude.... When the plane had reached a range of about 1000 to 1500 feet and an altitude of about 50 feet, it began a counter-clockwise turn with the obvious intention of re-attacking from dead ahead or on the starboard bow. The Captain began to maneuver the ship to try to keep the Val on the starboard beam. However, in a continuous, approaching sweep, the plane came in from a relative bearing of about 060, crashing into the upper forward section of the flying bridge at the Asdic hut level. The bulkhead was penetrated by the impact, and through a long hole, the aircraft embedded itself in the Asdic hut. There was an instantaneous explosion of high octane gasoline with resultant fire enveloping the entire upper part of the bridge and pilot house.[20]

After the fires were brought under control and she headed back to safety, she counted forty-eight dead and fifty-six wounded among her crew. On the casualty list was her CO Lt. Cmdr. C.F. Highfield and the ship's XO, Lt. S. A. Haavik, both of whom were seriously wounded. Her Gunnery Officer, Communication Officer, ASW/CIC Officer, and Supply Officer were on the bridge at the time of the crash. All four of them perished.

Shortly after *Bowers* was struck, *Harding DMS 28* came under attack by two Vals. The high-speed minesweeper had been sent to accompany *Shea DM 30* at Radar Picket Station No. 14. She shot the first Val down to port at 0958 and then shifted her attention to the second plane which was attacking her starboard beam. Her gunners hit the plane numerous times and it crashed in the water just short of its target. Water and debris showered the ship and the Val's bomb exploded underwater, holing her hull. The speed of the ship caused her to scoop water into the hole and within minutes she was listing severely to port. Once the ship lost headway she began to right herself but was still down by the head and listing ten degrees to port. She was able to make it back to Kerama Retto under her own power after transferring her casualties. She had twenty-two dead and ten wounded.[21]

The oiler *Taluga AO 62* was one of those floating bombs. Her cargo of 300,000 gallons of aviation fuel would make a devastating explosion if it were to go off. Fortunately for her, the kamikaze that struck her bridge, spun off and crashed into her forward well deck and did not set off the gas. Her fires were quickly extinguished to the relief of all ships in the area, but she had twelve men injured.

The damage to *Bowers DE 637* after the kamikaze crash of 16 April 1945. U.S.S. *Bowers (DE-637)* Serial No. 001. *Damage, Detailed Report of.* 29 April 1945. Enclosure (S), No. 8.

The carriers of Task Force 58 had cruised north to attack the kamikaze's airfields on Kyushu and then returned to the area of Okinawa. *Intrepid CV 11* was a part of Task Group 58.4, steaming east of Okinawa on 16 April. The carrier went to general quarters at 1327 as incoming flights of enemy aircraft were spotted close to the ships.

> The first plane approached the Intrepid from dead ahead and it was shot down just off the starboard bow. It was identified as a Tony. A few seconds after a second plane attacked, approaching from ahead. This was a Zeke and was shot down by fire from the entire Task Group; just off the port quarter. The third plane attacked from astern, changed its course, and dived at the Missouri. It was shot down prior to completing its attack. At 1336 two planes attacked the Intrepid from astern, the first of which was shot down and crashed to starboard. The second plane was hit but continued its run and crashed on the flight deck. The engine and parts of the plane pierced the flight deck crashing on the hangar deck carrying what was estimated to be a 250 kilogram [551 lbs.] APA bomb. The bomb dished the armored hangar deck about 4", then apparently exploded about 3 feet above the deck forward of its first contact. This explosion pierced the armor leaving a hole 5 × 5 feet. The hole in the flight deck was 12 × 14 feet. The crash and bomb explosion started large fires on the hangar deck among planes parked there. The fire was extinguished in about one hour. However, 40 planes on the hangar deck were ruined by the explosion, fire and salt water drenching of the sprinkler system. No. 3 elevator was damaged beyond repair.[22]

The indomitable carrier resumed station. Although damage to her was slight, she had ten dead and eighty-seven wounded. *Missouri*, operating nearby, had a close call when the Zeke mentioned above clipped her stern crane and crashed just off her stern with a violent explosion. It showered the aft end of the ship with debris, but there was little damage and no casualties.

Of the many battles at the Okinawan radar picket stations, the one at RP No. 1 on 16

April was among the most intense. Pitted against the kamikazes that day were *Laffey DD 724* and *LCS(L)s 51* and *116*. By the end of the day, all three ships would be hit and forty-three men would be dead, with an additional eighty-four wounded. Although the station was covered by a combat air patrol of VF-10 Corsairs from *Intrepid CV 11*, there were so many kamikazes in the area that they were just outnumbered. Attacks on *Laffey* began around 0827 when a raid of approximately fifty planes approached the station. At 0830 lookouts on *Laffey* spotted four Vals about eight miles from the ship. Her gunners opened fire and the group split in two, approaching from each side of the ship. Two were shot down to starboard at ranges of 3,000 and 9,000 yards and the other two shot down to port, with an assist by an LCS(L). Simultaneously, two Judys dove on the ship, one on each beam. The one to port strafed the ship on the way in and wounded several men. Both were shot down, but the one to port exploded near the number two stack causing some minor damage. At 0839 another Val attacked from the port bow. Hit by fire from the 5" gun and the port machine guns, it struck a glancing blow on top of gun mount three and crashed in the water. Six minutes elapsed before another Judy was shot down on the starboard beam, but another Judy came in from the port bow and crashed into the gun mounts of group 23, putting both the No. 43 and 44 20mm mounts out of commission. Gasoline covered the area and started fires. Moments later *Laffey* was struck by a Val, putting her No. 3 5" mount out of commission. The plane's bomb exploded, starting fires and wounding a number of men.

> This plane was followed by another on the starboard quarter which dropped bomb two feet inboard of deck edge to starboard aft of mount three and then crashed into the side of mount three. Shortly thereafter an unidentified Jap plane came out of the sun in a steep glide, then leveled off when just above the water and dropped bomb which landed on the port quarter above the propeller guard, possibly an attempt at skip bombing. Plane was under brief fire by after 20MM mount of group 24 but the plane made his escape apparently unharmed. The bomb struck the ship at or just below the deck edge and exploded in 20MM magazine C-310M. Flying fragments from this explosion ruptured hydraulic leads in the steering gear room and jammed the rudder while it was 26 degrees to port. After that, evasive maneuvers were confined to rapid acceleration and deceleration, as the ship swung through tight circles with full engine power still available.[23]

Two more kamikazes followed, both hitting the after deckhouse. An Oscar, with a Corsair in hot pursuit, sped over the ship and clipped the SC antenna, knocking it off. The Oscar, having been hit by fire from *Laffey*, crashed to starboard. With his plane damaged in the melee, the Corsair pilot bailed out and his plane went down. A Judy crashed close board and the explosion from the plane and its bomb knocked out electric power to the No. 2 5" mount.

The crew of *Laffey* had a brief respite, but the next attacks were not far off. As they tended to their ship, its wounded and dead, another Val dropped a bomb just off the port side at 0906, causing additional damage. The CAP quickly shot him down. Within seconds, another Val made a run on the ship from the starboard bow and dropped its bomb, wiping out the 20mm Group 21 guns. Fire from the ship caused him to overshoot and he went down under fire from the CAP. CAP fighters followed another Judy in from the port bow and he flamed under the combined fire from the ship and a Corsair, splashing close to the destroyer. This was the final attack of the day and *Laffey* had survived, although most of her guns had been damaged or put entirely out of commission. Cmdr. Julian Becton, the CO of the ship, summed up the situation:

> During the eighty minute action the ship was attacked by a total of twenty-two planes, being struck by eight enemy planes, seven of which were with suicidal intent, the eighth being the Val who dropped a bomb on the fantail and then knocked off the starboard yardarm as he passed over the ship.
>
> Five of the seven planes which struck the ship inflicted heavy personnel and material damage.

Besides the planes which crashed into the ship with their bombs still aboard, four bombs were dropped on the ship, three of which struck the fantail. The ship's gunnery personnel shot down nine of these twenty-two attacking planes.[24]

Laffey was taken in tow by *Macomb DMS 23*. *PCE 851* evacuated the wounded and later transferred them to a hospital ship. *Pakana ATF 108* took over the tow at 1430, and *Tawakani ATF 114* came alongside to assist in pumping out the injured destroyer. She had suffered thirty-one dead and seventy-two wounded in the battle.

LCS(L) 51 also saw her share of the action that day. At 0815, as *Laffey* was under attack, a Val made a run on the gunboat. Taken under fire by the *51*'s 20mm and 40mm guns, the plane hit the water near her. At 0850 she shot down another Val that was diving toward *Laffey* as the plane passed in front of the ship. Still another plane crossed her stern heading for *Laffey*, and this was also shot down by the gunboat's sharp-shooting gun crews. Fifty minutes later the *51* took another Val under fire as it dove on her port bow and sent it to a watery grave. Another Val attacked the gunboat at 1010. This plane came in low on the port side, and fire from the ship blew it apart only about twenty-five away. Its engine continued on and struck the ship just under the deck bead where it became embedded. Twenty minutes later the gunboat's lookouts spotted a Zeke to starboard heading for *Laffey*. They shot it down promptly and then watched as *Laffey* took its last hit from another Japanese plane. *LCS(L) 51* had a lucky day; she had shot down six kamikazes and had no wounded or dead among her complement. Her only real damage was a souvenir Val engine embedded in her hull. She cruised the area picking up men who had been blown overboard from the *Laffey* and assisting the destroyer as she reorganized for the trip back to the anchorage.[25]

Bryant DD 665 had been patrolling on Radar Picket Station No. 2 and came to the aid of *Laffey*. She soon found herself in the midst of the brawl. At 0934, as she headed toward *Laffey*, she was attacked by six Zekes. She shot one down and the second was seen smoking as it crashed into her bridge area. Its bomb penetrated her hull causing a great deal of damage to the interior departments of the bridge area, but her hull was still sound. Her crew's attempts at firefighting were successful and, within a short time, the fires were out. She sustained casualties numbering thirty-four dead and thirty-three wounded. For her the war was over. She soon headed back to the states for repairs.[26]

LCS(L) 116 was not so lucky. She fired on her first Val at 0840, but it was out of range. At 0905 three Japanese planes made a run on the gunboat. Two were turned away by the ship's gunfire, but the third crashed into her aft twin 40mm gun. Its bomb went off, killing and injuring men in the area. Two more planes attacked the *116*. A Hellcat from the CAP had one blazing as it headed toward the ship, and the gunners on *116* finished it off. It hit the water 200 yards away. The second plane clipped the antenna as it flew over. Numerous hits from the ship's guns sent it into the water one hundred yards to starboard. With the action over, the officers and crew assessed the damage. Wounded men were transferred to *Macomb DMS 23*. *LCS(L) 32* began to tow the ship back to the anchorage and *ATR 51* completed the mission. *LCS(L) 116* had suffered twelve dead and twelve wounded.[27]

Patrolling on Radar Picket Station No. 14 on 16 April 1945 were *Pringle DD 477*, *Hobson*, *DMS 26*, *LSM(R) 191*, and *LCS(L) 34*. A radar picket patrol consisting of two VMF-323 Corsairs and a CAP of four Corsairs from VMF-224 covered the ships from overhead. *Pringle*'s CIC picked up incoming enemy aircraft about 0815. Fifteen minutes later the ships spotted a Zeke at about 12,000 yards making a run on the destroyer. They took evasive action and a 5" round from *Pringle* connected. It went down 2,000 yards from the ship. At 0910 three Vals were spotted approaching the ships and were taken under fire. One low flying Val crashed after flying through a shell splash which evidently confused or startled the would-be kamikaze. A second Val made it through a hail of gunfire from the rapidly turning ships and crashed *Pringle* behind

LCS(L) 116 had damage to her aft 40mm gun tub after a kamikaze attack. NARA 80G 342581.

The engine from a Japanese Zeke protrudes from the side of *LCS(L) 51* after she was attacked at Radar Picket Station No. 1 on 16 April 1945. Official U.S. Navy Photograph.

The *Aichi D3A Type 99* carrier bomber was code named Val. Photograph courtesy the National Archives.

The *Yokosuka D4Y Suisei*, or Judy, was frequently used in kamikaze attacks at Okinawa. NARA 80G 169285.

the base of her No. 1 stack. The ensuing explosion from the Val's 1,102 lb. bomb was the death blow; the force of the blast buckled *Pringle*'s keel, breaking her in half. Lt. Cmdr. J. L. Kelley, Jr., the ship's CO, gave the order to abandon ship and she went down within five minutes in 500 fathoms of water. *Pringle*'s casualties were sixty-five dead and 110 wounded.

Hobson, cruising nearby, had managed to shoot down one of the planes but could not save her companion. Shortly after *Pringle* was hit, a Val made a run on the mine sweeper. *Hobson*'s gunners blew it apart close aboard but its bomb, estimated at 250 lb., penetrated the minesweeper amidships, exploding inside. The ship was still afloat and functioning although damaged. She lost four men with another eight wounded.

The support ships, *LCS(L) 34* and *LSM(R) 191*, came under attack as they headed for *Pringle* and *Hobson*. Three Vals made a run on the *34* which drove off one and shot down two. *LSM(R) 191* accounted for one kamikaze and drove off another. The support ships commenced rescuing survivors when the action subsided. *PCE(R) 852* arrived at the station and began the task of transferring survivors from the other ships.

Kikusui No. 3 had been costly. *Pringle* had been sunk. *Bowers* and *Laffey* were seriously damaged. Twelve additional ships had been hit by the kamikazes with varying degrees of damage. A total of 171 men had died and 299 were wounded.

The Suicide Boats Return

Both the Japanese navy and army had demonstrated the use of their suicide boats during the campaign for the Philippines. The interrogation of captured Japanese boat operators in that area had indicated the presence of large numbers of such boats at Okinawa.[28] Accordingly, the American navy decided that destruction of these boats prior to the invasion was imperative. It was known that many of the boats were in the Kerama Retto area, a group of islands that would have other valuable uses as well. As a part of the capture of Kerama Retto, just prior to the actual invasion of Okinawa proper, it was determined that all efforts should be made to suppress the Japanese attempt to launch suicide boats. Numbers of the small amphibious gunboats, such as LCS(L)s, LCI(G)s, LCI(M)s, and LCI(R)s were involved in the effort.

Although the initial landings at Okinawa had taken place two weeks before, there were still plenty of suicide boats remaining in the area to cause problems. From 15 to 16 April *LCI(G) 659* was on patrol near the town of Naha. She reported:

> At 2335 (K), 15 April and again at 0225 (K), 16 April, 1945, this ship contacted and sank two Japanese small suicide craft. The first was detected by a cruiser initially and shortly afterwards by this vessel. We approached to about 300 yards of the boat and then illuminated the target and opened fire with two 20 MM's and one .50 caliber machine gun. The boat, underway and proceeding at a slow but increasing speed in the opposite direction, caught fire almost immediately and a few seconds later exploded and sank, the explosive charges it carried presumably causing the explosion.
>
> The second boat was contacted by radar at 0218 (K); we closed the target and when about 250 yards from it, illuminated it and opened fire. Three 20 MM's and two .50 caliber machine guns riddled the boat, but it did not catch fire or explode as the previous one had, and at first it attempted evasive action to keep out of our lights. It suddenly disappeared altogether from sight and from the radar screen and was assumed to have sunk as no further trace of it could be found.[29]

Benham DD 796 was operating as a radar picket for TG 58.6 along with six other destroyers. They were east of Okinawa on 17 April when they came under attack. A large raid of about fifteen to twenty planes headed for the pickets. The CAP was controlled by *Cushing DD 797* which soon accounted for several of the enemy planes. This action caused the remaining raid to split and head in different directions. At 0824 two Georges approached the ship but were shot down by the CAP. At 0940 the combined fire of the destroyers brought down another plane which crashed inside the formation. *Benham* then came under attack. At 0945 a George dove on *Colahan DD 658*, leveled off at the last minute, and headed for *Benham*'s bridge. *Benham* turned sharply to left to bring her guns to bear and went to flank speed. After it was hit numerous times by fire from the destroyer, the plane began to slip out of control,

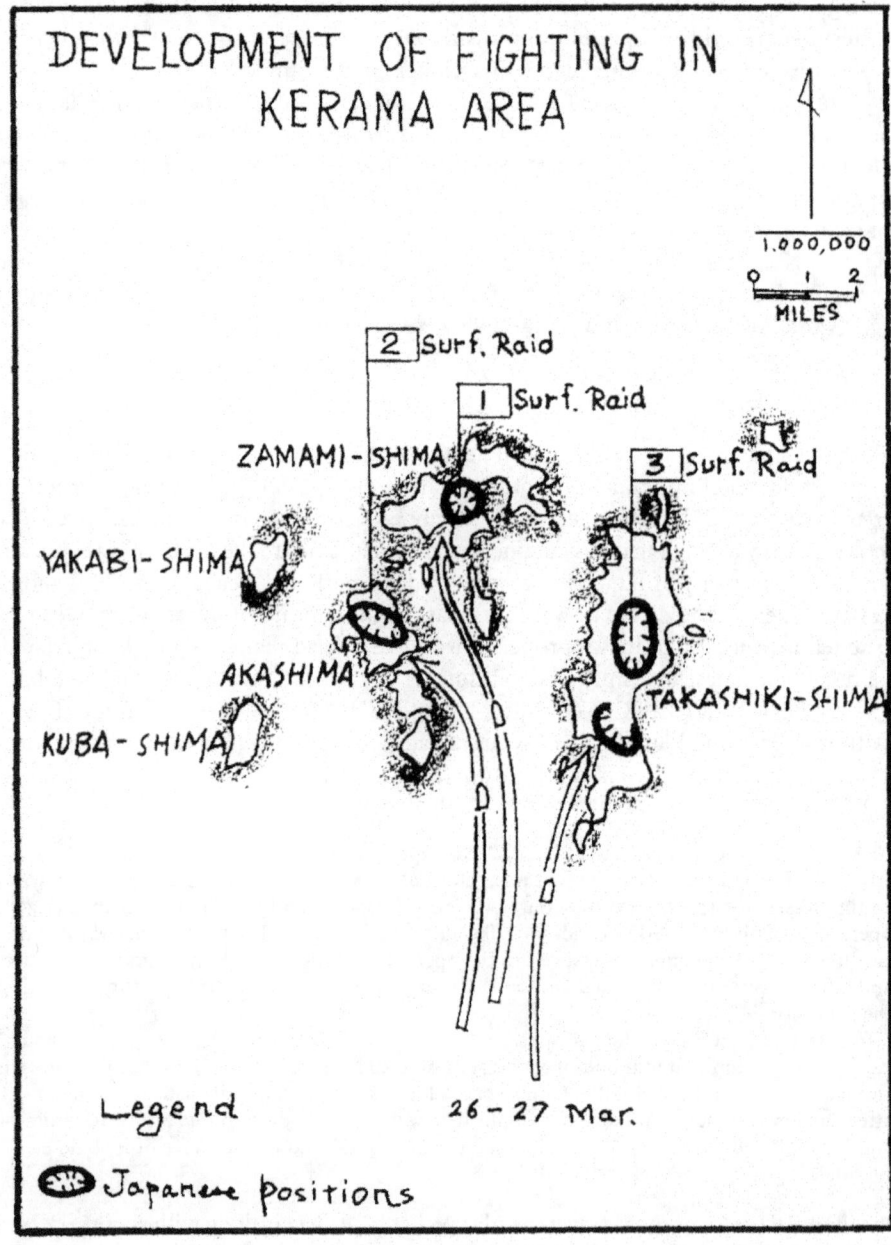

This map of the Kerama Retto islands shows the location of the Naval Surface Raiding Squadrons. Military History Section — General Headquarters Far East Command Military Intelligence Section General Staff. *Japanese Monograph No. 135 Okinawa Operations Record*, p. 154.

LCS(L) crewmen examine a captured *Shinyo* at Kerama Retto. Photograph courtesy Ed Castelberry.

and finally hit the water fifty feet off *Benham*'s fantail, exploding on impact. The explosion blew the pilot into the air and opened his parachute. As *Benham*'s crew watched, his lifeless body drifted down into the sea. *Benham*'s gunners continued firing as the plane approached the ship. A shell from the 5"/38 guns exploded close to the ship and the shrapnel killed one man and wounded eight.[30]

Isherwood DD 520 was operating west of Kerama Retto on an anti-submarine screen on 22 April. At about 1725 she picked up an incoming raid on her radar at a distance of eleven miles. Shortly thereafter, three Vals approached the ships. Two dove on other ships in the area and missed, but one picked *Isherwood* as its target. It was taken under fire at 11,000 yards and turned off, only to appear on the starboard beam a few minutes later. *Isherwood* maneuvered radically to keep her guns bearing on the plane, but the Val continued to evade her gunfire, making its final run at only thirty feet off the water. It struck the destroyer's No. 3 gun mount causing numerous fires. Nearby depth charges were engulfed in flame, and attempts to put out the fires were to no avail. At 1816 several of them cooked off and caused extensive damage to the aft end of the ship. Forty-two of her men died and forty-one were injured by the Val's crash. With her fires under control and the flooding stopped, *Isherwood* headed back to Kerama Retto under her own power. At 1857 she fired on a Zeke, but was unable to stop it from crashing *Swallow AM 65*. The hit was perfect, just at the starboard waterline amidships. *Swallow* flooded, took a forty-five degree list, and a few minutes later went under in eighty-five fathoms of water. Among her crew only two died and nine were injured.[31] About the same time that *Isherwood* encountered her kamikaze, *Wadsworth DD 516* came under attack. A Judy made a run on her at 1829 and was hit by her 20mm and 40mm fire. The plane was driven off course and crashed into the water fifteen feet off her starboard side. A second Judy was taken under fire and flew away smoking. She had minor damage to her hull, but only one man was injured.[32]

Hudson DD 475 was a lucky ship. She managed to get through the war without losing

A Marine stands guard near *Shinyo* found on Aka Jima, Kerama Retto. These *Shinyo* were hidden in caves and then transported to the water on trailers. The trailer can be seen under the nearest *Shinyo*. Official USMC photograph.

any of her crew. The nearest she came was on 22 April when a kamikaze passed over her before crashing close aboard. On its way past, it clipped one of her chiefs in the head. He was her sole casualty of the war and he was only wounded.[33] *Ransom AM 283* had a close call when a Val made a run on her. Her gunners hit the plane when it was 200 yards out and it was burning on the way in. A hard right turn at the last moment caused the Val to miss the ship and splash fifteen feet off the port beam. Its bomb went off and damaged the ship but not seriously. She had no casualties.

On 22 April 1945 the ships patrolling Radar Picket Station No. 14 were *Wickes DD 578, Van Valkenburgh DD 656, LSM(R) 195,* and *LCS(L)s 15, 37,* and *83*. At about 1700 incoming raids were picked up approaching the station. Ten CAP Corsairs from the MAG-31 field at Yontan on Okinawa were overhead on patrol and were sent to intercept the incoming enemy aircraft. Several were shot down by the Corsairs, however, one Val managed to slip through and made a run on *Wickes*. It was shot down by the destroyer. At 1828 another Val slipped by and also headed for *Wickes*. Hit by gunfire from the destroyer, it changed course and picked *LCS(L) 15* as its target. It crashed into the port side of the gunboat and its bombs went off mortally wounding her. Within seconds she took a thirty degree list to starboard as fires spread throughout the ship. At 1832 the word was given to abandon ship and she went under, stern first, at 1834. Wounded men clung to whatever floating debris could keep them up. The other ships at RP No. 14 picked up the survivors. Fifteen men had died and another eleven were wounded.

Although *Maru-re* and *Shinyo* boats were of a specific design, occasionally other varieties of boats were used in the attacks. This became the case as the standard suicide boats began to diminish in number due to American air and naval attacks. One such boat attacked *LCI(R) 763* on the evening of 26–27 April 1945. At 0501 on 27 April the gunboat spotted a boat about 400 yards off her port quarter and set out to investigate. While it was illuminated by the ship's searchlight, it began to move away and then turned to make a run on the *763*. The CO of the *763*, Lt. H. H. Goff, increased the ship's speed at the last moment and the suicide boat passed ten yards behind it. Circling around, the gunboat took the suicide boat under fire with its 40mm and 20mm guns, setting it afire and sinking it. The two occupants of the boat were killed in the engagement. It is probable that the occupants of the boat planned to attack American ships with rifle fire and grenades. At this point in the Okinawa campaign, many of the original suicide boats had been destroyed and the Japanese would use whatever was at hand to attack their enemy.

At 0013 on 28 April, *LCI(G) 347* sighted a boat several hundred yards off her port side. It was travelling slowly, as *Shinyo* did, so as not to arouse suspicion. At first the lookouts thought it was just a whitecap but, upon further investigation, found it was an enemy small boat. After it was hit with a number of 40mm and .50 caliber rounds, it went dead in the water about thirty-five yards off the ship. The ship's gunners took aim and let loose again. The result was a massive explosion which shook the gunboat and knocked out power for a few seconds. Fortunately, the ship was not damaged.

Operating in Nakagusuku Bay was the 27th SBB, commanded by Capt. Shigemi Ikabe. Later Japanese estimates indicate that "just before the commencement of the operation, about

This photograph shows a *Shinyo* variant found in the Naha estuary on 6 July 1945. The device on the bow may have been used as a net cutter, allowing this craft to open American defenses and allow other boats through. NARA 80G 325336.

280 vessels were available (only one company of the 29th Sea Raiding Squadron arrived; its main body was left on Amami Oshima because of the sinking of its transport). Of these, 124 craft sortied and presumably hit enemy vessels."[34] The remaining craft fell victim to aerial and gunboat attacks as they lay on shore. The battalion launched a strike of fifteen boats on 25 April 1945, but lost most of them to defensive fire from the American ships in the bay.

The 27th SBB, commanded by Capt. Shigemi Okabe, launched another attack from their base at Tomigusuku on Nakagusuku Bay late in the evening of 27 April. The dark night made it difficult for most of the fourteen boats to get through, however, some did. The destroyer *Hutchins DD 476* was in Nakagusuku Bay conducting harassing bombardment that night. She had just anchored when one of her lookouts heard a muffled engine sound to port but could not spot anything.

> At 0435 ½ a very fast and very small skimmer type craft was observed making a high speed turn away from the ship about 25 feet out from 40 MM No. 4. Lookout on 40 MM No. 1 saw it although vision was partially blocked by gig hanging in davits.... At 0436 about twenty seconds after boat swerved away from ship a large explosion occurred in vicinity of forward port depth charge throwers.[35]

The force of the blast threw men against bulkheads and knocked many down. Multiple cases of sprains and bruises were reported, with two men possibly suffering broken backs. The after engine room had absorbed much of the damage and was flooding at the rate of 2,000 gallons per minute. Quick work by the crew got the flooding under control and they set about to assess the damage. *Hutchins* was injured but not mortally. The next morning *Preston DD 795* accompanied her back to Kerama Retto where she underwent repairs.

LCS(L) 37 had been assigned to patrol the shoreline in Nakagusuku Bay, along with *LCI(L) 679* and *LCS(L)s 24, 38,* and *39*, in search of suicide boats. Ships operating in the bay were under constant threat from them, as they were hidden in the dunes in the area and could easily be launched from the beach at night. In the area known as China Saki, the ships fired on various objects on the beach but were not sure if they had destroyed any suicide boats.

Kikusui No. 4 began on 27 April and ended the following day. Heading for the ships at Okinawa were 115 kamikazes plus their escorts and conventional attack aircraft. Although a number of ships would be hit, the casualty toll would not be as great as in previous raids.

At 2145 *Canada Victory* fell victim to a kamikaze. She was anchored off Hagushi Beach and covered by smoke from the small boys in the area. A clearing in the smoke made her visible to a cruising kamikaze which spotted her and attacked. Her Armed Guard's action report detailed the attack.

> At or about the hour of 1930 on 27 April 1945 all personnel were called to general quarters after enemy aircraft had been reported by radio in the vicinity. The small craft was assigned to throw out a smoke screen over the SS CANADA VICTORY. At about 2115 on the same date the vessel assigned for smoke screening ran out of fog oil and proceeded ashore to replenish its supply. At that hour darkness had set in with only a slight moon showing. A Japanese plane came in on a noiseless glide using the moon to outline the silhouette of the ship. The plane was not visible except for a split second before it crashed into the after mast and dropped rearward into No. 5 hold, at the same time exploding.... The explosion blew out the side of the ship and caused it to settle in the water.
>
> Abandon ship order was given [by the ship's Master, William MacDonald] about 2200 and all survivors left the vessel. They were picked up by small craft in the vicinity and such first-aid as was necessary was given.
>
> In the explosion two (2) naval personnel were killed. W. C. Noah S1c 849 35 39 USN-I died as a result of burns and was buried in the Army Cemetery in Okinawa. Edward O. Johnston S1c 850 15 61 USN-IO was killed in action. Johnston's decapitated remains were seen and identified by members of the Armed Guard crew. The remains were left aboard ship at the time of the sinking.[36]

Canada Victory went down stern first. Three men had died in the attack and five were wounded.

Late in the evening of the 27th, while *Rathburne APD 25* patrolled as part of the transport screen off the Hagushi beach area, she came under attack. She was on alert when, at 2207, one of a group of six enemy aircraft crashed into her port bow. Both the plane's engine and its 220-lb. bomb passed directly through the ship, the bomb exploding underwater on the ship's starboard side. The forward section of the ship was covered with burning gasoline, but the fires were quickly extinguished. After hitting the ship, the bulk of the plane went over the port side and sank. *Rathburne* had a close call but she was alright. Her speed had to be kept to around seven knots because of the hole in her bow, but she made it back for repairs on her own. *Ralph Talbot DD 390* was also screening off Hagushi when two kamikazes attacked her at 2040. One struck her in the starboard side aft and the other crashed close aboard. The ship began to flood, but it was quickly brought under control and the destroyer headed to Kerama Retto for repairs. Her casualties were five dead and nine wounded.

At about 0028, on 28 April, lookouts on *LCS(L) 37* spotted what they believed to be a navigation can about a thousand yards from the ship. As the ship began to approach the object, it began its high speed run from dead ahead. Unfortunately, a signalman tripped, knocking the communications wire loose from the gunnery officer's phones and delaying the response. The order to fire was shouted to the gun crew, but the *Maru-re* had already come close enough so that the guns could not depress enough to hit it. The pilot dropped his two depth charges on the port side, turned and sped away. Both went off under the ship. Gunners on the ship exploded the boat as it sped away, killing the driver. A second man, who had been blown out of the boat, was machine gunned and killed. The entire episode had only taken a few minutes. *LCS(L) 37* was afloat and three of her crew had suffered minor injuries, but she had sustained serious damage. Her main engines were damaged beyond repair and her rudder jammed, but she survived the attack. *LCI(R) 648*, patrolling nearby, came to her assistance and picked up one of her men who had been blown overboard by the initial blast. The next day she was towed to Kerama Retto for repairs.[37] Japanese reports claimed a destroyer and a transport sunk that night, but the only casualty was *LCS(L) 37*.

Although the gunboats were doing a creditable job in keeping the *Maru-re* at bay, they could not stop them all. The cargo ship *Bozeman Victory* had a close call at 0210 on 28 April when she was hit by one of the explosive speedboats while at anchor. Her hull plates were damaged along with her bearings and other parts of the ship. While the damage was serious, she was not holed and her crew was not injured. Several of the main bearings on her port propeller shaft were cracked, which basically immobilized the ship. This attack had the potential for great destruction, as the ship was carrying a cargo of 6,000 tons of ammunition.[38]

Later that morning, at 0545, *LCS(L) 40* patrolled near the beach at China Saki Point and spotted a number of small boats near the seawall. She took them under fire and destroyed eight small craft on the beach. In all likelihood these were suicide boats. The next day, at 0520, she destroyed another four boats on the beach near Chinen Misaki. For the next week, the area was abuzz with suicide boats and swimmers, but they were all sunk or dispatched quickly.

The hospital ships *Pinkney APH 2* and *Comfort AH 6* both suffered kamikaze crashes on 28 April. As non-combatants it was expected that they would not be subject to enemy action, but the assumption was wrong. *Pinckney APH 2,* anchored at Kerama Retto, was hit at 1931 when a Val struck the aft end of her superstructure, setting the ship ablaze and killing a number of her patients. The crash blew a hole thirty feet in diameter in her deck and she began to take on water. Rescue tugs and other small ships assisted in the firefighting, but the flames took three hours to extinguish. She was temporarily repaired at Kerama Retto and headed back to the states on 9 May for permanent repairs.[39] Between her crew and patients she had thirty-five dead and twelve wounded. Among the wounded was her CO, Cmdr. A. A Downing.[40] It is possible that her standard navy grey paint job may have confused the kamikaze pilot who may have mistaken her for an attack transport. Apparently, the Japanese pilot had followed a PBM back to its base at Kerama Retto in order to avoid detection. No such confusion could be claimed by the pilot who crashed into *Comfort* at 2041. She was steaming due south of the southern tip of Okinawa and brightly lit when she was hit. The plane passed over her at masthead height, circled around, gained altitude, and crashed into her superstructure deck. The plane and its bomb penetrated the hull and did considerable damage to the operating room. "At the time of the attack, the entire surgical staff of the Army hospital unit aboard and the Naval medical officer of the ship's company, were in surgery, operating on casualties recently evacuated from Okinawa. As the entire surgery was demolished, everyone working there was killed instantly, with the exception of one Army surgeon, who was suffering from shock."[41] Minor fires broke out and the ship took a slight list, but these problems were soon remedied. Included in the casualty list were doctors, nurses, crew, and patients. In all, thirty were killed and forty-eight wounded.

Ralph Talbot DD 390 was on patrol off the Hagushi beaches when she came under attack by two Japanese planes. According to her action report:

> At 2201, the roar of a plane's motor as heard close aboard, and a single-engined fighter appeared dead ahead, at about 100 feet altitude, headed directly for the bridge in a 40° dive, at high speed. At this moment, left standard rudder was on, and the ship was moving to the left in its zig-zag plan. It is believed that this movement saved the superstructure from a direct crash. The plane flashed past the starboard wing of the bridge at an estimated speed of 300 to 400 knots, within 25 feet of the bridge, and crashed on the starboard side aft at frame 165, just forward of number 4 gun. One wing sheared off and swept past number 4 gun, causing numerous casualties, and crumpling against the depth charge racks and after smoke generators. The engine and fuselage struck the side of the ship near the waterline, causing a hole of about 14 x 16 feet, rupturing fuel tanks, magazines, and living compartments. A small fire was started on the fantail from gasoline-soaked wreckage of the wing, but was quickly extinguished by the survivors of the crew of gun number 4 using a fire hose. No bomb or belly tank was observed as the plane flashed past the bridge, and the absence of any explosion indicates that no bomb was carried, and that gasoline supply was low. The major part of the wreckage was washed clear of the ship, and a large fire broke out in the wake of the ship.[42]

Three minutes later, a second kamikaze came in on her starboard quarter and crashed only twenty-five feet off the ship. Her fires were soon put out and her flooding controlled by 2213, but she suffered five dead and nine wounded. She made it to Kerama Retto for repairs under her own power.

The ships on the radar picket stations around Okinawa were once again in the line of fire. Patrolling on RP No. 1 on 27 April were *Aaron Ward DM 34*, *Mustin DD 413*, *LCS(L) 11*, and *LSM(R) 191*. Late in the evening of 27 April, incoming enemy aircraft were picked up on *Aaron Ward's* radar. At 2130 *Ward* shot one down. Fifteen minutes elapsed before the next raid arrived, but gunfire from the ships turned the intruders away. This pattern of attack, ship firing, and raids turning away from the ship continued periodically until early in the morning on 28 April. Finally at 0240, two twin-engine Bettys flying from the field at Kanoya, bombed the ships at RP No. 1, but all the bombs missed. The Bettys then tried to crash into *Aaron Ward*, but both were shot down during their final approach. The line up at RP No. 1 changed on the 28th with *Bennion DD 662* and *Ammen DD 527* relieving *Aaron Ward* and *Mustin* respectively. *LCS(L) 23* relieved *LCS(L) 11*. Most of the day was relatively quiet, but at 1830 the action heated up. *Bennion* picked up incoming raids and vectored her CAP to intercept them, they shot down twelve planes. In spite of their valiant effort, some planes made it through. An Oscar dove on *Bennion* and, in spite of being hit by the ship's fire, managed to clip the destroyer's No. 2 stack before splashing off the starboard side. Damage to the ship was minimal and there were no casualties.

Radar Picket Station No. 2 was patrolled by *Daly DD 519* and *Twiggs DD 591*. At 1700 the ships picked up a raid estimated at between eight and ten planes. A half hour later two flights of Vals appeared, one to port and one to starboard. *Daly*'s gunners made short work of three of the Vals, but a fourth took aim at her bridge. Ordnance flew from *Daly*'s 20mm and 40mm guns but could not deter the kamikaze's plunge. It clipped *Daly*'s No. 2 torpedo tube and continued on to splash and explode twenty-five yards to port of the destroyer. Within a few minutes *Daly* shot down another attacker off her stern. Although damage to the ship was minimal, *Daly* had two men killed and fifteen wounded. *Twiggs* shot down two planes, however, they exploded too close to the ship and opened her seams. She made it back to safety under her own power with only two men wounded.

Wadsworth DD 516 was patrolling RP No. 12 with *LSM(R)s 190* and *192* on 28 April. The ships had their hands full with a kamikaze attack at 2007. One was shot down by *LSM(R) 190* and a Kate went down under *Wadsworth*'s guns. However, a second Kate narrowly missed the ship but clipped the ship's gig before exploding close off the side of the ship. No casualties resulted from the near miss, but the ship incurred minor damage. *Wadsworth* shot down two more aircraft in the following two hours but none got through to her.

Shortly after *Wadsworth* encountered her kamikaze, *LCI(G) 580* suffered a hit. She was heading for her anti-small boat patrol station west of the Okinawa beaches and was about half way between Okinawa and Kerama Retto when she came under attack. Her attacker made a run on her from north to south, but the ship's gunners could not spot the plane until it was heading away. A few minutes later at 2048, after the plane had circled around, it came in and crashed her starboard side. Its bomb exploded close aboard wounding gunners in her 40mm gun tub. It could have been worse since small combatants such as the LCI gunboats were not that large and were relatively thin-skinned. A single kamikaze hit could easily sink them, in fact several such craft went under after kamikaze hits. In spite of the crash *LCI(G) 580* was relatively unscathed, counting numerous shrapnel holes in her hull and superstructure. The fires that were started were soon extinguished, and the ship headed back to Kerama Retto to transfer her wounded and effect repairs. She had six men wounded, most of whom were in the forward gun tub.[43]

The last two days of April held no rest for the ships at Okinawa. The constant threat of a kamikaze attack kept many at general quarters. *Haggard DD 555*, *Uhlmann DD 687*, and *Hazelwood DD 531* were part of the screen for RAdm. A. W. Radford's Task Group 58.4 carriers on 29 April. At 1627 the ships went to general quarters with bogeys reported in the area. Three aircraft approached the ships, but as soon as they were within firing range they turned away. At 1653 four Zekes made their approach and were taken under fire by *Uhlmann* who reported to *Haggard*, "Four Zekes in our vicinity, heads up. Two Zekes are diving on you."[44] Lookouts on *Haggard* immediately spotted a Zeke 52 closing on her stern with four Hellcats on its tail. *Haggard* opened fire with a combination of 20mm and 40mm guns but could not score any hits. The Zeke continued on its course with one Hellcat in pursuit. It ran a parallel course to the ship and when abeam, turned directly into *Haggard*, strafing on the way in. At about 1657, the Zeke crashed *Haggard*'s starboard beam just below the waterline. A minute later, a second Zeke 52 plunged toward the ship, crashed ten feet off the bow, and exploded. Water and debris covered the ship's bridge. *Haggard* was flooding and had fires to put out but had assistance. *San Diego CL 53*, *Hazelwood*, and *Walker DD 517* came to help. *Walker* took her in tow and they headed back to Kerama Retto. *Haggard* had eleven dead and forty wounded.

This photograph shows the damage to *Hazelwood DD 531* after the kamikaze attack of 29 April 1945. Official U.S. Navy photograph.

Shortly after *Haggard* was hit, *Hazelwood* was ordered to stand by her for protection. At 1720 additional enemy planes appeared on the scene. One made a dive on *Hazelwood* and crashed close aboard her port quarter. Ten minutes later a second plane came in on her from astern. Strafing on the way in, its right wing hit the after stack and gun No. 44 director and finally crashed the ship's superstructure. Its bomb exploded on deck and the area was engulfed with flames. *McGowan DD 678*, *Melvin DD 680*, *Colahan DD 658*, *Flint CL 97*, and *San Diego* came to her aid, picking up survivors and casualties who had been thrown overboard. *McGowan* and *Melvin* came alongside and played water on the fires.[45] The toll on *Hazelwood* had been heavy; forty-six killed, including her CO, Cmdr. V. P. Douw. Twenty-six more of her crew were wounded. She was taken in tow by *McGowan*, but by next morning was able to proceed to Kerama Retto on her own, albeit slowly.

In the early morning hours of 30 April two more American ships were hit, a liberty ship and a minelayer. The *S. Hall Young*, sailing under Master Peter F. Butler, was anchored in Nago Bay when she was hit by a kamikaze at 0345 in the morning. Included in her cargo were gas and explosives, but the crew extinguished the fires before they were set off. She was holed and in need of repair, but her casualty list was light; only one man was injured. *Terror CM 5* was anchored at Kerama Retto when she was crashed at 0400. Ships around her had spotted the plane and the Coast Guard cutter *Bibb* fired on it, but the plane made it through to crash *Terror*'s starboard side. One of its bombs exploded on the communications deck and the other penetrated the deck to explode below. Damage to the ship was significant, but the fires did not reach her magazine. *Bibb* quickly sent her medical officer to assist, but he was injured while trying to board *Terror* and had to return to his own ship. Another doctor was sent to assist *Terror*, which had suffered forty-eight dead and 123 wounded. She underwent temporary repairs at Okinawa and headed to Saipan for permanent repairs on 8 May.[46]

14. "...We Cleaned Up the Bodies..."

The 27th Suicide Boat Battalion's final attack came on the evening of 3 May 1945, but had limited success in spite of grandiose claims. The cargo ship *Carina AK 74* was anchored in Nakagusuka Bay on the evening of 3–4 May. At 0114 on the morning of 4 May, a nearby minesweeper spotted a suicide boat and illuminated it with her searchlight. Within a few minutes the boat crashed into an LCVP which was tied up next to *Carina*. The explosion opened her seams but the LCVP had taken most of the impact from the explosion. Nonetheless, cracks in the ship's deck and hull were discovered the next day and the ship's CO reported that "the *Carina* is not seaworthy and would break up in a moderate sea."[1] About a half-hour later, at 0156, *Paducah Victory* had a close call when a suicide boat slipped past her guards and brushed alongside her. Either her depth charges were duds and failed to detonate or her pilot lost nerve. When last seen, she was heading away from the ship at high speed and disappeared into the gloom.[2] With that sortie, the 27th depleted its supply of boats and afterward made only sporadic attacks using canoes, a practice which soon led to its extinction.[3]

It had been difficult to combat the suicide boats, particularly since they attacked at night. During the day the best possibility was to spot them on the beach and destroy them there. This method presented its own difficulties. *LCS(L)113* reported:

> Boats are cleverly concealed. It is necessary to gaze intently at one spot for some time before a boat can be detected. They are generally hidden along a sandy beach. Small sand dunes are made use of and you may be able to just see a small part of the boat sticking up from behind a small rise in the sand. Most of the boats were placed with the bows headed towards the beach. The enemy cuts off palmetto and fills the boat up with it as well as pushing it into palmetto clump. If you see a low row of palmetto within a palmetto clump you must keep looking for some time before you can suspect that a boat is hidden there. If you suspect the presence of a boat or have any doubts you had best open fire and clear some of the palmetto away with gun fire. It is rather dangerous for the man, but it is best to have at least one lookout in the mast for better spotting.
>
> ... Enemy generally places a number of boats in one place. When approaching a sandy beach it is a good idea to look for paths leading down to the beach and notice grass to see if it is well worn and scuffed. If it is then this is likely a skunk nest.[4]

The third of May saw the beginning of *Kikusui* raid No. 5, which would include 125 kamikazes plus their supporting aircraft. Patrolling Radar Picket Station No. 9 were *Bache DD 470*, *Macomb DMS 23* and *LCS(L)s 89, 111,* and *117.* At 1810 *Bache* picked up incoming bogeys and the ships went to general quarters. Control of the Combat Air Patrol was passed from the amphibious command ship *Mount McKinley AGC 7* to *Macomb*. The turnover caused some difficulties in communication, and the Combat Air Patrol reached their interception

Japanese suicide boat units camouflaged their boats on shore to protect them from air attack and ship fire. This camouflaged boat was discovered on Zamami Jima in the Kerama Retto islands off Okinawa on 10 April 1945. NARA 80G 314031.

point too late to catch the incoming Japanese planes. At 1829 the first kamikaze appeared, a Tony. It crashed off *Bache*'s port quarter. A minute later a second Tony crashed into *Macomb*'s gun No. 3. Its bomb passed into the hull of the mine sweeper and exited the port side where it exploded in the water. As a result, damage was limited and the fires started by the crash were soon extinguished. *Macomb* counted four dead, three missing and fourteen wounded.[5]

Little DD 803, *Aaron Ward* DM 34, LSM(R) 195, and LCS(L)s 14, 25, and 83 were on patrol at Radar Picket Station No. 10 on 3 May. *Little* and *Ward* were separated from the support gunboats by a distance of about five miles. Without supporting firepower, their chances of survival were lessened. Since the Officer in Tactical Command (OTC) was usually on the fighter director destroyer, the responsibility for placement of the various ships fell under his command. Two bogeys were spotted on radar at a distance of twenty-seven miles and the CAP, consisting of four Hellcats, was sent to intercept them. The two managed to slip past the CAP and were soon spotted making a run on *Aaron Ward* with the Hellcats in hot pursuit. Both of the enemy aircraft were Val dive bombers, one of which was quickly shot down. Parts of the destroyed plane ricocheted off the water and landed on the destroyer's deck. The second Val was shot down in flames 1,200 yards from the ship. The distraction caused by the two Vals allowed a Zeke, previously undetected, to slip through the ship's fire and crash into *Ward*. Its bomb went off and the after engine room and fire rooms were set on fire and began to flood. Many men were killed and wounded. The ship sustained serious damage from the impact and began to slow down. In addition to her other damage, her rudder had been jammed, causing her to circle to port. At 1859 additional enemy planes attacked the station. *Aaron Ward* shot down a Val and a Betty. Still another Val made a run on her and, damaged by her gunfire, clipped her stack and crashed close aboard. Within minutes another Val appeared and headed for the minelayer. In spite of being hit repeatedly by the ship's fire, it crashed into the main deck. Its bomb exploded just off the port beam, holing the ship. Seconds later, another Val successfully crash dived on the ship, followed by a Zeke at 1916. Burning gasoline spread over the deck, igniting 40mm ammunition and hindering efforts to fight fires and tend to the wounded. Having sustained crashes from two Vals and two Zekes, the *Aaron Ward* was dead in the water. Her ordeal was not over. Obscured by smoke and fire, another enemy plane slipped through at 1921, crashing into the superstructure deck at the base of the number 2 stack.

> This plane carried a bomb. The force of the explosion blew the plane, number 2 stack, searchlight, and guns 26 and 28 into the air, the mass falling across the superstructure deck just aft of number 1 stack above the main deck, as there were several large holes blown in the main deck over the after fire room.
>
> This was the last hit on the AARON WARD. She suffered five direct hits from the Kamikazes—three of whom carried bombs—plus the hit on number 1 stack which caused little damage. In addition, 4 planes had been shot down.[6]

Ward's crew struggled mightily and managed to keep her afloat.

Little sustained her first kamikaze strike on her port side at 1843, followed by another a few minutes later. Between the two crashes she managed to shoot down one other plane. About 1945 two Zekes crashed her simultaneously, one from starboard and another from overhead. Bombs from the aircraft broke her keel and she took a starboard list. Her CO, Cmdr. Madison Hall, Jr., gave the order to abandon ship. At 1855 she sank beneath the waves, another victim of the special attack forces. She had been hit by four kamikazes and had shot down two others. *LCS(L) 83* and *Nicholson DD 442* cruised the area and picked up survivors.[7] *Little*'s casualties were thirty dead and seventy-nine wounded.

While the attacks on *Aaron Ward* and *Little* were going on, the support gunboats headed in their direction to lend fire support. *LSM(R) 195* lost her starboard engine and fell behind, making her an isolated target for the enemy. Designed as a rocket ship to bombard the enemy shore prior to an amphibious assault, she was not the best choice for anti-aircraft support. Two twin-engine planes attacked from port and one made it through the hail of fire to crash into the port side of the ship. Rockets and munitions exploded, adding to the damage and spreading fires. The water mains had been knocked out by the impact and fire and rocket explosions continued to spread. At 1920 her CO, Lt. W. E. Woodson, gave the order to abandon ship. *LSM(R) 195* sank about twenty-five minutes later. Shortly after she went under, flames reached her 5" powder magazine and set off a tremendous underwater explosion. At about 2145 *Bache DD 470* arrived and began rescuing survivors.[8] *LSM(R) 195*'s casualties were eight dead and sixteen wounded.

The three LCS(L) gunboats also had their share of the action. *LCS(L) 25* was the target as a kamikaze made a run on her at 1909. *LCS(L) 14* helped her splash it astern of the *25*. Pieces of the plane ricocheted off the water and broke the mast, while other parts showered the ship with debris. One man was killed, eight wounded, and two blown over the side. At 1916 two planes dove on the *LCS(L) 83*; both missed and crashed into the sea. The *83* continued toward the sinking ships and was soon attacked by another kamikaze which she promptly shot down. As she maneuvered to pick up survivors the gunboat had to fight off an Oscar. The ship's gunners sent out a torrent of fire and the plane crashed close aboard the gunboat. In all, it had been a disastrous day for the ships at RP No. 10.

Shannon DM 25, which had been on screen nearby, was sent to aid *Aaron Ward*. She arrived at RP No. 10 at 2100 to find that, in addition to the damage sustained by *Aaron Ward*, *Little* and *LSM(R) 195* had been sunk and *LCS(L)25* had been damaged as well. *Aaron Ward* was towed back to Kerama Retto by *Shannon DM 25*. In the attacks, forty-five of her men had been killed and forty-nine wounded.

From 3 to 4 May *Morrison DD 560*, *Ingraham DD 694*, *LSM(R) 194*, and *LCS(L)s 21, 23, and 31* were patrolling Radar Picket Station No. 1. Aware of the disaster at RP No. 10, they were particularly watchful, but they would suffer the same fate. By mid-afternoon bogeys began to appear on the radar screens. *Morrison* directed the CAP toward two Dinahs around 1600 and they sent both flaming into the sea. The remainder of the evening was uneventful, with bogeys occasionally showing up on radar, but none nearing the station. At 0150 the next morning the situation changed. *Ingraham* escaped an enemy bomb and was unable to fire on the plane in the darkness. A number of enemy aircraft continually approached the area, keeping the ships at general quarters till dawn. At 0540, twelve VF-9 Hellcats from *Yorktown* reported to the area for CAP duty. Corsairs from VMF-224 at Okinawa and additional Hellcats from *Yorktown* soon joined the group, placing around thirty-two American fighters over the area.

At 0715 the first bogey approached the station and *Morrison* sent a division of Corsairs

Yorktown CV-10 fighter squadrons took their toll of would-be kamikazes at Okinawa. One of the better known fighter squadrons was VF-9. One of VF-9s divisions was led by Lt. Eugene Valencia. The division, flying their Hellcats, became known as the "Flying Circus." Here they pose for a publicity photograph after their score of Japanese planes totaled fifty. From left to right are Lts. Harris Mitchell (10 kills), Clinton Smith (16 kills), James French (11 kills), and Eugene Valencia (23 kills). NARA 80G 700016.

after it. They reported splashing one Oscar. A Val, initially spotted on radar, managed to slip past the Corsairs and made a beam run on *Morrison*'s port side. Hit repeatedly by the destroyer's guns and the Corsairs, it passed over the ship and crashed in the water only twenty feet away from the ship. By 0732 the sky was full of Nicks, Nans, and Vals engaged in dogfights with the CAP or being shot down as they bore in toward the destroyers and their support gunboats. *Morrison* radioed back for additional help because of the size of the enemy force and, within a short time, the CAP numbered forty-eight planes. A Val made a run on *Morrison* at 0745 and was caught between the ship's fire and that of the CAP. The same thing occurred soon after and another Val was shot down at 0810. Firing on the enemy planes became problematic for the American ships as they were wary of hitting their own aircraft. *Morrison* came under attack again when a Zeke made a run on her, followed by Corsairs. The Zeke was shot down fifty yards from the ship by the combined gunfire of both the destroyer and the CAP. By this time, radio reports indicated that the CAP had shot down an Oscar, six Vals, two Zekes, two Nicks, a Frances and a Myrt. *Morrison*'s luck ran out at about 0825 when two Zekes made a run on her. The first Zeke was hit by the ship's guns and afire, however, it still managed to get through and crash into the base of the forward stack. The second Zeke was hit repeatedly and managed to get through also, crashing into the main deck after first hitting the No. 3 5" gun. Seven twin-float biplanes appeared on the scene and joined in the attack. VT fuses would not detonate near these craft as they were constructed of canvas over wood frames. Although their speed was slow, they were maneuverable and kept up with *Morrison*'s evasive maneuvers. At 0834 the first hit the destroyer's 40mm gun No. 45 and 5" gun No. 3. The impact ignited powder in the handling rooms and caused a huge explosion and fire ball, killing and wounding many men. The 5" gun was blown off its foundation and landed nearby on the deck. Within minutes a second bi-plane, chased by Corsairs, landed in the ship's wake, taxied forward, took off, and crashed into the No. 4 5" gun, causing another massive explosion. With so much damage, the stern went under and the ship rolled on its starboard side. *Morrison*'s skipper, Cmdr. James R. Hansen, gave the order to abandon ship. She pointed her bow to the sky and slid beneath the waves at 0840 in 325 fathoms of water.[9] One hundred fifty-nine men had died and 102 were wounded.

The next ship sunk that day at RP No. 1 was *LSM(R) 194*. Commanded by Lt. Allen M. Hirshberg, the rocket ship had little chance to defend herself with so many kamikazes overhead. The problem for the LSM(R) was her armament. Whereas the other ships had radar-directed fire control and twin and quad mounted 40MM guns, the LSM(R) only had two single 40mm mounts and a single 5" gun, neither of which were director controlled. At 0838 a single Tony with a bomb managed to evade fire from *LCS(L) 21* and the LSM(R) and crash into the stern of the rocket ship.

> Fires were started in the aft steering and engine room. The boiler blew up. The handling room was in flames. Fire and flushing system was ruptured. Sprinkler systems all turned on but it is questionable that much water was forthcoming. The after damage control party were all badly burned and Commanding Officer called forward damage control to proceed aft and take over. The ship immediately started to settle by the stern with a list to starboard before the hose could be rigged to pump out, the ship had settled too far to save, with water washing up on main deck aft. The order was given to abandon ship for all except 40 mm gun crews. Then ordered 40 mm gun crews to abandon ship, following which Commanding Officer abandoned ship. Ship settled straight down stern first. About 5 minutes after she went down a terrific explosion occurred.[10]

The underwater explosion knocked out the gyro compass, sprung water mains and split several seams on *LCS(L) 21* which was coming to her assistance. *Ingraham*'s action report for the day noted that the LSM(R) "sank with her guns blazing as she went down."[11] The rocket ship had thirteen dead and twenty-three wounded.

Ingraham came under attack shortly after *Morrison*. At 0822 she shot down a Val off her starboard bow. In the space of the next few minutes she accounted for another three planes. At this point *Morrison* and *LSM(R) 194* had been sunk and *Ingraham* became the prime target. She managed to shoot down four more kamikazes before a Zeke slipped through and crashed her port side at the waterline. Its bomb exploded inside the ship's forward diesel room, seriously damaging the ship and leaving a thirty foot gash in the port side. The fireroom began to flood and the crew set about doing the work necessary to save their ship. Heroism in the crew was not lacking.

> The two men on duty in the forward diesel room were literally blown to bits, and the seven men in the I.C. room and Plot were believed lost. There were two fire-controlmen, however, who were unwilling to take this for granted. While the ship was still settling and was thought to be sinking, James E. Vaught, FCR3c, and Charles J. Pittenger, FC3c, worked their way below through a mass of twisted and jagged metal, through dense fumes and smoke, in water and oil up to their shoulders, to the I.C. room, where Richard E. O'Connor, EM3c, stunned by the blast of the explosion, and burned, was trapped. By dint of great perseverance they succeeded in freeing the injured man and bringing him up on deck.[12]

With the flooding under control, *Ingraham* headed back to Ie Shima. She was met by a tug on the way back, which took her under tow and a PCE(R) which took off her wounded. *Ingraham* had fourteen dead and thirty-seven wounded.

The LCS(L) gunboats had a busy day. *LCS(L) 21* took her first plane under fire at 0817, as *Morrison* was being attacked. She hit the Val and it crashed 800 yards from the ship. She then spotted a Zeke heading for *Morrison* and shot it down astern of the destroyer. Still another kamikaze headed for the gunboat and it was shot down 2,000 yards out. At that point a Val made a run on the gunboat. Shells from the *21*'s 40mm guns hit the plane, setting it afire. It turned away and crashed into the stern of *LSM(R) 194*, dealing it the fatal blow.

LCS(L) 21 searched the area and crowded 187 survivors on board from *Morrison* and fifty from *LSM(R) 194*. Added to her regular complement of seventy-one men, this placed 308 men on board the diminutive gunboat, which measured only 158' in length with a beam of 23'. It was so crowded that the crew could barely man their guns. In the midst of all this, *LCS(L) 23* shot down four enemy aircraft and was credited with an assist on three more.

LCS(L) 31 took her first kamikaze attack at 0822 when a Zeke made a dive on her port beam. It got no closer than 2,000 yards from the gunboat before it was hit repeatedly. It passed closely over the ship, clipping the ensign off the mast before crashing into the water fifty feet to starboard. A minute later another Zeke made a run from the port bow. Although it was hit many times it did not alter course. It passed between the ship's conning tower and the forward twin 40mm gun tub. The wings hit both the gun tub and the conning tower. Two men were killed in the gun tub and one was injured. Its engine tore off the starboard 20mm gun and the remains exploded off the starboard beam, killing three men and injuring two. A significant portion of the gunboat's fire power had been wiped out in the course of a couple of minutes. This did not help, as shortly thereafter a Val made a run directly at the conning tower from the port beam. The *31*'s gunners scored many hits on it and drove it off course. Unfortunately, it was not far enough off course and crashed into the main deck aft the deck house. Burning gasoline spread throughout the area. Two men were killed, three injured and two blown overboard from the impact. As crewmen worked to put out the flames, gunners on the starboard 20mm gun spotted a Zeke headed for *Ingraham* and took it under fire. They shot it down only twenty-five yards off their port quarter. Another enemy plane fell under the guns of the *31* at 0855. As a result of the action, *LCS(L) 31* had eight dead and eleven wounded. She headed back to the Hagushi anchorage for repairs.

On Radar Picket Station No. 2 *Lowry DD 770* had a close call at 0834 when an incoming kamikaze crashed close off her port bow. The ship sustained minor damage, but two men were killed and twenty-three wounded.

At RP No. 10, *Cowell DD 547* came under attack by two Vals. She shot down one which attempted a crash, but pieces of the plane landed on her, damaging her No. 4 Mk. 51 director and the gyro action of the Mk. 14 sight. *Gwin DM 33* managed to down eight, but one got through and crashed her after deck house. There was little damage to the high-speed minesweeper but she counted two dead and nine injured. *LSM(R) 192*, one of the support ships on the station, had a close call as a plane missed her conning tower, clipped some of the rocket launchers and went over the side. One crewman was injured.

Nearby, on Radar Picket Station No. 12, *Luce DD 522*, *LSM(R) 190*, and *LCS(L)s 81, 84*, and *118* were on patrol. Early in the morning on 4 May, enemy aircraft were reported heading for the station. At 0145 *Luce* fired on and turned away a pair of enemy aircraft which were heading toward her. With daybreak CAP aircraft appeared, giving some comfort to the sailors on the ships below. At around 0730 enemy raids were reported incoming and the CAP was vectored out to meet them. They reported splashing a number of enemy aircraft, however, some managed to slip through. At 0805 lookouts on *Luce* spotted two fighter type aircraft approaching her and the ship went to twenty-five knots. The two aircraft split apart and lined up for runs on opposite sides of *Luce*. The destroyer took them under fire but both managed to make it through. The first crashed 100 feet off her starboard beam knocking out power momentarily and cutting some power to her guns. Immediately after the first plane hit the water, the second crashed into *Luce*'s port side aft disabling her port side engine, her 5" mounts Nos. 3, 4 and 5, and several of her 20mm and 40mm guns. She began to flood aft and within three minutes had a heavy list to starboard. It was obvious that she was going to sink and the order to abandon ship was given as she settled by the stern. At 0815 her bow pointed skyward and she disappeared beneath the waves. The rapidity of her sinking, combined with the damaged interior communications in the ship, trapped many men below. They went down with the ship. Three minutes after her sinking one of her depth charges went off underwater, causing injury to many survivors in the water. *Luce* had 149 dead and 94 wounded.[13]

LSM(R) 190, supporting *Luce* on the picket station, was also sunk that day. About the same time that *Luce* came under attack, a Dinah flew over the *LSM(R) 190*'s stern and dropped a bomb which missed. It was taken under fire and damaged. This may have been an instance of the pilot recognizing that his fate was sealed and becoming a kamikaze on the moment. The Dinah did a wing over and crashed into the ship's 5/38 mount, setting it ablaze. The crash seriously injured a number of men, including the ship's CO, Lt. R. H. Saunders. The ship's Communications Officer, Ens. Tennis, took command of the ship. Broken fire mains hampered firefighting and the flames continued to spread. At this point the ship suffered her second kamikaze hit of the day as a Val crashed into her port beam igniting fires in her engine room. Several other planes attempted to bomb her, and one struck in the area of the Mk. 51 director tub. It was at this point that *Luce* sank. *LSM(R) 190* was beginning to list heavily to port and the fires were out of control. The CO was carried from the conn, and after consultation with his surviving officers, decided to abandon ship. The rocket ship sank at 0850. *LCS(L) 84* began the task of picking up survivors but the *LSM(R) 190* had thirteen dead and eighteen wounded.[14]

Radar Picket Station No. 14 was patrolled by *Shea DM 30*, *Hugh W. Hadley DD 774*, *LSM(R) 189*, and *LCS(L)s 20, 22*, and *64*. Although it was a bright, sunny day, smoke from the anchorage area had drifted to the station and cut visibility to about 2,000 yards. Nearby and overhead, numerous aircraft engaged in dogfights as American fighters shot down many enemy aircraft. *Shea*'s action report indicates:

At 0959 (-9) a Japanese piloted rocket bomb was sighted close aboard to starboard and headed directly for SHEA. This bomb emerged from haze to westward at very high speed and hit the SHEA between 3–5 seconds after first sighting. During this brief interval, only one 50-caliber, one 20mm, and one twin mount 40mm were able to open fire. The appearance of this bomb was exactly as pictured in JICPOA Intelligence bulletin No. 40 of 16 April 1945, and the bomb was at very low altitude in about a 10° glide when it hit the ship. Speed can only be estimated as very fast.[15]

An *Oka* struck *Shea* on the starboard side of her bridge, passed through the ship and exploded in the water fifteen feet off the side of the ship. She suffered a great deal of damage to her port side hull plating from the explosion, as well as various interior spaces where the fuselage of the plane had passed through. Twenty-seven of her men died and ninety-one were wounded, but the ship was afloat. It was surmised that the relatively thin hull plating of the ship saved her as the *Oka* was designed to penetrate much thicker armor prior to exploding.

While the radar picket ships had their fill of action, ships elsewhere were in peril as well. *Idaho BB 42* was attacked by two Vals and three Kates at 1452 on 3 May. She shot them all down, but one exploded close off her port quarter. Another crashed close aboard her port quarter and exploded, flooding her blisters. Shrapnel was sent flying over her deck but the ship had only minor damage.

Hopkins DMS 13 had a close call on 4 May when she was narrowly missed by a kamikaze that crashed close aboard. She had left the anchorage at Kerama Retto at 0630 along with *Gayety AM 239*, and *YMSs 89, 327, 331,* and *427*. Their assignment was to sweep for mines off the island of Tori Shima. *Hopkins* had the assignment as acting as fire support for the group and its CO, Cmdr. T. F. Donahue, was also the OTC. At about 0730 the group received notice of approaching enemy air raids and went to general quarters. The first Japanese plane, a Betty, was spotted at 0816 as it passed south of the formation. A minute later a Val was seen diving on *Hopkins'* port beam. It was taken under fire by the ships and passed closely over *Hopkins*, clipping her superstructure wiring, and it crashed twenty yards off *Hopkins'* starboard beam. A second Val closely followed the first and appeared heading for *Gayety*. Gunfire from the minesweeper disrupted the pilot's aim and he crashed close aboard *Gayety*'s stern. The near proximity of the crash forced several men overboard and the YMSs maneuvered to pick them up. At 0942 another plane was picked up on radar. This one was a Betty carrying an *Oka*. It came to within six miles from the ships and dropped its manned bomb at 0945. As it turned away it was caught by American fighters and shot down. The *Oka* seemed to target *YMS 331*, but the minesweeper maneuvered out of its way. Unable to follow the small ship's movement, it singled out *Gayety* for its attack. Her action report detailed the event.

At 0947: the Baka Bomb [*Oka*] approached Task Group at terrific speed, estimated at 350 to 400 knots, and decreasing altitude steadily. GAYETY executed hard turn to port, at same time taking the Baka under fire with all automatic weapons as they could be brought to bear. The Baka Bomb next appeared to be making low altitude run on the YMSs.... As the Baka passed over leading YMS (nearest to GAYETY) and increased altitude slightly to avoid hitting the YMSs's mast, it became clear that its objective was not YMS but GAYETY. Bursts from port guns were now seen to be hitting the Baka which continued its low level straight run on port quarter of GAYETY. At a range of about 500 yards a cowling or nose ring appeared to fly from the Baka and fall into the sea. A few seconds later the Baka Bomb appeared to disintegrate very rapidly, turned end over end, and crashed into the water at an estimated 15 yards off GAYETY's port 40mm gun; it did not detonate.... Parts of the Baka bomb passed over this vessel from port to starboard striking the starboard 40mm gun in several places, damaging it beyond repair. Human flesh (presumed to be that of the pilot) and pieces of Baka Bomb debris (plywood and aluminum) were scattered over the boat deck at the 40mm guns and over the fantail. The starboard 40mm gun was the only material casualty.[16]

Debris from the disintegrated *Oka* rained down on the ship's deck, wounding three of her men. It had been a close call but the ship was basically undamaged.

The escort carrier *Sangamon CVE 26* had put into Kerama Retto for supplies on 3 May and then headed out to rejoin Task Unit 52.1.3 the following day. An incoming raid at 1902 supplied targets for Marine Corsairs from the fields on Okinawa, but one got through to make a run on *Sangamon*, narrowly missing the carrier. At 1925 *Fullam DD 474* picked up an incoming raid and vectored nearby night fighters to intercept it. The plane, a Nick, managed to slip past the night fighters and made it to *Sangamon*, where it crashed into her flight deck at 1933. It released a bomb just prior to the crash which penetrated the flight deck and exploded. *Sangamon* became a ball of fire and attracted the attention of nearby ships which came to her aid. *Hudson DD 475*, *LSM 14*, and *LCS(L)s 13, 16*, and *61* pulled alongside and began playing water on the fires even as her crew fought them topside. Fires raged below deck and on deck, cooking off 20mm and 40mm ammo, as well as .50 caliber rounds from the aircraft. *LCS(L) 13* broke her mast in a collision with *Sangamon*'s flight deck but no one was injured. She then assisted the carrier's crew in jettisoning burning planes by attaching lines to several and pulling them over the side of the flight deck. One plane landed on *Hudson*'s fantail, near the depth charges. Her crew quickly shoved it over the side before they could go off. The destroyer also sustained damage from the carrier's overhanging flight deck. In addition, two of her 40mm mounts were rendered inoperable by the encounter with the carrier. After laying water on her for about fifteen minutes *Hudson* moved off and the LCS(L)s and *LSM 14* continued firefighting. By 2230 most of the fires were out, *Sangamon* had survived. Damage to her was extensive, however, and so were her casualties. She had forty-six dead and 116 wounded.

In the evening of 3–4 May 1945, *LCS(L) 12* was on skunk patrol south of the Hagushi anchorage as part of Task Unit 52.19.3. At about 0220 in the morning on 4 May her lookouts

Sangamon CVE 26 had severe damage to her deck and elevator after the kamikaze attack of 4 May 1945. NARA 80G 336257.

The Kawasaki Ki-45 KAIa Army Type 2 fighter carried the Allied code name "Nick." NARA 80G 129458.

spotted two suicide boats lying dead in the water about 2,500 yards from the ship. The gunboat made its approach, turning so as to place her starboard bow toward the boats. Star shells, fired by nearby ships, illuminated the area and the LCS(L) challenged the two boats unsuccessfully. The suicide boats got underway on different courses and evaded the gunboat, which was in pursuit. Finally, at 0230, one of the boats was taken under fire at a range of 500 yards as it made a run on the gunboat. It was driven away and *LCS(L) 12* lost sight of it. Reports from nearby ships indicate the she had disabled it and it was dead in the water. One of them sank it.

Birmingham CL 52 was anchored off Hagushi on 4 May. Around 0835 a formation of enemy planes was reported heading for the area sixty miles out. American fighters shot down a number of them but several made it through to threaten the anchored ships. An Oscar with a bomb dove on *Birmingham* from directly overhead and crashed through her main deck. Its bomb exploded in the cruiser's sick bay, killing or wounding everyone in the area. It took a half hour to extinguish the fires started by the plane's explosion. Her main deck had a hole fifteen by eighteen feet and the deck in the area was blown upward. *Birmingham*'s hull was bulged outward on the starboard side, adjacent to the blast. It was a successful strike for the kamikaze. He took with him fifty-one dead and eighty-one wounded.

Suicide boats were still a threat. At 0040 on the morning of 4 May, *Spectacle AM 305* sighted one but was unable to engage it. However, at 0200, she spotted several and opened fire. The first was hit at 0232 when her shells hit the suicide boat's explosive charge and it detonated. Even though the explosion was over 700 yards away, *Spectacle*'s 185' hull was shaken by the blast. Shortly after 5 in the morning she fired on and sank two small canoe type boats.

These were frequently used by Japanese soldiers to close in on a ship so that they could throw hand grenades, virtually a suicide mission.[17]

LCS(L) 53 was on anti-small boat patrol on the evening of 4–5 May 1945. Her station was north of Naha and west of Kezu Saki and was roughly two miles long. At 0105 on May 5, she spotted two suicide boats near shore. Reefs in the area made her cautious in her approach. *AGM 305*, cruising nearby, fired on one of the boats. The second headed for open water, but the *53* lost its radar track due to interference. At 0207 she sighted the suicide boat about 400 yards to seaward and sank it with 40mm fire. Eleven minutes elapsed and two more blips showed on the *53*'s radar screen. These were to the south and the gunboat headed in their direction. Star shells were used to illuminate the area and the boats were spotted about 1,200 yards off. One was hit by the ship's fire and sank, but the other made a speedy getaway.[18]

On 6 May *Pathfinder AGS 1* suffered a kamikaze crash on her after gun platform. Damage to the survey ship was light, but one man was killed in the attack. On 8 May, the seaplane tender *St. George AV 16*, operating at the seaplane base at Kerama Retto, fell victim to a kamikaze which crashed her seaplane crane, killing three and wounding thirty.

Oberrender DE 344 was operating in the outer screen north of Kerama Retto on 9 May. At 1840 enemy aircraft were reported to be in the area and the ship went to general quarters. Soon a bogey was reported heading for her and she went to flank speed at 1850. *Oberrender* maneuvered to bring her guns to bear on the plane and took it under fire. One of her 5" gun bursts loosened the plane's port wing and it flapped in the air as the plane closed on the ship, finally coming off when the plane was only 250 yards away. This caused the plane to swerve to the right, but not sufficiently to miss the ship. At 1852 it struck and demolished gun tub No. 25. The plane's bomb penetrated her hull and exploded in the forward fireroom, disabling the ship which went dead in the water. *PCE(R) 855* came alongside and took off her casualties. *Tekesta ATF 93* towed her in to Kerama Retto.[19] *Oberrender*'s navy career was over. She was damaged so badly that she was declared a total loss and decommissioned on 11 July 1945. Her casualties were eight dead and fifty-three wounded.

The same day, *England DE 635* was patrolling station B11, which was northwest of Kerama Retto. At 1951 she picked up a raid of three bogeys closing on her position and went to flank speed. Three Vals headed for her position and one made a dive on her. At 1855 it crashed into her superstructure just as the CAP was shooting down the other two. Her action report for the day said:

> The Val that hit contained 2 Japs wearing parachutes and carried bombs. The plane had been seriously damaged by ship's gunfire before it hit. One wheel had been shot off and the plane was burning and smoking around the engine and the pilot in the forward cockpit was slumped over his controls as if dead, while the one in the after cockpit apparently was in control.... Flying bridge and signal bridge were completely surrounded by smoke and flames; and, for a while, it seemed that all hands there were completely trapped. Consequently some of the men stationed on the signal bridge and some of those who had come from combat, jumped over the side, taking with them several wounded who probably would not have been saved otherwise. Some of the men from the bridge, including the acting executive officer who had been in combat, went to the main deck by climbing down No. 2 life raft and swinging down from there, while men below sprayed them with water.... Due to the smoke and fire the Commanding Officer gave the order to clear the bridge, although at the time no way was seen to accomplish this. Most of those on the flying bridge escaped by getting on top of the sound shack and jumping to No. 3 and 34 20mm guntubs.[20]

Heat from the fires cooked off 20mm shells as the men commenced firefighting. The ship was still at flank speed, not knowing that the other Vals had been shot down. At 1919 *Vigilance AM 324* was observed closing on the ship. *England* stopped to contact her since her communications were out. *Vigilance* was also able to help in firefighting and picking up survivors who had gone overboard. At 2200 *Gherardi DMS 30* arrived to assist with firefighting and sent her doctor and a medical party aboard to help with the wounded. The tug *Gear AT 34* arrived at 2300 to tow her. Although *England* was capable of steaming on her own, her commanding officer, Lt. Cmdr. J. A. Williamson, correctly assessed the situation. She was still ablaze and had many wounded aboard. Attempting to get back into the harbor at Kerama Retto without radar, charts, or gyro compass at night would have been too risky. In addition, the harbor was covered by a thick blanket of smoke to protect ships from the kamikazes. *Gear* towed her back to safety and the ship anchored about 0130 the next morning. Thirty-five of her crew had died and twenty-seven were wounded in the kamikaze attack.

Kikusui Raid No. 6 was scheduled for 10 to 11 May. A total of 150 special attack planes, seventy from the navy and fifty from the army, would head for Okinawa along with their escorts. The radar picket ships would be prime targets. In spite of their heavy losses, it was obvious that the kamikazes had not lost their spirit. Flight PO 1/c Isao Matsuo, of the 701st Air Group at Miyazaki Air Base, wrote his last letter to his parents:

> Dear Parents,
> Please congratulate me. I have been given a splendid opportunity to die. This is my last day. The destiny of our homeland hinges on the decisive battle in the seas to the south where I shall fall like a blossom from a radiant cherry tree. How I appreciated this chance to die like a man. Think well of me and know that I also died for our country. May my death be as sudden and clean as the shattering of crystal.
> Written at Miyazaki on this day of my sortie.
> Isao[21]

Patrolling Radar Picket Station No. 15 were *Evans DD 552*, *Hugh W. Hadley DD 774*, *LSM(R) 193*, and *LCS(L)s 82, 83*, and *84*. A combat air patrol of sixteen VF-85 Corsairs from *Shangri-La* covered the station. Two additional Corsairs from VMF-323 flew radar picket patrol above the station. Radar picket patrol usually involved two to four Corsairs from the Marine air groups at either Kadena or Yontan fields on Okinawa. Their task was to remain close to the picket ships in case any kamikazes slipped through the combat air patrol, which usually tried to intercept them at a distance of twenty-five to fifty-miles from the ships. At 1935 on 10 May, the destroyers fired on and destroyed an enemy plane. The radar picket station was active all night from the 10th to the 11th as enemy aircraft passed through the area, keeping the ships at general quarters for most of the time. Around 0740 on May 11, bogeys were reported heading for the station. Shortly thereafter, a Jake from the seaplane base at Ibusuki on Kyushu, made a run on the ships and was shot down by *Hadley*. Additional incoming raids appeared on radar and *Hadley* vectored combat air patrol Corsairs to intercept them. Estimates of the number of planes heading for the station ran to 156. Basically the entire *Kikusui* raid was headed straight at the ships at RP No. 15, making it the largest air battle at the radar picket stations that would take place during the campaign.

By 1755 reports from the CAP indicated that they had shot down from forty to fifty of the enemy planes, but that still left over one hundred enemy aircraft to attack the ships. Some of these planes would bypass the station but many would not. With so many enemy planes in the area, it was impossible for the CAP to stay near the ships. At times the dogfights were ten to twenty miles away, leaving little protection for the picket ships.

> From this time on the Hadley and the Evans were attacked continuously by numerous enemy aircraft coming at us in groups of four to six planes on each ship. During the early period, enemy aircraft were sighted trying to pass our formation headed for Okinawa. These were flying extremely low on both bows and seemingly ignoring us. The Hadley shot down four of these.... The tempo of the engagement and the maneuver of the two destroyers at high speed was such as to cause the Hadley and the Evans to be separated by distances as much as two and three miles.

This resulted in individual action by both ships. Three times the Hadley suggested to the Evans to close for mutual support and efforts were made to achieve this but each time the attacks prevented the ships from closing each other. The Hadley closed the four small support ships several times during the engagement.[22]

After initially splashing four of the planes passing by, *Hadley* came under direct attack. From 0830 to 0900 her gunners shot down twelve more kamikazes as they made runs on her from all directions. *Evans*, in the meantime, had been hit and was out of action and unable to assist her. *Hadley* requested that the CAP return to the area as the ships were being overwhelmed. For the next twenty minutes *Hadley* was alone and surrounded by enemy planes. They came at her from all sides and she shot down ten more, but some got through. "As a result of this attack, the *Hadley* was (1) Hit by a bomb aft (2) By a BAKA bomb seen to be released from a low flying BETTY (3) Was struck by a suicide plane aft (4) Hit by suicide plane in rigging."[23] The CAP came to the rescue and shot down numerous enemy planes as *Hadley* lay dead in the water. She was flooding rapidly and fires raged throughout the ship, setting off munitions. Her CO, Cmdr. Baron J. Mullaney, gave the order to prepare to abandon ship. The wounded and most of the crew were put over the side. Remaining on board was a group of fifty officers and crew who made a last ditch effort to save the rapidly listing ship. Although the odds were heavily against them, they succeeded and the ship remained afloat. She was towed back to Ie Shima and eventually to the United States. Her condition was such that she was decommissioned and scrapped. Twenty-eight of her men had died and another sixty-seven were wounded in action, but they had shot down twenty-three kamikazes, including the ones that crashed the ship. Mullaney summed up the experience of his crew:

> No Captain of a man of war ever had a crew who fought more valiantly against such overwhelming odds. Who can measure the degree of courage of men who stand up to their guns in the face of diving planes that destroy them? Who can measure the loyalty of a crew who risked death to save the ship from sinking when all seemed lost? I desire to record that the history of our Navy was enhanced on 11 May 1945. I am proud to record that I know of no record of a Destroyer's crew fighting for one hour and thirty-five minutes against overwhelming enemy aircraft attacks and destroying twenty-three planes. My crew accomplished their mission and displayed outstanding fighting abilities.[24]

The fury of the aerial assault had forced the destroyers to go to high speed, separating them from each other and from the support gunboats by two to three miles and negating the possibility of mutual fire support. While *Hadley* was undergoing her ordeal, so was *Evans*. At 0753 the destroyer took an approaching Jake under fire.. After being hit numerous times the plane exploded about 1,000 yards off the starboard quarter. The magnitude of the explosion indicated that the plane was carrying a bomb. For about another half hour *Evans* was not threatened. However, at 0830 her radar began tracking three Kates approaching from the port quarter. All three were shot down within the next few minutes. Enemy aircraft continued to appear and, over the span of another fifteen minutes, the destroyer splashed a combination of seven Tonys, Kates, Jills, and Zekes. Another Kate under fire and burning managed to get off a torpedo aimed at *Evans*. Her CO, Cmdr. Robert J. Archer, ordered hard left rudder, and the torpedo passed twenty-five yards across her bow. It had been a close call. Immediately thereafter, a Tony went down under the guns of both *Hadley* and *Evans* and crashed at 3,500 yards. A Val made the next suicide attempt, but gunfire from the ship made him lose control and he passed over and crashed 2,000 yards off the starboard bow. An Oscar dropped a bomb which missed, then was shot down as it attempted a crash into the ship. An Oscar and Jill attacked from the port side and both were shot down close aboard. Within minutes a Tony made a run and went down under *Evan's* guns. The destroyer took its first hit at 0907 when a Judy crashed into her port bow at the waterline, holing the ship. *Evans* began to flood in the forward crew compartment. Another Tony was shot down at 8,000 yards when it suffered a direct hit from one of the destroyer's 5" guns. At 0911 *Evans* took her second kamikaze hit when a plane crashed into her just below the waterline on her port side. As the ship began to flood in the after engine room, two more kamikazes hit her. The first was an Oscar which hit her from overhead and released a bomb that penetrated the deck and exploded inside. This bomb blew out both of the forward boilers. A second Oscar hit the ship from the starboard side, starting fires and causing additional damage. As a result of these successful kamikaze crashes *Evans* was dead in the water. The final kamikaze attack for *Evans* came at 0925 when two Corsairs chased an enemy plane into the destroyer's guns. Fire from the CAP and the ship caused it to overshoot and it passed over the bridge to crash close aboard. *LCS(L) 84* closed on the *Evans* and began to assist in fighting the fires. LCS(L)s had extra firefighting equipment aboard and this was of great benefit to many ships that they accompanied. *LCS(L) 82* and *Harry E. Hubbard DD 748* came alongside to assist, picking up survivors, transferring wounded and lending equipment. For the support gunboats, 11 May was also hazardous. In the ensuing melee, *LCS(L) 82* shot down three kamikazes and assisted in the destruction of two more. Up until around 0900 most of the attacks had been aimed at the two destroyers. This was still the case when the gunboat spotted a Jill with a torpedo heading for *Evans* at 0837. She took it under fire at 3,500 yards and scored several hits. The flight of the Jill became erratic, it dropped its torpedo, which missed the *Evans* and slowly crashed into the sea. At 0845 she assisted the *LCS(L) 84* in splashing a Tony which approached from her port side. All around her aircraft crashed into the water, falling victim to the guns of the CAP, destroyers, and other gunboats. An Oscar headed for the ship from the starboard bow and the ship's gunners began scoring hits at around 1,000 feet. As the plane passed over the ship it broke in half, with the wings and engine falling toward the ship. Lt. Peter G. Beierl, the CO of the *82*, ordered flank speed and the pieces fell into the ship's wake. At 0940, *LCS(L) 82* faced a direct attack when a Val, chased by the CAP, approached her from astern. She scored hits at a range of 400 yards and the plane passed by and narrowly missed *Evans*. A few shells from the gunboat hit the forecastle of *Evans* and started fires. The *82* came alongside and began to assist in firefighting.[25]

LCS(L) 83 found herself in the middle of the action.

> Several planes were reported coming in astern. One of them came around our starboard side but was driven off. They then attacked from all directions and altitudes. The destroyers were much closer now running roughly south east. Several planes attacked them from high altitudes. We fired at these and knocked one down astern of one of the destroyers. Another plane came in astern, climbed and made a dive at the 84 on our starboard quarter. Our guns took this one under fire. The tail was knocked off. It crashed slightly to starboard of the 84. We next took two planes under fire over the DD 774. They got away I believe. A plane made a run on the DD 552 low from astern, dropped a bomb, climbed then went very low. The destroyer and LCS 82 were firing at it. It glided for a while and finally crashed. We were firing at a plane making a dive on the DD 774 when we discovered a plane coming in on us dead ahead. The forward guns switched to it. It immediately burst into flames and exploded. The gasoline fumes blinded us on the conn. Another plane came in after the 82 astern of us. We took it under fire. It broke up and fell astern of the 82. All ships were maneuvering independently by this time. Corsairs arrived for air cover. The destroyers had been hit several times and were separating.... LSM 193 and LCS 83 headed for the DD 774. The LCS's 82 and 84 headed for the DD 552.[26]

Working in conjunction with the destroyers and the other gunboats, *LCS(L) 83* shot down three Zekes and a Tojo between 0900 and 0939. She then moved in to pick up survivors and assist *Evans*. *LCS(L) 84* spotted a Zeke making a dive on her at 0858. Her gunners made short work of it and it crashed only ten feet off her starboard bow. Damage to the ship was negligible and one man was wounded.

Although LSM(R)s were not noted for their anti-aircraft abilities, the gunners on *LSM(R) 193* demonstrated that they were the equal of any others on RP No. 15 that day. At 0845 a Kate made a dive bombing run on *Evans* but missed. It peeled off and headed for *LSM(R) 193* in an apparent crash attempt. It was shot down by a combination of 5" and 40mm fire. At 0859 her gunners spotted a Kate to starboard gaining altitude for a crash dive on the rocket ship. Hits from the 5" and 40mm guns caused it to splash. Thirteen minutes later *193* shot down a Hamp to starboard and a few minutes later destroyed a second. Another plane dove on *Hadley* and she helped shoot it down. With the immediate action over, the LSM(R) went to the assistance of *Hadley*, helping put out fires and tending to the wounded. At 1401 she began to tow the destroyer back to the anchorage, assisted by *ATR 114*. *LCS(L) 83* remained alongside the destroyer to assist as needed.[27]

With her condition stabilized, *Evans* was towed back to the anchorage at Ie Shima by *Arikara ATF 98* and *Cree ATF 84*. She had lost thirty men and twenty-nine more were wounded in the attacks. *Evans'* score for the day was fourteen enemy aircraft.[28]

Harry F. Bauer DM 26 was patrolling Radar Picket Station No. 5 along with *Douglas H. Fox DD 779* on 11 May. Supporting them with additional firepower were *LCS(L)s 52, 88, 109* and *114*, along with *PGM 20*. As daylight arrived so did the enemy planes. By 0800 the picket ships were under attack. *Harry F. Bauer* opened fire on a Dinah that closed her position from the northwest and drove it off. The CAP of four Marine Corsairs from VMF-441 at Yontan caught up with it in short order. Second Lt. Willis A. Dworzak shot it down. One Zeke attempted a crash and left its wingtip on board *Bauer* as it crashed just off the side of the ship. At 0822 another Zeke clipped the depth charge rack and lines before splashing thirty yards off the starboard quarter. Its bomb catapulted off the plane and landed 200 feet away in the water. The ships continued to fire on incoming aircraft and hit another. However, a second plane crashed close aboard *LCS(L) 88*, killing the CO, Lt. Casimir L. Bigos, and seven others. Nine others among the officers and crew were wounded, two of whom would later expire. The gunboat had damage to her aft 40mm gun tub and rudder; she was out of the war. *PGM 20* came to her assistance. Lookouts on *Harry F. Bauer* spotted four more enemy planes coming in from the starboard quarter. The first, believed to be a Tojo, was shot down. Immediately after, a Zeke made its run from the starboard beam. *Bauer's* gunners took it under fire as both ship and plane maneuvered violently. The Zeke went down in flames thirty yards off the ship's starboard quarter. At 0833 another Zeke made its run on the ship. *Bauer's* action report states:

> Opened fire on ZEKE closing from north (on starboard beam) at range about 8000 yards. Hits were observed, but again the poor functioning of VT ammunition hindered in effecting a splash. Toward the end of the run he dipped his starboard wing and with it knocked a depth charge on the forward port K-gun onto the main deck. His wing caught in the life line on the port side of the superstructure deck snapping it and catapulting his bomb about two hundred feet clear of the port side. A burst from the 40 mm hit his tail as he approached the ship, blasting it from the plane. He splashed seconds later clear of the side to port.... During the last three runs, the CAP reported splashing the fourth fighter type plane (a ZEKE). Thus of the seven attacking planes in the area, none got away. Neither FOX nor support craft fired in latter attacks, shooting at planes overhead which were believed part of CAP. None was splashed.[29]

Harry F. Bauer had escaped with only one injury and superficial damage. *LCS(L) 88* was towed back to Kerama Retto by *Ute ATF 76*.

It had been a productive day for the pilots of VMF-221. They had flown off *Bunker Hill CV 17* at 0700 that morning and headed out to fly CAP over the radar picket ships. In the course of the day's action, the seven F4U-1D Corsairs had encountered a number of enemy aircraft menacing the picket ships at Radar Picket Station No. 15. Below them were *Hugh W. Hadley, Evans, LSM(R) 193*, and *LCS(L)s 82, 83*, and *84*. Between their arrival at 0800 and

LCS(L) 88 suffered significant damage in the kamikaze attack of 11 May 1945. Official U.S. Navy Photograph courtesy Art Martin.

their departure from the area at about 0915, they shot down a Betty carrying an *Oka*, one Frances and one Jill. They regrouped and headed back to *Bunker Hill* just in time to see it come under attack. Their action report indicated:

> At approximately 0915 the two flights rendezvoused over reference point Tare and proceeded back to base [*Bunker Hill*]. They were orbiting the base at 1500' when Captain Swett sighted two planes almost over the Bunker Hill and about 3000' above his flight. He turned toward them and one of the planes began to dive toward the Bunker Hill. Captain Swett called out over the radio to the CU that two kamikazes were diving at her. The ship however did not fire at the first plane and he crashed into the planes on the after end of the flight deck. (Time app. 1020.)
>
> In the meantime Lieutenant Glendinning's section had started after the second plane but despite full power was unable to close on him. They therefore opened fire out of range but their fire was ineffective. The plane immediately dove on the center section of the Bunker Hill. (The fwd. port bank of 20mm on the Bunker Hill scored many hits on the second plane and he was flaming as he hit the deck.)
>
> At this time they sighted a 3rd bandit but were unable to close before he was splashed by the D.D. screen. Captain Baldwin's division immediately joined the C.A.P. while Captain Swett directed his division to circle the survivors in the water (which they did from 1020 to 1130) and dropped dye marker to assist D. D.s in their rescue missions.[30]

With *Bunker Hill* severely damaged, the VMF-221 Corsairs had to land on *Enterprise CV 6*, touching down at 1130.

The attack on *Bunker Hill* caused the greatest number of casualties of any kamikaze attack in World War II. Killed in the attack were 396 men, with another 264 wounded. The kamikazes that struck *Bunker Hill* were a part of the total of thirty-seven Zekes that sortied from the bases at Kanoya and Kokubu on Kyushu.[31] The first Zeke was piloted by Yasunori Seizo. Seizo's plane strafed the ship on its way down. The 551-pound bomb he released just prior to the crash passed through the deck and the side of the ship, exploding overboard. Shrapnel from the bomb blast killed and wounded many men aboard the carrier. The second plane was piloted by Kiyoshi Ogawa. Ogawa's plane was hit on the way in and crashed into the ship while on fire. His bomb blew a hole in the deck that was fifty feet in diameter and extended three decks below the flight deck.[32]

Seamam 1/c Al Perdeck had just climbed into his bunk, three decks below the flight deck. Perdeck was a plane captain and his job was to look after his Curtiss SB2C Helldiver. Twice that morning there had been two calls to general quarters and two for torpedo defense and he had headed to his plane, which was his general quarters station. As he lay in his bunk, he recalled:

> I don't know how to describe it, it wasn't like a bang, not like a boom, it was a noise. I didn't know what the hell it was. A gush of air came through the compartment.... Then I went forward, trying to go up that double hatch and as I got my head above the deck, I says, "I'm not going up here." The folded wings of the planes each have three machine guns in the wings and those machine guns were firing ... so my better judgment told me I ain't going up this way.[33]

Perdeck eventually made his way aft, along the way crawling through thick black smoke and over the bodies of some of his dead shipmates. He emerged from the stern area and came up on the deck. What he saw shocked him, bodies were everywhere and the fires were raging. The kamikazes had done their job well. When the fires had subsided, the odious task of collecting the bodies began. Perdeck remembered, "And then we cleaned up the bodies, they brought them up from three decks below, two decks below and they laid them out on the hangar deck and it was an ugly, ugly sight — they got mutilated, their arms with no flesh on them, we had them in a few rows — about five rows I think — and then they had a burial at sea."[34]

Bunker Hill CV 17's burned and melted aircraft and damaged elevator are in evidence after the kamikaze attack of 11 May 1945. NARA 80G 259964.

Bunker Hill's fires were intense after she was struck by two kamikazes. NARA 80G 274266.

With so many dead, the medics soon ran out of body bags and had to put two men in each bag, weighted down with a shell casing. In spite of her heavy casualties, *Bunker Hill* survived the attack.

While major attacks from above plagued the ships at Okinawa, individual suicide swimmers were still active below. Early in the morning on 11 May the cargo ship *C. W. Post* was anchored off Ie Shima when she noted the presence of five enemy swimmers in her vicinity

Bunker Hill burns as *The Sullivans DD 537* stands by in foreground. NARA 80G 274264.

Crewmen and firefighting crews scramble to save their ship after it was hit by two kamikazes. NARA 80G 323712.

Bunker Hill crewmen look over the bodies of their shipmates after the kamikaze attack of 11 May 1945. NARA 80G 323708.

along with a small boat. The would-be suiciders were dispatched by gunfire from a nearby patrol craft.[35] Shortly thereafter, the crew of *C. W. Post* watched in horror as a kamikaze made a successful attack on another cargo ship nearby, the *M. S. Tjisadane*.

Ship's Master J. Naerabout had anchored *M. S. Tjisadane* near *C. W. Post* and *Panamint AGC-13* on 10 May 1945. At 0904, observers on *M.S. Tjisadane* saw *Panamint* open fire on an aircraft that was approaching her. At this point they realized that this was just one of three that were headed directly at *M. S. Tjisadane*. The first was a Jill which was taken under fire but managed to launch a torpedo which first missed *M. S. Tjisadane* and then curved around and missed *Panamint*. At this point a second Jill was taken under fire and crashed forward of *Tjisadane*. Meanwhile, the first Jill continued its attack, making a low altitude run on the ship which ended in its crash into the booms of the number two hold, erupting in a ball of flame. Parts of the plane were scattered over the deck and some went over the side. Moments later a Betty made a run on the cargo ship but was shot down 900 yards astern. Fire fighting on the cargo ship was effective and, by 0918 the flames had been extinguished. She had not suffered significant damage, but four men were killed and nine wounded in the attack.[36] Although the invasion was in its sixth week, there was no safe haven at Okinawa.

15. A Miserable May

Although the first eleven days of May had seen numerous attacks by the kamikazes, the remainder of the month would prove just as deadly. During this period the Japanese launched two more of their *Kikusui* attacks from 24 to 25 May and again from 27 to 28 May. Two ships would be sunk and many others would be hit. The toll of dead and wounded continued to rise.

New Mexico BB40 was returning from Kerama Retto to the Hagushi anchorage at 1903 on 12 May 1945 when a bogie was reported in her area. She went to general quarters at 1910 and a minute later fired on an incoming George, which was strafing the ship. A shell from one of her 5" guns exploded under the plane, lifting it up at the last moment and causing it to miss the battleship. However, its bomb went off, showering the ship with shrapnel. It crashed near her stern. A few minutes later a Frank, which took advantage of the distraction caused by the George, hit her amidships on the gun deck near the base of the stack. Fires caused by the explosion were quickly extinguished and *New Mexico* dropped anchor at 1920. The battleship had fifty-four dead and 119 wounded.

The destroyer escort *Bright DE 747* was patrolling an anti-submarine screen off Okinawa. At 1325 she had relieved *Sims APD 50* and was on station Baker 12. An incoming raid was reported at 1918 and the crew, already at general quarters, spotted a single engine plane low on the water making a run on her port beam. Fire from *Bright* struck the plane and damaged its engine and port wing, however, it was not sufficient to stop it. At about 1840 it crashed into the ship's fantail and exploded. *Bright*'s rudders were jammed at hard left and she had to cut her speed to five knots to avoid collisions with other ships in the area. Two of her men in the aft steering area were severely injured. *McClelland DE 750* came to her aid and stood by for assistance. Her crew managed to get the fires out and *Gear ARS 33* towed her into Kerama Retto. She remained there for several days undergoing temporary repairs and then joined a convoy headed for Ulithi on 21 May for further work.[1]

Ever wary of the possibility of a suicide boat attack, anti-small boat screens were constantly on patrol near the anchorages at Okinawa. Such a screen was in operation the evening of 12–13 May 1945. Patrolling to the south and west of the Hagushi beach anchorage at Okinawa was Task Unit 52.19.3, which consisted of seven LCS(L) gunboats, the *19, 53, 82, 83, 84, 86,* and *111*. Four of the ships, *LCS(L)s 19, 82, 84,* and *86*, patrolled on a line southwest of the anchorage. At 2330 *LCS(L) 84* made contact with a small craft and went to general quarters. She sent out a request for illumination, and within a short time, starshells went off overhead exposing the suicide boat. Reports indicate that it was about twenty feet long and held four men in an open cockpit. The *84* fired on the boat and it swerved away and headed toward *LCS(L) 19* which was patrolling on an adjacent station. *Thomas E. Fraser DM 25* was notified and picked up the boat with her arc light, illuminating it so that the gunboats were able to spot it. This was much more effective than the small signal lights on the LCS(L)s and enabled them to spot the suicide boats at a greater range. The *19* increased her speed and turned so that she was broadside to the small craft and let go with her 20mm and 40mm guns. At 0012 on 13 May, she scored hits on the boat and it sank a few minutes later. Fifty-two minutes later, at 0104, the gunboat spotted another *Shinyo* crossing her bow 800 yards dead ahead. As the distance closed to 600 yards she turned to port and let go with a broadside. The *Shinyo* was hit by 20mm fire and sank at 0112.[2]

LCS(L) 82 made its first suicide boat contact at 2353 on 12 May when her commanding officer, Lt. Peter G. Beierl, spotted a boat about seventy-five yards dead ahead. He gave the order to go to flank speed and hard left rudder in order to set his gunners up for a starboard broadside against the boat. The ship's twelve inch signal light illuminated the boat which then picked up speed and headed for the gunboat's starboard bow. For a while the boat was obscured by smoke from the guns, but soon appeared about fifteen feet off the ship's bow and then swerved toward the ship. The gunboat's speed was greater and the *Shinyo* passed behind the ship and headed for open water. The *82* gave chase and was finally able to spot the boat at a range of about 300 yards. By this time a nearby APD had managed to illuminate the boat with its arc light. Both ships fired on the boat and it went dead in the water and began to burn about 0019. It sank soon after.[3] Suicide boats continued to plague the area and *Spectacle AM 305* reported sinking six the night of 14–15 May.

On 13 May *Bache DD 470* was patrolling Radar Picket Station No. 9 along with *Cowell DD 547, LSM(R) 198,* and *LCS(L)s 23, 56,* and *87.* The ships came under attack at 1745 as three Petes approached the station. The two Marine Corsairs flying Combat Air Patrol made short work of them. An hour later the ships were under attack again. Three Vals were the attackers this time. Two made simultaneous runs on *Bache* from both sides and were promptly shot down near the ship. The third Val made it through the ship's fire. Its wing struck the ship near the No. 2 stack and the plane bounced along the deck and exploded. Its bomb, jarred loose by the impact, bounced off the deck and exploded a few feet in the air. The ship lost steam and electric power and the guns had to be handled manually. Other kamikazes tried to get at her but were prevented by the Combat Air Patrol and the support ships. Once her fires were under control at 1912, she transferred off her most seriously wounded to the LCS(L)s for treatment. *LCS(L) 56* began the task of towing her back to Kerama Retto for repairs and *Lipan ATF 85* took over. She had forty-one killed and thirty-two wounded.[4]

Enterprise CV 6, commanded by Capt. G. B. H. Hall, was still operating as part of Task Force 58. Along with the other carriers of the force she had been attacking the airfields on Shikoku and Kyushu. Early in the morning of 14 May the carriers came under attack as they headed back to Okinawa. A large raid of twenty-six enemy planes descended on the carriers and one Zeke chose *Enterprise* as its target. The large carrier maneuvered in an attempt to evade the plane and took it under fire with its five inch guns. The plane ducked in and out of cloud cover, evading the ship's fire. The carrier's action report describes the maneuvers of the kamikaze:

> The dive was very shallow, not at any time exceeding 30°. Previously his speed, as indicated by computer solution, had been in the vicinity of 250 knots. As the ship turned, his relative bearing increased to 185 or 190. No evasive tactics were employed although slight changes in the attitude of the plane indicate the pilot was correcting his point of aim as the ship turned. At an estimated distance of 100–200 yards from his point of impact flipped over in a left hand snap roll ending up on his back. When the plane passed Air Defense Forward a distance of 140 feet from

the terminal point the pilot had steepened his inverted dive so that he finally struck in a 40°–50° dive.

When the plane issued from the cloud all the guns that could effectively bear opened fire immediately.... The bomb explosion in No. 1 elevator pit caused fires to break out on 5 inch groups I and II (forward starboard and port respectively), and the forward starboard 20MM battery. The fire was extinguished in approximately thirty minutes, the abandoned guns remanned, and jettisioned ammunition replaced.[5]

The Zeke's bomb penetrated the carrier's deck and exploded below. Parts of the forward elevator were blown 400 feet in the air. This crash caused the death of thirteen of her crew and the wounding of another sixty-eight. Eight men, who had been blown overboard, were picked up by *Waldron DD 699*. However, the attacks were not finished. Two more Zekes attacked at 0803 and were shot down. Ten minutes later *Enterprise* assisted in shooting down a Zeke that was making a suicide run on *Bataan CVL 29*. The final attack came at 0817 when another Zeke came at the carrier from dead astern and was driven off by the ship's guns. At the time of these attacks "the big E" had thirteen planes aloft. They landed safely on the other carriers. *Enterprise* rejoined her task group for refueling and further service.

Douglas H. Fox was patrolling Radar Picket Station No. 9 along with *Van Valkenburgh* and *LCS(L) 53, 65, 66,* and *67* on 17 May when she encountered kamikazes. At 1926, four Oscars flying from the field at Karenko South on Taiwan attacked the radar pickets. Two went down under the combined firepower of the ships and *Douglas H. Fox* accounted for a third. However, a fourth made it through and hit *Fox's* deck near her No. 1 and 2 5"/38 mounts. Mount No. 1 was totally destroyed and No. 2 was damaged badly. Fires started by the explosions were fought successfully and were completely out fifteen minutes later. The swarm of kamikazes had done their best, but in the end *Fox* claimed five, *Van Valkenurgh* three and *LCS(L) 53* one. On board *Douglas H. Fox* nine men had died and thirty-five were wounded.[6]

Sims APD 50 was screening west of the Hagushi area on 18 May when a Tony attacked her. The plane came in on her port bow and was taken under fire. At 200 yards, *Sims'* gunners knocked its port wing off. At about the same time a second plane dove on her starboard quarter and also sustained damage from the ship's guns. Both went down just off her port side. The explosion shook the ship and caused minor damage, but there were no casualties. *Sims* had a lucky day.

LST 808 had been hit by a torpedo on 18 May

A Zeke, carrying a 551 pound bomb, rolls over on its back just prior to crashing into the flight deck of *Enterprise CV 6* on 14 May 1945. USS Enterprise CV 6 Serial 0273. *Action Report of USS Enterprise—CV6—in Connection with Operations in Support of Amphibious Landings at Okinawa 3 May to 16 May 1945—Phase III.* 22 May 1945, p. 26.

while anchored at Ie Shima. Her damage had been serious, and two tugs towed her to shallow water nearby where she came to rest on a reef. At 1837 on 20 May a Japanese plane crashed into her forward superstructure, penetrated her decks and set the ship afire. On board was a five man security team which had one man injured. The tugs *Tekesta ATF 93*, *YTB 404*, and *YTL 488* came to her assistance and put out the fires. At that point she was damaged beyond repair and the navy salvaged equipment that was still useable.

At the same time that *LST 808* was under attack, nearby *John C. Butler DE 339* was also attacked. At 1831 two Zekes passed by the ship, circled around near Motobu Peninsula, and

Parts of *Enterprise*'s elevator may be seen after being blown high over the carrier after she was hit by a Zeke with a 551 pound bomb on 14 May 1945. This photograph was taken from *Bataan CVL 29*. USS Enterprise CV 6 Serial 0273. *Action Report of USS Enterprise—CV6—in Connection with Operations in Support of Amphibious Landings at Okinawa 3 May to 16 May 1945—Phase III*. 22 May 1945, p. 28.

Enterprise CV 6's crew fights fires after the kamikaze crash on 14 May 1945. *NARA 80G 274352.*

headed for the ships near Ie Shima. Seven more planes appeared off her starboard side and split into two groups. *Butler*'s anti-aircraft fire brought down five planes and crippled another before one got close enough to cause damage. Fortunately, it only clipped her antennae and crashed close aboard the starboard beam. Three of her crew had minor injuries.

A short while later at 1950 the liberty ship *Uriah M. Rose* was attacked by an Oscar while in Nakagusuku Bay. The ship's gunners scored on it along with gunners from neighboring ships. It came in sixty feet over the ship and tried to crash but hit the water fifty feet off the port side. The ensuing explosion jarred the ship and caused some minor damage but no casualties. She had escaped destruction.

On 20 May *Chase APD 54* was underway five miles north of Kerama Retto when she was attacked at 1915 by a Zeke carrying two 220-lb. bombs. The plane did not hit her but crashed in the water about ten yards off her starboard beam. Its bombs went off under water and parts of the plane showered the aft end of the ship. Her starboard shaft was damaged and her steering was jammed. *Chase*'s after engine room began to flood and had to be abandoned. As she lay dead in the water, another plane dove at her but was driven away by her gunfire. *Impeccable AM 320* came to her aid. By 1941 the ship was listing seven degrees to starboard and the list increased to ten and one half degrees by 1950. *Chase* was informed that *Shackle ARS 9* was on the way from Kerama Retto to take her in tow. With *PCE(R) 852* and *Converse DD 509* standing by, her commanding officer decided that she had to be abandoned. At 2018 she was listing sixteen degrees to starboard and it looked as though she could not be saved. All non-essential personnel were ordered aboard *Impeccable*. Finally, with her list at nineteen degrees, all remaining personnel were transferred to *Impeccable*. *Converse* came alongside and stood by. Miraculously, the list stopped increasing and a skeleton repair party returned to the ship with additional pumps from *Converse*. *Shackle* arrived with more pumps and by 2300 the flooding was under control. *Shackle* towed her back to Kerama Retto where she underwent emergency repairs.[7] Although no one was killed in the attack, thirty-five of her men had been injured.

Thatcher DD 514 was patrolling in the outer screen at Okinawa on 20 May. *O'Neill DE 188* patrolled to her southwest and *Fair DE 35* to her northwest. At 1835 raids were reported heading for the area. *John C. Butler DE 339* reported that she was under attack by four aircraft and *Anthony DD 515* went to her aid. At 1920 an Oscar was spotted off *Thatcher*'s port bow making a run on her at a low altitude. The plane passed down the port side of the destroyer and circled around her stern. A couple of minutes later it crashed into *Thatcher*'s main deck aft the superstructure. Explosions rocked the destroyer and fires broke out. Immediately on the heels of the Oscar, two more planes came in on *Thatcher*'s port quarter but were driven off by her gunfire. *Boyd DD 544* and *Pavlic APD 70* came alongside to assist with firefighting. At 2030, with her fires under control, *Thatcher* headed for Kerama Retto. She reported:

> It is thought that the OSCAR type aircraft which struck the THATCHER carried two bombs, estimated at 500 pounds each. One of these detonated on contact, carrying away the lower part of the mast, destroying the radar transmitter room and CIC, damaging the forward part of the deck house and number one stack, and the after part of the bridge superstructure. The other bomb is thought to have entered the water just short of the ship and exploded in close proximity to hull or at instant of penetration causing the rupture in the hull, destroying the diesel generator room.... Deckhouse forward of one stack demolished. After part of bridge superstructure and forward part of number one stack and searchlight platform badly damaged.[8]

Thatcher had fourteen dead and fifty-three wounded.

Register APD 92 had arrived at Okinawa on 19 May and the next day was assigned to the screen. Ten Zekes headed in her direction at 1923. Four of them gave their attention to the APD, with two heading in from her starboard side, one from astern, and one from dead ahead. Under fire from her guns, two of the planes were shot down and a third driven off smoking. However, the plane making a run on her from her bow clipped the kingpost on the port side and crashed close aboard. The kingpost was damaged by the hit and struck the No. 3 40mm gun tub, severely damaging the ship. None of her crew died, but twelve were injured, including her commanding officer.[9]

Kikusui No. 7 ran from 24 to 25 May. Included in the attacks would be 165 kamikazes from both army and navy.

William C. Cole DE 641 came under attack twice from 24 to 25 May. An Oscar attacked her as she patrolled off Ie Shima and nearly crashed the ship. Its gunners hit it with anti-aircraft fire and the plane grazed the torpedo tubes, passed over the ship, and crashed close aboard the starboard beam. The action report for the event indicated that:

The entire hull was littered with debris of the plane, including engine parts, fuselage, and partial pieces of human flesh. The pilot, just prior to the planes crashing, was thrown clear and aft in such a way that his parachute opened partially. During his short descent the body had a limp appearance. From a post action inspection of the quantities of internal organs and flesh that were strewn about the ship in the vicinity of the crash, it is safe to assume the pilot was dead prior to hitting the water.[10]

The ship suffered some mild shock damage from the explosion but nothing serious. Later in the day she shot down a Tony which hit the water 1,000 yards from the ship.

The EC(2) type cargo ship *Segundo Ruiz Belvis* had a close call while anchored at Ie Shima. At 0130 on May 25, a kamikaze made a run on her, heading directly toward her bow. Accurate fire from a pair of LCIs nearby shot the plane down only 100 yards from the ship. Her decks were strewn with shrapnel and debris from the plane but no serious damage occurred and she suffered no casualties.

At 0142 on 25 May, a twin engine bomber passed over *Cowell DD 547* as she was patrolling Radar Picket Station No. 16. The plane clipped her mast and antenna and crashed close aboard, showering the ship with debris and wounding two men. Damage to the ship was minimal, a rare event for the radar picket ships. *Stormes DD 780* did not fare as well. She was patrolling Radar Picket Station No. 15 along with *Drexler DD 741, Ammen DD 527* and *LCS(L)s 52, 61, 85,* and *89*. The ships had been continually threatened by enemy aircraft from the preceding evening until the time *Stormes* was hit. At about 1900 the ships went to general quarters. This was a precautionary move as it was near the time the combat air patrol fighters usually began to return to their bases. Japanese airmen were aware of this and frequently planned their attacks for the evening hours and before daylight so as to avoid the presence of the Hellcats, Corsairs, and Wildcats. As if on pre-arranged signal, the kamikazes appeared around 2000, with many of them heading toward the ships at Hagushi. Several remained in the area of the radar pickets and began to attack them. At 1905 lookouts on *Stormes* observed a Tojo making a dive on *Ammen* and took it under fire. "Stormes opened fire with 5" and automatic weapons. The plane then did a half loop and came down on its back in a near vertical dive on the STORMES' after torpedo mount. The impact was followed by violent shaking of the ship and heavy fires billowed aft from the torpedo mount and 5" mount three."[11] The torpedo mount was demolished in the crash and the plane's bomb penetrated her deck and exploded in her after 5" magazine. Force from the explosion went upward and damaged the deck, as well as downward, where it tore a hole in the bottom of the ship. The aft end of *Stormes*' keel was blown off and her struts were bowed slightly. Flooding was brought under control, but when it was over, the destroyer was down three and one-half feet at the stern. *Stormes*' crew quickly put out the fires and *Sproston DD 577* escorted her back to base. Her CO, Cmdr. W. N. Wylie, paid tribute to his adversary:

> The enemy pilot was an excellent flyer. He handled his plane quickly and executed an attack which presented an ever changing deflection problem at difficulty position angles. He took full advantage of his tremendous speed without ever losing control of his plane. He executed a half roll to insure a hit in the last 500 feet of his dive.[12]

Early in the morning of 25 May, at 0025, *O'Neill DE 188* came under attack at the Hagushi anchorage by a Japanese plane described in her action report as an "advanced army trainer, type 15."[13] The plane appeared out of the smoke, circled *O'Neill*, and made a run on her from dead ahead. The destroyer escort took it under fire, and one of her 5" shells exploded the plane close aboard her starboard bow. Its explosion sent the plane's engine into the forecastle and the superstructure was splattered with shrapnel. Sixteen of *O'Neill*'s crew were wounded. Two of the more fortunate ships that day were *Guest DD 472* and *Sims APD 50*. Both had planes splash close aboard. *Guest* had no casualties and *Sims* suffered eleven wounded, but both ships had only minor damage.

Least fortunate of the ships hit that day was *Barry APD 29*. She had only been at Okinawa about ten days when she was attacked by two Vals while on patrol off Okinawa. One made it through her anti-aircraft fire to crash near her bridge, and the other passed over the ship and was soon shot down by other ships in the area. Severe fires broke out and threatened her magazines. The ship was abandoned, but flooding eventually put an end to the threat to her magazines and she was re-boarded and saved. However, her condition was such that she was too far gone and was decommissioned. Thirty of her men were wounded in the attack. Her hulk would be sunk later in an attempt to use her as bait for the kamikazes.[14] In his endorsement of the ship's action report, Capt. J. N. Hughes, Commander Transport Division 102, noted the vulnerability of the older destroyers:

1. To present date a total of six of these old APD's (ex "four stacker" destroyers) have been hit by suicide aircraft. The basic report illustrates how ill-equipped to meet present day problems in the forward area these old ships are. The average age of ships in this division (including APD-36) is over 26 years.
2. Japanese aviators have repeatedly shown a preference for attacking types that give ineffective opposition on account of their light armament and unwieldy turning circle. On this account the old APD's, with their antiquated design and consequent sluggish handling characteristics are select targets for enemy airmen.
3. The very large turning circle of the "four stacker" destroyer types is well known to the high command. When these old ships are a part of a composite unit under attack their sluggish handling proves mutually embarrassing to and embarrassed by the modern ships and thereby actually increases the hazard to the newer vessels.
4. It is recommended that such of the old APD's as have survived be withdrawn to rear areas for escort and training duties. The men who bring these ships into the forward area feel that they are being given a job to do but nothing to do it with.[15]

Spectacle AM 305 was operating as part of the suicide boat and submarine screen between Ie Shima and Okinawa on 25 May. Early in the morning, about 0505, her after engine governor failed and it became necessary for her to operate on her forward engine while she repaired the problem. At 0805, as the repairs were underway, she came under attack. A kamikaze attempted a run on a nearby destroyer escort but missed it and crashed into the water. Moments later a George also headed for the DE, pulled up and headed for *Spectacle*. As the George attacked the 185' minesweeper, her CO, Lt. G. B. Williams, ordered flank speed and a hard turn to starboard to give his gunners maximum opportunity to bear on the plane, which was coming in from astern. In spite of *Spectacle*'s maneuvers the plane crashed just aft of her starboard beam. Its engine and bomb went through the hull and into the after engine room. The explosion and subsequent fires cooked off ammo in the 40mm magazines and set the depth charges on fire. A number of men were blown overboard and were further imperiled by the ship. Its rudder had been jammed to full right by the blast and the ship circled around, narrowly missing the men in the water. Firefighting measures were instituted and the fires were brought under control. *LSM 135, LCI(M) 353* and several other ships came to her assistance, picking up crewmen from the water and helping with the firefighting. In the midst of all this, another plane crashed into *LSM 135* and a fourth was driven away after making an attempt on one of the ships. It was hit by gunfire and flew off smoking. *LCI(M) 353* took wounded aboard and headed back to Ie Shima. *Spectacle* had suffered twenty-nine dead and six wounded. She was towed in by *Tekesta ATF 93*. Her action report for the day indicated that:

> The crash demolished the crew's and CPO's heads, the two 40mm magazines amidships on the main deck, general workshop, laundry, all of these between frames 52 and 62, also blew up and

ripped open the boat deck (01) between those frames, bulged out hull on both sides, demolished the port 40mm gun, mount and foundation, smashed the motor whaleboat and put starboard 40mm out of action. In the after engine room the main engine was ruined, all piping and accessories near the point of penetration were ripped and torn. The bulkheads at frame 52, main deck, were bulged forward, all hatches in the amidship passageway leading forward were blown out except for one at frame 44 leading into the mess hall. The hatch, starboard side leading to the after main deck, was blown out, and all other hatches in the vicinity were bulged out from force of explosion. Six bodies were recovered from the wreckage and one in the engine room were nude. Due to this fact, and to the general disruptive force, and due to the lack of widespread gasoline fires, it is believed this plane carried a small bomb which exploded on impact. [16]

At 0810 *LSM 135* had been ordered to assist *Spectacle* which was on fire three miles southeast of Ie Shima. She arrived on the scene and began rescuing survivors from the mine sweeper when she was attacked by two Tonys. Her action report stated:

> At approximately 0845 the ramp was being raised when two planes identified as Jap Tonys suddenly appeared out of the low hanging clouds and approached from dead astern at low angle (almost mast head height) and continued in face of the fire of our 20 MM. guns. One plane hit the conn and parts of the plane and possibly a bomb continued by force into the starboard side forward crew's compartment, and through to the bottom spraying the well deck and the weather deck with gasoline and parts of the plane. The other plane veered off. The conn was enveloped in flames immediately. At the same time the forward crew's compartment was engulfed in flames and burning oil due to the puncturing of the forward fuel tanks and escaping of oil into the compartment. Due to the instantaneous fire of the burning fuel oil completely enveloping the compartment it was impossible to save those survivors of the AM 305 and those members of ship's company there assisting them.[17]

Water mains had been broken by the explosions and firefighting was impossible. With fires raging and the ship beginning to list to starboard, it was obvious that she was not going to be saved. Burning oil leaked out of the ship and surrounded her and she was abandoned. *William C. Cole DE 641* and *Tekesta ATF 93* rescued most of the survivors. Her commanding officer, Lt. H. L. Derby, Jr., and ten of her crew were dead, with ten more of her crew wounded in the attack. The ship drifted onto a reef off Ie Shima and was declared a total loss.

Sims APD 50 had suffered some minor damage from a close miss on 18 May. Again on 25 May she had a similar experience. At 0033 in the morning, an unidentified plane attacked her and crashed close aboard her starboard beam. The ship had little damage, but the explosion of the plane and its bomb wounded eleven men.

The high speed transport *Roper APD 20* ran afoul of the kamikaze horde at 0921 on 25 May. She was patrolling the screen with *Abercrombie DE 343* and two other destroyer escorts. At 0703 she transferred ten men from her engineering force to *Barry APD 29*, which had suffered a kamikaze strike at 0100 that morning. She then resumed patrol and was near *Abercrombie* when she was hit. A Zeke, with three Corsairs in hot pursuit, broke through the clouds four miles away. In all probability the Zeke had not set out from its base on a kamikaze mission. However, with little chance of escaping the Corsair, the Zeke picked *Roper* as a target and made its run. Certain that the Zeke would fall victim to the Corsairs, *Roper* held fire but the plane made it through to crash her forecastle.

> When the plane struck the forecastle, its gasoline exploded throwing a sheet of flame up about 200 feet, the port wing entered the starboard side making a hole roughly six feet square, five feet above the water line. The motor hit No. 1 3" 50 Cal. Gun mount, and with the starboard wing or part of the fuselage glanced into the air and exploded about 30 feet over the water and 50 feet from the port side near the stern. Several fragments which appeared to be pieces of the motor block were found on the after deck, and it is believed to be one of these fragments which killed the First Lieutenant, who was crouching just forward of the after deck house ordering the men in the repair parties to hit the deck.... The Pilot's flying helmet, pieces of his leather jacket, and small pieces of his anatomy were left hanging on Gun No. 1.[18]

The fires started by the explosion were extinguished by 1030. *Roper* transferred her injured to *Relief AH 1* and headed back to Kerama Retto escorted by *Abercrombie* and two Corsairs where temporary repairs were completed by 30 May. *Roper* had one dead and ten wounded.

Bates APD 47 was on patrol two miles south of Ie Shima and had a busy night from 24 to 25 May. Continual calls to general quarters occurred between 2000 and 0430, and she fired on planes along with *Shannon DM 25* which was cruising nearby. At 0700 she was relieved by *William Seiverling DE 441* and headed back toward Ie Shima. Constantly under general quarters from 0800 to 0845, she fired on a plane about 0900. At 1115 three Vals, at first thought to be American planes landing on Ie Shima headed for *Bates*. *William Seiverling* and *Bates* took them under fire, but one approached *Bates* from port and dropped a bomb, which exploded close aboard her starboard side, opening her seams. Moments later it crashed into *Bates*' fantail on the starboard side. The second Val crashed into *Bates*' wheelhouse on the port side. Gasoline fires spread instantly and *Bates* lost power. Minutes later, just as *Bates* was beginning to recover, the third Val bombed her. It missed the ship, but the bomb exploded so close aboard the port side that *Bates* incurred additional severe damage. Fuel oil leaked out and was ignited by the existing fires. Soon the burning oil had spread over the side and the ship was in the midst of a sea of fire. *Gosselin APD 126* attempted to close on *Bates*, but had to back off due to the extreme fires on the water. With the fires continuing to spread and the water mains out, the order to abandon ship was given. *Cree ATF 84* managed to get a line on her later in the afternoon and towed her burning hulk to the anchorage at Ie Shima, but it was too late. At 1923, the burning ship rolled over and went under in twenty fathoms.[19] Twenty-one of her men had died and thirty-five were wounded.

At 0233 on 25 May, *Guest DD 472* was patrolling off the Hagushi anchorage, just north of Yontan airfield, when she came under attack by a single engine plane. It struck her mast and hit the water fifty yards off her starboard beam. She had minor damage and no casualties.

Forrest DMS 24 was on patrol in Nakagusuku Bay on 26 May when she was hit by a kamikaze. She had cut her speed and was in the process of slowing the ship when, at 2249, a Val with a 551 pound bomb struck her on the starboard side just below the main deck. According to her action report:

> Evidently the bomb was broken by impact and the forward half bounced across to settle against the hull, first platform deck, above the after port corner of the chill box. When it exploded, apparently with delayed nose fuse, it created a depression in the first platform deck at that point, split the main deck athwartships from port side to midships and turned the two pieces back against the adjacent stanchions, made a hole in the port side, and bulged the forward and after bulkheads of the forward mess hall. The explosion created one heavy black cloud of smoke approximately twenty feet in diameter, but no noxious fumes or gasses were observed.[20]

Tawakoni ATF 114 came immediately to her aid and the process of firefighting and pumping her out commenced. She was down by the head but made it to Kerama Retto on her own twenty-seven hours later where she tied up alongside *Nestor ARB 6* for repairs. Her casualties were five dead and thirteen wounded.

PC 1603 was moored at Taka Shima on 26 May when she came under attack. Apparently the ship was not aware that there were enemy aircraft in the area. A Tony crashed her port bow and buried itself below, its tail protruding from the ship. Now alerted, the crew spotted another incoming kamikaze but they were too late. It crashed their starboard side and gasoline from its tanks erupted in a ball of fire. It was fortunate for the crew that the bombs carried by the planes did not go off. So thin were the sides of the PC that the bombs passed right through without exploding. Her casualties were three dead and fifteen wounded. She was towed back to Kerama Retto and declared a total loss.[21]

Kikusui No. 8 ran from 27 to 28 May and would include 110 special attack aircraft, sixty from the navy and fifty from the army. Conventional escorts and attack planes would also participate in the attacks.

Braine DD 630 was patrolling Radar Picket Station No. 5 along with *Anthony DD 515* and LCS(L)s 13, 82, 86, and 123 on 26 May. Covering the ships was a CAP of army air force Thunderbolts. Foul weather forced them to return to base around 0700, leaving the picket ships unguarded. Several Vals approached the station and began their attack. *LCS(L) 123* shot down one as it attempted a run on *Braine*. It crashed close aboard the destroyer. A second Val headed for *Anthony* and was hit by anti-aircraft fire from *Anthony* and *Braine*. *Braine* took a third Val under fire without realizing that the second had regained control and was heading right for her. It crashed into her number 2 handling room. Moments later another Val crashed her amidships and its bomb penetrated her deck. Interior damage to the ship, as well as her bridge, was caused by this attack. So many fires broke out from the two kamikaze crashes that the ship was effectively divided into three parts. Communication between them was destroyed, and men in each section were on their own in determining how to save their ship.[22] *Braine*'s rudder was jammed, and with the lack of communications, the ship circled continually at about ten knots, putting men in the water in peril. Other ships in the area had to take evasive measures so that they would not collide with her. Hot on the heels of the first two Vals, a third made its attack. This one went after *LCS(L) 86* but was shot down by the combined fire of the support ships. At about the same time, a Val made its attack on *Anthony* but was shot down close aboard. The pilot's body along with other debris from the plane showered down on *Anthony*, but damage to the destroyer was minimal, and she had no casualties.

On board *Braine*, many men had been killed and wounded. A number went into the shark infested waters. Walter C. Gaddis, a machinist mate on board *Braine*, survived the blast from the two planes and wound up in the water. The LCS(L) gunboats came to the destroyer's aid, picking up their men and shooting at the sharks which were attacking them.[23] Gaddis was rescued and "looked back and saw a shark hit someone in the water and throw him into the air."[24] *Anthony* and the gunboats came alongside *Braine* and assisted with firefighting and the rescue of survivors. A number had been killed by sharks. John Rooney, a yeoman on board *LCS (L) 82*, recalled, "We recovered one who had not made it, hanging pale and lifeless in his Mae West, a leg torn away, the other arm gone, gutted by the sharks. He had escaped the terror of incineration on his ship."[25]

Enemy aircraft continued to threaten the ships. At one point *Anthony* and the LCS(L)s had to cast off from *Braine* in order to combat enemy planes. In the midst of the fray, ten men in the water were carried away by the current and drifted out of sight of the ships. They were fortunate, as a call had been made to the "Dumbo" patrol of *Hamlin AV 15* at Kerama Retto. At 0917, Lt. M. W. Kouns set his PBM-5 Mariner down in the choppy waters and rescued the men. One of them died en route to safety. *Anthony* began to tow *Braine* back to Kerama Retto and was relieved of the chore by *Ute ATF 76*. *Braine*'s casualties were sixty-six dead and seventy-eight wounded.

Loy APD 56 was hit by a kamikaze at 2320 on 27 May while on anti-submarine patrol off Okinawa. At 2332 her lookouts spotted a Jill circling the ship and lining up for a suicide run. As the plane approached the ship, *Loy*'s gunners let loose with a barrage of 40mm and 20mm fire and the plane crashed just off the starboard side of the ship. Pieces of the plane made a number of small holes in her side and some flooding in the engine room was experienced. Hot shrapnel from the explosion pierced some drums of fog oil and gasoline on the fantail, and major fires engulfed the aft end of the ship. Within a short time the fires were under control and the flooding stopped. *Loy* headed back to Hagushi under her own steam to transfer casualties and lick her wounds.[26] Three of her crew had been killed and fifteen wounded.

Rednour APD 102 had been on anti-submarine screen off Okinawa near *Loy* and observed the attack on her. She was soon under attack herself. At 2345 an Oscar made a run on her from her starboard quarter and crashed into her fantail on the starboard side. The plane's explosion blew a ten foot hole in the deck and engulfed the area in a fireball. Within ten minutes the fires were under control. Depth charges were jettisoned as a precaution and the flooding in the aft compartment was stopped. *Pavlic APD 70* came to her aid and sent its medical officer on board to assist in treating casualties. At 0030 another plane menaced the ship but was turned away by her gunfire. She made it back to Hagushi to transfer her wounded at 0145.[27] Three of her men had died and thirteen were wounded.

The hydrographic ship *Dutton AGS-8* had arrived at Okinawa on 1 April along with the invasion fleet. Her job had been to survey various bodies of water, determining safe passages, good anchoring ground, and suitable locations for amphibious landings. On 27 May she was en route from Nakagusuku Wan to Kimu Wan when she came under attack. It was a cloudy, wet day, with intermittent rain and low visibility. At 0735 bogeys were reported in the area and the ship was put on alert. Five minutes later three Vals were spotted heading toward Okinawa, but they changed course as American fighters headed to attack them. Their new course put them on path to fly near *Dutton*. One passed by *Dutton*'s stern and was taken under fire by the ship with no hits scored. It turned off and headed for a nearby destroyer escort. The second plane dove on *Dutton*'s port beam. *Dutton*'s gunners hit the plane and probably killed the pilot, causing the plane to lift up and crash into the forward section of the bridge. The remaining parts of the plane crashed into the starboard forecastle and went over the side. Debris from the crash and a shower of water came down on *Dutton*'s deck, but she had not suffered a mortal wound. Her CO, Lt. Frederick E. Sturmer, aware of his ships limited anti-aircraft capability, headed for the company of other ships in order to protect his vessel against the increasing number of bogeys overhead. As they headed away from the area, a muster of the crew revealed that one man had been blown overboard and was missing. *Dutton* returned to the scene of the attack and searched for thirty minutes and could not find him. *SC-1338* took over the search and *Dutton* left the area. The crewman was never found and presumed dead.[28]

LCS(L) 52 was on patrol at Radar Picket Station No. 15A on 27 May, along with *LCS(L)s 55, 56,* and *61*. They were the support group for *Ammen DD 527* and *Boyd DD 544*. During the daylight hours the ships had driven off several would-be kamikazes. Neither destroyer was damaged, but at 2047, a Zeke made a run on *LCS(L) 52*. *LCS(L)s 61* and *82* both hit it with their fire and the plane crashed only twenty yards off the starboard quarter of *LCS(L) 82*. The explosion damaged the gunboat, killed one officer and wounded another. Nine of the crew were also injured. She headed back to Hagushi for repairs with *61* as an escort. Along the way a Betty bomber circled the two ships and came in astern the *52*. It passed over and was hit by shells from the gunboat but continued on course heading for the conn of *LCS(L) 61*. The *61*'s aft 40mm battery took it under fire and literally lifted the aircraft upward as it passed directly over the gun tub. A hard left turn at the last second, ordered by the CO Lt. Jim Kelley, saved the ship as the bomber crashed twenty feet off her port bow. A section of the tail bounced back off the water and landed on the ship, injuring Bosun's Mate Joe Columbus. Aside from one man injured, the *61* escaped unscathed.

The sinking of another destroyer on a radar picket station was not far away. Patrolling RP No. 15A on 28 May were *Drexler DD 741, Lowry DD 770,* and *LCS(L)s 55* and *56*. By this time it was standard practice to have at least two destroyers and four support gunboats on each radar picket station, however, with the damage to the *LCS(L) 52* the previous day and the assignment of *LCS(L) 61* as her escort, that left only two support gunboats on the station.

Drexler's radar picked up six twin-engine Franceses approaching the station about 0643.

The two radar picket patrol Corsairs from VMF-322 went after them, shot down two and damaged two others. Another plane from the group slipped by and made a run at *Lowry*.

> The DREXLER came left sharply and opened fire immediately at about 12,000 yards range, firing directly over the U.S.S. LOWRY as the plane closed. The plane appeared to be making its suicidal dive on the LOWRY which was 800 yards on the starboard beam of the DREXLER as a result of our turn. This plane was hit but came on in, missed the LOWRY by a few feet passing directly over her, and looked as if it was going to crash; however, it recovered and seemed to stumble into this vessel striking between the main deck and waterline ... just slightly forward of the starboard 40MM Quad mount. The ship in this vicinity was sprayed with gasoline which started a fire, but the fire was quickly brought under control.[29]

The impact knocked the 40mm quad off its mount and ruptured steam lines in the ship. Almost immediately another Frances dove on *Lowry* and was shot down by a hit from one of *Drexler*'s 5" guns. At this point, *Drexler* was dead in the water and an easy target for still another Frances that came in on her starboard bow. The Corsairs drove it off but did not shoot it down. It circled and made another run on the destroyer, which scored numerous hits on it with 40mm and 20mm gunfire. Although the plane appeared about to crash, the pilot recovered control and came back at the ship for a third run. This time he was successful and crashed into *Drexler* on the port side. Its bomb went off inside the ship and *Drexler* rolled over to starboard, pointed her bow skyward, and slipped beneath the surface. Less than a minute had elapsed between the kamikaze hit and *Drexler*'s sinking. The quick roll-over of the ship prevented many men below from getting out. One hundred fifty-eight died and fifty-one were wounded. *Lowry* had shot down two enemy aircraft. The LCS(L)s patrolled the area rescuing survivors.

Transports and cargo ships were important targets for the kamikazes. Keeping supplies from the American forces would slow down their advances on the Japanese army on Okinawa. On 28 May several of them suffered kamikaze attacks.

Brown Victory was anchored off Ie Shima carrying 1,000 tons of gas and trucks when she was crashed by a kamikaze at 0745 on 28 May. Fortunately, the kamikaze that hit her did not score a direct hit on the hull or superstructure. It crashed into the victory ship's after mast and broke in two, with a major portion of the plane hitting the water to starboard. Its bombs exploded, starting fires and killing four men and injuring sixteen more. Damage to the ship was minor and she continued operations.

Mary A. Livermore's cargo was a mundane mix of cement, lumber, and machinery. She was anchored in Nakagusuku Bay when she was attacked. Her assailant was a float plane that maneuvered its way toward the ship and crashed into the chart room at 0515. Its bomb destroyed the area around the chart room and the captain's quarters. Fires damaged various areas of the ship and killed her master, James A. Stewart. Along with Stewart, ten men perished and six were injured. The ship survived the attack and, with temporary repairs, made it back to San Francisco for an overhaul. Anchored nearby was *Josiah Snelling*, carrying a similar cargo. At 0800 a kamikaze made a run on *Sandoval APA 194*, missed and then crashed *Josiah Snelling*. However, it experienced a similar fate as other kamikazes which went after cargo ships. Heavy masts and booms for shifting cargo were part of the deck furniture on these ships and it was hard to crash into the ship's bridge or deck without running afoul of these. The kamikaze hit her forward winches and then her booms before it went through the deck. Fires broke out below, but the cement was non-flammable and the fires were quickly extinguished. Twenty-five of her men were injured.[30]

Sandoval APA 194 was carrying a SeaBee unit and its equipment. She anchored in Nakagusuku Bay on 27 May and began to offload her troops and cargo. She had just resumed her offloading at 0737 the following morning when she was crashed by a Tony which hit her wheelhouse. As she fought the fires, another kamikaze dove on her and missed, splashing 2,000 yards off the ship. Her XO was one of eight men killed, and her CO was among the twenty-six wounded.

LCS(L) 119 had been assigned skunk patrol on the north side of the Hagushi Anchorage. She arrived at her patrol station at 1830 on 27 May. Early the next morning she was attacked by three Japanese aircraft. A Betty made a run at 0007 and was taken under fire by the ship's 20mm and 40mm guns. The plane flamed and lost its right wing, causing it to splash in the water only fifteen feet from the ship. Its bomb went off and the ship was covered with gas and shrapnel. At 0015 a Rufe was spotted on the port quarter making a run at the gunboat. It went to flank speed and opened fire, but the Rufe made it through and crashed her starboard quarter. The center of the ship was transformed into a mass of fire and communications within the ship were down. Her fire mains had been broken by the crash and it was impossible to fight the fires. As she struggled to launch her life rafts, another Rufe made a run and dropped two depth charges but did not crash the ship. No further damage was sustained from this incident, but it was too late. Her CO, Lt. E. Saroch, Jr., gave the order to abandon ship. *LCS(L) 119* had fourteen dead and eighteen wounded. She was towed in to Kerama Retto where she was cannibalized to provide parts for other ships as she was being repaired. On 14 June *Ute ATF 76* towed her to the Marianas. Eventually she made it back to Treasure Island, California, for a complete overhaul.[31]

Two ships were hit by kamikazes on 29 May. One was *Shubrick DD 639*, operating on Radar Picket Station No. 16A, and the other was *Tatum APD 81* serving on a picket station off the Hagushi beaches. In the early evening, *Tatum* came under attack by four enemy aircraft. She fired on the first which crashed close aboard. Its bomb, released by the impact, went

The *Nakajima A6M2-N Navy Type 2* fighter seaplane carried the Allied code name Rufe. It was developed along the same lines as the Zeke. NARA 80G 169840.

through the ship's side; fortunately, it was a dud. The mass of the plane bounced off the water then off *Tatum's* side but fell back harmlessly into the sea, causing a few dents in her side plating. She then drove off another plane with her fire and shot down the third close aboard. The fourth plane made its run on *Tatum* and was hit by many shells from the fast transport. It hit the water only thirty feet from its port bow. The plane's bomb went off underwater, rocking the transport, but she held together. The accumulation of several close misses by the aircraft had damaged the transport, and she was repaired later after she was relieved.

Shubrick DD 639 was underway for Radar Picket Station No. 16A at 2357 and had just been relieved by *Bradford DD 545* at Radar Picket Station No. 11A when a two plane raid approached the ships. *Bradford* made short work of her attacker splashing it 200 yards astern. *Shubrick* spotted the second plane and slowed to decrease her wake so that she could not be spotted. The ships at RP No. 11A took the plane under fire but failed to hit it. It spotted *Shubrick* and made a run on the destroyer but was shot down 3,500 yards off the ship. A few minutes later at 1012 another kamikaze hit her starboard quarter. This one had slipped in unseen by anyone. Its 551 lb. bomb blew a thirty foot hole in the ship's deck and blew out her starboard side. In short order the ship began taking on water in her aft engine and fire rooms. Topside, ammo in the 20mm and 40mm gun tubs began to explode, and at 1029 one of her depth charges went off. The explosion blew out most of the fires but also killed one of the crew and injured several others. She was listing three degrees to port and down by the stern as *Van Valkenburgh DD 656* and *Pavlic APD 70* came to her assistance, taking off her wounded and helping with the firefighting. The tug *Menominee ATF 73* arrived at 0400 and took her in tow back to Kerama Retto. *Shubrick* had thirty-two killed and twenty-eight wounded.

Thus ended the month of May at Okinawa. Seventy-four ships had been hit by airborne kamikazes of which nine were sunk. In addition, two were hit by suicide boats, one of which sank. In the kamikaze attacks of May 1945, 1,620 men had died and 2,073 were wounded.

16. The War Winds Down

On 1 June 1945, Task Unit 32.19.12, consisting of *LCS(L)s 61, 62, 65, 81, 82,* and *90* departed the Hagushi area for patrol. They circled the southern part of Okinawa and entered Nakagusuku Wan on the southeastern part of the island. Their targets were suicide boats and swimmers. By this time many of the suicide boat units had lost their boats to American gunfire, and the remaining personnel frequently attacked by using canoes or by swimming. At 2230 on 5 June, *LCS(L) 62* picked up a nearby boat on radar. Star shells revealed a solidly built twenty foot dugout canoe. On board were six Japanese wearing breech cloths and two of them were wearing swimming goggles. They had gear piled in the bottom of the canoe and covered by a tarp. The commander of the task unit, Lt. Cmdr. B. D. Voegelin, ordered them to take prisoners if possible. After circling the canoe for several minutes they used the bullhorn to order the Japanese to surrender. When their order was ignored, they fired on the boat and the swimmers went overboard. Small arms were issued to the crew and they killed five of the men. The sixth tried to swim away, but fire from the ship stopped him and he was dragged aboard. As the crew was about to tie him up, he went over the side and tried to escape. He swam back to the canoe and could not be enticed back on board the gunboat. Having enough of this, the CO ran over the canoe, thus ending the life of the Japanese swimmer.

It was difficult to capture Japanese soldiers since one could never trust that the individual they encountered was not on a suicide mission. In the same area on 4 May, *LCS(L) 40* had encountered a swimmer. According to the ship's action report:

> 0608: Sighted enemy swimmer about 600 yards northwest of Chinen Misaki. Closed him and attempted to bring him aboard, but when alongside he drew a hand grenade from out of his shirt and attempted to throw it at the men rescuing him. He was dispatched with small arms fire. This man was in full uniform less helmet and life jacket. He spoke English and on our approach asked us to help him.
>
> 0639: Sighted second enemy swimmer about 1600 yards east of Yonabaru. This man was in full uniform including helmet and wore a life jacket but had removed his shoes. Remembering the experience of the previous swimmer he was dispatched at a distance of 300 yards with small arms fire.[1]

Thus, the CO of a ship had to quickly determine if the individual was truly in need of rescue and could be captured or if he was a threat to the ship and its crew. Most preferred to err on the side of caution.

Kikusui No. 9 was scheduled for 3 to 7 June 1945. Twenty navy and thirty army special attack planes would undertake kamikaze missions at Okinawa. The number of aircraft available for these missions was beginning to decline by this time. Accompanying the *Kikusui* raid would be additional planes flying escort for the kamikazes, as well as others flying conventional missions.

At anchor in Chimu Wan was *LCI(L) 90*. Her task in the area was to act as the harbor entrance control unit. Around 1340 a Val appeared out of the clouds and seemed to be making a run on a small Marine encampment on the nearby island of Taka Hanare. It spotted the anchored LCI(L) and changed its purpose. In his action report for the day the ship's CO, Lt. (jg) J.A. Spear, questioned whether it was an actual suicide attack or a pilot error that caused the Val to crash his ship. He noted that the plane strafed on the way in, dropped a bomb fifty yards to starboard of the ship and struck a glancing blow on the aft section of the conn. It almost seemed as if he was trying to pull up when he hit. However, this type of attack was not inconsistent with kamikaze crash methods, so the incident is open to question. The ship had its number one gun manned, but since the plane came in from astern, the ship was unable to fire on it. It was also unclear if there were air raid warnings broadcast for the area, as the signalman on watch was killed in the crash and the records destroyed. Damage to the landing craft was serious and she had one dead and seven injured on her casualty list.[2]

Mississippi BB 41 and *Louisville CA 28* were operating off the southwestern tip of Okinawa to prevent the escape of Japanese personnel by boat or small craft. At about 1933 on 5 June, two Tony's roared in and made an attack on them. One chose *Mississippi* and the other went for *Louisville;* both were successful. *Mississippi* was making about six knots and in the process of making a 180 degree turn when she was hit. Both of the planes had been picked up on radar and mistakenly identified as Corsairs. The Tony crashed into her starboard quarter and both of its bombs went off. However, the sides of the battleship were too thick for them to penetrate. *Mississippi*'s hull was buckled inward in two places, one where each of the bombs had hit. After the plane and the bombs exploded, there were small fires on board the ship, but they were quickly extinguished. Damage to her was minor, although one man had been killed and eight wounded. *Mississippi* continued on her patrol.[3] At about the same time that *Mississippi* was hit, the second Tony crashed into *Louisville*. This plane approached from the island and came out of cloud cover. Its low approach put it in line with several LCI gunboats and it "hedge-hopped" over them to get at the cruiser. It struck on the port catapult, demolishing a SC-1 Seahawk observation plane and cutting through the after half of the No. 1 stack before skidding over the side of the ship. The number 1 stack was demolished and other parts of the ship suffered minor damage in the area. Casualties were high, with eight men killed and thirty-seven wounded.[4]

In spite of the efforts of the patrolling ships around Okinawa, suicide boats were still considered a threat. In addition, the Japanese also had the ability to use landing barges to move troops or to escape from tight corners as the American troops closed in on them in southern Okinawa. *J. William Ditter DM 31* and *Harry F. Bauer DM 26* were on flycatcher patrol on 6 June, along with several LCI gunboats. At 1708 the ships went to general quarters with notification that several enemy planes were approaching their position. *Harry F. Bauer*'s gunners took aim at an incoming Betty and hit it numerous times. The twin-engine bomber passed over the ship in flames and crashed 2,000 yards to starboard. Moments later a Val was taken under fire and crashed only ten yards off the ship's starboard beam and passed under the ship. This attack caused some minor damage to the minelayer but she suffered no casualties.[5] Minutes after *Harry F. Bauer* was damaged, *J. William Ditter* came under attack. She was not as fortunate as her companion: a kamikaze crashed her No. 2 stack at 1714, and a second plane crashed her port side below the main deck at 1723. The second crash opened a hole in her hull that was five by fifty feet. Fires broke out and were soon extinguished. Her main problem was flooding of her forward engine room and after fire room. The minelayer went dead in the water with a two degree list to port. *Harry F. Bauer* came to her aid to cover her. *LSM 708* came alongside to render aid. With the flooding stopped, she was towed to Kerama Retto by *Ute ATF 76*. She suffered ten dead and twenty-seven wounded in the attack.[6]

Natoma Bay CVE 62 was operating off Okinawa on 7 June when she suffered a kamikaze strike. At 0635 she was approached by two Zekes. The first came in from astern, strafed the ship, and made a wing over into the flight deck. Its bomb exploded below decks and resulted in a twelve by twenty foot hole in the deck. Immediately thereafter, its companion was taken under fire by the ship's gunners and crashed close aboard. The escort carrier was damaged, but not mortally. She had one killed and four wounded, but her fires were out quickly and she resumed operations later that evening.[7]

Anthony DD 515 was on patrol at Radar Picket Station No. 15A on 7 June, along with *Walke DD 723, Bradford DD 545* and *LCS(L)s 18, 66, 86,* and *94*. The ships had been at general quarters frequently on 6 June and had shot down an Oscar near *Walke*. They went to general quarters again late in the afternoon of the 7th with the approach of enemy aircraft, which subsequently fell victim to the CAP. Her action report indicated:

> Visitors came again during afternoon and evening. At Battle Stations 1427–1505, during which time our CAP splashed three planes.
> Dusk attacks commenced about 1850 on many stations. Our destroyer group went to 25 knots. At 1855 visually sighted two planes (NATES or VALS) approaching out of low haze from starboard quarter. Went to maximum speed with hard right rudder. At 1858 one plane splashed by 40MM at about 2,000 yards while in an almost straight approach. Other plane must have had instructions to get in from port side, for he continued in an end around stern chase, finally crossing stern, came up port side at about 1,500 yards, banked sharply and came in. We couldn't figure what held him up, for the machine gun fire of this ship and BRADFORD could be seen hitting and taking chunks out of plane. He splashed alongside to port just forward of No. 1 5" mount, and part of plane flipped over the forecastle and ended up in the water to starboard. Dished in side between frames 24 and 27, with one 4" × 5" hole in CPA quarters, carried away lifelines and stanchions for 25' on port side. The whole forward part of ship, including bridge and director got one big slug of water and burning gasoline. Fortunately the water was sufficient to put out the fire, and after all gas ran off forecastle there was no fire on board. Much wreckage came aboard, including parts of the pilot.[8]

Five of *Anthony*'s men were either washed overboard or blown overboard by the crash. Three of them were injured but none seriously. *LCS(L)s 66* and *86* recovered them and returned them to *Anthony*. The tradition for such service by the gunboats was to reward them with a supply of ice cream. The small LCS(L)s could not make or store this treat but larger ships such as a destroyer could. At 1904, *Anthony* fired on an approaching Val off her starboard beam and alerted the CAP, which shot it down.

On 10 June Radar Picket Station No. 15A was patrolled by *William D. Porter DD 579, Aulick DD 569, Cogswell DD 651,* and *LCS(L)s 18, 86, 94,* and *122*. *William D. Porter* served as the fighter director for the station. A radar picket patrol of two planes circled the ships and a CAP of eight Corsairs from VMF-212 and VMF-314 flew nearby. At 0823 the VMF-314 division observed Val a mile and half away. Their efforts to shoot it down were in vain as it slipped through their fire and crashed just off *Porter*'s stern. It exploded underwater, lifting the stern of the destroyer and dropping it again in a violent movement. Cmdr. C. M. Keyes later wrote:

> It is not known whether the explosive was carried within the plane or in a bomb which might have been released, but it is believed that the explosion occurred nearly directly under the ship, under the after engine room or slightly aft of it. All the events of this paragraph occurred within a space of seconds. Pertinent to the failure of any ship in company to make radar contact on this plane until it had closed to 7000 yds., and the failure of this ship to make radar contact at all was a later report from one of the LCS's which had recovered parts of the plane, that paper and wood appeared to have been used extensively in its construction.[9]

The description of the recovered pieces may be explained by the fact that Vals had fabric covered control surfaces.

The after engine room and fire room began to flood rapidly and steam lines were ruptured, causing the area to fill with steam and effectively cutting power to the rest of the ship. The four LCS(L)s came to *Porter*'s assistance and two tied up on either side of the ship to aid in pumping. By 0836 the ship had an eight degree starboard list and the stern was below water. Topside gear, torpedoes, depth charges and other weighty items were jettisoned in an attempt to keep the ship afloat, but the list continued to increase and more of the stern slipped under. Sixty-one men had received minor injuries in the blast and they were transferred off the ship and onto the LCS(L)s. The *18, 94,* and *122* were ordered to stand off and the *86* remained tied to the destroyer. By 1108 it was obvious that nothing could be done to save the ship, which at that time had a twenty-five degree starboard list with the stern about sixteen feet under water. *LCS(L) 86* took the CO and the remainder of the ship's company on board and cast off. At 1120 the ship pointed her bow skyward and slipped beneath the waves. She was more fortunate than most ships, none of her crew died and those who were injured had relatively minor ones.

LCS(L) 122, which assisted *Porter* as she was in her death throes, was soon to be a target herself. Commanded by Lt. Richard M. McCool, she resumed radar picket duty at the station along with *Ammen DD 527, Aulick DD 569, Cogswell DD 611,* and *LCS(L)s 19, 86,* and *94*. The following day at *1845, Ammen,* the fighter director ship, picked up incoming enemy planes at a distance of forty-two miles and the ships went to general quarters. Two Vals appeared, making a run on the ships at 1900. Both planes were shot down by their combined fire. One crashed in the water, however, the second was able to crash into the conning tower of the

William D. Porter DD 579 being assisted by *LCS(L)s 86* and *122* prior to her sinking after being hit on Radar Picket Station No. 15A. NARA 80G 490024.

William D. Porter DD 579 goes under stern first as LCS(L) support ships stand by rescuing survivors. NARA 80G 490028.

LCS(L) 122. Commanding Officer McCool was knocked unconscious by the blast and wounded. He quickly recovered and, in spite of his wounds, rescued a number of his men and rallied the ship's crew. McCool directed firefighting measures that saved his ship. Finally when the ship was stable, he and a number of other wounded men were removed from the ship for transport back to a hospital ship. Eleven men had died and twenty-nine were wounded. *LCS(L) 86* began to tow the *122* back to port. For his bravery and leadership that day McCool was awarded the Congressional Medal of Honor.

The liberty ship *Walter Colton* arrived at Okinawa on 29 May. On 11 June, as she was at anchor in Nakagusuku Bay, she was attacked by a Val. It first made a run at *LSD 6*, then gained altitude and headed for *Walter Colton*. Under intense fire from ships in the area, it passed in front of her bow, circled around and made a run at the ship's bridge. It missed the bridge, but struck her No. 3 boom and crashed close aboard. Anti-aircraft fire from other ships in the area hit *Colton*, but overall, she escaped serious damage. Although her damage was light and no one was killed, several of the men on board reported injuries.[10]

Twiggs DD 591 was a veteran of the infamous radar picket lines at Okinawa. She had taken a kamikaze hit on 28 April and was back in action. She had just come off duty at Radar Picket Station No. 2 and was sent to the area off Naha to bombard remnants of the Japanese army. At 2030 on 16 June she came under attack by a Jill. It launched its torpedo, which was right on target. It struck *Twiggs* port side and her No. 2 magazine went off. Not satisfied with his success, the pilot circled around and crashed his Jill into the ship. In spite of valiant efforts by Capt. George Philip and his crew, *Twiggs* was doomed. In a short time the fires had reached the after magazine which blew up, effectively finishing the ship. *LCS(L) 14* attempted to close the destroyer to assist in firefighting, but the fires were too intense. *Twiggs* went under, taking with her 184 men, including her CO. An additional thirty-four of her men were wounded.

President Harry S Truman presents the Congressional Medal of Honor to Lt. Richard M. McCool for his actions during the kamikaze attack on his ship, *LCS(L) 122*, at Okinawa. Official U.S. Navy Photograph courtesy Capt. Richard M. McCool USN (Ret.).

On 21 June *LSM 59* and *Lipan ATF 85* were in the process of towing *Barry APD 29* out of Kerama Retto. She had been damaged so extensively in a kamikaze attack on 25 May that she was decommissioned. The plan was to anchor her offshore where she would be a decoy for kamikazes. Unfortunately, the kamikazes would have one more chance at her and would take another ship with her. At 1841 a kamikaze crashed *LSM 59* on her starboard side aft. Moments later, *Barry* also took a kamikaze hit. "The plane that hit the U.S.S. LSM 59 went through the tank deck into the engine room and tore a large hole in the bottom of the ship. The stern was engulfed in flame and smoke and began to settle immediately. All electrical power and both main engines were knocked out when the plane hit."[11] The fires started by the crash were put out in short time, but the rapidly flooding LSM was beyond saving. Her CO, Lt. D. C. Hawley, gave the order to abandon ship. At 1846 her bow rose in the air and at 1854 she went under stern first. From the time she was hit by the kamikaze until she went under, only thirteen minutes had elapsed. She had two dead and eight wounded. *Barry* was also crashed during this attack and finally went under a short while later.

About the same time that *LSM 59* and *Barry* were under attack, the seaplane tenders *Curtis AV 4* and *Kenneth Whiting AV 14* were also hit. They were anchored in the seaplane area at Kerama Retto when two planes, either Franks or Georges, made a high speed run on the ships. "The first plane struck the CURTISS on the starboard side; the second plane pulled up into a climb and was believed to be getting in position for a run on the port side of the CURTISS prior to being hit by AA fire and crashing close aboard the KENNETH WHITING

(AV14)."[12] *Kenneth Whiting* had a close call, but her damage was minimal. None of her crew members were killed and only five were injured. On board *Curtiss* fires raged below decks and threatened the ship's magazine. Executive Officer, Lt. Cmdr. J. W. Coghlin, ordered three hoses lowered down the dumbwaiter, and at 1925 four tugs, *Shackle ARS 9*, *Chickasaw ATF 83*, *ATA 124* and *ARS 73* came alongside and added water to the area. By 2200 it appeared as though the fires were nearly out and the ship was listing to port. The tugs were ordered away, but *Shackle* had to return at 0625 the next day to help extinguish a difficult fire. By 1000 all fires were out and *Curtiss* began the task of tending to her casualties, of which there were forty-one dead and twenty-eight wounded. A gruesome reminder of the horror of a kamikaze attack was noted in the XO's report when he recommended that: "All belts worn about the waist should be stenciled on the inside, in at least two places, and preferably with one inch letters if possible. Since many of the casualties were found without arms, legs, or heads, the only immediate means of identification were their belts, which were invariably in excellent condition, and required merely cutting to be removed and read."[13]

Halloran DE 305 had a close miss on 21 June when a Nick made a run on her. It strafed her midships area and was shot down close aboard without hitting the ship. However, its bomb sent shrapnel flying all over the ship killing three men and wounding twenty-four.

The last of the *Kikusui* raids, No. 10, ran from 21 to 22 June. Thirty navy and fifteen army special attack planes would fly their last missions to Okinawa. Accompanying them would be other army and navy aircraft on conventional missions. The situation at this point was obvious to the Japanese, and they would save their special attack plans to combat the invasion of the Japanese home islands which was predicted for the near future.

Ellyson DMS 19 was screening with *Foreman DE 633* on 22 June. The ships came under attack and a Zeke crashed fifty feet off *Ellyson*'s bow. She had one man killed and four wounded, but damage to the ship was minimal.

Also hit on 22 June was *LSM 213*, which was crashed while in Kimmu Bay. Her damage was severe and her casualties included three dead and eight wounded. At Nakagusuku Bay *LST 534* was unloading supplies when a Zeke roared in and struck her forecastle area. Its bomb penetrated the deck and blew a hole in her bottom. Fires raged and were eventually put out, but the ship settled by the bow and grounded in twelve feet of water. She had three killed and thirty-five wounded.

Thatcher DD 514 was in Nakagusuku Bay, having ridden out a typhoon. At 1950 on 19 July, two Oscars came out of the overcast sky and one made a dive on *Thatcher*. The two had just passed down the starboard side of the ship when one suddenly made a wingover and crashed into the port side of the ship just above the waterline. It was a glancing blow and the ship did not sustain any serious damage. The plane lost a wing, which remained on the ship, and sank about twenty feet off the port bow. Two of *Thatcher*'s men were wounded but the ship was basically unscathed.

American forces had become aware of the existence of the *Kaiten*. As a result, it became increasingly difficult for Japanese submarines to conduct operations against anchorages. Sub commanders were wary of taking unnecessary risks under such circumstances. Targeting an anchored ship did not take as much skill as attacking a convoy, but in time the *Kaiten* pilots and sub commanders began to acquire the necessary skills.

> Attack operations with "Kaiten" were frequently conducted. Although the attack procedure was primarily to assault enemy vessels at anchorage, as a result of training, skill was steadily acquired in attacking cruising vessels. The Submarine Force insisted on positive tactics in connection with cruising vessels and, although the Combined Fleet opposed it, this tactic was adopted.
>
> The reason advanced for advocating attacks on cruising vessels was that it had become more

and more difficult to effect surprise attacks on anchored vessels because of the enemy's countermeasures. Security near the anchorage was very strict and "Kaiten" attacks only increased the losses to mother submarines. The possibility of explosion of "Kaiten" before reaching their target became greater because of enemy antisubmarine measures at anchorages.

Those opposing the attack on cruising vessels held that it was difficult to attack in rough seas using a periscope with a low line of visibility. In addition, further training was required for the "Kaiten" crews before cruising vessels could be successfully attacked.[14]

The American attack on Southern Kyushu on 18 March 1945 and the invasion of Okinawa soon after, made it imperative to change strategies. Henceforth, attacks on cruising vessels would be attempted in order to head off attacks on the home islands.

Leaving the base at Otsujima between 14 July and 8 August 1945 was the *Kaiten* Group *Tamon*, consisting of six subs, the *I-47, I-53, I-58, I-363, I-366,* and *I-367*. The *I-53*, under Lt. Cmdr. Saichi Oba, left its home base on 14 July 1945. On board were six *Kaiten* and their pilots, Flight POs 1st Class Tsutomo Kawajiri, Masahiro Arakawa, Takahashi, and Sakamoto, Ens. Toyooki Seki, and Lt. (jg) Jun Katsuyama. She encountered an American convoy on 24 July about 285 miles east of Cape Engano, Luzon which was bound from Okinawa to Leyte. Escorted by *Underhill DE 682*, the convoy consisted of five patrol craft, three sub chasers a reefer and several LSTs. The convoy had been shadowed by a Japanese reconnaissance plane which reported its position to *I-53*.

The skipper of the *Underhill*, Cmdr. R. M. Newcomb, USNR, was notified that the convoy was under surveillance. *I-53* and its *Kaiten* lay in wait. At 1415 lookouts on *Underhill* spotted a mine which the DE took under fire. Within minutes her sonar detected submarine activity and the battle was on. *PC 804* picked up the sound of the sub's screws and *Underhill* laid depth charges in the area, believing that she was dealing with only one sub. She did not realize that *I-53* had launched two *Kaiten* piloted by Katsuyama and Arakawa. Reports indicate that *Underhill* rammed and sank one *Kaiten*, although this is unproven. Aiming to ram a second sub, she apparently ran into one of the *Kaiten*. Its 3,000 lb. warhead exploded, blowing the forward half of *Underhill* completely off and killing her CO. The forward section sank immediately, taking with it many men. The senior surviving officer of the ship, Lt. (jg) Elwood M. Rich, later reported:

> I then heard the lookout report another periscope. Then I heard the range reported from somewhere as 700 yds. Shortly after that we got the word "Stand By To Ram." I went to the Log Room and braced myself and I felt two slight jars as though the ship had scraped something. Then came the explosion. There were two explosions in quick order, the second one seemed to be the biggest. The light went out with the explosion, and I lost my phones. In feeling around for my phones, I felt water coming into the log room and decided to go out on deck. I started to go forward and ran into steam and spraying oil, so I went aft. When I got out on deck I found the ship was still afloat. I was trying to get in touch with control when I realized that the whole forward half of the ship had been blown off, just aft of the bridge.[15]

Underhill had been finished off by a *Kaiten*, making her the first warship so destroyed. *PCs 803* and *804*, cruised the waters picking up survivors. Of the 238 men on board the destroyer escort, 112 died, including her commanding officer. It was a solitary but successful victory for the *I-53* and her manned torpedoes.

Although there had been numerous sorties for the better part of a year, only two noted successes were achieved. In spite of grandiose claims in their action reports, only two verifiable sinkings had been achieved at the loss of eight Japanese submarines, their *Kaiten*, and their crews.

Even though the war was nearly over, occasional kamikaze attacks continued right to the end. Patrolling Radar Picket Station No. 9A on 29 July were *Callaghan DD 792, Pritchett DD 561, Cassin Young DD 793,* and *LCS(L)s 125, 129,* and *130*. One of the interesting things about the kamikaze experience is that some ships took numerous serious hits, such as *Laffey*, and did not sink, while others such as the *William D. Porter* would be sunk by only one attacker. This would also be the case with *Callaghan*.

The CO of *Callaghan* was Cmdr. C. M. Bertolf. Also on board was the Commanding Officer of Destroyer Squadron Fifty-Five, Capt. A. E. Jarrell. At about 0030 a bogey was picked up at a distance of thirteen miles. The plane's speed was estimated to be about ninety knots and seemed to indicate that it was one of the biplane trainers that the Japanese had begun using as kamikazes. This was a navy Willow intermediate trainer, one of about a dozen that had flown from Taiwan that evening. Their relatively slow speed and maneuverability made it possible for them to readily adjust to changes in ship position or course. This one proved no exception. Although it was taken under fire by both *Pritchett* and *Callaghan*, it managed to crash into the main deck of *Callaghan* in a vital spot. Although the biplane could not carry a very heavy bomb, its 220 pounder did the trick. It penetrated the deck of *Callaghan* and exploded in the after engine room putting it out of commission and jamming the ship's rudder. Capt. Jarrell later wrote:

> When I got outside, the entire after half of the ship appeared to be in flames. Actually the ship was in flames from about frame 118 to about frame 150; this is from just abaft number 2 stack to approximately the forward depth charge throwers. I was informed that there was no fire main pressure forward and that many key repair personnel had been knocked out when the second, or major explosion occurred. These personnel had been very prompt in initiating firefighting measures immediately after the first explosion occurred, and many were eliminated when the second explosion occurred very shortly after they arrived on the scene. The LCS's were ordered by blinker tube to close *Callaghan* and fight fires. The stern of the after end of *Callaghan* was submerged, with main deck under water, up to the forward depth charge throwers, which were awash.[16]

Wounded men were lying on the deck and Capt. Jarrell tried to notify the CO, Cmdr. Bertolf, that he should abandon ship. He found that Bertolf had already given the order and the process was underway. By 0150 the wounded and most non-essential personnel had been transferred to the LCS(L)s. It was felt at that time that the ship might still be saved and towed back to port. However, at 0155 ammunition below decks began to explode and the intensity of the explosions increased, making further salvage efforts impossible. The remaining personnel abandoned ship and she went under stern first at 0234 in 600 fathoms. Her casualties were forty-seven dead and seventy-three wounded.

In the midst of the maneuvering, after *Callaghan* was hit, another Willow approached the ships and struck *Pritchett*, causing minor damage. The plane had been hit by fire from *Pritchett* and, within minutes, she shot down another. Meanwhile, *Cassin Young* shot down a biplane that was approaching her for a run. Several others were driven away by gunfire from the ships.

LCS(L) 130, skippered by Lt. William H. File, Jr., headed toward *Callaghan* to lend assistance. Along the way she picked up twenty-seven survivors from the ship that had been blown overboard. At 0110 she came alongside the stern of the destroyer and began fighting fires. She was ordered to stand off at 0135, and ten minutes later spotted a Willow approaching the formation. Her 20mm and 40mm guns managed to take chunks out of the plane's flimsy fuselage and it crashed into the water about 400 yards to her port. She then returned to *Callaghan* and, with her bow practically touching the destroyer, continued to assist in firefighting. Her efforts contributed materially to saving the ship. As a result her CO, Lt. File, was awarded the Silver Star.

Cassin Young took aboard the survivors from *Callaghan* and, in the company of *LCS(L) 129*, brought them back to the Hagushi Anchorage where they were transferred to *Crescent City APA 21*. *Cassin Young* was now in a seemingly safe location back at the anchorage. However, this was not to be the case. That evening she was assigned to screen a station at the entrance to Nakagusuku Bay on the southeast part of Okinawa. At 0300 on 30 July, bogeys were picked up on the radar screens. Two planes approached the ship and were fired upon. One made it through and crashed into the destroyer's starboard side. Cmdr. J. W. Ailes, III, CO of *Cassin Young*, later wrote:

> As a result of the explosion which accompanied crashing of the plane, much damage was done to the forward superstructure and enclosed equipment from the director level to the main deck and all the deckhouse forward of the galley including the uptakes of No. 1 and 2 boilers and No. 1 stack were damaged beyond repair. Blast effect downward caused extensive damage to the forward fireroom and machinery therein necessitating abandoning of the fireroom but personnel were trapped by the sealing of both accesses. Broken steam lines in the forward engine room necessitated abandoning of that station which was so ordered with instructions to secure all machinery. Subsequently turbines, reduction gears and bearings overheated and were damaged due to the absence of lubrication.[17]

Aulick DD 569, patrolling nearby, came to the aid of *Cassin Young*. Her wounded were transferred and brought back to *Cascade AD 16* and *Hamul AD 20* for care. As a result of the attack, twenty-two men died and forty-five were injured. It was one of the last successful kamikaze attacks of the war, and it took its toll.

Horace A. Bass APD 124 was operating as part of the anti-submarine screen off Hagushi on 30 July. At 0230 a biplane came out of the dark and made a dive on her. It had been spotted on radar some time earlier but lookouts were unable to pick it up. The suddenness of its attack made it impossible to train the ship's guns on it. Fortunately, the pilot aimed too high and passed over the ship, taking with him parts of the life raft and some davits. It struck the water close aboard the port side and its bomb went off with a bright orange flash. Men on the ship were knocked over and fragments from the bomb killed one man and wounded fifteen others.[18]

The carriers of Task Force 38 had spent several days sending their planes to attack targets in Northern Honshu. *Borie DD 704*, *Hank DD 702*, *John W. Weeks DD 701* and *Benner DD 807* were on Tomcat patrol fifty miles southwest of Task Force 38 on 9 August. The pickets came under attack about 1456 when a Val crashed *Borie*, hitting her between her mast and five inch gun director. Its bomb passed through the ship and exploded close aboard with shrapnel causing damage to the starboard side and killing and wounding a number of her men. Control of the ship from the bridge was lost and steering was shifted to the secondary conn. It only took twenty minutes to bring the fires under control, but the fires continued to cook off 40mm ammo from the gun tubs near the crash. *Borie* was able to resume formation but several of her guns had been disabled. Killed in the crash were forty-eight of her crew, with sixty-six wounded. The ship returned to the safety of the task force where medical officers from *Alabama BB 60* and *Abbot DD 629* came aboard to assist with her wounded. The following day her wounded were transferred to the hospital ship *Rescue AH 18*.[19]

Hank came under attack next. At 1522 a Zeke dove on her from dead ahead and crashed off her port quarter. Debris from the plane showered the deck and caused injuries. At 1549 a Frank made its dive on the ship and was also shot down close aboard after losing a wing. Once again *Hank* received a shower of debris and gasoline but no serious damage to the ship. She had one death and five injuries from the attacks. The remainder of her day was spent searching for men from *Borie* who had been blown overboard in the crash.[20]

Lagrange APA 124 had the dubious distinction of being the last ship struck by a kamikaze in World War II. She was anchored in Nakagusuku Bay on 13 August when she was crashed by a kamikaze. According to her action report for the day:

> At 1947 ½ enemy plane first noticed approaching directly on ship, 165°T, 1000 yards, position angle 10°, dive angle 10°, speed estimated 300 m.p.h., low-wing monoplane, single radial engine,

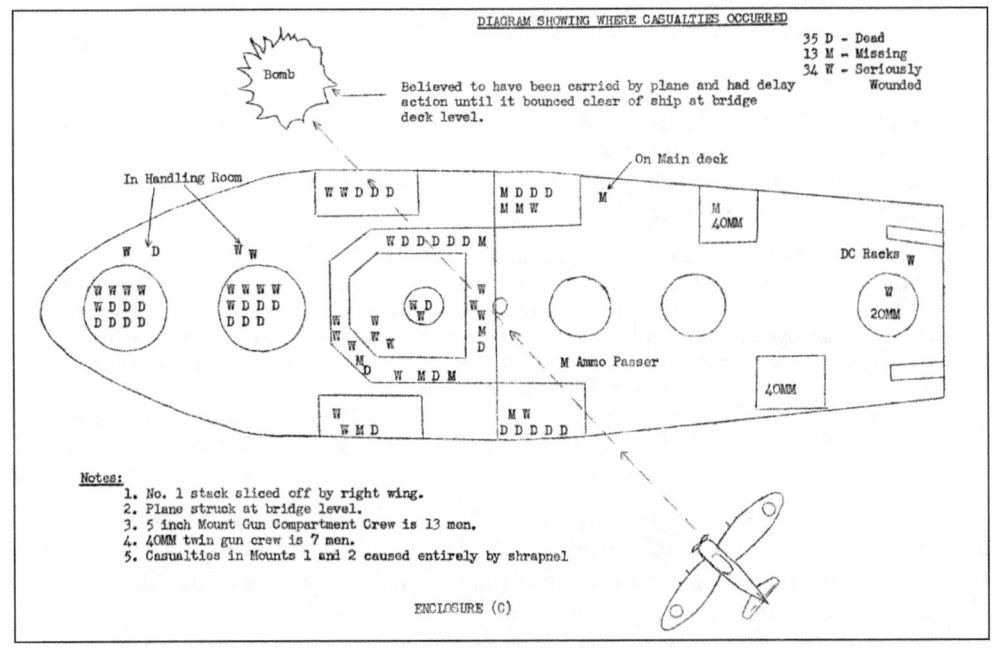

This diagram shows the attack on *Borie DD 704* on 9 August 1945. *U. S. S. Borie (DD704)* Serial 0222-45. *Action Report Operations During the Period 2 July 1945 to 15 August 1945. 15 August 1945,* Enclosure (C).

Lagrange APA 124 was the last American ship to be hit by a kamikaze during World War II. Damage from the crash is shown in the photograph above. NARA 80G 331974.

Lagrange APA 124 after the kamikaze crash. *Lagrange APA 125* Serial 043. *War Damage Report.* 29 August 1945.

identified as a Tojo or Zeke. Plane passed 25 feet over No. 3 hatch, starboard wing hitting starboard No. 3 forward boom, left wing hitting port kingpost. 1948 plane crashed into after port side of superstructure cabin deck, causing explosion and large fires rising 200 feet into the air, resulting in immediate loss of all electric power and the use of steam fire pumps, all ventilation, inter-ship and intra-ship communication, main propulsion unit, fresh water system, and auxiliary condensing system; damage resulting from simultaneous explosion of plane and inwardly carried bomb.[21]

A few minutes later a second plane hit her kingpost and hit the water twenty yards to port. Its explosion showered the ship with debris, water and gas. Damage to the cargo ship was significant and her casualties were twenty-one dead and eighty-nine wounded. With these two crashes, the damage to American ships ended. However, a third plane approached *LaGrange* but was driven off by other ships in the area. It was not to be the last sortie by the divine wind fliers. They would continue to fly against American ships until several days after the official end of the war, albeit unsuccessfully.

The announcement of the surrender of Japan by the Emperor was greeted with mixed emotions by the men of the Imperial Japanese Army and Navy. Some wept in silence and accepted the "unbearable," while others swore to continue the battle. Conflicts tore through the minds of many as to whether to disobey an Imperial decree and continue the struggle or to end their lives in traditional, honorable ways. For those in the higher command who had sent many young men to their deaths, the thought of living on after them was unacceptable, and a number of high-ranked officers committed suicide. Some, not so quick to end their own lives, were captured alive, tried as war criminals, and executed.

VAdm. Matomi Ugaki, who had commanded the First Mobile Base Air Force, was one such military man who struggled with the Emperor's decision. On 11 August 1945, as the end of the war approached and talk of surrender circulated, he wrote in his diary:

> Though an emperor's order must be followed, I can hardly stand to see us suspending attacks while still having this fighting strength. I think many things remain to be done after consulting with those brave men willing to die. When and how to die as a samurai, an admiral, or a supreme commander, a subject I have long resolved in my mind, should be seriously studied for the sake of the future of the Japanese nation. I renewed a resolution today of entrusting my body to the throne and defending the empire until death takes me away.[22]

A couple of days later, on 15 August 1945, Ugaki and the rest of Japan listened to the Emperor's message of capitulation. Realizing that he would not receive official orders to surrender for several hours, Ugaki prepared himself for a final kamikaze mission. He noted, "We haven't yet received the cease-fire order, so there is no room for me to reconsider. I'm going to follow in the footsteps of those many loyal officers and men who devoted themselves to the country, and I want to live in the noble spirit of the special attack."[23]

At 1600 VAdm. Matome Ugaki bid farewell to his men, boarded a *Suisei* (Judy) dive bomber and flew to his doom over Okinawan waters. Accompanying him were twenty-three other men of the 701st Air Group flying ten more *Suiseis*. American records do not show any kamikaze attacks at Okinawa that day, so it is likely that the planes simply crashed into the sea.

17. *Ketsu Go*: Defending the Homeland

Preparations for defense of the Japanese home islands revolved around the plan that the Japanese termed *Ketsu Go*. Included in this plan were estimations of how the United States would attack Japan. It was generally assumed that the attack would come on the southernmost of the main islands, Kyushu, with a later attack in the Kanto Plains area near Tokyo and Yokohama.

A significant portion of this plan involved the use of special attack weapons. The declining situation had forced the Japanese to the realization that conventional warfare was not an option. Only by use of special attack methods could they hope to stave off the American offensive directed against their homeland. Decades of militarization of the Japanese school system had regenerated the traditions of the samurai class and made it possible for them to accept the promulgation of these methods. A brief recollection of their history indicated to the leadership of Japan that this was a long-accepted method of fighting.

> The concept of special attack tactics (the tactic of resorting to one-way or suicidal missions for certain destruction of the target) was not entirely new in the history of the Japanese Army and Navy. The Port Arthur blockade in the Russo-Japanese War, the demolition mission of the three demolition tube heroes (Nikuden-Sanyushu) in the China Incident and the midget submarines employed at Pearl Harbor, all possessed some features of special attack tactics. There are also many instances in the history of Japan in which men voluntarily acted in a manner similar to a special attack mission, but these acts were not specifically ordered by their superiors. The attacks carried out by the Kamikaze Special Attack Unit and the Type "A" Midget Submarine Unit (Cebu) during the operations in the Philippines area, during and after October 1943, were probably the first attack missions that were planned and ordered by competent commanders. The results achieved by these special attack units were unexpectedly good in comparison to the small force committed.... These desperate attack tactics employed by field forces were inevitably reflected in the policies adopted by those concerned with war preparations.[1]

Success in the use of kamikaze aircraft and explosive speedboats in the Philippines and at Okinawa had demonstrated to the Japanese that a minimal investment in men and equipment could pay dividends that far surpassed the abilities of their meager resources. This resulted in an increased demand for the production of special attack weapons. With the fall of the Philippines and Iwo Jima it became clear to the Japanese high command that the invasion of the home islands was imminent. Okinawa would prove to be a stepping stone toward that eventuality. The production of *Shinyo*, *Maru-re*, and *Kaiten* was accelerated, as well as the development of newer types of special attack aircraft such as the Nakajima *Kikka*, Kawanishi *Baika*, Nakajima *Ki-115 Tsurugi* and the Mitsubishi *J8M Shusei*. The navy alone planned to

Under development at the end of the war by the Japanese navy was the *Mitsubishi J8M1 Shusei* or Sword Stroke. It was a rocket powered interceptor modeled after the German *Messerschmitt ME 163B*. The development of this plane was necessitated by the need for an interceptor that could successfully defend against the B-29. NARA 80G 193477.

This Japanese twin-engine jet, the *Nakajima Kikka* (Orange Blossom), is shown under construction at the Nakajima factory on Honshu on 6 October 1945. NARA 111-SC-225102.

Status of Aircraft for the "Ketsu-Go" Operation

Type of Aircraft	3d Air Fleet Allot	3d Air Fleet Opnl	5th Air Fleet Allot	5th Air Fleet Opnl	10th Air Fleet Allot	10th Air Fleet Opnl	Total Allot	Total Opnl
"Ko"-type Fighters	312	200	242	141	119	75	673	416
"Otsu"-type Fighters (Interceptor)	137	50	136	55	3	2	276	107
"Hei"-type Fighters (Night fighter)	133	91	28	16			161	107
Bombers			88	60	166	111	254	171
Carrier-bombers	157	113	119	99	99	65	375	277
Carrier-based Attack Planes	90	80	52	44	65	24	207	148
Land-based Bombers	40	32	49	40			89	72
Land-based Attack Planes	25	12	60	48	112	63	197	123
Land-based Recon Planes	49	31	55	16			104	47
Seaplanes	152	120	71	69			223	189
Intermediate Trainer	478	275	1,106	978	659	445	2,243	1,698
"Shiragiku" Utility Trainer	167	131	238	174	19	15	424	320
Total	1,740	1,135	2,244	1,740	1,242	800	5,226	3,675

Abbreviations: Allot -- Allotment   Opnl -- Operational

Military History Section, Army Forces Far East. *Japanese Monograph No. 174 Outline of Naval Armament and Preparations for War Part VI*, p. 12.

have at lease 5,000 special attack planes ready to meet the invasion. By 1 March 1945, plans were in force to shift the entire strategy of the naval air forces to one which the special attack method was the primary means of combating the enemy.[2]

According to navy planning, a number of training aircraft were to be converted so that they could carry bombs on special attack missions.

Type of Aircraft	Bombs (kg)	Number
Type-93 Intermediate Trainer (Willow)	250 [551 lbs.]	1
Type-2 Intermediate Trainer (Cypress)	250	1
Shiragiku Utility Trainer	250	2
Type-94 Reconnaissance Seaplane (Alf)	250	2
Type-95 Reconnaissance Seaplane (Dave)	250	1
Type-Zero Reconnaissance Seaplane (Jake)	250	2
Type-Zero Observation Plane (Pete)	250	1
Type-Zero Training Fighter (Zeke)	250	1
Type-Zero Carrier Fighter (Zeke)	250 or 500 [1,102 lbs.]	1[3]

Many of these converted aircraft would make their first appearance during the battle for Okinawa and they took a terrible toll. The training aircraft, particularly the biplanes constructed of fabric over wood frames, were hard to detect and just as hard to shoot down as the American VT fuses were designed to explode upon proximity to metal. Even a direct hit on these aircraft would cause little damage, as the shell would pass right through the fabric and continue on its path.

Japanese estimates were that the earliest invasion of their home islands would not come before September of 1945. As a result, their planning used that date as a target for completion of their preparations. They correctly surmised that the invasion would be in Kyushu and would consist of at least ten divisions transported by 1,000 transport ships. Their estimations of needed special attack aircraft to sink at least half of these transports would be 3,000, with additional aircraft to be used against carriers and other warships. If that many transports, and their troops could be sunk, then the invasion could be stopped. All available aircraft that could be used as kamikazes were to be repaired as soon as possible, and the development of the newer types was scheduled.

Construction Schedule of Special Planes (Projected/Actual)

The first number given is the projected figure as of 20 June 1945, and the second is the actual production as of 15 July 1945. Figures for months including August and later are estimates of production.

Special Attack Plane	May	June	July	Aug.	Sept.	Oct.	Nov.	Dec.
Oka Model 22	6	49/48	30/5	50/20	60/40	60	60	
Oka Model 43			2	10/8	22/12	38	65	80
Kikka (Aeronautical Dept.)	Experimental	12	0/2					
	Manufacture		13	125	0/20			
	Final		11					
Kikka (Naval Technical Dept.)				10	40			
Shusei		35/1	90/12	145/37	225/88			
Ki 115 Tsurugi				0/40	10/10	150	320	400[4]

In order to accommodate the vast numbers of aircraft, existing fields would be repaired and a number of other fields constructed. Aircraft would have to be hidden from sight in various ways, including underground and in makeshift shelters. These did not have to be elaborate structures as the battle would be considered decisive. Either the Japanese would prevail with their massed special attack forces or they would face annihilation by landed American forces. Existing in Japan by summer of 1945 were seventy airfields and twenty-four seaplane bases. These were referred to by the Japanese as "pasture ground" in order to disguise their true

By the end of the war the Japanese had managed to place various special attack weapons throughout their country, many in residential areas. Here a woman passes by an *Oka* stored in a revetment. The photograph was taken in September 1945, shortly after the end of the war. NARA 80G 375010.

nature. Some of the bases were designed with special catapults that could launch the *Oka*, since the previous method of having them carried to the target by a Betty bomber was not feasible. These would be located at Izu Peninsula, Southern Boso Peninsula, Eastern Boso Peninsula, Tsukuba, Miura Peninsula, Oi, Tanabe, and Toba and were slated for completion between July and November 1945. Collectively they would have forty-seven catapults and sheds for 270 *Oka*.

In reviewing their experiences at Okinawa and in the Philippines, the Japanese discovered that an adjustment in their methods of aerial attack might be in order. Since larger ships were not usually disabled or sunk by a single crash they determined to modify their attack methods. The Chief of the First Bureau, Naval General Staff stated in a letter that American ships did not have armor plating below the water line. Notably important was the area near the stern, which was particularly vulnerable. If a kamikaze could crash into the water in such a manner as to have his bomb explode under the ship, it was felt that there was a good chance that the ship would be disabled or sunk.[5] *William D. Porter DD 579* met her fate at Okinawa in just such a manner. Her CO, Cmdr. C.M. Keyes, reported:

> The plane struck the water close aboard to port, abreast the after engine room. There was a single violent, but almost silent explosion, which seemed to lift the ship bodily and drop it again in a quick movement. The Commanding Officer who had been asleep in the sea cabin was awakened by the explosion, and coming out on the bridge was informed by the Officer of the Deck that the ship had been struck by a Val. It is not known whether the explosive was carried within

Both seaplanes and biplane trainers were to be important parts of the special attack effort as the invasion of Japan by the Americans commenced. These aircraft, found at Otsu Naval Air Base on Lake Biwa after the war, would have been essential elements of the campaign. This photograph was taken on 16 October 1945 and shows a number of the aircraft disassembled and ready for destruction. NARA 111-SC 218696.

This *Tachikawa Ki-9* "Spruce" army trainer is shown at the end of the war in kamikaze configuration. Biplane trainers of this sort were being prepared for use as kamikazes against the expected American invasion of the home islands. To amplify the destruction caused by the plane's impact, a fifty-five gallon drum of gasoline was strapped into the back seat of the aircraft. This is visible in the photograph. The plane was assigned to the *21 Hikoshidan Shireibu Hikodan* or 21st Air Brigade which was stationed at Kikuchi, Japan. In the middle of the chrysanthemum painting on the rudder is the Japanese *hiragana* character for *To*, which was short for *Tokko-tai* or Special Attack Corps.

the plane or in a bomb which might have been released, but it is believed that the explosion occurred nearly directly under the ship, under the after engine room or slightly aft of it.[6]

The explosion opened the seams of the ship's hull and resulted in rapid flooding of the engine room as well as damage to the starboard propeller shaft. Three hours and five minutes after the initial underwater explosion *Porter* pointed her bow skyward and went to the bottom.

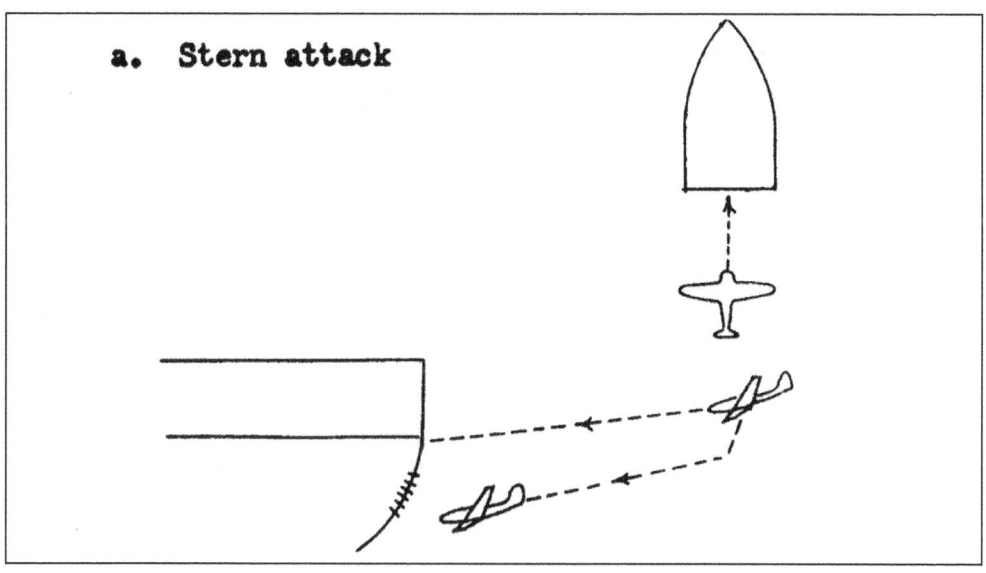

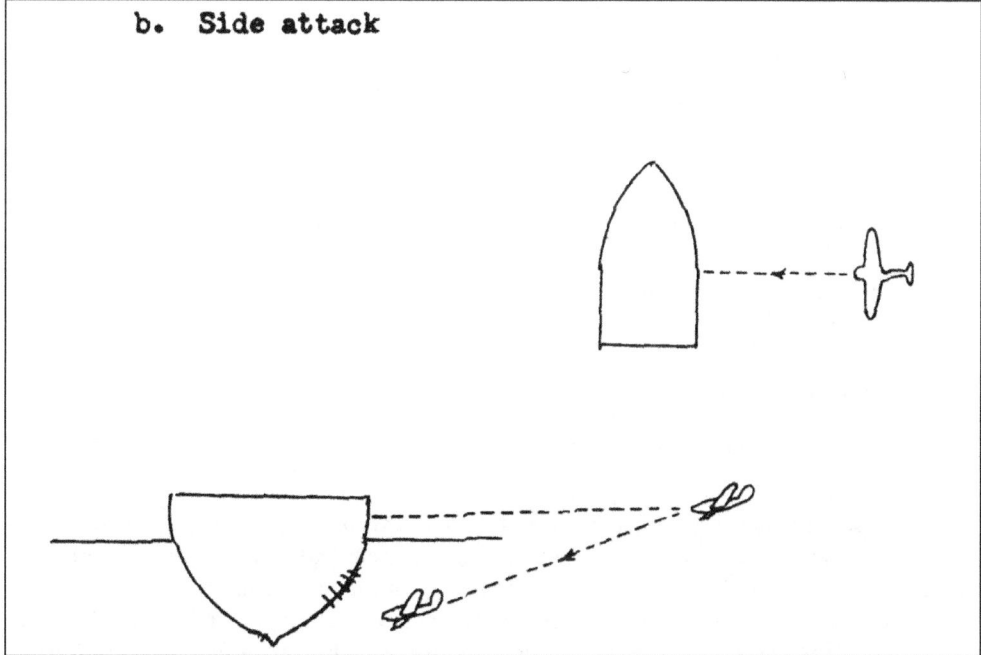

After studying reports of kamikaze actions in Okinawa, the Naval General Staff recommended that future kamikaze attacks attempt to crash under the stern of an American ship in order to create maximum damage. Military History Section, Army Forces Far East. *Japanese Monograph No. 174 Outline of Naval Armament and Preparations for War Part VI*, pp. 39–40.

Methods of increasing the effect of a kamikaze crash were also suggested. The newly designed *Ki-115 Tsurugi*, which was planned as a special attack weapon from the onset, could achieve greater impact speed if the wings could be jettisoned as the plane began its final dive. This would prevent the plane from spiraling out of control if an American fighter or anti-aircraft fire damaged one wing. Plans to implement the changes to the *Tsurugi* were put into action. Additional studies would include "testing of explosive charges ... producing a more powerful bursting effect, to be employed by the special attack plane by loading it with liquid oxygen, hydrogen peroxide or yellow phosphorous, be studied and tested."[7] Tests were soon conducted at Takeyama and Kure with positive results, and recommendations were made to produce new bombs for the special attack planes.

Once the American campaign at Okinawa was underway, invasion of the home islands was of great concern to the Japanese. To defend against the coming invasion, the Japanese began to hold back on the expenditure of their forces toward the end of the Okinawa campaign. In addition to aircraft, numerous *Shinyo* and *Maru-re* units were stationed throughout Japan at her remaining bases in preparation for the assault on Japan proper. Listed below is the distribution of *Koryu, Kaiten, Kairyu,* and *Shinyo* as of 27 July 1945, a scant two and one-half weeks before the Japanese surrendered.

DISPOSITION OF SURFACE AND UNDERWATER SUICIDE UNITS AS OF 27 JULY 1945*

Location	Koryu	Kairyu	Kaiten	Shinyo
Yokosuka Naval District Including Hachijoshima	0	180	36	775
Osaka Guard District	0	24	4	50
Kure Naval District	48	24	32	225
Sasebo Naval District	4	24	46	1,000
Maizura Naval District	3	0	0	0
Chinkai-Wan Guard District	0	0	0	100
Chichi Jima Base	0	0	0	150
Haha Jima Base	0	0	0	80
Oshima Defense District	1	0	0	225
Miyako Surface Escort Unit	0	0	0	50
Ishigaki Surface Escort Unit	0	0	0	200
Takao Guard District	3	0	0	325
Mako Base	0	0	0	125
Chushan Surface Escort Unit	0	0	0	175
Hainan Guard District	0	0	0	125
Hong Kong Base	0	0	0	125
Amoy Base	0	0	0	100
Combined Fleet	18	0	0	0
Totals	77	252	118	3,830[8]

*These figures represent the actual disposition of these weapons. Additional units had been produced but not delivered to operational forces.

Japanese estimates of the effectiveness of these four types of suicide weapons were typically optimistic. *Koryus* and *Kairyus* had sufficient maneuverability and range to intercept enemy transports 200–300 miles from the shore. The *Kaiten* was limited in this sense, and the high command felt that they would be wasted in attacking transports. Instead, they were to be used against escort ships, which would be a more suitable target for them. For *Koryus, Kairyus,* and *Shinyos,* the most important targets would be the transports which carried troops and equipment for the invasion landing. Attack plans called for the Japanese to mount a massed attack the first evening that the transports were anchored. Ideally this would be supported by air special attack forces in order to create maximum confusion in the American fleet. According to them, "Loss of surface and underwater special attack forces was expected to be ten percent and the probability of success was estimated at 2:3 for 'KORYUS,' 1:3 for 'KAITENS' and 'KAIRYUS,' and 1:10 for 'SHINYOS.' The results would be about 60 ships by 'KORYUS,' 120 by 'KAIRYUS' and 'KAITENS,' and 90 by 'SHINYOS,' or a total of approx. 260 transports."[9]

The increased emphasis on these types of weapons indicated pragmatism on the part of

The magnitude of the special attack submarine effort can be seen in this photograph of the midget submarines found at Kure Naval Base at the end of the war. NARA 80G 351875

Sasebo, one of the major naval bases on the island of Kyushu, was also home to a large number of *Shinyo*. This photograph, taken after the war, shows suicide boats that were positioned there to counter American landings. NARA 127GW 1523-140564.

the Japanese. They were aware of their inability to produce first rate weapons so they turned to the only practical solution. Japanese reports indicated:

> In light of the national production capacity sinking with the fall of the PHILIPPINES and OKINAWA, our efforts were concentrated on the mass production of "underwater special attack weapons" which required only a comparatively simple process to manufacture as well as in the mobilization of planes already made. Furthermore, the mass production of special planes such as "KIKKA" [twin engine jet similar to the German Me 262] and TYPE "KI"—115 [*Tsurugi*] was taken up to increase our fighting strength notwithstanding the sceptical opinions in some quarters.[10]

The establishment of bases throughout Japan was imperative, and the Japanese set about to complete as many as possible before the expected invasion date. Manned torpedoes, suicide boats and midget submarines, as well as *Okas* and other special attack craft, were delivered to these bases as rapidly as possible. "Human torpedo bases were being built on the southern coast of Kyushu, the southern coast of Shikoku and the coast extending from Izu Peninsula to Bose Peninsula, where enemy landings were anticipated. Submarines I-56, I-57, I-58, I-59 and I-62 were charged with the mission of delivering human torpedoes to these bases."[11]

Location of Special Attack Bases, 15 August 1945

By mid–August 1945 the plan to emphasize special attack tactics in the defense of the home islands was in evidence throughout Japan. These three maps show the locations of the bases devoted to utilizing water-borne special attack weapons, including suicide boats, human torpedoes, and midget subs. Many of the bases had provisions for more than one type of weapon and the symbols on the maps indicate the major weapon to be used at the base. By 15 August 1945 many of the bases had been supplied with special attack weapons while others were in readiness awaiting delivery. The list below indicates the number of weapons at each base as of 15 August 1945. In this list, MS stands for Midget Submarine, HT for Human Torpedo, and Sc for Surface Crash Boat. It should be noted that a number of bases had the capability to support more than one type of weapon. In some cases there is a double listing, such as the use of MS twice. This indicates that two types of midget subs were planned for the base.

Kyushu Bases
Aburatsu MS × 0, HT × 10
Daidotsu HT × 3, Sc × 74
Gamae HT × 0, Sc × 0
Hinatadomari HT × 0
Hosojima HT × 12, Sc × 26
Ibusuki Sc × 0
Intsuji Sc × 0
Karatsu MS × 0, HT × 0, Sc × 26
Kataura Sc × 0
Kawatana Sc × 285
Kojimaura Sc × 0
Kyodomari Sc × 52
Madomari HT × 0, Sc × 0
Makinoshima Sc × 52
Matsushima Sc × 26
Mimisu Sc × 0
Mogushi Sc × 52
Nakamagoshi MS × 0, Sc × 0
Nokonoshima Sc × 0
Nomaike Sc × 0
Okami HT × 16
Saeki MS × 7

Sasebo MS × 4, Sc × 50
Sendaikawaguchi Sc × 0
Shinjo Sc × 0
Sotonoura HT × 7, Sc × 25
Tainoura Sc × 52
Tomariura Sc × 0
Tomioka Sc × 26
Totoro Sc × 71
Tsuno Sc × 26
Uchinoura HT × 6, Sc × 0
Ushibuka Sc × 0
Utsumi Sc × 0
Yamakawa Sc × 0
Yatake MS × 0

Shikoku Bases
Kashiwajima HT × 0, Sc × 18
Komatsujima MS × 24, HT × 4, Sc × 50
Moroto MS × 0
Mugigaura HT × 8, Sc × 0
Shimizu HT × 0, Sc × 19
Sukumo MS × 0

Suzaki HT × 12, Sc × 32
Tachibanaminato MS × 0, HT × 0
Teyuki Sc × 0
Tomariura HT × 0, Sc × 3
Urado HT × 12, Sc × 94
Usa Sc × 0

Honshu Bases
Aburatsubo MS × 42, Sc × 0
Ajiro HT × 0
Anamizu MS × 0
Anamizu MS × 0
Arari MS×0, Sc × 0
Arasaki HT × 0
Ego MS × 0
Ena Sc × 0
Enoura MS × 17, HT × 0, Sc × 0
Futaijima HT × 0
Gokanosho MS × 0, Sc × 0
Hachinoe Sc × 0
Hagihama MS × 0

Hata MS × 0
Hazama HT × 0
Hikari HT × 30
Iinuma SC × 26
Inatori Sc × 6
Iwaibukuro Sc × 49
Kasado MS × 1, HT × 22
Katana Sc × 0
Katsuryama × MS × 11
Katsuura MS × 0
Katsuura MS × 0
Koajiro Sc × 0
Koamikurahama HT × 0
Kominato Sc × 26
Kure MS × 29, HT × 22, MS × 9
Maizuru MS × 6
Manazura HT × 0
Matoya MS × 0
Mihogaseki MS × 0
Minato Sc × 45
Moriya Sc × 0
Nagatsuro Sc × 18
Nanaruiura MS × 0
Nonohama MS × 0

Obana HT × 0
Obuchi Sc × 0
Odawa HT × 0
Ohima MS × 4
Oi HT × 0
Okitsu HT × 0, Sc × 0
Omaezaki Sc × 0
Ona Sc × 0
Onahama MS × 10, SC × 26
Oura MS × 104
Otsushima Sc × 11
Sanenoura Sc × 0
Sasagawa Sc × 25
Shigeura MS × 0
Shimisu Sc × 0
Shimoda MS × 12, Sc × 38
Shimonoseki MS × 22
Shimozu Sc × 0
Shinjomura Sc × 0
Sotokawa Sc × 52
Sunako Sc × 25
Sunosaki Sc × 0
Tago MS × 1, Sc × 0
Tanabe Sc × 0
Tatamiishiura Sc × 0

Toba MS × 0, HT × 0, SC × 100
Tohi HT × 0
Uhara Sc × 52
Uraga MS × 3
Yokohama MS × 4
Yokosuka MS × 73 (MS × 4)
Yoshimi MS × 0, HT × 0, Sc × 0
Yura Sc × 0
Yuyawan HT × 0

Small Island Bases

Amami O Shima MS × 0, Sc × 150
Hachijojima HT × 8, Sc × 50
Saishuto Sc × 100
Shodoshima MS × 0
Tainoura Sc × 52
Takeshiki MS × 0

Other Bases

Bonin Islands — Sc × 91
ChuShantao Is. Sc about 100
Korea — Chinkai MS × 0
Miyako Is. Sc about 200
Taiwan Sc about 300

LOCATION OF SPECIAL ATTACK BASES
15 AUGUST 1945

Chart 12-c

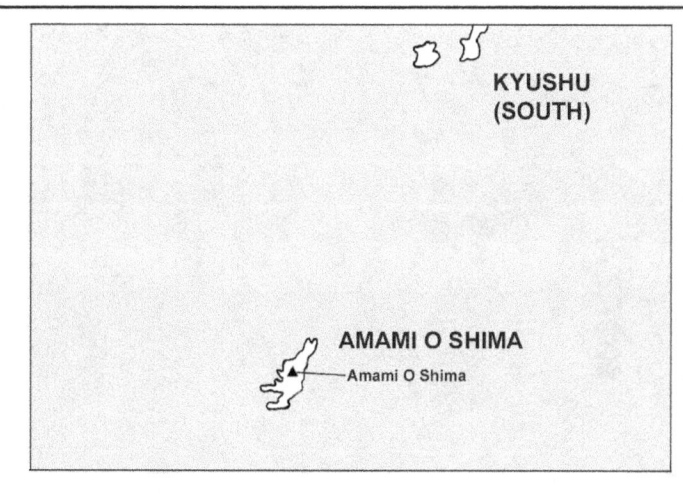

★ Main Base for Special Attack Unit

● Midget Subs

▲ Surface Crashing Craft (*Shinyo*)

♦ Human Torpedo

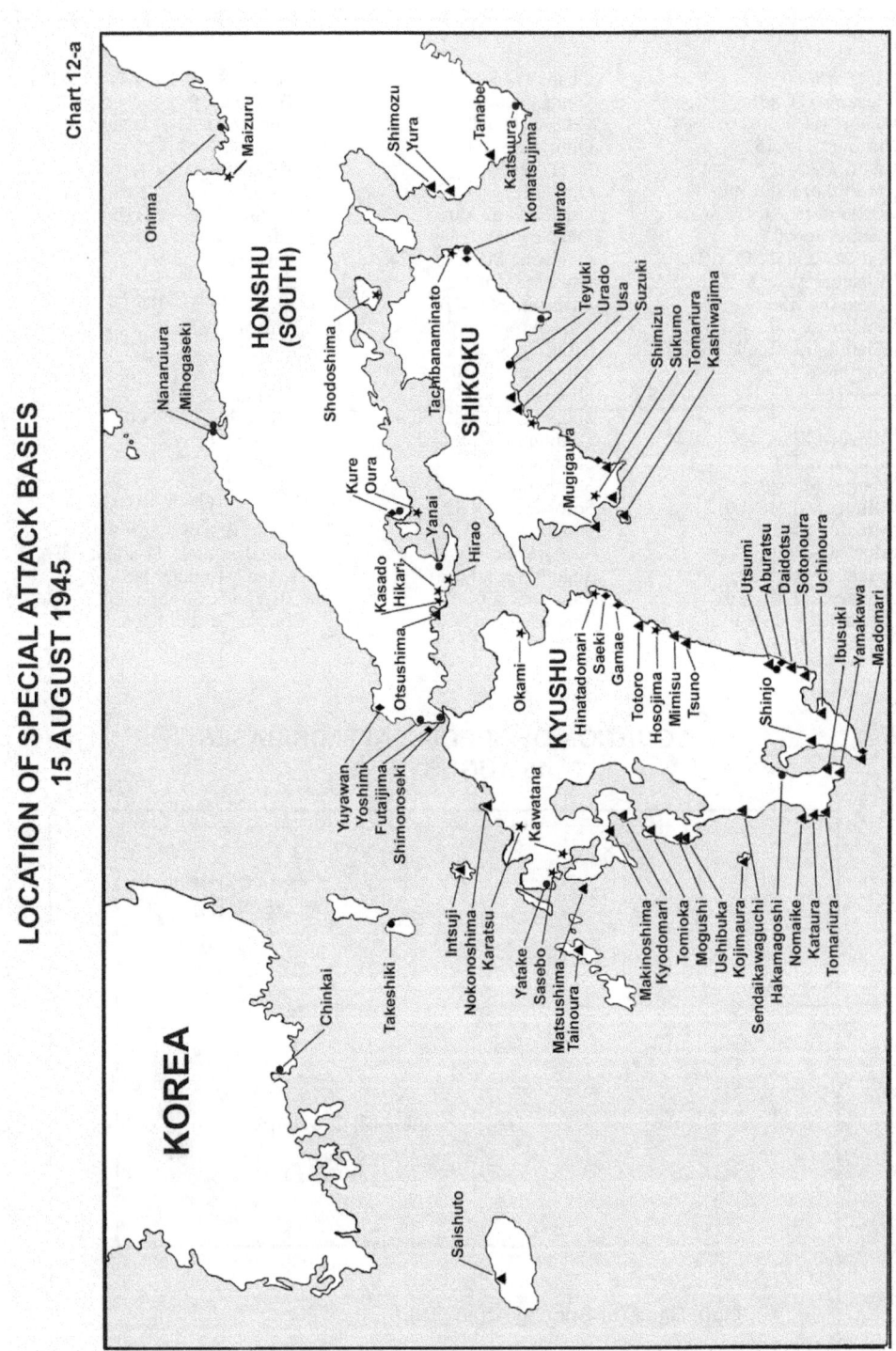

Above, previous, and opposite page: These three maps give an indication of the extent of planned use for the water-borne special attack squadrons. Bases for midget submarines, *Kaiten*, and suicide boats were scattered throughout Japan in preparation for the American invasion. Adapted from Military History Section, Army Forces Far East. *Japanese Monograph No. 174 Outline of Naval Armament and Preparations for War Part VI*, pp. 48–50.

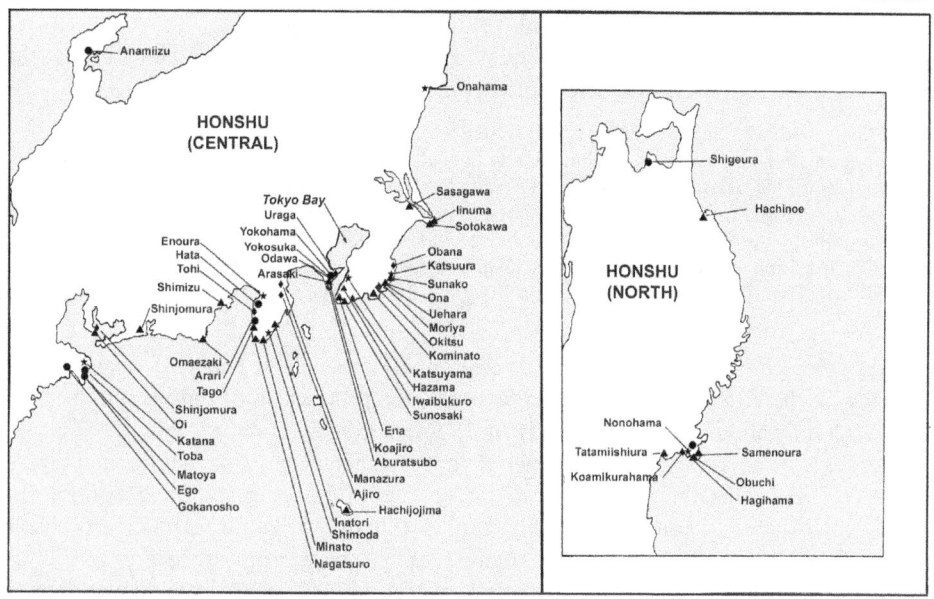

**LOCATION OF SPECIAL ATTACK BASES
15 AUGUST 1945**

Chart 12-b

The *Fukuryu* Underwater Attack Units

Although most of the special attack weapons had required much technical expertise to develop there were some that did not. The *Fukuryu* or "crawling dragons" fell into that category. The concept for these early underwater warriors did not arise until the last year of the war as the invasion of Japan proper loomed on the horizon. Although the Japanese had used frogmen and suicide swimmers during the war, these *Fukuryu* were to operate underwater using self-contained breathing devices, in some ways similar to contemporary scuba equipment. In tests near the end of the war, Lt. Masayuki Sasano reported that he was able to remain underwater at a depth of from three to eight meters for nearly eight and one half hours.[12] In April 1945, development of these forces was placed under the command of Capt. K. Shintani, a former destroyer commander. He was the commander of the 71st *Totsugekitai* (*Arashi*), headquartered at Yokosuka.

In a manner similar to the recruitment of *Kaiten* pilots, the navy drew upon air corps trainees. As noted before, the shortage of aircraft for special attack missions had led to a surplus of pilots, many of whom could be used in other ways. Although volunteers were used at first, by the end of the war, at least half of the men in the *Fukuryu* force were draftees. Planned for the fall of 1945, the *Fukuryu* force was to number 6,000 men by 30 September 1945, with combat readiness to be completed two weeks after that. Two other units, the 81st *Arashi* at Kure and the *Kawatana* unit at Sasebo were also planned, but they were not organized by war's end. However, when the war ended on 14 August 1945, the Japanese had completed the training of 1,200 *Fukuryu* in the 71st at Yokosuka, with another 2,800 ready to begin training. Two battalions of 650 men each with another four battalions in training were to be stationed at Yokosuka and ready for combat in Tokyo Bay.

The entire process was slowed by the difficulties in producing the appropriate diving suits and equipment. Each *Fukuryu* wore a complete diving suit and helmet similar to a "hard hat diver." Strapped to his back were two tanks of compressed oxygen, each holding 214 cubic inches. Weights attached to a belt helped him to remain on the bottom. No swim fins were used. The "crawling dragon" was supposed to walk along the bottom and attack enemy shipping with a mine mounted on the end of a pole. Thrusting the pole into the underside of the ship would set off the contact charge and blow up an enemy landing craft. The *Fukuryu* would die in the explosion and hopefully would sink the invading landing craft.

The pole mounted explosive device was the Type 5 Attack Mine, which had some similarities to pole charges used by suicide infantry troops against tanks.

> The Type 5 Attack (Suicide) Mine was essentially a charge of explosive mounted on a stick equipped with a contact fuse.... Immediately behind the charge was a floating chamber. The weapon could be balanced so that it was readily handled underwater. Its use was simple. The diver rammed the front end against the bottom or side of a boat. He was, of course, destroyed.... Computations indicated that a charge of 20 kg [44 lbs.] of TNT or TNA would be safe to another man at a 40 meter distance. Based upon tests made upon a target boat of double-bottomed construction, it was decided that a 10 kg [22 lbs.] charge would accomplish the desired result.[13]

Although plans for the force included the production of at least 10,000 of the mines, none were ready by the end of the war. In like manner, the production of diving suits had been slowed, with only about a thousand ready on 15 August 1945.

In order to be effective, the *Fukuryu* would have to be in place prior to the actual invasion attempt. To achieve this, the construction of underwater pillboxes was planned. Some of these would be constructed of concrete and then sunk, while others would be built into obsolete or damaged merchant vessels that would then be sunk at the appropriate locations. Pillboxes or sunken ships would have compartment space of around 1440 square feet and would be able

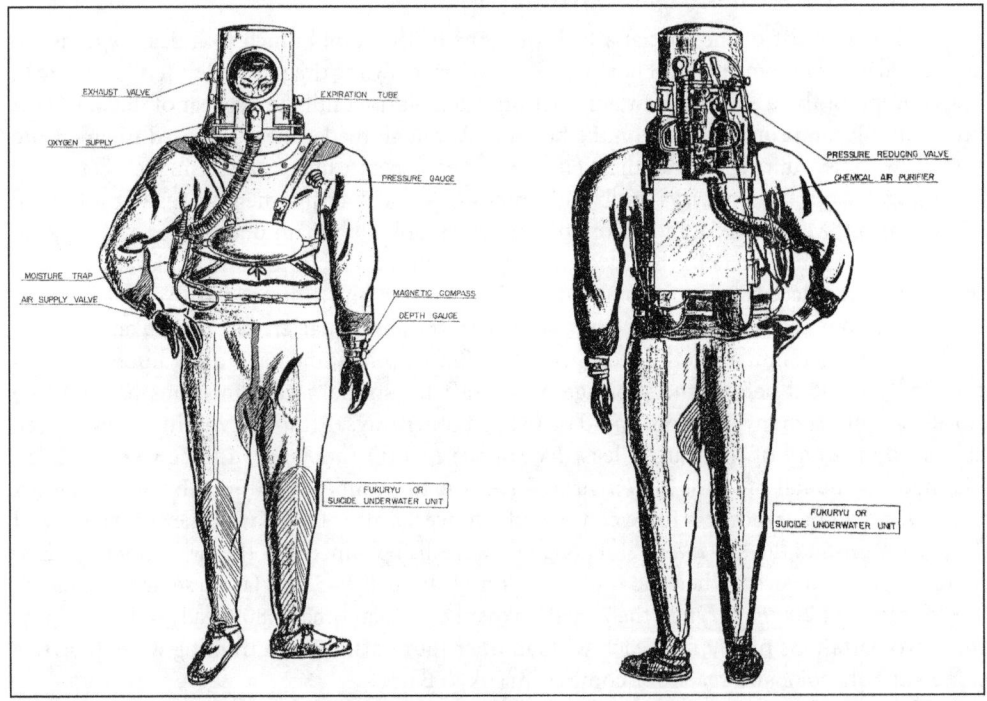

Fukuryu, or crawling dragons, wore dry type underwater suits and hard diving helmets. Air was supplied by two tanks on their back containing compressed oxygen. No swim fins were used as the *Fukuryu* was supposed to walk on the bottom of the bay. U.S. Naval Technical Mission to Japan. Target Report — *The Fukuryu Special Harbor Defense and Underwater Attack Unit—Tokyo Bay*. January, 1946, pp. 11–12.

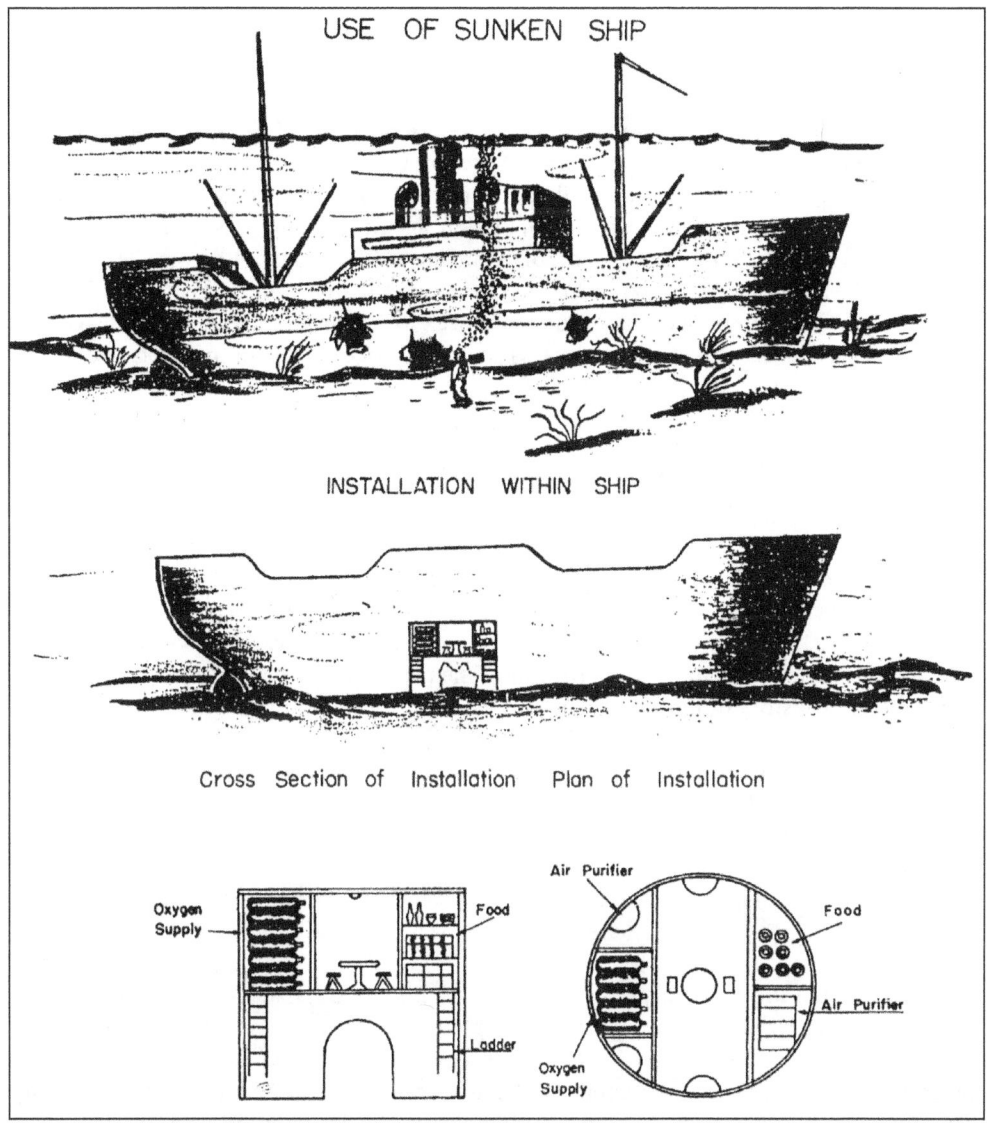

Plans for the use of the *Fukuryu* included underwater bases. One would be concrete pillboxes sunk to the bay floor, while others would be obsolete merchant ships with built in compartments. These would be sunk to the bay floor as well. Forty to fifty men could stay for up to ten days in such an underwater base. U.S. Naval Technical Mission to Japan. Target Report — *The Fukuryu Special Harbor Defense and Underwater Attack Unit—Tokyo Bay.* January, 1946, p. 15.

to accommodate forty to fifty men. A tour of duty in such an underwater living space would be about ten days, at which time the men would be rotated out. Each living space would have food, water, air, and other necessities to sustain life. It is not clear if any of these were actually in place by the end of the war. Japanese naval officers denied that any had been constructed, however, a sonar search of likely locations in Tokyo Bay turned up four possible sites. It had been expected that they would be at a depth of less than one hundred feet, but these were at about 180 feet. The hazards of working at these depths led the U.S. Navy to call off further investigation.

What Might Have Been

At the end of the war President Harry Truman made the decision to use the power of the atomic bomb against the Japanese homeland. Many historians debate the effect that the bombs had on terminating the war, as well as the rationale for using them. The author has no desire to enter into the discussion over the appropriateness of that decision. The work presented herein has demonstrated the willingness of the Japanese military man to die for his country. What percentage of the civilian population shared their fervor is debatable. Had the invasion of the Japanese home islands occurred in late 1945, it is obvious from the foregoing that the Japanese military was committed to utilize special attack methods as their first line of defense. The number of lives that would have been lost on both sides in that endeavor has always been speculative. What seems obvious is that the price in human suffering would have been high.

The Special Attack Forces: A Continuation of Tradition

It is common to think of the kamikaze or special attack corps as a solitary phenomena linked to the Japanese airman of World War II. However, as investigation has shown, the practice of special attack was common throughout the Japanese armed forces in and before World War II. Evidence exists that it was practiced in modern warfare as far back as the Russo-Japanese war in 1904. The concept of giving up one's life for the cause since it was not the individual's property antedates modern times. The tradition can be seen in many instances over the lengthy history of the samurai class. I would suggest that the continuance of the tradition has another meaning.

Japan, faced with the prospect of conflict between the values of the modern world and those that were considered Japanese traditions, struggled continually to find a position that would allow them to retain their unique "Japan-ness" in the face of modern influences from the west.

This is not to suggest that the creation of the *Tokko-tai* was a deliberate effort to reinforce the tradition. Rather it was simply one more manifestation of the struggle within the Japanese mind.

How this tradition was displayed is part of the history of Japanese military exploits in the twentieth century. That this spirit was amply displayed by the members of the armed forces of Japan who willingly gave their lives for their state and emperor gives evidence of the survival of tradition in the face of modern pressure. In that sense, the special attack program may be viewed as a success even though it did not stop the American juggernaut.

Appendix I: U.S. Navy and Merchant Marine Ships Damaged or Sunk by Kamikaze Attacks, 1942–1945

Compiling a list of ships damaged or sunk in kamikaze attacks has presented several problems. First of all there is the question of inclusion. Numerous ships suffered close calls and had only minor damage, such as the loss of a mast or antenna. Others ships not actually touched by the kamikaze airplane were severely damaged or sunk. Many not struck by the airplane or other weapon suffered casualties from explosions in close proximity to the ship. Some ships suffered kamikaze attacks on several occasions. If the attacks took place on different days they are considered to be separate incidents. Ships falling into that category are listed more than once.

I have taken a broad view of kamikaze attacks and included every ship that suffered direct or indirect damage or casualties as a result of a kamikaze attack. The attacks were committed by aircraft, manned torpedoes, suicide boats, and suicide swimmers.

Secondly, I have every confidence that there are additional ships damaged by kamikazes that I have not been able to find in spite of several years of dedicated research on the subject. Here and there in action reports I found mention of ships that may have been damaged in the attacks, but no further information. These are not great in number, however, I am sure that there are probably a few ships that I have missed. That having been noted, I believe this to be the most complete and comprehensive list yet developed by any historian dealing with the subject.

It will be noted that the list begins with several attacks that predate the unofficial formation of the naval kamikaze units on 19 October 1944 and their first sorties two days later. These have been identified in official American reports as kamikaze attacks and therefore have been included.

A third problem with constructing this list relates to the number of casualties. For most of the ships there are action reports, war diaries, or ship logs that give casualty figures. However, the lists of killed and wounded in those documents cannot be considered accurate. Many sailors were transferred off their ship after an attack with the expectation of surviving, only to pass away from complications later on. Others, whose prognosis was terminal, managed to survive. In some cases, there are no statistics available for the attack and I have simply inserted a dash to indicate the lack of information. Some action reports note that "several" or "numerous" casualties occurred and I have included that wording in the list as there are no other data available. As a result, the list below must be considered an approximation of the numbers of dead and wounded resulting from kamikaze attacks in World War II.

Ship	Location	Date	Cause	Killed	Wounded
1942					
Smith DD 378	Battle of Santa Cruz	26 October	Air Attack	28	23
1944					
Franklin CV 13	Taiwan	13 October	Air Attack	1	10
Reno CL 96	Taiwan	14 October	Air Attack	0	9
David Dudley Field	Philippines	24 October	Air Attack	0	4
Augustus Thomas	Philippines	24 October	Air Attack	0	2
Sonoma ATO 12*	Philippines	24 October	Air Attack	7	36
LCI(L) 1065*	Philippines	24 October	Air Attack	13	8+
Santee CVE 29	Philippines	25 October	Air Attack	16	27
Suwanee CVE 27	Philippines	25 October	Air Attack	46	55
Kitkun Bay CVE 71	Philippines	25 October	Air Attack	1	20
White Plains CVE 66	Philippines	25 October	Air Attack	0	11
St. Lo CVE 63*	Philippines	25 October	Air Attack	114	-
Kalinin Bay CVE 68	Philippines	25 October	Air Attack	5	55
Suwanee CVE 27	Philippines	26 October	Air Attack	30	83
Benjamin Ide Wheeler	Philippines	27 October	Air Attack	2	3
Intrepid CV 11	Philippines	29 October	Air Attack	10	6
Belleau Wood CVL 24	Philippines	30 October	Air Attack	92	54
Franklin CV 13	Philippines	30 October	Air Attack	56	14
Ammen DD 527	Philippines	1 November	Air Attack	5	21
Abner Read DD 526*	Philippines	1 November	Air Attack	22	56
Anderson DD 411	Philippines	1 November	Air Attack	16	20
Claxton DD 571	Philippines	1 November	Air Attack	5	23
Matthew P. Deady	Philippines	3 November	Air Attack	61	104
Cape Constance	Philippines	4 November	Air Attack	0	1
Lexington CV 16	Philippines	5 November	Air Attack	50	132
Leonidas Merritt	Philippines	12 November	Air Attack	3	6
Thomas Nelson	Philippines	12 November	Air Attack	136	88
Jeremiah M. Daily	Philippines	12 November	Air Attack	106	43
William A. Coulter	Philippines	12 November	Air Attack	0	69
Morrison R. Waite	Philippines	12 November	Air Attack	21	43
Alexander Majors	Philippines	12 November	Air Attack	2	15
Egeria ARL 8	Philippines	12 November	Air Attack	0	21
LCI(L) 364	Philippines	12 November	Air Attack	-	-
Achilles ARL 41	Philippines	12 November	Air Attack	33	28
Matthew P. Deady	Philippines	12 November	Air Attack	0	0
Alpine APA 92	Philippines	18 November	Air Attack	5	12
Nicholas J. Sinnett	Philippines	18 November	Air Attack	0	0
Gilbert Stuart	Philippines	18 November	Air Attack	6	11
Alcoa Pioneer	Philippines	19 November	Air Attack	6	13
Cape Romano	Philippines	19 November	Air Attack	0	0
Mississinewa AO 59*	Ulithi	20 November	Kaiten	62	95
James O'Hara APA 90	Philippines	23 November	Air Attack	0	0
Essex CV 9	Philippines	25 November	Air Attack	15	44
Intrepid CV 11	Phillippines	25 November	Air Attack	69	35
Hancock CV 19	Phillippines	25 November	Air Attack	0	2
Cabot CVL 28	Philippines	25 November	Air Attack	36	16
Colorado BB 45	Philippines	27 November	Air Attack	19	72
SC 744*	Philippines	27 November	Air Attack	6	7
St. Louis CL 49	Philippines	27 November	Air Attack	16	43
Montpelier CL 57	Philippines	27 November	Air Attack	0	11
Maryland BB 46	Philippines	29 November	Air Attack	31	30
Saufley DD 465	Philippines	29 November	Air Attack	1	0
Aulick DD 569	Philippines	29 November	Air Attack	32	64
Marcus Daly	Philippines	5 December	Air Attack	65	49
LSM 20*	Philippines	5 December	Air Attack	8	9

Ships Damaged or Sunk, 1942–1945 (by date)

Ship	Location	Date	Cause	Killed	Wounded
LSM 23	Philippines	5 December	Air Attack	8	7
Drayton DD 366	Philippines	5 December	Air Attack	6	12
Mugford DD 389	Philippines	5 December	Air Attack	8	16
John Evans	Philippines	5 December	Air Attack	0	4
Ward APD 16*	Philippines	7 December	Air Attack	0	several
Mahan DD 364*	Philippines	7 December	Air Attack	6	31
Liddle APD 60	Philippines	7 December	Air Attack	36	22
Lamson DD 367	Philippines	7 December	Air Attack	4	17
LSM 318*	Philippines	7 December	Air Attack	several k & w	
LST 737	Philippines	7 December	Air Attack	2	4
Marcus Daly	Philippines	10 December	Air Attack	0	8
William S. Ladd*	Philippines	10 December	Air Attack	0	10
Hughes DD 410	Philippines	10 December	Air Attack	14	26
LCT 1075	Philippines	10 December	Air Attack	2	9
PT 323*	Philippines	10 December	Air Attack	2	11
Reid DD 369*	Philippines	11 December	Air Attack	Appx. 150 dead	
Caldwell DD 605	Philippines	12 December	Air Attack	33	40
Haraden DD 585	Philippines	13 December	Air Attack	14	24
Nashville CL 43	Philippines	13 December	Air Attack	133	190
Howorth DD 592	Philippines	15 December	Air Attack	0	0
Ralph Talbot DD 390	Philippines	15 December	Air Attack	0	1
Marcus Island CVE 77	Philippines	15 December	Air Attack	1	1
LST 738*	Philippines	15 December	Air Attack	1	10
LST 472*	Philippines	15 December	Air Attack	6	several
LST 605	Philippines	15 December	Air Attack	0	several
PT 75	Philippines	17 December	Air Attack	0	4
PT 300*	Philippines	18 December	Air Attack	8	7
LST 605	Philippines	21 December	Air Attack	5	11
Juan De Fuca	Philippines	21 December	Air Attack	2	17
LST 460*	Philippines	21 December	Air Attack	-	-
LST 749*	Philippines	21 December	Air Attack	-	-
Foote DD 511	Philippines	21–22 December	Air Attack	0	0
Bryant DD 665	Philippines	22 December	Air Attack	0	1
Francisco Morazan	Philippines	28 December	Air Attack	0	3
William Sharon	Philippines	28 December	Air Attack	11	11
Unidentified Army FS Ship	Philippines	28 December	Air Attack	lost all but 1 man	
John Burke*	Philippines	28 December	Air Attack	68	0
William Ahearn	Philippines	28 December	Air Attack	-	-
PT 332	Philippines	28 December	Air Attack	0	0
Gansevoort DD 608	Philippines	30 December	Air Attack	17	15
Pringle DD 477	Philippines	30 December	Air Attack	11	20
Orestes AGP 10	Philippines	30 December	Air Attack	59	106
Porcupine IX 126*	Philippines	30 December	Air Attack	7	8
1945					
Orca AVP 49	Philippines	2 January	Air Attack	0	6
Cowanesque AO 79	Philippines	3 January	Air Attack	2	1
Ommaney Bay CVE 79*	Philippines	3 January	Air Attack	93	65
Lewis L. Dyche*	Philippines	4 January	Air Attack	69	0
Helm DD 388	Philippines	5 January	Air Attack	0	6
Apache ATF 67	Philippines	5 January	Air Attack	0	3
LCI(G) 70	Philippines	5 January	Air Attack	6	9
Stafford DE 411	Philippines	5 January	Air Attack	2	12
Manila Bay CVE 61	Philippines	5 January	Air Attack	22	56
Savo Island CVE 78	Philippines	5 January	Air Attack	0	0
Louisville CA 28	Philippines	5 January	Air Attack	1	59
Louisville CA 28	Philippines	6 January	Air Attack	36	56
Allen M. Sumner DD 692	Philippines	6 January	Air Attack	14	19
Richard P. Leary DD 664	Philippines	6 January	Air Attack	0	1
New Mexico BB 40	Philippines	6 January	Air Attack	30	87
Walke DD 723	Philippines	6 January	Air Attack	12	34

Ship	Location	Date	Cause	Killed	Wounded
Long DMS 12*	Philippines	6 January	Air Attack	1	35
Brooks APD 10	Philippines	6 January	Air Attack	3	11
O'Brien DD 725	Philippines	6 January	Air Attack	0	0
Minneapolis CA 36	Philippines	6 January	Air Attack	0	2
California BB 44	Philippines	6 January	Air Attack	45	151
Newcomb DD 586	Philippines	6 January	Air Attack	2	15
Columbia CL 56	Philippines	6 January	Air Attack	13	44
Southard DMS 10	Philippines	6 January	Air Attack	0	6
Palmer DMS 5*	Philippines	7 January	Air Attack	26	38
LST 912	Philippines	8 January	Air Attack	4	4
Kadashan Bay CVE 76	Philippines	8 January	Air Attack	0	3
Callaway APA 35	Philippines	8 January	Air Attack	29	22
Kitkun Bay CVE 71	Philippines	8 January	Air Attack	17	36
LCI(G) 404	Palau Islands	8 January	Suicide Swimmers	0	0
Hodges DE 231	Philippines	9 January	Air Attack	0	0
Columbia CL 56	Philippines	9 January	Air Attack	24	68
Mississippi BB 41	Philippines	9 January	Air Attack	26	63
Hodges DE 231	Philippines	9 January	Air Attack	0	0
Du Page APA 41	Philippines	10 January	Air Attack	32	157
LeRay Wilson DE 414	Philippines	10 January	Air Attack	6	7
War Hawk AP 168	Philippines	10 January	Suicide Boat	61	32
Robinson DD 562	Philippines	10 January	Suicide Boat	"No serious injuries"	
LST 548	Philippines	10 January	Suicide Boat	0	0
LST 610	Philippines	10 January	Suicide Boat	0	0
LST 925	Philippines	10 January	Suicide Boat	1	8
LST 1028	Philippines	10 January	Suicide Boat	0	14
LCI(M) 974*	Philippines	10 January	Suicide Boat	-	-
LCI(G) 365	Philippines	10 January	Suicide Boat	0	4
Eaton DD 510	Philippines	10 January	Suicide Boat	1	14
Pontus H. Ross	Hollandia	11 January	Kaiten	0	0
Elmira Victory	Philippines	12 January	Air Attack	0	6
Otis Skinner	Philippines	12 January	Air Attack	0	2
Edward N. Wescott	Philippines	12 January	Air Attack	0	11
Kyle V. Johnson	Philippines	12 January	Air Attack	130	9
David Dudley Field	Philippines	12 January	Air Attack	0	8
Gilligan DE 508	Philippines	12 January	Air Attack	12	13
Richard W. Suesens DE 342	Philippines	12 January	Air Attack	0	11
Belknap APD 34	Philippines	12 January	Air Attack	38	49
LST 700	Philippines	12 January	Air Attack	2	8
LST 700	Philippines	13 January	Air Attack	2	2
Zeilin APA 3	Philippines	13 January	Air Attack	8	32
Salamaua CVE 96	Philippines	13 January	Air Attack	15	88
Ticonderoga CV 14	Taiwan Area	21 January	Air Attack	143	202
Maddox DD 731	Taiwan Area	21 January	Air Attack	7	33
PC 1129*	Philippines	31 January	Suicide Boat	1	several
Army FS 309	Philippines	1 February	Suicide Boat	0	0
LCS(L) 7*	Philippines	16 February	Suicide Boat	2+	-
LCS(L) 26	Philippines	16 February	Suicide Boat	25	8
LCS(L) 27	Philippines	16 February	Suicide Boat	2	23
LCS(L) 49*	Philippines	16 February	Suicide Boat	24	22
Bismarck Sea CVE 95*	Iwo Jima	21 February	Air Attack	119	99
LST 477	Iwo Jima	21 February	Air Attack	9	5
LST 809	Iwo Jima	21 February	Air Attack	0	0
Lunga Point CVE 94	Iwo Jima	21 February	Air Attack	0	11
Saratoga CV 3	Iwo Jima	21 February	Air Attack	123	192
Randolph CV 15	Ulithi	11 March	Air Attack	25	106
Intrepid CV 11	Kyushu	18 March	Air Attack	2	43
Wasp CV 16	Kyushu	19 March	Air Attack	0	0
Halsey Powell DD 686	Kyushu	20 March	Air Attack	12	29
Kimberly DD 521	Okinawa	26 March	Air Attack	4	57

Ships Damaged or Sunk, 1942–1945 (by date)

Ship	Location	Date	Cause	Killed	Wounded
Robert H. Smith DM 23	Okinawa	26 March	Air Attack	0	0
Biloxi CL 80	Okinawa	26 March	Air Attack	0	2
O'Brien DD 725	Okinawa	27 March	Air Attack	50	76
Foreman DE 633	Okinawa	27 March	Air Attack	0	1
Gilmer APD 11	Okinawa	27 March	Air Attack	1	3
Nevada BB 36	Okinawa	27 March	Air Attack	11	47
Dorsey DMS 1	Okinawa	27 March	Air Attack	3	2
Callaghan DD 792	Okinawa	27 March	Air Attack	0	0
LCI(G) 558	Okinawa	29 March	Suicide Boat	0	0
LSM(R) 188	Okinawa	29 March	Air Attack	15	32
LCI(G) 560	Okinawa	29 March	Air Attack	0	1
Indianapolis CA 35	Okinawa	31 March	Air Attack	9	20
Adams DM 27	Okinawa	1 April	Air Attack	0	0
Alpine APA 92	Okinawa	1 April	Air Attack	16	19
Hinsdale APA 120	Okinawa	1 April	Air Attack	16	39
LST 884	Okinawa	1 April	Air Attack	24	21
LST 724	Okinawa	6 April	Air Attack	0	0
West Virginia BB 48	Okinawa	1 April	Air Attack	4	23
Dickerson APD 21*	Okinawa	2 April	Air Attack	54	97
Goodhue APA 107	Okinawa	2 April	Air Attack	24	119
Henrico APA 45	Okinawa	2 April	Air Attack	49	125
Achernar AKA 53	Okinawa	2 April	Air Attack	5	41
LCI(G) 568	Okinawa	2 April	Air Attack	1	4
Telfair APA 210	Okinawa	2 April	Air Attack	1	16
Tyrrell AKA 80	Okinawa	2 April	Air Attack	0	0
Hambleton DMS 20	Okinawa	3 April	Air Attack	0	0
LST 599	Okinawa	3 April	Air Attack	0	21
LCT 876	Okinawa	3 April	Air Attack	0	2
Wake Island CVE 65	Okinawa	3 April	Air Attack	0	0
LCI(G) 82*	Okinawa	4 April	Suicide Boat	8	11
Bush DD 529*	Okinawa	6 April	Air Attack	94	32
Colhoun DD 801*	Okinawa	6 April	Air Attack	35	21
Howorth DD 592	Okinawa	6 April	Air Attack	9	14
Hyman DD 732	Okinawa	6 April	Air Attack	10	40
Leutze DD 481	Okinawa	6 April	Air Attack	7	34
Morris DD 417	Okinawa	6 April	Air Attack	13	45
Mullany DD 528	Okinawa	6 April	Air Attack	30	36
Newcomb DD 586	Okinawa	6 April	Air Attack	40	51
Haynsworth DD 700	Okinawa	6 April	Air Attack	14	20
Witter DE 636	Okinawa	6 April	Air Attack	6	6
Fieberling DE 640	Okinawa	6 April	Air Attack	0	0
Emmons DMS 22*	Okinawa	6 April	Air Attack	57	71
Facility AM 233	Okinawa	6 April	Air Attack	0	0
Rodman DMS 21	Okinawa	6 April	Air Attack	16	20
Defense AM 317	Okinawa	6 April	Air Attack	0	9
San Jacinto CVL 30	Okinawa	6 April	Air Attack	1	5
LST 447*	Okinawa	6 April	Air Attack	5	17
Logan Victory*	Okinawa	6 April	Air Attack	15	9
Hobbs Victory*	Okinawa	6 April	Air Attack	13	2
YMS 331	Okinawa	6 April	Air Attack	1	2
Wesson DE 184	Okinawa	7 April	Air Attack	8	23
Hancock CV 19	Okinawa	7 April	Air Attack	62	71
Maryland BB 46	Okinawa	7 April	Air Attack	31	38
Bennett DD 473	Okinawa	7 April	Air Attack	3	18
YMS 81	Okinawa	7 April	Air Attack	0	0
Gregory DD 802	Okinawa	8 April	Air Attack	0	2
Sterrett DD 407	Okinawa	9 April	Air Attack	0	9
Charles J. Badger DD 657	Okinawa	9 April	Suicide Boat	0	0
LCS(L) 36	Okinawa	9 April	Air Attack	0	5
Starr AKA 67	Okinawa	9 April	Suicide Boat	0	4
Enterprise CV 6	Okinawa	11 April	Air Attack	0	18
Samuel Miles DE 183	Okinawa	11 April	Air Attack	1	0

Ship	Location	Date	Cause	Killed	Wounded
Hank DD 702	Okinawa	11 April	Air Attack	3	1
Kidd DD 661	Okinawa	11 April	Air Attack	38	55
Missouri BB 63	Okinawa	11 April	Air Attack	0	1
Bullard DD 660	Okinawa	11 April	Air Attack	0	0
Minot Victory	Okinawa	12 April	Air Attack	0	5
Riddle DE 185	Okinawa	12 April	Air Attack	1	9
Stanly DD 478	Okinawa	12 April	Air Attack	0	3
Walter C. Wann DE 412	Okinawa	12 April	Air Attack	0	1
Tennessee BB 43	Okinawa	12 April	Air Attack	22	73
Idaho BB 42	Okinawa	12 April	Air Attack	0	13
Rall DE 304	Okinawa	12 April	Air Attack	21	38
Whitehurst DE 634	Okinawa	12 April	Air Attack	37	37
Lindsey DM 32	Okinawa	12 April	Air Attack	52	60
Zellars DD 777	Okinawa	12 April	Air Attack	29	37
Purdy DD 734	Okinawa	12 April	Air Attack	13	27
Cassin Young DD 793	Okinawa	12 April	Air Attack	1	59
LCS(L) 33*	Okinawa	12 April	Air Attack	4	29
LCS(L) 57	Okinawa	12 April	Air Attack	2	6
Jeffers DMS 27	Okinawa	12 April	Air Attack	0	0
Mannert L. Abele DD 733	Okinawa	12 April	Air Attack	79	35
LSM(R) 189	Okinawa	12 April	Air Attack	0	4
Gladiator AM 319	Okinawa	12 April	Air Attack	0	0
Connolly DE 306	Okinawa	13 April	Air Attack	0	0
New York BB 34	Okinawa	14 April	Air Attack	0	2
Sigsbee DD 502	Okinawa	14 April	Air Attack	22	74
Hunt DD 674	Okinawa	14 April	Air Attack	0	5
YMS 331	Okinawa	16 April	Suicide Boat	0	0
Wilson DD 408	Okinawa	16 April	Air Attack	5	3
LCI(G) 407	Okinawa	16 April	Air Attack	0	1
LCS(L) 51	Okinawa	16 April	Air Attack	0	0
LCS(L) 116	Okinawa	16 April	Air Attack	12	12
Laffey DD 724	Okinawa	16 April	Air Attack	31	72
Intrepid CV 11	Japan Area	16 April	Air Attack	10	87
Bryant DD 665	Okinawa	16 April	Air Attack	34	33
Hobson DMS 26	Okinawa	16 April	Air Attack	4	8
Missouri BB 63	Okinawa	16 April	Air Attack	0	2
Harding DMS 28	Okinawa	16 April	Air Attack	22	10
YMS 331	Okinawa	16 April	Suicide Boat	0	0
Taluga AO 62	Okinawa	16 April	Air Attack	0	12
Bowers APD 40	Okinawa	16 April	Air Attack	48	56
Pringle DD 477*	Okinawa	17 April	Air Attack	65	110
Benham DD 796	Japan Area	17 April	Air Attack	1	8
Wadsworth DD 516	Okinawa	22 April	Air Attack	0	1
LCS(L) 15*	Okinawa	22 April	Air Attack	15	11
Isherwood DD 520	Okinawa	22 April	Air Attack	42	41
Hudson DD 475	Okinawa	22 April	Air Attack	0	1
Swallow AM 65*	Okinawa	22 April	Air Attack	2	9
Ransom AM 283	Okinawa	22 April	Air Attack	0	0
Ralph Talbot DD 390	Okinawa	27 April	Air Attack	5	9
Hutchins DD 476	Okinawa	27 April	Suicide Boat	0	20
Rathburne APD 25	Okinawa	27 April	Air Attack	0	0
Canada Victory*	Okinawa	27 April	Air Attack	3	5
Bozeman Victory	Okinawa	28 April	Suicide Boat	0	6
LCS(L) 37	Okinawa	28 April	Suicide Boat	0	3
LCI(G) 580	Okinawa	28 April	Air Attack	0	6
Comfort AH 6	Okinawa	28 April	Air Attack	30	48
Pinkney APH 2	Okinawa	28 April	Air Attack	35	12
Bennion DD 662	Okinawa	28 April	Air Attack	0	0
Twiggs DD 591	Okinawa	28 April	Air Attack	0	2
Daly DD 519	Okinawa	28 April	Air Attack	2	15
Wadsworth DD 516	Okinawa	28 April	Air Attack	0	0
Haggard DD 555	Okinawa	29 April	Air Attack	11	40

Ships Damaged or Sunk, 1942–1945 (by date)

Ship	Location	Date	Cause	Killed	Wounded
Hazelwood DD 531	Okinawa	29 April	Air Attack	46	26
LCS(L) 37	Okinawa	29 April	Suicide Boat	0	4
S. Hall Young	Okinawa	30 April	Air Attack	0	1
Terror CM 5	Okinawa	30 April	Air Attack	48	123
Macomb DMS 23	Okinawa	3 May	Air Attack	7	14
Little DD 803*	Okinawa	3 May	Air Attack	30	79
Aaron Ward DM 34	Okinawa	3 May	Air Attack	45	49
Idaho BB 42	Okinawa	3 May	Air Attack	0	0
LSM(R) 195*	Okinawa	3 May	Air Attack	8	16
LCS(L) 31	Okinawa	4 May	Air Attack	5	2
Ingraham DD 694	Okinawa	4 May	Air Attack	14	37
Morrison DD 560*	Okinawa	4 May	Air Attack	159	102
LSM(R) 194*	Okinawa	4 May	Air Attack	13	23
Hopkins DMS 13	Okinawa	4 May	Air Attack	1	2
Gayety AM 239	Okinawa	4 May	Air Attack	0	3
Lowry DD 770	Okinawa	4 May	Air Attack	2	23
LCS(L) 25	Okinawa	4 May	Air Attack	1	8
Gwin DM 33	Okinawa	4 May	Air Attack	2	9
LSM(R) 192	Okinawa	4 May	Air Attack	0	1
Luce DD 522*	Okinawa	4 May	Air Attack	149	94
Sangamon CVE 26	Okinawa	4 May	Air Attack	46	116
LSM(R) 190*	Okinawa	4 May	Air Attack	13	18
Cowell DD 547	Okinawa	4 May	Air Attack	0	0
Carina AK 74	Okinawa	4 May	Suicide Boat	0	6
Shea DM 30	Okinawa	4 May	Air Attack	27	91
Birmingham CL 62	Okinawa	4 May	Air Attack	51	81
Pathfinder AGS 1	Okinawa	6 May	Air Attack	1	0
St. George AV 16	Okinawa	8 May	Air Attack	3	30
England APD 41	Okinawa	9 May	Air Attack	35	27
Oberrender DE 344	Okinawa	9 May	Air Attack	9	51
Army FS 225*	Philippines	10–11 May	Suicide Boat	–	–
Evans DD 552	Okinawa	11 May	Air Attack	30	29
LCS(L) 84	Okinawa	11 May	Air Attack	0	1
Bunker Hill CV 17	Okinawa	11 May	Air Attack	396	264
LCS(L) 88	Okinawa	11 May	Air Attack	7	9
Harry F. Bauer DM 26	Okinawa	11 May	Air Attack	0	1
Hugh W. Hadley DD 774	Okinawa	11 May	Air Attack	28	67
M. S. Tjisadane	Okinawa	11 May	Air Attack	4	9
New Mexico BB 40	Okinawa	12 May	Air Attack	54	119
Bache DD 470	Okinawa	13 May	Air Attack	41	32
Bright DE 747	Okinawa	13 May	Air Attack	0	2
Enterprise CV 6	Kyushu	14 May	Air Attack	13	68
Douglas H. Fox DD 779	Okinawa	17 May	Air Attack	9	35
Uriah M. Rose	Okinawa	18 May	Air Attack	0	0
Sims APD 50	Okinawa	18 May	Air Attack	0	0
LST 808	Okinawa	20 May	Air Attack	0	1
Chase APD 54	Okinawa	20 May	Air Attack	0	35
Thatcher DD 514	Okinawa	20 May	Air Attack	14	53
Register APD 92	Okinawa	20 May	Air Attack	0	12
John C. Butler DE 339	Okinawa	20 May	Air Attack	0	3
Guest DD 472	Okinawa	25 May	Air Attack	0	0
Stormes DD 780	Okinawa	25 May	Air Attack	21	6
O'Neill DE 188	Okinawa	25 May	Air Attack	0	16
Cowell DD 547	Okinawa	25 May	Air Attack	0	2
William C. Cole DE 641	Okinawa	25 May	Air Attack	0	0
Barry APD 29	Okinawa	25 May	Air Attack	0	30
Bates APD 47*	Okinawa	25 May	Air Attack	21	35
Segundo Ruiz Belvis	Okinawa	25 May	Air Attack	0	0
Roper APD 20	Okinawa	25 May	Air Attack	1	10
Spectacle AM 305	Okinawa	25 May	Air Attack	29	6
LSM 135*	Okinawa	25 May	Air Attack	11	10

Ship	Location	Date	Cause	Killed	Wounded
Sims APD 50	Okinawa	25 May	Air Attack	0	11
PC 1603	Okinawa	26 May	Air Attack	3	15
Forrest DMS 24	Okinawa	26 May	Air Attack	5	13
Braine DD 630	Okinawa	27 May	Air Attack	66	78
Dutton AGS 8	Okinawa	27 May	Air Attack	0	1
Anthony DD 515	Okinawa	27 May	Air Attack	0	0
Rednour APD 102	Okinawa	27 May	Air Attack	3	13
LCS(L) 119	Okinawa	27 May	Air Attack	12	6
Loy APD 56	Okinawa	27 May	Air Attack	3	15
LCS(L) 52	Okinawa	27 May	Air Attack	1	10
LCS(L) 61	Okinawa	27May	Air Attack	0	1
Drexler DD 741*	Okinawa	28 May	Air Attack	158	51
Sandoval APA 194	Okinawa	28 May	Air Attack	8	26
Mary A. Livermore	Okinawa	28 May	Air Attack	11	6
Brown Victory	Okinawa	28 May	Air Attack	4	16
Josiah Snelling	Okinawa	28 May	Air Attack	0	25
LCS(L) 119	Okinawa	28 May	Air Attack	14	18
Shubrick DD 639	Okinawa	29May	Air Attack	32	28
Tatum APD 81	Okinawa	29 May	Air Attack	0	3
LCI(L) 90	Okinawa	3 June	Air Attack	1	7
Mississippi BB 41	Okinawa	5 June	Air Attack	1	8
Louisville CA 28	Okinawa	5 June	Air Attack	8	37
J. WilliamDitter DM 31*	Okinawa	6 June	Air Attack	10	27
Harry F. Bauer DM 26	Okinawa	6 June	Air Attack	0	0
Anthony DD 515	Okinawa	7 June	Air Attack	0	3
Natoma Bay CVE 62	Okinawa	7 June	Air Attack	1	4
William D. Porter* DD579	Okinawa	10 June	Air Attack	0	61
LCS(L) 122	Okinawa	11 June	Air Attack	11	29
Walter Colton	Okinawa	11 June	Air Attack	0	76
Twiggs DD 591*	Okinawa	16 June	Air Attack	184	34
Thatcher DD 514	Okinawa	19 July	Air Attack	0	2
Kenneth Whiting AV 14	Okinawa	21 June	Air Attack	0	5
Halloran DE 305	Okinawa	21 June	Air Attack	3	24
LSM 59*	Okinawa	21 June	Air Attack	2	8
Barry APD 29*	Okinawa	21 June	Air Attack	0	0
Curtiss AV 4	Okinawa	21 June	Air Attack	41	28
Ellyson DMS 19	Okinawa	22 June	Air Attack	1	4
LSM 213	Okinawa	22 June	Air Attack	3	10
LST 534	Okinawa	22 June	Air Attack	3	35
Thatcher DD 514	Okinawa	19 July	Air Attack	0	2
Underhill DE 682	Philippines Area	24 July	Kaiten	112	-
Callaghan DD 792*	Okinawa	29 July	Air Attack	47	73
Pritchett DD 561	Okinawa	29 July	Air Attack	0	0
Cassin Young DD 793	Okinawa	29 July	Air Attack	22	45
Horace A. Bass APD 124	Okinawa	30 July	Air Attack	1	15
Hank DD 702	Japan Area	9 August	Air Attack	1	5
Borie DD 704	Japan Area	9 August	Air Attack	48	66
Lagrange APA 124	Okinawa	13 August	Air Attack	21	89
				6,830	9,931

The number of ships damaged in kamikaze attacks was 407. Of this number, sixty were sunk.
*Ships marked with an asterisk were either sunk outright by a kamikaze attack or deemed unsalvageable or a hazard to navigation and sunk by American gunfire or torpedoes.
Casualty figures marked with a dash (-) indicate that there are no data available.

Appendix II: Ship Types

American Ship Classes

Throughout the text ships are identified by name, type, and number. For instance, the designator BB indicates that the type of ship is a battleship and the number following it identifies the particular ship. The numbers would also identify the particular class of ship. Accordingly, *U. S. S. New Jersey BB 62*, is a battleship belonging to the *Iowa* Class which carried the numbers *BB 61* through *BB 66*. Larger ships were named, but smaller ships such as LSTs, LCI(L)s and others were not named and only known by their hull numbers.

Listed below are the official type designations and their meanings.

AD — Destroyer Tender
AGM — Auxiliary Ship
AGP — Motor Torpedo Boat Tender
AGS — Surveying Ship
AH — Hospital Ship
AK — Cargo Ship
AKA — Cargo Ship (Attack)
AM — Fleet Minesweeper
AO — Fuel Oil Tanker
APA — Transport (Attack)
APD — High Speed Transport
APH — Transport Fitted for Evacuation of Wounded
ARB — Repair Ship (Battle Damage)
ARL — Repair Ship (Landing Craft)
ARS — Salvage Vessel
ATF — Ocean Tug (Fleet)
ATO — Ocean Tug (Old)
ATR — Ocean Tug (Rescue)
AV — Seaplane Tender
BB — Battleship
CA — Heavy Cruiser
CL — Light Cruiser
CM — Coastal Minelayer

CV — Aircraft Carrier
CVE — Escort Carrier
CVL — Aircraft Carrier, Light
DD — Destroyer
DE — Destroyer Escort
DM — Light Minelayer
DMS — High Speed Minesweeper
FS — Army Freight and Supply Ship
LCI(G) — Landing Craft Infantry (Guns)
LCI(L) — Landing Craft Infantry (Large)
LCI(M) — Landing Craft Infantry (Mortars)
LCS(L) — Landing Craft Large (support)
LCT — Landing Craft Tank
LSD — Landing Ship (Dock)
LSM — Landing Ship Medium
LSM(R) — Landing Ship Medium (Rockets)
LST — Landing Ship (Tank)
PC — Patrol Craft
PCE(R) — Patrol Craft (Rescue)
PGM — Patrol Motor Gunboat
PT — Motor Torpedo Boat
SC — Sub Chaser
SS — Submarine
YMS — Motor Minesweeper

Appendix II

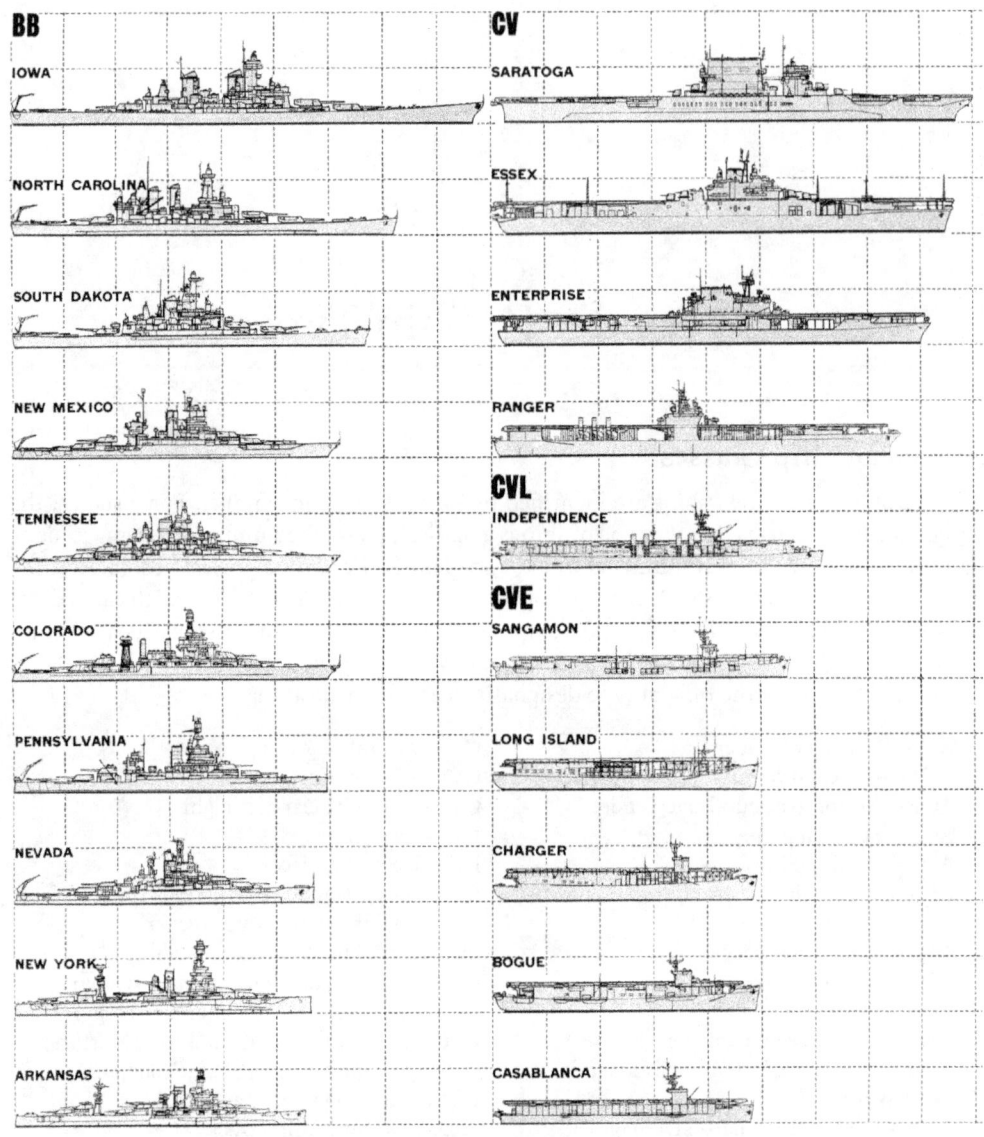

Scale: One square equals 100 feet.*

Ship Types

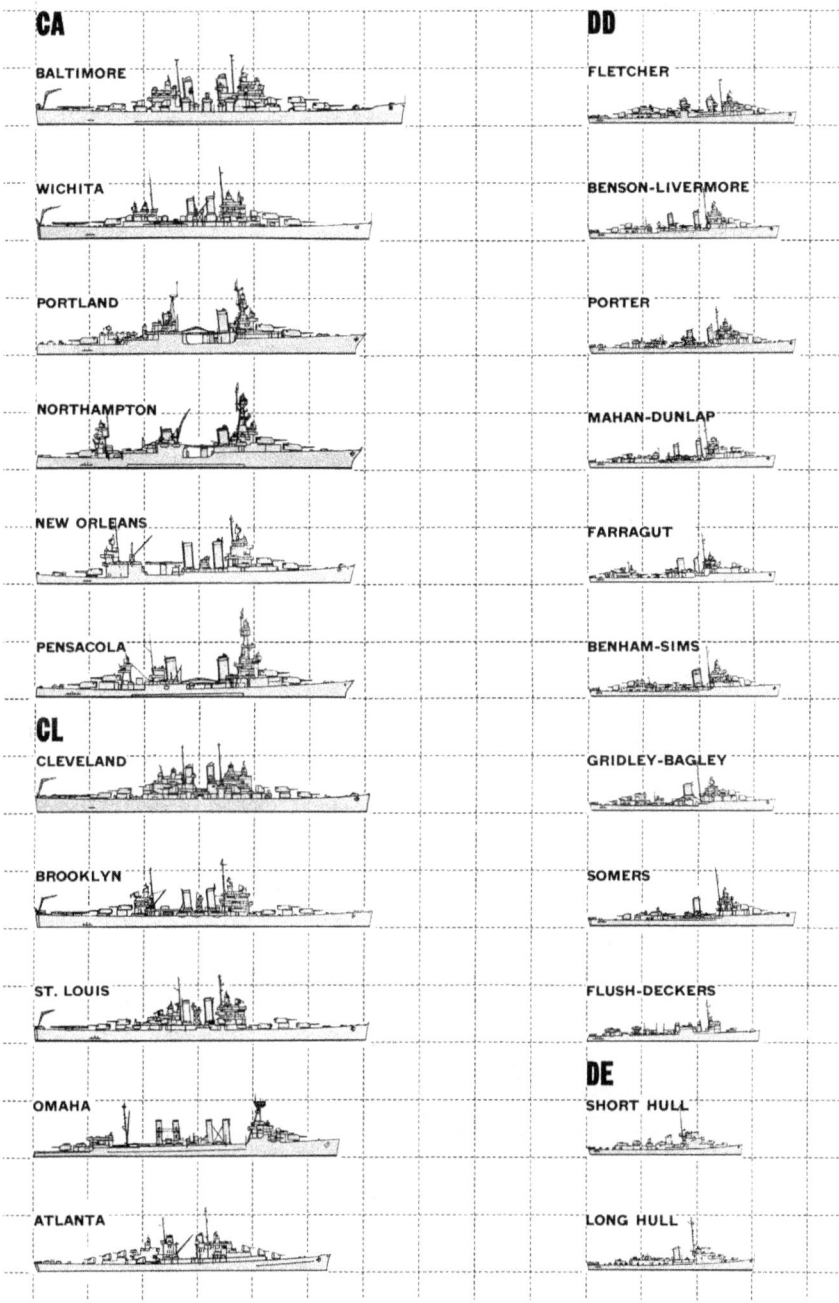

Scale: One square equals 100 feet.

Appendix II

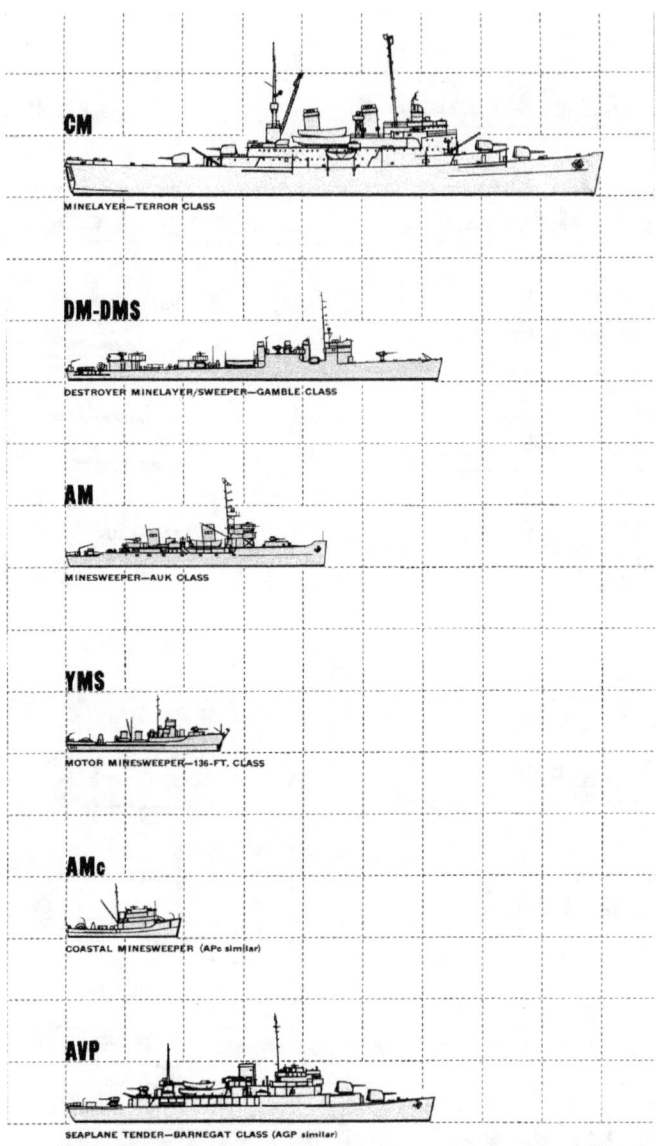

One square equals 50 feet.

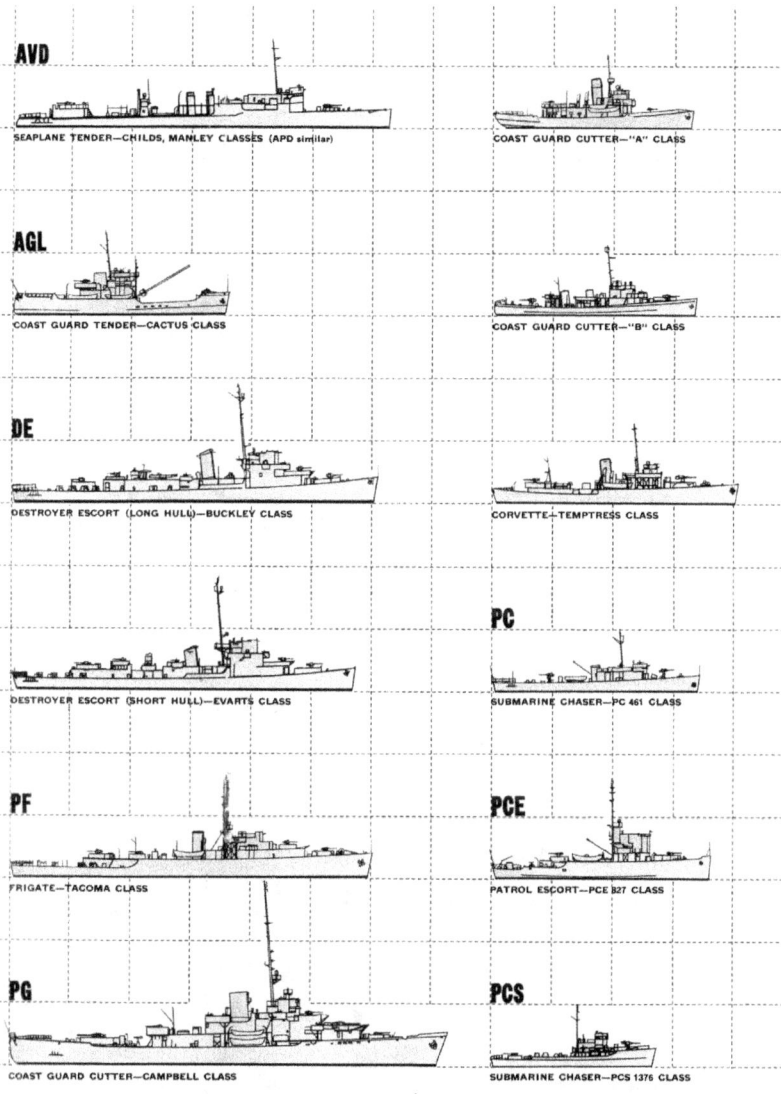

Scale: One square equals 50 feet.

Appendix II

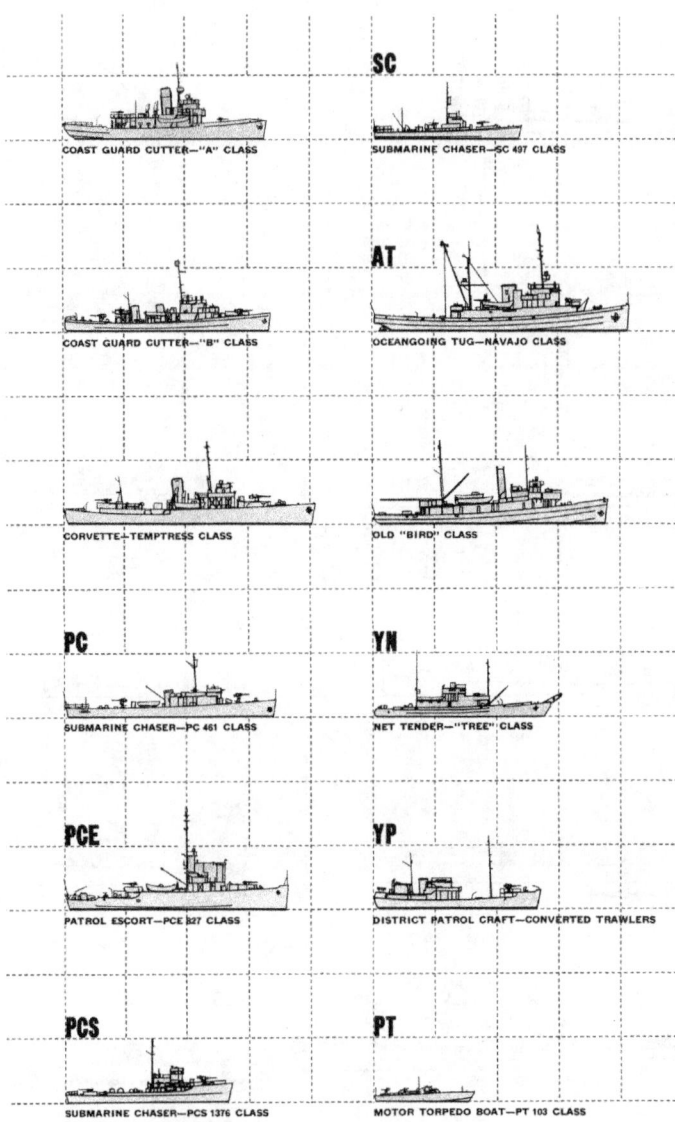

Scale: One square equals 50 feet.

Ship Types

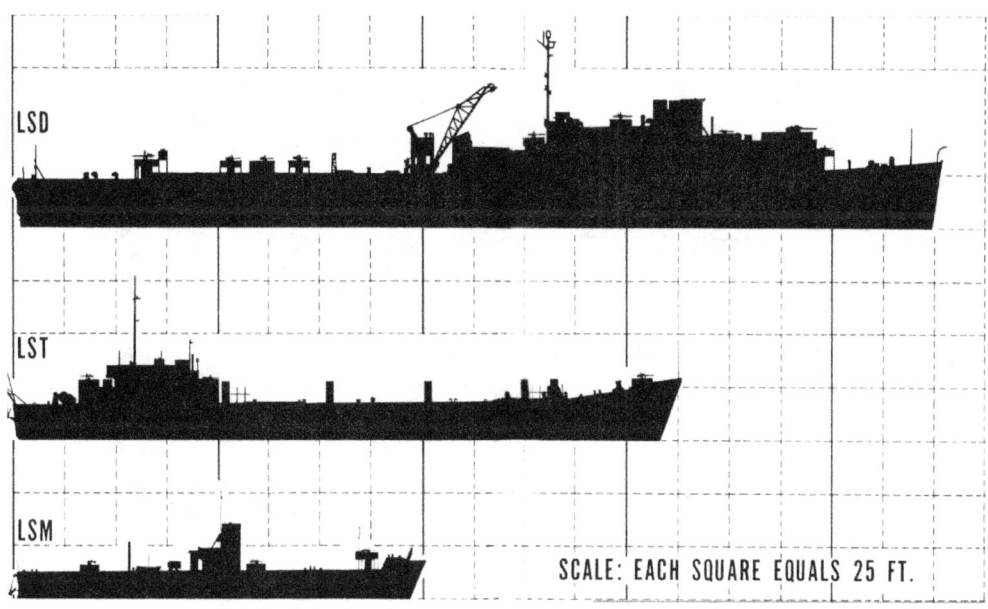

SCALE: EACH SQUARE EQUALS 25 FT.

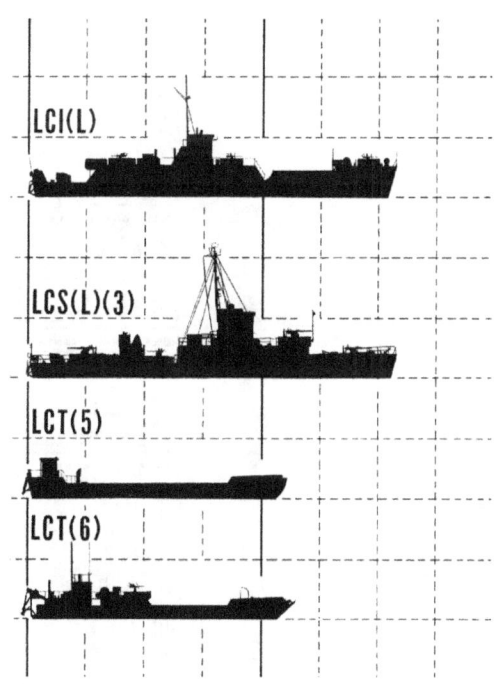

Scale: One square equals 25 feet.

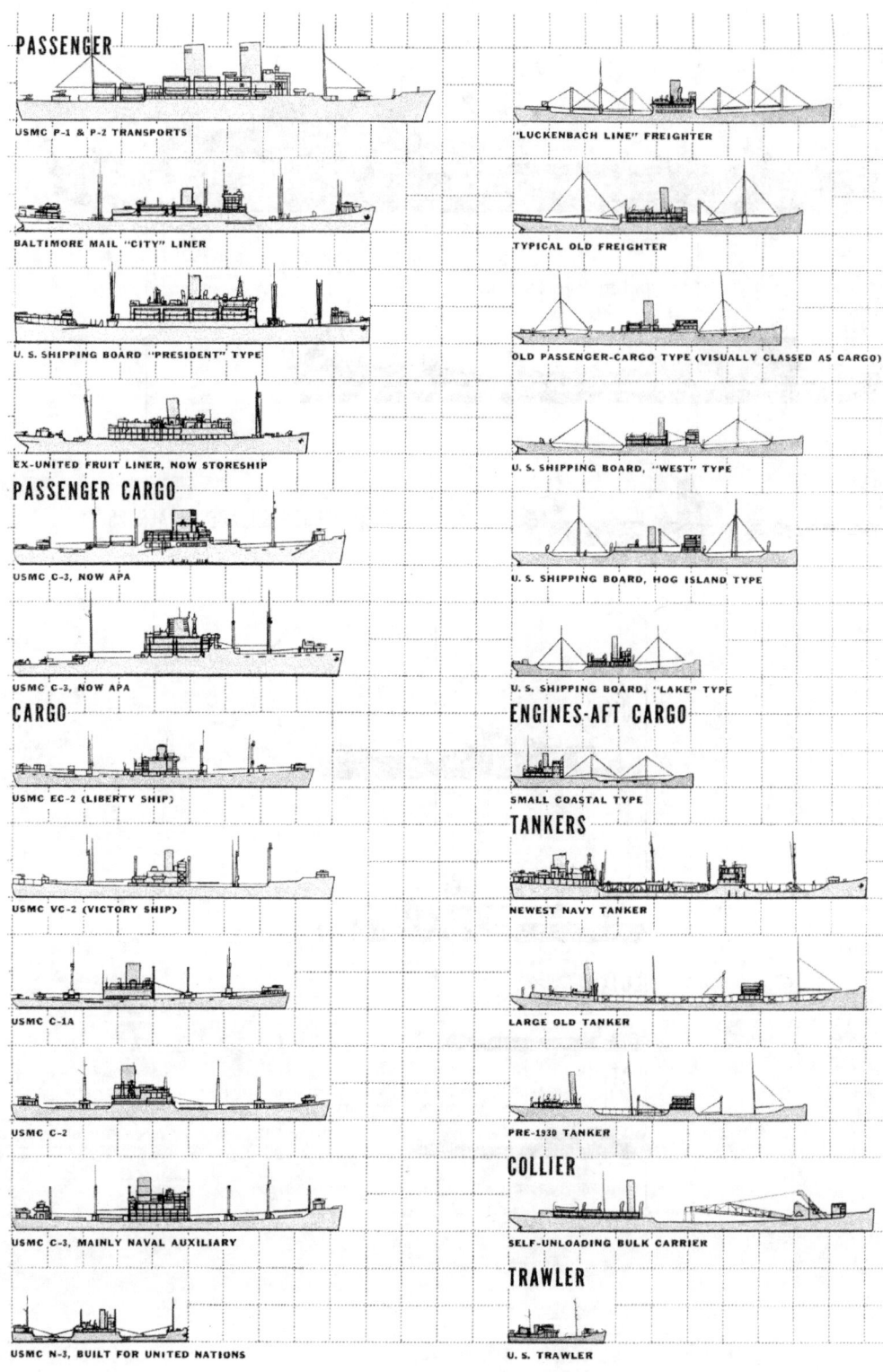

Scale: One square equals 50 feet.

*The charts in this appendix come from several issues of the *U.S. Army–Navy Journal of Recognition*. In each case they were drawn on a different scale, so a direct visual comparison of ships of different types is not possible. The scale of the drawings is indicated at the bottom of each graphic. The sources are:

- U.S. Naval Vessels: Bureau of Aeronautics of the U.S. Navy, *U.S. Army-Navy Journal of Recognition*, No. 1, September 1943, pp. 26–27.
- Minor U. S. Warships: Bureau of Aeronautics of the U.S. Navy, *U.S. Army-Navy Journal of Recognition*, No. 5, January, 1944, pp. 26–27.
- Landing Ships and Craft: U.S. War and Navy Departments, *Recognition Journal*, No. 17, January 1945, pp. 26–27.
- Merchant Vessels: U.S. War and Navy Departments, *Recognition Journal*, No. 10, June 1944, pp. 26–27.

Most of the ship types and classes mentioned in the text are contained in these graphics, as well as some that are not. It should be noted that the first two charts, U.S. Naval Vessels, were developed in September 1943 and do not show ship development at the end of the war. Some ships, like the Sumner-Gearing destroyers, are thus omitted.

Appendix III:
American and Japanese Aircraft

Presented here are silhouettes of American and Japanese aircraft, most of which are mentioned in the text. The number of American aircraft is much smaller as bombers and transports were not used to combat kamikaze aircraft. Japanese aircraft depicted herein are more numerous as virtually any aircraft capable of flying to the intended targets were pressed into service as kamikazes. The planes used as kamikazes ranged from trainers to bombers and fighters.

The ability of American and Allied forces to differentiate their own aircraft from that of the enemy was of paramount importance. Failure to do so could allow an enemy to slip through or for an Allied plane to be brought down by friendly fire. To aid in identifying various aircraft and ships, recognition manuals and journals were published by the Allied forces and disseminated throughout the war zone as an aid.

Identifying Japanese aircraft types had proven problematic in the early stages of the war. In the beginning months of 1942, members of the Directorate of Intelligence, Allied Air Forces, Southwest Pacific Area devised a code name system to assist in identifying Japanese aircraft. These code names used male and female first names as well as the names of trees and birds. Within a short period of time the code names had proven acceptable throughout the U. S. armed forces. By early 1943 the names had been published officially in the War Department's *Recognition Pictorial Manual FM 30-30* and shortly thereafter in the *U. S. Army–Navy Journal of Recognition*. The latter publication put forth its first monthly edition in September of 1943 and continued to the end of the war. Male first names were used for fighter aircraft and reconnaissance seaplanes. Bombers of various sizes and types from single engine to quadruple engine were designated by the use of female first names. Reconnaissance aircraft not equipped with floats also used female first names as did flying boats. Tree names were used for trainers and the names of various birds were used for gliders. Transports were given female first names beginning with the letter "T." The code name designators were quickly put into use and remained the primary method of identification until the end of the war.

Occasional exceptions to the rule were observed as the *Nakajima Ki-42-II* was nicknamed Tojo and the Zeke was more popularly known as the Zero. A few aircraft, such as the Willow and *Shiragiku* trainers, did not have silhouettes published in the recognition manuals and journals as their appearance in the war zones did not occur until near the end of the war.

Since aircraft profiles depicted in this appendix came from several sources, there is no common scale. Accordingly, no direct visual comparison of size is possible.

American Aircraft

U.S. Army

P-40 "WARHAWK"

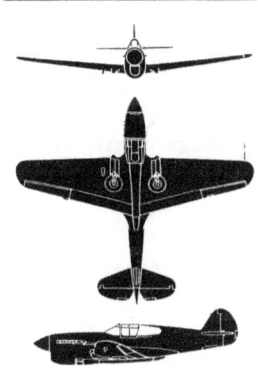

SPAN: 37 ft. 4 in.
LENGTH: 31 ft. 9 in.
APPROX. MAX. SPEED: 360 m.p.h.
SERVICE CEILING: over 30,000 ft.

P-39 "AIRACOBRA"

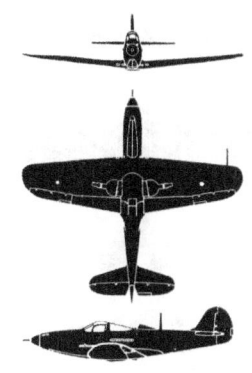

SPAN: 34 ft.
LENGTH: 30 ft. 2 in.
APPROX. MAX. SPEED: over 360 m.p.h.
SERVICE CEILING: over 30,000 ft.

P-38 "LIGHTNING"

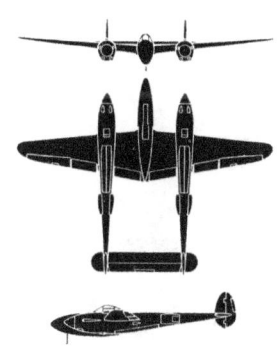

SPAN: 52 ft.
LENGTH: 37 ft. 10 in.
APPROX. MAX. SPEED: over 400 m.p.h.
SERVICE CEILING: over 30,000 ft.

P-61 BLACK WIDOW

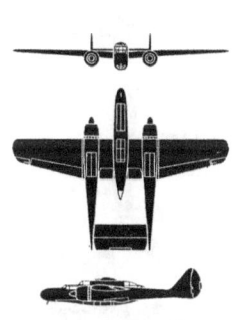

SPAN: 66 ft. 0 in.
LENGTH: 49 ft. 6 in.
APPROX. MAX. SPEED: Over 300 m.p.h.
SERVICE CEILING: About 30,000 ft.

P-51 "MUSTANG"

SPAN: 37 ft.
LENGTH: 32 ft. 3 in.
APPROX. MAX. SPEED: 390 m.p.h.
SERVICE CEILING: over 30,000 ft.

P-51 MUSTANG

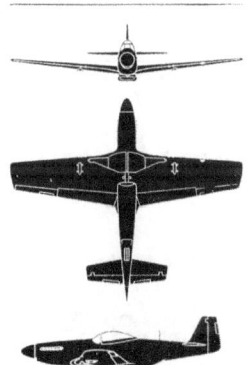

SPAN: 37 ft. 0 in.
LENGTH: 32 ft. 3 in.
APPROX. MAX. SPEED: 449 m.p.h. at 30,000 ft.
SERVICE CEILING: 43,700 ft.

P-47 "THUNDERBOLT"

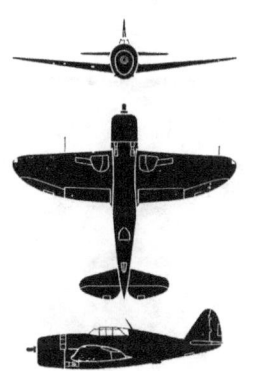

SPAN: 40 ft. 10 in.
LENGTH: 35 ft. 4 in.
APPROX. MAX. SPEED: over 390 m.p.h.
SERVICE CEILING: over 38,000 ft.

P-47 THUNDERBOLT

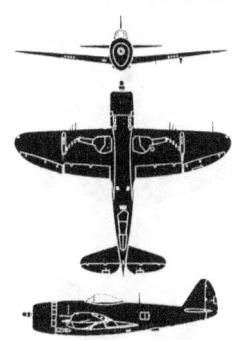

SPAN: 40 ft. 8 in.
LENGTH: 36 ft. 1 in.
APPROX. MAX. SPEED: 430 m.p.h. at 30,000 ft.
SERVICE CEILING: Over 40,000 ft.

P-47N

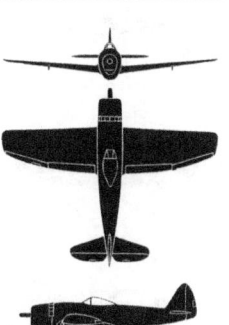

SPAN: 35 ft. 4 in.
LENGTH: 31 ft. 8 in.
APPROX. MAX. SPEED: 350 m.p.h.
SERVICE CEILING: 37,500 ft.

Appendix III

U.S. Navy

F4F "WILDCAT"

SPAN: 38 ft.
LENGTH: 28 ft. 11 in.
APPROX. MAX. SPEED: over 310 m. p. h.
SERVICE CEILING: about 35,000 ft.

F6F "HELLCAT"
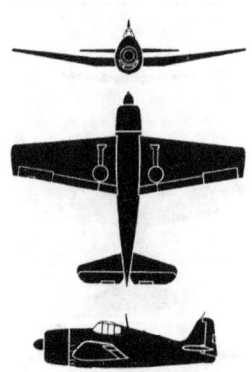
SPAN: 42 ft. 10 in.
LENGTH: 33 ft. 6¼ in.
APPROX. MAX. SPEED:
SERVICE CEILING:

F4U "CORSAIR"
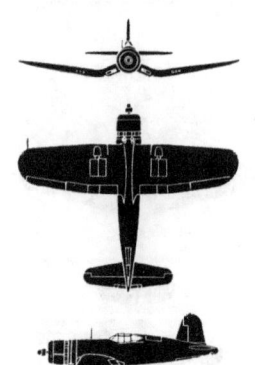
SPAN: 41 ft.
LENGTH: 33 ft. 4 in.
APPROX. MAX. SPEED: 365 m. p. h.
SERVICE CEILING: over 34,000 ft.

F4U-4 "CORSAIR"

SPAN 41 FT.   LENGTH 33 FT. 4 IN.
AIRSCOOP DEEPENS NOSE OF THE CORSAIR

PBM "MARINER"

SPAN: 118 ft.
LENGTH: 80 ft.
APPROX. MAX. SPEED: 205 m. p. h.
SERVICE CEILING: 17,000 ft.

DUCK J2F
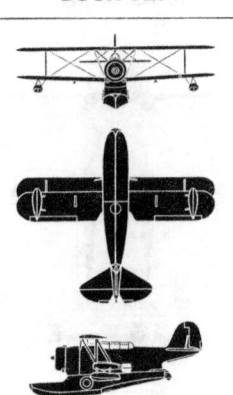
SPAN: 39 ft.
LENGTH: 34 ft.
MAX. SPEED: 176 m. p. h. at 3,200 ft.
SERVICE CEILING: 18,900 ft.

KINGFISHER OS2U (Seaplane)

SPAN: 35 ft. 11 in.
LENGTH: 33 ft. 10 in.
MAX. SPEED: 164 m. p. h. at 5,500 ft.
SERVICE CEILING: 13,000

SEAGULL SO3C (Seaplane)
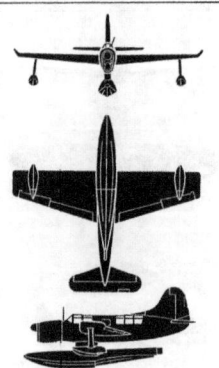
SPAN: 38 ft.
LENGTH: 35 ft.
MAX. SPEED: 183 m. p. h. at 12,000 ft.
SERVICE CEILING: 15,200 ft.

SB2C "HELLDIVER"
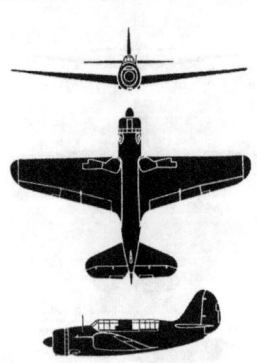
SPAN: 49 ft. 9 in.
LENGTH: 36 ft. 8 in.
APPROX. MAX. SPEED: over 300 m. p. h.
SERVICE CEILING: over 25,000 ft

Japanese Army

"NATE" TYPE 97 F

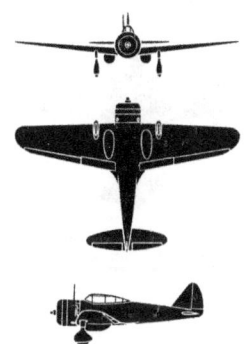

SPAN: 35 ft. 10 in.
LENGTH: 24 ft. 4 in.
APPROX. SPEED: 280 m.p.h. at 13,000 ft.
SERVICE CEILING: 33,000 ft.

OSCAR

SPAN: 37 ft. 7 in.
LENGTH: 28 ft. 7 in.
MAX. SPEED: 317 m.p.h. at 16,000 ft.
SERVICE CEILING: 37,500 ft.

TONY

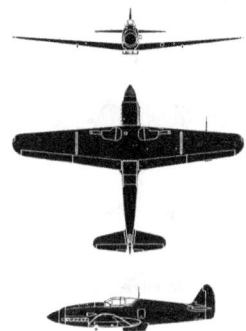

SPAN: 39 ft. 4 in.
LENGTH: 30 ft. 0 in.
MAX. SPEED: 356 m.p.h. at 17,000 ft.
SERVICE CEILING: 35,100 ft.

TOJO

SPAN: 31 ft. 0 in.
LENGTH: 29 ft. 2 in.
MAX. SPEED: 376 m.p.h. at 17,200 ft.
SERVICE CEILING: 36,500 ft.

FRANK 1

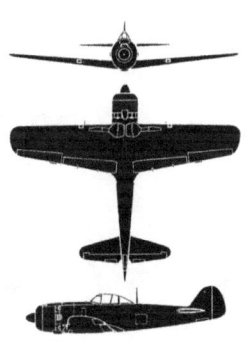

SPAN: 37 ft., 1 in.
LENGTH: 32 ft., 4 in.
APPROX. MAX. SPEED: 422 m.p.h.
SERVICE CEILING: 39,000 ft.

SONIA

SPAN: 39 ft. 10 in.
LENGTH: 30 ft. 2 in.
MAX. SPEED: Estimated 250 m.p.h.

DINAH

SPAN: 50 ft. (est.)
LENGTH: 38 ft. (est.)
MAX. SPEED: 343 m.p.h. at 13,000 ft.
SERVICE CEILING: 34,700 ft.

DINAH III

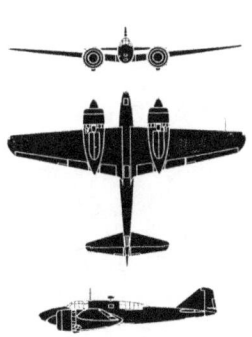

SPAN: 48 ft. 4 in.
LENGTH: 36 ft. 3 in.
MAX. SPEED: 341 m.p.h. at 17,600 ft.
SERVICE CEILING: 36,300 ft.

NICK

SPAN: 49 ft. 6 in.
LENGTH: 34 ft. 6 in.
MAX. SPEED: 357 m.p.h. at 18,500 ft.
SERVICE CEILING: 35,300 ft.

PEGGY 1

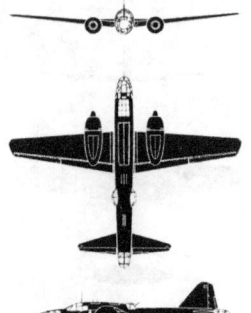

SPAN: 73 ft., 10 in.
LENGTH: 61 ft., 4 in.
APPROX. MAX. SPEED: 350 m.p.h.
SERVICE CEILING: 30,000 ft.

"SALLY" TYPE 97 MB

SPAN: 72 ft.
LENGTH: 47 ft. (approx.)
APPROX. MAX. SPEED: 245 m. p. h. at 8,000 ft.
SERVICE CEILING: about 23,500 ft.

SALLY III

SPAN: 74 ft. 8 in.
LENGTH: 52 ft. 0 in.
MAX. SPEED: 283 m.p.h. at 14,500 ft.
SERVICE CEILING: 29,900 ft.

LILY

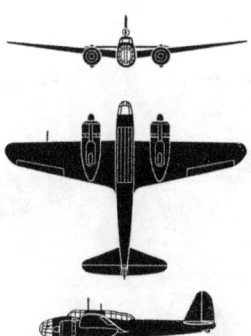

SPAN: 56 ft. 11 in.
LENGTH: 47 ft. 3 in.
ESTIMATED SPEED: 278 m. p. h. at 10,000 ft.
SERVICE CEILING: 28,200 ft. with normal load.

HELEN

SPAN: 68 ft. 0 in.
LENGTH: 54 ft. 0 in.
MAX. SPEED: 299 m.p.h. at 19,700 ft.
SERVICE CEILING: 29,200 ft.

Japanese Navy

"ZEKE" (ZERO) TYPE 0 MK. 1 F

SPAN: 39 ft. 5 in.
LENGTH: 30 ft. 3 in.
APPROX. SPEED: 326 m.p.h. at 16,000 ft.
SERVICE CEILING: 38,500 ft.

HAMP

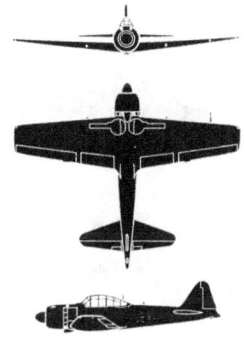

SPAN: 36 ft. 5 in.
LENGTH: 29 ft. 10 in.
MAX. SPEED: 348 m.p.h. at 20,600 ft.
SERVICE CEILING: 35,900 ft.

JACK

SPAN: 35 ft., 4 in.
LENGTH: 31 ft., 8 in.
APPROX. MAX. SPEED: 350 m.p.h.
SERVICE CEILING: 37,500 ft.

GEORGE 11

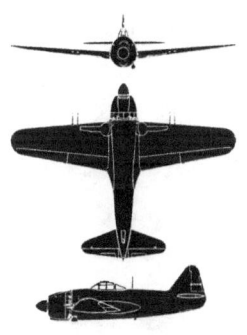

SPAN: 39 ft., 4 in.
LENGTH: 29 ft. 7 in.
APPROX. MAX. SPEED: 407 m.p.h.
SERVICE CEILING: 40,000 ft.

JILL

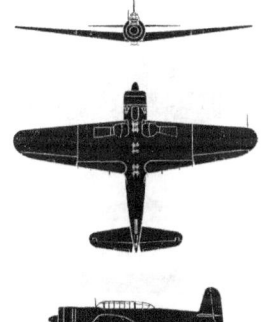

SPAN: 48 ft. 6 in.
LENGTH: 35 ft. 0 in.
MAX. SPEED: 329 m.p.h. at 13,500 ft.
SERVICE CEILING: 35,100 ft.

"KATE" TYPE 97 MK. 3 TB

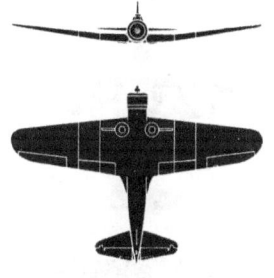

SPAN: 52 ft.
LENGTH: 34 ft.
APPROX. SPEED: 225 m.p.h. at 8,000 ft.
SERVICE CEILING: 27,500 ft.

KATE III

SPAN: 51 ft. 0 in.
LENGTH: 33 ft. 6 in.
MAX. SPEED: 222 m.p.h. at 8,500 ft.
SERVICE CEILING: 18,800 ft.

MYRT 11

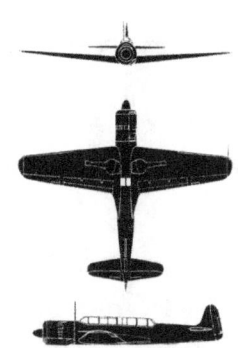

SPAN: 41 ft., 1 in.
LENGTH: 36 ft., 6 in.
APPROX. MAX. SPEED: 370 m.p.h.
SERVICE CEILING: 34,000

JUDY 33

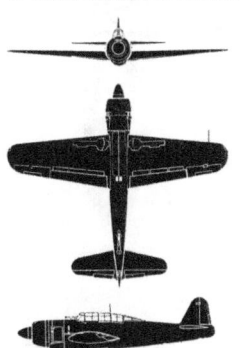

SPAN: 37 ft., 10 in.
LENGTH: 33 ft., 6 in.
APPROX. MAX. SPEED: 376 m.p.h.
SERVICE CEILING: 38,300 ft.

JUDY

SPAN: 37 ft. 10 in.
LENGTH: 33 ft. 7 in.
MAX. SPEED: 332 m.p.h. at 16,000 ft.
SERVICE CEILING: 30,000 ft.

"VAL" TYPE 99 DB

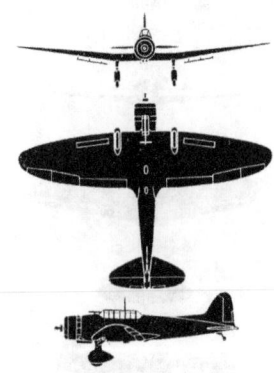

SPAN: 47 ft. 7 in.
LENGTH: 32 ft. 10 in.
APPROX. SPEED: 220 m.p.h. at 7,500 ft.
SERVICE CEILING: 27,000 ft.

VAL II

SPAN: 47 ft. 8 in.
LENGTH: 33 ft. 9 in.
MAX. SPEED: 254 m.p.h. at 13,000 ft.
SERVICE CEILING: 29,800 ft.

GRACE 11

SPAN 47 FT. 3 IN.   LENGTH 37 FT. 7 IN.
NEW JAP TORPEDO BOMBER (TENTATIVE)

FRANCES II

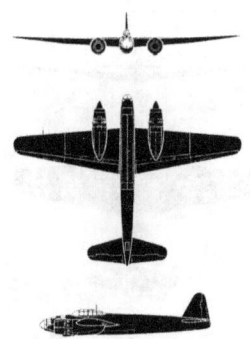

SPAN: 65 ft. 7 in.
LENGTH: 49 ft. 2 in.
APPROX. MAX. SPEED: 350 m.p.h.
SERVICE CEILING:

IRVING II

SPAN: 55 ft. 9 in.
LENGTH: 40 ft.
APPROX. MAX. SPEED: 315 m.p.h.
SERVICE CEILING: 30,500 ft.

"NELL" TYPE 96 MK. 4 MB

SPAN: 82 ft.
LENGTH: 54 ft.
APPROX. SPEED: 225 m.p.h. at 7,000 ft.
SERVICE CEILING: 28,000 ft.

"BETTY" TYPE 1 MB

SPAN: 79 ft. 8 in.
LENGTH: 64 ft. (approx.)
APPROX. SPEED: 288 m.p.h. at 13,500 ft.
SERVICE CEILING: 30,000 ft.

BAKA

SPAN 16 FT. 5 IN.   LENGTH 19 FT. 10 IN.
JAP SUICIDE PLANE IS ROCKET-PROPELLED

Japanese Aircraft

JAKE

SPAN: 47 ft. 6 in.
LENGTH: 35 ft. 4 in.
MAX. SPEED: 216 m. p. h. at 7,500 ft.
SERVICE CEILING: 24,400 ft.

14 EXPERIMENTAL

SPAN: 42 ft. 0 in.
LENGTH: 35 ft. 7 in.
MAX. SPEED: Estimated 275 m.p.h. at 19,000 ft.

"DAVE" TYPE 95 O-F/P

SPAN: 36 ft.
LENGTH: 28 ft. 4 in.
APPROX. SPEED: 155 m. p. h. at 12,000 ft.
SERVICE CEILING: 23,000 ft.

"PETE" TYPE 0 O-F/P

SPAN: 37 ft.
LENGTH: 34 ft. 6 in.
APPROX. SPEED: 198 m. p. h. at 3,200 ft.
SERVICE CEILING: 29,000 ft.

"RUFE" TYPE 0 MK.1 F-F/P

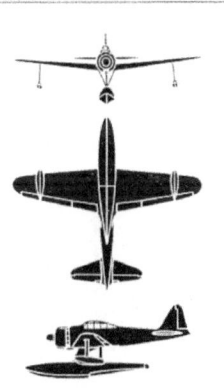

SPAN: 39 ft. 5 in.
LENGTH: 34 ft. 10 in.
APPROX. SPEED: 277 m. p. h. at 15,200 ft.
SERVICE CEILING: about 36,500 ft.

Source: Training Division, Bureau of Aeronautics, *War Department FM 30-30: Recognition Pictorial Manual* (Washington, D.C.: Navy Department, 1943), with Supplement No. 1 of November 1943 and No. 2 of August 1944.

Chapter Notes

Chapter 1

1. Far Eastern Bureau, British Ministry of Information, Japanese Translation Series No. 121, November 13, 1943, *The General Counter-offensive and the Divine Wind,* translated by Edward Band from the editorial in the *Asahi Weekly,* 5 September 1943.
2. Inspectorate General, Army Air Force, *Suicide Force Combat Methods Training Manual,* February 1945, translated as CinCPac-CinCPOA Bulletin No. 129–45, *Suicide Force Combat Methods Special Translation Number 67,* 27 May 1945, p. 2.
3. Far Eastern Bureau, British Ministry of Information, *Japanese Translation Series No. 167,* November 9, 1944, Shigeki Oka, The Air Defense of Japan, trans. Edward Band.
4. John Morris, *Traveller from Tokyo* (London: The Book Club, 1945), p. 47.
5. Shigeo Imamura, *Shig: The True Story of an American Kamikaze* (Baltimore: American Library Press, Inc., 2001), pp. 34–35.
6. Ibid., p. 17.
7. Ibid., p. 29.
8. Teruyuki Okazaki, interview, 21 February 2009.
9. Teruyuki Okazaki, interview, 6 September 2003.
10. G. Cameron Hurst III, *Armed Martial Arts of Japan Swordsmanship and Archery* (New Haven: Yale University Press, 1998), pp. 164–165.
11. Imamura, p. 33.
12. For a more detailed description of how the military managed to control the mind of the average Japanese citizen see: Saburo Ienaga, *The Pacific War* (New York: Pantheon Books, 1978); also Toshio Iritani, *Group Psychology of the Japanese in Wartime* (New York: Kegan Paul International, 1991), pp. 19–76.
13. Cabinet Information Board, Op-16-FE Translation No. 264 WDC 38549, *Kamikaze Special Attack Force,* 9 July 1945, p. 3.

Chapter 2

1. Hatsusho Naito, *Thunder Gods: The Kamikazes Tell their Story* (Tokyo: Kodansha International, 1989), p. 115.
2. Nihon Senbotsu Gakusei Kinen-Kai (Japan Memorial Society for the Students Killed in the War–Wadatsumi Society), *Listen to the Voices from the Sea (Kike Wadatsumi no Koe),* trans. Midori Yamanouchi and Joseph L. Quinn (Scranton: The University of Scranton Press, 2000), p. 225. Hereafter *Listen to the Voices....*
3. *Suicide Weapons and Tactics Know Your Enemy!* CinCPac-CinCPOA Bulletin 126–45, 29 May 1945, p. 21.
4. Shigeo Imamura, *Shig: The True Story of an American Kamikaze* (Baltimore: American Library Press, Inc., 2001), p. 78.
5. Naito, p. 114.
6. Richard J. Smethurst, *A Social Basis for Prewar Japanese Militarism: The Army and the Rural Community* (Berkeley: University of California Press, 1974), p. 153.
7. Andrew Adams, ed., *The Cherry Blossom Squadrons: Born to Die,* by the Hagoromo Society of Kamikaze Divine Thunderbolt Corps Survivors, intro. Andrew Adams, ed. and suppl. by Andrew Adams, trans. Nobuo Asahi and the Japan Technical Company (Los Angles: Ohara Publications), 1973, p. 15.
8. Commander Fifth Amphibious Force, *Translation of a Japanese Letter,* 11 June 1945.
9. Allied Translator and Interpreter Section South West Pacific Area, *Report No. 76: Prominent Factors in Japanese Military Psychology Research,* Part IV, 7 February 1945, pp. 6–7.
10. Ibid., p. 7.
11. Yukihisa Suzuki, "Autobiography of a Kamikaze Pilot," *Blue Book Magazine,* Vol. 94, No. 2 (December 1951), pp. 92–107, Vol. 93, No. 3 (January 1952), pp. 88–100, and Vol. 93, No. 4 (February 1952), p. 107.
12. *Listen to the Voices...,* pp. 229–230.
13. Naito, p. 114.
14. Vice Adm. Matome Ugaki, *Fading Victory: The Diary of Admiral Matome Ugaki 1941–1945,* trans. Masataka Chihaya (Pittsburgh: University of Pittsburgh Press, 1991), p. 485.
15. Ryuji Nagatsuka, *I Was a Kamikaze: The Knights of the Divine Wind,* trans. from the French by Nina Rootes (New York: Macmillan, 1973), p. 102.
16. Haruko Taya Cook and Theodore F. Cook, *Japan at War: An Oral History* (New York: The New Press, 1992), p. 160.
17. Lt. Gen. Masakazu Kawabe, USSBS Interrogation No. 277, 2 November 1945.

18. See Rikihei Inoguchi and Tadashi Nakajima, *The Divine Wind* (New York: Bantam Books, 1978). It is unfortunate that too few sources about the kamikazes have been published in English. Most of those extant have been of three types: (1) translations of work by pilots and officers who seek to justify their participation in the program, (2) publications with a leftist flavor, tending to discredit Japan's participation in the war, and (3) journalistic writings by Western bushidophiles seeking to glorify the exotic aspects of Japanese culture.
19. See *Listen to the Voices from the Sea.*
20. See Emiko Ohnuki-Tierney, *Kamikaze, Cherry Blossoms and Nationalisms: The Militarization of Aesthetics in Japanese History* (Chicago: The University of Chicago Press, 2002).
21. Jean Larteguy, ed., *The Sun Goes Down: Last Letters from Japanese Suicide-Pilots and Soldiers* (London: William Kimber, 1956), pp. 141–143.
22. *Listen to the Voices...*, p. 215.
23. Ibid., p. 128.
24. Adams, p. 75.
25. Larteguy, p. 148.
26. Suzuki, p. 95.
27. Nagatsuka, p. 172.
28. Ibid., p. 197.
29. Shogo Hattori, "Kamikaze Japan's Glorious Failure," *Air Power History*, Spring 1996, Vol. 43, No. 1, p. 17.
30. Suzuki, p. 92.
31. Superior Pvt. Guy Toko, USSBS Interrogation No. 386, 20 November 1945, p. 5.
32. Maj. Gen. Miyoshi, USSBS Interrogation No. 352, 9 November 1945, p. 6.
33. First Class PO Takao Musashi, *ADVATIS Interrogation Report No. 15,* circa 1945, p. 9.
34. Imamura, pp. 99–100.
35. Ibid.
36. Adams, p. 153.
37. Ibid., p. 180.
38. Sonarman 2d Class John Huber, *USS Cogswell DD 651, Personal Diary,* 1944–45, p. 48.
39. Quartermaster 2d Class Robert F. Rielly, *LCS(L) 61,* interview, 19 May 2001.
40. Pharmacists Mate Charles Brader, *LCS(L) 65, LCS Men in a Spectacular Part of Okinawa Campaign,* typescript, undated, p.1.
41. Sonarman 1st Class Jack Gebhardt, *USS Pringle DD 477,* Naval Historical Foundation Oral History Program, *Recollections of Sonarman 1st Class Jack Gebhardt USN,* 7 November 2000.
42. Saburo Ienaga, *The Pacific War 1931–1945: A Critical Perspective on Japan's Role in World War II* (New York: Pantheon Books, 1978), p. 183.
43. *USS Aaron Ward DM 34 Serial 005 Action Report 13 May 1945,* pp. 8–9.

Chapter 3

1. Air Intelligence Group Division of Naval Intelligence, *Observed Suicide Attacks By Japanese Aircraft Against Allied Ships,* OpNav-16-V No. A106, 23 May 1945, p. 87.
2. Lt. Cmdr. Ohira, *USSBS Interrogation No. 457,* 2 November 1945.
3. Andrew Adams, ed., *The Cherry Blossom Squadrons: Born to Die,* by the Hagoromo Society of Kamikaze Divine Thunderbolt Corps Survivors, intro. Andrew Adams, ed. and suppl. Andrew Adams, trans. Nobuo Asahi and the Japan Technical Company (Los Angles: Ohara Publications, 1973), p. 144.
4. Ibid., pp. 162–163.
5. CinCPac-CincPOA Bulletin No. 170–45, *Translations Interrogations Number 35,* 7 July 1945, p. 101.
6. Hatsuho Naito, *Thunder Gods: The Kamikaze Pilots Tell Their Story,* trans. Mayumi Ichikawa (Tokyo: Kodansha International, 1989), p. 114.
7. *VF-30 Action Report No. 17–45,* 21 March 1945.
8. Naito, pp. 141–144.
9. Yukihisa Suzuki, "Autobiography of a Kamikaze Pilot," *Blue Book Magazine,* Vol. 93, No. 3 (Jan. 1952), p. 92.
10. *VMF-323 Action Report No. 10,* 16 April 1945.
11. National Security Agency, *Magic Far East Summary No. 385,* 9 April 1945, p. 52.
12. National Security Agency, *Magic Far East Summary No. 475,* 8 July 1945, pp. 7–8.
13. For a closer comparison of the three aircraft, see Rene J. Francillon, *Japanese Aircraft of the Pacific War* (Annapolis: Naval Institute Press, 1979). The Dinah is discussed on pp. 168–177, the Peggy on pp. 186–191, and the Frances on pp. 462–467.
14. *Technical Air Intelligence Center Summary No. 31 Baka* (Anacostia, D.C.: Technical Air Intelligence Center, June 1945), p. 3.
15. Director Air Intelligence Group, *Statistical Analysis of Japanese Suicide Effort Against Allied Shipping During OKINAWA Campaign,* 23 July 1945, p. 6.
16. National Security Agency, *Magic Far East Summary No. 451,* 14 June 1945, pp. 7–8.
17. Rene J. Francillion, *Japanese Aircraft of the Pacific War* (Annapolis: Naval Institute Press, 1979), pp. 241–243.

Chapter 4

1. Ens. Sadao Nakamura, *ADVATIS Interrogation Report No. 1,* p. 4.
2. Saburo Sakai with Martin Caidin and Fred Saito, *Samurai!* (New York: ibooks, Inc., 2001), p. 308.
3. Capt. Mitsuo Fuchida, Doc. No. 49259 in General Headquarters Far East Command Military Intelligence Section, General Staff, *Statements of Japanese Officials on World War II (English Translations) Volume 1,* 1949–1950, p. 123. Hereafter *MIS Statements Vol 1.*
4. *U.S.S. Smith DD 378,* Serial 00327, *Action Report, U.S.S. Smith, October 26, 1942,* 2 November 1942, p. 3.
5. Bureau of Ships Navy Department, Destroyer Report—*Gunfire Bomb and Kamikaze Damage Including Losses in Action 17 October, 1941 to 15 August 1945.*
6. Lt. Col. Koji Tanaka, Doc. No. 49807 in General Headquarters Far East Command Military Intelligence Section, General Staff, *Statements of Japanese Officials on World War II (English Translations) Volume 4,* 1949–1950, pp. 159–161.
7. Lt. Gen. Torashiro Kawabe, Doc. No. 49258 in General Headquarters Far East Command Military Intelligence Section, General Staff, *Statements of Japanese Officials on World War II (English Translations) Volume 2,* 1949–1950, p. 68.
8. Col. Manjiro Akiyama, Doc. No. 58512, *MIS Statements Vol. I,* p. 16.
9. United States Strategic Bombing Survey Naval Analysis Division, *Japanese Air Power* (Washington, D.C.: U.S. Government Printing Office, 1946), p. 64.
10. General Headquarters, Far East Command Military Intelligence Section, Historical Division, *Interro-*

gations of Japanese Officials on World War II (English Translations), Vol. 1, 1949, p. 237.

11. Lt. Col. Naomichi Jin, *USSBS Interrogation No. 356,* 29 October 1945, p. 2.

12. Ron Surels, *DD 522: Diary of a Destroyer: The action saga of the USS Luce from the Aleutian and Philippines Campaigns to her Sinking off Okinawa* (Plymouth, NH: Valley Graphics, 1996), pp. 104–105.

13. Emiko Ohnuki-Tierney, *Kamikaze, Cherry Blossoms and Nationalisms: The Militarization of Aesthetics in Japanese History* (Chicago: The University of Chicago Press, 2002), pp. 163, 252–253.

14. Albert Axell and Hideaki Kase, *Kamikaze, Japan's Suicide Gods* (London: Pearson Education Limited, 2002), pp. 164–168.

15. Col. Ichiji Sugita, Doc. No. 58512 in General Headquarters Far East Command Military Intelligence Section, General Staff, *Statements of Japanese Officials on World War II (English Translations) Volume 3,* 1949–1950, p. 342.

16. Capt. Toshikazu Omae, Doc. No. 50572 in General Headquarters Far East Command Military Intelligence Section, General Staff, *Statements of Japanese Officials on World War II (English Translations) Volume 4,* 1949–1950, p. 319.

17. Cmdr. Yoshimori Terai, Doc. No. 50572 in General Headquarters Far East Command Military Intelligence Section, General Staff, *Statements of Japanese Officials on World War II (English Translations) Volume 4,* 1949–1950, p. 321.

18. Cmdr. Yoshimori Terai, RAdm. Sadatoshi Tomioka, and Capt. Mitsuo Fuchida, Doc. No. 50572 in General Headquarters Far East Command Military Intelligence Section, General Staff, *Statements of Japanese Officials on World War II (English Translations) Volume 4,* 1949–1950, p. 317.

19. Headquarters Far East Command Military History Section, *Imperial General Headquarters Navy Directives Volume II, Directives No. 316–No 540 (15 Jan 44–26 Aug 45) Special Directives No. 1–No. 3 (2 Sep 45–12 Sep 45),* p. 143.

20. Ibid., pp. 161–162.

21. Saburo Sakai with Martin Caidin and Fred Saito, pp. 29–32.

22. Yukihisa Suzuki, "Autobiography of a Kamikaze Pilot," *Blue Book Magazine,* Vol. 94, No. 3 (January 1952), pp. 98–99.

23. Shigeo Imamura, *Shig: The True Story of an American Kamikaze* (Baltimore: American Library Press), p. 68.

24. CincPac-CincPOA Bulletin No.170–45, *Translations Interrogations No. 35,* 7 July 1945, pp. 95–100.

25. United States Strategic Bombing Survey Naval Analysis Division, *Interrogations of Japanese Officials Vol. II* (Washington, D.C.: U.S. Government Printing Office, 1945), p. 533.

26. *Report From Captured Personnel and Material Branch Military Intelligence Service, U.S. War Department,* Interrogation of Prisoner of War No. 1376, 12 March 1945.

27. *USS LCS(L)(3) 115 Serial 42 Action Report 16 April 1945,* p. 5.

28. Yasuo Kuwahara and Gordon T. Allred, *Kamikaze* (New York: Ballantine Books, 1957), p. 61.

29. Ibid., p. 33 ff.

30. Ryuji Nagatsuka, *I Was a Kamikaze: The Knights of the Divine Wind,* trans. from the French by Nina Rootes (New York: Macmillan, 1973), p. 44 ff.

31. Col. N. Brunetti, "The Japanese Air Force," typed report in National Archives RG 38 Records of the Chief of Naval Operations, Office of Naval Intelligence, Monograph Files Japan 1939–46, pp. 1001–1015.

32. Nagatsuka, p. 164.

33. Col. Junji Hayashi, USSBS Interrogation No. 357, 2 November 1945, p. 5.

Chapter 5

1. *USS Ingraham DD 694 Serial 004 Action Report 8 May 1945,* p. 19.

2. Air Intelligence Group Division of Naval Intelligence, *Observed Suicide Attacks by Japanese Aircraft Against Allied Ships,* OpNav-16-V No. A106, 23 May 1945, p. 6.

3. *USS Pritchett DD561 Serial 037 Action Report 10 July 1945,* p. 10.

4. Inspectorate General, Army Air Force, *Suicide Force Combat Methods Training Manual,* February 1945, translated as CinCPac-CinCPOA Bulletin No. 129–45, *Suicide Force Combat Methods Special Translation Number 67,* 27 May 1945, pp. 17–18. Hereafter SFCMTM.

5. *SFCMTM,* pp.13–14.

6. *U.S.S. Bennion (DD 662) Serial 153 Action Report 9 June 1945,* enclosure T, 28 April 1945.

7. *SFCMTM,* pp. 8–13.

8. Air Intelligence Group Division of Naval Intelligence, *Observed Suicide Attacks by Japanese Aircraft Against Allied Ships,* OpNav-16-V No. A106, 23 May 1945, p. 5.

9. Yasuo Kuwahara and Gordon T. Allred, *Kamikaze* (New York: Ballantine Books, 1957), p. 127.

10. *U.S.S. Gregory (DD 802) Serial 0109 Action Report 10 May 1945,* p. 19.

11. *SFCMTM,* p. 13.

12. *USS LCS(L)(3) No. 85 Serial 22 Action Report 26 July 1945,* p. 2.

13. *USS Ingraham DD 694 Serial 004 Action Report 8 May 1945,* pp. 19–20.

14. *USS Douglas H. Fox DD 779 Serial 004 Action Report 24 May 1945,* pp. 1, 6.

15. *USS Shannon DM25 Serial 021-45 Action Report 15 July 1945,* VIII, p. 1.

16. *U.S.S. Isherwood (DD 520) Serial 0098 Action Report 1 May 1945,* Enclosure (A), p. 19.

17. Capt. Rikihei Inoguchi, IJN in USSBS *Interrogations of Japanese Officials Volume I,* p. 60.

18. *Suicide Weapons and Tactics Know Your Enemy!* CinCPac-CinCPOA Bulletin 126–45, 29 May 1945, pp. 15–17.

19. National Security Agency, *Magic Far East Summary No. 381,* 5 April 1945, pp. 1–3.

20. National Security Agency, *Magic Far East Summary No. 394,* 18 April 1945, p. 7.

21. United States Fleet Headquarters of the Commander in Chief Navy Department, Washington D.C. *Effects of B-29 Operations in Support of the Okinawa Campaign From 18 March to 22 June 1945,* 3 August 1945, p. 1.

22. Lt. Gen. Masakazu Kawabe, USSBS Interrogation No. 277, 2 November 1945, p. 4.

23. National Security Agency, *Magic Far East Summary No. 404,* 28 April 1945, pp. 1–2.

24. National Security Agency, *Magic Far East Summary No. 423,* 17 May 1945, pp. 2–3.

25. National Security Agency, *Magic Far East Summary No. 421,* 15 May 1945, pp. 6–8.

26. Maj. Gen. Kazuo Tanikawa, Doc. No. 59121 in General Headquarters Far East Command Military Intelligence Section, General Staff, *Statements of Japanese Officials on World War II (English Translations) Volume 4,* 1949–1950, p. 216.
27. Ibid., p. 216.
28. National Security Agency, *Magic Far East Summary No. 445,* 6 June 1945, B p.6.
29. National Security Agency, *Magic Far East Summary No. 444,* 7 June 1945, p. 7.
30. National Security Agency, *Magic Far East Summary No. 451,* 14 June 1945, pp. 3–4.
31. National Security Agency, *Magic Far East Summary No. 452,* 15 June 1945, pp. 5–6.

Chapter 6

1. U.S. Naval Technical Mission to Japan, *Japanese Suicide Craft,* January 1946, p. 1.
2. Reports of General MacArthur, *Japanese Operations in the Southwest Pacific Area, Volume II,* compiled from Japanese Demobilization Bureau Records, Facsimile Reprint, 1994, pp. 572–573.
3. Maj. James E. Bush, et al., *Corregidor— February 1945,* typescript (Fort Leavenworth, KS, 1983), pp. 3–6.
4. Commander Task Force Seventy-Eight, Serial 0907, *Action Reports, Mariveles— Corregidor Operation, 12–16 February 1945,* 12 April 1945, Enclosure (G), *Japanese Suicide Boats,* pp. 1–3.
5. Allied Translator and Interpreter Section South West Pacific Area, *Prisoner of War Preliminary Interrogation Report: Chief Petty Officer Yoshio Yamamura,* 4 March 1945, p. 2.
6. Commander Task Force Seventy-Eight, Serial 0907, *Action Reports, Mariveles— Corregidor Operation, 12–16 February 1945,* 12 April 1945, Enclosure (G), *Japanese Suicide Boats,* pp. 1–3.
7. Lt. Col. Masahiro Kawai, *The Operations of the Suicide-Boat Regiments in Okinawa,* National Institute for Defense Studies (undated), p. 1.
8. Kawai, p. 2.
9. Allied Translator and Interpreter Section South West Pacific, *Research Report No. 125,* 27 March 1945, pp. 1–2. Hereafter *ATIS RR No. 125.*
10. Allied Translator and Interpreter Section South West Pacific, *Spot Report No. 195,* 27 February 1945, pp. 6–7. Hereafter *ATIS Spot Rept. No. 195.*
11. Allied Translator and Interpreter Section South West Pacific Area, *Interrogation Report No. 749, Corporal Nobuo Hayashi,* pp. 6–7.
12. *ATIS RR No. 125,* p. 20.
13. Ibid., p. 14.
14. Ibid.
15. *ATIS Spot Rept. No. 195,* pp. 5–6.
16. *ATIS RR No. 125,* pp. 13–14.
17. Kawai, p. 3.
18. Ibid.
19. Ibid., pp 3–9.
20. *Japanese Monograph No. 52 History of the 10th Area Army, 1943–1945,* p. 53. Hereafter *JM No. 52.*
21. Ibid., pp. 50–53.
22. Yutaka Yokota with Joseph D. Harrington, *Suicide Submarine!* (New York: Ballantine Books, 1961), pp. 24–33.
23. U.S. Naval Technical Mission to Japan, *Japanese Suicide Craft,* January 1946, pp. 22–24.
24. Ibid., p. 27.
25. Yokota, pp. 13–19.

26. Ibid., p. 21.
27. This estimate is compiled from information on the website of the All Japan Kaiten Pilot's Association.
28. Shizuo Fukui, *Japanese Naval Vessels at End of War* (Japan: Administrative Division, Second Demobilization Bureau, 1947), pp. 12, 27, 33.
29. The chart is based on information in Mark Stille, *Imperial Japanese Navy Submarines 1941–45* (New York: Osprey Publishing Ltd., 2007) and Shizuo Fukui, *Japanese Naval Vessels at End of War* (Japan: Administrative Division, Second Demobilization Bureau, 1947).
30. Fukui, p. 197.
31. Ibid., p. 198.
32. Ibid., p. 204.
33. Allied Translator and Interpreter Section South West Pacific, *Enemy Publications No. 405 Antitank Combat Reference,* 24 September 1945, p. 1.
34. War Department Military Intelligence Division, *Intelligence Bulletin* Vol. III, No. 7, March 1945, pp. 64–66.
35. War Department Military Intelligence Division, *Intelligence Bulletin* Vol. III, No. 5, July 1945, p. 3.
36. War Department Military Intelligence Division, *Intelligence Bulletin* Vol. III, No. 11, January 1945, p. 15.
37. War Department Military Intelligence Division, *Intelligence Bulletin* Vol. III, No. 4, December 1944, p. 19.
38. Allied Land Forces South East Asia, *Weekly Intelligence Review No. 14,* For
    Week Ending 5 January 1945, p.7.
39. *LCI(L) Flotilla Thirteen War Diary for January 1945,* 2 February 1945, p. 3.

Chapter 7

1. How closely the American military plans in the Pacific followed the original plans is subject for much discussion. For an in-depth study of War Plan Orange and its varieties see the comprehensive work by Edward S. Miller, *War Plan Orange: The U.S. Strategy to Defeat Japan, 1897–1945* (Annapolis: Naval Institute Press, 1991).
2. *U.S.S. Franklin (CV13),* Serial 0036, *Report of Action with Japanese Aircraft on 13 October 1944,* 20 October 1944, p. 2.
3. *U.S.S. Sonoma (ATO-12),* Serial 113, *Action Report,* 3 November 1944, p. 2.
4. Armed Guard Unit *SS Augustus Thomas, Report of Voyage, SS Augustus Thomas From Langemak Bay, New Guinea to Leyte,* p. I, 5 May 1945, pp. 2–4.
5. Samuel E. Morison, *History of United States Naval Operations in World War II, Volume Twelve, Leyte, June 1944–January 1945* (Edison, NJ: Castle Books, 2001), p. 243.
6. *USS Santee CVE 29,* Serial 0018, *Action Report— Leyte, Philippines Operation,* Enclosure A-3, p. 2.
7. *USS Kitkun Bay CVE 71,* Serial 005, *Surface Action Report Submission of— Covers Battle off Samar on 25 October 1944 in Task Unit 77.4.3,* 28 October 1944, p. 2.
8. *USS Kalinin Bay CVE 68* Serial 0102, *Action Report of 25 October 1944 — Engagement With Enemy Units East of Leyte,* p. I., Supplement to, 4 November 1944, Enclosure (A).
9. *U.S.S. Suwannee CVE 27,* Serial 008, *Action Report, Leyte Operation,* 6 November 1944.
10. Navy Department, Office of the Chief of Naval Operations, *Memorandum for File — Summary of Statements by Survivors of the SS Benjamn Ide Wheeler,* 8 March 1945, p. 1.

11. General Staff, Supreme Commander for the Allied Powers, *Reports of General MacArthur, Japanese Operations in the Southwest Pacific Area Vol. II — Parts 1 & II*, Facsimile Reprint, 1994, p. 405.

12. Bureau of Ships Navy Department, *Destroyer Report — Gunfire Bomb and Kamikaze Damage Including Losses in Action 17 October, 1941 to 15 August, 1945*, 25 January 1947, p. 96.

13. Ibid., pp. 96–98.

14. *U.S.S. Anderson (DD411)* Serial 00139, *Action Report — LEYTE Operation, 26 October–8 November 1944*, 9 November 1944, pp. 2–4.

15. This is given as a representative number. In the Armed Guard reports, which all contain rosters of the Armed Guard members, the numbers vary between twenty-six and twenty-eight, plus an officer in charge.

16. Armed Guard Report *SS Matthew P. Deady, Report of Voyage S.S. Matthew P. Deady, K. D. Frye, Master*, 5 January 1945, pp. 3–4.

17. *U.S.S. Lexington CV 16* Serial 0390, *Attacks on Luzon Island on 5 and 6 November 1944 (East Longitude Dates) — Action Report of*, 22 November 1944, p. 3.

18. *S.S. Thomas Nelson, Enemy Action Report, S.S. Thomas Nelson*, 12 February 1945, pp. 1.

19. Leading Petty Officer, U.S. Naval Armed Guard Unit *S.S. Jeremiah M. Daily, Disaster, report of*, undated, circa November 1944, p. 1.

20. Navy Department, Office of the Chief of Naval Operations, *Memorandum for File, Summary of Statements by Survivors of the SS Jeremiah M. Daily*, 20 January 1945, pp. 1–2.

21. 500th Bombardment Squadron (M) AAF, *Commendation of Armed Guard*, 20 November 1944, p. 1.

22. Armed Guard Unit *SS Alexander Majors, Report of Voyage Hollandia, Dutch New Guinea to Leyte, Philippine Islands*, 6 December 1944, pp. 1–3.

23. James A. Mooney, Ed., *Dictionary of American Naval Fighting Ships*, Vol. I, Part A (Washington, D.C.: Naval Historical Center, 1991), p. 220.

24. Navy Department, Office of the Chief of Naval Operations, *Memorandum for File, Summary of Statements by Survivors of the SS Gilbert Stuart*, 30 March 1945, pp. 1–2.

25. Lt. Cdr. Andrew W. Gavin, USNR (inactive), Master *SS Alcoa Pioneer* to CO Armed Guard Center, 12th Naval District, Treasure Is., San Francisco, Calif., letter of 19 November 1944, pp. 1–2.

26. Robert M. Browning Jr., *U.S. Merchant Vessel War Casualties of World War II* (Annapolis: Naval Institute Press, 1996), pp. 455–457.

27. *USS James O'Hara APA 90* Serial 062, *Action Report Period 3 November to 24 November 1944*, 29 November 1944, pp. 1–2.

28. *U.S.S. Intrepid (CV11)*, Serial 0249, *War Diary, U.S.S. Intrepid (CV11) — Month of November 1944*, 7 December 1944, p. 38.

29. *U.S.S. Cabot CVL 28*, Serial 0058, *War Damage Report*, 9 December 1944, pp. 1–4.

30. *USS Hancock CV 19*, Serial 0136, *Action Report 25 November 1944*, 29 November 1944, p. 2.

31. *U.S.S. Essex (CV-9)*, Serial 0244, *Action Report — Action off Luzon 25 November 1944*, 9 December 1944.

32. Theodore R. Treadwell, *Splinter Fleet: The Wooden Subchasers of World War II* (Annapolis: Naval Institute Press, 2000), pp. 191–192.

33. Ibid., pp. 196–197.

34. *USS Colorado BB 45*, Serial 1093, *Anti-Aircraft Action Report*, 5 December 1944, Enclosure (F), p. 2.

35. *U.S.S. St. Louis CL 49*, Serial 0030, *Action Report, Anti-Aircraft — 27 November 1945*, 9 December 1945, pp. 2–3.

36. *USS Aulick DD 569*, Serial 00170, *Report of Action on 29 November 1944, Forwarding of*, 8 December 1944, Enclosure (B), p. 1.

Chapter 8

1. Robert M. Browning, Jr., *U.S. Merchant Vessel War Casualties of World War II* (Annapolis: Naval Institute Press, 1996), p. 463.

2. Armed Guard Report *S.S. John Evans, Report of Voyage, S.S. John Evans*, 14 December 1944, pp. 2–3.

3. Special Staff U.S. Army Historical Division, *Japanese Monograph No. 12 — 4th Air Army Operations, 1944–1945*, p. 50.

4. *USS Drayton DD 366*, Serial l084, *Action Report*, 9 December 1944, p. 2.

5. *USS LSM 23*, Serial 085, *Antiaircraft Action Report*, 9 December 1944, pp. 4–5.

6. *USS Mahan DD 364*, Serial 007, *Report of Action — Amphibious Landing, Ormoc Bay, 7 December 1944*, 11 December 1944, p. 3.

7. *USS Ward APD 16*, Serial 8249, *Report of Action — Ormoc Bay Amphibious Operation, 7 December 1944*, 16 January 1945, p. 2.

8. *U.S.S. Lamson (DD367)*, Serial 02, *Action Report — Ormoc Bay Operation — 6-7 December 1944*, 13 December 1944, p. 4.

9. Ibid., Enclosure (D) p. 1.

10. Robert J. Bulkley, Jr., *At Close Quarters: PT Boats in the United States Navy* (Annapolis: Naval Institute Press, 2003), pp. 394–395.

11. *USS LST 737*, Serial 142, *Action Report, Amphibious Assault on Western Coast of Leyte Island, Philippine Islands*, 9 December 1944, pp. 1–3.

12. *USS LSM 318*, Serial 007, *Report of Action — Ormoc Bay, p. I, Amphibious Operation, 7 December 1944*, 16 January 1944, p. 3.

13. Navy Department, Office of the Chief of Naval Operations, *Memorandum for File, Summary of Statements by Survivors of the SS William S. Ladd*, 20 February 1945, pp. 1–2.

14. Armed Guard Unit S. S. *Marcus Daly, Heroism and Bravery of gun crew, Recommendation for*, 26 December 1944, pp. 3–4.

15. *USS Reid DD 369*, No Serial, *U.S.S. Reid (DD369) Amplifying Report of Action on 11 December 1944*, 3 February 1945, pp. 1–3.

16. Capt. Walter Karig, Lt. Cmdr. Russell L. Harris and Lt. Cmdr. Frank A. Manson, *Battle Report Victory in the Pacific* (New York: Rinehart and Company, Inc., 1949), pp. 105–107.

17. *USS Nashville CL 43*, Serial 06, *Report of Anti-Aircraft Action 13 December 1944 — Forwarding of*, 8 January 1945, p. 5.

18. Karig, p. 110.

19. *USS Haraden DD 585*, No Serial, *Action Report — Forwarding of, Covers Action on 13 December 1944 in Sulu Sea, In Task Unit 77.12.7*, 25 December 1945, p. 4.

20. *USS Caldwell DD 605*, Serial 003, *Report of Action with the Enemy, Ormoc Bay, Philippine Islands, December 11–12, 1944*. 15 December 1944, p. 3.

21. *U.S.S. L.S.T. 738*, No Serial, *Preliminary Action Report: Submission of, Covers Air Attack While Maneuvering off San Jose Sector, Southwestern Mindoro, on 15 December 1944*, 29 December 1944, p. 1.

22. Ibid., p. 2.

23. *U.S.S. L.S.T. 472*, No Serial, *Report of Action of the USS LST 472 from 17 November 1944 to 15 December 1944, Culminating in Its Loss on 15 December 1944*, 29 December 1944, p. 2.
24. *USS Howorth DD 592*, Serial 0106, *Special Action Report Anti-Aircraft Action by Surface Ships, Submission of*, 15 December 1944, p. 2.
25. *USS Ralph Talbot DD 390*, Serial 081, *Actions by Surface Ships— Report of*, 23 December 1944, pp. 1–3.
26. *USS PT 75*, No Serial, *Action Report— PT 75— 17 December 1944*, 15 January 1945, p. 1.
27. *USS PT-300*, Serial 0105, *Loss of USS PT-300, 18 December 1944, Report of*, 20 December 1944, pp. 1–2.
28. Samuel Eliot Morison, *The Liberation of the Philippines Luzon, Mindanao, the Visayas 1944–1945* (Edison, NJ: Castle Books), p. 34.
29. Browning, p. 467.
30. *U.S.S. Bryant (DD665)*, Serial 059, *Anti-Aircraft Action Report— Submission of*, 22 December 1944, pp. 1–2.
31. Browning, p. 470. I have tried in vain to discover the hull number of this ship. The reports of CTG 77.11 below, as well as other reports, do not identify the ship by hull number.
32. Commander Task Group 77.11 (Commander LCI(L) Flotilla 24), Serial 004, *Action Report 27 December to 31 December 1944 Leyte-Mindoro p.I*, 4 January 1945, p. 3.
33. *U.S.S. Gansevoort DD 608*, Serial 008, *Action Report, Uncle Plus 15, Mindoro Resupply Echelon, 27 Through 31 December 1944*, 1 January 1945, p. 11.
34. *USS Porcupine IX 126*, No Serial, *Action Report Covers AA Action en Route & In Landing Area Mindoro Culminating in Sinking of Ship 30 December 1944*, 17 January 1945, p. 2.
35. *Porcupine*, p. 2.

Chapter 9

1. *U.S.S. Louisville (CA28)*, Serial 005A, *Action Report, U.S.S. Louisville (CA28) in Seizure and Occupation of Luzon Area, 2 January to 12 January 1945*, 12 January 1945, p. 2.
2. *U.S.S. Louisville (CA28)*, Serial 005A, *Action Report, U.S.S. Louisville (CA28) in Seizure and Occupation of Luzon Area, 2 January to 12 January 1945*, 12 January 1945, First Endorsement, p. 2.
3. *U.S.S. Manila Bay (CVE-61)*, Serial 001, *U.S.S. Manila Bay Action Report: Operations in Support of the Landings at Lingayen, p. I (1–19 January 1945)*, Part I Narrative, pp. 2–3.
4. *USS California BB-44*, Serial 0030, *War Damage, Report of— Report of Damage Sustained by Ship During Enemy Aircraft Attack at 1720(I) 6 January while en route to Lingayen Gulf Landings, Suicide Plane Crash the Cause*, 25 January 1945, pp. 1–2.
5. Ibid., p. 2.
6. *USS Walke DD 723*, Serial 06, *Action Report for 2–10 January 1945*, 18 January 1945, Part V, p. 3.
7. *U.S.S. Columbia CL 56*, Serial 06 of 23, *Action Report— Lingayen Gulf, Luzon, p. I,— Period 1–9 January 1945*, 22 January 1945, Enclosure A, p. 2.
8. *U.S.S. New Mexico BB 40*, Deck Log, 6 January 1945, pp. 20–22.
9. *U.S.S. Minneapolis CA 36*, Serial 005, *U.S.S. Minneapolis (CA36) Report of Participation in Bombardment of Lingayen Gulf, p.I. 6–10 January 1945, inclusive*, 17 January 1945, pp. 1–6.

10. *U.S.S. Louisville CA 28*, Serial 0003, *Action Report, U.S.S. Louisville (CA28) in Seizure and Occupation of Luzon Area, 2 January to 12 January 1945*, 6 March 1945.
11. *U.S.S. Richard P. Leary (DD-664)*, Serial 0125, *Action Report for period 6 January 1945 to 18 January 1945*, 20 January 1945, pp. 1–2.
12. *USS Palmer DMS 5*, Serial 0003, *AA Action Report— Forwarding of*, 14 January 1945, p. 2.
13. *USS Palmer DMS 5*, Serial 0004, *Action Report of U.S.S. Palmer (DMS-5)— Forwarding of*, 12 January 1945, pp. 1–8.
14. Robert F. Heath, *With the Black Cat USS LCI Flotilla 13* (Chico, CA: The Technical Education Press, 2003), p. 75.
15. *U.S.S. LST 912*, Serial 013, *Action Report— Anti-Aircraft Action 8–9 January 1945, Lingayen Gulf Operation, San Fabian Attack Force— Blue Beach Unit*, 12 January 1945, p. 2.
16. *U.S. S. Columbia CL 56*, Serial 06 of 23, *Action Report— Lingayen Gulf, Luzon, p. I — Period 1–9 January 1945*, 22 January 1945, Enclosure A, p. 3.
17. *USS Mississippi BB 41*, Serial 015, *Action Report— Bombardment Operations in Lingayen Gulf, Luzon, Philippine Islands During Period 6–9 January 1945 and Including Collateral Supporting Actions and Operations During Period 3–18 January 1945*, 30 January 1945, p. 10.
18. James L. Mooney, Ed., *Dictionary of American Naval Fighting Ships Volume VIII* (Washington, D.C.: Naval Historical Center, 1981), p. 98.
19. *U.S.S. LST 1028*, Serial 9, *War Diary: Narrative account of USS LST 1028 from time of damage by enemy Torpedo Boat 10 January 1945, until towed off Beach 28 January 1945*, 29 January 1945, p. 2.
20. *USS LCI (G) 365*, No Serial, *Action Report, Submission of, Covers Fire Support Activity for Lingayen Landings on 9 and 10 January 1945*, 12 January 1945, pp. 2–4.
21. *U.S.S. Eaton (DD510)*, Serial 08, *Action report for period 4–14 January 1945*, 23 January 1945, p. 5.
22. *Eaton*, pp. 5–6.
23. *USS Robinson DD 562*, Serial 03, *Action Report— Amphibious Assault on Luzon, Philippine Islands at Lingayen Gulf, Period 31 December 1944 to 15 January 1945*, 20 January 1945, p. 12.
24. Allied Translator and Interpreter Section South West Pacific Area, Serial No. 938, *Interrogation Report No. 775*, 1 September 1945, p. 3.
25. Robert M. Browning, Jr., *U.S. Merchant Vessel War Casualties of World War II* (Annapolis: Naval Institute Press, 1996), pp. 478–479.
26. *U.S.S. Richard W. Suesens (DE 342)*, Serial No. 003, *Action Report, Lingayen Operation*, 18 January 1945, pp. 2–3.
27. *U.S.S. Belknap (APD34)*, Serial No.002-45, *Action Report— Lingayen Guf Operation, Luzon Island, Philippine Islands*, 15 March 1945, p. 6.
28. Lt. (j.g.) Roy Abshier (D), USNR, Commanding Officer, Naval Armed Guard, *Report of Voyage, SS Kyle V. Johnson from Houston, Texas to San Francisco, California*, 16 March 1945, pp. 2–5.
29. Browning, pp. 479–481.
30. *USS LST 700*, Serial 209, *Action Report, Covers Anti-Aircraft Actions While Retiring from Landings at Lingayen Gulf on 12–13 January 1945*, 19 January 1945, p. 2.
31. *U.S.S. Salamaua (CVE-96)*, Serial No. 002, *Action Report for Period of 27 December 1944 to 18 January 1945*, 5 February 1945, pp. 3–4.
32. Captain Rikihei Inoguchi, Commander Tadashi

Nakajima, and Roger Pineau, *The Divine Wind: Japan's Kamikaze Force in World War II* (New York: Bantam Books, 1978), pp. 103–108.
33. Earl Griffiths, Jr., CS/2 *PC 1129*, interview October 21, 2009.
34. *U.S.S. Lough (DE 586)*, Serial No. 75-45, *War Diary of the U. S. S. Lough DE-586) for the month of February 1945*, 3 March 1945, p. 1.
35. Samuel E. Morison, *History of United States Naval Operations in World War II: The Liberation of the Philippines Luzon, Mindanao, the Visayas 1944–1945* (Edison, NJ: Castle Books, 2001), pp. 191–192.
36. Robert J. Bulkley Jr., *At Close Quarters: PT Boats in the United States Navy* (Annapolis: Naval Institute Press, 2003), pp. 420–422.
37. *USS LCI(G) 558*, No Serial, *Action Report—Nasugbu—Luzon—P.I. Landing Operation of*, 5 February 1945, p. 3.
38. Commander Task Force Seventy-Eight, *Action Report, Mariveles—Corregidor Operation, 12–16 February, 1945*, 12 April 1945, Enclosure (G), p. 2.
39. Claude Haddock, S 1/c, *LCS(L) 49*, interview 24 July 2008.
40. Dean Bell, S 2/c, *LCS(L) 26*, interview 11 August 2007.
41. Harry G. Meister, Lt. Cmdr. USNR (Ret.), *USS LCS(L)3-27: A WWII Amphibious Landing Craft Support Vessel* (Vancouver, WA: Harry & Gene Meister, 2002), p. 16.
42. Commander Task Unit 78.2.58 (Commander LCS(L) Flotilla One), Serial 057, *Davao Gulf Operations—11 to 19 May 1945*, 20 May 1945, pp. 1.

Chapter 10

1. Capt. Rikihei Inoguchi, Cmdr. Tadashi Nakamima and Roger Pineau, *The Divine Wind: Japan's Kamikaze Force in World War II* (New York: Bantam Books, 1978), pp. 116–117.
2. Samuel Elion Morison, *History of United States Naval Operations in World War II: The Liberation of the Philippines Luzon, Mindanao, the Visayas 1944–1945* (Edison, NJ: Castle Books 1959), p. 179.
3. Inoguchi, pp. 117–121.
4. *U.S.S. Ticonderoga (CV-14)*, Serial 020, *Action Report of Operations in Support of Amphibious Operations in Lingayen Gulf Area of Luzon, p. I, for period 3 through 21 January 1945*, 27 January 1945, p. 2.
5. *USS Maddox DD731*, Serial 0010, *Action Report 21 January 1945—Forwarding of—Covers Damage as a Result of Suicide Plane Crash Aboard While on Picket Duty in Task Group 38.1, 26 January 1945*, Enclosure A, pp. 3–4.
6. Inoguchi, pp. 122–124.
7. *U.S.S. Lunga Point (CVE 94)*, Serial 020, *Action Report—Occupation of IWO JIMA, 10 February 1945 to 11 March 1945*, 11 March 1945, pp. 3–4.
8. *USS Bismarck Sea (CVE 95)*, Serial 001, *Action Report USS Bismarck Sea off Iwo Jima 21 February 1945, including Circumstances of the Resultant Sinking of the Ship*, 25 February 1945, p. 2.
9. *U.S.S. Saratoga (CV3)*, Serial 007, *U.S.S. Saratoga (CV3) Action Report for period 0900 (K) to 2130 (K), 21 February 1945*, 26 February 1945, p. 3.
10. *U.S.S. LST 477*, Serial 38, *Battle Damage—First Report of*, 4 March 1945, p. 3.
11. *USS LST 809*, Serial 03, *Anti-Aircraft Action Report*, 6 March 1945, p. 4.

12. For a more detailed discussion of these missions see Michael Mair, *Oil, Fire, and Fate: The Sinking of the USS Mississinewa (AO-59) in WWII by Japan's Secret Weapon* (Platteville, WI: SMJ Publishing, 2008), pp. 268–341.
13. There is no substantive way to determine which of the four *kaiten* actually hit the *Mississinewa*, however, Japanese sources attribute it to Nishina.
14. The aircraft code named "Frances" by the allies was the Yokosuka P1Y1 Navy bomber *Ginga*. It had a top speed of 340 mph at 19,355 feet and a normal range of 1,036 nautical miles. It could carry a 2,205-lb. bomb load and mounted a flexible 20mm cannon in the nose and one rear-firing 20mm cannon.
15. Adm. Matome Ugaki, *Fading Victory: The Diary of Admiral Matome Ugaki 1941–1945*, trans. by Masataka Chihaya (Pittsburgh: University of Pittsburgh Press, 1991), pp. 547–551.
16. *USS Randolph CV 15*, Serial 004, *Action Report for 11–12 March 1945, Attack by Enemy Plane at Ulithi*, 20 March 1945, p. 3.

Chapter 11

1. Col. Ichiji Sugita. Doc. No. 58512 in General Headquarters Far East Command Military Intelligence Section, General Staff, *Statements of Japanese Officials on World War II (English Translations) Volume 3*, 1949–1950, p. 342.
2. Capt. Toshikazu Omae, Doc. No. 50572 in General Headquarters Far East Command Military Intelligence Section, General Staff, *Statements of Japanese Officials on World War II (English Translations) Volume 4*, 1949–1950, p. 319.
3. Cmdr. Yoshimori Terai, Doc. No. 50572 in General Headquarters Far East Command Military Intelligence Section, General Staff, *Statements of Japanese Officials on World War II (English Translations) Volume 4*, 1949–1950, p. 321.
4. Cmdr. Yoshimori Terai, RAdm. Sadatoshi Tomioka, and Capt. Mitsuo Fuchida. Doc. No. 50572 in General Headquarters Far East Command Military Intelligence Section, General Staff, *Statements of Japanese Officials on World War II (English Translations) Volume 4*, 1949–1950, p. 317.
5. Headquarters Far East Command Military History Section, *Imperial General Headquarters Navy Directives Volume II, Directives No. 316–No. 540 (15 Jan 44–26 Aug 45) Special Directives No. 1–No. 3 (2 Sep 45–12 Sep 45)*, p. 143. Hereafter *Navy Directives Vol. II*.
6. Ibid., pp. 161–162.
7. RAdm. Sadatoshi Tomioka, Doc. No. 50572 in General Headquarters Far East Command Military Intelligence Section, General Staff, *Statements of Japanese Officials on World War II (English Translations) Volume 4*, 1949–1950, p. 326.
8. *Navy Directives Vol. II*, p. 164.
9. Second Demobilization Bureau, *Monograph No. 141 (Navy) "Okinawa Area Naval Operations" Supplement Statistics on Naval Air Strength* (General Headquarters Far East Command Military Intelligence Section, General Staff, 1949) and United States Strategic Bombing Survey (Pacific), *The Campaigns of the Pacific War* (Washington, D.C.: United States Government Printing Office, 1947), p. 328.
10. *Headquarters XXI Bomber Command Tactical Mission Report, Missions No. 46 and 50, 27 and 31 March 1945*, 30 April 1945, p. 2.

11. Robin L. Rielly, *Kamikazes, Corsairs, and Picket Ships: Okinawa 1945* (Philadelphia: Casemate Publishers, 2008), Appendix IV, pp. 369–371.

12. National Security Agency, *Magic Far East Summary Number 400*, 24 April 1945, pp. 1–2.

13. Maj. Gen. Ryosuke Nakanishi, USSBS Interrogation No. 312, 4 November 1945.

14. Military History Section — General Headquarters Far East Command Military Intelligence Section General Staff, *Japanese Monograph No. 51 Air Operations on Iwo Jima and the Ryukyus*, p. 24.

15. Ibid., p. 27.

16. *CINCPAC PEARL Dispatch AI 58199*, 3 May 1945.

17. Based on *Japanese Monograph No. 135 Okinawa Operations Record (8th Air Division)*, p. 249; CinCPac-CinCPOA Bulletin No. 102–45, *Translations Interrogations Number 26 Airfields in Formosa and Hainan*, 25 April 1945, p. 6; *CinCPac Pearl Dispatch AI88009*, 18 June 1945.

18. Director Air Intelligence Group, *Statistical Analysis of Japanese Suicide Effort Against Allied Shipping During OKINAWA Campaign*, 23 July 1945, p. 4.

19. *USS Pritchett (DD 561)*, Serial 045, 6 August 1945.

20. Director Air Intelligence Group, *Statistical Analysis of Japanese Suicide Effort Against Allied Shipping During OKINAWA Campaign*, 23 July 1945, p. 4.

21. Capt. Minoru Genda, USSBS Interrogation No. 329, 12 November 1945.

22. *U.S.S. Wasp CV 18*, Serial 0104, *Action Report*, 5 April 1945, Enclosure (A), pp. 4–5.

23. *USS Halsey Powell DD 686*, Serial 007, *USS Halsey Powell (DD686) Action Report for the Period 14 March to 25 March 1945 Inclusive (Annex A)*, 4 April 1945, pp. 4–5.

24. *USS O'Brien DD 725*, Serial 048, *Action Report, U.S.S. O'Brien (DD725) 21 March–4 April 1945, Operating in Task Group 51.1 During Landing and Support of U.S. Army and Marine Corps Troops on the Island of Kerama Retto in the Nansei Shoto Group of the Ryukyu Islands*, 12 April 1945, p. 9.

25. *USS Nevada BB 36*, Serial 028, *Anti-Aircraft Action Report*, 5 April 1954, p. 1.

26. *USS Dorsey DMS 1*, Serial 082, *Action Report*, 12 April 1945, pp. 2–3.

27. *USS LCI(G) 558*, No Serial, *Report of Capture of Okinawa Gunto, Phases 1 and 2*, 21 July 1945, pp. 2–3.

Chapter 12

1. *U.S.S. Alpine (APA-92)*, Serial No. 081, *Okinawa Shima, Nansei Shoto Operation — 1–6 April 1945 — Report of*, 10 April 1945, enclosure (A), p. 16.

2. James L. Mooney, ed., *Dictionary of American Naval Fighting Ships Volume I, Part A* (Washington, D.C.: Naval Historical Center, 1991), p. 53. Hereafter *DANFS*.

3. Earl Blanton, *Boston-To Jacksonville (41,000 Miles by Sea)* (Seaford, VA: Goose Creek Publications, 1991), p. 58.

4. *U.S.S. Hinsdale APA 120*, Serial 073-45, *Action Report — Period 16 March–23 April 1945*, 23 April 1945, pp. 1–3.

5. *U.S.S. West Virginia (BB 48)*, Serial (00254), *Action Report — Bombardment and Fire Support of Landings on Okinawa Island and Adjacent Islands, 21 March 1945 to 24 April 1945, inclusive*, 28 April 1945, pp. 12–13.

6. Robin L. Rielly, *Kamikazes, Corsairs, and Picket Ships: Okinawa 1945* (Philadelphia: Casemate Publishers, 2008), p. 58.

7. *USS Dickerson APD-21*, No Serial, *Loss of USS Dickerson, 2–4 April 1945*, 10 April 1945, Enclosure (A), pp. 1–2.

8. *USS Henrico APA 45*, Serial 004, *Action Report Covers Suicide Plane Attack on 2 April 1945 While Underway in Night Retirement Course West of Kerama Retto, Okinawa Gunto, Report Covers 26 March–1 April 1945*, 23 April 1945, p. 1.

9. *U.S.S. Telfair (APA-210)*, Serial 004, *Action Report for 2 April 1945, submission of*, 14 April 1945, pp. 1–2.

10. *USS LCI(G) 568*, Serial 5-45, *Anti-Aircraft Action Report by USS LCI(G) 568*, 7 April 1945, pp. 1–2.

11. *USS LCI(G) 82 Action Report*, No Serial, 14 April 1945, p. 3.

12. *U.S.S. Wake Island CVE 65*, Serial 064, *Action Report — Ryukyus Operation — 21 March 1945 to 6 April 1945 — Inclusive Dates*, 9 April 1945, Part III, pp. 2–3.

13. *War Diary VMF-322, 1 April to 30 April 1945*, Appendage: Report of Maj. Edward F. Camron, Commanding Officer (Ground) Assault Echelon, VMF-322.

14. *U.S.S. Newcomb DD 586*, Serial 0018, *Action Report for 6 April 1945 Covers Heavy Damage Received as Result of Four Suicide Plane Crashes Aboard on 6 April 1945*, 14 April 1945, p. 5.

15. *USS Leutze DD 481*, Serial 0080, *War Damage Report, 6 April 1945*, 5 May 1945, pp. 1–2.

16. *Defense (AM-317) Deck Log*, 6–7 April 1945, pp. 17–18.

17. *U.S.S. Witter (DE636)*, Serial 038, *Action Report (Advance Copy) — Okinawa Shima, 6 April 1945*, 6 April 1945, Enclosure (B), pp. 1–3.

18. *USS Morris (DD417)*, Serial 001, *Action Report — Okinawa Jima Operation — (1 April 1945 to 7 April 1945)*, 17 April 1945, pp. 3–6.

19. *U.S.S. Mullany (DD528)*, Serial 020, *Action Report — Preparation for, and Landing on Okinawa Gunto, Nansei Shoto, from 15 March 1945 to 6 April 1945*, 16 April 1945, p. 7.

20. *U.S.S. Emmons (DMS 22)*, Serial (None), *Action Report and sinking of USS Emmons (DMS 22), 6 April 1945*, 12 April 1945, p. 2.

21. Armed Guard Report *S. S. Hobbs Victory*, *Report of Voyage of S.S. Hobbs Victory*, 8 May 1945, pp. 2–3.

22. Samuel E. Morison, *History of United States Naval Operations in World War II, Volume Fourteen — Victory in the Pacific 1945* (Boston: Little Brown and Company, 1960), pp. 195–196.

23. This was the site of American landings and adjacent to the former airfields at Yontan and Kadena. Lying off shore in this area were numerous warships, supply ships, and troop transports. It was a prime target for kamikaze attacks during the campaign and thus was heavily guarded by American aircraft and ships.

24. *USS Maryland BB46*, Serial 0100, *Action Report — Operations Against Okinawa Island — Nansei Shoto — 21 March 1945–14 April 1945*, 23 April 1945, Enclosure (E), pp. 16–18.

25. Rielly, pp. 351–353.

26. *USS Colhoun DD 801*, No Serial, *Action Report, Invasion and Occupation of Okinawa Nansei Shoto, April 1 to April 6, 1945, and loss of the USS Colhoun (DD801)*, 27 April 1945, p. 8.

27. *U.S.S. Cassin Young (DD793)*, Serial 002, *Action Report, Capture of Okinawa Gunto Phases One and Two*, 21 July 1945, p. 6.

28. *USS Hyman DD 732*, Serial 028, *Action Report — Assault and Occupation of Okinawa Gunto — Nansei*

Shoto — 27 March–14 April 1945 — Including Attack and Damage of USS Hyman by Japanese Planes on 6 April 1945, 21 April 1945, pp. 7–14.
   29. *DANFS Volume VIII,* 1981, p. 206.
   30. *U.S.S. Sterrett (DD 407),* Serial 0139, *Return from Combat Area with Battle Damage, Report of,* 8 May 1945, p. 1.

Chapter 13

   1. Lt. Col. Masahiro Kawai, *The Operations of the Suicide-Boat Regiments in Okinawa* (National Institute for Defense Studies, undated), p. 6.
   2. *USS Charles J. Badger DD 657,* Serial 002, *Action Report of USS Charles J. Badger (DD657) for 9 April 1945,* 19 May 1945, p. 5.
   3. Samuel Eliot Morison, *History of United States Naval Operations in World War II, Volume XIV, Victory in the Pacific 1945* (Boston: Little Brown and Company, 1960), pp. 217–218.
   4. *USS Kidd DD 661,* Serial 002-45, *Action Report — 11 April to 15 April 1945,* 16 April 1945, p. 2.
   5. *USS Missouri BB-63,* Serial 087, *Action Report Covering Operations Against Kyushu, 18–19 March; Shore Bombardment of Okinawa, 24 March Against Okinawa, 25 March–6 May 1945,* 9 May 1945, Enclosure (C-1).
   6. *U.S.S. Enterprise CV-6, Deck Log,* 10–13 April 1945, pp. 391–399.
   7. *U.S.S. Cassin Young (DD793),* Serial 002, *Action Report, Capture of Okinawa Gunto, Phases One and Two,* 21 July 1945, p. 6.
   8. *USS Stanly DD 478,* Serial 087, *Occupation of Okinawa Gunto — 25 March–13 April 1945,* 17 April 1945, p. 3.
   9. *U.S.S. Mannert L Abele (DD733),* No Serial, *Action Report from 20 March through 12 April 1945, including damage to and loss of ship,* 14 April 1945, Enclosure (B), p. 2.
   10. *USS Rall DE 304,* Serial 0016, *Action Report, First Phase of the Occupation of the Nansei Shoto (Okinawa Shima),* 26 April 1945, pp. 1–5.
   11. *USS Lindsey DM 32,* No Serial, *Action Report — Okinawa Operation,* No Date, p. 22.
   12. Armed Guard Report *S.S. Minot Victory, Report of the Voyage, S.S. Minot Victory from Okinawa, Japan to San Pedro, California,* 25 May 1945, p. 2.
   13. *USS Zellars DD 777,* Serial 0033, *Report of Capture of Okinawa, Phase One and Two,* 1 May 1945, p. 7.
   14. Ibid., p. 11.
   15. *USS Tennessee BB 43,* Serial 0121, *Amplifying Report of the Heavy Coordinated Air Attack on the Tennessee 12 April 1945,* 16 May 1945, Enclosure (A), p. 8.
   16. *USS Whitehurst DE 634,* Serial 0087, *Anti-Aircraft Action Report of 12 April — Forwarding of,* 21 April 1945, pp. 1–4.
   17. *USS Sigsbee DD 502,* Serial 045, *Action Report — Operations in Support of the Invasion of Okinawa — Period 14 March 1945–20 April 1945,* 29 April 1945, Enclosure (A), pp. 15–27.
   18. *U.S.S. YMS 331,* Serial 4559, *Action Report,* 17 April 1945, p. 1.
   19. *USS LCI (G) 407,* No Serial, *Anti-Aircraft Action Report,* 16 April 1945, p. 1.
   20. *U.S.S. Bowers (DE-637),* Serial No. 003, *Action Report of The U.S.S. BOWERS (DE-637), 1–24 April 1945,* 15 May 1945, Enclosure (A), pp. 9–10.

   21. *USS Harding DMS-28,* Serial 006, *War Damage Report 14 June 1945,* pp. 1–2.
   22. *U.S.S. Intrepid (CV11),* Serial 0046, *War Diary, U.S.S. Intrepid (CV11) — Month of April 1945,* 22 June 1945.
   23. *U.S.S. Laffey (DD724),* Serial 023, *Report of Operations in Support of Landings by U.S. Troops in Kerama Retto — Okinawa Area March 25 to April 22 1945, Including Action Against Enemy Aircraft on April 16, 1945,* 29 April 1945, p. 25.
   24. *U.S.S. Laffey (DD724),* Serial 023, p. 26-A.
   25. *U.S.S. LCS(L) 51,* No Serial, *Anti-Aircraft Action, Okinawa, 16 April 1945,* 20 April 1945, pp. 1–2.
   26. *U.S.S. Bryant DD 665,* Serial 025, *Action Report — Amphibious Assault on Okinawa Gunto,* 28 April 1945, pp. 11–14.
   27. *U.S.S. LCS(L) 116,* Serial 1, *Action Report, Operations in Vicinity of Okinawa, 1 April to 16 April, 1945,* 18 April 1945, pp. 1–2.
   28. Allied Translator and Interpreter Section South West Pacific Area, *Research Report No. 125, Liaison Boat Units,* 27 March 1945.
   29. *USS LCI(G) 659,* No Serial, *Action Report, Report of Action Night of 15 and 16 April 1945,* 19 April 1945, pp. 2–3.
   30. *U.S.S. Benham (DD796),* Serial No. 033, *AA Action Report, USS Benham (DD796) of 17 April 1945,* 24 April 1945, pp. 1–3.
   31. *U.S.S. Swallow (AM65),* No Serial, *Action Report,* 25 April 1945, pp. 1–3.
   32. *USS Wadsworth DD 516,* Serial 028, *Action Report for the Invasion of Okinawa Jima,* 24 June 1945, p. 31.
   33. James L. Mooney, ed., *Dictionary of American Naval Fighting Ships Volume III* (Washington, D.C.: Naval Historical Center, 1968), p. 386. Hereafter *DANFS.*
   34. Military History Section — General Headquarters Far East Command Military Intelligence Section General Staff, *Japanese Monograph No. 135 Okinawa Operations Record,* p. 119.
   35. *USS Hutchins DD 476,* Serial 019, *Action Report Okinawa Operations Phases One and Two,* 7 May 1945, p. 7.
   36. Commanding Officer, Armed Guard Unit, *SS Canada Victory, Disaster Report SS Canada Victory,* 1 June 1945, p. 1.
   37. *USS LCS(L) 37 Action Report of 28 April 1945,* Revised 14 May 1945, p. 2.
   38. Armed Guard Unit *S.S. Bozeman Victory, Report of Voyage, S.S. Bozeman Victory,* 9 June 1945, pp. 1–2.
   39. *DANFS Volume V,* p. 311.
   40. *U.S.S. Pinckney (PH-2), Deck Log,* 27–28 April 1945, pp. 117–118.
   41. *U.S.S. Comfort (AH-6),* Serial C-68, *Aerial attack and Resultant Damage — report of,* 1 May 1945, p. 7.
   42. *U.S.S. Ralph Talbot (DD390),* Serial 043, *Action by Surface Ships — Report of,* 9 May 1945, Enclosure (A), p. 3.
   43. *USS LCI(G) 580,* No Serial, *Action Report — Okinawa Operation,* 1 July 1945, pp. 2–4.
   44. *USS Haggard DD 555,* Serial 056, *Report of Anti-Aircraft Action by Surface Ships,* 12 May 1945, p. 1.
   45. *USS Hazelwood DD 531,* Serial 0065, *Report of Action Against Japanese Suicide Planes — 2–9 April 1945,* Enclosure (A), p. 1.
   46. *U.S.S. Terror CM 5,* Serial 0125, *AA Action Report,* 9 May 1945, pp. 1–3.

Chapter 14

1. U.S.S. *Carina AK 74*, Serial 09-45, *Action Report*, 21 May 1945, p. 2.
2. Armed Guard Unit S.S. *Paducah Victory, Report of Voyage, SS Paducah Victory*, 4 June 1945, p. 2.
3. Lt. Col. Masahiro Kawai, *The Operations of the Suicide-Boat Regiments in Okinawa* (National Institute for Defense Studies, undated), p. 7.
4. U.S.S. *L.C.S. (L) (3) 113, Action Report*, 16 May, 1945, p. 3.
5. USS *Macomb DMS 23*, Serial 103, *Anti-Aircraft Action of 3 May 1945, Report of*, 5 May 1945, pp. 1–2.
6. USS *Aaron Ward DM 34*, Serial 005, *Action Report for 3 May 1945*, 13 May 1945, p. 6.
7. USS *Little DD 803*, No Serial, *Report of Action Between U.S.S. Little (DD 803), and Enemy Aircraft on May 3, 1945* (E. L .D.), 7 May 1945, pp. 3–5.
8. USS *LSM(R) 195*, Serial F9-05, *Action Report — Battle of Okinawa, 3 May 1945*, 5 May 1945, p. 2.
9. USS *Morrison DD 560*, Serial 030, *Action Report of USS Morrison on Air Engagement 4 May 1945*, 10 May 1945, pp. 1–4.
10. U.S.S. *LSM(R) 194*, Serial F9-6, *Action Report — Battle of Okinawa — 4 May 1945*, 6 May 1945, p. 1.
11. USS *Ingraham DD-694*, Serial 0010, *Iceberg Operation, 4 May 1945*, 17 June 1945, p. 2.
12. Ibid., p. 3.
13. USS *Luce DD 522*, No Serial, *Action Report on Ryukyus Operation, 24 March–4 May 1945*, 4 May 1945, pp. 5–21.
14. USS *LSM(R) 190*, Serial F9-04, *Action Report — Battle of Okinawa, 4 May 1945*, 18 August 1945, pp. 1–5.
15. U.S.S. *Shea (DM30)*, Serial 004, *Battle Damage Incurred 4 May 1945 — Report of*, 15 May 1945, p. 2.
16. U.S.S. *Gayety (AM 239)*, Serial 037, *Action with Enemy Suicide Planes on 4 May 1945, Report of*, 10 May 1945, pp. 2–3.
17. USS *Spectacle AM305, War Diary, May 1–31, 1945*, p. 1.
18. U.S.S. *LCS(L)(3) 53*, Serial No. 051, *Action Report of Anti-Small Boat Patrol on the Night of 4 to 5 May 1945*, 1 June 1945, p. 1.
19. U.S.S. *Oberrender (DE 344)*, Serial 006, *Action Report on Okinawa Operation, Phases I and II, from 9 April 1945 to 10 May 1945*, 18 May 1945, pp. 3–4.
20. U.S.S. *England (DE-635)*, Serial No. 005, *Okinawa Operation — Action report of*, 13 June 1945, pp. 17–18.
21. Translation of letter written by Flight PO 1/c Isao Matsuo, 11 May 1945.
22. USS *Hugh W. Hadley DD 744*, Serial 066, *Action Report, Action Against Enemy Aircraft Attacking This Ship, While on Radar Picket Station Number Fifteen, Off Okinawa, Nansei Shoto, 11 May 1945*, 15 May 1945, p. 2.
23. USS *Hugh W. Hadley DD 744*, Serial 066, p. 3.
24. Ibid., pp. 5–6.
25. U.S.S. *LCS(L)(3) 82*, Serial 72-45, *Action Report, Okinawa Campaign, USS LCS(L) 82*, 26 July 1945, Enclosure (A), pp. 1–3.
26. U.S.S. *LCS(L) (3) 83*, Serial 020-45, *Action Report of Okinawa Campaign, 16 April to 21 June*, 26 July 1945, Enclosure (h), p. 1.
27. U.S.S. *LSM(R) 193*, Serial 007, *Action Report, Battle of Okinawa 11 May 1945*, 13 May 1945, pp. 2–3.
28. U.S.S. *Evans DD 552*, Serial 004, *Action Report, Anti-aircraft Action off Okinawa 11 May 1945*, 22 May 1945, pp. 6–9.
29. U.S.S. *Harry F. Bauer (DM26)*, Serial 006, *Report of Capture of Okinawa Gunto, Phases I and II, 25 March to 11 June 1945*, 12 June 1945, p. 38.
30. VMF-221 *Aircraft Action Report No. 63*, 11 May 1945.
31. Military History Section — General Headquarters Far East Command Military Intelligence Section General Staff, *Japanese Monograph No. 141*, "Okinawa Area Naval Operations" Supplement Statistics on Naval Air Strength, Chart A.
32. Maxwell Taylor Kennedy, *Danger's Hour: The Story of the USS Bunker Hill and the Kamikaze Pilot Who Crippled Her* (New York: Simon & Schuster, 2008), pp. 284–292.
33. Interview with Albert Perdeck, S 1/c U.S.S. *Bunker Hill CV 17*, 13 August 2009.
34. Ibid.
35. Armed Guard Unit *SS C. W. Post, Report of Voyage, SS C. W. Post from Oakland Callifornia to Ie Shima*, 23 May 1945, pp. 1–2.
36. Armed Guard Unit *M. S. Tjisadane, Report of Voyage M. S. Tjisadane*, 15 June 1945, pp.1–3.

Chapter 15

1. U.S.S. *Bright (DE-747)*, Serial 028, *War Diary for period ending 31 May 1945*, 5 June 1945, p. 5.
2. USS *LCS(L)(3)19*, Serial No. 0-4, *Action Report*, 18 May 1945, pp. 1–2.
3. U.S.S. *LCS(L)(3) 82*, No Serial, *Action Report, USS LCS(L)(3) 82 of 12–13 May 1945*, Enclosure (A), pp. 2–3.
4. USS *Bache DD 470*, Serial 0126, *Action Report — Okinawa Jima Operation, 16 March 1945 to 2 June 1945*, 2 June 1945, Enclosure (A), p. 7.
5. USS *Enterprise CV 6*, Serial 0273, *Action Report of USS Enterprise — CV6 — in Connection With Operations in Support of Amphibious Landings at Okinawa 3 May to 16 May 1945 — Phase III*, 22 May 1945, pp. 15–16.
6. U.S.S. *Douglas H. Fox (DD779)*, Serial 004, *Action Report — Action against enemy aircraft attacking this ship while on Radar Picket Station Number Nine off Okinawa, Nansei Shoto, May 17, 1945*, 24 May 1945, pp. 1–3.
7. USS *Chase APD 54*, Serial No. 005, *War Damage Report*, 10 June 1945, pp. 1–3.
8. U.S.S. *Thatcher (DD 514)*, Serial 0121, *Action Report, U.S.S. Thatcher (DD514), Okinawa Gunto, 16–20 May 1945*, pp. 6–7.
9. U. S. S. *Register (APD-92)*, Serial No. 031, *Action Report, Suicide Air Attack night of 20 May 1945*, 26 May 1945, pp. 1–4.
10. U.S.S. *William C. Cole DE 641*, Serial No. 022, *War Diary for Month of May 1945*, 4 June 1945.
11. USS *Stormes DD 780*, Serial 072, *Action Report*, 1 June 1945, p. 2.
12. Ibid., p. 9.
13. USS *O'Neill DE 188*, Serial 044, *Action Report — Operations at Okinawa, Nansei Shoto, From April–June 1945*, 10 June 1945, p. 3.
14. James L. Mooney, ed., *Dictionary of American Naval Fighting Ship Vol. I A-B* (Washington, D.C.: Naval History Center, 1991), p. 101.
15. U.S.S. *BARRY (APD-29)*, Serial: 024, *Anti-Aircraft Action Report*, First Endorsement, 3 June 1945, pp. 1–2.
16. U.S.S. *Spectacle (AM305)*, Serial 042, *Anti-Aircraft Action Report — Japanese Plane Suicide Attack, Ie Shima, 25 May 1945*, 1 June 1945, pp. 2–3.

17. U.S.S. LSM 135, No Serial, *Action Report—Attack by Japanese Suicide Plane 25 May 1945, Ie Shima, Ryukyu Rhetto, Resulting in Loss of Ship— U.S.S. LSM 135*, 1 June 1945, p. 1.
18. U.S.S. Roper (APD 20), Serial 022, *Action Report—Suicide Plane Crash on U.S.S. ROPER (APD-20) 25 May 1945*, 31 May 1945, pp. 6–7.
19. U.S.S. Bates (APD 47), No Serial, *Action Report—Attack and Bombing by Japanese Suicide Planes May 25, 1945—Okinawa—Resulting in Loss of Ship*, 1 June 1945, pp. 1–3.
20. USS Forrest DMS-24, Serial 001, *War Damage Report, Report of Damage Sustained From Suicide Plane Crash Aboard, Ship in Task Group 51.5 Patrolling off Okinawa*, 12 June 1945, p. 1.
21. William J. Veigele, *PC Patrol Craft of World War II* (Santa Barbara, CA: Astral Publishing Co., 1998), p. 222.
22. U.S.S. Braine (DD630), Serial 0013, *U.S.S. BRAINE Action Report—Engagement with Japanese Aircraft off the Island of Okinawa on 27 May 1945*, pp. 1–5.
23. John Rooney, *Mighty Midget U.S.S. LCS 82* (Phoenixville, PA: John Rooney, 1990), p. 140.
24. USS Braine DD 630 website, *http://www.ussbrainedd630com/witness.htm*, p. 4.
25. Rooney, p. 140.
26. U.S.S. Loy (APD 56), Serial 16, *Ships Damage Report—Summary of*, 30 May 1945, pp. 1–2.
27. U.S.S. Rednour (APD 102), Serial 022, *General Action Report, 26 April to 8 June 1945—submission of*, 11 June 1945, pp. 2–4
28. USS Dutton AGS 8, Serial 62-45, *Action Report of Attack by Enemy Suicide Plane*, 28 May 19345, pp. 1–2.
29. U.S.S. Drexler (DD741), Serial 01, *Action Report, Involving Loss of U.S.S. Drexler (DD741)*, 26 June 1945, pp. 1–2.
30. Robert M. Browning, Jr., *U.S. Merchant Vessel War Casualties of World War II* (Annapolis: Naval Institute Press, 1996), pp. 514–515.
31. USS LCS(L) 119, Serial 00201, *Action Report*, 2 June 1945, pp. 3–4.

Chapter 16

1. USS LCS(L) 40, Serial 202, *Action Report on*, 8 August 1945, pp. 6–7.
2. USS LCI(L) 90, No Serial, *Action Report of Operations of 3 June 1945*, 8 June 1945, pp. 1–2.
3. USS Mississippi BB-41, Serial 004, *War Damage, Suicide Plane Attack, 5 June 1945*, 8 July 1945, pp. 1–3.
4. U.S.S. Louisville CA 28, Serial 0014, *Report of War Damage Sustained as a Result of Japanese Suicide Plane Hit, June 5, 1945*, 11 June 1945, pp. 1–6.
5. U.S.S. Harry F. Bauer DM 26, Deck Log, 6 June 1945, pp. 442–443.
6. U.S.S. J. William Ditter DM 31, Deck Log, 6 June 1945, pp. 376–378.
7. James L. Mooney, ed., *Dictionary of American Naval Fighting Ships*, Vol. V (Washington, D.C.: Naval History Division, 1970), p. 23.
8. U.S.S. Anthony (DD515), Serial 042, *U.S.S. Anthony (DD515)—Action Report, Okinawa Campaign, 28 May–24 June 1945*, 26 June 1945, p. 2.
9. USS William D. Porter DD-579, Serial 00236, *Report of Loss of USS William D. Porter, 10 June 1945*, 18 June 1945, p. 3.
10. Armed Guard Unit *S.S. Walter Colton, Report of Voyage, S. S. Walter Colton from March 28, 1945 to 24 July, 1945*, 26 July 1945, pp. 2–4.

11. USS LSM 59, No Serial, *Action Report—Sinking of the U.S.S. LSM 59 by Japanese Suicide Plane on 21 June 1945*, 23 June 1945, p. 1.
12. U.S.S. Curtiss (AV4), Serial 0010, Action Report, 1 July 1945, p. 2.
13. Ibid., Enclosure A, p. 3.
14. Military History Section Headquarters, Army Forces Far East, *Japanese Monograph No. 184 Submarine Operations in the Third Phase Operations Parts 3, 4, and 5*, 1960, p. 144.
15. Action Report, No Serial, *LTJG Elwood M. Rich, USN, Senior Surviving Officer— USS Underhill (DE682)*, 30 July 1945, p. 22.
16. Commander Destroyer Squadron 55, Serial 0023, *Anti-Aircraft Action Report for Action of 29 July, 1945—Loss of U.S.S. Callaghan (DD792)*, 7 August 1945, Enclosure (A), p. 5.
17. USS Cassin Young DD-793, Serial 003, *Iceberg Operation Memorandum Report of Radar Picket Duty off Okinawa—Under Kamikaze Attack 29 and 30 July*, 1 August 1945, p. 2.
18. U.S.S. Horace A. Bass (APD 124), Serial 024, *Action Report, Defense of Okinawa, 30 July 1945*, 9 August 1945, p. 2.
19. U.S.S. Borie (DD704), Serial 0222-45, *Action Report—Operations During the Period 2 July 1945 to 15 August 1945*, 15 August 1945, pp. 1–2.
20. USS Hank DD 702, Serial 046, *USS Hank (DD702) Action Report—Operations with Task Force 38 Against Japanese Empire During Period 1 July–16 August 1945*, 20 August 1945, pp. 2–3.
21. USS Lagrange APA 124, Serial 040, *Action Report—Forwarding of*, 22 August 1945, pp. 1–2.
22. VAdm. Matome Ugaki, *Fading Victory: The Diary of Admiral Matome Ugaki 1941–1945*, trans. Masataka Chihaya (Pittsburgh: University of Pittsburgh Press, 1991), p. 659.
23. Ugaki, p. 664.

Chapter 17

1. Military History Section Headquarters, Army Forces Far East, *Japanese Monograph No. 174 Outline of Naval Armament and Preparations for War, Part VI*, pp. 8–9. Hereafter *JM No. 174*.
2. Ibid., p. 12.
3. *JM No. 174*, p. 13.
4. *JM No. 174*, pp. 28–29.
5. *JM No. 174*, pp. 39–40.
6. U.S.S. William D. Porter (D579), Serial 00236, *Report of Loss of USS William D. Porter, 10 June 1945*, 18 June 1945, pp. 2–3.
7. *JM No. 174*, p. 20.
8. Military History Section Headquarters, Army Forces Far East, *Japanese Monograph No. 85 Preparations for Operations in Defense of the Homeland, Jul. 1944–Jul. 1945*, Annexed Sheet # 3. Hereafter *JM No. 85*.
9. Ibid., p. 28.
10. *JM No. 85*, p. 15.
11. History Section Headquarters, Army Forces Far East, *Japanese Monograph No. 184 Submarine Operations in the Third Phase Operations Parts 3, 4, and 5*, p. 162.
12. U.S. Naval Technical Mission to Japan, Target Report: *The Fukuryu Special Harbor Defense and Underwater Attack Unit—Tokyo Bay*, January 1946, p. 9.
13. Ibid., p. 7.

Bibliography

The bibliographic section for this work is quite extensive. In order to fully document the numerous kamikaze attacks on American ships during World War II it was necessary to check as many records as possible. This included ship logs, action reports, and assorted government reports dealing with the kamikazes, their organization, and activities. As an aid to other researchers the numerous primary source materials have been listed according to the facility in which they were found. Where possible, particularly for materials from the National Archives and Records Administration in College Park, Maryland, the various records groups have been listed as an aid to further expedite the research of others.

The textual record groups of particular use at the National Archives were:

RG 18: WWII USAAF Mission Record Index-Fighter Groups and Squadrons
RG 19: Records of the Bureau of Ships
RG 24: List of Logbooks of U.S. Navy Ships, Stations and Miscellaneous Units, 1801–1947
RG 38: Records of the Chief of Naval Operations
RG 127: Records of the United States Marine Corps—Aviation Records Relating to World War II
RG 165: War Department General and Special Staffs
RG 243: Records of the United States Strategic Bombing Survey
RG 457: Records of the National Security Agency

The photo archive groups used were:
RG 19: Records of the Bureau of Ships, Series Z
RG 80G: General Records of the Dept. of the Navy, 1941–1945
RG 80 JO: General Records of the Dept. of the Navy, 1789–1947
RG 111: SC Records of the Army Signal Corps, 1941–1945
RG 127 MC: Records of the US Marine Corps
RG 306 NT: United States Information Agency, New York Times Paris Bureau Collection
RG 342 FH: Records of the U.S. Air Force Commands, Activities, Organizations

Photographs obtained from the National Archives all have the credit beginning with the letters NARA and followed by the specific record group such as 80G, 111-SC and so forth. Photographs from the Naval History and Heritage Command in Washington, D.C., are preceded with the letters NH.

Materials listed as being miscellaneous are in the author's collection. They may be available at the National Archives or other facilities, but they came into my possession in various ways not associated with any formal collections. Primary source materials and their locations are listed by location. Specific reports in each category are listed in the end notes for each chapter. It should be noted that official reports from the era display a wide variety of formats. In some instances parts or all of the document title may appear in capital letters while in other similar documents, they do not. The use of periods, commas, and hyphens is also fairly diverse. I have listed them here in their original form.

Primary Sources

AIR FORCE HISTORICAL RESEARCH AGENCY, MAXWELL AIR FORCE BASE

Records of the 7th Fighter Squadron January 1941–March 1945. Microfilm Publication A0716.
Records of the 8th Fighter Squadron January 1942–August 1947. Microfilm Publication A0718.
Records of the 9th Fighter Squadron January 1941–August 1947. Microfilm Publication A0719.
Records of the 49th Fighter Group January 1941–June 1946. Microfilm Publication B0143.
Records of the 318th Fighter Group. Microfilm Publication BO522-2309.

Records of the 318th Fighter Group Narrative. Microfilm Publication BO239-2078.
Records of the 431st Fighter Squadron September 1944–August 1945. Microfilm Publication A0807.
Records of the 432nd Fighter Squadron May 1943–April 1945. Microfilm Publication A0807.
Records of the 433rd Fighter Squadron May 1943–June 1945. Microfilm Publication A0808.
Records of the 475th Fighter Group May 1943–July 1945. Microfilm Publication B0632.

LIBRARY OF CONGRESS

Archival Manuscript Collection. Deyo, Morton L. Papers of VAdm. M. L. Deyo USN 1911–1981. Call Number 0535S.
Deyo, VAdm. M. L. *Kamikaze*. Typescript, circa 1955.
Military History Section — General Headquarters Far East Command Military Intelligence Section General Staff. Microfilm Records, Shelf 8489, Reels 1, 5, 7, 10, 13, 14.
Japanese Monograph No. 6. 35th Army Operations, 1944–1945 (Reel 1).
Japanese Monograph No .7. Philippines Operations Record, Phase III Jan.–Aug. 1945 (Reel 1).
Japanese Monograph No. 8. Philippines Operations Record, Phase III Dec. 1944–Aug. 1945 (Reel 1).
Japanese Monograph No. 12. 4th Air Army Operations 1944–1945 (Reel 1).
Japanese Monograph No. 51. Air Operations on Iwo Jima and the Ryukyus (Reel 5).
Japanese Monograph No. 52. History of the 10th Area Army, 1943–1945 (Reel 5).
Japanese Monograph No. 53. 3rd Army Operations in Okinawa March-June, 1945. Army Defense Operations (Reel 5).
Japanese Monograph No. 85. Preparations for Operations in Defense of the Homeland, Jul. 1944–Jul. 1945 (Reel 7).
Japanese Monograph No. 86. War History of the 5th Air Fleet (The Ten Air Unit) Operational Record from 10 February 1946 to 19 August 1945 (Reel 7).
Japanese Monograph No. 135. Okinawa Operations Record (Reel 10).
Japanese Monograph No. 141. (Navy) Okinawa Area Naval Operations Supplement Statistics on Naval Air Strength. August, 1949 (Reel 10).
Japanese Monograph No. 174. Outline of Naval Armament and Preparations for War, Part VI (Reel 13).
Japanese Monograph No. 184. Submarine Operations in the Third Phase Operations Parts 3, 4, and 5 (Reel 14).

MISCELLANEOUS MATERIALS

Allied Land Forces Southeast Asia Weekly Intelligence Review. No. 1. "More Suicide Tactics." For week ending 5th January, 1945. p. 7.
Bureau of Ships Navy Department. *Destroyer Report — Gunfire Bomb and Kamikaze Damage Including Losses in Action 17 October, 1941 to 15 August 1945*.
Bureau of Ships Navy Department. NAVSHIPS A-3 (420) *Summary of War Damage to U.S. Battleships, Carriers, Cruisers, Destroyers and Destroyer Escorts 8 December 1943 to 7 December 1944*. Washington, D.C.: U.S. Hydrographic Office, 1945.
Bureau of Ships Navy Department. NAVSHIPS A-4 (424). *Summary of War Damage to U.S. Battleships, Carriers, Cruisers, Destroyers and Destroyer Escorts 8 December 1944 to 9 October 1945*. Washington, D.C.: U. S. Hydrographic Office, 1945.
Cabinet Information Board. Op-16-EE Translation No. 264. "Kamikaze Special Attack Force." *Weekly Report of 8 November 1944*.
CINCPAC PEARL *Dispatch AI 58199*. 3 May 1945.
Fukui, Shizuo. *Japanese Naval Vessels at End of War*. Japan: Administrative Division, Second Demobilization Bureau, 1947.
Headquarters Far East Command Military History Section. *Imperial General Headquarters Navy Directives Volume II. Directives No. 316- No. 540 (15 Jan 44–26 Aug 45) Special Directives No. 1–No. 3 (2 Sep 45–12 Sep 45)*.
Industrial Department Scientific & Test Group, Puget Sound Navy Yard. *War Damage Report — USS Sterrett (DD 407) Action of 9 April 1945*.
U.S. Naval Technical Mission to Japan. *Japanese Suicide Craft*. January 1946.
_____. *Target Report — The Fukuryu Special Harbor Defense and Underwater Attack Unit — Tokyo Bay*. January 1946.
War Department Military Intelligence Division. *Intelligence Bulletin*. Various volumes and dates from November 1944 through August 1945. Specific articles are listed in the chapter endnotes.

NATIONAL ARCHIVES AND RECORDS ADMINISTRATION, COLLEGE PARK, MD

RG 18: WWII USAAF Mission Record Index—Fighter Groups and Squadrons

USAAF Squadron and Groups Mission reports and Squadron and Group Histories for the: 1st, 19th, 21st, 34th, 333rd, 418th (N) and 548th (N) Fighter Squadrons and the 318th and 413th Fighter Groups.

RG 19: Records of the Bureau of Ships

BuShips General Correspondence 1940–1945 LSM(R)/L 11–3 to C-LSM(R)/S 29–2.
BuShips General Correspondence 1940–1945 LSM(R)/S87 to LSM(R) 188–189/S 17.
BuShips General Correspondence 1940–1945 LSM(R)/S87 to LSM(R) 188–189/S 17.
BuShips General Correspondence 1940–1945 C-DD 552 to DD 553.
BuShips General Correspondence 1940–1945 C-DD 734/L 11–1 (350-C-44LIL).
BuShips General Correspondence 1940–1945 DD 741–C-DD 742.

RG 24: List of Logbooks of U.S. Navy Ships, Stations, and Miscellaneous Units, 1801–1947

Ship Logs
Amphibious command ships: *Ancon AGC 4, Biscayne AGC 18, Eldorado AGC 11, Panamint AGC 13*.

Carriers: *Belleau Wood CVL 24, Bennington CV 20, Block Island CVE 106, Chenango CVE 28, Essex CV 9, Franklin CV 13, Hancock CV 19, Hornet CV 12, San Jacinto CVL 30, Wasp CV 18, Yorktown CV 10.*

Destroyer escorts: *Bowers DE 637, Edmonds DE 406.*

Destroyers: *Alfred A. Cunningham DD 752, Ammen DD 527, Anthony DD 515, Aulick DD 569, Bache DD 470, Barton DD 722, Beale DD 471, Bennett DD 473, Bennion DD 662, Boyd DD 544, Bradford DD 545, Braine DD 630, Brown DD 546, Bryant DD 665, Bush DD 529, Callaghan DD 792, Caperton DD 650, Cassin Young DD 793, Charles Ausburne DD 570, Claxton DD 571, Cogswell DD 651, Colhoun DD 801, Compton DD 705, Converse DD 509, Cowell DD 547, Daly DD 519, Douglas H. Fox DD 779, Drexler DD 741, Dyson DD 572, Evans DD 552, Foote DD 511, Frank E. Evans DD 754, Fullam DD 474, Gainard DD 706, Gregory DD 802, Guest DD 472, Harry E. Hubbard DD 748, Heywood L. Edwards DD 663, Hudson DD 475, Hugh W. Hadley DD 774, Ingersoll DD 652, Ingraham DD 694, Irwin DD 794, Isherwood DD 520, James C. Owens DD 776, John A. Bole DD 755, Kimberly DD 521, Knapp DD 653, Laffey DD 724, Lang DD 399, Laws DD 558, Little DD 803, Lowry DD 770, Luce DD 522, Mannert L. Abele DD 733, Massey DD 778, Moale DD 693, Morrison DD 560, Mustin DD 413, Nicholson DD 442, Picking DD 685, Preston DD 795, Pringle DD 477, Pritchett DD 561, Purdy DD 734, Putnam DD 757, Richard P. Leary DD 664, Rowe DD 564, Russell DD 414, Shubrick DD 639, Smalley DD 565, Sproston DD 577, Stanly DD 478, Sterett DD 407, Stoddard DD 566, Stormes DD 780, Van Valkenburgh DD 656, Wadsworth DD 516, Walke DD 723, Watts DD 567, Wickes DD 578, Wilkes DD 441, Willard Keith DD 775, William D. Porter DD 579,* and *Wren DD 568.*

Fleet minesweeper: *Defense AM 317.*

Fleet tugs: *Arikara ATF 98, Cree ATF 84, Lipan, ATF 85, Menominee ATF 73, Pakana ATF 108, Tekesta ATF 93, Ute ATF 76.*

High speed minesweepers: *Butler DMS 29, Ellyson DMS 19, Emmons DMS 22, Forrest DMS 24, Gherardi DMS 30, Hambleton DMS 20, Harding DMS 28, Hobson DMS 26, Jeffers DMS 27, Long DMS 12, Macomb DMS 23, Rodman DMS 21,* and *Southard DMS 10.*

High speed transports: *Barber APD 57, Clemson APD 31, Frament APD 77, Ringness APD 100.*

Landing crafts support (large): *11* through *22, 31, 32, 34* through *40, 51* through *57, 61* through *67, 68, 70, 71, 74, 76, 81* through *90, 92* through *94, 97* through *105, 107, 109, 110, 111, 114* through *125,* and *128* through *130.*

Landing ships medium: *14, 82, 167, 222, 228, 279.*

Landing ships medium (rockets): *189, 191, 192, 193, 196, 197, 198, 199.*

Landing ships tank: *472, 477, 534, 554, 605, 610, 700, 724, 737, 738, 750, 778, 808, 809, 912, 925, 1025, 1028.*

Light mine layers: *Aaron Ward DM 34, Gwin DM 33, Harry F. Bauer DM 26, Henry A. Wiley DM 29, J. William Ditter DM 31, Lindsey DM 32, Robert H. Smith DM 23, Shannon DM 25, Shea DM 30, Thomas E. Fraser DM 24.*

Patrol craft: *PC 1129.*

Patrol crafts rescue: *PCE(R)s 851, 852, 853, 854, 855, 856.*

Patrol motor gunboats: *PGM 9, PGM 10, PGM 17, PGM 20.*

Specific log references are listed in the chapter end notes.

RG 38: Armed Guard Reports

For the merchant ships *Alcoa Pioneer, Alexander Majors, Augustus Thomas, Benjamin Ide Wheeler, Bozeman Victory, Canada Victory, C. W. Post, George Von L. Meyer, Gilbert Stuart, Hobbs Victory, James O'Hara, Jeremiah M. Daily, John Evans, John S. Burke, Juan de Fuca, Kyle V. Johnson, Logan Victory, Marcus Daly, Matthew P. Deady, Morrison R. Waite, Minot Victory, M. S. Tjisadane, Paducah Victory, Segundo Ruiz-Blevis, Thomas Nelson, Walter Colton, William A. Coulter, William S. Ladd,* and *William Sharon.*

RG 38: Records of the Chief of Naval Operations—Office of Naval Intelligence

Monograph Files—Japan 1939–1946 1001–1015

Air Branch, Office of Naval Intelligence. *Naval Aviation Combat Statistics World War II.* OPNAV-P-23V No. A 129. Washington, D.C.: Office of the Chief of Naval Operations Navy Department, 17 June 1946.

Air Intelligence Group, Division of Naval Intelligence. *Air Operations Memorandum No. 81.* 18 May 1945.

Air Operations Memorandum No. 82. 25 May 1945.

Air Operations Memorandum No. 83. OpNav-16-V # S234. 1 June 1945.

Air Operations Memorandum No. 88. 6 July 1945.

Brunetti, Col. N. *The Japanese Air Force* (undated).

Chain of Command of Naval Air Forces Attached to the Combined Fleet (as of August 15th 1945).

Data Table—Japanese Combat Aircraft.

Director Air Intelligence Group. *Statistical Analysis of Japanese Suicide Effort Against Allied Shipping During OKINAWA Campaign.* 23 July 1945.

Japanese Suicide Effort Against Allied Shipping During OKINAWA Campaign, Statistical Analysis of. OP-16-VA-MvR. Serial 001481916. 23 July 1945.

Observed Suicide Attacks by Japanese Aircraft Against Allied Ships. OpNav-16-V # A106. 23 May 1945.

Photographic Interpretation Handbook—United States Forces. Supplement No. 2. Aircraft Identification. 15 April, 1945.

Secret Information Bulletin, No. 24.

Technical Air Intelligence Center. *Summary # 31 Baka.* OpNav—16-V # T 131. June 1945.

United States Fleet Headquarters of the Commander in Chief Navy Department, Washington D.C. *Effects of B-29 Operations in Support of the Okinawa Campaign From 18 March to 22 June 1945.* 3 August 1945.

U. S. Naval Technical Mission to Japan. Index No. *S-02 Ships and Related Targets Japanese Suicide Craft.*

_____. *O-01-1 Japanese Torpedoes and Tubes Article I Ship and Kaiten Torpedoes.* April 1946.

RG 38: Records of the Chief of Naval Operations—Records Relating to Naval Activity During World War II

Action Reports

Amphibious command ships: *Ancon AGC 4, Biscayne AGC 18, Eldorado AGC 11, Panamint AGC 13.*

Attack transports: *Alpine APA 92, Callaway APA 35, Du Page APA 41, Goodhue APA 107, Henrico APA 45, Hinsdale APA 120, James O'Hara APA 90, Lagrange APA 124, Sandoval APA 194, Telfair APA 210, Zeilin APA 3.*

Battleships: *California BB 44, Colorado BB 45, Maryland BB 46, Mississippi BB 41, Missouri BB 63, Nevada BB 36, New Mexico BB 40, New York BB 34, Tennessee BB 43, West Virginia BB 48.*

Cargo ship: *Carina AK 74.*

Cargo ship attack: *Achernar AKA 53, Starr AKA 67.*

Carriers: *Belleau Wood CVL 24, Bennington CV 20, Bunker Hill CV 17, Cabot CVL 28, Essex CV 9, Enterprise CV 6, Franklin CV 13, Hancock CV 19, Hornet CV 12, Intrepid CV 11, Lexington CV 16, Randolph CV 15, San Jacinto CVL 30, Saratoga CV 3, Ticonderoga CV 14, Wasp CV 18, Yorktown CV 10.*

Cruisers: *Biloxi CL 80, Birmingham CL 62, Columbia CL 56, Indianapolis CA 35, Louisville CA 28, Minneapolis CA 36, Montpelier CL 57, Nashville CL 45, Reno CL 96, St. Louis CL 49.*

Destroyer escorts: *Bowers DE 637, Bright DE 747, England DE 635, Fieberling DE 640, Gilligan DE 508, Halloran DE 305, Hodges DE 231, John C. Butler DE 339, LeRay Wilson DE 414, Lough DE 586, Oberrender DE 344, O'Neill DE 188, Rall DE 304, Richard W. Suesens DE 342, Samuel Miles DE 183, Stafford DE 411, Walter C. Wann DE 412, Whitehurst DE 634, William C. Cole DE 641, Witter DE 636, Underhill DE 682, Wesson DE 184, Witter DE 636.*

Destroyers: *Abner Read DD 526, Allen M. Sumner DD 692, Ammen DD 527, Anderson DD 411, Anthony DD 515, Aulick DD 569, Bache DD 470, Beale DD 471, Benham DD 796, Bennett DD 473, Bennion DD 662, Borie DD 704, Boyd DD 544, Bradford DD 545, Braine DD 630, Brown DD 546, Bryant DD 665, Bullard DD 660, Bush DD 529, Caldwell DD 605, Callaghan DD 792, Caperton DD 650, Cassin Young DD 793, Charles J. Badger DD 657, Claxton DD 571, Cogswell DD 651, Colhoun DD 801, Converse DD 509, Cowell DD 547, Daly DD 519, Douglas H. Fox DD 779, Drayton DD 366, Drexler DD 741, Dyson DD 572, Eaton DD 510, Evans DD 552, Foote DD 511, Frank E. Evans DD 754, Fullam DD 474, Gainard DD 706, Gansevoort DD 608, Gregory DD 802, Guest DD 472, Haggard DD 555, Halsey Powell DD 686, Hank DD 702, Haraden DD 585, Harry E. Hubbard DD 748, Haynsworth DD 700, Hazelwood DD 531, Heywood L. Edwards DD 663, Howorth DD 592, Hudson DD 475, Hughes DD 410, Hugh W. Hadley DD 774, Haraden DD 585, Helm DD 388, Hutchins DD 476, Hyman DD 732, Ingersoll DD 652, Ingraham DD 694, Irwin DD 794, Isherwood DD 520, John A. Bole DD 755, Kidd DD 661, Killen DD 593, Kimberly DD 521, Knapp DD 653, Lamson DD 367, Lang DD 399, Laffey DD 724, Laws DD 558, Leutze DD 481, Little DD 803, Lowry DD 770, Luce DD 522, Maddox DD 731, Mahan DD 364, Mannert L. Abele DD 733, Massey DD 778, Morris DD 417, Morrison DD 560, Mugford DD 389, Mullany DD 528, Mustin DD 413, Newcomb DD 586, O'Brien DD 725, Preston DD 795, Pringle DD 477, Pritchett DD 561, Purdy DD 734, Putnam DD 757, Ralph Talbot DD 390, Reid DD 369, Richard P. Leary DD 664, Robinson DD 562, Rowe DD 564, Russell DD 414, Sampson DD 394, Saufley DD 465, Shubrick DD 639, Sigsbee DD 502, Smalley DD 565, Smith DD 378 Sproston DD 577, Stanly DD 478, Sterrett DD 407, Stoddard DD 566, Stormes DD 780, Taussig DD 746, Thatcher DD 514, Twiggs DD 591, Van Valkenburgh DD 656, Wadsworth DD 516, Walke DD 723, Watts DD 567, Wickes DD 578, Wilkes DD 441, William D. Porter DD 579, Wilson DD 408, Wren DD 568, Zellars DD 777.*

Escort carriers: *Bismark Sea CVE 95, Kadashan Bay CVE 76, Kalinin Bay CVE 68, Kitkun Bay CVE 71, Chenango CVE 28, Lunga Point CVE 94, Manila Bay CVE 61, Marcus Island CVE 77, Natoma Bay CVE 62, Ommaney Bay CVE 79, Salamaua CVE 96, Sangamon CVE 26, Santee CVE 29, Savo Island CVE 78, St. Lo CVE 63, Suwannee CVE 27, Wake Island CVE 65, White Plains CVE 66.*

High speed transports: *Barr APD 29, Bates APD 47, Belknap APD 34, Bowers APD 40, Brooks APD 10, Chase APD 54, Dickerson APD 21, England APD 41, Gilmer APD 11, Horace A. Bass APD 124, Liddle APD 60, Loy APD 56, Rathburne APD 25, Register APD 92, Sims APD 50, Tatum APD 81, Ward APD 16.*

Landing craft infantry (large): 90.

Landing craft infantry (mortars): 974.

Landing craft infantry (rockets): 763.

Landing crafts infantry (guns): 70, 82, 365, 407, 558, 568, 580, 659.

Landing crafts support (large): 7, 11 through 21, 26, 27, 31, 32, 34 through 40, 48, 49, 51 through 57, 61 through 67, 68, 81 through 90, 94, through 109, 110, 111, 113,114 through 117, 119 through 125, 129, 130.

Landing ships medium: 14, 20, 23, 28, 59, 82, 135, 167, 213, 216, 222, 228, 279, 318,477 809.

Landing ships medium (rockets): 188, 189, 190, 192, 193, 194, 195, 197.

Landing ships tank: 447, 460, 472, 534, 548, 599, 610, 700, 737, 738, 749, 778, 808, 884, 912, 925, 1025, 1028.

Light mine layers: *Aaron Ward DM 34, Adams DM 27, Gwin DM 33, Harry F. Bauer DM 26, Henry A. Wiley DM 29, J. William Ditter DM 31, Lindsey DM 32, Robert H. Smith DM 23, Shannon DM 25, Shea DM 30, Thomas E. Fraser DM 24.*

High speed minesweepers: *Butler DMS 29, Dorsey DMS 1, Ellyson DMS 19, Emmons DMS 22, Forrest DMS 24, Hambleton DMS 20, Harding DMS 28, Hobson DMS 26, Hopkins DMS 13, Jeffers DMS 27, Macomb DMS 23, Palmer DMS 5, Rodman DMS 21, Southard DMS 10.*

High speed transports: *Barber APD 57, Barry APD 29, Bates APD 47, Belknap APD 34, Chase APD 54, Clemson APD 31, Dickerson APD 21, Horace A. Bass APD 124, Liddle APD 60, Loy APD 56, Rathburne APD 25, Rednour APD 102, Register APD 92, Ringness APD 100, Roper APD 20, Sims APD 50, Ward APD 16.*
Hospital ships: *Comfort AH 6, Pinckney APH 2.*
Minelayer: *Terror CM 5.*
Minesweepers: *Defense AM 317, Facility AM 233, Gayety AM 239, Gladiator AM 319, Ransom AM 283, Spectacle AM 305, Swallow AM 65, YMS 331.*
Motor torpedo boats: *PT 75, 300.*
Oilers: *Cowanesque AO 79, Taluga AO 62.*
Patrol crafts rescue: *PCE(R)s 851, 852, 853.*
Patrol motor gunboats: *PGM 10, PGM 20.*
Repair ship—landing craft: *Egeria ARL 8.*
Seaplane tenders: *Curtiss AV 4, Hamlin AV 15, Kenneth Whiting AV 14, Orca AVP 49, St. George AV 16.*
Sub chaser: *SC 699.*
Survey ship: *Dutton AGS 8.*
Transport: *War Hawk AP 168.*
Tugs: *Apache ATF 67, Arikira ATF 98, Cree ATF 84, Lipan ATF 85, Menominee ATF 73, Pakana ATF 108, Sonoma ATO 12, Tawakoni ATF 114, Tekesta ATF 93, Ute ATF 76.*
Unclassified vessel: *Porcupine IX 126.*
Various serials and dates were used for each ship. Specific reports are listed in the chapter end notes.

CINC-CINCPOA Bulletins
Airfields in Kyushu. Bulletin No. 166–45, 15 August 1945.
Airways Data Taiwan Chiho Special Translation No. 36, 1 June 1945.
Daito Shoto Bulletin No. 77–45, 20 March 1945.
Digest of Japanese Air Bases Special Translation No. 65, 12 May 1945.
Suicide Force Combat Methods Bulletin No. 129–45, 27 May 1945.
Suicide Weapons and Tactics Know Your Enemy! Bulletin No. 126–45, 28 May 1945.
Translations Interrogations Number 26. Bulletin No. 102–45, 25 April 1945.
Translations Interrogations Number 35. Bulletin No. 170–45, 7 July 1945.

CinCPac, 5th Fleet, Task Force, Task Group and Task Unit Records, Reports, Communiques
Amphibious Forces Pacific Fleet (TF 52) Serial 000166 16 March 1945 Operation Order A6–45.
CinCPac Adv. Hdqtrs. 17 April 1945.
CinCPac United States Pacific Fleet Serial 0005608 *War Diary for the Period 1 March through 31 March 1945.* 11 April 1945.
_____. 0005643 *War Diary for the Period 1 April through 30 April 1945.* 13 May 1945.
_____. 0005685 *War Diary for the Period 1 May through 31 May 1945.* 13 June 1945.
_____. 0005748 *War Diary for the Period 1 June through 30 June 1945.* 15 July 1945.
_____. 0005801 *War Diary for the Period 1 July through 31 July 1945.* 9 August 1945.
_____. 0005849 *War Diary for the Period 1 August through 31 August 1945.* 9 September 1945.

Commander Fifth Amphibious Force CTF-51 and CTF-31 Serial 0268 *Report of Capture of Okinawa Gunto Phases I and II.* 17 May 1945–21 June 1945. 4 July 1945.
Commander Fifth Amphibious Force letter of 11 June 1945. *Translation of a Japanese Letter.*
Commander Fifth Fleet. Serial 0333 *Action Report, RYUKYUS Operation through 27 May 1945.* 21 June 1945.
Commander Task Force Fifty-One. Commander Amphibious Forces U.S. Pacific Fleet. Serial 01400 *Report on Okinawa Gunto Operation from 17 February to 17 May,* 1945.
Commander Task Force 54. Serial 0022 *Action Report—Capture of Okinawa Gunto, Phase II 5 May to 28 May 1945.* 4 June 1945.
Commander Task Force SEVENTY-EIGHT. Serial 0907. *Action Reports, MARIVELES—CORREGIDOR Operation, 12–16 February 1945.* 12 April 1945.
CTF 31 to TF 31, TG 99.3, 29 May 1945.
CTF 51 to TF 51 16 April 1945.
CTF 51 to TF 51 24 April 1945.
CTU 52.9.1 OUTGOING MESSAGE OF 17 APRIL 1945.
Task Force 51 Communication and Organization Digest, 1945.

Destroyer Division, Mine Division, LSM, LCS Flotilla, Group, Division Reports, War Diaries, and Histories
Commander Destroyer Division 92 Serial 0192. *Action Report.* 23 July 1945.
Commander Destroyer Division 112 Serial 030. *Action Report Amphibious Assault on Okinawa Gunto.* 18 April 1945.
Commander Destroyer Division 120 Serial 002. *Action Report—Okinawa Gunto Operation, for Period from 29 April through 4 May 1945.* 6 May 1945.
Commander Destroyer Division 126 Serial 08. *Action Report, Attack by Japanese Aircraft off Okinawa Gunto on Hyman—6 April, 1945, and on Purdy, Cassin Young, Mannert L. Abele and Supporting Gunboats on 12 April 1945.* 15 April 1945.
Commander Destroyer Squadron 2 Serial 00551. *Action Report, Okinawa Gunto Operation 1 March to 17 May 1945.* 1 June 1945.
Commander Destroyer Squadron 24 Serial 0118. *Iceberg Operation, 23–27 May 1945.* 29 May 1945.
Commander Destroyer Squadron 24 Serial 0155. *Invasion of Okinawa Jima, 19 April–28 May 1945.* 18 June 1945.
Commander Destroyer Squadron 24 Serial 0166. *Invasion of Okinawa Jima, 28 May to 27 June 1945.* 28 June 1945.
Commander Destroyer Squadron 45 Serial 00138. *Report of Capture of Okinawa Gunto Phases 1 and 2, Commander, Destroyer Squadron Forty-Five for the Period 27 March to 21 June 1945.* 27 June 1945.
Commander Destroyer Squadron Forty-Nine. Serial 0011. *Action Report—OKINAWA CAMPAIGN—9 March 1945 to 23 June 1945.* 28 June 1945.
Commander Destroyer Squadron 55. Serial 0023.

Anti-Aircraft Action Report for 29 July, 1945 Loss of U.S.S. Callaghan (DD792). 7 August 1945.
Commander Destroyer Squadron Sixty-Four. Serial 032. *Report of Capture of Okinawa Gunto, Phases 1 and 2.* 25 June 1945.
Commander LCS(L) Flotilla THREE Serial 621. *LCS(L) Flotilla THREE Staff—Factual History of.* 21 November 1945.
Commander LCS(L) Flotilla FOUR Serial 25–46. *War History, Commander LCS(L) Flotilla FOUR.* 6 January 1946.
Commander LCS(L)(3) Group 11 Serial 0138. *Action Report Capture and Occupation of Okinawa Gunto Phases I and II.* 30 July 1945.
Commander LSM Flotilla Nine Serial 006. *War Diary for the Month of March 1945.*
Commander LSM Flotilla Nine Serial 021. *War Diary for the Month of April 1945.*
Commander LSM Flotilla Nine Serial C010. *Action Report—Ie Shima and Southeastern Okinawa, 2 April through 20 April 1945.* 21 April 1945.
Commander Mine Division 58 War Diary. April 1945.
Commander Mine Division 58 War Diary. May 1945.
Commander Mine Squadron Three Serial 078. *Action Report, Capture of Okinawa Gunto, Phase I and II, 9 March to 24 June 1945.* 5 July 1945.
Commander Mine Squadron Twenty Serial 0106. *Action Report.* 3 July 1945.
Commander Seventh Fleet (Commander Task Force 77) Serial 00302-C. *Report of Operation for the Capture of Leyte Island Including Action Report of Engagements in Surigao Strait and Off Samar Island on 25 October 1944—(King Two Operation).* 31 January 1945.
Commander Task Flotilla 5 Serial 0894. *Action Report, Capture of Okinawa Gunto 26 March to 21 June 1945.* 20 July 1945.
Commander Task Force 78 Serial 0907. *Action Report—Mariveles-Corregidor Operation—12–16 February 1945.* 18 April 1945.
Commander Task Force 78 (Commander Seventh Amphibious Force) Serial 00911. *Leyte Operations—Report On.* 10 November 1944.
Commander Task Group 77.12 (Commander Battleship Division 4). Serial 0297. *Report of the Operations of Heavy Covering and Carrier Group in the Support of "L-3."* 25 December 1944.
Commander Task Unit 77.4.1 (Commander Escort Carrier Force) Serial 00161. *Action Report of Commander Task Unit 77.4.1 for Lingayen, Luzon, Philippine Islands Operation.* 27 January 1945.
Commander Task Unit 77.4.2 Commander Carrier Division 24 Serial 00114. *Reoccupation of Leyte Island in the Central Philippines During the Period from 18 October 1944 to 29 October 1944, Including the Air-Surface Engagement with Major Units of the Japanese Fleet on 25 October 1944.* 2 November 1944.
Commander Task Unit 78.2.58 Serial 057. *Davao Gulf Operations—11 to 19 May 1945.* 20 May 1945.
Commander Task Unit 78.3.8. Commander LCS(L) Flotilla One. Serial 04. *Action Report—Special—Suicide Boat Attack Mariveles, P.I. 16 February 1945.* 25 February 1945.

DD-475 Dispatch 5 June, 1945.
LCI(L)(3) Flotilla Thirteen. *War Diary for January 1945.* 2 February 1945.
LCS Group Nine Operation Order No. *1–45 Annex Dog Fighting Instructions.*
LCS Group Eleven Serial 0138 *Composite Action Report Okinawa Gunto 1 April 1945–21 June 1945.*
LCS(L)(3) Flotilla Five Confidential Memorandum No. 5–45, 10 July 1945.

Navy Carrier Air Group and Individual Squadron Histories, War Diaries and Aircraft Action Reports
For CAG-40, 46, 47, 82, VBF-17, VC-8, 83, 85, 90, 93, 96, VF-9, 10, 12, 17, 23, 24, 29, 30, 31, 33, 40, 45, 82, 84, 85, 86, 87, and 90(N). Various dates.

War Diaries
Amphibious command ships: *Ancon AGC 4, Biscayne AGC 18, Eldorado AGC 11, Panamint AGC 13.*
Destroyers: *Anthony DD 515, Bryant DD 665, Lowry DD 770, Wadsworth DD 516, Wickes DD 578.*
Fleet tug: *Arikara ATF 98.*
High speed minesweeper: *Macomb DMS 23.*
Landing ships medium: *14, 82, 167, 222, 228,* and *279.*

RG 38: Records of the Naval Security Group, Crane, Indiana
Kamikaze Attacks at Okinawa, April–June 1945. 6 May 1946.

RG 127: Records of the United States Marine Corps-Aviation Records Relating to World War II
Tenth Army Tactical Air Force Records
Air Defense Command (Fighter Command) Operation Plan 1–45.
Air Defense Command Intelligence Logs Nos. 1 through 5, 7 April to 27 November 1945 inclusive.
Air Defense Command Intelligence Section—Daily Intelligence Summaries for 12, 15, 16, 17, 22, 23, 24, 29 April, 1, 4, 5, 7, 10, 11, 12 May 1945.
Commanding General Tactical Air Force Tenth Army No Serial 12 July 1945 Action Report—Phase 1—Nansei Shoto. Covers Period 1 April–30 June 1945.
Fighter Command Okinawa Intelligence Section—Daily Intelligence Summary for 12, 13, 14, 16, 18, 26, 27, 28, 29 May, 4, 12, 23 June, 1945.
Tactical Air Force Score Board 7 April–12 July 1945.
Tactical Air Force, Tenth Army Action Report, Phase I Nansei Shoto Period 8 December 1944 to 30 June 1945 Inc.
Tactical Air Force Tenth Army Operation Plan No. 1–45.
Tactical Air Force Tenth Army Periodic Reports Periodic Reports April-June 1945.
Tactical Air Force, Tenth Army War Diary for 1 May to 31 May 1945.
Tactical Air Force, Tenth Army War Diary for 1 June to 30 June 1945.

US Marine Corps Unit War Diaries, Daily Intelligence Summaries, Aircraft Action Reports and Unit Histories 1941–1949
For 2nd MAW, MAG-14, 22, 31, 33, VMF-112, 113, 123, 212, 221, 222, 223, 224, 311, 312, 314, 322, 323,

351, 422, 441, 451, 511, 512, 513, 533(N), 542(N), 543 (N), and VMTB-232. Various dates.

RG 165: War Department General and Special Staffs

Captured Personnel and Material Reports Far Eastern Bureau, British Ministry of Information. *Japanese Translations— No. 9–28*, 121, 146–169.

Report from Captured Personnel and Material Branch, Military Intelligence Service, U.S. War Department. Reports A(Air) 22 of 10 March 1945, A-220 of 20 July 1945, A (Air)— 32 11 August 1945.

Reports: *(Air) 20–22 Japanese Interrogations 1945* through *A (Air) 186–192 Japanese Interrogations* + *(A) 193 -204 Japanese Interrogations through AL 1–39 German, French and Dutch Interrogations*, 1944.

RG 243: Records of the United States Strategic Bombing Survey

243.4.2 Records of the Intelligence Branch — Microfilm Publication M-1654 Transcripts of Interrogations of Japanese Leaders and Responses to Questionnaires, 1945–46. (9 rolls).

Interrogations of: Lt. Gen. Saburo Endo, Lt. Col. Kazumi Fuji, Col. Heikichi Fukami, Cmdr. Fukamizu, Capt. Minoru Genda, Maj. Gen. Hideharu Habu, Lt. Col. Maseo Hamatani, Col. Hiroshi Hara, Col. Junji Hayashi, Capt. Gengo Hojo, Maj. Gen. Asahi Horiuchi, Capt. Rikibei Inoguchi, Lt. Kunie Iwashita, Lt. Col. Naomichi Jin, Col. Katsuo Kaimoto, RAdm. Seizo Katsumata, Lt. Gen. Masakazu Kawabe, Maj. Toshio Kinugasa, Lt. Gen. Kumao Kitajima, Cmdr. Mitsugi Kofukuda, Col. M. Matsumae, Col. Kyohei Matsuzawa, Capt. Takeshi Mieno, Gen. Miyoshi, Lt. Gen. Ryosuke Nakanishi, Lt. Cmdr. Ohira, Capt. Toshikazu Ohmae, Cmdr. Masatake Okumiya, Capt. Tonosuke Otani, Maj. Iori Sakai, Maj. Hideo Sakamoto, Lt. Cmdr. Takeda Shigeki, Lt. Gen. Michio Sugawara, Maj. O. Takahashi, Maj. O. Takauchi, Capt. T. Takeuchi, Col. Shushiro Tanabe, Col. Isekichi Tanaka, RAdm. Toshitanea Takata, Cmdr. Oshimori Terai, Superior Pvt. Guy Toko, Maj. Gen. Sadao Yui.

JANIS 84–2. *Air Facilities Supplement to JANIS 84. Southwest Japan (Kyushu Island, Shikoku Island, Southwestern Honshu Island).* Joint Intelligence Study publishing Board. June 1945. Microfilm Publication 1169, Roll 10.

JANIS 87 *Change No. 1.* Joint Intelligence Study Publishing Board, August, 1944. Microfilm Publication 1169, Roll 14.

Supplemental Report of Certain Phases of the War Against Japan Derived From Interrogations of Senior Naval Commanders at Truk. Naval and Naval Air Field Team No. 3, USSBS. Microfilm Publication M1655, Roll 311.

Tactical Mission Reports of the 20th and 21st Bomber Commands, 1945. Microfilm Publication M1159, Rolls 2, 3.

RG 457: Records of the National Security Agency

Explanatory Notes on the KAMIKAZE Attacks at Okinawa, April-June 1945. 6 May 1946.

Intelligence Reports from U.S. Joint Services and other Government Agencies, December 1941 to October 1948.

SRMD — 007. *JICPOA Summary of ULTRA Traffic, 1 April-30 June 1945, 1 July-31 August 1945.*

SRMD — 011. *JICPOA Estimate of Japanese Army and Navy Fighter Deployment 8 August 1944–23 April 1945.*

SRMD — 015. *Reports and Memoranda on a Variety of Intelligence Subjects January 1943–August 1945.*

Magic Far East Summaries 1945–1945
SRS341 (24-2-45)–SRS 410 (4-5-45).
SRS411 (5-5-45)–SRS 490 (23-7-45).
SRS491 (24-7-45)–SRS547 (2-10-45).

Special Research Histories (SRHS)
SRH-52 *Estimated Japanese Aircraft Locations 15 July 1943–9 August 1945.*
SRH-53 *Estimates of the Japanese Air Situation 23 June 1945.*
SRH-54 *Effects of B29 Operations in Support of the Okinawa Campaign 18 March–22 June 1945.*
SRH-55 *Estimated Unit Locations of Japanese Navy and Army Air Forces 20 July 1945.*
SRH-103 *Suicide Attack Squadron Organizations July 1945.*
SRH 183 *Location of Japanese Military Installations.*
SRH-257 *Analysis of Japanese Air Operations During Okinawa Campaign.*
SRH-258 *Japanese Army Air Forces Order-Of-Battle 1945.*
SRH-259 OP-20G *File of Reports on Japanese Naval Air Order of Battle.*

United States Navy Records Relating to Cryptology 1918 to 1950
SRMN 013 *CINCPAC Dispatches* May–June 1945.

PRINCETON UNIVERSITY— FIRESTONE LIBRARY

Wartime Translations of Seized Japanese Documents. Allied Translator and Interpreter Section Reports, 1942–1946. Bethesda, MD: Congressional Information Service, Inc., 1988. (Microfilm).

ADVATIS Bulletins 405, 656

ADVATIS Interrogation Reports
1, 601. Ens. Sadao Nakamuara.
11. Superior Petty Officer Ichiro Tanaka.
13. 1st Class Petty Officer Hirokazu Maruo.
15. 1st Class Petty Officer Takao Musashi.
17, 694. 1st Class Petty Officer Tadayoshi Ishimoto.
27, 775. Probational Officer Toshio Taniguchi.
603. Lt (jg) Takahiko Hanada.
650. Leading Pvt. Masakiyo Kato.
727. Sgt. Jyuro Saito.
749. Cpl. Nobuo Hayashi.

Preliminary Interrogation Report: Seaman 1st Class Ryusuki Hirao.
Preliminary Interrogation Report: Chief Petty Officer Yoshio Yamamura.
Preliminary Interrogation Report: 2nd Class Petty Officer Ichiro Ashiki.
Preliminary Interrogation Report: Leading Seaman Takao Mae.

Enemy Publications
No. 391. Data on Navy Airplanes and Bombs.
No. 405. Antitank Combat Reference.

Research Reports
No. 76. Self-Immolation as a Factor in Japanese Military Psychology.
No. 125. Liaison Boat Units.
Spot Report No. 193.
Spot Report No. 195.

THE TAILHOOK ASSOCIATION

Allowances and Location of Naval Aircraft 1943–1945.
Navy Individual Squadron Histories for VF-9, 10, 17, 23, and 90(N).

UNITED STATES ARMY MILITARY HISTORY INSTITUTE, CARLISLE, PENNSYLVANIA

Allied Translator and Interpreter Section South West Pacific Area A.T.I.S. Publication. *Japanese Military Conventional Signs and Abbreviations*. 4 March 1943.
CinCPac-CinCPOA Bulletin 120-45. *Symbols and Abbreviations for Army Air Units.* 21 May 1945.
Commander in Chief Navy Department. *CominCh P-0011 Anti-Suicide Action Summary.* 31 August 1945.
Commander in Chief United States Fleet. *Antiaircraft Action Summary Suicide Attacks.* April 1945.
General Headquarters, Far East Command Military Intelligence Section, Historical Division. *Interrogations of Japanese Officials on World War II (English Translations) Vol. I & II.* 1949.
_____. *Statements of Japanese Officials on World War II (English Translations).* Vols. 1–4. 1949–1950.
Headquarters Far East Command Military History Section. *Imperial General Headquarters Navy Directives.* Volume II, Directives No. 316–No. 540 (15 Jan 44–26 Aug 45) Special Directives No. 1–No. 3 (2 Sep 45–12 Sep 45).
_____. *Imperial General Headquarters Navy Orders.* Orders No. 1–No. 57 (5 Nov. 41–2 Sep 45).
Joint Intelligence Study Publishing Board. *Air Facilities Supplement to JANIS 86 Nansei Shoto (Ryukyu Islands).* May 1945.
Trabue, Lt. Col. William. G.S.C. *Observers Report The Okinawa Operation (8 February 1945 to 2 June 1945).* Headquarters United States Army Forces Pacific Ocean Areas G-5. 15 June 1945.

UNITED STATES NAVY HISTORY AND HERITAGE COMMAND, WASHINGTON, D.C.

Naval Foundation Oral History Program. "War in the Pacific: Actions in the Philippines including Leyte Gulf, as well as the battles of Iwo Jima and Okinawa, 1943–45." Recollections of Sonarman 1st Class Jack Gebhardt, *USS Pringle DD 477.* Ed. Senior Chief Yeoman (YNCS) George Tusa. 7 November 2000.

Operational Archives Branch—*L. Richard Rhame Collection—Papers of the National Association of USS LCS(L)(3) 1–130,* 1940s.
Assorted documents and personal memoirs. Individual Ship Histories for LCS(L)s.

Interviews, Correspondence, Personal Papers, Diaries

Ball, Donald L. *LCS(L) 85.* Interview. 18 September 2002.
Barkley, John. L. *USS Rowe DD 564* E-Mails 25, 26 November 2002.
Barnby, Frank. *LCS(L) 13.* Collected papers and photographs.
Baumler, Raymond. *LCS 14.* Letter of 4 March 2003.
Blanton, Earl. *LCS(L) 118.* Interview. 19 September 2002.
Bell, Dean. *LCS(L) 26.* Interview 11 August 2007.
Bennett, Otis Wayne. 333rd Fighter Squadron. Interview. 8 October 2002.
Bletso, William E. Radioman *USS Gregory.* Diary, correspondence, November 2008.
Blyth, Robert. *LCS(L) 61.* Interview. 25 August 1995.
Burgess, Harold H. *LCS(L) 61.* Interview. 25 August 1995.
Cardwell, John H. *LCS(L) 61.* Collected papers.
Christman, William R. *LCS(L) 95.* Letter of 9 April 2003.
Davis, Franklin M., Sr. *LCS(L) 61.* Interview. 25 August 1995.
Davis, George E. *USS Pakana ATF 108.* E-mail of 6 April 2003.
Dean, Mel. *USS Lough DE 586.* Interview. 26 August 2009.
Diary of Philip J. Schneider Signalman 1st Class USS Boyd.
Dworzak, W. A. Bud. VMF-441. Interview. 21 July 2003.
Fenoglio, Melvin. *USS Little* Interview. 3 September 2003.
Gauthier, David. *USS Knapp.* E-mails to the author, 22 December 2000, 16, 19 March 2001.
Griffis, Earl O. *PC 1129.* Interview. 21 October 2009.
Haddock, Claude. *LCS(L)(3) 49.* Interview. 24 July 2008.
Hoffman, Edwin Jr. *USS Emmons* e-mails 23, 24 December 2003, 30 January 2004.
Howell, Linda. Letter to Ray Baumler March 27, 1992.
Huber, John. *USS Cogswell DD 651.* Personal Diary. 1944–45.
Hudson, Hugh. LSM-49, LSM 467. Collected papers and Photographs.
Katz, Lawrence S. *LCS(L) 61.* Diary, Interview. 25 August 1995.

Kaup, Harold. *LCS(L) 15*. Interview. 29 September 1996.
Kelley, James. W. Commanding Officer *LCS(L) 61*. Interview. 18 December 1995.
Kennedy, Doyle. *USS Little*. Interview. 3 September 2003.
Landis, Robert W. *LSM(R) 192*. Interview. 14 February 2002.
Leitch, Richard. *Hyman DD 732*. Letter of 2 January 2009.
Mahakiam, Carl. Marine Air Warning Squadron 8. Interview 9 September 2009.
McCool, Richard M. Capt. USN (Ret). CO *USS LCS(L) 122*. Interview 21 May 1997, Letter to the author with narrative of 23 May 1997.
Moulton, Franklin. *LCS(L) 25*. Collected papers and photographs.
Okazaki, Teruyuki. Interviews. 6 September 2003, 2 February 2009.
Pederson, Marvin letter to the editor of LCS Assn. newsletter undated.
Perdeck, Albert. *USS Bunker Hill CV 17*. Interview 13 August 2009.
Peterson, Phillip E. *LCS(L) 23*. Collected papers and photographs.
Portolan, Harry. *LCS(L)(3) 38*. Interview 25 July 2008.
Rielly, Robert F. *LCS(L) 61*. Interview of 20 September 2001.
Robinson, Ed. Letter to Lester O. Willard. 10 January 1991.
Rooney, John. *Sailor*. (Interview with Julian Becton, CO of *Laffey*.)
Russell, L. R. *LSM(R) 191*. Letters of 18 July, 22 July 2003.
Selfridge, Allen. *LCS(L) 67*. Collected papers and photographs.
Sellis, Mark. Executive Officer *LCS(L) 61*. Interview. 25 August 1995.
Spargo, Tom. *USS Cogswell DD 651*. E-mails to the author, 15 April, 21 May 2001.
Sprague, Robert. *LCS(L) 38*. Letter of 29 September 2002.
Staigar, Joseph. *LCS(L) 61*. Interview. 14 July, 1995.
Tolmas, Harold. *LCS 54*. Letter of 5 December 2002.
Wiram, Gordon H. *LCS(L) 64* letter to Ray Baumler, 13 April 1991.
Wisner, Robert. *LCS 37* Interview 15 August 2001.

Books, Official Histories and Unpublished Histories

Adams, Andrew, ed. *The Cherry Blossom Squadrons: Born to Die*. By the Hagoromo Society of Kamikaze Divine Thunderbolt Corps Survivors. Intro. by Andrew Adams. Edited and supplemented by Andrew Adams. Translation by Nobuo Asahi and the Japan Technical Company. Los Angeles: Ohara Publications, 1973.
Andrews, Lewis M., Jr., et al. *Tempest, Fire and Foe: Destroyer Escorts in World War II and the Men Who Manned Them*. Vancouver, B.C.: Trafford Publishing, 2004.
Astor, Gerald. *Operation Iceberg: The Invasion and Conquest of Okinawa in World War II*. New York: Donald I. Fine, Inc., 1995.
Axell, Albert, and Hideaki Kase. *Kamikaze: Japan's Suicide Gods*. London: Pearson Education, 2002.
Ball, Donald L. *Fighting Amphibs: The LCS(L) in World War II*. Williamsburg, VA: Mill Neck Publications, 1997.
Becton, F. Julian. *The Ship That Would Not Die*. Missoula, Montana: Pictorial Histories Publishing Company, 1980.
Billingsley, RAdm. USN Edward Baxter (Ret.). *The Emmons Saga*. Winston-Salem, NC: USS Emmons Association, 1989.
Blanton, Earl. *Boston to Jacksonville (41,000 Miles by Sea)*. Seaford, VA: Goose Creek Publications, 1991.
Boyd, Carl, and Akihiko Yoshida. *The Japanese Submarine Force and World War II*. Annapolis: Naval Institute Press, 2002.
Brader, Pharmacists Mate Charles, *LCS(L) 65*. *LCS Men in a Spectacular Part of Okinawa Campaign*. Typescript, undated.
Browning, Robert M., Jr. *U.S. Merchant Vessel War Casualties of World War II*. Annapolis: Naval Institute Press, 1996.
Bulkley, Robert J., Jr. *At Close Quarters: PT Boats in the United States Navy*. Annapolis: Naval Institute Press, 2003.
Bush, Maj. James E., et al. *Corregidor—February 1945*. Fort Leavenworth, Kansas. Typescript, 1983.
Calhoun, C. Raymond. *Tin Can Sailor: Life Aboard the USS Sterett, 1939–1945*. Annapolis: United States Naval Institute, 1993.
Causemaker, GM 3/c Richard, *LCS 84*. *Duty with the LCS(L)(3) 84*. Typescript, undated.
Chickering, Lt. CO H. D., *LCS(L) 51*. *World War II*. Typescript, undated.
Committee on Veterans Affairs, U.S. Senate, Medal of Honor Recipients: 1863–1973. Washington, D.C.: Government Printing Office, 1973.
Conway, Paul L. *A Fiery Sunday Morning*. Warren, PA: Paul L. Conway, 2002. (Unpublished typescript).
Cook, Haruko Taya, and Theodore F. Cook. *Japan at War: An Oral History*. New York: The New Press, 1992.
Costello, John. *The Pacific War 1941–1945*. New York: Atlantic Communications, Inc., 1981.
Craig, William. *The Fall of Japan*. New York: The Dial Press, 1967.
Craven, Wesley Frank, and James Lea Cate, eds. U.S. Air Force, USAF Historical Division. *The Army Air Forces in World War II, Vol. 5, The Pacific: Matterhorn to Nagasaki, June 1944 to August 1945*. Chicago: University of Chicago Press, 1953.
Fergusen, S. W., and William K. Pascalis. *Protect & Avenge: The 49th Fighter Group in World War II*. Atglen, PA: Schiffer Publishing Ltd, 1996.
Foster, Simon. *Okinawa 1945: Final Assault on the Empire*. London: Arms and Armour Press, 1994.
Francillon, Rene J. *Japanese Aircraft of the Pacific War*. Annapolis: Naval Institute Press, 1979.
Frank, Benis M. *Okinawa: The Great Island Battle*. New York: Talisman/Parrish Books, Inc., 1978.

Frank, Benis M., and Henry I. Shaw, Jr. *Victory and Occupation: History of U. S. Marine Corps Operations in World War II Vol. V.* Historical Branch, G-3 Division, Headquarters, U. S. Marine Corps. Washington: U. S. Government Printing Office, 1968.

Frank, Richard B. *Downfall: The End of the Imperial Japanese Empire.* New York: Penguin Books, 2001.

General Staff, Supreme Commander for the Allied Powers. *Reports of General MacArthur. Japanese Operations in the Southwest Pacific Area Vol. II — Parts 1 & II.* Facsimile Reprint, 1994.

_____. *Reports of General MacArthur. MacArthur in Japan: The Occupation: Military Phase Volume I Supplement.* Facsimile Reprint, 1994.

_____. *Reports of General MacArthur. The Campaigns of MacArthur in the Pacific Volume I.* Facsimile Reprint, 1994.

Gibney, Frank B., ed. *The Japanese Remember the Pacific War.* Armonk, New York: An Eastgate Book, 1995.

Grover, David. H. *U.S. Army Ships and Watercraft of World War II.* Annapolis: Naval Institute Press, 1987.

Halsey, Fleet Admiral William F., and Lieutenant Commander J. Bryan III. *Admiral Halsey's Story.* New York: McGraw-Hill Book Company, Inc., 1947.

Hata, Ikuhiko, and Yasuho Izawa. *Japanese Naval Aces and Fighter Units in World War II.* Trans. Don Cyril Gorham. Annapolis: Naval Institute Press, 1989.

Hata, Ikuhiko, Yasuho Izawa, and Christopher Shores. *Japanese Army Air Force Fighter Units and Their Aces 1931–1945.* London: Grub Street, 2002.

Haughland, Vern. *The AAF against Japan.* New York: Harper & Brothers Publishers, 1948.

Heath, Robert F. *With the Black Cat USS LCI Flotilla 13.* Chico, CA: The Technical Education Press, 2003.

Hess, William N. *49th Fighter Group Aces of the Pacific.* New York: Osprey Publishing Ltd., 2004.

Hurst, G. Cameron III. *Armed Martial Arts of Japan Swordsmanship and Archery.* New Haven: Yale University Press, 1998.

Ienaga, Saburo. *The Pacific War, 1931–1945: A Critical Perspective on Japan's Role in World War II.* New York: Pantheon Books, 1978.

Ike, Nobutaka. "War and Modernization," in *Political Development in Modern Japan.* Robert E. Ward, ed. Princeton: Princeton University Press, 1968. pp. 189–211.

Imamura, Shigeo. *Shig: The True Story of An American Kamikaze.* Baltimore: American Library Press, Inc., 2001.

Inoguchi, Rikihei. *The Divine Wind: Japan's Kamikaze Force in World War II.* New York: Bantam Books, 1958.

Iritani, Toshio. *Group Psychology of the Japanese in Wartime.* New York: Kegan Paul International, 1991.

The Japanese Air Forces in World War II: The Organization of the Japanese Army & Naval Air Forces, 1945. New York: Hippocrene Books, Inc., 1979.

Kaigo, Tokiomi. *Japanese Education; Its Past and Present.* Tokyo: Kokusai Bunka Shinkokai, 1968.

Karig, Capt. Walter, Lt. Cmdr. Russell L. Harris, Lt. Cmdr. Frank A. Manson. *Battle Report: The End of an Empire.* New York: Rinehart and Company, Inc., 1948.

_____. *Battle Report: Victory in the Pacific.* New York: Rinehart and Company, Inc., 1949.

Kaup, RM3/c Harold J., *LCS(L) 15. The Death of a Ship.* Typescript, Undated.

Keenleyside, Hugh L. *History of Japanese Education and Present Educational System.* Ann Arbor: Michigan University Press, 1970.

Kemp, Paul. *Underwater Warriors.* Annapolis: Naval Institute Press, 1996.

Kennedy, Maxwell Taylor. *Danger's Hour: The Story of the USS Bunker Hill and the Kamikaze Pilot Who Crippled Her.* New York: Simon & Schuster, 2008.

King, Ernest J. *U.S. Navy at War 1941–1945.* Washington: United States Navy Department, 1946.

Knight, Rex A. *Riding on Luck: The Saga of the USS Lang (DD-399).* Central Point, Oregon: Hellgate Press, 2001.

Kuwahara, Yasuo, and Gordon T. Allred. *Kamikaze.* New York: Ballantine Books, 1957.

Larteguy, Jean, ed. *The Sun Goes Down: Last Letters from Japanese Suicide-Pilots and Soldiers.* London: William Kimber, 1956.

Lory, Hillis. *Japan's Military Masters: The Army in Japanese Life.* New York: The Viking Press, 1943.

Mair, Michael. *Oil, Fire, and Fate.* Platteville, Wisconsin: SMJ Publishing, 2008.

Martin, Signalman Arthur R. *History of the U.S.S. LCS 88.* Typescript, Undated.

Mason, William. *U.S.S. LCS(L)(3) 86: The Mighty Midget.* San Francisco: By the author, 1993.

Meister, Lt. Cmdr. USNR Harry G. (Ret.). *USS LCS(L) 3-27: A WWII Amphibious Landing Craft Support Vessel.* Vancouver, Washington: Harry & Gene Meister, 2002.

Miller, Edward S. *War Plan Orange: The U.S. Strategy to Defeat Japan, 1897–1945.* Annapolis: Naval Institute Press, 1991.

Millot, Bernard. *Divine Thunder: The Life & Death of the Kamikazes.* Trans. Lowell Bair. New York: The McCall Publishing Company, 1971.

Mission Accomplished: Interrogations of Japanese Industrial, Military, and Civil Leaders of World War II. Washington, D.C.: Government Printing Office, 1946.

Monsarrat, John. *Angel on the Yardarm: The Beginnings of Fleet Radar Defense and the Kamikaze Threat.* Newport, Rhode Island: Naval War College Press, 1985.

Mooney, James A., ed. *Dictionary of American Naval Fighting Ships* (9 Vols.). Washington, D.C.: Naval History Center, 1959–1981.

Morison, Samuel Eliot. *History of United States Naval Operations in World War II, Volume VI: Breaking the Bismarck's Barrier 22 July 1942–1 May 1944.* Boston: Little, Brown and Company, 1950.

_____. *History of United States Naval Operations in World War II, Volume VII: Aleutians, Gilberts and*

Marshalls June 1942–April 1944. Boston: Little, Brown and Company, 1951.

_____. *History of United States Naval Operations in World War II, Volume VIII: New Guinea and the Marianas March 1944-August 1944.* Boston: Little, Brown and Company, 1984.

_____. *History of United States Naval Operations in World War II, Volume XII: Leyte June 1944–January 1945.* Boston: Little, Brown and Company, 1958.

_____. *History of United States Naval Operations in World War II, Volume XIII: The Liberation of the Philippines, Luzon, Mindanao, the Visayas 1944–1945.* Boston: Little, Brown and Company, 1968.

_____. *History of United States Naval Operations in World War II, Volume XIV: Victory in the Pacific 1945.* Boston: Little, Brown and Company, 1968.

Morris, John. *Traveller from Tokyo.* London: The Book Club, 1945.

Morse, Philip M., and George E. Kimball. *Methods of Operations Research.* First Edition Revised. Cambridge, Massachusetts: The M. I. T. Press, 1970.

Nagatsuka, Ryuji. *I Was a Kamikaze: The Knights of the Divine Wind.* Trans. Nina Rootes. New York: Macmillan, 1973.

Naito, Hatsusho. *Thunder Gods: The Kamikaze Pilots Tell Their Story.* Tokyo: Kodansha International, 1989.

Navy Department Communiques 601–624 May 25, 1945 to August 30, 1945 and Pacific Fleet Communiques 373 to 471. Washington: United States Government Printing Office, 1946.

Nihon Senbotsu Gakusei Kinen-Kai (Japan Memorial Society for the Students Killed in the War-Wadatsumi Society). *Listen to the Voices from the Sea (Kike Wadatsumi no Koe).* Trans. Midori Yamanouchi and Joseph L. Quinn. Scranton: The University of Scranton Press, 2000.

Nitobe, Inazo. *Bushido: The Soul of Japan.* Tokyo: Charles E. Tuttle Company, 1969.

Norman, E. Herbert. *Soldier and Peasant in Japan: The Origins of Conscription.* Vancouver: University of British Columbia, 1965.

Ohnuki-Tierney, Emiko. *Kamikaze, Cherry Blossoms, and Nationalisms: The Militarization of Aesthetics in Japanese History.* Chicago: University of Chicago Press, 2002.

_____. *Kamikaze Diaries: Reflections of Japanese Student Soldiers.* Chicago: University of Chicago Press, 2006.

Osterland, Lt. Cmdr. Frank C. *Dolly Three.* Typescript, August 28, 1993.

Prados, John. *Combined Fleet Decoded The Secret History of American Intelligence and the Japanese Navy in World War II.* Annapolis: Naval Institute Press, 1995.

Prunty, GM 1/c Jonathan G. *My Days in the U.S. Navy 1944 to 1946.* Typescript, December, 1998.

Rielly, Robin L. *Kamikazes, Corsairs, and Picket Ships: Okinawa 1945.* Philadelphia: Casemate Publishers, Inc, 2008.

_____. *Mighty Midgets at War: The Saga of the LCS(L) Ships from Iwo Jima to Vietnam.* Central Point, Oregon: Hellgate Press, 2000.

Rooney, John. *Mighty Midget: U.S.S. LCS 82.* Pennsylvania: By the author, 1990.

Roscoe, Theodore. *United States Destroyer Operations in WWII.* Annapolis: Naval Institute Press, 1953.

Safier, Joshua. *Yasukini Shrine and the Constraints on the Discourses of Nationalism in Twentieth-Century Japan.* Dissertation.com, 1997.

Sakai, Saburo, with Martin Caidin and Fred Saito. *Samurai!* New York: ibooks, Inc. 2001.

Sakaida, Henry. *Imperial Japanese Army Air Force Aces 1937–45.* Oxford: Osprey Publishing Limited, 1997.

_____. *Imperial Japanese Navy Aces 1937–45.* Oxford: Osprey Publishing Limited, 1999.

Sakaida, Henry, and Koji Tanaka. *Genda's Blade: Japan's Squadron of Aces 343 Kokutai.* Surrey, England: Classic Publications, 2003.

Sherrod, Robert. *History of Marine Corps Aviation in World War II.* Washington: Combat Forces Press, 1952.

Smethurst, Richard J. *A Social Basis for Prewar Japanese Militarism: The Army and the Rural Community.* Berkeley: The University of California Press, 1974.

Stanaway, John. *475th Fighter Group.* New York: Osprey Publishing Limited, 2007.

_____. *P-38 Lightning Aces of the Pacific and CBI.* London: Osprey Publishing Limited, 1997.

_____. *Possum, Clover & Hades: The 475th Fighter Group in World War II.* Atglen, PA: Schiffer Publishing Ltd., 1993.

Stanley, W.H. *Kamikaze: The Battle for Okinawa, Big War of the Little Ships.* By the author, 1988.

Staton, Michael. *The Fighting Bob: A Wartime History of the USS Robley D. Evans (DD-552).* Bennington, VT: Merriam Press, 2001.

Stewart, CO James M. *LSM(R) 189 Autobiography.* Typescript, Undated.

Stille, Mark. *Imperial Japanese Navy Submarines 1941–1945.* New York: Osprey Publishing Ltd., 2007.

Stone, Robert P. *USS LCS(L)(3) 20: A Mighty Midget.* By the author, 2002.

Sumrall, Robert F. *Sumner-Gearing Class Destroyers: Their Design, Weapons, and Equipment.* Annapolis: Naval Institute Press, 1995.

Surels, Ron. *DD 522: Diary of a Destroyer.* Plymouth, NH: Valley Graphics, Inc., 1996.

Tagaya, Osamu. *Imperial Japanese Naval Aviator 1937–45.* Oxford: Osprey Publishing, 1988.

_____. *Mitsubishi Type 1 Rikko Betty Units of World War 2.* Oxford: Osprey Publishing, 2001.

Thomas, Charles. *Dolly Five: A Memoir of the Pacific War.* Chester, VA: Harrowgate Press, 1996.

Timenes, Nicolai, Jr. *An Analytical History of Kamikaze Attacks against Ships of the United States Navy During World War II.* Arlington, VA: Center for Naval Analyses, Operations Evaluation Group, 1970.

_____. *Defense Against Kamikaze Attacks in World War II and Its Relevance to Anti-Ship Missile Defense.* Arlington, VA: Center for Naval Analyses, Operations Evaluation Group, 1970.

Treadwell, Theodore R. *Splinter Fleet: The Wooden Subchasers of World War II*. Annapolis: Naval Institute Press, 2000.

Ugaki, VAdm. Matome. *Fading Victory: The Diary of Admiral Matome Ugaki 1941–1945*. Trans. Masataka Chihaya. Pittsburgh: University of Pittsburgh Press, 1991.

The United States Strategic Bombing Survey Naval Analysis Division. *Air Campaigns of the Pacific War* (Washington, D.C.: U.S. Government Printing Office, 1947).

_____. *The Campaigns of the Pacific War* (Washington, D.C.: U.S. Government Printing Office, 1946).

_____. *The Fifth Air Force in the War Against Japan*. (Washington, D.C.: U.S. Government Printing Office, 1947).

_____. *Interrogations of Japanese Officials Volume I* (Washington, D.C.: U.S. Government Printing Office, 1945).

_____. *Interrogations of Japanese Officials Volume II* (Washington, D.C.: U.S. Government Printing Office, 1945).

_____. *Japanese Air Power* (Washington, D.C.: U.S. Government Printing Office, 1946).

_____. *The Seventh and Eleventh Air Forces in the War Against Japan* (Washington, D.C.: U.S. Government Printing Office, 1947).

_____. *Summary Report (Pacific War)* (Washington, D.C.: U.S. Government Printing Office, 1946).

Veigele, William J. *PC Patrol Craft of World War II*. Santa Barbara, CA: Astral Publishing Co., 1998.

War Department. *Handbook on Japanese Military Forces: War Department Technical Manual TM-E30-480 October 1944–September 1945*. 1 October 1944.

Warner, Denis, and Peggy Warner with Commander Sadao Seno. *The Sacred Warriors: Japan's Suicide Legions*. New York: Van Nostrand Reinhold Company, 1982.

Wilson, William Scott, translator. *Budoshoshinshu: The Warrior's Primer of Daidoji Yuzan*. Burbank, California: Ohara Publications, Inc., 1984.

_____. *The Ideals of the Samurai Writings of Japanese Warriors*. Burbank, California: Ohara Publications, Inc., 1982.

Yamamoto, Tsunetomo. *Hagakure: The Book of the Samurai*. Trans. William Scott Wilson. Tokyo: Kodansha International Ltd., 1979.

YBlood, William T. *The Little Giants: U.S. Escort Carriers Against Japan*. Annapolis: U.S. Naval Institute Press, 1987.

Yokota, Yutaka, with Joseph D. Harrington. *Suicide Submarine!* New York: Ballantine Books, 1961.

Articles

Coox, Alvin D. "The Rise and Fall of the Imperial Japanese Air Forces." *Air Power and Warfare Proceedings of the Eighth History Symposium USAF Academy* (1978): 84–97.

Fukuya, Hajime. "Three Japanese Submarine Developments." *United States Naval Institute Proceedings*. Annapolis: United States Naval Institute (August 1952), pp. 863–867.

Hackett, Roger F. "The Military—Japan." In *Political Modernization in Japan and Turkey*, edited by Robert E. Ward and Dankwart A. Rustow, pp. 328–351. Princeton: Princeton University Press, 1964.

Hattori, Shogo. "Kamikaze: Japan's Glorious Failure." *Air Power History*. Volume 43, Number 1 (Spring 1996): pp. 14–27.

Henry, John R. "Out Stares Jap Pilot After Ammo Runs Out." *Honolulu Advertiser*, April 27, 1945.

Ike, Nobutaka. "War and Modernization." In *Political Development in Modern Japan*, edited by Robert E. Ward, pp. 189–211. Princeton: Princeton University Press, 1968.

Inoguchi, Captain Rikihei, and Commander Tadashi Nakajima. "The Kamikaze Attack Corps." In *United States Naval Institute Proceedings*. Annapolis, MD: United States Naval Institute (September 1953): pp. 993–945.

Kawai, Lieutenant Colonel Masahiro. *The Operations of the Suicide-Boat Regiment in Okinawa: Their Battle Result and the Countermeasures Taken by the U.S. Forces*. National Institute for Defense Studies, undated.

McCurry, Justin. "We Were Ready to Die for Japan.": *Guardian* (Manchester, UK), 28 February 2006. Online at www.guardian.co/uk/world/2006/feb/28/world dispatch.secondworldwar.

Nagai, Michio. "Westernization and Japanization: The Early Meiji Transformation of Education." In *Tradition and Modernization in Japanese Culture*, edited by Donald H. Shively, pp. 35–76. Princeton: Princeton University Press, 1971.

Rooney, John. "Sailor." *Naval Institute Proceedings* (Unpublished Article). Rooney's interview of Rear Admiral F. Julian Becton, conducted in Wynewood, PA, Fall 1992.

Scott, J. Davis. "No Hiding Place—Off Okinawa," *US Naval Institute Proceedings* (Nov. 1957): pp. 208–13.

Suzuki, Yukihisa. "Autobiography of a Kamikaze Pilot." *Blue Book Magazine*, Vol. 94, No. 2 (December 1951): pp. 92–107; Vol. 93, No. 3 (January 1952): pp. 88–100; Vol. 93, No. 4 (February 1952).

Torisu, Kennosuke, assisted by Masataka Chlihaya. "Japanese Submarine Tactics." *United States Naval Institute Proceedings*. Annapolis: United States Naval Institute (February 1961): pp. 78–83.

Trefalt, Beatrice. "War, Commemoration and National Identity in Modern Japan, 1868–1975." In *Nation and Nationalism in Japan*, edited by Sandra Wilson, pp. 115–134. London: RoutledgeCurzon, 2002.

Turner, Adm. Richmond K. "Kamikaze." *United States Naval Institute Proceedings*. Annapolis: United States Naval Institute (March 1947): pp. 329–331.

Vogel, Bertram. "Who Were the Kamikaze?" *United States Naval Institute Proceedings*. Annapolis: United States Naval Institute (July 1947): 833–837.

Wehrmeister, Lt. (jg) R. L. "Divine Wind Over Okinawa." *United States Naval Institute Proceedings*. Annapolis: United States Naval Institute (June 1957): 632–641.

Yokoi, RAdm.Toshiyuki. "Kamikazes and the Okinawa Campaign." *United States Naval Institute Proceedings*. Annapolis: United States Naval Institute (May 1954): 504–513.

Yokota, Yutaka, and Joseph D. Harrington. "Kaiten ... Japan's Human Torpedoes." *United States Naval Institute Proceedings*. Annapolis: United States Naval Institute (January 1962): 54–68.

Web Sites

Web sites listed were active at the time of the author's research.

USS *Aaron Ward DM 34*, http://www.ussaaronward.com/.

USS *Alfred A. Cunningham DD 752*, http://home.infini.net/~eeg3413/index.htm.

All Japan Kaiten Pilot's Association, http://www2s.biglobe.ne.in/~kyasuto/kaiten/album-kikusui.htm.

USS *Arikara ATF*, http://ussarikara.com.

USS *Boyd DD 544*, http://www.destroyers.org/DD544-Site/DD544.htm.

USS *Braine DD 630*, http://www.ussbrainedd630.com/witnes.htm.

USS *Bush DD*, http://www.ussbush.com.

USS *Callaghan DD 792*, http://www.destroyers.org/DD792-Site/index.htm.

USS *Cogswell DD 651*, USS-Cogswell@destroyers.org.

USS *Evans DD 552*, http://www.ussevans.org.

The 503rd P.R.C.T. Heritage Battalion Online, http://corregidor.org.

USS *Freemont APA 44*, USSFreemont.org/index.html.

Haze Gray and Underway, http://www.hazegray.org.

USS *Little DD 803*, http://skyways.lib.ks.us/history.dd803/info/picket.html.

USS *Macomb DMS 23*, http://www.destroyers.org/bensonlivermore/ussmacomb.html.

USS *Mississinewa AO*, http://USSMississinewa.com/B.

National Association of Fleet Tug Sailors, http://www.nafts.com.

NavSource, http://www.NavSource.org.

USS *Purdy DD 734*, http://www.destroyers.org/uss-purdy/.

Tin Can Sailors, http://www.destroyers.org.

USS *Underhill DE682*, www.ussunderhill.org.

U.S. Merchant Marine, http://usmm.org.

Index

Numbers in **_bold italics_** indicate pages with illustrations.

Aaron Ward DM 34 27, 250, 254–255, 256, 323
Abbot DD 629 297
Abdill, Capt. Everett W. 146
Abercrombie DE 343 118
Abner Read DD 526 125, 318, 321
Achernar AKA 53 208
Achilles ARL 41 131
Adachi, Capt. Mutsuo 88, 227
Adams DM 27 206, 321
Adelman, Ens. William 144
AGM 305 263
Aguni Shima 233
Ailes, Cmdr. J. W. III 297
Airbases, American: Kadena 227, 265; Yontan 227, 264, 267, 282; *see also* Airbases, Japan
Airbases, Japan: Akino 45; Amakasa 194; Amami-O-Shima 195; Atsugi 52; Bansei 197; Chiran 23, 26, 53, 194, 197; Fukuoka **_189_**, 194, 197; Gifu 53; Hachijo-Jima 188; Hakata 193, 194; Hamamatsu 45, 188; Hiro 51; Hokoba 45; Hotoyoshi 193; Hyakurigahara 31, 49; Ibusuki 193, 194; Iwakawa 193; Iwaki 188; Izuki 194; Izumi 34, 193, 194; Kadena 188, 208; Kagohara 52; Kagoshima 193, 194; Kanoya 34, 35, 37, 50, 52, 62, **_67_**, 188, **_189_**, 192, 193, 194, 231; Karesahara 53, 197; Kasanohara 193, 194; Kasumigaura 194, 199; Katori 178; Kikaiga-Shima **_193_**, 195, 197; Kikuchi 194; Kisaratsu 194; Koichi 188; Kokubu 193, 194; Komatsu 37, 194; Konoike 34; Kumamoto 194, 197; Kumanosho 194, 197; Kushira 193, 194, 223; Matsuyama West 37, 194; Mie 49; Miho 194; Miyakonojo 34, 193, 194, 197; Miyakonojo East 188; Miyazaki 193, 194, 264; Nagoya, 49; Nara 93; Niijima 188; Nittagahara 188, **_189_**, 194, 197; Oita 34, 50, 67, 188, 193, 194; Omura 67, 193, 194; Oshima 188; Otsu **_306_**; Ozuki 52; Saishu-To 188; Saeki 194; Tachiarai 67, 188, 194, 197; Takume 194; Tanegashima 188; Togani 188; Tokuno Shima 195, 197, 208; Tomitaka 34, 194; Tsuchiura 93; Tsuiki 193; Usa 34, 193, 194; Yabuki 188; Yokoshiba 188; Yonatan 188; *see also* Airbases, American
Airbases, Korea: Gunzan (Genzan) 188, 194, 195, 197; Keijo 188, 189, 195, 197
Airbases, Philippines: Cebu 26; Mabalacat 29, 45, 46, 118, 156, 168; Manila 45; Nichols 42, 162; Tuguegarao 163
Airbases, Taiwan: Choshu 194; Ensui 194, 197; Giran 191, 194, 197; Hachikai 194; Heito 194; Kagi 194, 197; Karenko 194, 275; Kobi 191; Mato 194; Matsuyama (Taipei) 191, 194, 197, 211; Ryutan 194; Shinchiku 176, 191, 194; Shoka 194; Taichu 176, 191, 194, 197; Tainan 176, 191; Takao 115, 191, 194; Tansui 194, 197; Toen 194
Aircraft Armament 56
Aircraft Units, Japanese Army: 5th Air Army 189, 194, 195; 6th Air Army 197; 6th Air Brigade 197; 7th Air Regiment 188; 8th Air Division 189, 194; 8th Fighter Brigade 195; 16th Fighter Regiment 195; 20th *Shimbu* Unit 195, 197; 21st Air Brigade 306; 21st *Shimbu* Unit 195; 23rd *Shimbu* Unit 195; 51st Training Flying Division 53; 59th Air Regiment 197; 65th Air Regiment 197; 66th Air Regiment 197, 208; 90th Fighter Regiment 195; 98th Air Regiment 188; 101st Air Brigade 197; 102nd Air Brigade 197; 103 Air Regiment 197, 208; 105th Air Regiment 211; 105th Fighter Flying Unit 26; *Fugaku* Special Attack Unit 138
Aircraft Units, Japanese Navy: 1st Air Fleet 45, 51, 176, 189, 191, 223; 1st Attack Flying Unit 49; 1st Cherry Blossom Unit 34; 1st *Shimpu* Special Attack Unit 138; 3rd Air Fleet 67, 189, 191, 192; 3rd Cherry Blossom Squadron 31; 5th Air Fleet 67, 189, 191, 192; 10th Air Fleet 47, 67, 69, 189, 191, 192; 26th Air Flotilla 45; 30th Flying Group 26; 201st Air Group 45, 118, 168; 293rd Naval Air Unit 42; 405th *Kokutai* 29; 601st Air Group 178; 701st Air Group 264, 300; 721st Naval Air Corps (*Jinrai Butai*) 30, 31, 34, **_35_**; 722 Naval Air Corps (*Tatsumaki Butai*) 16, 25, 27, 34, 37; *Azusa* Special Attack Unit 185; *Niitaka* Unit 176; *Shinpui* Special Attack Unit 18, 25, 46; Showa Special Attack Unit 25
Aka Jima 87
Akagi 42
Akamatsu, Capt. Yoshitsugu 88
Akeno Army Flight School 45
Alabama BB 60 297
Alcoa Pioneer 131, 132, 318
Alexander Majors 128, 130, 318
Allen M. Sumner DD 692 159, 319
Allied Land Forces S.E.A. Weekly Intelligence Review 103
Alpine APA 92 131, 205–206, 318, 321
AM 232 217
Amami-O-Shima 193, 194
Ammen DD 527 125, 250, 279, 284, 291, 318
Amphibious Group 8 169
Anami, Gen. Korechika 45
Anderson DD 411 125, 170, 318
Anderson, Master Nels F. 145
Anthony DD 515 66, 278, 283, 290, 324
Anti-Tank Combat Reference 101
Anti-tank tactics *see* suicide soldier
Anzio CVE 57 178, 223
Apache ATF 67 158, 319
Arakawa, Flight PO1c Masahiro 295

Index

Araki, Haruo 23
Archer, Cmdr. Robert J. 265
Archerfish SS 311 34
Ariga, Capt. Kosaku 220
Arikara ATF 98 213, 267
Arima, RAdm. Masafumi 45
Armed Guard *126*, 129, 132, 152, 167, 218, 219
Army Air Academy (Japan) 26
Army Air Force Units (US): 9th Fighter Squadron 111; 36th Fighter Squadron 141; 49th Fighter Group 111; 305th Airdrome Squadron 111; 421st Night Fighter Squadron 111; 475th Fighter Group 111, 114
Army FS 225 173, 323
Army FS 309 320
Army Ground Units (US): 19th Regimental Combat Team 152; 24th Division 152; 77th Division 132, 138, 192, 208, 209; 305th Regimental Combat Team 209; 536th Amphibious Tractor Battalion 144; 718th Amphibious Tractor Battalion 144
The Army-Navy Joint Central Agreement on Air Operations 48
Arnow, Lt. (jg) Theodore 210
ARS 73 294
Arunta H.M.A.S. 125, 156
Asashimo 220
ATA 124 294
ATR 114 267
ATR 31 143
ATR 51 240
ATR 80 219
Augustus Thomas 115, 117, 318
Aulick DD 569 55, 136, 137, 290, 291, 297, 318
Australia H.M.A.S. 157, 160, 163

Bache DD 470 253, 274, 323
Baka see *Oka*
Baker, S1c Gilbert C. 132
Bakufu 5
Barnett, Lt. J. T. 147
Barry APD 29 280, 281, 293, 323, 324
Barton DD 722 159, 161, 204
Bataan CVL 29 275
Bates APD 47 282, 323
Battle of Santa Cruz 5, 42, *43*
Beale DD 471 212
Becton, Cmdr. Julian 239
Beierl, Lt. Peter G. 266, 274
Belknap APD 34 165, 167, 320
Bell, S2c Dean 171–172
Belleau Wood CVL 24 37, 114, 115, *123*, *124*, 223, 320
Benham DD 796 243–246, 322
Benjamin Ide Wheeler 122–123, 318
Benner DD 807 297
Bennett DD 473 211, 224, 321
Bennington CV 20 17, 220, 223
Bennion DD 662 57, 59, 125, 234, 250–251, 322
Bertoli, Cmdr. C. M. 296
Bibb 252
Bigos, Lt. Casimir L. 267
Biloxi CL 80 114, 200, 321

Binubusan 84
Birmingham CL 62 262, 323
Bismarck Sea CVE 95 178–180, 320
Black DD 666 227–228
Blakley, Lt. John L. 149
Bogan, RAdm. Gerald F. 123, 132
Boise CL 47 125
Bong, Maj. Richard I. *112*, 114
Borie DD 704 297, *298*, 324
Bowers APD 40 237, *238*, 243, 322
Boyd DD 544 278, 284
Bozeman Victory 249, 322
Brader, Charles 27
Bradford DD 545 287, 290
Braine DD 630 283, 324
Breese DM 18 161
Bright DE 747 273, 323
Brittin, B. H. Lt. 228
Brodie, Cmdr. Robert A. Jr. 219
Brogger, Lt. Cmdr. L. C. 144
Brooks APD 10 160, 320
Brown Victory 285, 324
Brown, Gordon 219
Brunetti, Col. N. 52
Brush DD 745 177
Bryant DD 665 125, 147, 151, 240, 319, 322
Buckner Bay see Nakagusuku Bay
Bullard DD 660 228, 322
Bunch APD 79 208–209
Bunker Hill CV 17 123, 229, 267–*268*, *269*, *270*, *271*, *272*, 323
Burns, Lt. Cmdr. E. S. 150
Burns DD 588 154
Bush DD 529 125, 152, 177, 211, 223–*224*, 321
bushido 5, 8–9, 25, 64
Bushido the Soul of Japan 9
Butler, Master Peter F. 252

C. W. Post 270, 272
Cabot CVL 28 123, 133, 135, 318
Caldwell DD 605 145, 146, 147, 319
California BB 44 125, 154, 159, 320
Callaghan DD 792 200, 295–296, 321, 324
Callaway APA 35 161, 320
Campbell, Cmdr. E. G. 141
Canada Victory 248–249, 322
Cape Constance 128, 318
Cape Engano 295
Cape Romano 131, 132, 318
Caplin, Lt. Stanly 160
Caraley, S1c Otis B. 132
Caribou IX 114 131, 136
Carina AK 74 253, 323
Carson, Lt. Cmdr. M. V. 163
Cascade AD 16 297
Case DD 370 184
Cassin Young DD 793 65, 223–224, 229, 295–297, 322, 324
Chambers, Cmdr. C. E. 233
Champion AM 314 233
Chandler DMS 9 161
Chandler, RAdm. Theodore E. 161
Chapde, GM Lloyd Earl 132
Charles J. Badger DD 657 83, 227, 321
Chase APD 54 277–278, 323
Chenango CVE 28 117
Chester CA 27 184

Chickasaw ATF 83 116, 132, 294
Chimu Wan 289
Chinen Misaki 249, 288
Chowanoc ATF 100 162
Chung-Hoon, Cmdr. G. P. 235
Clamp ARS 33 232
Claxton DD 571 125, 170, 318
Cofer APD 62 143
Coghlan DD 606 145
Cogswell DD 651 27, 290, 291
Colahan DD 658 145
Cole, Capt. W. M. 143
Colhoun DD 801 4, 211, 223–224, *225*, 321
Colorado BB 45 135, 136, 154, 318
Columbia CA 56 136, 160, 162–163, 320
Columbus, Bosun's Mate Joe 284
Colvin, Lt. Cmdr. Almer P. 151
Combs, S1c Don Taylor 219
Comfort AH 6 249–250, 322
Conklin DE 439 182
Conolly, RAdm. R. L. 168
Connolly DE 306 235, 322
Converse DD 509 278
Conway DD 507 136
Cony DD 508 136
Conyngham DD 371 42, 145, 169
Coolbaugh DE 217 117
Corregidor 74, 75, 76, 77, 79, 170–171, *172*, *173*
Coughlin, Lt. Cmdr. J. W. 293
Cowanesque AO 79 152, 319
Cowell DD 547 259, 274, 279, 323
Cree ATF 84 267, 284
Crescent City APA 21 296
Crosley APD 87 235
Curtis AV 4 293–294, 324
Cushing DD 797 42, 246

Daly DD 519 251, 322
Dashiell DD 659 146, 235
Davao Gulf 74
David Dudley Field 117, 167, 318, 320
Davis, Cmdr. George F. 159
Davison, RAdm. Ralph E. 114, 123
Defense AM 317 211, 212, 321
Demarest, Lt. B. M. 62–63
Dennis DE 405 118, 120
Denver CL 57 136
DeSirant, Dean 161
DesRon 5, 143
Deyo, RAdm. Morton L. 202
Dickerson APD 21 208–209, 321
Divine Wind 5, 9
Doi, Lt. (jg) Saburo 232
Donahue, Cmdr. T. F. 260
Dorsey DMS 1 202–203, 321
Douglas H. Fox DD 779 62, 63, 267, 275, 323
Douw, Cmdr. V. P. 252
Dowling, Lt. Cmdr. Arthur L. 221
Downing, Cmdr. A. A. 250
Drayton DD 366 138, 139, 140, 319
Drexler DD 741 279, 284–285, 324
Driver, GM2c Grady 219
Du Page APA 41 165–166, 320
Dulag 108, 114, 128, 144, 152
Dunckel, BGen. William C. 146, 152
Durgin, RAdm. Calvin T. 178
Durnford, 1st Lt. Dewey F. Jr. 38

Dutton AGS 8 284, 324
Dworzak, Lt. Willis A. 267
Dyson DD 572 55

Eaton DD 510 136, 165, 320
Ebert, Lt. (jg) James D. 208
Edmunds DE 406 117
Educational Reform of 1941 (Imperial Ordinance No. 1483) 10
Educational system, military training in 9, 10, 16
Edward N. Wescott 167, 320
Edwards DD 619 143, 145, 152
Egeria ARL 8 131, 318
Elder, Lt. Franklin L. 171
Eldorado AGC 11 62
Ellyson DMS 19 210, 217, 294, 324
Elmira Victory 167, 320
Emmons DMS 22 210, 217–218, 321
England APD 41 263–264, 323
Enterprise CV 6 42, 114, 115, 123, 274–275, **276**, **277**, 321, 323
Ernst, Lt. (jg) Gerhardt E. 152
Essex CV 9 114, **133**, **134**, **135**, 318
Eta Jima 49, 85, 86, 87, 165
Evans DD 552 264–267, 323
Eversole DE 789 117
Evjen, S1c Russel LeRoy 219
Execute AM 232 216–217

Facility AM 233 219, 321
Fair DE 35 278
Fanshaw Bay CVE 70 118, 120
Far East Air Forces (FEAF) 111
farewell ceremony 21–**22**
Fieberling DE 640 219, 321
File, William H. Jr. Lt. 296
First Mobile Base Air Force 193, 300
fishing battalion *see* suicide boats
Fleming, Capt. R. W. 160
Flint CL 97 252
Flusser DD 368 138, 140, 143, 169, 175
Foote DD 511 147, 151, 319
Foreman DE 633 203, 294, 321
Foristel, Lt. (jg) J. W. 45
Forrest DMS 24 282, 324
Foss, Lt. Cmdr. Eugene N. 217
France, Capt. W. C. 209
Francisco Morazan 152, 319
Franklin CV 13 45, 114, 115, **123**, 318
Franks DD 554 118
French, Lt. James 256
Frye, Master K. D. 126
Fugaku Special Attack Unit 138
Fujinagata 99
Fujisaki, Flying Officer 26
Fujisaki, Lt. (jg) Toshihide 37
Fukuda, Lt. (jg) Hitoshi 183
Fukuryu 311, **314**–315
Fullam DD 474 261
Fun, Sgt. 1c Park Ton 47
Funshiki 40
Fuyutsuki 220

Gaddis, MM Walter C. 253
Gage APA 168 167
Gambier Bay CVE 73 117, 118
Gansevoort DD 608 152–153, 319
Gavin, Lt. Cmdr. Andrew W. 132
Gayety AM 239 260–261, 323

Gear ARS 34 264, 273
Gebhardt, Sonarman 1/c Jack 27
Genda, Capt. Minoru 199
General Fleischer 132
Gherardi DMS 30 217
Gilbert Stuart 131, 318
Gilligan DE 508 166–167, 320
Gilmer APD 11 202, 321
Gladiator AM 319 236, 322
Glendinning, Lt. 268
Glienke, Lt. A. P. 51
Goff, H. H. Lt. 247
Goldman, S1c Roy Cleo 219
Goodhue APA 107 208, 209, 321
Gosselin APD 126 282
Grabowski, Lt. Leon 212
Grapple ARS 7 152
The Great Principles of Education (1879) 10
Gregory DD 802 61, 213, 214, 226, 321
Griffin APD 38 214
Griffin, Lt. John J. Jr. 217
Griffis, Earl O. Sr. 169
Grigchy, S1c Edward Larcy 132
Guest DD 472 279, 282, 323
Guidelines Pertaining to Military Operations Covering Small Islands 81
Gwin DM 33 201, 259, 323

Hachimaki 16, 17, **18**
Haddock, S1c Claude 171
Haggard DD 555 251–252, 323
Hagushi anchorage 206, 208, 232, 248, 249, 250,261, 273, 275, 282, 283, 286, 288, 296
Hailey DD 556 118
Hakoate 99
Hale DD 642 220
Hall, Capt. G. B. H. 274
Hall, Cmdr. Madison Jr. 255
Halloran DE 305 185, 294, 324
Halsey Powell DD 686 199–200, **201**, 320
Halsey, Adm. William F. 117, 154, 176
Hamakaze 220
Hamamatsu Army Flight School 45
Hambleton DMS 20 210–211, 321
Hamlin AV 15 283
Hamly, J. R. 157
Hamul AD 20 297
Hancock CV 19 123, 135, 199, 220, 318, 321
Hank DD 702 228, 297, 322, 324
Hanson, Cmdr. James R. 257
Hara, Lt. (jg) Atsuro 166
Haraden DD 585 146–147, 150, 319
haramaki see sennin-bari
Harbor Construction Battalions *see* suicide boats
Harding DMS 28 237, 322
Harris APA 2 163
Harrison, RM2c William H. 45
Harrison DD 573 235
Harry E. Hubbard DD 748 266
Harry F. Bauer DM 26 267, 289–290, 323, 324
Hasegawa, Capt. Minoru 208
Hatsushimo 220

Hattori, Prof. Shogo 26
Hawley, Lt. D. C. 293
Hayashi, Col. Junji 53
Hayashi, Cpl. Nobuo 81, 85, 169
Hayashi, Lt.(jg)Tohimasa 18
Hayashi, Lt. 163
Hayashikane 99
Haynsworth DD 700 219, 321
Hazelwood DD 531 117, 251–**252**, 323
Heath, S1c Robert F. 161
Heermann DD 532 118, 120
Helm DD 388 158, 319
Hendrikx Master Charles 218
Henrico APA 45 208, 209, 321
Henry A. Wiley DM 29 28, 204
Herbert APD 22 208
Heywood L. Edwards DD 663 125
Hickman, Charles 219
Hickman, Lt. K. K. 140
Hicks, Capt. R. L. 156
Hidatsa ATF 102 102
High, Cmdr. P. L. 151
Highfield, Lt. Cmdr. C. F. 237
Hill, Col. Bruce C. 146
Hinsdale APA 120 206, 321
Hirano, Lt. Akira 34
Hiryu 42
Hitachi Army Flight School 45
Hitachi 98
Hobbs Victory 218–219, 321
Hobson DMS 26 209, 240, 243, 322
Hoctor, Lt. (jg) John M. 164
Hodges DE 231 162, 320
Hoel DD 768 118
Hokoda Army Flight School 45
Hollandia 126, 138, 144, 166, 182
Holmes, Cmdr. R. H. 57
Honma, Capt. Toshio 88
Hopkins DMS 13 161, 260, 323
Horace A. Bass APD 124 297, 324
Horikawa, Lt. (jg) 76, 77
Hornet CV 12 223
Hovey DMS 11 160
Howard DE 346 175
Howorth DD 592 149–150, 211–212, 225, 319, 322
Huber, Sonarman 2/c John 27
Hudson DD 475 245–246, 261, 322
Hugh W. Hadley DD 774 259, 264–267, 323
Hughes, Capt. J. N. 280
Hughes DD 410 143, 145
Hunt DD 674 235, 322
Hutchins DD 476 248, 322
Hyen, 2nd Lt. Takkyon 47
Hyman DD 732 214, 224–225, 321

Ichijima, Yasuo 25
Ichikawa, Motoji 27
Ichishima, Lt. Yasuo 17
Idaho BB 42 260, 322, 323
Ie Shima 38, 237, 258, 265, 270, 276, 277, 280, 281, 286
Ienaga, Saburo 27
I-Go 41
Ikabe, Capt. Shigemi 247–248
Imamura, Lt. (jg) Shigeo 10, 18, 26, 49
Imanishi, Ens. Taichi 182
imon ningyo see *masukotto ningyo*
Impeccable AM 320 278

Index

Imperial General Headquarters, Army Department Directive No. 1336 of 26 May 1945 71
Imperial Headquarters Naval Information Department 10
Imperial Precept for the Military (1882) 8
Imperial Rescript on Education, The (1890) 10, 23
Independence CVL 22 123, 199
Indianapolis CA 35 204, 321
Ingraham, Lt. Cmdr. W. T. 62
Ingraham DD 694 54, 63, 159, 256, 258, 323
Innoshima 99
Inoguchi, Capt. Rikihei 25, 47, 64
Intrepid CV 11 **123**, 132, 133, 199, **200**, 228, 229, 238, 239, 318, 320, 322
Isherwood DD 520 63, 245, 322
Ishigaki Shima 191, 194
Ishikawa, Lt. 76
Isokaze 220
Itagaki, Capt. Takashi 75
Itoh, Keichi 25
Itoman 227
Izant, Master Kenneth F. 218

J. William Ditter DM 31 289–290, 324
James C. Owens DD 776 67
James O'Hara APA 90 132, 318
Japanese Air Power 190
Japanese Monograph Series No. 52 89, 190
Japanese pilot training 49–53
Japanese superstitions: *Jippogure* 21; *To Shi Bi* 21
Jarrell, Capt. A. E. 296
Jeffers DMS 27 232–233
Jenkins DD 447 136
Jensen, Master A. 233
Jeremiah M. Daily 128, 129, 318
Jicarilla AT 104 168
Jin, Lt. Col. Naomichi 47
John Burke 4, 152, 153, 319
John C. Butler DE 339 118, 120, 152, 276–277, 278, 323
John Evans 138, 319
John W. Weeks DD 701 297
Johnson, Cmdr. Frank L. 217
Johnston, S1c Edward O. 248
Johnston DD 821 118
Josiah Snelling 285, 324
Juan De Fuca 147, 319
judo 12

Kadashan Bay CVE 76 118, 162, 320
Kairya, Lt. Cmdr. Tsutomu 16
Kairyu **93**, **98**, **99**, **308**
Kaiten **91**, **92**, **95**, 294, 301, 308; development of 90–92; missions 95–96, 181–185, 294–295; training 93–95
Kaiten Group Tamon 295
Kalinin Bay CVE 68 118, 120, 318
Kamakura Court 7
Kameda, Flight PO2c Naokichi 23
Kamibeppu, Lt. Yoshinori 182
kamikaze training 11, 49–53, 54
Kanemoto, Lt. Cmdr. Nobuo 182
Kasumi 220

Kasumigaura Naval Flying School 9, 26, 49
Katsuyama, Lt. (jg) Jun 295
Kawabe, Lt. Gen. Masakasu 25, 45, 69, 195
Kawajiri, Flight PO 1/c Tsutomo 295
Kawakubo, Lt. (jg) Teruo 166
Kawanishi: *Baika* 301
Kawasaki 98
Kawashima, Lt. 26
Kelley, Cmdr. J. L. Jr. 243
Kelley, Lt. James 284
kendo 11, *12*, *13*
Kenneth Whiting AV 14 293–294, 324
Kenney, Lt. Gen. George C. 107, 108, 191
Kenney, Lt. R. L. 228
Kerama Retto 80, 200, 206, 208, 209, 211, 212, 213, 214, 217, 218, 219, 225, 230, 232, 235, 236, 237, **244**, 245, 249, 250, 251, 252, 253, 256, 260, 261, 263, 264, 267, 273, 274, 278, 282, 293
Ketsu Go 301
Key DE 348 175
Keyes, Cmdr. C. M. 290, 305
Kezu Saki 263
Kidd DD 661 227–229, 322
Kiefer, Capt. Dixie 177
Kiehl, Capt. E. 209
Kikusui Attacks 1 211ff, 222, 226; *4* 22, 248; *5* 253; *7* 70, 278; *8* 283; *9* 288; *10* 37
Killen DD 593 125
Kimberly DD 521 223, 320
Kimu Wan 284
Kincaid, VAdm. T. C. 154
Kirk, S1c Leroy Vincent 132
Kirokomi Tai see suicide soldier
Kitakami 96
Kitkun Bay CVE 71 118, 120, 162, 318, 320
Kobayashi, Tsunenobu 27
Kobe 98
Kocardora, S1c Edward Henry 132
Kojiki 10
Kondo, Ens. Kazuhiko 182
Kondo, Ens. Yoshihiku 182
Korean kamikaze pilots 47
Koryu **96**, **97**, 98, 308, **309**
Kouns, Lt. M. W. 283
Kube, Lt. (jg) Carl Mather 129
Kublai Khan 7
Kumagaya Army Flying School 52
Kure Naval Base 90, 98, 99
Kurita, VAdm. Takeo 117, 118
Kuroki, Lt. (jg) Hiroshi 90, 95
Kuwahara, Cpl. Yasuo 51, 61
Kyle V. Johnson 167, 320

Laffey DD 724 136, 239–240, 243, 296, 322
Lagrange APA 124 297, 298, 299, 300, 324
Lamon Bay 74
Lamson DD 367 138, 139, 141, 143, 319
Lang DD 399 136, 226, 231
Langley CVL 27 37, 199, 229
Las Vegas Victory 218
LaVallette DD 448 140
Lawrence, Lt. Risley 172

LCI(G) 21 175
LCI(G) 22 175
LCI(G) 70 158, 319
LCI(G) 72 116
LCI(G) 73 170
LCI(G) 79 209
LCI(G) 82 209, 210, 321
LCI(G) 347 209, 210, 247
LCI(G) 365 164–165, 320
LCI(G) 404 105, 161–162, 320
LCI(G) 407 236–237, 322
LCI(G) 442 165, 170, ***171***
LCI(G) 452 202, 203, 225
LCI(G) 453 209
LCI(G) 455 209
LCI(G) 461 202, 216
LCI(G) 465 209
LCI(G) 558 170, 203–***204***, 321
LCI(G) 559 203
LCI(G) 560 203, 204, 321
LCI(G) 567 20
LCI(G) 568 209, 321
LCI(G) 580 251, 322
LCI(G) 659 243
LCI(G) 725 209
LCI(L) 90 289, 324
LCI(L) 364 131, 318
LCI(L) 430 131
LCI(L) 442 164, 165
LCI(L) 676 165
LCI(L) 679 248
LCI(L) 977 131
LCI(L) 1065 115, 318
LCI(M) 353 280
LCI(M) 588 225
LCI(M) 974 164, 320
LCI(R) 646 204
LCI(R) 648 249
LCI(R) 763 247
LCS(L) 7 170–173
LCS(L) 8 170–172
LCS(L) 11 55, 67, 232, 250
LCS(L) 12 261–262
LCS(L) 13 232, 261, 283
LCS(L) 14 254, 255, 292
LCS(L) 15 246, 322
LCS(L) 16 65, 66, 261
LCS(L) 18 290, 291
LCS(L) 19 67, 273, 274
LCS(L) 20 55, 259
LCS(L) 21 256, 257, 258
LCS(L) 23 250, 256, 258, 259, 274
LCS(L) 24 226, 248
LCS(L) 25 254, 255, 256, 323
LCS(L) 26 170–175, 320
LCS(L) 27 170–***174***, 320
LCS(L) 31 231, 256, 258, 323
LCS(L) 32 240
LCS(L) 33 4, 229, 231, 322
LCS(L) 34 240, 243
LCS(L) 36 226, 321
LCS(L) 37 226, 246, 248, 249, 322, 323
LCS(L) 38 226, 248
LCS(L) 39 224, 238
LCS(L) 40 226, 249, 288
LCS(L) 48 170
LCS(L) 49 170–174, 320
LCS(L) 51 239–***241***, 322
LCS(L) 52 231, 267, 279, 284, 324
LCS(L) 53 263, 273, 275

LCS(L) 54 65, 66
LCS(L) 55 284
LCS(L) 56 274, 284
LCS(L) 57 229, 230–231, 322
LCS(L) 61 27, 261, 279, 284, 288, 322
LCS(L) 62 288
LCS(L) 64 223–224, 259
LCS(L) 65 27, 275, 288
LCS(L) 66 275, 290
LCS(L) 67 275
LCS(L) 81 259, 288
LCS(L) 82 264, 266, 267, 273, 274, 283, 288
LCS(L) 83 65, 66, 246, 254, 255, 264, 266, 267, 273
LCS(L) 84 65, 66, 224, 259, 264, 266, 267, 273–274, 323
LCS(L) 85 61, 279
LCS(L) 86 273, 283, 290, 292
LCS(L) 87 67, 224, 274
LCS(L) 88 267, 264, **268**, 323
LCS(L) 89 253, 279
LCS(L) 90 288
LCS(L) 92 55
LCS(L) 94 290, 291
LCS(L) 109 224, 267
LCS(L) 110 224
LCS(L) 111 224, 253, 273
LCS(L) 113 253
LCS(L) 114 224, 227, 230, 231, 267
LCS(L) 115 51, 206, 227, 231
LCS(L) 116 206, 231, 239, **241**, 322
LCS(L) 117 253
LCS(L) 118 206, 259
LCS(L) 119 206, 286, 327
LCS(L) 122 55, 290, 291–292, 324
LCS(L) 123 283
LCS(L) 125 295
LCS(L) 129 295, 296
LCS(L) 130 295
LCT 876 211, 321
LCT 1075 145, 319
Lee, S1c Carl Winton 132
Leland E. Thomas DE 420 175
Leonidas Merritt 128, 318
LeRay Wilson DE 414 118, 163, 320
Leutze DD 481 125, 163, 164, 211, 212, **215**, 321
Lewis L. Dyche 156, 319
Lexington CV 16 128, **129**, **130**, 318
Liberty Ships 4, 125–126, **127**, 252
Liddle APD 60 143, 144, 319
Liloan 136
Lindsey DM 32 210, 233, 234, 322
Lipan ATF 85 293
Little DD 803 254–255, 323
Logan Victory 321
Long DMS 12 160, 230
Loud, Cmdr. Wayne R. 156
Lough DE 586 169, 170
Louisville CA 28 156, 160–161, 289, 319, 324
Loundsbury, Lt. Cmdr. Ralph F. 208
Lowry DD 770 67, 258–259, 284, 285, 323
Loy APD 56 283, 324
LSD 6 292
LSM 14 261
LSM 18 194
LSM 19 144
LSM 20 140, 319

LSM 21 115
LSM 23 140, 319
LSM 34 140
LSM 59 293
LSM 135 280–281
LSM 138 131
LSM 213 294, 324
LSM 318 144, 319
LSM 708 290
LSM(R) 188 204, 321
LSM(R) 189 204, 231, 232, 259, 322
LSM(R) 190 231, 251, 252, 323
LSM(R) 191 67, 240, 243, 250
LSM(R) 192 251, 259, 323
LSM(R) 193 264, 267
LSM(R) 194 256, 257, 258, 323
LSM(R) 195 246, 254, 255, 256, 323
LSM(R) 197 231
LSM(R) 198 231, 275
LST 268 167, 168
LST 447 211, 219, 321
LST 460 147, 151, 321
LST 472 147, 148, **149**, 150, 319
LST 477 180, 230
LST 479 147, 151
LST 534 294, 324
LST 548 165, 320
LST 599 211, 321
LST 605 147, 319
LST 610 164, 165, 320
LST 700 167, 168, 320
LST 724 206, **207**, 321
LST 735 164
LST 737 144, 319
LST 738 147–148, 319
LST 749 319
LST 750 152
LST 808 275–276, 323
LST 809 180–181
LST 884 206, **207**
LST 911 168
LST 912 162, 320
LST 925 163–164, 320
LST 1028 164, 320
Luce DD 522 47, 259, 323
Lunga Point CVE 94 178–**179**, 320

M. S. Tjisadane 272, 323
MacArthur, Gen. Douglas 68, 107
MacDonald, Master William 248
Macomb DMS 23 217, 240, 253–254, 323
Maddox DD 731 177–**178**, 320
Maeda, VAdm. Minoru 191
Mahan DD 364 42, 140–142, 143, 319
Maizuru 98
Makin Island CVE 93 154, 178
Manila Bay CVE 61 118, 157–**158**, 319
Manila Bay Entrance Defense Force 75
Mannert L. Abele DD 733 39, 231–232, 322
Marcus Daly 138, 145, 318, 319
Marcus Island CVE 77 118, 144, 147, 162, 319
Marine Corps Air Units: MAG-31 246; MAG-45 183; VMF-212 290; VMF-221 268; VMF-224 37, 240, 256; VMF-314 37; VMF-322 211, 285; VMF-323 38, 240, 264; VMF(N) 543 208

Mariveles Harbor 170–**174**
Maru-re 4, 73, 80, **81**, **82**, 89, 163, 165, 168, 169, 202–203, 204, 247, 249, 301; deployment 86–89; development of 80–81; formations **83–85;** training 85–86
Maru-re units: *1st* 80, 87; *2nd* 80, 87; *3rd* 80, 88; *4th* 80; *9th* 87; *11th* 169; *12th* 169; *13th* 169; *15th* 169; *16th* 169; *17th* 169; *18th* 169; *19th* 84, 85, 168–169; *20th* 169; *26th* 80, 87, 88, 227; *27th* 80, 87, 88, 247, 248, 253; *28th* 80, 87, 88; *29th* 80, 87, 88, 248; *105th* 169; *106th* 169; *107th* 169; *111th* 169; *112th* 169; *114th* 169; *115th* 169; *117th* 169; *118th* 169
Mary A. Livermore 285, 324
Maryland BB 46 136, 137, 211, 220–221, 318, 321
Massey DD 778 67
masukotto ningyo 16, **20**
Matsueda, Lt. (jg) Yoshihisa 76, 170
Matsuo, Flight PO1c Isao 18, 264
Matthew P. Deady 126, 128, 318
McCambell, Cmdr. David **113**, 114
McCandless, Cmdr. Bruce 61
McCarty, Cmdr. W. P. 156
McClelland DE 750 273
McCool, Lt. Richard M. 291–292, **293**
McCord DD 539 117
McCornock, Cmdr. Samuel A. 145
McCoy Reynolds DE 440 182
McEwen, Lt. A. G. 209
McGowan DD 678 252
McGuire, Maj. Thomas B. **113**, 114
McGuire, MM Mac 169
McGuirk Lt. W. E. 161
McNair DD 679 228
McNealy, S1c Chester Lee 219
McNeese, S1c William H. 130
Meister, Lt. (jg) Harry G. 172
Melvin DD 680 252
Miami CL 89 235
midget submarine *see* Kairyu and Koryu
Miki, Lt. Cmdr. Tadanao 29–30
Mikuriya, Lt. (jg) Takuji 25
Miller, Ens. J. G. 37
Mindoro Resupply Unit 152
Mindoro 149–153, 154
Minneapolis CA 36 136, 160, 320
Minot Victory 232, 322
Mississinewa AO 59 19, 182–**184**, 185, 318
Mississippi BB 41 124, 152, 160, 163, 288, 320, 324
Missouri BB 63 228–**229**, 238, 322
Mitate Unit No. 2 178
Mitchell, Lt. Harris **256**
Mitsubishi *Shusei* 301, **302**, 304
Mitsugi, Tadanao 30
Mitsuhashi, Lt. Kentaro 16, **17**
Miwachi, Tsuko 20
Miyagi, Yoshi 25
Miyako Jima 191, 194
Miyazaki, Maj. Gen. Shuichi 45
Miyoshi, Maj. Gen. 26
M-kanemono 99
Moale DD 693 147, **148**

Mobile CL 63 185
Moebus, Capt. L. A. 180
Momm, Cmdr. Albert O. 217
Monadnock CM 9 168
Mongol invasion 7, 8
Montpelier CL 57 135–136, 318
Moore, Cmdr. H. G. 228
Moosebrugger, Capt. Frederick 217
Morris, John 10
Morris DD 417 211, 212, 213, 214, **216**, 321
Morrison DD 560 54, 62, 256–257, 258, 323
Morrison R. Waite 128, 130, 318
Mount McKinley AGC 7 253
Mount Olympus AGC 8 168
Mugford DD 389 140, 319
Mullaney, Cmdr. Baron J. 265
Mullany DD 528 206, 211, 214–217, 321
Munsee AT 107 235
Murakami, Lt. (jg) Katsutomo 182
Muramatsu, CPO Minoru 166
Musashi, Miyamoto 9
Musashi, PO1c Takao 26
Musashi 117
Mustin DD 413 136, 250

Nachi 128
Naerabout, Master J. 272
Nagasaki 98
Nagatsuka, Flying Officer Ryuji 23, 52, 53
Nago Bay 252
Naha 88, 227
Nakagusuku Bay 80, 87, 88, 247, 248, 282, 284, 285, 288, 292, 294, 297
Nakajima, Lt. (jg) Kenjiro 76, 79, 170
Nakajima, Cmdr. Tadashi 168
Nakajima *Tsurugi* **41**, 301, 304, 307
Nakajima *Kikka* 301, **303**, 304
Nakamura, 1st Lt. 86
Nakamura, Ens. Sadeo 42
Namikaze 96
Nashville CL 43 125, 146, 319
Nasugbu 169, 171
Natoma Bay CVE 62 118, **157**, 290, 324
Navy Air Units (U.S.): CAG-13 123; CAG-18 123; CAG-19 128; CAG-21 123; CAG-40 66; CAG-80 176; VC-5 120; VC-90 38; VF-9 **256**; VF-10 239; VF-13 115; VF-15 114; VF-17 37; VBF-17 37; VF-30 37; VF-85 67, 264; VF-86 37
Navy Directive No. 513 (1 March 1945) 48
Navy Directive No. 513 (20 March 1945) 48, 188
Navy Directive No. 516 (8 April 1945) 188
Navy Directive No. 540 48
Navy Directive No. 5410 (March 1945) 188
Nestor ARB 6 282
Nevada BB 36 **202**, **203**, 321
New Mexico BB 40 136, 152, 158–159, 160, 273, 319
New Orleans CA 32 114
New York BB 34 235, 322

Newcomb, Cmdr. R. M. 295
Newcomb DD 586 125, 161, 211–212, **213**, **214**, 295, 320
Nicholas DD 449 136
Nicholas J. Sinnet 131, 318
Nicholson DD 442 255
Nihon Shoki 10
Niigata 98
Nimitz, Adm. Chester 107
Nishimura, VAdm. Shoji 117
Nishina, Lt. (jg) Sekio 90, 183–184
Nitobe, Inazo 9
Noah, S1c W. C. 248
Noda, Capt.Yoshihiko 87
Nonaka, Lt. Cmdr. Goro 31, **35**, 36

O'Brien DD 725 142, 161, 200–202, 320, 321
O'Connor, EMC 3/c Richard E. 258
O'Neill DE 188 278, 279, 323
Oba, Cmdr. Saichi 295
Oberrender DE 344 118, 263, 323
Ogawa, Kiyoshi 267, 268–269
Ohira, Lt. Cmdr. 31
Ohnuki-Tierney, Emiko 25
Ohta, Lt. (jg) Mitsuo 29–30
Oikawa, Adm. Koshiro 48, 188
Oka 17, 27, 231, 232, 260, 261, 268, 304, 305; development 29–30; K-I trainer 31, 32 missions 37, 38, 39; testing 30; Model 11 30, **32**, **33**, **34**, **35**, **36**, 304; Model 22 33, 304
Okabe, Flight CPO Konichi 34, 49
Okabe, Capt. Shigami 49, 88
Okamura, Cmdr. Motoharu 22, 31
Okazaki, Teruyuki 10
Okubo, Masazo 34
Oldendorf, VAdm. Jesse B. 117, 154, 159
Omae, Capt. Toshikazu 48, 187
Ommaney Bay CVE 79 118, 154, **156**, 319
Onishi, VAdm. Takajiro 22, 45, **46**, 191
Ono, Sgt. 44
Orca AVP 49 154, 319
Orestes AGP 10 153, 319
Orita, Lt. Cmdr. Zenji 183
Ormoc Bay 138, 145, 146
Otis Skinner 167, 320
Otsujima 93, 183
Otsuka, Lt. (jg) Akio 22
Outline of the Operations Plan of the Imperial Army and Navy 187
The Outline of the Operations Plan of the Imperial Army and Navy (1945) 47
Oyamada, Lt. Cmdr. Shoichi 76, 170
Ozawa, VAdm. Jisaburo **69**, 70, 115

Paducah Victory 253
Pakana ATF 108 240
Palmer DMS 5 4, 161, 320
Panamint AGC 13 272
Parker, Cmdr. A. E. 232
Pathfinder AGS 1 262, 323
Patoka AO 49 184
Pavlic APD 70 278, 284, 287
PC 623 169
PC 803 295

PC 804 295
PC 851 240
PC 853 233
PC 1129 169–170, 320
PC 1603 282, 324
PCE(R) 852 243, 278
PCE(R) 855 263
Pennsylvania BB 38 125, 152
People's Rights Movement 10
Perdeck, S1c Al 269
Petrof Bay CVE 80 117, 118, 122, 229
PGM 10 217
PGM 11 217
PGM 20 267
Phil, Capt. Kim San 47
Philip, Capt. George 292
Philip DD 498 152, 153, 163, 164
Phoenix CL 46 125
pilot training (Japan) 49–53
Pinkney APH 2 232, 249, 322
Pittenger, FC3c Charles J. 258
Pontus H. Ross 95, 182, 320
Pope, Lt. A. J. 115
Porcupine IX 126 153, 319
Porter DD 800 42, 306
Porterfield DD 682 212
Portland CA 33 42
Potts, Col. Ramsey D. 69
Pratt, Capt. J. L. 180
Presley DE 371 169
Preston DD 795 42
Pringle DD 477 27, 136, 152, 240–243, 319, 322
Pritchett DD 561 55, 198, 295–296, 324
PT 75 151, 319
PT 77 151
PT 84 147, 151
PT 106 175
PT 223 151
PT 224 151
PT 230 151
PT 297 **150**
PT 298 151
PT 300 147, 151, 319
PT 323 144, 319
PT 332 152, 319
PT 335 175
PT 342 175
PT 343 175
PT 532 144
Purdy, Cmdr. A. M. 125
Purdy DD 734 125, 217, 227, 229–**230**, 231, 322
Putnam, Cpl. W. H. 234

Quapaw ATF 110 116

Radar Picket Stations **222**; *1* 59, 223, 229, 231, 238–239, 250, 256; *2* 67, 223, 224, 231, 240, 251, 292; *4* 224, 226; *5* 267; *9* 55, 62, 223, 253, 274, 275; *9A* 198, 295; *10* 254, 256, 259; *11A* 65, 287; *12* 232, 251, 254; *14* 231, 237, 240–241, 246, 259; *15* 267, 279; *15A* 284, 290; *16* 279; *16A* 286–287
Radford, RAdm. A. W. 199, 251
Rall DE 304 185, 232, 322
Ralph Talbot DD 390 147, 150–151, 248, 250, 319, 322

Randolph CV 15 185, 186, 320
Ransom AM 283 245, 322
Rathburne APD 25 248, 322, 324
Rawlings, VAdm H. B. 69
Raymond DE 341 118, 120
Reber, Ens. J. V. Jr. 37
Rednour APD 102 284
Register APD 92 278, 323
Reid DD 369 145–146, 319
Relief AH1 282
religion (Japanese) 23–25
Reno CL 96 115, 318
Renraku Tai 73
Renshaw DD 499 136
Rescue AH 18 297
Rich, Lt. (jg) Elwood M. 295
Richard M. Rowell DE 403 117
Richard P. Leary DD 664 125, 161, 213, 319
Richard S. Bull DE 402 117
Richard W. Suesens DE 342 118, 166–167, 169, 320
Riddle DE 185 322
Rielly, QM2c Bob 27
Robert H. Smith DM 23 65, 200, 321
Robinson DD 562 125, 163, 164, 320
Rodman DMS 21 210, 211, 217–**218**, 321
Rooks DD 804 225
Rooney, Yeoman John 283
Roosevelt, Pres. Franklin 107
Roper APD 20 281–282
Ruddock, RAdm. Theodore D. Jr. 136, 146
Rudyerd Bay CVE 81 178
Russell DD 414 169
Russo-Japanese War 10

S. Hall Young 252, 323
Saginaw Bay CVE 82 117, 178
St. George AV 16 263, 323
St. Lo CVE 63 118, 119, **120**, 318
St. Louis CL 49 135, 136, 137, 211, 318
Sakai, Saburo 42, 49
Sakamoto, Flight PO1c 295
Sakishima Gunto 191
Sakura Jima 99
Salamaua CVE 96 168, 320
Salt Lake City CA 25 204
Sampson DD 394 44–45
Samuel B. Roberts DE 823 118
Samuel Miles DE 183 229, 321
samurai 5
San Bernadino Strait 117
San Diego CL 53 251, 252
San Fabian 165
San Jacinto CVL 30 114, 115, 123, 220, 223, 321
San Jose 108, **141**, 152
San Juan CL 54 42
San Pedro Bay 115, 117, 126, 143, 145, 152, 160
Sandoval APA 194 285–286
Sangamon CVE 26 117, **261**, 323
Santee CVE 29 117, 118, 122, 318
Sarangani Bay 74
Saratoga CV 3 180, 181, 320
Saroch, E. Jr. Lt. 286
Sasaki, Hachiro 25
Sasano, Lt. Masayuki 311
Sato, Flight PO1c Katsumi 183

Sato, Lt. (jg) Akira 166, 183
Saunders, Lt. R. H. 259
Saunter AM 295 142
Savo Island CVE 78 118, 154, 157, 319
SC 699 45
SC 744 136, 318
SC 1338 284
Schmidt, Cmdr. L. E. 63
Schmitz, Lt. Paul J. 219
Scout AM 296 142
Segundo Ruiz Belvis 279, 323
Seizo, Yasunori 268
Seki, Ens. Toyooki 295
Seki, Lt. Yukio 45, 118, 295
sennin-bari 16, 18, **19**
71st Totsugekitai 311
Shackle ARS 9 278, 294
Shamrock Bay CVE 84 162
Shangri-La CV 38 265
Shannon DM 25 63, 201, 208, 255–256, 282
Shaw DD 373 138, 139, 169
Shea DM 30 237, 259–260, 323
Sherman, RAdm. Frederick C. 128, 135
Shima, Capt. Katsuo 47
Shima, VAdm. Kiyohide 117
Shimamura, Flight PO1c Ataru 36
Shimbu Tokubetsu-Kogekitai 8
Shimoyama, Lt. Gen. Takuma 195
Shimpu Tokubetsu-Kogekitai 8
Shinano 34
Shinkai 99, **100**
Shintani, Capt. K. 311
Shinyo 4, 73–80, **77**, **78**, **79**, **80**, **89**, 236, **245**, **246**, **247**, **254**, 262, 274, 301, **304**; deployment 74–80, 88, **243**, 308; development 74; technical drawings **75–76**; units *9th* 76, 170; *10th* 76; *11th* 76; *12th*; 76, 78, 163, 170, 173; *13th* 76, 77; *22nd* 80; *24th* 80
Shiokaze 96
Shoemaker, Capt. J. M. 115
Shropshire H.M.A.S. 125, 160
Shubrick DD 639 286–287, 324
Sigsbee DD 502 235–**236**, 322
Sims APD 50 273, 275, 279, 281, 323, 324
Sino-Japanese War 10
Smethurst, Richard J. 19
Smith DD 378 5, 42, **43**, **44**, 143, 145, 318
Smith, Lt. Clinton **256**
Smith, Lt. Harry L. 171, 230
Smith, Ens. W. H. Jr. 37
Sonoma ATO 12 45, 115–**116**, 318
South Dakota BB 57 42–43
Southard DMS 10 147, 161, 320
Spear, Lt. (jg) J.A. 289
Special Attack Corps 8, 20–21, 25, 26, 27, 47, 52, 63
Special Attack Force *see* Special Attack Corps
Spectacle AM 305 262–263, 280–281, 323
Spencer WPG 36 152
Sprague, RAdm. Clifton A. F. 46, 118
Sprague, RAdm. Thomas L. 363, 117
Sproston DD 577 279

Stadler, Lt. (jg) Herbert 144
Stafford DE 411 158, 319
Stanly DD 478 146, 231, 322
Starr AKA 67 227, 321
Stephen Potter DD 538 200
Sterrett DD 407 152, 214, 225, **226**, 321
Stevens, S1c Patrick Henry 132
Stevens DD 479 152
Stewart, Master James A. 285
Stormes DD 780 279, 323
Stroetzel, Lt. Donald S. 136
Struble, RAdm. A. D. 141, 142, 146
Stump, RAdm. Felix B. 118, 157
Sturdevant, Lt. (jg) H. W. 37
Sturmer, Lt. Frederick E. 283
Submarines, Japanese: *I-8* 96; *I-15* 183; *I-36* 96, 182; *I-37* 96, 181, 182; *I-44* 96, 181; *I-47* 96, 97, 166, 182, 183, 295; *I-48* 96, 181; *I-53* 96, 97, 295; *I-56* 96, 81, 310; *I-57* 310; *I-58* 97, 295, 310; *I-59* 310; *I-62* 310; *I-156* 96; *I-157* 96; *I-158* 96; *I-159* 96; *I-162* 96; *I-165* 96, 181; *I-361* 96; *I-363* 96, 295; *I-366* 96, 295; *I-367* 96, 295; *I-368* 96, 181; *I-370*; 96, 181; *I-372* 96; *I-373* 96
Success AM 310 219
Suffolk AKA 69 209
Sugawara, Lt. Gen. Michio 70, 188, 194, 195, 197
Sugita, Col. Ichiji 47, 187
Suicide Force Combat Methods Training Manual 9, 57, 61
suicide soldiers **102**, **103**, **104**
suicide swimmers 103, 105
Surigao Strait 117
The Sullivans DD 537 200, **271**
Suwanee CVE 27 117, 118, **122**, 318
Suzukawa, Hiroshi 90
Suzuki, Lt. Gen. 80
Suzuki, Yukihisa 21, 26, 99
Suzutsuki 220
Swallow AM 65 245, 322
Swett, Capt. 268

Tacloban 74, 108, **110**, **111**, 114, 126, 128, 136
Taffy 1, 2, 3 *see* Task Units 77.4.1, 77.4.2, 77.4.3
Tahara, Lt. 163
taiatari o kurawasu 9
Taka Hamare 236
Taka Shiki Island 87
Taka Shima 282
Takahashi, Capt. Isao 163
Takahashi, Flight PO1c 295
Takata, Maj. 44
Take 96
Takata, Lt. Col. Koji 43, 45
Tamano 98
Tan Operation 48, 185
Tanaka, Lt. Col. Koji 43, 45
Taniguchi, Probational Officer Toshio 165
Tanikawa, Maj. Gen. Kazuo 69
Tanzla, Col.V. J. 209
Task Force 38 132, 176, 297
Task Force 54 202, 220, 232, 234
Task Force 58 34, 185, 220, 238, 274
Task Force 61 42

Index

Task Force 77 154
Task Force 79 162
Task Group 38.2 123, 132
Task Group 38.3 128, 135
Task Group 38.4 114, 123
Task Group 51.5 232
Task Group 52.6.3 236
Task Group 53.4 209
Task Group 58.1 37
Task Group 58.3 227
Task Group 58.4 199, 228, 238, 251
Task Group 58.6 243
Task Group 58.8 235
Task Group 70.1.4 151
Task Group 77.1 124, 125
Task Group 77.12 150
Task Group 77.2 35, 136, 154, 161
Task Group 77.2.1 160
Task Group 78.3 138, 146, 150
Task Group 78.3.13 151
Task Group 78.3.15 152
Task Unit 32.19.12 288
Task Unit 50.18.7 228
Task Unit 51.7 208
Task Unit 51.92 209
Task Unit 52.1.3 261
Task Unit 52.19.3 261, 273
Task Unit 52.2.4 180
Task Unit 77.12.7 *139*
Task Unit 77.2.1 158
Task Unit 77.4.1 (Taffy 1) 117, 118, 122
Task Unit 77.4.2 (Taffy 2) 117, 118, 157
Task Unit 77.4.3 (Taffy 3) 118
Task Unit 78.2.9 115
Task Unit 78.3.8 145
Task Unit 78.34 147
Tatum APD 81 286–287, 324
Tawakoni ATF 114 233, 240, 282
Taylor, Lt. Cmdr. C. B. Jr. 232
Technical Air Intelligence Center 30
Tekesta ATF 93 212, 276, 280, 281
Telfair APA 210 208, 209, 321
Ten-go 47, 48, 67, 70, 187, 188, 211
Tennessee BB 43 234, 322
Tennis, Ens. 259
Terai, Cmdr. Yoshimori 48, 187
Teramoto, Lt. Cmdr. Iwao 182
Teraoka, VAdm. Kimpei 178, 191
Terror CM 5 252, 323
Thatcher DD 514 294, 323, 324
Third Fleet 154
Thomas E. Fraser DM 24 65, 274
Thomas Nelson 128, 318
Thunderbolt Corps *see* Aircraft Units, Japanese Navy; 722 Naval Air Corps
Ticonderoga CV 14 176–*177*, 320
Tokashiki Island 88
Tokko-tai 4, 7, 8, 25, 204, 316
Toko, Pvt. Guy 26
Tokubetsu-Kogekitai see Tokko-tai
Tokugawa 8
Tokuno Shima 193, 195, 197, 208
Tomioka, RAdm. Sadatoshi 188
Tomonaga, Lt. Cmdr. 42
Tori Shima 260

Toyoda, Adm. Soemu 17, 70, 188, *191*, 192, 195
Toyozumi, Lt. (jg) Kazuhisa 182
TP 114 136
Tracy DM 19 209–210
Trathen DD 530 117
Treasure Island 286
Truman, Pres. Harry S *293*, 316
Tsuchiura Navy Fliers School 49, 93
Tsurumi 74
Tulagi CVE 72 158
Twiggs DD 591 146, 212, 251, 291, 322, 324
Tyrrell AKA 80 208, 321
Tyus, Louis C. 129

Uehara, Pvt. 2c Tokusaburo 103
Uemura, Lt. Masahisa 20
Ugaki, VAdm. Matome 185, 192, 193, 300
Uhlmann DD 687 251
Ujina 85, 86
U-kanemono 99, **100**
Ulithi Atoll 48, 177, 178, *182*, 185, 186, 228, 229, 232
Umezawa, Capt. Hiroshi 87
Underhill DE 682 95, 182, 295–296, 324
Underwater Demolition Team No. 8 158
United States Strategic Bombing Survey (USSBS) 190, 211
Uraga 99
Uranosaki 99
Uriah M. Rose 277, 323
Ute ATF 76 267, 283, 286, 290
Utsunomiya, Ens. Hidieichi 182

Valencia, Lt. Eugene **256**
Van Valkenburgh DD 656 206, 246, 275, 287
Vaught, FCR 3/c James E. 258
Vayda, Ray 161
Victory ships 126
Vigilance AM 324 235, 263
Voegelin, Lt. Cmdr. B. D. 288

Wadsworth DD 516 245, 250, 322
Wake Island CVE 65 211, 321
Waldron DD 699 275
Walker DD 517 251
Walker DD 723 141, 159, 290, 319
Waller DD 466 136
Walter C. Wann DE 412 118, 231, 322
Walter Colton 292, 324
War Hawk AP 168 164, 320
War Plan Orange 107
Ward APD 16 **142**, 319
Warren, Cmdr. J. T. 159, 160
Wasp CV 18 199, 320
Watanabe, Ens. Kozo 183
Watch Hill 160
Weaver DE 741 185
Webb, Capt. Richard 147
Weller, Capt. O. A. 199
Wesson DE 184 225–226, 321

West Virginia BB 48 136, 152, 160, 206–208, 321
Westralia H.M.A.S. 162
Weyler, RAdm. G. L. 125
White Plains CVE 66 118, 120, **121**, 318
Whitehurst DE 634 235, 322
Wickes DD 578 246
Wilkinson, VAdm. T. S. 162, 168
William A. Coulter 128, 131 318
William Ahear 319
William C. Cole DE 641 278–279, 281, 323
William D. Porter DD 579 4, 290, **291**, **292**, 296, 305, 324
William S. Ladd 144–145, 319
William Seiverlling DE 441 282
William Sharon 147, 152, 319
Williams, Col. L. O. 209
Williams, Lt. G. B. 280
Williamson, Lt. Cmdr. J. A. 264
Willmarth DE 638 219
Wilson, Cmdr. G. R. 224
Wilson DD 408 152, 153, 236, 322
Winfield, Lt. (jg) Murray 37
Winterberry AN 56 182
Witter DE 636 211, 212–213, 321
Woods, Lt. Edgar H. 143
Woodson, Lt. W. E. 255
Wylie, Cmdr. W. N. 279

Yahagi 220
Yamaki, Capt. 9, 49
Yamamoto, Maj. Gen. Kenji 194
Yamamoto, Capt. Hisanori 88
Yamamoto, 2d Lt. Nishi 208
Yamamura, Flight CPO Keisuke 37
Yamana, Masao 30
Yamato 219–220, **221**, 234
Yamato daimashii 69
Yamazaki, Lt. (jg) Shigeo 76
Yasukuni Shrine 22, 23, **24**, 25, 36, 47
YMS 31 236, 260, 321, 322
YMS 47 168
YMS 81 321
YMS 89 260
YMS 327 260
YMS 331 236, 260, 321, 322
YMS 427 260
Yokohama 98, 99
Yokosuka 74, 98, 99, 311
Yokosuka First Naval Air Technical Arsenal 31
York, S1c William Ellis 132
Yorktown CV 10 199, 228, 256
Yoshikawa, Eiji 9
Yoshimoto, Lt. (jg) Kentaro 182
YTB 404 276
YTL 488 276
Yukikaze 220
Yume ATF 94 209
Yunokawa, Lt. Morimasa 34

Zamami Jima 87, 254
Zampa Misaki 204, 232
Zeilin APA 3 168, 320
Zellars DD 777 234, 322

www.ingramcontent.com/pod-product-compliance
Lightning Source LLC
Chambersburg PA
CBHW081534300426
44116CB00015B/2631